The Development of Textlinguistics in the Writings of Robert Longacre

SIL International
Publications in Translation and Textlinguistics
4

Publications in Translation and Textlinguistics is a peer-reviewed series published by SIL International. The series is a venue for works concerned with all aspects of translation and textlinguistics, including translation theory, exegesis, pragmatics, and discourse analysis. While most volumes are authored by members of SIL, suitable works by others will also form part of the series.

Series Editors
Bryan Harmelink
George Huttar

Volume Editor
Shin Ja J. Hwang

Volume Managing Editor
Lana Martens

Production Staff
Bonnie Brown, Managing Editor
Lois Gourley, Compositor
Patrick Gourley, Cover Design

The Development of Textlinguistics in the Writings of Robert Longacre

Edited by
Shin Ja J. Hwang

SIL International
Dallas, Texas

© 2010 by SIL International
Library of Congress Catalog No: 2009943660
ISBN: 978-1-55671-246-3
ISSN: 1550-588X

Printed in the United States of America

All Rights Reserved.

No part of this publication may be reproduced, stored in a retrieval system, or transmitted in any form or by any means—electronic, mechanical, photocopy, recording, or otherwise—without the express permission of SIL International. However, short passages, generally understood to be within the limits of fair use, may be quoted without permission.

Copies of this and other publications of SIL International may be obtained from

International Academic Bookstore
SIL International
7500 W. Camp Wisdom Road
Dallas, TX 75236-5699

Voice: 972-708-7404
Fax: 972-708-7363
Email: academic_books@sil.org
Internet: http://www.ethnologue.com

Contents

1	Why we need a vertical revolution in linguistics	1
2	A spectrum and profile approach to discourse analysis	25
3	Two hypotheses regarding text generation and analysis	49
4	Some interlocking concerns which govern participant reference in narrative	97
5	The dynamics of reported dialogue in narrative	115
6	The paragraph as a grammatical unit	135
7	The discourse structure of the flood narrative	155
8	Building for the worship of God	201
9	Genesis as soap opera: Some observations about storytelling in the Hebrew Bible	231
10	Exhortation and mitigation in First John	239
11	A top-down, template-driven narrative analysis, illustrated by application to Mark's gospel	281
12	Mark 5.1-43: Generating the complexity of a narrative from its most basic elements	311
13	The discourse strategy of an appeals letter	339
14	Holistic Textlinguistics	361
15	Some hermeneutic observations on textlinguistics and text theory in the humanities	409

Acknowledgements

We are grateful to the original publishers for permission to reprint the articles and chapters in this volume. Original publication details are provided below.

1. "Why we need a verbal revolution in linguistics" from the *Fifth LACUS Forum*, Wolfgang Wolck and Paul L. Garvin (eds.), 1979, pp. 247-270. Columbia, SC: Hornbeam Press. Reprinted by permission.

2. "A spectrum and profile approach to discourse analysis" from *Text* 1.4, 1981, pp. 337-359. Reprinted by permission of Mouton de Gruyter.

3. "Two hypotheses regarding text generation and analysis" from *Discourse Processes* 12.4, 1989, pp. 413-460. Reprinted by permission of Ablex Publishing Corporation.

4. "Some interlocking concerns which govern participant reference in narrative" from *Language Research* 31.4, 1995, pp. 697-714. Seoul National University. Reprinted by permission.

5. "The dynamics of reported dialogue in narrative" from *Word* 45, 1994, pp. 125-143. Reprinted by permission.

6. "The paragraph as a grammatical unit" from *Discourse and Syntax (Syntax and Semantics 12)*, Talmy Givón (ed.), 1979, New York: Academic Press, pp. 116-134. Reprinted by permission of Elsevier.

7. "The discourse structure of the Flood Narrative" from *Journal of the American Academy of Religion* 47.1, Supplement B, 1979, pp. 89-133. Reprinted by permission.

8. "Building for the worship of God: Exodus 25:1-30:10" from *Discourse Analysis of Biblical Literature*, Walter Bodine (ed.), 1995, Atlanta, GA: Scholars Press, pp. 21-49. Reprinted by permission.

9. "Genesis as soap opera: Some observations about storytelling in the Hebrew Bible" from *Journal of Translation and Textlinguistics* 7, 1995, pp. 1-8. SIL.

10. "Exhortation and mitigation in First John" *Selected Technical Articles Related to Translation* 9, 1983, pp. 3-44. SIL.

11. "A top-down, template-driven narrative analysis, illustrated by application to Mark's Gospel" from *Discourse Analysis and the New Testament*, Stanley E. Porter and Jeffrey T. Reed (eds.), Sheffield: Sheffield Academic Press, 1999, pp. 140-168. Reprinted by permission of Sheffield Academic Press.

12. "Mark 5:1-43: Generating the complexity of a narrative from its most basic elements" from *Discourse Analysis and the New Testament*, Stanley E. Porter and Jeffrey T. Reed (eds.), Sheffield: Sheffield Academic Press, 1999, pp. 169-196. Reprinted by permission of Sheffield Academic Press.

13. "The discourse strategy of an appeals letter" from *Discourse Description: Diverse linguistic analyses of a fund-raising text*, W. C. Mann and S. A. Thompson (eds.), 1992, Amsterdam, Philadelphia: John Benjamins. pp. 109-130. Reprinted by permission of John Benjamins.

14. "Holistic textlinguistics" , posted in 2003 by SIL at http://www.sil.org/silewp/2003/silewp2003-004.pdf.
(Also appears in *Linguistics Today: facing a greater challenge*, CD-Rom attachment, Piet von Sterkenburg (ed.), 2004, Amsterdam, Philadelphia: John Benjamins, pp. 1-48.)

15. "Some hermeneutic observations on textlinguistics and text theory in the humanities" from *Functional Approaches to Language, Culture and Cognition: Papers in honor of Sydney M. Lamb*, David G. Lockwood, Peter H. Fries, and

Acknowledgements

James E. Copeland (eds.), 2000, Amsterdam, Philadelphia: John Benjamins, pp.169-183. Reprinted by permission of John Benjamins.

16. Longacre feels that this is a good place to voice a disclaimer on his part regarding his being the pioneer in discourse analysis in North America. That place, he believes, properly should go to Henry A. Gleason, Jr. (obit Jan. 13, 2007). While teaching at the Kennedy School of Missions, Hartford Theological Seminary in the nineteen sixties and seventies, Gleason developed three essential components of discourse analysis: mainline vs. background, the tie-in of verb morphology to discourse structure, and the study of connectives. All this was in full swing in Gleason's work when a student, Mildred Larson, came to the Kennedy School of Missions in 1964. I will let her speak for herself in the following private communication:

> As a graduate student in linguistics, I found that Dr. Henry Gleason opened up a whole new area of research for me and all of his students. Until I studied under him my understanding of grammatical research had been limited to sentence and paragraph notions. Gleason taught us to analyze and described the structure of whole texts.
>
> He had been to Papua New Guinea where he collected texts from one of the indigenous languages [Longacre: Kate]. These he used as examples in class lectures and in our assignments. We learned, for example, to chart and describe how participant reference is handled throughout a total text. This process of charting also included the grammatical markers of tense and aspect and how they were used throughout the time line of the text, the various functions and types of connective devises, and other grammatical markers. This detailed charting was the key to doing a good analysis and a more accurate description of the grammar at all levels of grammatical description from morpheme to total text.

A careful examination for published articles and books, by Henry Gleason, Joseph Grimes, and myself, and the publication dates—which I cannot give here—further establishes the priority for Gleason.

After the Hartford Seminary years, Gleason moved to the University of Toronto in or around 1968. He was the fifth president of the Linguistic Association of Canada and the United States.

Introduction

The current book, *The development of textlinguistics in the writings of Robert Longacre*, brings together Robert Longacre's articles on textlinguistics and discourse analysis scattered through many journals and books which are not readily accessible to the student of discourse analysis. To fill this need, Longacre himself carefully selected fifteen papers on his theory and its application published during the twenty-five years between 1979 and 2004.

    The term *textlinguistics* was and is still primarily used by European linguists like van Dijk, Petöfi, and Enkvist. Textlinguists take the whole text as the necessary scope of studying the language; early publications include the Research in Text Theory series (de Gruyter) in Germany. American linguists whose primary interests are in discourse tend to use the expression, *discourse analysis*, rather than *textlinguistics*. *Discourse*, however, may refer to only spoken data for some and dialogue for others, as in conversational analysis. Whether you use the term *textlinguistics* or *discourse analysis*, it is a linguistic study of texts, whether written or spoken, monologue or dialogue. Specifically, Longacre's theory of textlinguistics focuses on the areas of the intersection of the morphosyntax and the discourse structure. He states in an article included here (2000:170): "The goal of the textlinguist is to confront the morphosyntax of a language with the structure of texts in that language to the mutual elucidation of both. This leads not only to a better understanding of the linguistic structure of a language, but also to a kind of text hermeneutic." He urges us to study the structure of the text as a whole while analyzing the parts of the text in light of the whole.

For many scholars in functional approaches, discourse along with pragmatics provides the explanations and motivations for the use of language in its natural habitat. It is a fruitful approach, but to them the analysis of discourse or text as a linguistic unit on its own is secondary.

Longacre has developed a theory of textlinguistics by approaching discourse as a linguistic unit at the highest level of the grammatical hierarchy; his approach is similar in vein to that of textlinguists in Europe. His approach, however, is not to view and study the language only as a whole unit of discourse, but also study it at all the possible interfaces with lower levels of grammar from morpheme and word to phrase, clause, sentence, and paragraph. Hence his paper on mystery particles and morphemes functioning at discourse (1976). The *grammar of discourse* (1983; 2nd ed. 1996) is the foundational monograph of his textlinguistics theory with discourse as a level of grammar. It presents discourse typology and plots with peak(s). Two important theoretical concepts, spectrum (also called saliency scheme) and profile, are delineated in relation to lower-level grammatical features such as tense, aspect, and modality of the verb, and unusual peak-marking features of grammar that define the shape of the profile. In other words, in all his studies, the parts are analyzed in the context of the whole (text), while the whole is determined by the intricately interwoven features of the parts. His theory of textlinguistics is thus profoundly anchored on morphosyntax as it interfaces with the text and discourse. The book also covers case roles and clauses, interclausal and intersentential (paragraph) relations, focusing on those lower levels of grammar but always reminding the reader of the need for the holistic perspective of discourse.

As a book on textlinguistics, this volume does not include his papers on other aspects of linguistics. It would be a multiple-volume set if we were to include them all. For over fifty years, Longacre has contributed to a variety of subfields of linguistics. With his in-depth research in Trique while translating the New Testament into the language in the 1940's and 50's, his early studies have been on tones and phonology, morphosyntax, and historical-comparative linguistics (his dissertation published in 1957). He was the first linguist to provide evidence that a language may have five contrastive levels of tone (1952).

His areas of research gradually expanded to the higher levels of grammar beyond morphosyntax. In the 1960's he started to catalog all possible semantic interclausal relations in human language, such as coupling, alternation, and contrast, when clauses combine into sentences, with workshops in the Philippines and Papua New Guinea, culminating in several volumes of publication. His name is so closely associated with the description of clause chaining structure (such as those in PNG and South America) that no article or book on clause chaining fails to refer to his work.

Beyond the level of the clause, which is basic and atomic in language, and the level of the sentence as a combination of clauses, he moved to concentrating on yet higher level structures found in the paragraph and discourse in the 70's, far ahead of many whose primary concerns are now on discourse analysis.

Within the area of textlinguistics proper, this volume has fifteen representative papers divided into five parts: I. Theory of textlinguistic analysis, II. Application to Biblical Hebrew, III. Application to the Greek New Testament, IV. Application to contemporary English, and V. L'Envoi: Broader horizons in the humanities.

Part I includes six articles on the theory, starting from the need for discourse analysis, to the presentation of basic concepts of textlinguistics based on the two building blocks of language which are the VPs and NPs, and to reported dialogue and the paragraph.

The first paper, "Why we need a vertical revolution in linguistics" (1979), presents arguments why any linguistic study needs to have discourse perspective. That is, why bother with discourse analysis? Longacre says that discourse analysis is "a rock bottom necessity," rather than simply possible or desirable, in studying such topics as pronouns, deictics, tense/aspect/mode/voice, and word order variation. The discourse revolution he referred to in the title is in fact with us: all morphosyntactic elements in languages are being (re)analyzed in light of discourse. Beyond the description of linguistic units, we pursue their functions in discourse in order to understand their appropriate use.

"A spectrum and profile approach to discourse analysis" appeared in 1981 in the first volume of the journal Text edited by van Dijk. It presents two main concepts that uniquely define Longacre's approach to textlinguistics, i.e., verb/salience ranking and peak in profile. Using the metaphor of spectrum, he shows that the analysis of narrative reveals a cline of information from the most dynamic elements to the most static. His ideas are similar to those stated in the influential article by Hopper and Thompson (1980) in recognizing the distinct types of information, but Longacre goes beyond their binary division of foreground and background. The cline involves multiple levels of relevance or significance to the text, which is further developed with more detailed data in his "Two hypotheses" paper . The cline of levels is marked by surface structure features of tense and aspect, particles, and word order. The peak, a concept vital to his approach to the text as a whole unit, helps to explain the unusual, unexpected, off-norm features that occur in a section of the text. The peak episode is often a zone of analytical difficulty with unusual features and corresponds to the climax or denouement of a story in a horizontal view. Thus tense shifts to the present or person shifts to second or first person in a third person story, or shifts to more dialogue or drama are not anomalous features that cannot be explained, but are reflections of a higher level call to mark the excitation and tension. Such peak episodes may occur once or twice to mark the climax and denouement in relation to actions and events, or it may mark a thematic peak.

"Two hypotheses regarding text generation and analysis" (1992) presents detailed salient schemes in eight languages, including English, Totonac, and Biblical Hebrew, based on morphosyntactic features of texts at the global level. At the local level of paragraph, he shows how salient schemes are tied into the analysis of paragraph. The sentences that mark the mainline of the discourse, high in a salient scheme, are labeled "thesis" in the paragraph analysis. Other sentences that lack such features are marked differently, and they are ancillary and supportive to the thesis, in distinct relations as paraphrase, reason, or comment.

The next article, "Some interlocking concerns which govern participant reference in narrative" (1995), deals with nominal features, such as a noun phrase, pronoun, verb agreement, or zero anaphora, that refer to participants. Three interlocking concerns are resources in language (e.g. does it have verb agreement as in Greek or Spanish?), ranking of participants (central, major, or minor), and discourse operations (first mention, routine tracking, restaging, etc.). The third concern of discourse operations, in particular, was never systematically presented before his work, although many researchers have tackled the issue of participant reference and identification (Givón 1983, Gundel et al., 1993, Chafe 1994).

"The dynamics of reported dialogue in narrative" (1994) looks at variations in quotation formulas in four languages (e.g., *John said to her, he said*, or *said John*) and their positions relative to the quotation as preposed or postposed or interposed. The thesis of the article is that the excessive use of quotation formulas is "indexical of the intensity of participant interaction in dialogue." It is well documented with illustrative texts.

One of the most quoted and referenced articles of his, "The paragraph as a grammatical unit" (1979), deals with a controversial topic, well indicated by the title itself: Is paragraph a grammatical unit? His answer to this question is "Yes," while most linguists of the period viewed such a unit as semantic at best. He argues that the paragraph is by its very nature a looser structure than the sentence. It is like a network structure which is harder to pinpoint, but it does have grammatical features and is thus a grammatical unit. The closure is marked by surface features as an ice-breaker or terminus. The thematic unity can also be grammatically marked. This is the article where he lays out a possible etic list of paragraph types, with further variants conditioned by stylistic factors, discourse types, or running quotes. He finishes with an illustrative analysis of a paragraph having six sentences.

The next two parts include his research in Old Testament Biblical Hebrew and New Testament Greek. As a graduate of a seminary before earning his degrees in linguistics in the mid 1950's, he has continued to analyze biblical texts applying the theory and insights that he has developed in linguistics. His versatility in these two fields, biblical and linguistic, uniquely equip him to be able to view 'old' data from the Bible with a new pair of linguistic glasses. It has been phenomenal to see him at home in either a seminary or linguistics department and to see how biblical scholars have been pursuing him and his textlinguistic theory as much as linguists have. He could initiate linguistic analysis almost as a new paradigm for the study of the Bible by focusing on minute details of the data as they occur in discourse context.

Part II includes three articles applying his theory to Biblical Hebrew. Longacre has written extensively about Biblical Hebrew, especially during the last thirty years: books on Joseph from Genesis (1989, 2nd ed. 2003a), on Biblical Hebrew grammar (Longacre and Bowling, in press), and numerous articles on a variety of types of discourse, such as procedural/instructional texts (1994), functions of distinct tense, aspect, and modality for each discourse type (2003b), and Psalm 19 (2003c), just to name a few. The readers for this category of his writings are probably more in biblical scholarship than in linguistics, but he had both groups in mind as readers when writing them - not an easy task for any writer. His book on Joseph and other articles have established him as a solid and great scholar in the field of Biblical Hebrew. He is a scholar who deals with the detailed linguistic features of the Old Testament language. In this collection, three papers are selected, those dealing with the Flood narrative, instructional discourse in Exodus about building the tabernacle, and Genesis as soap opera.

"The discourse structure of the Flood Narrative" (1979) in *Journal of the American Academy of Religion*, is primarily for theological scholars, while a later article "Interpreting biblical stories," somewhat different and shorter, appears in a volume aimed at linguists (edited by a linguist van Dijk 1985). In his abstract, the first sentence reads: "This paper approaches the Genesis Flood Narrative from the standpoint of contemporary discourse analysis" (p. 89). The article applies Longacre's theory to Genesis 6:9b-9:17, especially in terms of the eventline vs. supportive material, the peak episode (coinciding with the destruction by the flood as a remorseless mechanism of judgment) vs. prepeak and postpeak episodes, and embedded non-narrative material in God's speeches. Finally, he argues for the unity of the Flood narrative through its varied linguistic features as an elegantly structured text rather than being the result of editorial patchwork from different sources.

"Building for the worship of God: Exodus 25:1-30:10" (1995) appeared in *Discourse analysis of Biblical literature*, edited by biblical scholar W. Bodine and published by The Society of Biblical Literature. The articles in that book try to bring in theories of discourse analysis to the understanding of the Old Testament. Longacre states in his abstract that "contemporary textlinguistic methodology is brought to bear on these five and a half chapters" of Exodus. Describing instruction as a distinct type of discourse in biblical Hebrew, the author shows the discourse unity by positing macrostructure (the gist or abstract) and macrosegmentation, and presents the structure of the text progressing towards the peak.

The contemporary artistic and stylistic device of breaking off a story at a high suspension point is compared with breaks in Genesis in "Genesis as soap opera: some observations about storytelling in the Hebrew Bible" (1995). After Genesis 37 where Joseph is sold and goes to Egypt as a slave, the story is abruptly interrupted and we hear the story of Judah and Tamar in Genesis 38 before continuing on with Joseph from chapters 39 to 50. Two other places of discontinuity are also discussed: chapter 26 and chapter 14. Such discontinuities are viewed as the work of a superb storyteller, rather than the result of poor work by an author/editor. They are compared to the television dramas of today, which direct the viewers to put their questions on hold and tune in again next week.

Part III includes three articles relating to the Greek New Testament: 1 John, a hortatory text, Marks's gospel as a narrative in a holistic view, and Mark 5:1-43.

"Exhortation and mitigation in First John" (1983) was published as an issue of *Short Technical Articles related to Translation*. A shorter version with a slightly different focus was published in 1992 as "Towards an exegesis of 1 John based on the discourse analysis of the Greek text" in *Linguistics and New Testament interpretation*. It focuses on the surface structure clues to the natural outline structure of 1 John, clues such as the distribution of vocatives (e.g. 'beloved', 'little children') and the verb 'to write'. The longer study included in this volume presents both the discourse and paragraph level analyses directly using the Greek data. All sentences in the five chapters of 1 John are interconnected with the surrounding sentences, related to each other in ways such as 'thesis' and 'antithesis'. The epistle has been known to be notoriously difficult to outline, but Longacre shows natural seams, displayed in the data by presenting three main sections and subsections: Introduction (chapters 1-2), Body (3:1-5:12), and Closure (5:13:21). That this text is hortatory is an important basis for him for seeking the schema consisting of problem, command, and motivation. Two peaks, ethical and doctrinal, occur both in the long introduction and in the body in a chiastic, reverse order. Also presented is the chiastic structure found in 3:23, where the key of the chiasmus is the summary of the whole book: 'believe in Jesus Christ and love one another.' It is remarkable how he clearly leads us to come to the main theme and macrostructure of 1 John.

The next two articles are about Mark's Gospel, both published in *Discourse analysis and the New Testament* (1999) edited by biblical scholars Stanley Porter and Jeffrey Reed. The two articles are very different in kind. In "A top-down, template-driven narrative analysis, illustrated by application to Mark's Gospel," all sixteen chapters of the Mark's Gospel are analyzed into discourse-level slots on the narrative template from aperture and stage, to six episodes. Longacre points out that Episode 4 (8.27-9.50) is central and pivotal to the gospel with the theme, "Who is He?", while Episode 6 (11.1-16.8) includes both a didactic peak (11.12-13.37), dealing with Jesus' teachings amid controversy, and an action peak (chs. 14, 15, and 16.1-8) with events culminating in the crucifixion and resurrection. All episodes except the first (1.9-13) are shown to have layers of embedded structure with subepisodes. This paper is an excellent illustration of textlinguistic analysis showing the discourse organization of the gospel as a whole.

Whereas the above article shows the overview of the whole gospel, "Mark 5:1-43: generating the complexity of a narrative from its most basic elements" details how the parts of discourse need to be and can be analyzed at the interclausal level in stepped-in tree diagrams. Thus the diagram for the account of the healing of the Gadarene demoniac details how clauses and sentences in Mark 5.1-20 are combined in semantically distinct ways, e.g., evidence and conclusion, or plan and execution. Also included are dialogue relations such as IU (Initiating Utterance) and RU (Resolving Utterance) as a pair in a question and answer. Two intricately interwoven structures in Mark 5.21-43 are similarly analyzed where the story of the raising of Jairus's daughter is bracketing the story of the woman with the issue of blood. Finally, the article discusses how the stories can be generated from their abstracts, first starting with clauses having aorist verbs and then those with historical present and those with imperfects, resulting in a salience scheme of verbs and clauses in New Testament Greek.

Part IV includes two articles applying the theory to contemporary English, one to a hortatory text and the other to a narrative text. These two types of discourse selected here and in Part III are universal to all cultures. (It is difficult to imagine a group of people with no stories to tell or no advice to give. They are thus the most common in our everyday discourse and in the Bible.) Expository discourse (explaining themes and topics) and procedural discourse (featured in Part II with the text from Exodus) are rarer in comparison, and even more so in some cultures with no written form of language.

"The discourse strategy of an appeals letter" (1992) deals with a fund-raising letter from an organization called Zero Population Growth. The editors, William Mann and Sandra Thompson, solicited articles analyzing the same letter from different discourse analysts for their book *Discourse description: diverse linguistic analyses of a fund-raising text*. The result is the book with two sections (seven articles on text organization and five on lexico-grammatical approaches), which show how 'diverse' their analyses indeed are. The section on text organization allows the reader to readily compare diverse approaches, such as RST (Rhetorical Structure Theory), SSA (Semantic Structure Analysis), Longacre's theory, and a model with a complex network diagram (by Jordan). Longacre's article first discusses distinct discourse-type specific moves for five different discourse types. He develops his analysis based on the fact that the letter is of a hortatory type and that it has hortatory schema with three moves. The letter consisting of 30 segments (sentences and sentence fragments as given by the editors) is divided along natural seams into three paragraphs that correspond to the three moves of credibility claim, problem, and motivated appeal. Each paragraph/move is further analyzed as to how each sentence is grammatically and semantically related to the other in the microsegmentation analysis. Each move is shown to contribute to the macrostructure, the main message of the letter, which culminates in Segment 22: *Please make a special contribution to Zero Population Growth today*. It is remarkable to note that Longacre is the only author in the whole book to anchor his analysis on the type of discourse, which is hortatory. Other linguists, of course, noted that it is a fund-raising letter, but since a letter can be of any type of discourse, such as telling a story or urging you to act in a certain way, it is crucial to identify the particular discourse type in analyzing the tense or aspect, for example.

Fifteen years earlier, a book of similar type was published as the first volume in the Research in Text Theory series, *Grammars and descriptions: studies in text theory and text analysis*, edited by van Dijk and Petöfi 1977. The book has thirteen articles analyzing the same fable by James Thurber, *The lover and his lass*, a story that was distributed as the common text to be analyzed. It is noteworthy that Longacre was one of only four American linguists among the seventeen contributors mostly from Europe. The articles in the book are in English, German, and French. Only two linguists, Longacre and Halliday, are in both of these books separated by fifteen years.

"Holistic textlinguistics" (2004) presents an analysis of discourse and paragraph from a contemporary English novel, *The final diagnosis* by Arthur Hailey. Longacre argues that textlinguistics "knits up the many loose ends left from the morphosyntax" and is "the completion and fulfillment of linguistics." Again the emphasis is on the fact that a text is a *whole* (with concerns of text types, macrostructures, profiles, etc.) and that the textual concerns are interlaced with morphosyntactic features of the lower levels. The examples illustrate not only narrative paragraphs but also dialogue paragraphs which are analyzed with the methodology he has developed in terms of utterances (initiating, continuing, and resolving) and exchanges. The analyses at the local paragraph span are shown to be tied in with the narrative salience scheme for

English so that the thesis sentence that is dominant at the local span belongs to the highest level of salience at the discourse level.

For the final part, L'Envoi: broader horizons in the humanities, Longacre selected his article from 2000, "Some hermeneutic observations on textlinguistics and text theory in the humanities." This article discusses how textlinguistics and text theory can be applied to music, painting, and architecture. Just as texts have moves from introduction to climax and denouement, musical compositions have parts in sequence. They have a mainline of development in dominant musical themes and a background in echoes of variations. A painting as a whole has an overall macrostructure to which the details must conform, and it has a hierarchical, constituent structure. A building is similarly a cohesive whole with lines and details that support the main thrust. The keystone of an arch may be compared to the center of chiastic structure in literary text. He concludes that "the study of texts and the study of the arts can mutually illuminate each other."

There are fifteen of Robert Longacre's articles included in thi book. We note, however, that the book includes only a selection from a vast amount of research material he has published. We also note that he continues to present papers at conferences and write for journals and edited volumes.

We wish him to continue to have a healthy long and productive life!

References

Chafe, Wallace L. 1994. *Discourse, consciousness, and time.* Chicago: University of Chicago Press.
van Dijk, Teun A. and Janos Petöfi, eds. 1977. *Grammars and descriptions: studies in text theory and text analysis.* New York: W. de Gruyter. (Research in Text Theory, v. l.)
Givón, Talmy, ed. 1983. *Topic continuity in discourse.* Amsterdam: Benjamins.
Gundel, Jeanette K., Nancy Hedberg, and Ron Zacharski. 1993. Cognitive status and the form of referring expressions in discourse. *Language* 69:274–307.
Hopper, Paul J. and Sandra A.Thompson. 1980. Transitivity in grammar and discourse. *Language* 56:251–299.
Longacre, Robert E. 1952. Five phonemic pitch levels in Trique. *Acta Linguistica Academiae Scientarum Hungaricae* 7:62–81.
Longacre, Robert E. 1957. *Proto-Mixtecan.* Indiana University Research Center in Anthropology, Folklore and Linguistics Publication 5. International Journal of Linguistics 23:4, part 3.
Longacre, Robert E. 1976. "Mystery" particles and affixes. *Chicago Linguistic Society* 12: 468–475. Chicago: Chicago Linguistic Society.

Longacre, Robert E. 1985. Interpreting biblical stories. In Teun A. van Dijk (ed.), *Discourse and literature*, 169-185. Amsterdam: Benjamins.

Longacre, Robert E. 1992. Towards an exegesis of 1 John based on the discourse analysis of the Greek text. In David A. Black (ed.), *Linguistics and New Testament interpretation: essays on discourse analysis*, 271–286. Nashville: Broadman Press.

Longacre, Robert E. 1994. *Weqatal* forms in Biblical Hebrew prose: a discourse-modular approach. In Robert Bergen (ed.), *Biblical Hebrew and discourse linguistics*, 50–98. Dallas: Summer Institute of Linguistics.

Longacre, Robert E. 1996 [1st ed. 1983]. *The grammar of discourse*. 2nd ed. New York: Plenum Press.

Longacre, Robert E. 2003a [1st ed. 1989]. *Joseph, a story of divine providence: a text theoretical and textlinguistic analysis of Genesis 37 and 39–48*. 2nd ed. Winona Lake, IN: Eisenbrauns.

Longacre, Robert E. 2003b. Complementarity: verb types and discourse types in Biblical Hebrew. *LACUS Forum* 29:123–133.

Longacre, Robert E. 2003c. A textlinguistic analysis of Psalm 19: general and special revelation. In Mary Ruth Wise, Thomas N. Headland, and Ruth M. Brend (eds.), *Language and life: essays in memory of Kenneth L. Pike*, 383–393. Dallas: SIL International.

Longacre, Robert E. and Andrew Bowling. In press. *Discourse modular grammar of Biblical Hebrew*. Dallas: SIL international.

1

WHY WE NEED A VERTICAL REVOLUTION IN LINGUISTICS

Robert E. Longacre

The University of Texas at Arlington

and

The Summer Institute of Linguistics

    The word revolution is used here in the title of this paper to signify a radical reorientation in one's thinking in regard to a science or some other discipline. A favorite figure here is the replacement of the ptolemaic conception of the universe with the copernican conception, i.e., the replacement of an established theory in which the earth was the center of the universe with the theory in which the sun is the center at least of the solar system--only to be shown in turn that out solar system must take its place among many other systems in its galaxy and the galaxy must in turn take its place among the countless galaxies out in the depths of space. This radical reorientation of astronomy has been termed the copernican revolution.

    A good starting place here is to consider the practical outcome of what has been referred to as the Chomskyian revolution in linguistics. The foment which Noam Chomsky began in 1957 has now all but quieted down. Nevertheless, that the field was profoundly shaken by him and those associated with him, cannot be denied. What may be some of the abiding results of the Chomskyian revolution? 1) Chomsky banished the specter of naive empiricism. The latter was put to me in a sociology class in my college days years ago as "find, filter, focus, follow facts". There was a good deal of this naive empiricism in U.S. linguistics of the 1940's and early '50's. Chomsky replaced this attitude with the much more adequate point of view in which there was insistence that one must have a good theory of language before one can sit down to work on any given language or any part of a language. 2) The Chomskyian approach made syntax feasible for the rank and file of linguists where it had not been feasible before.[1] I recall a remark of George Lane's in the early 1950's "Syntax--that stepchild of descriptive linguistics". In those days prior to the mid-fifties, a structural grammar of an American Indian language typically consisted of phonology and morphology with maybe two or three pages on syntax at the end of the entire volume. Nobody knew how to handle syntax in those days. 3) The Chomskyian revolution left behind it the ideal of explanatory power, i.e., we should not simply describe a language, but we should explain its features in some insightful way.

Nevertheless, there were some serious blind spots in the Chomskyian framework. These as a whole were blind spots that he inherited from Bloomfield and never challenged. For this reason, Talmy Givon (unpublished materials) has recently fallen to talking about the "Crypto-Bloomfieldian nature of Chomskyian linguistics".

The greatest of these hangups inherited from Bloomfield was inherent in the definition of grammar as a device for generating sentences. This perpetuated the Bloomfieldian blindspot in which the independence of the sentence from its context was over emphasized. Thus Bloomfield said, "It is evident that the sentences in any utterance are marked off by the mere fact that each sentence is an independent linguistic form, not included by virtue of any grammatical construction in any larger linguistic form." (1933, p. 170) This definition effectively ruled out the possibility of grammar beyond the sentence.

There were, nevertheless, occasional voices raised against this Bloomfieldian-Chomskyian restriction. In Europe there was a triangle of interaction between Prague school linguists, the Danish linguist Louis Hjelmslev, and the British linguist Rupert Firth, all of which had a certain interest in the analysis of text. Early American structuralists occasionally published an analyzed text. Unfortunately, however, this was almost exclusively an accounting for the morphological structure of words in the discourse and no attempt was made to explain the structure of the discourse itself. Zellig Harris in the late 40's evolved a methodology which he called discourse analysis (1952, 1957, 1963) which got at the content structure of a discourse but did not really approach its grammar. All these treatments of text left something to be desired.

A new beginning was made in 1958 when a young man fresh from the jungles of Peru, Jim Loriot, wrote an article "Shipibo Paragraph Structure". This was a genuine piece of discourse grammar. It discussed ties of various sorts which gave cohesion to the discourse and features which mark beginning and end of paragraphs. The article, unfortunately, was not published until 1970 when it appeared as a joint article with Barbara Hollenbach. Nevertheless, Loriot's article influenced many people who were studying South American Indian languages at that time. Meanwhile, Pike was insisting that we can and should go beyond the sentence (1964) and in the same year Gleason wrote a very significant article in which he stated that the grammar of a Papua New Guinea language, Kate, could better be written as a discourse grammar than as a sentence grammar. I myself got into discourse research in 1965 when three colleagues who were students of Totonac and I began to study Totonac discourse (Reid and others, 1968). This led in turn to field workshops which I held in the Philippines (1967-68), Papua New Guinea (1970), and Colombia (1974-75).

Kenneth L. Pike was also holding workshops abroad in which discourse was featured, especially in Africa (1965-66), and in India-Nepal (1972). All this rather extensive fieldwork was showing the feasibility of discourse grammars-although the right questions were not necessarily coming to the fore. Grimes in his National Science Foundation program in which he visited Brazil, Papua New Guinea, and the Philippines in the same year (1970-71) was zeroing in on some of the basic questions better than the rest of us, I feel.

Meanwhile, in Europe, men educated in the formalism of the transformational generative approach and of generative semantics in particular were getting interested in discourse. I note especially here van Dijk in Amsterdam, Petöfi in Biefield (West Germany) and Dressler in Vienna. A belated contribution was Prop's work which although written much earlier (1928) was not translated into English until 1958. Inspired by this and other sources, the tradition of European structuralism arose--although somewhat out of the domain of linguistics proper.

I think that much of the work cited above can be considered the opening guns of a revolution whose thesis can be stated as follows: It is not simply that systematic analysis and study of units larger than the sentence is possible, nor even that such analysis is desirable, but rather that discourse analysis is a rock bottom necessity, i.e., all linguistic structure must ultimately be related to the structure of context. In brief, to a text linguist or a discourse grammarian of this persuasion, discourse analysis is not a luxury but a necessity. It is something which we have done without too long to the detriment and impairment of the whole field.

1. In this section I want to go into the matter of tasks that a discourse grammar can accomplish that a sentence grammar cannot accomplish. Before going into this I want to pay respects to the ambiguity of the term grammar. Grammar can be used to refer to the whole study of a language in all of its aspects, or it can be used in reference to grammar proper. I intend to use it in the second sense here. Nevertheless, while I do not go into phonology in this paper, it is instructive to note what happened in the phonology of the 1940's and early 50's in the U.S., i.e., in the heyday of Bloch-Trager and Trager-Smith linguistics. An attempt was made to analyze the phonology of a language as a simple linear sequence of phonemes. In order to make this work there was resort to juncture phonemes to account for seams of phonological units, such as the syllable, phonological words, phonological clauses and sentences, and even the intonational run down found at the end of paragraphs and discourses. Here there were many clues that the phonology of a language was not a simple linear sequence, but rather involved pyramiding units in phonological hierarchy so that in the end the study of phonological context was of the greatest importance. We might too notice that, as argued by van Dijk, assignment of intonation and stress is

impossible to a sentence without taking account of its context.

We may also while we are at it think in terms of the problem of lexical structure. It seems well established by now that a lexical item has meaning only in context and that its meaning is to a large degree a function of its interplay with context. This is so strong that it can be rationally argued that the meaning of a word is not deducible within the boundaries of single sentences.

2. Now in regard to grammar proper I want to especially show some of the tasks that a sentence grammar cannot do and which require the contruction of discourse grammars.

2.1 Definitivization and use of deictics

To put this as a question, when do we say a dog, when do we say the dog, and when do we say that dog, and what is the function of a, the, and that in sentences within English? Obviously, we need context to account for the meaning and function of these words. Consider the following three sentence sequence: As I stepped out of my front door, I saw a dog coming down the sidewalk. Before I knew what was happening the dog had bitten me. That dog, I learned later, had bitten three people before I came on the scene. Here we see that the dog is introduced with the indefinite article as object in the first sentence. Already, however, by the second sentence this participant has become thematic and as such is now referred to as the dog. In the third sentence the speaker of the paragraph makes a comment regarding the dog, which has already been identified and made thematic. In making this comment he refers to him as that dog--since this is an appropriate structure in such comments. Here we've had to use a three sentence sequence to explain varied handlings of the same noun in terms of the meaning and function of accompanying articles and deictics.

Patterns of this sort can be highly language specific--even if certain overall universal features are found. Thus for Bahasa Indonesian Don Barr (1976) says that three steps are necessary to establish a participant in a Bahasa Indonesian narrative discourse. "1) A participant is introduced by formula: se-orang, 'one-person', plus noun phrase, often further described in clauses introduced by yang (a relative particle). 2) The next reference is usually by noun phrase plus ini ('this'). 3) A further reference is by noun phrase plus itu ('that')." Thus, in a narrative about a woman's falling into the hands of thieves, she is first introduced as

se-orang	perempuan	yang	berbadan	kecil	molek	berdandan
one-person (num. class. for people)	female	who	had body	small	pretty	dressed

bagus	dan	beperhiasan	cukup,
well	and	wearing jewelry	enough

After being referred to as above in the first sentence of the discourse, in the next sentence she is referred to as

<u>perempuan yang baru datang ini,</u>
woman   who   just came   this

and later on in the same sentence is referred to as

<u>perempuan itu.</u>
woman   that

In these three stages the woman is established as a major participant in the narrative. English does this in two stages, <u>a dog</u> and <u>the dog</u>. In Bahasa Indonesian it is a three stage affair with the demonstratives not being saved for special functions such as narrator comment (as in English). Continuing further references to a participant such as the one introduced above is varied and consists of pronouns, noun phrase plus <u>itu</u>, affixing of -<u>nya</u> to the participant, and use of certain further particles. It is not within the scope of this paper to go into these matters in detail, but they can be accounted for by resort to the on-going structure of the discourse.

2.2 Pronominalization

The linguist is considerably cramped when he tries to explain the occurrence of pronouns within the limits of a single sentence, although some very important work has been done in this direction by such people as Langacker within the transformational generative tradition. The difficulty is that pronominalization chains commonly run through several sentences. Furthermore, the paragraph is the natural unit of such anaphoric chaining in English. Thus, we may start off with <u>John Smith</u> and have in successive sentences <u>he, his, him</u>, down to the end of the paragraph, while sometimes the pronominalization chain may continue across the paragraph boundary, although it is not at all uncommon for the noun to be reintroduced at the onset of a new paragraph.[2]

One rather puzzling phenomenon in English and a phenomenon which cannot be accounted for at all within the boundaries of a single sentence is that of backward pronominalization. Thus, when is it appropriate to say <u>When he came to power, Augustus</u>. . . versus <u>When Augustus came to power, he</u>. . .? There certainly is no ambiguity in either case, but again we must appeal to the context to know which to use. Robert Kantor (1976) has recently pointed out that if we say <u>When he came to power, Augustus</u>. . . we then proceed in this sentence and in the following sentences to establish <u>Augustus</u> as thematic. We talk about what he has done or what he did while he had the power. If, on the other hand, we say <u>When Augustus came to power, he</u>. . ., we proceed not to make Augustus thematic in the paragraph, but rather some other noun, i.e., his, works, his program, the progress of the empire under him, etc.

In languages other than English, i.e., in languages where there is an indication of the person and number (and even sometimes of the gender) of the subject on the verb itself, pronouns are not used at all in the way that they are used in English. Pronouns are simply not needed for continuing participant reference. Rather, pronouns when used, have other more specialized functions such as topicalization and contrast. Thus, if one takes a short story in Spanish and compares it with a good translation of the same story in English one finds at least four times as many pronouns indicating subject in the English version as one finds in the Spanish version.

Spanish has however, frequent use of pronouns to indicate direct and indirect objects in conjunction with the verb. One has to look at non-Indo-European languages which mark faithfully person, number (and sometimes gender) of both subject and object to find examples of systems which get on with even less use of pronouns. Such a language is Totonac of Mexico (data from Aileen Reid). In Totonac pronouns are not used at all as in English, i.e., they are not used for continuing anaphoric reference. This is taken care of rather by features of the verb morphology. Instead, Totonac uses pronouns for special function and in fact such special function is almost entirely limited to the vicinity of quotations and the quote formulas which accompany them. If a narrative has no reported speech or dialogue it will get on without pronouns. If it has reported speech and dialogue then it will employ pronouns extensively. The use of the pronouns will correlate with such factors as relative emotional intensity of the dialogue, dominance of one speaker over the other, and marking of thematic participant in the dialogue paragraph.

Guambiano of Colombia (data from Thomas Branks) is a further example of a language which uses pronouns in a very different way from English. Guambiano, like so many languages of the same area of the world, keeps track of same subject versus different subject in successive clauses, whether in or across sentence boundaries by affixes on the verb. In a simple narrative discourse with two participants (i.e., a protagonist and an antagonist) one and only one participant is referred to pronominally. If it is a first person narrative, the narrator refers to himself as 'I'; if it is a third person narrative, the central participant (the protagonist) is referred to in a third person pronoun. Very important, however, to the structure of such Guambiano narratives is the relative directness of the narrative. Thus, if the person narrating the story heard it from another person, then the 'I''s of the original story will become third person in the narrator's version of the story. This transformation of first to third person is not entirely complete, however, in that there is an occasional use of first person in a structure that is somewhat intermediate between a direct and an indirect quote. If, on the other hand, the story is third or fourth hand, the first person pronoun will not occur at all--unless in a direct quote--and the third pronoun will refer only to the central character, i.e., in such a story the central character will be referred to by third person pronoun and the antagonist will be referred to entirely by noun and never pronominalized. So it is evident that in Guambiano to use pronouns correctly one must know the slate of participants for a discourse--with identification of the central character within that slate of participants--and one must also know the relative closeness of the narrator to the events which he is retelling.

2.3 Use of tense, aspect, mode, and voice

While the preceding two considerations deal with details of participant reference, and hence with the use of noun and pronoun in connected discourse, the present section deals with features of verb structure and their relation to context.

The analysis of verb morphology in a language which is under study for the first time may be a formidable and time consuming job. Sorting out the markers of the various tenses, aspects, and modes, the various allomorphs of each marker, as well as the co-occurrence privileges of these morphemes and allomorphs can be a long and difficult task. When such analysis is complete, one is presumably able to form correctly the verb structures of the language. But then the further question arises 'When does one use one form in preference to another?' While one can learn something from this by the study of isolated sentences, an adequate understanding of the uses of various forms of the verb in a given language must take into account structures other than those found within a single sentence.

This is true even of a language such as English which has a relatively simple tense-aspect-mood system. Compare the following paragraph of a contemporary novel (The Final Diagnosis, Arthur Hailey, p. 31):

> Now McNeil slipped on his own gloves and went to work with Pearson. By this time, moving swiftly, the older man had peeled back the chest flap and, hacking the flesh loose with a larger knife, exposed the ribs. Next, using the sharp levered rib cutters, he cut his way into the rib cage, exposing pericardium and lungs. The gloves, instruments, and table were now beginning to be covered with blood. Seddons, gloved also, on his side of the table, was cutting back the lower flaps of flesh and opening the abdomen. He crossed the room for a pail and began to remove stomach and intestines, which he put into the pail after studying them briefly. The odor was beginning to be noticeable. Now Pearson and Seddons together tied off and cut the arteries so the undertaker would have no trouble when it came to embalming. Taking a small tube from a rack above the table, Seddons turned

on a tap and began to siphon blood that had escaped into
the abdomen and, after a nod from Pearson, did the same
thing for the chest.

A variety of tense forms are used in the above paragraph:
past, past progressive, pluperfect, conditionals which refer to
the future, participles, gerunds, and infinitives. Of these
tenses, however, there is a position of privilege given to the
past tense. In English as in many other languages, there is a
special tense in which a story is customarily told. In English
(aside from use of the historic present in special discourses and
special contexts within discourses) a story is customarily told in
the past tense. The past tense forms can be considered therefore
to be the backbone of English narration. Thus, in the above paragraph this backbone or event line is marked by the verbs <u>slipped</u>,
<u>went</u> (to work), <u>cut</u>, <u>crossed</u>, <u>began</u> (to remove), <u>put, tied off</u>,
<u>cut, turned on, began</u> (to siphon), and <u>did</u>. The other tenses that
occur are doing more specialized jobs. Thus, pluperfects mark
activities and events that occurred earlier in the procedure and
which now are reported out of chronological sequence: <u>The older
man had peeled back the chest flap. . .and (had) exposed the ribs.</u>
And <u>later in the paragraph: . . .Seddons. . .began to siphon blood
that had escaped into the abdomem.</u> The past progressives mark
concomitant happenings and activities: <u>The gloves, instruments,
and table were now beginning to be covered with blood. Seddons. .
.was cutting back the lower flaps of flesh and was opening the
abdomen. . .The odor was beginning to be noticeable.</u> One sentence
contains references to a course of action which is future in reference to the procedure described in the paragraph (an autopsy):
<u>. . .so the undertaker would have no trouble when it came to em-
balming.</u> Here the grammar of the language requires a modified
future <u>would have</u> and a subjunctive which is homophonous with the
past, <u>came</u>. A few participles and gerunds (all -<u>ing</u> forms) round
out the sentences of the paragraph: <u>moving, hacking, using, ex-
posing, studying, embalming</u>--as well as some infinitives. These
verbals (non-finite forms) act as attributives, nominals, and
verb complements within the sentences where they are found.

In analyzing such paragraphs as above the crucial move is,
however, to identify the backbone or event line as opposed to
other parts of the narrative. Tense does not, however, do this
trick too well in English. Particularly diagnostic of background
and descriptive material in many languages is use of the verb <u>to
be</u> even if in past tense, i.e., even if in the regular form of the
event line verb. Furthermore, even though background verbs can be
past progressive, there are some verbs which reject this form even
when background. For example, we get <u>he knew</u> rather than <u>he was
knowing</u> and <u>he felt</u> rather than <u>he was feeling</u>. There is therefore some residual ambiguity in the use of such a verb as <u>he knew</u>,
i.e., does the writer or speaker mean <u>he came to know, he realiz-
ed</u>, or is he describing a state of mind? Conceivably, coming to
know something could be an important event in a story.

Longacre WHY WE NEED A VERTICAL REVOLUTION IN LINGUISTICS   255

Latin, Greek, Romance, and Slavic use tense/aspect in a more consistent way than English to distinguish backbone versus background. Wallace Reid (1976) and P. Hopper (1977) have pointed out that the function of the much discussed French imperfect is to background non-event line material. Hopper has further pointed out that this is the regular function of imperfects or imperfectives in such languages as those cited above.

Consider the following rather lengthy passage from Spanish (Cervantes, in Flores, 1960, p. 64-66).

En Toledo, una noche de las calurosas del verano, regresaban de dar un paseo cerca del río, un anciano hidalgo con su mujer, un niño pequeño, una hija de edad de diez y seis años, y una criada. La noche era clara, la hora las once y el camino solitario. Con la seguridad que promete la mucha justicia y la bien intencionada gente de aquella ciudad, venía el buen hidalgo con su honrada familia sin temor de que le pudiera ocurrir nada malo. Sin embargo en aquel momento coincidió en pasar por allí un mancebo de aquella ciudad, llamado Rodolfo, de unos veinte y dos años de edad, cuya riqueza, viles instintos, sangre ilustre, demasiada libertad y malos compañeros, le habían estimulado a hacer cosas que desdecían de su calidad y le daban renombre de atrevido. Rodolfo, pues, con cuatro amigos, todos mozos, todos alegres y todos insolentes, bajaba por la misma cuesta que el hidalgo subía--así es que las ovejas se encontraron con los lobos.

Con deshonesta desenvoltura Rodolfo y sus camaradas, cubiertos los rostros, miraron los de la madre, y de la hija, y de la criada. El viejo se alborotó y les reprochó su atrevimiento. Ellos le respondieron con muecas y burlas, y pasaron adelante. Pero aquel rostro tan hermoso de Leocadia, que así se llamaba la hija, despertó en Rodolfo tal deseo de gozarla que en un instante comunicó su pensamiento a sus camaradas que en seguida decidieron volver y robarla para darle gusto a su amigo; pues siempre los ricos por ser ricos hallan quien apruebe sus desafueros y califique por buenos sus malos gustos. Cubriéronse los rostros y, desenvainadas las espadas, volvieron y pronto alcanzaron al hidalgo y su familia que habían acabado de dar gracias a Dios por haberlos librados de las manos de aquellos atrevidos. Arremetió Rodolfo con Leocadia y, cogiéndola en brazos, huyó con ella.

In the above passage, noting the distribution of preterites or simple past tense versus other types of tense, we can see at a glance that the first paragraph is mainly background material, while the second features events. Thus, in the first paragraph there are only two simple past tenses occurring about paragraph medial and at the end of the paragraph: coincidió (en pasar) 'chanced (to pass)' and se encontraron 'met up with'. Imperfects in this paragraph describe the background: regresaban 'were returning', era 'was', venía 'was coming', desdecían 'detracted', daban 'gave', bajaba 'was going down', subía 'was going up'. There is one pluperfect in the paragraph habían estimulado 'had provoked' which refers to incidents in the life of Rodolfo before this story starts. There is a present tense promete early in the paragraph which makes a general statement as to the security of the city. There is a past subjunctive form pudiera 'could' which is appropriate to its immediate context.

By contrast with the above paragraph, much is going on in the part of the second paragraph which is reported here. There are a great many verbs which refer to event line material: miraron 'looked on', alborotó 'got indignant', reprochó 'scolded', respondieron 'answered', pasaron 'passed on', despertó 'aroused', comunicó 'told', decidieron 'decided', cubrieronse 'covered', volvieron 'returned', alcanzaron 'caught up with', arremetió 'siezed', huyó 'fled'. Only one imperfect occurs: se llamaba 'was named' in an obvious aside from the story line. A pluperfect occurs to mark an action again reported out of chronological sequence: habían acabado 'had finished (giving thanks to God for delivering them)'. Again a present tense occurs in a general statement which is an author comment: hallan 'find'(in the statement 'thus the rich always find those who will approve of their misdeeds and account as good their bad actions'). A couple of subjunctives appropriate to the local context occur in the sentence just referred to. Notice it is the movement of the story and the type of information involved that dictates the choice of tenses here even to a greater degree than in English.

As to the school book definition of the imperfect as continuous action in past time, while this is a frequent function of the imperfect, in that it describes material off the event line, such a definition by no means summarizes all uses of the imperfect in narrative. Consider the following brief passage from a short story (L'aventure de Walter Schnaffs) by de Maupassant in French.

> Soudain quelque chose remua contre lui. Il eut un sursaut épouvantable. C'était un petit oiseau qui, s'étant posé sur une branche, agitait des feuilles mortes. Pendant près d'une heure, le coeur de Walter Schnaffs en battit à grands coups pressés.

In this paragraph, the verbs in the passé simple, which marks the backbone of the discourse, are remua, eut, and battit. The verbs était and agitait in the imperfect fulfill their customary function of background material, i.e., they fill in the reader as to the nature of the event which so startled the character in the story. Notice, however, the inadequacy of attempting to define

Longacre WHY WE NEED A VERTICAL REVOLUTION IN LINGUISTICS 257

the choice of tense in the above passage in terms of the type of activity, i.e., punctiliar versus continued activity. The imperfect verb agitait does not necessarily indicate a continued action. On the other hand, the passé simple verb battit in the last line certainly represents an action which went on for some time, because we are told very explicitly that 'for the better part of an hour the heart of Walter Schnaffs beat in great hurried strokes'.

The need for a discourse oriented theory of tense/aspect is even more acute in languages with more complicated systems of tense/aspect than are found in most European languages. Thus, in the Camsa language of Colombia, Linda Howard (Longacre and Woods, 1977.2.273-296) reports three distinct forms of past tense verbs. This distinction correlates with the distribution of these forms in the backbone material of three distinct types of narrative. In the legend narrative, which deals with events in the remote past, background verbs are prefixed with yoj-. In the historic narrative, which deals with events within the recollectable past, backbone verbs have toj. . .an- prefixes. In the contemporary narrative, backbone verbs have toj- prefixes. Quite distinct from all these verb forms which are found in the backbone of narrative discourses, is the type of verb found in procedural discourse, whether giving how something was done in orderly stages or how it is to be done in orderly stages. Verbs in the backbone of discourses such as these have prefixes j. . .na- and are termed by Howard 'infinitives'. It is also possible to specify to some degree the type of material which is found in non-backbone material in Camsa as well, but I cannot go into detail here. Suffice it to say that what marks the backbone in one discourse type may prove to be off the backbone in another discourse type.

The matter of distribution of voice also calls for a discourse interpretation. While there have been many ingenious suggestions made for the meaning and function of passive voice in English, the simplest and most adequate one has to do with the needs to preserve thematicity in discourse, i.e. the twin stratagems of (1) making what would have been the object the subject of a passive verb (and hence thematic) and (2) the desire to omit mention of the agent (who is presumably non-thematic).

While English uses genuine passive voice to preserve thematicity, a language such as Totonac (data from Reid) in Mexico uses an affix which suppresses the identity of the subject so that in effect we have 'someone did this' or 'someone did that'. Thus the Totonac suffix -ca/-can is of paramount importance in matters of establishing and preserving thematicity in Totonac discourse.

The moral of all this is that the study of the distribution and function of tense, aspect, mode, and voice in discourse can enable us to come up with a theory of considerable explanatory power. The various forms of verbs can be shown to be subservient to the needs of discourse and occasioned by those needs.

2.4 Word order phenomena

Word order variation within a language cannot be adequately described without resort to discourse considerations. That this is true has been evidenced in the work of Prague school linguists such as Firbas and Daneš for some time (Daneš, 1974). They have shown that in some languages such as Czech there is a distribution of elements in the clause according to the amount of 'communicative dynamism' that each part of the clause conveys. The less dynamic parts are put earlier in the clause and the more dynamic are put later. Thus old information regularly goes in the beginning of the clause and new information toward the end, according to the familiar theme-rheme division of these linguists. Obviously, whether one knows whether a given item is old information or new information or whether a certain item is relatively important or less important to the communication situation requires resort to context.

Most Otomanguean languages of Mexico have a basic VSO word order with a possibility of rotating either subject or object to the fore of the verb. Obviously the permutation of the noun phrase to the fore of the verb has some sort of topicalization or thematization function. It is, however, quite rare in some languages and reserved for special purposes. Thus in Trique a frequent use of the preposed noun phrase is to highlight some unexpected participant. There is a text where a man is pushed into an underground pit by his wife and stays there for seven years. Suddenly we are told that crows lowered him down things to eat--and 'crows' is moved to the fore of the verb. It is evident here that the crows constitute a minor participant in the discourse in that they are mentioned only in this clause and nowhere else in the entire story. Furthermore, when first mentioned here they are entirely rhematic and new. In fact this passage may even be a digression from the event line of the story--a digression whose purpose is to tell how the man managed to eat during the years of his being in the pit. At any rate, it does not seem to carry the event line of the story forward. Further on in the story, the man's rescuer appears and asks him how he came to be in the cave. The man answers 'it was my <u>wife</u> who brought me here and left me'. The fronting of the word 'wife' here both harks back to an earlier stage of the story and also in the context of quotation in which it occurs highlights the wife in a rather unwonted and surprising role, i.e., it is not (fortunately) the usual thing for wives to attempt to murder their husbands.

There are certain Cayapa texts (language of Ecuador, data from Neil Wiebe) which show still another function of word order permutations. Cayapa is an SOV language, like most of the languages of this part of South America. There is a series of texts in which various animals one by one beat the tiger in various contests. The animals are all unlikely victors such as a fly, a snail, etc. These texts are essentially two participant stories. In such stories rather consistently the tiger or his protagonist are moved to a position following the verb. What is interesting in these discourses is the fact that usually the protagonist of the tiger is rotated to the post verb position early in the discourse while the tiger himself crops up in post verb position late in the discourse. The permutation seems to have to do with which is featured as the under dog in the conflict. As long as the tiger is the aggressor (and because of his weight and ferocity the probable victor), it is his protagonist who is featured in post verbal. But as soon as the tide begins to turn, and the tiger is to be defeated, then the tiger himself will crop up in post verbal position. In one or two of these discourses at the point where the conflict is squarely joined, both participants are permuted to post verbal so that in place of the SOV order which is normative, we get a VOS order. In such cases there is a special phonological juncture after the VO and before the S--a feature which labels this as an unusual word order.

Hopper in a recent paper (1977) has made some very interesting observations about event line versus supportive material in Anglo Saxon and has shown how this is marked by word order. Event line clauses are those in which the verb is peripheral to the clause, i.e., it is either initial or final. This, I assume, means that we find event line clauses to be either VSO or SOV. Background material, however, has the subject before the verb and presumably includes SVO clauses. Of interest here is the fact that the chain of backbone clauses begins with the VSO order and evidently continues with the SOV order. Here we have a way in which the beginning of a chain of clauses is marked with a special structure in the initial clause. It is the converse of languages of Papua New Guinea and many at the northern tip of South America where we find a special kind of verb (often called the 'final verb') which marks the end of a chain of clauses.

Hebrew presents a further variation on word order conditioned by discourse considerations. Hebrew has a special event line form of the verb, the so-called waw- consecutive which has been recognized since 1910 by Gesenius (p. 326) as a narrative tense. When this tense is used, the word order is VSO or occasionally VOS. What this backbone tense does not tolerate is the preposing of any noun to the verb. When any noun is preposed to the verb, we must revert to some other tense. My own studies in Hebrew discourse of the Old Testament (Longacre, 1976a, 1977) have convinced me that the clauses which have initial nouns (whether subject or object) are off the event line of a story. Thus we find VSO order (or occasionally VOS) on the event line, but SVO or OVS off the event line. The distinction correlates with what was called by the Arab grammarians nominal clauses versus verbal clauses, i.e., the verbal clause has an initial verb and a nominal clause has an initial noun. In terms of the dynamics of narrative discourse, a clause with an initial verb is featuring the action and is on the event line, while a clause with an initial noun is featuring some participant and is a digression from the event line in order to talk about that participant.

2.5 Use of location and temporal expressions

Attention in the above section has centered in the positions of verb, subject, and object relative to each other. Obviously, clauses have other elements as well, not the least of which are expressions of location and time. We may consider that the verb, subject, and object are nuclear to the clause and that the location and temporal expressions (along with such further units as manner) are optional and peripheral. But to call them optional obscures entirely their discourse function. In terms of the function of connected discourse, such phrases are not optional, but are called for at certain places in the discourse.

Thus, temporal expressions may serve to move a discourse forward in time as a story sweeps through progressive time horizons. Similarly, a series of locational expressions may indicate a trajectory of a travelogue or the march of an army. In either case, whether a series of successive times are indicated in various parts of the discourse, or a series of locations, such elements belong to the fundamental framework of the entire discourse and occur in various component clauses of that discourse as the design of the whole requires their occurrence.

2.6 Uses of adverbial clauses

In most languages subordinate clauses which are adverbial in thrust occur along with the independent clauses on which they depend (cf. Thompson and Longacre, 1978). Some of these clauses are preposed to the main clause, others are postposed. A few such clauses in discourse have merely local relevance, i.e., they have to do only with the sentence in which they are found and add to that sentence some detail, but are not echoed or referred to elsewhere in the entire discourse. For example, in a scientific essay adverbial clauses which are chiefly bibliographical in reference, are of this nature, e.g., <u>as X (date) has shown</u>, or as <u>X and Y (date) have observed</u>. On the other extreme from this, some adverbial clauses function clearly to preserve discourse movement and perspective. Thus in a travel book on Mexico adverbial clauses in various functions are used by the author to constantly remind the reader of the you-are-on-a-journey perspective of the entire discourse. Thus we have adverbial clauses like <u>as you walk through these huge chambers</u>, after seeing this underground fairyland, <u>as your car moves on</u>, wherever you go in Taxco, <u>as you browse about the village</u>, and as <u>you prowl up and down the narrow streets</u>. These adverbial clauses and other similar features of the discourse serve to preserve the pseudo-procedural form of the whole, i.e., the discourse is given as if you were on a guided tour through the regions and towns which are mentioned.

Adverbial clauses may also be used to give cohesion between successive paragraphs of a discourse. A frequent device here is what might be called tail-head linkage, i.e., something mentioned in the last sentence of the preceding paragraph is referred to by means of backreference in an adverbial clause in the following paragraph. Thus one paragraph might end, <u>Finally, exahusted with trying to figure the situation out,</u> John drifted off to sleep. The next paragraph might begin, <u>When he had been asleep only a short time</u>. . . Very similar to this is summary head linkage, i.e., the first sentence of a successive paragraph has a clause which summarizes the preceding paragraph. Thus one paragraph may involve description of a variety of activities and the next paragraph may begin <u>When he had done all these things</u> or something to that effect. Or we may be in an explanatory discourse where an argument is presented in one paragraph and the following paragraph begins <u>As the preceding argument indicates</u>.

Especially relevant is the function of adverbial clauses in connecting sentences within the same paragraph. Here there is such a variety of connections that we can give only a brief sample of a few possibilities. A backreference by means of a when clause may serve to connect a sentence to previous context in the same paragraph. In many languages of the Philippines and Papua New Guinea the use of such backreference is so common that each successive sentence in a sequence paragraph builds on the preceding by some such device as 'having x-ed', or 'when he had x-ed', or 'after he had x-ed, he y-ed'. English has such a variety of conjunctions that is not as dependent on backreference as are some languages in other areas of the world. It therefore uses backreference with much more discrimination. A backreference in an English paragraph is more likely to mark something special, often the climactic sentence of the paragraph.

In the same way, a while clause may be used in the ensuing sentence to refer back to the preceding sentence and thereby make the action of both sentences simultaneous. Thus we have a paragraph like: <u>Mary came home, put the hamburgers on to fry, put the french fries to warm in the oven, and set the tea kettle on the back of the stove. While doing all this she kept nervously watching the clock</u>. Here the <u>While doing all this</u>, summarizes the actions described in the preceding sentence. Cause clauses can be used for similar linkage in sentences, e.g., what is expressed in a cause clause in the first sentence, can be amplified in the following sentence, as in the following paragraph translated from Dibabawon: 'But it was the same as if he had recovered from his illness, because he became famous by riding in an airplane. There is no other old man who has ridden in an airplane; he's the only one.' Here the second sentence amplifies 'because he became famous by riding in an airplane' of the first sentence.

While this is but a sampling of the function of adverbial clauses in providing various sorts of cohesion within discourse, these examples should serve to make the point that if we are to understand the function of adverbial clauses we must look at more than isolated sentences, but must see their function in on-going contexts.

2.7 Sequence signals and conjunctions

It seems evident that conjunctions and sequence signals, whose job is to fit a sentence or a sequence of sentences into a broader context, can never be explained simply as part of the sentence to which they happen to belong. Indeed it may be argued that they are mainly phonologically part of their sentences more than grammatically part of them and that they more properly belong to the larger context. English has not only such conjunctions as <u>and</u>, <u>but</u>, <u>however</u>, <u>nevertheless</u>, and <u>therefore</u> which serve to fit sentences into context, but also many other signals (often phrasal, or sentence adverbs) such as <u>obviously</u>, <u>on the other hand</u>, <u>alternatively</u>, <u>consequently</u>, etc.

An experiment of mine several years ago in generating a discourse from its abstract (Longacre 1976b) was very instructive in regard to the role of conjunctions in discourse. I first reduced a short text to its general idea, which I expressed as a line of symbolic logic. Then I tried to generate the entire discourse from this abstract by a set of ordered generative rules. In my first compilation I generated each sentence more or less indepently of the others and I left for a later stage the job of conjunction insertion. I found to my consternation, however, that it was impossible to insert the conjunction at a later stage of the rules--since I had not already provided for their introduction earlier. I had to go back then and provide for conjunction insertion very early in the generation of the component paragraphs of the discourse. Conjunctions, then, are no trivial additions to a paragraph and certainly are not after thoughts. They belong to the central structure of paragraph and discourse.

2.8 Nominalization and topicalization

Most languages provide ways to nominalize a verb or for that matter a whole clause. Languages differ greatly, however, in the frequency and function of nominalization. Thus, in English discourse sometimes the purpose of nominalization seems to be to shunt something off the event line or to in some way push it away from the spotlight. In keeping with this it is not to be wondered at that backreference in English sentences often prefers a nominalized form of the verb to a full verb. Thus we may have a two sentence sequence <u>John took off in his piper cub promptly at 9:00 a.m.</u> The next sentence may go on to say <u>After he took off he noticed that the engine of the plane was not acting normal.</u> But it seems somewhat more frequent and natural in English to use such nominalizations as <u>After taking off</u>. . . or <u>After the take off</u>. ... or even <u>While in flight</u>. . . than to use the finite verb

After he took off. . . for the backreference.

The function of nominalization in the Tucanoan languages of Colombia is very different, however. In these languages nominalization is not as common as in English and when it does occur, its function is not to shunt an event away from the spotlight, but to spotlight it. In keeping with this Nate Waltz (1976) notes that we often find nominalization at the peak of a story, i.e., at its high point.

Nominalization sometimes appears to be especially characteristic of certain genres in a language. Thus an Aguaruna expository discourse has as its backbone nominalized forms. To quote Larson (1978, 133), "The classifiers form the backbone of the network. Actually they may be actors, i.e., they classify a thing as having the characteristics of a certain action. In the surface they are realized by nominal forms, even though an action is referred to. It seems clear, after studying numerous expository texts in Aguaruna, that the deep structure concept is that of 'one who does such and such' and therefore the term classifier." Similarly, in Tarahumara expository and procedural discourse (data from Don Burgess) we also find nominalized forms of verbs to be an important part of the backbone structure.

Topicalization devices, while they have been described in detail for some time in contemporary linguistics, have lacked explanation as to contextual appropriateness. Thus, why is it strategic at a certain point in a travelogue discourse to say, <u>It was Cortez who discovered the silver and started the mines which made this village thrive and still keep it going,</u> rather than just saying Cortez discovered the silver and started the mines. .? Why is it similarly appropriate in the following paragraph to say <u>But it was José de la Borda who made a real town out of the mining camp of Cortez's day</u>. . .and in the next sentence of the same paragraph <u>It was also Borda who built the huge church whose twin spires tower above all the other village buildings?</u> It seems that in the context referred to above, one of the aims of topicalization is to contrast Cortez's role with José de la Borda's role in building of the town of Taxco. Linda Jones (1977) has recently made a good beginning at explaining the role of such devices as those exemplified above in marking thematicity in various hierarchical layers of a discourse. Obviously, such devices as those exemplified here must be explained as to contextual appropriateness. Otherwise, the linguist who simply taxonomically-transformationally describes such structures is in the position of one who is able to discribe the verb forms of a language without any knowledge of their function.

2.9 Variation in reported speech

Reported speech, whether in isolated speech acts or (as is more common) developed as dialogue, is important to narrative structure in most languages. While in some languages the form of recorded speech, whether in isolated utterance or in dialogue, is very stereotyped, in others there is considerable variety. To begin with there is the question of direct versus indirect quote which is an option available in most languages--although by no means in all. There are some languages (e.g., Agta of the Philippines and some Zapotec dialects of Central America) where only direct quotes are possible. Then there is the matter of the presence or absence of the quote formula (<u>he said</u>. . .). There is a further question in many languages of the position of the quote formula. Is the quote formula preposed to the quotation? Or is it postposed? Or is it both preposed and postposed? Or may the quotation itself be broken and the quote formula interlarded? ("<u>Fine</u>", <u>he said</u>, "<u>Let's go</u>.") How do all three possible quote positions relate to each other? Finally, there is the intricate matter of the nature of the quote formula. In a language such as Totonac (data from Aileen Reid) where the verb marks in its morphology both subject and object, there are six possible options for a quote formula. 1) verb, 2) verb plus noun indicating speaker, 3) verb plus noun indicating addressee, 4) verb plus nouns which indicate both speaker and addressee, 5) verb plus suffix <u>ca/can</u> (which means 'indefinite, unspecified subject of the clause'), and 6) verb plus <u>ca/can</u> plus noun indicating addressee. Only a theory of discourse can sort out these many variations in reported speech according to the parameters mentioned above.

Thus, in a language where there is frequent use of both direct and indirect quote, the contextual conditions under which one is used rather than the other, must be specified. Similarly, the presence or absence of quote formula must also be examined according to its contextual appropriateness. We often find, for example, that a story may be characterized by rather careful use of quote formulas until we get to the peak of the story at which point the story may drop the quote formulas and report the speech in what is, in effect, a more dramatic style. Or we may find that quote formulas are used early in a dialogue until the identity of the alternating speakers is established, after which point the quote formulas are dropped.

The matter of the position of the quote formula also calls for contextual specification. We may find for instance that the use of a postposed quote formula closes more than simply the quotation itself, i.e. that it may also close a section of dialogue, or even an episode of the story.

Finally, there comes the difficult question of the nature of the quote formula itself. Current work into the nature of the quote formula in Totonac shows that at least the following factors must be taken into account. (a) The nature of the dialogue. Is it a highly emotional dialogue or a comparatively placid one? (b) Does one participant dominate the dialogue or are both participants on an equal footing with each other? (c) Are we at the beginning or at the end of a stretch of dialogue, and do the quote formulas as used indicate some of these transitional features? Thus, in regard to the first factor, the nature of the dialogue, if the dialogue is highly emotional we can expect to have both preposed and postposed quote formulas and the speakers will be identified by a noun in both. As to the second factor above, the dominance of the speaker or addressee, the dominant person in the dialogue will be mentioned frequently and the other person only seldomly. As to the third factor above, it can also be noted that at the beginning of a dialogue the identity of the speaker may be suppressed by means of a <u>ca</u> or <u>can</u> on the Totonac verb so as to make plain that the addressee is thematic in the dialogue which follows. Or if the speaker is introduced first and then his identity is suppressed by means of a <u>ca</u> or <u>can</u> on the Totonac verb and the addressee identified, this indicates that the two speakers are on somewhat equal footing in the dialogue. At the conclusion of a dialogue if a quote formula suppresses the identity of the speaker in favor of the identity of the addressee, this is an indication that the speaker will not be thematic in the following section, but the addressee will be thematic (oral communication from Aileen Reid).

2.10 Variation in the length of syntactic units

A further consideration is variation in the length of syntactic units, especially of the sentence itself. Thus, out of context we find we may cite very short sentences or we may cite very long sentences. Are there contextual features which dictate choice of sentence length?

In many New Guinea highland languages where there is a feature of clause chaining which may consist of a great many medial verbs in medial clauses followed by a final verb in a final clause, there is a striking difference in discourse genre at this point. For example, in narrative and procedural discourse in such languages as Foré and Waffa we find extremely long chains with a final verb at the end. (In some such languages, notably Foré, the chain is so long that it really patterns as a paragraph rather than as a sentence and certain sub-chains within pattern as sentences). But in expository and hortatory discourse in the very same languages, chains are not built to any great length but may consist of only one or two clauses. The difference is so pronounced that one is almost tempted to wonder if he is in the same language. Somewhat the same situation is true of certain South American languages which also have pronounced chaining characteristics, noticeably Aguaruna of Peru (Larson, 1978, p. 159).

Sentence length may also be conditioned by placement in the discourse. Thus, Hemingway is known for his short crisp sentences, yet he may at the high point of a story write a sentence that can go for half a page. Thus at the climax of Hemingway's story 'The Short Happy Life of Francis Macomber' the central participant's wife (accidentally?) shoots him dead as he faces an on-coming bull.

This is reported in the following sentence.

> Wilson, who was ahead was kneeling shooting, and Macomber, as he fired, unhearing his shot in the roaring of Wilson's gun, saw fragments like slate burst from the huge boss of the horns, and the head jerked, he shot again at the wide nostrils and saw the horns jolt again and fragments fly, and he did not see Wilson now, and aiming carefully, shot again with the buffalo's huge bulk almost on him and his rifle almost level with the on-coming head, nose out, and he could see the little wicked eyes and the head started to lower and he felt a sudden white-hot, blinding flash explode inside his head and that was all he ever felt.

A similar way of marking the peak, i.e., by resort to a long run-on sentence has been observed in a New Guinea language, Wojokeso. The opposite possibility, namely resort to short crisp sentences which contrast with former long sentences can also be documented in some language as a feature marking peak.

2.11 Mystery Particles and Affixes

Many times in studying a language we find that there are certain particles of uncertain meaning which cannot be defined by the language helper, who nevertheless, insists that he wants them used at certain points and not used at others. Almost invariably such particles of apparently random distribution are subject to discourse constraints.

The Guajiro language (Mansens, 1976) of Colombia has a system of auxiliary verbs, which seem, on initial investigations to be rather vague in their meaning. Two of these auxiliaries are especially important to the structure of discourse. Thus, the auxiliary verb calacá, when it occurs on the verb of a clause, marks an important event of the story. It does not occur in a paraphrase of that main event. Thus, if we are told in a piece of folklore 'The tree thickened back to the thickness that it was before' the verb 'thickened' will have the auxiliary calacá on it. That is an important event in the progress of the story. If, however, the next sentence goes on to say 'In fact, it grew to be thicker than it had been in the first place', this further added information will not merit an occurrence of calacá. Similarly, in a dialogue where two people are talking to each other and what they say is considered important to the progress of the story, if one of them speaks an aside to a third person and the aside is of comparative unimportance, then the verb 'say' (of the quote formula) will not have a calacá in that situation. But the verb 'say', which introduces quotes from the characters whose dialogue is on the main line of the discourse, will be characterized by occurrence of calacá. The auxiliary verb taa similarly has discourse functions. It marks the subject of whatever verb it occurs with as the thematic participant of the paragraph. The rules governing its use are too intricate and detailed to state here. The two auxiliary verbs together serve to keep track of the main events and the participant reference structure.

In Totonac there is a mystery particle tza? (data from Ruth Bishop) which has a rather different function. Tza? does not mark either of the two functions mentioned for auxiliary verbs in Guajiro in the past paragraph. Rather tza? marks important background information that is not on the event line, but on which an event of the event line builds. So tza? marks background material of a specially privileged status.

Occurrence of such particles as here exemplified for Guajiro (of South America) and Totonac (of Mesoamerica) are by no means rare. The linguist who encounters them in a given language, if he has not seen similar particles marking discourse functions in other languages, will initially be tempted to feel that such particles are randomly distributed. Actually, however, one of the hardest thesis to prove in all linguistics is that 'there is no structure at this point'. Patient discourse analysis will uncover discourse function of particles of the sort which we have here illustrated.

3. Conclusion

This paper has tried to document on a broad front the thesis that understanding of many details of linguistic structure is dependent on the analysis of discourse. Discourse analysis is, I believe, one of the most exciting frontiers of contemporary linguistics. What I would like to suggest is that all of us from various backgrounds and linguistic traditions unite in the common enterprise of discourse analysis. We can bring to bear in this enterprise all the tools and insights of various schools of grammar: transformational-generative grammar, stratificational grammar, tagmemics, systemics, computational linguistics, and even artifical intelligence. The common task will in fact, carry us beyond the frontiers of linguistics itself and land us at the crossroads of linguistics, sociology, psychology, and perhaps several other disciplines. In view of the challenge of the new frontier, continued preoccupation with differences between us seems to be anachronistic. The discourse grammarian typically finds that he has more in common with another discourse grammarian of a different approach than his own, than he does with someone of his own approach who is not interested in the study of discourse.

We have, in effect, a new continent to explore and subdue. In the exploration of this continent I believe that all our theories and approaches to linguistics are going to be tested and suffer modification. Maybe, when we know enough about discourse

structure in various languages of the world, all the present
theories will be replaced by a still more adequate one which
will become the framework of the future. In that more adequate
theory bits and pieces of our present approaches may survive,
but find their proper place in the larger structure of the whole.

FOOTNOTES

[1] Another approach which made syntax feasible for the rank and
file of linguists but which found acceptance only with a minority of linguists was tagmemics as developed by Pike and his
colleagues. As one who participated in the latter foment I recall
vividly how suddenly one summer all of us were trying our hand at
syntax while the summer before syntactic analysis had not been a
live option. Pike's development of tagmemics came to crest in
the late 1950's and was like Chomsky's, symptomatic of a profound
dissatisfaction with U.S. structuralism as dominant in that and
the preceding decade.

[2] In English, the reintroduction of a noun which is not needed for
disambiguation (and hence where a pronoun would do) marks either
the onset of a new paragraph or some important seam within the
paragraph. The latter is often a climactic or summary sentence
in the development of a paragraph. It is not uncommon for a noun,
when thematic in a paragraph, to be mentioned in the first and
the last sentences, thus providing a bracketing feature (or
inclusio).

ACKNOWLEDGEMENTS

I acknowledge gratefully the permission granted to quote from The
Final Diagnosis (p. 31) by Arthur Hailey. Copyright © 1959 by
Arthur Hailey. Used by permission of Doubleday and Co., Inc.
I also acknowledge similar permission to quote from La Fuerza de
la Sangre by Miguel de Cervantes in Great Spanish Stories (pp. 64-
66) edited by Angel Flores. Hardback edition, 1956, The Modern
Library. Paperback edition, 1960, Bantam Book. Currently out of
print but to be reissued in 1979 by Gordian Press, New York. Copyright © Angel Flores. I am grateful again to Charles Scribner's
Sons for the right to quote once more from Hemingway's The Short
Happy Life of Francis Macomber in the third edition of Studies
in the Short Story (1968) (pp. 126-127) edited by Adrian H. Jaffe
and Vergil Scott.

Longacre WHY WE NEED A VERTICAL REVOLUTION IN LINGUISTICS 269

BIBLIOGRAPHY

Barr, Don
   1976   "The Use of Deictics to Identify Participants in Bahasa Indonesian", (ms.)

Bloomfield, Leonard
   1933   Language (New York: Henry Holt).

Cervantes, Miguel
   1960   "La Fuerza de la Sangre", Spanish Stories, ed. by Angel Flores (New York: Bantam Books), 62-89.

Daneš, František, ed.
   1974   Papers on Functional Sentence Perspective (Prague: Academia, Publishing House of the Czechoslovak Academy of Sciences).

Gleason, H.A., Jr.
   1964   "The Organization of Language: A Stratificational View", Georgetown University Monograph Series on Languages and Linguistics 17, 75-95.

Harris, Zellig S.
   1952   "Discourse Analysis", Language 28, 1-30.
   1957   "Co-occurrence and Transformation in Linguistic Structure", Language 33(3), 283-340.
   1963   Discourse Analysis Reprints (The Hague: Mouton).

Hopper, Paul J.
   1977   "Aspect and Foregrounding in Discourse", paper read at Symposium in Discourse and Syntax UCLA, November 1977.

Howard, Linda
   1977   "Camsá: Certain Features of Verb Inflection as Related to Paragraph Types", in Longacre and Woods (II), 273-296.

Jones, Linda Kay
   1977   Theme in English Expository Discourse (Lake Bluff, Illinois: Jupiter Press).

Kantor, Robert N.
   1976   "Discourse Phenomena and Linguistic Theory", (ms.).

Larson, Mildred
   1978   "The Functions of Reported Speech in Discourse", University of Texas, Arlington Ph.D. dissertation, reissued in SIL Publications in Linguistics.

Longacre, Robert E.
   1976a   "The Discourse Structure of the Flood Narrative", Society of Biblical Literature, 1976 Seminar Papers, ed. George MacRae (Missoula, Montana: Scholars Press).

1976b "Generating a Discourse from the Abstract", *Third LACUS Forum* (Colombia, South Carolina: Hornbeam Press).

1977 "Macro-structure and Overlay in the Flood Narrative", paper read at the San Francisco meeting of the Society of Biblical Literature, 1977.

Longacre, Robert E., and Frances Woods
1976-7 *Discourse Grammar: Studies in Indigenous Languages of Colombia, Panama, and Ecuador*, Three Parts (Summer Institute of Linguistics Publications in Linguistics 52) (Dallas: Summer Institute of Linguistics).

Loriot, James, and Barbara Hollenbach
1970 "Shipibo Paragraph Structure", *Foundations of Language* 6(1), 43-66.

Mansen, Richard, and Karis
1976 "The Structure of Sentence and Paragraph in Guajiro Narrative Discourse", in Longacre and Woods (I), 147-258.

Pike, Kenneth L.
1964 "Beyond the Sentence", *College Composition and Communication*.

Propp, Vladimir
1958 *Morphology of the Folktale* (Indiana University Research Center in Anthropology, Folklore, and Linguistics, publication 10), reissued 1968 (Austin: Texas University Press).

Reid, Aileen A., Ruth G. Bishop, Ella M. Button, and Robert E. Longacre
1968 *Totonac: From Clause to Discourse* (Summer Institute of Linguistics Publications in Linguistics 17)(Norman: Summer Institute of Linguistics and University of Oklahoma).

Reid, Wallis
1976 "The Quantitative Validation of a Grammatical Hypothesis: The Passé Simple and the Imparfait", *Papers of the North-Eastern Linguistic Society* 7.

Thompson, Sandra A., and Robert E. Longacre
1978 "Adverbial Clauses", to appear in *Language Typology and Syntactic Field Work*.

van Dijk, Teun A.
1972 *Some Aspects of Text Grammars* (The Hague: Mouton).
1977 *Text and Context* (London: Longman).

Waltz, Nathan E.
1976 "Discourse Functions of Guanano Sentence and Paragraph", in Longacre and Woods (I), 21-146.

2

A spectrum and profile approach to discourse analysis

ROBERT E. LONGACRE

Abstract

A text needs to be approached in terms of its situation (physical setting or social/intellectual milieu) in which it is composed, in terms of the addressee-interpreter's contribution *to the understanding of the text (schemata, scripts, and referential frames), and in terms of the text itself. The latter complex of considerations certainly includes at least the* macrostructure *(germinal idea or overall conception),* constituency *(embedded discourses, paragraphs, and sentences), and* texture. *This paper develops the third concern under the twin rubrics Spectrum and Profile. Until these terms are given more meaning in the body of this paper, suffice it to say here that both spectrum and profile have to do with the complementary concerns of cohesion and prominence in discourse structure; that spectrum has to do largely with continuing strands of information which at once unite a discourse and distinguish hierarchically the types of information within it; and that profile has to do with the linguistic reflexes of mounting and declining tension (or excitement) within a discourse.*

1. Spectrum

1.1. Following an early clue from Gleason, Grimes (1978) categorized types of information in narrative discourse. He pointed out that such a text not only contains information concerning *events* and *participants*, but also further sorts of information which he variously labeled *setting* (spatial-temporal, circumstantial, and introductory material especially appropriate to the onset of a story or of a section of a story), *background* (similar, but less bunched and hence more scattered through the narrative), *comment* (evaluation by the narrator), and *collateral* (alternatives, most quotations, and most negatives). Hopper (1979), following a lead from Reid (1976) and others, has described the grammatical base (choice of a particular tense/aspect/mode/voice, word order, marking by an affix or particle) for distinguishing *foregrounded* events in a story from *backgrounded* events, activities, and situations. Fleming's (1978) approach to discourse makes similar distinctions. Jones and Jones (1979), writing of 'multiple levels of information in discourse', distinguish not only an event-line for narrative, but cite data for languages that morphosyntactically mark a distinction of pivotal versus routine events on the one hand, and routine versus down-graded events on the other. The latter, down-graded events, merge with the other supportive information types. In turn, however, there may be resources to distinguish (on the basis of marking in certain languages) crucial supportive material from routine supportive material. The data underlying the study are drawn from ten Mesoamerican languages. In brief, categories of information which Grimes once distinguished largely on a semantic basis are more and more seen to correlate with distinctions made in the morphosyntax of the world's languages.

1.2. Before going further into the argument of this section, it is useful to stop and illustrate the general binary division (events versus nonevents, foregrounded versus backgrounded) which is indicated above, as well as the Jones and Jones claim that more than a simple dichotomy is involved here. Note the following paragraph from Mark Twain:

Example 1

In a minute a third slave was struggling in the air. It was dreadful, I turned away my head for a moment, and when I turned back I missed the king! They were blindfolding him! I was paralyzed; I couldn't move, I was choking, my tongue was petrified. They finished blindfolding him, they led him under the rope. I couldn't shake off that clinging impotence. But when I saw them put the noose around his neck, then everything let go in me and I made a spring to the rescue — and as I made it I shot one more glance abroad — by George! here they came, a-tilting! — five hundred mailed and belted knights on bicycles!

In this paragraph there is a certain amount of action along with a considerable amount of material which depicts the situation, describes the (fictitive) narrator's emotions, and portrays the scene when help finally arrives. We note the following simple past tenses — which are presumably candidates for the 'event-line' in the story: (1) 'turned (away my head)', (2) 'turned (back)', (3) 'missed (the king)', (4) 'finished (blindfolding him)', (5) 'led (him)', (6) 'saw (them put the noose)', (7) '(everything) let go (in me)', (8) 'made (a spring)', (9) 'made (it)', (10) 'shot (one more glance)'. Some rather graphic details are given in the past progressive: . . . 'a third slave was struggling in the air' . . . 'They were blindfolding him' . . . 'I was choking'. Still other clauses which contain the stative 'be' depict the narrator's emotions: 'It was dreadful'. . . . 'I was paralyzed' . . . 'my tongue was petrified'. Two clauses of similar semantic content use a modal and negative: 'I couldn't move' . . . 'I couldn't shake off that clinging impotence'. It seems possible that, in addition to the fact that clauses whose verbs employ the event-line past tense should be distinguished from supportive clauses which employ other sorts of verb forms, we could make a beginning at drawing distinctions among the latter as well. Thus, very probably the past progressive pictures a background activity that is secondary to the event-line in importance. Then clauses that have statives and negative modals probably rank lower in information relevance; as used here they are depictive of the narrator's emotions and his feeling of impotence.

But we must reexamine the putative event-line verbs just listed. Three of the simple past-tense action verbs are, it turns out, in adverbial clauses which serve to provide cohesion via back-reference. Thus, 'when I turned back' is a cohesive back-reference to the previous clause, 'I turned away my head for a moment'. Likewise, 'when I saw them put the noose around his neck' reflects the next step (in the hanging script) after (4) and (5): 'They finished blindfolding him', 'they led him under the rope'. So close is this predictable script connection that 'put the noose around his neck' is, in effect, a back-reference to 'under the rope'. Not too different is the sort of back-reference involved in 'as I made it', which builds on 'I made a spring to the rescue'.

What is the upshot of all this? The above analysis of the functions of the past-tense verbs (2), (6), and (9) in adverbial clauses shows that they are used in a secondary capacity. They do not so much announce new events as use references to past events for the purposes of cohesion. They can, therefore, be excluded from the event-line of this passage. In that they treat of script-predictable actions which closely ensue on event-line actions, they are still of a certain relevance to the story. They are, however, mainly cohesive in function. In information rank they should perhaps be ranked between the event-line proper and the past progressives (which are activities rather than events). Alternatively, we might consider that the past progressives encode activities that are less predictable (and hence more salient) than the events encoded in the adverbial clauses.

Another problem is illustrated by the very last simple past tense above: 'here they came, a-tilting'. Note that this clause is part of the narrator's report of what he saw (reported as 'I shot one more glance . . .'). Furthermore, it is evident that the action which is reported ('here they came . . .') is meant to be continuative -- which explains the 'a-tilting' which follows. This is, therefore, a past tense essentially of the rank of the past progressives or lower. This illustrates a fundamental ambiguity of English past-tense forms in some verbs. This is especially true of verbs of sensation and awareness. Thus 'I knew that something was wrong' could be, in appropriate context, event-line (i.e., equal to 'I concluded that something was wrong') or supportive-descriptive. Probably adverbial expressions help resolve this ambiguity in English, so that 'I knew right off that something was wrong' refers to an event, while 'I knew all the time that something was wrong' seems rather obviously to be a piece of supportive material.

The above paragraph illustrates the usefulness of a binary division in narrative discourse between the foregrounded event-line and supportive material. The former is correlated in English with independent clauses whose verb is past tense and not the verb 'be' nor a verb which is shown by other features (e.g., adverbial expressions) to be depictive. The further tense forms and verb types are indicative of supportive material. On the other hand, the wealth of differing forms which characterize the latter leads us strongly to suspect that even these forms can be arranged in some fashion in a hierarchy or cline. Diversity must *always* be explained. Differing forms of tense/aspect/mood/voice do not exist for nothing in a language. Our belief is that such variety serves the needs of discourse.

1.3. At this point, while agreeing largely with Jones and Jones on 'levels of information relevance in discourse', I want to invoke a new metaphor and derive from it a new term. The metaphor is from optics and the new term is 'spectrum'. Just as a spectographic analysis of white light separates out various hues (our perception of differing wave lengths) ranging from red to violet, so the analysis of a narrative text reveals a cline of information which ranges from the most dynamic elements of the story to the most static (depictive) elements; successive positions along the cline correlate well (as a whole) with distinctions among the verb forms of a language (i.e., with the tense/aspect/mode/voice system), but other features (word order, use of affixes, particles, or adverbs) must sometimes be invoked to round out the picture. Thus, the

English verb forms illustrated in the above paragraph could perhaps be arranged in the order: past tense (action verbs in independent clauses; sensation and awareness verbs properly qualified), past tense in subordinate clauses, past progressive, past tense in verbs whose adverbial qualifiers indicate that they are depictive, statives ('be') with or without modals. The English pluperfect presents special problems and is beyond the scope of this paper. It is probable that clines of this general sort are not limited to narrative discourse but characterize other discourse types as well (cf. 1.3.4. below).

1.3.1. Possibly Biblical Hebrew narrative is one of the clearest places to posit with confidence a spectrum which involves considerable diversity of verb and clause structure. Note Figure 1, which ranks Hebrew verbs and clauses according to a rank scheme.

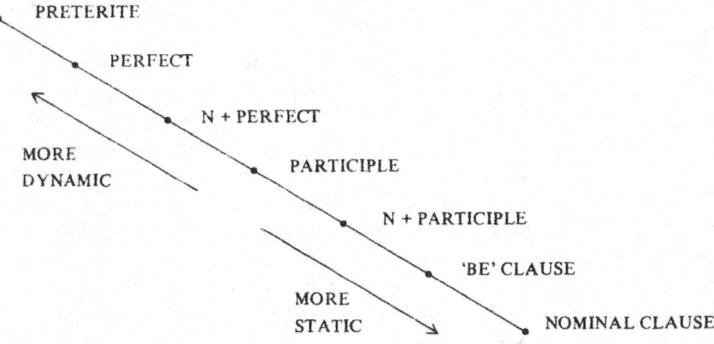

Figure 1. *A spectrum of Hebrew clause types (graded as to structural relevance in Biblical Hebrew narrative)*

Verbs and clauses at the upper left-hand side are the most dynamic; those at the lower right-hand side are the most static (depictive) and are, in fact, nominal clauses which contain no verb at all. The term 'preterite' is a summary way of referring to a special narrative tense which developed in Biblical Hebrew. This tense apparently consisted of a fused particle w^- 'and', which seemed to 'convert' an incompletive into a completive and was structurally distinct from the ordinary conjunctive 'and'. Actually, the form is not so summarily explained and has a very complex history which need not concern us here. Suffice it to observe that (1) this is a special 'narrative tense' even according to the Genesius-Kautsch-Cowley grammar of 1910 (Cowley, 1910: 326); (2) it must occur clause-initial and cannot tolerate a preposed noun or even the word *lō'* 'not'. Whenever there is a preposed noun or *lō'* 'not', we find not a preterite following it within the clause but rather another verb form, the suffixal verb, which is commonly called the perfect. All this makes good sense in terms of discourse structure. Clauses with initial verbs present actions and events, while clauses with initial nouns present participants or props. The latter are a step away from the event-line, which they compromise in the interests of presenting or highlighting a participant or a prop. This distinction correlates, in fact, with an old distinction drawn by the medieval Arabic grammarians, according to which all verb-initial clauses were called 'verbal clauses' and all clauses with initial nouns were called 'nominal clauses' (Cowley, 1910: 451).

To return, then, to the scheme represented in the diagram, preterites (exclusive of the preterite of *hayáh* 'be') represent the most dynamic elements of the narrative spectrum. Clauses which, while not preposing a noun, nevertheless abandon the preterite for a perfect are presenting *secondary actions* of some sort (e.g., a cause, a predictable result, or a pluperfect). Clauses which prepose a noun (usually subject, sometimes object) to the perfect are a peg lower in the spectrum; they are *action relative to a given participant*; hence they are often used to highlight temporarily a participant where the context is mainly about someone else, or to shift the spotlight back to and reintroduce a central participant. Still lower in the scheme are participles which present *background activities*, and clauses with noun plus participle which represent *background activities relative to a given participant*. Even lower still come equational clauses with 'be'; and finally, completely verbless clauses. 'Empty (was) the well. No water (was) in it.' The placement of negative clauses with perfects in the spectrum is still problematical, but they seem clearly not to be event-line.

Notice the operations of various Hebrew verbs and clauses in the following passage, Gen. 40: 20-23 (presented in transliterated Hebrew, with literal and free translations):

Example 2

(1)   wayĕhîy bayyôm haššĕlîyšiy yôm hulledet 'et-para' ōh
(2)   wayya' aś mišteh lĕcāl- 'ĕbādāyw.

(3) wayiśśa' 'et-rō'š śar hammašḳiym wě' et-rō'š śar hā'ōpiym bětok ěbādāyw.
(4) wayyāšeb 'et-śar hammašḳiym 'al mašḳēhû.
(5) wayyittēn haccôs 'al-cap para'ōh.
(6) wě'et śar hā' ōpiym tālah.
(7) ka' ěšer pātar lāhem yôsēp.
(8) wělō' zākar śar-hammašḳiym 'et-yôsēp.
(9) wayyiskāhēhû.

(1) And-it-happened on-the-day, the third, (the) day that-was-born Pharaoh,
(2) And-he-made (a) banquet for-all servants-his.
(3) And-he-raised the-head-of (the) chief-of the-cupbearers and-the-head-of (the) chief-of-the-bakers amidst servants-his.
(4) And-he-restored the-chief-of the-cupbearers to position-his.
(5) And-he-gave the-cup to-(the)-hand-of Pharaoh.
(6) But-the-chief of the-bakers (he) hanged
(7) as (he) interpreted to-them Joseph.
(8) And-not (he) remembered (the) chief-of the-cupbearers, Joseph.
(9) But-he-forgot-him.

(1) So it happened that on the third day, Pharaoh's birthday, (2) he made a banquet for all his court. (3) And he brought out the chief cupbearer and the chief baker and considered their cases before all his court. (4) Then he restored the chief cupbearer to his position, (5) so that he again handed the cup to Pharaoh. (6) But he hanged the chief baker. (7) All this happened just as Joseph had interpreted their dreams to them. (8) But the chief cupbearer didn't remember Joseph. (9) On the contrary, he forgot all about him.

In the above example, clauses 2,3,4,5, and 9 are on the event-line, by virtue of having verbs in the preterite in the required clause-initial position. Clause 1 is barred from the event-line according to a rule (common to many languages) that the verb *to be* is typically nonactive and descriptive; the *wayěhiy* 'and-it-happened' introduces a temporal phrase, has as its complement clause two, and is near the bottom of the cline which is represented in Figure 1. All the preterite of clauses 2-5 and 9 display the typical structure of a preterite with prefixed *wā-* and doubling of the first consonant (here a prefixal *y-* third person sg. masc.).

Clauses 6-9, the intervening clauses, contain off-the-line materials. In clause 6, the noun phrase, 'the chief baker', is clause-initial and the following verb *tālah* '(he) hanged' is a perfect (third from the top of the spectrum). Here local contrastive focus is put on the baker as opposed to the cupbearer. On the other hand, this clause has a perfect and is off the event-line of the story. This is plausible in that the baker here drops out of the story and his fate is irrelevant to the unfolding of subsequent events. The cupbearer, in spite of temporary failure, will by contrast prove crucial to subsequent events (the elevation of Joseph to the lordship of Egypt). Clause 7 is also off the event-line — as a subordinate clause and as a flashback (where English uses a pluperfect): 'as Joseph had interpreted to them'. The verb of this clause (*pātar* 'interpreted') is also a perfect (second from the top of the spectrum). Clause 8 is also off the event-line. First of all, it preposes *lō'* 'not' to the verb — which necessitates a shift to the perfect (*zākar* 'remember'). Second, it is a negative paraphrase of the event-line verb in 9. Finally, with clause 9, we return to the event-line. Participles and nominal clauses do not figure in this example.

1.3.2. For the Halbi language, an Indoeuropean language of India, Frances Woods (1980) posits the scheme presented in Figure 2. In the upper left-hand

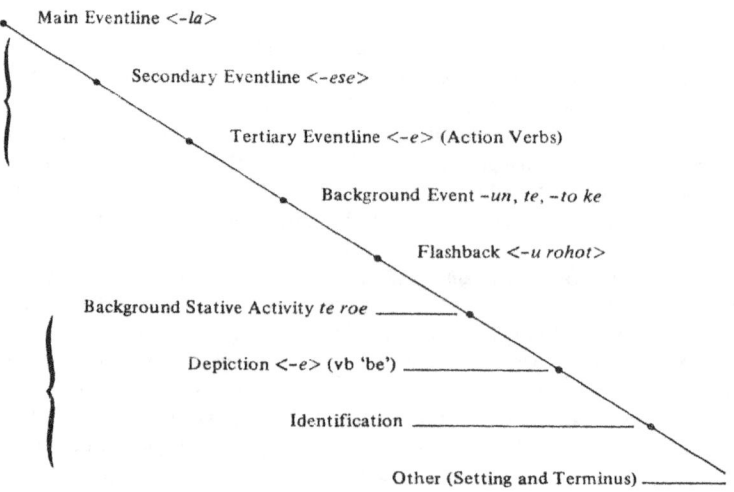

Figure 2. *Halbi: relative importance of events and nonevents (Woods, 1980)*

corner we find the main event-line, carried by verbs which are marked with [-*la*]person-number suffixes (-*l* occurs in every person and number). These verbs are characterized by Woods as 'completed action' verbs. First-order digressions from the event-line (continuing the temporal sequence of events but of less prominence) are marked by [-*ese*]person-number suffixes (-*s*- occurs in every person and number); these verbs are characterized by Woods as 'present incomplete'. She further observes that 'marking an event as less important (through the use of the present incomplete endings) indicates that either the event itself is not in focus or that the participant performing the activity lacks prominence' (Woods, 1980: 125). Her 'tertiary event-line' is a device for representing events that are presented as 'background and routine'; these are marked by [-*e*]person-number suffixes which indicate *only* person-number categories and have no tense-aspect component. To summarize the rest of the structures involved: backgrounded events (still more distant from the main lines of the story) are encoded as dependent verbs; flashback is indicated by a special main verb plus auxiliary complex; backgrounded stative activity by still another main plus auxiliary complex; depiction by the verb 'be' plus the [-*e*] endings; identification by another 'be' verb that is existential in import; and setting and terminus by still other more specialized and involved constructions. In overall outline we obtain a spectrum not so different from the Hebrew spectrum presented above, but the details are very different, in accordance with the markedly different tense-aspect systems of the two languages.

1.3.3. Still another language for which we may extrapolate such a spectrum (from published material: Bishop, 1979) is Northern Totonac (Mexico). See Figure 3.

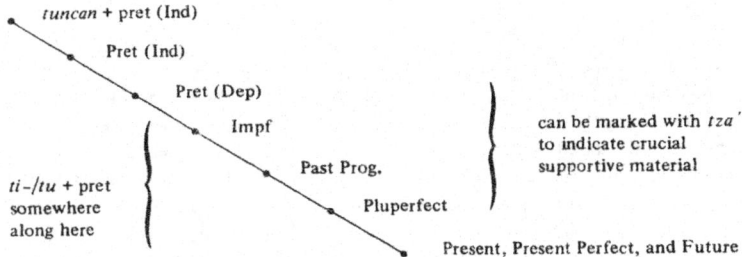

Figure 3. *Tentative spectrum for Northern Totonac (extrapolated from Bishop, 1979)*

Here the most pivotal events are encoded in a clause introduced with *tuncan* 'and then' and with an independent preterite as verb. Clauses without the special tagging conjunction but with an independent preterite represent more routine events. Dependent clauses with preterites are still lower (cf. English example above). Secondary events or activities encoded in clauses whose verbs are imperfect follow next; the imperfect is here a general backgrounding tense, much as in Romance and Slavic languages. Probably somewhat lower are clauses whose verbs are past progressives; here a background activity is certainly intended. Pluperfects possibly come next as events out of the line of succession in the story and therefore clearly background, rather than part of the ongoing narrative; they are used for flashback and for back-reference (cohesion). Somewhere down here also fit preterites which are prefixed with *tū-* 'negative' or *tī-* 'frustrative', 'in vain'. Such verbs represent actions that 'don't get off the launching pad'. Even further down come presents, present perfects, and futures, which figure in stories mainly in quotes and in awareness depiction. It is of considerable interest that clauses whose verbs are comparatively low in the spectrum – certainly not event-line – can be tagged with *-tza'* to mark them as especially crucial bits of background and supportive information.

1.3.4. I have referred previously to the possibility that discourse types other than narrative may have similar spectra of information relevance. In Hebrew predictive discourse the *waw* plus the perfect or suffixal tense (with the verb initial in its clause) is the most dynamic form of the verb, while the imperfect (prefixal) tense is next in rank. Next comes a clause with a preposed noun plus a verb in the imperfect. Participles and nominal clauses presumably rank lower still. Prediction is, however, broadly conceived as a kind of narration-in-the-future, so this general overall similarity to narrative should not surprise us.

What about hortatory discourse? It is rather well known that one of the features of hortatory discourse is the scale of mitigation/aggravation on which commands distribute themselves (Labov and Fanshell, 1977). Usually, however, a whole discourse has a certain tenor in this regard – a tenor quite regularly correlated with the age and social status of the speaker relative to those of the hearer. An employer speaking to his employee or an adult to his child may use bald imperatives, which would not be appropriate within his peer group. Possibly, however, some hortatory discourses display a scale of aggravation versus mitigation that is not unlike the dynamic-static spectrum of narrative discourse.

Expository discourse might also be investigated from this point of view. Linda Jones (1977) has indicated a scale of grammatical constructions which mark ever-inclusive domains of thematicity.

Alternatively, maybe the spectrum of dynamism constructed for narrative is of relevance everywhere, and other discourse types simply implement different parts of the same scheme. Thus, description typically implements forms from the lower parts of the spectrum (from the 'violet' instead of the 'red' end). Clearly, however, this is not of much help in hortatory discourse, since imperatives (and their surrogates) are not mentioned at all in the narrative spectrum.

2. Profile

Most discourse is not spoken or written on a uniform level of excitation and tension. Rather a discourse normally has a cumulative development which customarily occurs toward its end — or at least past its middle. The flow of discourse seems to quicken and grow more turbulent at such a point. To this point we can quite naturally apply the term 'peak'. I want to argue here for peak as (1) a structure which correlates with underlying notional categories; (2) something marked in the surface structure of the language; (3) a practical zone of analytical difficulty for the analyst; and (4) a feature which serves to give a Profile to a whole discourse which includes one or more such units.

2.1. Two sorts of peaks can occur in a narrative: action peaks and thematic (didactic) peaks. Action peaks relate to the underlying (notional) structure of a narrative in that a surface-structure peak correlates with the climax or with the denouement of a narrative. This assumes an underlying structure of the following sort: Exposition ('lay it out'); Inciting Incident ('get something going'), Mounting Tension ('keep heating it up'), Climax ('knot it all up proper'); Denouement ('loosen at some crucial point'), Lessening Tension ('keep on loosening it'), and Closure ('wrap it up'). What is chosen for marking as peak will conform, as has been said, with the spot of maximum tension (Climax) or the crucial event (Denouement) which makes possible the resolution of the plot.

If the story has but one action peak, then one or the other of these two crucial plot elements is chosen for surface-structure highlighting. Thus, if only the notional climax is featured as peak, then the notional denouement is treated simply as a postpeak episode in the surface structure. If, on the other

348   Robert E. Longacre

hand, only the denouement is featured as surface-structure peak, then the climax is treated simply as a prepeak episode in the surface structure. Finally, if both climax and denouement are featured as peaks in the surface structure, then we posit a peak and a peak' (with the possibility of one or more interpeak episodes). These possibilities are summarized in Figures 4 and 5.

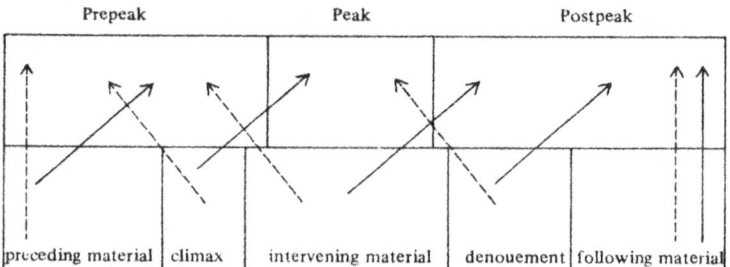

Figure 4.   Possibility 1 (with either climax or denouement featured as peak; not both)

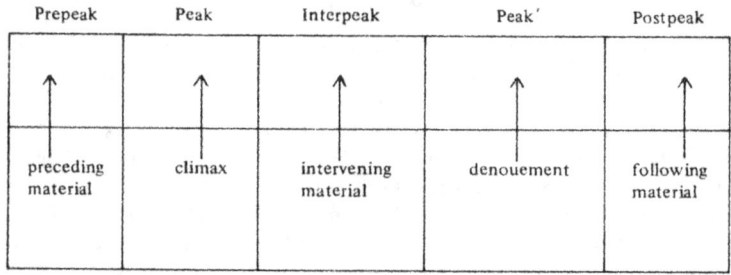

Figure 5.   Possibility 2 (with two action peaks)

A narrative may also have a thematic (didactic) peak. Since this was first suggested by Fran Woods in reference to Halbi, I reproduce here her table contrasting action peaks and didactic peaks (Woods, 1980: 281): see Table 1.

The didactic peak presumably occurs after the action peak of a narrative. Presumably, if a discourse were to have two action peaks and a didactic peak, the latter would follow the other two.

Table 1. *Didactic Peak contrasted with narrative Peak (from Woods, 1980)*

Didactic Peak	Narrative Peak
No chronological progression	Marked chronological progression
Cyclic structure	Forward movement
2 participants only and little description	Crowded with participants and much description
Crowded with props and extensive descriptions	Limited props and limited description
Dialogue	Events

According to Woods, chronological movement ceases at didactic peak and someone *talks*. While in her Halbi myth the talking takes the form of dialogue, it can be a monologue (speech by the main character) or even quotation of a written document. Whatever the case, the embedded material is nonnarrative and is either hortatory or expository. The cyclic structure (chiasmus) that she observes for the Halbi myth is probably specific to that text, but it is nevertheless not uncommon in well-composed hortatory and expository materials. The attention to props and description is common in didactic peaks, even if not universal.

In the sections that follow I will make little further reference to didactic peaks but will treat almost exclusively of action peaks.

2.2. Peaks are identified as such by a variety of means. The storyteller has, so to speak, a bag of tricks available for peak-marking. I have described these in detail elsewhere (Longacre, 1976). Consequently, I will summarize briefly at this point. Illustration of peak will be reserved for 2.3 below.

One of the commonest ways of marking a peak is *rhetorical underlining*, i.e., various devices are used to insure that the peak does not 'go by too fast.' Devices of repetition (somewhat cleverly disguised by a skillful writer) and paraphrase may be used. In general, this device is applicable to other discourse types as well as to narrative.

With narratives, however, rhetorical underlining can take some very specific forms. The narrator can in some manner *pack or extend the event-line*. Thus, he can report a lot of detail that would not be appropriate to routine narration. The camera is slowed down by focusing on the minutiae, the component actions of an overall action. This, in effect, is the answer to a problem raised by van Dijk: granted that the narrator cannot tell everything that happens, how much *does* he tell? (van Dijk, 1977: 108-111). In routine narration overmuch detail is distracting and obscures the mainline of the story, but at the peak of a narrative such detail can be introduced to mark the peak.

Thus, at the peak of a story it may be appropriate to describe in detail how a person deliberately rises out of a chair, i.e., how he shifts his weight forward to the balls of his feet, how he grasps the edge of the table where he is sitting, and how he deliberately pulls himself erect. If this preceeds a dramatic event such as, 'then, pointing his finger right under Duncan's nose, he said, "Duncan, it's no use, I've got enough evidence to convict you"' — it is quite appropriate. Such an amount of detail regarding particular body parts and muscular movements would not be appropriate in routine, nonpeak narration.

Such a packing of the event-line often results in a higher verb/nonverb ratio at the peak than for the story as a whole. Thus, for Ga'dang (Philippines) narrative, Walrod (1977) reports that while one/seven is the general ratio of verb to nonverb in his folklore material, one/three is the ratio at peak — where verb tumbles along after verb in rapid sequence. Such a development can also lead to a phasing-out of dialogue in favor of action at a peak; this is somewhat contrary to the use of dialogue (previously unused in a story) to mark peak (as described below).

The packing of the event-line can also take the form of reporting nonevents on the event-line as if they were events. This is true, e.g., of the peak of the Hebrew text of the Genesis flood narrative (Gen. 7: 17-24). Here the paraphrase of an event (such as 'the mountains were covered' or 'everything died' is reported as a preterite — *as if* it were a new event. Elsewhere (cf., e.g., the whole book of Ruth), the paraphrase of an event is reported off the line as a perfect instead of as a preterite (Longacre, 1979b).

Another basic device used to mark peak in narrative discourse is the *crowded stage*. In drama, a literal crowding of the stage usually characterizes the peak. In nondramatic narrative, there is often a similar concentration of participants at peak. Compare, e.g., the second trial of Charles Darnay in *The Tale of Two Cities* (Dickens). The question can also be raised here as to whether a concentrated interweaving of themes in expository discourse constitutes a nonnarrative peak-marking device which parallels the concentration of participants as a peak-marking device in narrative.

In addition to the basic narrative devices of the packed event-line and the crowded stage (with their possible nonnarrative counterparts), there are some more specialized devices which involve shifts along several surface-structure parameters. One such shift is to a higher person-number category on the agency hierarchy, e.g., a shift from third person to first person plural (from 'he' and 'they' to 'we'), or from third person to second person (when the narrator addresses a participant in the story). Shifts of tense also occur (e.g. past to historical present); some such shifts are discussed in 2.3 below. There may also be a shift along a parameter with four values; narrative, pseudodialogue, dialogue, drama. Clearly, if a story has had little or no dialogue in prepeak, a shift to dialogue can serve to mark the peak. Pseudodialogue includes apostrophe and rhetorical questions, which liven up narrative and resemble dialogue but do not evoke answers. By 'drama' I indicate dialogue without the use of quotation formulas. Thus a story which has employed dialogue freely in prepeak episodes can (by dropping the formulas of quotation) shift into drama at peak. There may also be change of sentence length at peak. Sentences of a normal length which the hearer/reader has learned to associate with a given speaker/writer can give way at peak to either (a) short crisp sentences or (b) long rolling sentences. There may also be increased use of onomatopoeia (or in some texts profanity and obscenity) at the peak of a story.

2.3. Peaks also emerge as points of typical analytical difficulty in the linguistic analysis of texts. If one is beginning the study of the narrative spectrum in a body of texts in a given language, the peak is the worst of all places to begin such a study. Conversely, if one has begun to understand the uses of various forms in the narrative spectrum, the analysis of the peak of a story can on first impression seem to uncover features which run counter to the analysis.

The reason for the above analytical difficulties is simply that spectral lines can shift at peak, so that the various verb forms that regularly mark differing sorts of information can occur in a distribution other than would be anticipated from previous parts of the narrative. Any other features that contribute to the distinction between spectral lines can likewise suffer shift. Or to change the metaphor, peak is a zone of turbulence in the otherwise placid flow of discourse.

A Totonac folktale (in Reid, et al., 1968) illustrates well some of the rather unusual things that can happen at peak. The story 'When our God walked on earth' pictures God going about in human form, pretending to be a simple laborer, and humbling the proud. In one incident of the story, he comes to a blacksmith shop where a sign has been posted to the effect that no one can shoe horses as well and as rapidly as this blacksmith. The (presumed) laborer asks for work and proceeds to shoe horses by cutting off a lower leg, putting on the horseshoe, and then sticking the leg back on the horse – all without

352   Robert E. Longacre

spilling a drop of blood. After working half a day the laborer gets his noonday meal and wages, then leaves. At this point the following paragraph (Example 3), which is notional climax encoding as peak, occurs (I present the paragraph in Totonac with verb forms identified in parentheses in the matching translation: PRES=present, PRPR=present progressive, IMPF=imperfect, PAPF=past perfect, PRET=preterite, PAPR=past progressive, FUT=future, PRPF=present perfect, INJ=injunctive, and CONT=contrafactual):

Example 3 (from Reid, et al., 1968: 140)

31. (1) Lā$'_1$ a'xni'ca'tza$'_2$ i'xa'nī'ttza$'_3$, tuncan$_4$ nā$_5$ xla$'_6$ macacā'tēlh$_7$ nā$_8$ lakatin$_9$ cahuayuj$_{10}$. (2) Lā$'_1$ tuncan$_2$ tzuculh$_3$ sta'jni$'_4$ i'xka'lhni$'_5$ (3) Lā$'_1$ como$_2$ laktzī'li$_3$ que lēj$_5$ ī'sta'jmā$'_6$ i'xka'lhni$'_7$, lēj$_8$ lacapali$_9$ hui'līni'ko'lh$_{10}$ i'xmacalīca'n$_{11}$ huan$_{12}$ cahuayuj$_{13}$. (4) Lā$'_1$ tuncan$_2$ tiyājuani'cu'tulh$_3$ i'xmacan$_4$; tūlalhtza$'_5$ yāhuani'lh$_6$. (5) Lā$'_1$ tantu$_2$ tilali$_3$ tiyāhuani'cu'tulh$_4$ i'xmacan$_5$ lā$'_6$ tūlalhtza$'_7$ yāhuani'lh$_8$ i'xmacanī'n$_9$ huan$_{10}$ cahuayuj$_{11}$. (6) Lā$'_1$ tantu$_2$ tilali$_3$, pero$_4$ por$_5$ masqui$_6$ i'xpuhuan$_7$ a'nchī$_8$ i'xlīcāyāhuani'lh$_9$ i'xmacanī'n$_{10}$ lā$'_{11}$ tūlalhtza$'_{12}$ cāyāhuani'lh$_{13}$. (7) Tuncan$_1$ a'lh$_2$ māputzanīni'n$_3$ huan$_4$ chi'xcu$'_5$ a'ntī$_{14}$ a'xni'ca$'_{15}$ i'xmacacā'tē$_{16}$ lā$'_{17}$ como$_{18}$ xla$'_{19}$ tū$'_{20}$ ī'sta'ja$_{21}$ i'xka'lhni$'_{22}$ huan$_{23}$ cahuayuj$_{24}$.

31. (1) And$_1$ when$_2$ he had gone-PAPF$_3$, then$_4$ he$_6$ also$_5$ cut off the forefoot of-PRET$_7$ a$_9$ horse$_{10}$ also$_8$. (2) And$_1$ then$_2$ his blood$_5$ began-PRET$_3$ to flow-PRES$_4$. (3) And$_1$ since$_2$ he saw-PRET$_3$ that$_4$ his blood$_7$ was flowing-PAPR$_6$ very much$_5$, very$_8$ quickly$_9$ he finished putting on-PRET$_{10}$ the shoe of$_{11}$ the$_{12}$ horse$_{13}$. (4) And$_1$ then$_2$ he tried to put on-PRET$_3$ his forefoot$_4$; he could not-PRET$_5$ put it on-PRET$_6$. (5) And$_1$ so much$_2$ he tried-PRET$_3$ to put on-PRET$_4$ his forefoot$_5$ and$_6$ he could not-PRET$_7$ put on-PRET$_8$ the forefeet of$_9$ the$_{10}$ horse$_{11}$. (6) And$_1$ so much$_2$ he tried-PRET$_3$ but$_4$ although$_{5,6}$ IMPF-he thought about$_7$ how$_8$ he would put on-CONT$_9$ its forefeet$_{10}$ (and) yet$_{11}$ he could not-PRET$_{12}$ put them on-PRET$_{13}$. (7) Then$_1$ he went-PRET$_2$ to look for-PRES$_3$ the$_4$ man$_5$ who$_6$ had passed by to show him-PRET$_7$ how$_8$ IMPF-he cut the feet off$_9$ the$_{10}$ horse$_{11}$, and$_{12}$ how$_{13}$ he$_{14}$ when$_{15}$ IMPF-he cut off the feet$_{16}$ and$_{17}$ as for$_{18}$ him$_{19}$ the blood of$_{22}$ the$_{23}$ horse$_{24}$ IMPF-did not flow$_{20,21}$.

This paragraph starts off in a fairly routine way with a back reference verb in the past perfect (1_3), and following event-line preterites (1_7, 2_3, and 3_{10}). The first two preterites are preceded by *tuncan* 'and then', which as we saw in 1.3.3 and in Figure 3 marks pivotal events: the cutting off of the horse's leg, and the immediate flow of blood. A dependent predicate (3_3) is lower in cline or spectrum than either the independent preterites or the preterites reinforced with a preceding *tuncan*. Words 2 and 3 of sentence (1) each occur with a suffixed *tza'* which tags especially crucial (but non-event-line) information: 'And when-*tza'* he had gone-*tza'*...' So far the uses of tenses in the paragraph are quite routine — although we are warned that the departure of the miracle-working laborer is a fateful event!

With sentence (4), however, things take a different turn — and this is reflected in the structure of the verbs in this and the following sentences. The sentence starts with *lā' tuncan* 'and then', which is customarily used to mark pivotal events. But word 3 of this sentence is a preterite with *ti-* 'in vain', and word 5 is a preterite prefixed with *tū-* 'negative'. The sentence can be rendered 'and then he tried (in vain) to put its forefoot back on, but he couldn't put it on'. It is striking here that *tuncan*, which usually marks pivotal *preterites*, here occurs with preterites which are compromised by the occurrence of the *ti-* and *tū-* prefixes and are low on the spectrum. Sentence (5) is not too different: 'No matter how much he tried to put the leg back on he couldn't put on the forefoot of the horse' — with the same recurrence of *ti-* and *tū-* marked verbs. And so also sentence (6), which mainly adds the thought that no matter how much he tried to figure out how to do it, he just couldn't. Obviously, the story is not moving forward here; we are stuck with the blacksmith in his moment of truth. Furthermore, the high incidence of low-level compromised predicates (Grimes' collateral information), along with the rather unusual use of *tuncan* with such verbs in sentence (5), points to something special. Note, in addition, that (4_5), (5_7), and (6_{12}) — all instances of the verb 'he couldn't' — are suffixed with *tza'*, which is indicative of important *supportive* material. Note finally the repetition of the word for 'forefoot' — the crucial prop — in sentences (4)-(6). Clearly this paragraph is the peak (climax) of the embedded blacksmith narrative. The story is brought to a close with the blacksmith going to seek his employee of the morning and getting him to fix up the horse for him. The blacksmith narrative ends with a didactic peak in which 'Our God' (the laborer) gives the blacksmith a lecture on humility.

This story is followed by another embedded narrative in which 'Our God'

354   *Robert E. Longacre*

incognito finds a baker who has posted a sign 'There isn't another breadmaker like me.' Again the laborer asks for work and again he outdoes his employer in the quantity and quality of work (baked goods) which he produces. Finally, toward the end of the day, the laborer picked up an old woman, put her on the baking board, and slipped her into the (large, beehive) oven. After a short while he took her out and she had become the most beautiful woman in town. Then the laborer took his wages and left.

The baker, whose wife was somewhat old and haggard, decided to try the same procedure upon her. But the results were rather disastrous — at which point we pick up the Totonac text:

Example 4 (from Reid, et. al., 1968:145-146)

44. (1) Lā$'_1$ como$_2$ xlīti$_3$ mānūlh$_4$, lā$'_5$ a'xni'ca$'_6$ i'xmāxtu$_7$ con$_8$ huan$_9$ i'xpūmāxtucan$_{10}$ huan$_{11}$ lātasna$'_{12}$ de$_{13}$ pāntzi$_{14}$ lā$'_{15}$ i'xmākosū$_{16}$ lā$'_{17}$ a'nlhā$_{18}$ i'xmacachā'n$_{19}$ tapok$_{20}$ i'xmacachā'n$_{21}$ puro$_{22}$ lhca'ca'n$_{23}$ i'xmacachā'n$_{24}$.

44. (1) And$_1$ since$_2$ for a long time$_3$ he put her in (PRET)$_4$ and$_5$ when$_6$ he took her out (IMPF)$_7$ with$_8$ the$_9$ thing with which he took out$_{10}$ the$_{11}$ pans$_{12}$ of$_{13}$ bread$_{14}$, and$_{15}$ he threw her/it (IMPF)$_{16}$ and$_{17}$ where$_{18}$ (the) powder$_{20}$ landed (IMPF)$_{19}$ nothing but$_{22}$ ashes$_{23}$ landed (IMPF)$_{21,24}$.

45. (1) Lā$'_1$ tuncan$_2$ i'xa'mpala$_3$ ī'saca$_4$ lēj$_5$ lacapalh$_6$. (2) Lā$'_1$ tuncan$_2$ i'xtamacanūpala$_3$; ka'tlā'tusi$_4$ i'xka'lhīpala$_5$. (3) Tuncan$_1$ i'xmāxtupala$_2$ lā$'_3$ chu$_4$ i'xmākosūpala$_5$. (4) Lā$'_1$ a'xni'ca$'_2$ i'xchā'mpala$_3$ a'nlhā$_4$ i'xmacachā'n$_5$ tapok$_6$, i'xchā'mpala$_7$ puro$_8$ lhca'ca'n$_9$. (5) Lā$'_1$ tuncan$_2$ i'xa'mpala$_3$ ī'saca$_4$ lēj$_5$ lacapalh$_6$. (6) Lā$'_1$ tuncan$_2$ i'xtamacanūpala$_3$ na$_4$ i'xpūpāntzi$_5$ lā$'_6$ ka'tlā'tusi$_7$ i'xka'lhīpala$_8$. (7) Chu$_1$ tuncan$_2$ i'xmāxtupala$_3$ lā$'_4$ i'xmākosūpala$_5$. (8) Lā$'_1$ a'nlhā$_2$ i'xmacachā'mpala$_3$ a'xni'ca$'_4$ i'xmākosūpala$_5$ tapok$_6$, i'xchā'n$_7$ x'mān$_8$ lhca'ca'n$_9$; i'xlani'ni'pala$_{10}$. (9) Lā$'_1$ tū$'_2$ maktin$_3$ cāxtlōlh$_4$; de$_5$ tantu$_6$ i'xtlahuacu'tun$_7$ a'nchī$_8$ i'xmāsu'ni'canī't$_9$, hasta$_{10}$ que$_{11}$ mejor$_{12}$ a'lh$_{13}$ putzatakchoko$_{14}$ huan$_{15}$ chi'xcu$'_{16}$ a'ntī$_{17}$ temāsu'ni'lh$_{18}$ huanmā$'_{19}$ a'nchī$_{20}$ i'xcāxlōnī't$_{21}$ huan$_{22}$ to'kotzīn$_{23}$. (10) Lā$'_1$ de$_2$ tantu$_3$ i'xputzatlā'- huan$_4$, hasta$_5$ que$_6$ quīkaksli$_7$ huan$_8$ chi'xcu$'_9$ a'nlhā$_{10}$ i'xlatlā'huanacha$'_{11}$.

45. (1) And$_1$ then$_2$ he went again (IMPF)$_3$ very rapidly$_6$ to pick her/it up (IMPF)$_4$. (2) And$_1$ then$_2$ he put it in again (IMPF)$_3$; he waited again (IMPF)$_5$

a long while$_4$. (3) Then$_1$ he took it out again (IMPF)$_2$ and$_3$ he threw it again (IMPF)$_{4,5}$. (4) And$_1$ when$_2$ it landed (IMPF)$_3$ where$_4$ (the) powder$_6$ landed (IMPF)$_5$, nothing but$_8$ ashes$_9$ landed (IMPF)$_7$. (5) And$_1$ then$_2$ he went again (IMPF)$_3$ very$_5$ rapidly$_6$ to pick it up (IMPF)$_4$. (6) And$_1$ then$_2$ he put it in again (IMPF)$_3$ into$_4$ his oven$_5$ and$_6$ he waited again (IMPF)$_8$ a long while$_7$. So$_1$ then$_2$ he took it out again (IMPF)$_3$ and$_4$ he threw it again (IMPF)$_5$. (8) And$_1$ where$_2$ it arrived again (IMPF)$_3$ when$_4$ he threw again (IMPF)$_5$ (the) powder$_6$ only$_8$ ashes$_9$ arrived (IMPF)$_7$; it happened to him again (IMPF)$_{10}$. (9) And$_1$ he never fixed her (PRET)$_{2-4}$; although so very much$_{5,6}$ he wanted to do (IMPF)$_7$ as$_8$ he had been shown (PAPF)$_9$, in the end$_{10,11}$ (he thought) better$_{12}$ he should go (PRET)$_{13}$ look for (PRES)$_{14}$ the$_{15}$ man$_{16}$ who$_{17}$ had taught him (PRET)$_{18}$ this$_{19}$ how$_{20}$ he had fixed up (PAPF)$_{21}$ the$_{22}$ old woman$_{23}$. (10) And$_1$ so much$_{2,3}$ he walked looking for him (IMPF)$_4$, in the end$_{5,6}$ he went and found (PRET)$_7$ the$_8$ man$_9$ where$_{10}$ he was walking around (IMPF)$_{11}$.

The first paragraph (number 44 of the entire story) pictures the baker's initial frustration: when he draws his wife out of the oven and tosses her (like one would toss a lot of newly baked bread into a basket) all that lands there is a heap of powder and ashes! The main verb here (word 19) and its repetitions (words 21 and 24) are imperfects, i.e., the usual background tense is used rather than an event-line preterite.

Similarly the baker's repeated attempts and repeated frustrations are pictured in paragraph 45 as an unbroken series of nineteen imperfects in sentences (1)-(8). None of the verbs are marked with *ti-* and *tū-* as in the peak of the preceding story (where the blacksmith *can't* do what he *tries* to do); rather, the imperfects picture a repeated and fruitless round of activity — an impression which is reinforced by the occurrence of *-pala* 'again', 'another time', 15 times in the paragraph. Again, we are at the peak, the point of maximum tension of the story. And again, the verbs don't act 'properly'. Event-line preterites disappear; the background tense (imperfect) takes over; and furthermore *tuncan* 'and then' occurs with considerable frequency with the imperfect, in sentences (1), (2), (3), (5), (6), and (7). In effect here, nonevents (or at the best fruitless activity) are labeled as if they were pivotal. We have here another instance of a pseudo-event-line as pointed out for the peak of the flood story in Hebrew.

This story is brought to a close by the baker's going to seek the man who had worked for him. Once the baker finds him and gets him to return to the bakery, 'Our God' puts the pile of ashes into the oven and brings out the man's wife alive and well — but twice as ugly as before.

2.4. Once we are able to isolate one or more peaks in a discourse, we can then plot the profile of a discourse in terms of mounting tension toward the peak and loosening tension away from it. Since peak is a *zone* encountered in the discourse, we do not necessarily find peak-marking features beginning exactly at the onset of the episode that is so marked and phasing out exactly at its close. Rather, we find that episodes which are immediately contiguous to a peak may partially share in the peak-marking features. Numbering episodes back from the peak and forward from it, as in Figure 6, we can hold open the possibility that the concluding part of P − 1 and/or the beginning of P + 1 may share peak-marking features.

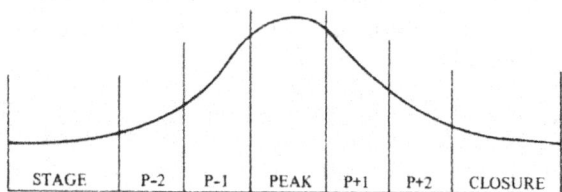

Figure 6. *Profile of a one-Peak discourse*

Looking again at Figure 6, we note that this is offered as the surface-structure morphology of a story. There are beginning and closing sections; and there are sections which precede and follow the central section. It is roughly analogous to a clause of SVO structure where the verb is the acknowledged central segment and the subject and object are distributed around it. Many narratives, and many discourses of other types, frequently have a profile of this sort. The two chief variations on this pattern are: (1) discourses in which peak is final, with no P + 1 and a very rudimentary (or absent) closure: (2) discourses in which the inciting incident of a story also has peaklike features. The latter gives a profile with a low rise and fall following the stage, then the major buildup to and from peak (cf. Konzime narrative discourse, Beavon, 1979).

Another sort of profile is that in which there is an action peak followed by a secondary didactic peak, as sketched in Figure 7 (closure may be merged with the didactic peak or can occur as a separate segment). This is the structure of the Genesis flood story, except that there are three prepeak episodes, and four postpeak episodes which precede the secondary peak.

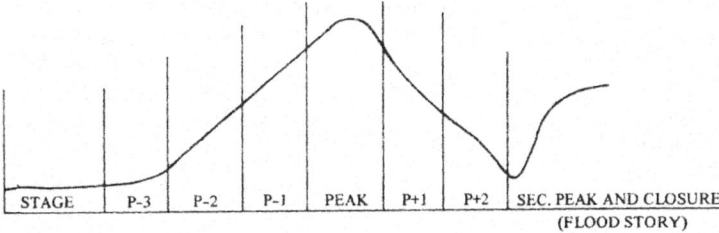

Figure 7. *Profile with a main Peak and final (didactic) Peak*

When both climax and denouement are marked as peaks, we get a structure like that symbolized in Figure 8. This is, roughly, the structure of the Joseph story in the book of Genesis. There are four prepeak episodes, beginning with the sale of Joseph into Egypt. In Gen. 41 we have the first action peak (climax), in which Joseph's rise to power is portrayed as a rapidly moving event-line which brackets both sides of his dialogue with Pharaoh.[1] The second action peak (denouement) (Gen. 43-45) records the second visit of Joseph's brothers to Egypt, his hazing and testing them, Judah's impassioned speech in defense of Benjamin, and Joseph's revelation of himself. There are an interpeak episode (Gen. 42), which maintains a rather consistently high level of excitement and suspense, and three postpeak episodes.

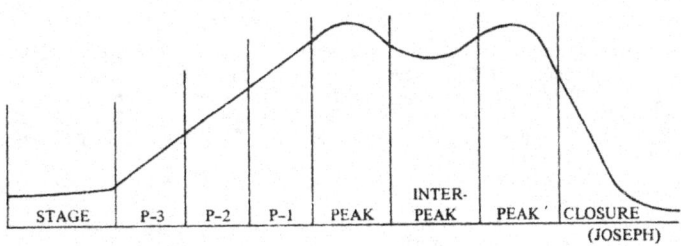

Figure 8. *Profile with double Peak*

358   Robert E. Longacre

Figures 6, 7, and 8 and the schemata that they portray are plausible constructs, if we recognize the importance of the surface-structure peak(s) in a discourse. When we keep in mind that the peak(s) also affect the spectral lines of the discourse and a number of other features as well, it is evident that much of the detail of a story — down to its morphosyntax, systems of nominal/pronominal reference, and linkage — can be explained relative to the twin concerns of spectrum and profile. They, of course, are not the whole analysis; we must also add further concerns, especially constituency analysis and macrostructure analysis — but these latter concerns are beyond the scope of this article.

Note

1. An interesting question emerges here: would it not be possible to suspend action midway in an action peak and run in a didactic discourse at that point, so that, in effect, an action peak and a didactic peak would be combined? There seems to be no good reason why this could not happen. This may in fact be what happens in the first peak of the Joseph story, i.e., the section of the story in which Joseph vaults from prison to be overlord of Egypt. Joseph's being called from prison, readied, and presented to Pharaoh is presented in a series of fast-moving event-line clauses — as is also the recital of the things which Pharaoh says and does to Joseph in installing him as grand vizier. In these respects the passage patterns as a typical action peak. But in between the two stretches of rapid-fire preterites comes Joseph's dialogue with Pharaoh and his interpretation of Pharaoh's dreams. The emphasis on divine providence in Joseph's speech would correlate well with the general idea of a didactic peak.

References

Beavon, Keith H. (1979). Studies in the discourse structure of Konzime — a Bantu language of Cameroun. Unpublished M.A. thesis, University of Texas at Arlington.
Bishop, Ruth (1979). Tense-aspect in Totonac narrative discourse. In *Discourse Studies in Mesoamerican Languages*, vol. 1, Linda K. Jones (ed.), 31–68. Summer Institute of Linguistics Publications 58. Dallas: Summer Institute of Linguistics and University of Texas at Arlington.
Cowley, A.E. (trans.) (1910). *Gesenius' Hebrew Grammar, as edited and enlarged by the late E. Kautzch*. Oxford: Clarendon.
Fleming, Ilah (1978). Discourse from the perspective of four strata. In the *Fifth Lacus Forum*, 307–317. Colombia, S.C.: Hornbeam.
Grimes, Joseph E. (ed.) (1978). *Papers on Discourse*. Summer Institute of Linguistics Publications in Linguistics 51. Dallas: Summer Institute of Linguistics and University of Texas at Arlington.

Hopper, Paul J. (1979). Aspect and foregrounding in discourse. In *Discourse and Syntax*, T. Givón (ed.), 213-242. New York: Academic Press.
Jones, Larry and Jones, Linda K. (1979). Multiple levels of information relevance in discourse. In *Discourse Studies in Mesoamerican Languages*, vol. 1, Linda K. Jones (ed.), 3-28. Summer Institute of Linguistics Publications 58. Dallas: Summer Institute of Linguistics and University of Texas at Arlington.
Jones, Linda K. (1977). *Theme in English Expository Discourse*. Lake Bluff, Illinois: Jupiter.
— (ed.) (1979). *Discourse Studies in Mesoamerican Languages*, vol. 1: *Discussion*, vol. 2: *Texts*. Summer Institute of Linguistics Publications 58. Dallas: Summer Institute of Linguistics and University of Texas at Arlington.
Labov, William and Fanshell, David (1977). *Therapeutic Discourse: Psychotherapy as Conversation*. New York: Academic Press.
Longacre, Robert E. (1976). *An Anatomy of Speech Notions*. Lisse: de Ridder.
— (1979a). The discourse structure of the Flood Narrative. *Journal of the American Academy of Religion* 47(1), Supplement (March, 1979) B: 89-113.
— (1979b). Towards a better understanding of Old Testament Hebrew narrative. Paper read at the meeting of the Evangelical Theological Society in St. Paul, Minnesota, December 1979.
Reid, Aileen, Bishop, Ruth G., Button, Ella M. and Longacre, Robert E. (1968). Totonac: from clause to discourse. *Summer Institute of Linguistics Publications in Linguistics and Related Fields* 17.
Reid, Wallis (1976). The quantitative validation of a grammatical hypothesis: the passé simple and the imparfait. *Papers of the Northeastern Linguistic Society* 7.
van Dijk, Teun A. (1977). *Text and Content: Explorations in the Semantics and Pragmatics of Discourse*. London: Longman.
Walrod, Michael R. (1977). Discourse grammar in Ga'dang. Unpublished M.A. thesis, University of Texas at Arlington.
Woods, Frances Margaret (1980). The interrelationship of cultural information, linguistic structure and symbolic representations in a Halbi myth. Unpublished Ph.D. dissertation, University of Texas at Arlington.

Robert E. Longacre has been teaching linguistics at the University of Texas at Arlington since 1972. Prior to that time he was a field linguist working with the Summer Institute of Linguistics in Mexico — where his name is associated with the study of Trique and comparative phonology in Otomanguean languages. He received his Ph.D. from the University of Pennsylvania (1955). As an international consultant for the SIL he has directed special research projects into the text structure of little known languages not only in Mexico (and Guatemala) but also in the Philippines (1967-1968), in Papua New Guinea (1970), and in Colombia (1974-1975 with attention to languages of Ecuador and Panama, as well). The latter three efforts were variously sponsored by the U.S. Office of Education, by the National Science Foundation, and by the National Endowment for the Humanities. He has also written or edited volumes on text structure in the latter three areas. Some of this is summarized in his *An Anatomy of Speech Notions*, Lisse: de Ridder (1976), and in his *The Grammar of Discourse* (in press). His present interests are text theory and methodology, and the discourse structure of Biblical Hebrew.

3

Two Hypotheses Regarding Text Generation and Analysis

ROBERT E. LONGACRE
University of Texas at Arlington

It is proposed here that in any language and for any discourse type within that language the verb forms/clause structures can be arranged in a rank scheme in which a mainline of discourse development is encoded by a characteristic construction (or a very limited set of constructions) while lines of subsidiary development, which represent progressive degrees of departure from the mainline, are encoded in other constructions. It is further proposed that this graded salience scheme can then provide guidelines for the analysis of local spans of text (paragraphs) so that sentences whose independent clauses have constructions which are high in the salience schemes are dominant over ancillary sentences which have constructions which are lower in the scheme. The first hypothesis has more to do with text generation, while the second has to do with text analysis. The two hypotheses are meant to yield salience schemes and constituent analyses which mutually corroborate and correct each other. These hypotheses and their reciprocity are illustrated here relative to narrative discourse in eight languages in five distinct linguistic areas.

A traditional scheme for parts of speech in grammars of American Indian languages has been an overall tripartite division into nouns, verbs, and particles. This simple scheme has a certain relevance for language in general and for text linguistics in particular. In analyzing a text in any language, several crucial concerns cluster around the textual functions of these word classes: (a) accounting for the textual functions of the various tense/aspect/mode verb forms of a language; (b) accounting for the apparatus of participant/thematic reference as marked by nouns, pronouns, verb affixes, and anaphoric zero; and (c) ascertaining the various discourse functions of particles (Longacre, 1976b). A further concern is the functional segmentation of a text. What can be termed *macrosegmentation* has to do with the gross divisions (chunks), and the relations of such parts to the whole and of the parts to each other. On the other hand, there are also concerns of *microsegmentation*, that is, of intersentential relations within local spans of the text.

This paper is concerned with (a) above, that is, accounting for the various tense/aspect/mode forms of the verb as they correlate with the textual functions of clauses and sentences (Hypothesis I)[1]. But this concern is intricately inter-

---

Correspondence and requests for reprints should be sent to Robert E. Longacre, Department of Foreign Languages and Linguistics, P.O. Box 19557, University of Texas, Arlington, TX 76019.

[1] In that this paper treats of the relative prominence among the verb forms of a text and the clause

woven with matters of microsegmentation and the relative dominance of one sentence over the other in local spans of text (Hypothesis II).

The verb system of any language exists to expedite discourse in that language. Therefore, the place to look for the meaning of tense/aspect/mode forms is to their discourse functions, whether in dialogue or monologue. The latter is especially enlightening in that it provides sufficient and prolonged context in which to study the varying verb forms. The textual functions of verb forms remain, however, a jumble unless some broad text types are posited and the verb functions analyzed relative to one type at a time. This paper restricts itself to the study of verb tense/aspect/mode in narrative discourse.

In analyzing textual functions of various verb forms in a given text type within a given language we encounter here—as everywhere in text analysis—the principle of relative prominence. Prominence can be semantic and/or structural. Structural prominence exists in its own right, although often correlating with semantic prominence. Thus, a story is not a story unless it presents sequential and punctiliar happenings. This *main line of development* is characteristically expressed by clauses and sentences given a particular tense/aspect/mode form appropriate to the language being studied plus inevitably some restrictions based on verb classification (e.g., active vs. stative and "be" verb). Thus, the line of sequential, punctiliar happenings is the main structural feature of the story. Other less prominent clauses/sentences characterize the story as well; this explains other tense/aspect/mode forms of the verb. Semantically, a narrative may have a weak storyline and the main semantic weight can be elsewhere. Nevertheless, the fact remains that the author chose to present his text in narrative form and its line of sequential, punctiliar forms is still the central *structural* feature.

I speak, therefore, of the main line of development appropriate to any text type and proceed to formulate hypothesis I as follows:

Hypothesis I: *It is assumed here that for any language each type of text has a main line of development and contains other materials which can be conceived of as encoding progressive degrees of departure from the main line.* This hypothesis has to do with the *generation* of a text from its abstract in that the main line of development is considered to be the central feature of the text of which other text features are essentially elaborations and additions; a text is generated from the main line by the addition of these further elements in ordered sequence. The different sorts of texts have differing main lines of development: Narrative text

---

types that correlate with such distinctions, I leave aside detailed consideration of the relative importance of the various strands of nominal/pronominal/affixal reference. In fact, however, some reference to participant/thematic reference is essential in that: (1) the more dynamic types of verbs typically involve more participants (e.g., object and/or indirect object as well as subject) than do the static (Hopper-Thompson, 1980, parameter 1); and (2) sometimes verbs of lesser salience call for participants of lesser status. Also it should be noted that discourse particles often function to reference to concerns (a) and (b) above in the body of this paper.

has a storyline; procedural text has a line of procedure; hortatory/persuasive text has a line of exhortation (which may, as a matter of fact, be very subtly concealed); and expository text has a line of exposition—to mention some basic distinctions.

It is further assumed that, for any given text type, in any language, once the implications of Hypothesis I have been followed out so as to yield a rank scheme of verb/clause types in that text type for that language, then *within local spans of text an intersentential analysis can be carried out so that the sentences whose main verb(s)/clause(s) are of highest rank are structurally dominant in the local span and those of lower rank are structurally ancillary*. This, the second Hypothesis of this paper (Hypothesis II), has to do more with text *analysis*.

In relating these two hypotheses to each other, Hypothesis I is the more basic in that it has to do with obtaining the abstract of a text (primarily from its main line) and "fleshing out" the abstract by progressively adding elements of lower rank. These concerns outrun somewhat the narrower concerns of Hypothesis II which is dependent upon the former. Nevertheless, the two can be a mutual check on each other: (a) Does Hypothesis I yield a scheme whose ranks correlate well with dominant versus ancillary concerns in intersentential relations? (b) Does the attempt to analyze according to Hypothesis II in a given language indicate deficiencies in the application of Hypothesis I? In brief, a good rank scheme of verbs/clauses should facilitate a good intersentential analysis; and a good intersentential analysis can confirm/modify the rank scheme.

This paper will test out these two interrelated hypotheses in narrative discourse in eight languages scattered around the world. More languages could be cited since a considerable amount of work is underway in this regard. Furthermore, more than narrative text could be cited since work on other sorts of texts is also proceeding apace. But the consideration of more languages and of other text types would necessarily take us beyond the confines of article-length treatment. On the other hand, a treatment at least as lengthy as that found in this article seems necessary to demonstrate that the two hypotheses here presented have empirical as well as *a priori* foundations.

I hasten to add here that the present approach and treatment bear several points of contact with the Hopper-Thompson transitivity hypothesis (1980). I differ from them, however, in trying to bring their various parameters to bear so as to yield a unified rank scheme. Furthermore, I attempt here to give more concrete content to their abstract idea of *salience* in discourse.

In the first section below, on the basis of available studies, rank schemes are presented for narrative texts in the following languages: English (as a convenient starting point), Totonac, Aguacatec, Kickapoo, Gujarati, Halbi, Ténhé, and Biblical Hebrew. In section two an attempt is made to generalize and to construct a universal theoretical instrument based on these various schemes. In section three, I use the appropriate rank schemes to guide illustrative paragraph analysis in English, Totonac, and Biblical Hebrew—thus illustrating Hypothesis II.

1. RANK SCHEMES IN PARTICULAR LANGUAGES

In this section I give in summary form (and diagrammatic representation) rank schemes that have been posited for narrative discourse in a variety of languages in accordance with Hypothesis I. Some rank schemes are more complete than others; all are, moreover, somewhat tentative. The validity of any such scheme can be tested against such considerations as are broached in section 2 (a generalization of Hypothesis I), that is, plausibility in terms of possible language universals, and in section 3, in terms of the usefulness of such a rank scheme for language X in the analysis of the constituent structure of local spans (paragraphs) in that language (i.e., in terms of Hypothesis II).

All schemes which are posited for narrative discourse proceed from the most dynamic to the most static elements. Usually a given verb tense/aspect/mode in a language can be considered to subsume a clause of which it is the center; in many languages, however, some of the most static clauses are nonverbal, that is, equative or descriptive clauses (here the verb is significantly absent).

1.1 The rank scheme I have posited for English (Longacre, in press) is represented in Table 1. I assume the following order of salience: Storyline–Background–Flashback–Setting–Irrealis–Evaluation–Cohesive elements. Within each of the seven bands I am not so sure of relative salience, but I have,

TABLE 1
English, Longacre

Band 1 Storyline	Past (S/Agent) Action, (S/Agent/Patient) Motion Past (S/Experience) Cognitive events (punctiliar adverbs) Past (S/Patient) Contingencies
Band 2 Background	Past Progressive (S/Agent) background activities Past (S/Experience) Cognitive states (durative adverbs)
Band 3 Flashback	Pluperfects (Events, activities, which are out of sequence) Pluperfects (Cognitive events/states that are out of sequence)
Band 4 Setting (expository)	Stative verbs/adjectival predicates/verbs with inanimate subjects (descriptive) "Be" verbs/verbless clauses (equational) "Be"/"Have" (existential, relational)
Band 5 Irrealis (other possible worlds)	Negatives Modals/futures
Band 6 Evaluation (author intrusion)	Past tense (cf. setting) Gnomic present
Band 7 Cohesive band (verbs in preposed/postposed Adverbial clauses)	Script determined Repetitive Back Reference

nevertheless, ranked elements internally in each band in what seems at present to be a plausible order.

The storyline band can be identified for the most part with the backbone of a narrative in English (aside from promotion and demotion as described below). The storyline is here a broad term to include a variety of *punctiliar, sequential happenings* which advance the narrative: (a) In some, the subject is agent and the actions are volitional; this certainly includes speech acts as well as other sorts of actions. These appear to be happenings of the highest order, but even here we may need to assume that motion verbs, as a subset of action verbs, have a somewhat subsidiary function, namely, to report the movement of a participant towards or away from the locus of the action proper. In motion verbs the subject is both agent and patient; when one goes somewhere he moves himself in that direction. (b) In other happenings we have cognitive/psychological/emotional events, that is, a moment of truth, falling in love, "swept by anger," and so forth. Here the subject is experiencer rather than agent. Since in English cognitive events are not regularly marked as distinct from cognitive states, we are especially dependent on the presence of *punctiliar adverbs* to indicate the former. Clearly, "I knew right off that something was bothering her" (a cognitive event) is distinct from "I knew all the time that something was bothering her" (background band, below). (c) There are also happenings in which the subject is simply patient: "We got caught in the rain" and "Jim fell off his chair." These are clearly events rather than actions. While I speak summarily here of S/Agent versus S/Experiencer versus S/Patient, I recognize, of course, the existence of grammatical transformations or alternative structurings in which the Agent or Experiencer or Patient may have some surface structure function other than subject.

The background band clearly includes background *activities* and cognitive *states*. The latter are illustrated above. Background activities are typically expressed with English past progressive: "Meanwhile Dr. Dugin was holding the dog down as if his life depended on it." Durative adverbs can figure here as well along with sequence markers such as "meanwhile." The background band represents *nonpunctiliar, nonsequential activities and states* that clearly do not move a story forward as do those reported in Band one, but which temporally overlap with one or more of the storyline actions/events.

Somewhat more remote from the storyline are the elements of Band three, the flashback band. While we here may reference to punctiliar actions/events, they are not sequential, that is, are not in regular sequence on the storyline. The English pluperfect permits a progressive stepping back through time in the same context: "He had gone there to inspect the kitchen. Dugin had ordered him to inspect it. Evidently, Dr. Dugin had come to suspect that all was not well with the food preparation." Only lexical probability leads us to decide that the example just given encodes *reason* structures with backstepping through time, while the following example encodes a sequence of events which is backset as a unit from the main sequence: "He had gone there to inspect the kitchen. He had carried out the inspection as best he could and hurried back to Dr. Dugin's office. He had given a report which thoroughly dismayed the doctor."

Still further removed from the storyline are expository and descriptive materials of the sort I call *setting* (following Grimes, 1975). This includes descriptives whose predicates are adjectives or participles (with use of *be* to preserve the canonical SVO form and to provide an element to hang the verb inflection on); here the subject is patient. Other descriptives consist of verbs with inanimate subjects: "The road glistened"; "The flags flapped in the wind." Other uses of *be, have,* and similar verbs in existential/locational clauses, relational clauses ("Mary had five children"), and in equative clauses (expressing set membership) occur in this band as well. It is important to note that such elements of setting are often somewhat important to the macrostructure of a story—they introduce participants and props and localize the text world in time and space. Nevertheless, they are further removed from the storyline than are elements of the bands above them.

The next band, *irrealis,* includes material that is not part of the text world but suggests possible alternative reconstruction of that world. Here occur potential actions/events which don't eventuate. This is reflected in the use of negatives and modals of various sorts: "Dr. Dugin didn't/should have/might have/almost answered the phone, but. . ."

Possibly some of the most clearly intrusive materials in a story are the author's evaluations of participants, props, or situations; such material, in the past tense, is often similar to setting: "But Dr. Dugin wasn't a man to give up easily." On the other hand, evaluation may employ a *gnomic present:* "Doctors are typically taciturn men." The first person of the narrator may even surface: "That part of town, from what I've seen of it, isn't the best place for a young doctor to hang out his shingle and begin his practice." Evaluations are clearly much more optional and even unnecessary to a narrative than either setting or irrealis (where alternative worlds are at least tangent to the text world). I feel that they clearly belong towards the bottom of the scheme of verb/clause salience in English.

In the final band I put cohesive elements that are more a part of the *connective tissue* of the text than any vital part of its content. Even here, however, we must be discriminating. Almost equivalent to a pure (*and*) *then* is such a preposed recapitulatory clause/phrase as that which begins the second sentence: "Paul took off in the Piper Cub promptly at 7:30 a.m. About as soon as he took off/immediately after the take-off, he noticed an abnormal sound in the engine."

Conceivably, however, the second sentence could have begun with "As he leveled off, he noticed an abnormal sound in the engine." Here we have implicit reference to a *flight script:* take off, ascend, level off, fly, descend, land. In that the recapitulatory element on the ensuing sentence after the one reporting the take off mentions the next event in the script—albeit highly predictable—I think we have to assume that script-referential back references have a higher significance to a story than do pure recapitulations.

The analysis of material in Band seven brings up the question as to whether the grammatical status of a clause need to be taken into consideration. As a whole, verb ranking concerns itself with verbs which are found in main clauses. Adverbial clauses of various sorts are often involved in cohesive functions (cf. Thompson & Longacre, 1985). What of other adverbial clauses? What of relative clauses? Note in this regard such not infrequent examples as "He [the little pig] was up in the tree when he saw the wolf coming." Here, "when he saw the wolf coming" is postposed to the main clause and is not a recapitulation of previous material in the story from which it is taken; it is in fact a further (cognitive) event. We can systematically put it on the storyline, if we recognize that the switch in linear order correlates with a grammatical inversion of storyline and setting elements, so that setting is now in the main clause and storyline is in the adverbial clause. The inversion is probably motivated by several concerns including thematicity: The thematic spotlight is now on the little pig, rather than on the wolf and his doings; consequently the latter is mentioned in a subordinate clause which is postposed and therefore of less prominence.

This grammatical inversion of storyline to the status of a subordinate clause must be regarded as part of a larger picture; it suggests that the practical working of rank scheme requires that we posit *promotion* and *demotion* as operations which can take place upon a rank scheme. Normally, adverbial "when" clauses are preposed and are in Band seven. When, however, there is inversion of the storyline with some other element, then the resultant subordinated clause must be regarded as *promoted* to Band one.

As for relative clauses, the restrictive relative clause must be considered to involve a radical demotion of the verbs that occur within it. This is because relative clauses are constituents of noun phrases and can therefore scarcely "pull rank" within the sentence much less within the paragraph. I assume that relativization demotes a clause by taking it out of the rank scheme entirely—or, at most, limiting it to some sort of cohesive function in Band seven. Even the latter, however, is not so plausible, since relative clauses function primarily in matters of participant reference and tracking, and figure therefore more on the noun phrase side than on the verb phrase side of the structure of text.

Relativization (whether restrictive or nonrestrictive) is, however, sensitive to broad considerations of the macrostructure of a story. Consider the following two sentences: "A Japanese family bought the lot next to ours three years ago. This past year they put a house on it." Here the two sentences with verbs *bought* and *put* are both Band one predications. We can, however, demote the first sentence to a relative clause: "The Japanese family that bought the lot next to ours three years ago put a house on the lot this past year." Under proper contextual conditions we might even want to relativize the original second clause: "The Japanese family that put a house on the lot next to ours this past year, actually bought the lot three years ago." Presumably two stories beginning in this alternative fashion are setting out to describe somewhat different courses of events. (1) If we keep the original sentence two as the main clause and relativize the first, we are going to tell a story beginning perhaps with putting the house on the lot about a year ago. (2) If on the other hand we keep the first sentence as the main clause and relativize the second, we are likely to tell a story of what has happened to the family since they originally bought the lot, that is, the course of events culminating in their putting a house on the lot. Demotion is thus sensitive to the whole macrostructure of the story.

Promotion in English may also be achieved by the use of punctiliar adverbs (or, on occasion, by less immediate contextual clues). The elements from bands two to five can be promoted to Band one by the use of the adverb "suddenly:"

'Suddenly, the patient's heart was beating again under those long slim fingers.'
'Suddenly, he had realized his life-long ambition.'
'Suddenly, he was whole again in body and soul.'
'Suddenly, he couldn't see a thing.'

Of special interest is promotion involving the pluperfect. Imagine such a three-sentence sequence as the following: "Dr. Dugin picked up the phone with both dread and anticipation. A voice on the phone spoke two brief sentences—all that Dugin needed to hear. Suddenly he had realized his life-long ambition of becoming the director of a hospital." Here *suddenly he had realized* is on the storyline along with *picked up* and *spoke*. Indeed, the resort to *suddenly* with the pluperfect (used somewhat as a perfective) probably marks this sentence as climactic in its paragraph.

We can also mark a sentence/embedded paragraph as climactic in an English sequence paragraph by using such an adverb as *finally*, or by putting a recapitulatory clause on the front of the climax sentence. This is of interest in that, while English has no pivotal storyline marking mechanism as in the other languages which are summarized below, it *does* clearly have a way of indicating the climax of a narrative sequence paragraph. Presumably such climaxes in paragraphs are pivotal to the storyline in these stories as well.

1.2 I turn now to the consideration of rank schemes in certain languages of Mesoamerica. For Totonac, a language related to the Mayan stock, we have good, text-tested data. For two Mayan languages proper, Aguacatec and Rabinal Achi, the data that we have are good but apparently incomplete.

1.2.1 The rank scheme for Totonac (Table 2) is based on the work of Ruth Bishop (1979), interpreted as "levels of information" by Jones and Jones (1979) in the same volume, and formulated as a rank scheme in Longacre (1981). The present scheme is that of the latter with some modifications.

The analysis of the upper ranks in Totonac narrative turns on the contrastive functions of the *preterite* and the *imperfect*. The function of the latter in Totonac is broadly similar to the function of the imperfect in such Romance languages as Spanish and French, that is, the imperfect is a general backgrounding tense used in reporting events that are not of top salience, are often only weakly sequential,

TABLE 2
Totonac, Bishop, 1979; Longacre, 1981

Band 1 Storyline	*tuncan* + Preterite: pivotal Preterite (Independent & nonirrealis)
Band 2 Secondary storyline grading into background	Imperfect (general backgrounding)
Band 3 Background activities	Past Progressive (specifically durative)
Band 4 Flashback	Pluperfect
Band 5 Irrealis	*ti-/tu-* preterites contrafactuals
Band 6 Setting?	Present, rare in narrative; not well understood
Band 7 Cohesion	Cohesive functions of Preterite or Imperfect in Adverbial clauses

Items in Band 2–Band 6 can be marked with *-tza'* (crucial background).

and therefore sometimes overlap temporally with the event reported in the preterite of the adjoining clause. In this respect the *imperfect* of Totonac (and Romance) is partially parallel to the *perfect* of Biblical Hebrew which also emerges as a backgrounding tense (described below)—in spite of the seeming incompatibility of the labels. The Totonac imperfect not only describes events which are relegated to a sort of secondary storyline, but also is used extensively in settings. I question, therefore, whether we should posit for Totonac a Band six, that is, a separate *setting* band (as in English) or a nominal/nonverbal clause band (as in Biblical Hebrew)[2]. Band six is tentatively posited to account for certain uses of the present tense in Totonac. The uses of the Totonac imperfect in setting-like functions are included in Band two.

The preterite is clearly the foregrounding tense/aspect in Totonac narrative; the storyline begins with the onset of the first preterite. A preterite may be promoted to a *pivotal event* by the use of *tuncan* "then" or *la' tuncan* "and then." My colleagues who study Totonac and I have made no attempt to sort out

---

[2]Actually Totonac does have four nonverbal clause types but their use in monologue (as opposed to dialogue) is so rare that I ignore them here.

nouns as to their case roles and verbs as to transitivity types as I have done in English (S/Ag vs. S/Ex vs. S/P). I suspect, however, that motion verbs again take a subsidiary position relative to action verbs.

Before leaving this discussion of the Totonac preterite vis-a-vis the imperfect, I mention a peculiar subtype of narrative discourse which Bishop refers to as a "cyclic" narrative, and explains as "short, condensed, parallel incidents" (1979:61). Thus, in the long text that she and others have analyzed there is in one section a series of parallel planting episodes, that is, the actions consist of the hero moving from one place to the next, asking workers what they are doing, and receiving a response, in accordance with which the workers see the results the next day (Reid, Bishop, Button, & Longacre, 1968). What is peculiar in these short parallel embedded discourses is the disappearance of the preterite from the text. The imperfect now carried the load of what is usually expressed as Band one plus Band two, that is, there is a collapsing of the distinction between foregrounded and backgrounded material (cf. the structure of a back-set narrative in English where foregrounded and backgrounded material are collapsed into the English pluperfect). A further characteristic of "cyclic" narrative is the more frequent occurrence there of the present tense—but not frequent enough to become a general backgrounding tense.

Totonac also has a specifically durative past tense, the past progressive, which encodes backgrounded *activities* of participants. It also has a pluperfect, which in general is parallel to the English pluperfect (much more work needs to be done on this tense in *both* languages). These tenses determine Bands three and four respectively.

The irrealis band especially has to do with two prefixes *ti-* "try in vain" and *tu-* negative. Either of these prefixes when affixed to a preterite verb encodes events that don't actualize and suggests alternative worlds from the text world which is presented in the story. Because the verbs thus affixed suggest alternative worlds I put them in Band five at considerable remove from the storyline (cf. English). The fact that these verbs, even though preterites, rank clearly somewhere below Band one can be argued from the distribution of *-tza'*. The latter particle is a promoter of background information. As such, it does not regularly occur with independent, nonrealis (uncompromised) preterites, while *-tza'* can mark dependent irrealis preterites.

Below this line I am not so sure of the relative ranking. The Totonac present tense has a few restricted uses in Totonac narrative. Some of these are grammatically predictable and well below the line of relevance, for example, the present tense can characterize the second verb of a verb phrase whose first verb is a preterite, and the present also occurs in awareness and speech quotes (where in fact *any* tense can occur). Aside from these grammatically specifiable usages the present can also occur in the narrative framework with a suffix *-telha* "goes around doing" to express, for example, the feelings of a participant. I take this to be a kind of setting and tentatively assign such *-telha* presents to Band six.

Perhaps they should go above the irrealis band, but we need to see more examples in text of -*telha* presents (and other uses of the present) to be sure that we have this matter sorted out correctly.

Band seven (Cohesion) is much as in English. I suppose that the distinction of script-determined back reference as opposed to purely repetitive back reference should hold here as well.

As to promoters and demoters in Totonac, two promoters are indicated in Table 2: (1) (*la'*) *tuncan* which promotes an independent, nonirrealis predicate to the position of pivotal storyline status, and (2) -*tza'* which promotes any piece of background (Bands 2–7) to crucial background (as high as Band 2?). A word about each.

Tuncan can be used discriminately by a good storyteller so that only crucial independent realis predicates are so marked. A less skilled storyteller may, however, make running use of "and then" to start every sentence. *Tuncan* has also a few special uses: For example, it occurs *at peaks* of story with imperfect verbs and irrealis preterites, even though the story is stalled and is not moving forward (cf. 3.3); here apparently it promotes these elements to status storyline (cf. 3.2. below).

As for -*tza'*, it is a sort of emphasizer, almost equal to extra high intonation in English. Nevertheless, its meaning should not simply be dissolved into "emphasis"; rather, as Bishop argues (1979:49) "When it [-*tza'*] occurs suffixed to a verb, the development of the story hinges on that action." She also notes its special prevalence around peak—but this is probably a further consideration.[3]

1.2.2 For Aguacatec, a Mayan language of Guatemala, we have data from Harry and Lucille McArthur. The data enable us to construct a partial rank scheme for a type of narrative which Harry McArthur calls the *definite event* narrative[4] (Table 3).

The upper ranks of the scheme turn on the distinction between what Harry McArthur (1979) calls *primary* and *secondary* events (Bands 1 and 2). Primary events have verbs with a zero aspect marker, that is, the "completed definite aspect." Secondary events are marked by what the McArthurs term *participles*—

---

[3]While -*tza'* apparently promotes independent verbs a peg or two in the scheme, difficulties arise when it is suffixed to a dependent verb. Shifting an independent preterite to a dependent preterite is a demotion device, as in English. But what is to be inferred when -*tza'* occurs on a dependent preterite? Maybe somewhere along the line we may have to assume that a difference between structural and semantic foregrounding occurs, with whatever restatement and adjustment that such a distinction would call for. This problem can probably be resolved only by resort to the analysis of a representative set of paragraphs in which -*tza'* figures prominently. Our return to Totonac in section 3, where salience in Totonac paragraphs is explored, will unfortunately leave the -*tza'* problem largely untouched.

[4]This is distinct from, for example, the immediate past narrative which is a loose recounting of experiences which have taken place on the same day that they are recounted. This latter narrative in effect collapses what is handled as Bands 1 and 2 above into a common form, the verb with *n-/m-* completed indefinite aspect.

TABLE 3
Aguacatec, McArthur, 1979

Band 1 Storyline	1.1 (1.2) or (2) marked by -tz (promoter), pivotal 1.2 Ø aspect primary (=completed definite aspect)
Band 2 Secondary storyline	2. Participle forms -e'n/-Vl
Band 3 Background	3.1 (3.2) marked with -tz (promoter); crucial background 3.2 Background: aspect/clause types other than (1) or (2) above

which may, however, occur in independent as well as in dependent clauses; essentially such verbs earmark their clauses as in some sense ancillary even though the clauses in which they figure constitute complete sentences. In preposed adverbial clauses their function is more like that of an English participle. Consider, by analogy, the participles of Biblical Hebrew which may also occur as verbs in independent clauses.

McArthur does not give us information regarding the structure of such elements as flashbacks and collateral. He describes a class of clauses which constitutes background information as clauses containing the existential verb *at* "there is/are," and verbless equative clauses which he calls topic-comment.

Of considerable interest here is a *-tz* suffix which attaches itself to the last occurring element of a VSO nucleus (i.e., only to the verb if S or O is not expressed, to the S in VS, and to the O in VSO). Lucille McArthur devotes an entire paper (1979) to discussion of *-tz* relative to various text types and uses within each type. Her paper and Harry McArthur's paper agree that *-tz*, added to a clause whose verb indicates primary or secondary storyline status (our Bands 1 and 2), results in a *promotion* (my terminology) of that clause to pivotal storyline status, which I indicate as Band 1. Likewise Band 3.2 can be promoted to 3.1, background matters of crucial importance, by the addition of *-tz*. A search of other Mayan languages to see if a similar particle can be found would be in order. If a Proto-Mayan particle such as *$*tx(V)$* occurred, it could be fruitfully compared with the Totonac *-tza'* of similar function.

1.2.3 For Rabinal Achi we have data from Carol Barrera conveyed to us by Larry and Linda Jones (1979). The data are too fragmentary to permit us to construct even a partial rank scheme but are nevertheless suggestive. In Rabinal Achi narrative the storyline verbs are in the completive aspect while background is incompletive. Semantic doublets (containing the template clause and its paraphrase) perform a function like *-tz* in Aguacatec, that is, the more pivotal mainline events are reported in such doublets while crucial (as opposed to ordinary) background is encoded in the same way. The chief value of this is its serving to alert us to the importance of paraphrase as figuring into schemes of storyline ranking in some language. Since Mayan languages abound in devices of para-

TABLE 4
Kickapoo, Jones, and Coleman, 1979

Band 1 Storyline	1.1 Doublets *1st Aorist Independent Indicative* + *2nd Aorist Conjunctive*: Pivotal 1.2 *2nd Aorist Conjunct Conjunctive*.
Band 2 background, Secondary storyline grading into crucial (?) background	2. *1st Aorist Conjunct Conjunctive*: "Demoted" events (routine or predictable); "Promoted" (descriptive of setting, participants)
Band 3 Background	3. *1st Aorist Independent Indicative*: Descriptive, setting, participants, mental/emotional states. Topic/participant prominent.
Band 4 Thematic	4. *3rd Aorist Conjunct Conjunctive*: Theme statements (to introduce/conclude a topic)

phrase and repetition, this clue might well guide future investigators in the discourse structure of Mayan languages.

1.3 We next consider a rank scheme for Kickapoo, a (Central) Algonquian language.[5] An immediate obstacle here in trying to summarize Kickapoo tense-aspect and mode relative to discourse is the extreme complexity of the verbal system and the equally forbidding complexity of the jargon in which Algonquian grammar has been described by Algonquianists. The Jones and Coleman paper (1979), on which this summary is based, conforms to typical Algonquian nomenclature (Voorhis, 1974), and attempts to explain, in textual terms, the *raison d'être* of such a system and of its various parts. While some discussion is made of Kickapoo modes and tenses as a whole (as they are distributed through various types of text), the discussion centers on *narrative*. As Jones and Coleman put it "We hope to demonstrate that one important function of these various modes and tenses in Kickapoo is to indicate the relative significance of a chunk of information within a narrative" (75).

Bands 1, 2, 3, 4 are characterized by the following Kickapoo mode-tense forms respectively (Table 4): conjunct conjunctive, second aorist; conjunct conjunctive, first aorist; independent indicative, first aorist; and conjunct conjunctive, third aorist. "Conjunct" versus "independent" is an inherited piece of inappropriate terminology in which it was formerly supposed that the conjunct modes (4 in Kickapoo) were somehow subordinate to or at least ancillary to the

---

[5]Although the data are from the Kickapoo dialect spoken by a band which ranges across the U.S.-Mexican border, Kickapoo is not, properly speaking, a Mesoamerican language; rather the Kickapoo are late immigrants to Mexico within historic times.

independent modes (indicative and dubitative in Kickapoo); the whole misapprehension may have simply been an egregiously poor result of the time-honored method of soliciting sentences in isolation. At any rate, it is the various tenses of the "conjunct conjunctive" that bear most of the weight in carrying a story forward in Kickapoo. Specifically, (1) storyline sentences have the conjunct conjunctive, second aorist; while (2) the conjunct conjunctive first aorist is a kind of secondary storyline (routine events) or is especially crucial background. In respect to the latter there is no promoter as in Totonac (*-tza'*) or in Aguacatec (*-tz*); rather, a distinctive tense is used. The conjunct conjunctive, third aorist, which I put in Band 4, has very special thematic/cohesive functions, that is, it can be "used to make thematic statements to begin a section of text or to summarize a section" (90). We are also told that this same construction marks themes in nonnarrative text types as well, and is characteristically associated with performance verbs: "what I did was . . . ", "what I said was. . . ." At any rate, such material by virtue of being thematic is at considerable distance from the storyline itself.

It remains to discuss the independent indicative, first aorist. This mode and tense is used in various kinds of setting and background, descriptions, introduction of participants, mental and emotional states. As such, it can also characterize the peak of a story (cf. the concept of a suspension point in Labov and Waletsky, 1967). It has a further very important use, that is, as a paraphrase of a conjunct conjunctive, second aorist in a *doublet*, to mark pivotal storyline status (my Band 1); cf. Rabinal Achi in 1.2.3 above.

1.4 Two languages of India have also been studied from this perspective, that is, Gujarati (Christian, 1983) and Halbi (Woods, 1980). Both belong to the Indo-Iranian branch of Indoeuropean. The latter language is comparatively obscure, but the former is better known.

1.4.1 Imanuel Christian (1987) specifically ties his discussion of Gujarati narrative into the general Indic features of *clause-chaining, verb-compounding,* and *ergativity*. Indic, as opposed to the other branches of Indoeuropean, has a (medial)^n + final pattern of clause sequence within the sentence such as found in Korean, Japanese, languages of Papua New Guinea, Ethiopia, languages of (northern) South America, and certain languages of the American Southwest (except that the Gujarati chain must have the same subject referent). Like these languages it has an SOV canonical order. Also, as in some of these languages, there has been a development in which certain medial-final verb combinations have coalesced into verb compounds (with grammaticalization of the second verb which becomes a sort of dummy auxiliary which receives the main inflections while the first verb carries the main lexical load). Also, a split ergative system characterizes Gujarati as well, that is, all past and perfective tense-aspects show ergative-absolutive structure, while other tense-aspects have nominative-accusative structure. Thus, characteristically, final verbs dominate over medial verbs in salience, compounds require evaluation as to salience, and ergative constructions (by virtue of their tense-aspect choice) dominate over nominative-accusative constructions.⁶

In presenting Christian's rank scheme for Gujarati I renumber his categories according to my band grouping. Otherwise, I follow his original distinctions with only some slight adaptations: (a) I change this *eventline* to *storyline* except in explicit quotations; (b) I group his categories 2.1 and 2.2 into a background activities band, and suggest that category 4 is setting or grades off into setting.

Christian's rank scheme (Table 5) turns on the following oppositions: punctiliar versus nonpunctiliar aspects, compound verbs versus simple verbs, and final verbs versus medials. At the top of the scheme he puts punctiliar aspect in compound verbs. Both verbs in such a compound are marked for completive aspect and in every case the compound verb is clause-final. In particular, a negative or a form of "be" does not follow the compound. As to the meaning of the forms on this band, Christian comments: "The emphasis in these types of compound verbs is not on aspect in the sense of punctiliar versus non-punctiliar, but rather on *suddenness* or *unexpectedness of the event,* or in some instances on the exhaustiveness of the activity" (p. 79). He also mentions that use of verbs on this band indicates "fast progress in the eventline . . . the eventline takes off and picks up speed" (p. 80). For the latter reason, he comments, "these compound verbs are never used at the beginning of a narrative" (p. 80).

Band 1.2, the secondary storyline, also has verbs in the punctiliar aspect, but has simple instead of compound verbs. Regarding the verbs in this band, Christian explains:

> The secondary eventline presents events that are significant for the overall plot structure. However, these events are not as crucial as the events on the primary eventline. . . These events are more or less expected from the contextual structure of the narrative . . . they do not present strikingly new or unexpected information (p. 81).

He further explains: "The main functions of the secondary eventline are to slow down the action and to add more detail" (p. 81). Apparently Bands 1 and 2 of the salience scheme for Gujarati encode information distributed over Bands 1–3 in Halbi (see next section).

Christian's next two categories—which I have grouped into Band 2, background actions/events—have to do with medial verbs.⁷ While previous writers on the grammar of Gujarati have considered medials marked with *-i* and those

---

⁶But even here we have to be cautious in analyzing compound verbs functionally. It is the *last* verb of a compound (which is sometimes a grammatical dummy) which determines ergative versus nonergative status regardless of the status of the preceding *lexically* dominating verb.

⁷Again, we need to remind ourselves that medial verbs cannot be considered simply straightforward parallels to subordinated clauses in nonchaining languages. When independent clauses are not coordinated as in English, a medial and a final can pattern much like coordinated clauses.

TABLE 5
Gujarati, Christian, 1983

Band 1 Storyline	1.1 Punctiliar aspect (-*i*-/-*y*-) + Compound verbs: Primary 1.2 Punctiliar aspect (-*y*-) + Noncompound verbs: Secondary
Band 2 Background Actions/events	2.1 Medial verbs with -*i*: ("Suppressed storyline") 2.2 Medial verbs with -*i* + *ne*: the how's and why's; minor actions/events
Band 3 Background activities	3.1 Nonpunctiliar aspect + compound verb: Primary 3.2 Progressive Perfect aspect -*t*- and -*t* + *y*-; Secondary
Band 4 Minor background (setting?)	4. Medial verbs -*i* and -*i* + *ne*

1. In many of these bands there are qualifications, for example, barring "be" from (1.1) & (3.1); barring negatives in some places.

2. (3.2) includes past progressive, past perfect, and present progressive final verb (noncompound).

3. (2.1) + (2.2) versus (4.); status of final verb (on-off status) determines medial which precedes.

marked with -*ine* to be free variants, Christian points out that they have different discourse functions. The medials with -*i* are "a suppressed event-line"; compare our notion of *demoting* a past tense in English by making it an adverbial clause. Clearly some such notion as *suppression* and *demotion* is in order here, for, as Christian observes, -*i* medials are on the "suppressed event-line" if they are dependent on a verb in the primary or secondary eventline. As we see below -*i* medials which are dependent on a verb from Bands 5 or 6 are background, like the verbs on which they depend. Regarding verbs in this category, Christian writes: "Events reported on this level are only weakly sequential and grade off into temporal overlap" (p. 82). Regarding the -*i* medials in one example he comments "They merely add detail to the narrative by describing step by step what happens" (p. 82). While all that has preceded argues that category 2.1 can indeed be considered to be a low level of the storyline (almost a semantic reflex of the grammatical transformation of an independent punctiliar verb to a medial), Christian also mentions that medial verbs can have a recapitulatory cohesive function which would cause me to relegate verbs which are used in this function to the lowest band of such a scheme (a cohesive band, not in Table 5). But—whether we deal with medials in a chaining language or adverbial clauses in a coranking language—the fact remains that some sort of split-level analysis of such constructions seems unavoidable; some add new information while others are purely cohesive.

Medials marked with -*ine* (2.2) are considered by Christian to encode minor events that are down a peg from the "suppressed eventline." Christian explains:

"These events are minor compared to the events presented by medial verbs with suffix -*i*. The latter are separate events informing the reader *what* happened before an event on the primary or secondary eventline took place, whereas events presented by medial verbs with the additional suffix -*ne* inform the reader *how* or *why* an event in the primary or secondary eventline took place" (p. 84). Nevertheless, as he points out, the how's and why's are minor events, not just background reasons. Again, the -*ine* medial must be dependent on a storyline verb if it is to count as storyline and not background (pp. 85–86).

Categories 3.1–3.2 are labeled background in Christian's scheme and background activities in my revision; category 3.1, his primary background, consists precisely of compound verbs which don't qualify for the primary storyline; they either have a -*wa* ending on the first verb or *r h* "remain" as the second verb. These mark duration in some sense, whether activity or state. Secondary background, Band 3.2 consists of three aspects which Christian does not attempt to rank relative to each other: past progressive, present progressive, and past perfect. Christian also puts here any compound verbs which are followed by a form of the verb "be" (p. 91). Christian summarizes "The progressive aspect, presents the information about the present situation, about the routine or habitual activities, or ongoing process. The perfective aspect, on the other hand, provides the background information about the activity of the participant in the past which has continuing effect in the present" (p. 94).

Minor background is encoded in any medial -*i* or -*ine* verb that is dependent on an independent verb that expresses background. This is essentially low-level material that rounds out the story.

1.4.2 Table 6, a rank scheme for Halbi, is taken with some adaptation from Woods (1980). Aside from minor terminological changes ('event-line' to storyline), I have tried to regroup elements of her scheme into bands which resemble what we find in other languages (without changing the relative order of salience). She originally grouped 1.1–3 under events, 4.1–5.1 under background and 5.2–5.4 under setting and terminus. I have regrouped 1.1–1.3 as storyline, 2 as background, 3 as flashback, 4.1–4.2 as setting, and 5.1–5.4 as cohesive and thematic.

The analysis of the storyline bands for Halbi turns on the ranking of three Halbi tense-aspect forms. The highest rank is assigned to completed action verbs, which are similar to the simple English past and have a characteristic -*l* in the person-number endings. Second rank is assigned to present incomplete verbs, which have an -*s*- in their person-number endings. Third rank is assigned to verbs which are action verbs but have "depictive" endings (which distinguish only person-number). We have here not merely primary and secondary storylines such as can be posited for Totonac, Aguacatec, Kickapoo, and Biblical Hebrew, but a three-way split into primary, secondary, and tertiary storylines.

Woods briefly describes the primary storyline as: "The verbs of the main

TABLE 6
Halbi, F. Woods, 1980 (adapted)

Band 1 Storyline	1.1 Primary storyline -l + ⟨-e, -is, -i/o, -u, -as, -a⟩ completed action in the past: (cf. English past) 1.2 Secondary storyline ⟨-s- + person/no. endings⟩ (actually = present incomplete but used with events/participants of secondary importance) 1.3 Tertiary storyline (depictive action verbs; only person/number endings; background/routine/weakly sequential)
Band 2 Background	2. Background actions/activities/events (dependent verb endings -un prior (cf. plup), -te incompletive; to-ke in "-ing" function; the latter two indicate temporal overlap with action in main verb)
Band 3 Flashback	3. Flashback Vb (-u conjunction "and" + auxiliary ro "be" + depictive endings: "to be in a state of having done X")
Band 4 Setting	4.1 Backgrounded static activity (main verb + -te (incomplete) + ro "be" + depictive endings 4.2 Depictive (with depictive endings: on nonaction verbs; on negative of action verbs; on repeated verbs [durative])
Band 5 Cohesive & thematic	5.1 Identification 5.2 Time (various) 5.3 Event (RhQ's & TC's) 5.4 Location *ase*, stative verb

eventline are all action verbs occurring in temporally sequenced strings" (123). She describes at length the secondary storyline: "While retaining and continuing the temporal sequence of the narrative, secondary events are less prominent than the backbone itself" (123). "Marking an event as less important (through the use of the present incomplete endings) indicates that either the event itself is not in focus or that the participant performing the activity lacks prominence. . ." (124). She mentions that a secondary storyline can "slow down the reporting of the action and build up suspense" (126), and can "have the effect of further specifying, clarifying, or augmenting the mainline events in the same way" (127).

The tertiary storyline is represented by Woods as "a device for indicating that an event (or series of events) is backgrounded and routine" (128). Her emphasis on "routine" and "habitual" (130) leads me to interpret her tertiary eventline as referring to script-predictable actions—which have a way of getting special treatment in some languages.[8] Woods also specifies that the verb forms themselves are "only weakly sequential, since they have no tense-aspect markers"—

---

[8] For example, in Camsa narrative (Howard, 1977) while a series of clauses with finite past tense is the backbone of a story, a script-predictable activity (e.g., the procedures involved in clearing a blocked road on a mountainside after an avalanche) is reduced to a string of nonfinite forms (infinitives) such as are used in procedural how-to-do-it discourse.

and in fact when not in *action* verbs (as here) figure in Band 4 below. The tertiary eventline is also used in some situations similar to the use of the secondary eventline, that is, "to indicate backgrounded action by a non-prominent partici-

I will dispose rather quickly of the remaining bands of the Halbi rank scheme as formulated by Woods and modified and renumbered in my own restatement. Her "backgrounded events" (Band 2) refer to dependent verbs with dependent verb endings in a chaining structure. These endings indicate that the action represented in the dependent verb antedates that of the main verb (*-un*), is simultaneous with the main verb (*-te*), or is meant to signal a new paragraph by introducing a new time horizon (*-take*) (but cf. 5.2 lower in the scheme). I suspect that some of these may be simply backreferential so that such constructions so used would properly figure under cohesion below. When, however, a dependent clause introduces a *new* event, it can be regarded as demoted by grammatical subordination to Band 2, as here indicated. Woods' next category is flashback, as used in the usual sense of that term (cf. the English pluperfect). Her categories 4.1 and 4.2, which I have separated from 5.1 as setting, have verb forms which she describes as "backgrounded static activity" ("something was occurring," 133) and "depictive" ("describes or delineates a participant.") The verb forms used for depiction must be resorted to in order to negate what would otherwise be a present incompletive on the secondary storyline—since the latter is never negated (135). Apparently, therefore, at least one irrealis construction is found in this band. (Other sorts of negatives and modals are not indicated and no irrealis band as such was set up). Woods' category 5.1, which I group along with her 5.2–5.4, is labeled identification and involves the use of an existential clause in a kind of topicalization. Categories 5.2, 5.3, and 5.4 include a variety of constructions, some of which are possibly so low-level as not to belong on a chart of this sort (e.g., time phrases in 5.2), some of which are dependent clauses in cohesive function, and others of which involve sentences in special text functions, for example, rhetorical questions, topic-comment sentences, alternative sentences) which help establish episode boundaries in narrative. I believe categories 5.1–5.4 can all be grouped into a cohesive and thematic band in that the constructions found here relate to overall text structure: that is, cohesion, thematization, and articulation of parts (cf. English and Kickapoo).
1.5 We turn now to Ténhé, a language of Ivory Coast (presumably a Gur or "Voltaic" language) with SVO structure. The data are from Inge Leenhouts (1983). I have adapted somewhat her salience scheme but the main outline is still hers.

One well-known feature of West African languages is the use of *serial verbs*. This term is a cover for constructions that apparently pattern all the way from a verb phrase to a sequence of clauses. Leenhouts sorts out three differing constructions in this general range and assigns each of them to a separate rank in her salience scheme. All are same subject constructions, *with tense-aspect marked only on the first verb but applying to the whole string.* The most cohesive such construction seems to be what Leenhouts calls the *potential aspect;* here a pronoun and tense-aspect marker precede the first verb with up to two or more verbs following (one or two modals and a main verb). Somewhat different is the *dynamic past* which has no tense-aspect marking on any verb, even the first, and repeats the subject pronoun before each verb. An object pronoun can also occur. Again modal verbs accompany a main verb. *Another type of serial verb is unmistakably a series of clauses. Again, however, tense-aspect is marked only on the first verb and the noun/pronoun subject of clause one is not repeated.* The conjunction *IE* "and" occurs between the clauses. Leenhouts calls this last construction *procedural* aspect.

As seen from the salience scheme which I offer here (Table 7)[9] the dynamic past and the simple past are especially crucial to telling a story in Ténhé. Regarding the first Leenhouts says, "This construction reflects highly dynamic activity. It is past completed action" (70). She goes on to explain, "All occurrences of the dynamic past, except for one . . . are non-quotes. They are important as framework of the story (73). There are no examples of this type in the introduction; the last four examples are in the epilogue" (73) [but she goes on to discuss some of the latter as doubtful]. Is it too much to see in the striking repetition of the pronoun a sort of "I came, I saw, I conquered" way of reporting events? In regard to the simple past, Leenhouts observes that such clauses (a) describe completed action, (b) report events in chronological sequence, and (c) when put together make a patchy abstract of the story [the addition of the dynamic past forms is needed to round out the abstract.] In regard to this interplay of a serial verb construction with a simple verb, compare Gujarati where the highest rank of dynamicity goes to a compound verb and the next rank to a simple verb. Compare also the role of doublets of clauses in Kickapoo and Rabinal Achi in marking top ranks in their salience schemes.

As nearly as I can understand Leenhouts' reasoning, she groups under 3 both simple clauses with one verb marked with the habitual aspect and also serial verbs joined with *IE* "and" when the first such verb is so marked. The latter amount to script-predictable parts of the story.[10] This may not be a far-fetched comparison with the tertiary event-line that Woods posits for Halbi where script-determinable sequences are also encoded. In that such sequences are *events,* but rather *predictable* ones, they should indeed rank comparatively lower than other events.

---

[9]I have made only one major change in Leenhouts' line-up: that of placing statives/nonverbals about the middle of the scheme instead of at its very bottom. I take complete responsibility for this change and do not assume that Leenhouts will necessarily concur with it.

[10]Where the script refers to an apparently all-too-routine procedure of grabbing a wife, beating her, and dropping her (twice in this text).

TABLE 7
Ténhé, Revision of Leenhouts, 1983

text world	1 Dynamic past: pr V_1 pr V_2 pr V_3 (unmarked aspect) 2 Simple past (marked aspect) 3 Procedural/habitual: N/pr cl_1 IE cl_2 IE cl_3 4 Stative/nonverbal (setting)
worlds within quotes	5 Present/Immediate future

alternative worlds	6 Irrealis:
	    Potential-Future
	    pronoun-aspect $V_1 V_2 V_3$
	    Conditional/Subjunctive

Note. Adapted from Leenhouts. My main change consists in moving the stative/nonverbal (which she ranks lowest) up to a position preceding both Present/Immediate future and the Irrealis constructions.

I put together the statives and nonverbals of Leenhouts' scheme and elevate them to category 4. My reason for doing this is that they are needed to complete the world of the narrative framework. They are depictive, existential-locative, and often introductory.

In category 5 we find tense-aspects that occur only in quotations, not in the framework of the narrative. Each quotation, as it were, opens a window into the world of the quotation which is complexly and often obliquely attached to the world of the narrative framework. What Leenhouts does here might well suggest similar expedients in other languages.

Finally, I put in category 6 irrealis material which Leenhouts internally differentiates with the Potential and Future ranking higher than the Conditional and the Subjective. All these constructions, it seems to me, present alternative worlds to the text world. It is quite probable the Leenhouts is justified in ranking the constructions as she does, but for the purposes of this paper, I consider all of them jointly. The variety of construction is such here that in a different discourse type they would probably sort out clearly according to salience for that type. Furthermore, some of the constructions may sort out according to sentence-level constraints; consider, for example, the structure of contrafactual sentences, even in narrative discourse.

Leenhouts simply divides her rank scheme for Ténhé into the broad bands: text-world, world within quotes, and alternative worlds. A suggested restatement of her bands and categories—to make them similar to the schemes already presented—would be to make her 1 and 2 primary and secondary storylines; to recognize in her category 3 background actions grading off into background activity; and to treat 6 as irrealis. Her category 5, the world within quotes, could, of course, be added to the rank scheme for narrative in any language. I have chosen rather to put speech verbs in the storyline—and, by implication, the content of what is said (which is often nonnarrative in discourse type).

1.6 We turn now to an ancient Semitic language for which there is a very large extant corpus of narrative text, that is, Biblical Hebrew. The rank scheme order suggested here and represented diagrammatically in Table 8 is based on my own studies of Biblical Hebrew narrative discourse as carried out over several years but the scheme given here differs somewhat from my previous schemes.

Every scholar in the field of Biblical Hebrew studies will readily admit that the preterite, as I term it (the *waw*-consecutive with the imperfect), is the backbone of Hebrew narration. Furthermore, it has been suggested since the time of the Medieval Arabic grammarians that in both Arabic and Hebrew, verb-initial clauses are *verbal*, that is, they describe actions, events, happenings, and the like, while clauses with initial nouns, regardless of the form of the verb, are in some sense *nominal*, that is, they are oriented towards the noun which begins the clause. These (rather ancient) insights have guided the formation of the scheme represented in Table 8, as has also the general notion that some such ranking as the following is to be expected: events/actions—activities—descriptions/existentials/equatives—modals.

Biblical Hebrew was a VSO language or at least a verb-initial one, if we are to go by the canonical form of the storyline clauses in narrative in that language. Thus, in category 1.1, we find *only* preterite verbs in verb-initial clauses; the fronting of a noun or the preposing of *lô* "not" is sufficient to drop a verb down into category 1.3 or 4. Clauses in 1.1 are under most conditions sequential and nonparaphrastic, that is, the *same* event is not normally referred to twice or more in a series of preterites.

Categories 1.2 and 1.3 involve a tense that has traditionally been called the perfect or sufformative tense (cf. Bailey, 1983). The perfect may occur in VSO clauses or in SVO or even OVS clauses. Sequences of two or more perfects are comparatively rare, are only weakly sequential,[11] and typically involve preposed nouns thrown into contrast. A VSO clause with an initial perfect encodes an action/event that is in some sense secondary, that is, preparatory to, or resultant from the main event represented in the preterite of another clause. It may also paraphrase an event represented by a verb in the preterite. It may on occasion be translated as a pluperfect. Furthermore, as said above, the fronting of a noun closes the option of using a preterite and necessitates a shift to the perfect. Here the noun is in some sense spotlighted or contrasted; sometimes it simply introduces a participant into the story. The narrator, as it were, steps off the storyline, to perform another one of his chores, that of introducing, tracking, contrasting,

---

[11]There may, for example, be a *gam* "also" introducing a perfect which follows another perfect. The particle *gam* does not as such mark time sequence but is an additive coordinator. None of my observations regarding the "only weakly sequential" nature of the perfect apply to the waw-consecutive perfect, which forms the mainline of procedural and prophetic text in Biblical Hebrew.

TABLE 8
Biblical Hebrew, Longacre

Band 1 Storyline	1.1 Preterite: primary 1.2 Perfect: Secondary 1.3 N + Perfect: Secondary with noun in focus	
Band 2 Backgrounded Activities	2.1 N + Imperfect: implicitly durative/repetitive 2.2 *hinnê* + participle 2.3 Participle. 2.4 N + Participle	explicitly durative
Band 3 Setting	3.1 Preterite of *hayâ* "be" 3.2 Perfect of *hayâ* "be" 3.3 Nominal clause (verbless) 3.4 Existential clause with *yeš*	
Band 4 Irrealis	4. Negation of verb in any band	
Band 5 Cohesion (back-referential)	(−/+ *wayhî* + Temp Ph/Cl)	5.1 General reference 5.2 Script-predictable 5.3 Repetitive

Note. 1. (1.1) demotes to 1.3 by preposing a *N*.
2. (1.1) demotes to (4.) by preposing *lô* "not"
3. *'ešer* relative clauses and *kî* causal clauses are demoted
4. (3.3) promotes to (3.1/3.2) by *hayâ* insertion
5. "significant negation" promotes (4.) to (1.2/1.3).

even phasing out of participants. Likewise negated verbs in a story come out here as *lô'* "not" plus a perfect (Band 4)—since preterites cannot be negated and remain preterites.

I had previously simply ranked all sorts of perfects, that is, the perfect VSO clauses, noun + a perfect, and *lô'* "not" plus a perfect in one band. According to this scheme N + perfect was outranked by the perfect in VSO clauses and the negated perfect was shunted *somewhere* off to the side. I now, however, place *all* negatives in an irrealis band towards the bottom of the scheme. At all events, it is necessary to give recognition to the special structural fact that in telling a Hebrew story, preterites cannot be negated while perfects may.

Before leaving this discussion of Biblical Hebrew preterite versus imperfect, I mention a further consideration, that of the transitivity classification of the verbs which encode as preterites. While I have made no general classification of this sort, I have reason to believe that motion verbs are not as salient as action verbs. Thus, given a succession of clauses with two preterites, when the first is a motion verb, it seems to function to move a participant onto the stage or across the stage so that he or she may participate in the action.

In Band 2 occur both imperfects and participles. Both are durative/repetitive. The imperfect is comparatively rare in the framework of narrative, but the participle is comparatively frequent. While in the total range of Hebrew discourse types the imperfect has a variety of meanings (present, future, and modal) in the framework of a narrative discourse it is durative in past time. Perhaps it can be regarded as indicating a more implicitly durative/repetitive aspect while the participle is more explicitly durative (and has become the present tense in contemporary Hebrew). Participles are adjective-like and agree with the nouns which they modify in gender and number. The occurrence of the particle *hinnê* "behold" with the participle labels it, presumably, as especially significant. In terms of discourse salience I rank it above other uses of the participle.

The setting band (Band 3) includes for the most part what we find in many languages: clauses with "be" verbs—whether descriptive, equative, or existential—and nominal clauses. The latter, as verbless clauses, can suffer the insertion of *hāyâ* "be." Presumably this raises slightly the status of such clauses by promoting them from the bottom of Band 3 to somewhere near its top. In accordance with this is the fact that, in some contexts, A *hāyâ* B is ambiguous as to "A was B" or "A became B," while "A ø B" is purely equative. I also believe that the preterite of *hāyâ* outranks the perfect by parallelism to the primary and secondary storylines in Band one. The preterite form *wayhî* "and-it-happened" can take a noun like *ra'ab* "famine" as subject: "And there was a famine" (Ruth 1:1).

The irrealis band (Band 4) includes the negation of any forms from the secondary storyline on down. Most negations simply present an alternative world to the story world. A *momentous* negation[12] can be considered to be promoted by virtue of its implication for the rest of the story which follows it. Should modal imperfects be uncovered in the narrative framework (not just in quoted speech within the story), then such modal imperfects would belong here as well.

As for Band 5, Hebrew has a complement construction: *wayhî* "and it happened that. . ." which is followed by a variety of constructions all temporal in thrust and which is in turn followed quite regularly by something from Band one. This use of *wayhî* (invariable as to person, number, and gender) is distinct from its use in setting above. Here the *wayhî* is mainly an element which accompanies the temporal phrase, which can, on the other hand, occasionally occur without it. Sometimes the temporal expression is very general: *wayhî 'aḥar haddĕbarîm hā'ēllê* "and it happened after these things/affairs that. . . ." Somewhat more rarely, the temporal expression is back-referential, where it may be repetitive or script-predictable. But in either case it seems that this ratherrare resort to back reference underlines the importance of the storyline element that follows it and raises it to an action/event of pivotal status (*not* shown on Table 8).

---

[12]Note, in the context of the Genesis Flood Narrative, the failure of the dove to return to the ark in Genesis 8:21. We infer that Noah took the failure of the dove to return as indicative that the flood waters were abated. If so, this in turn led to the opening of the ark and the disembarcation—but (at all events) not until specially commanded to do so by God.

2. COMPARISON AND GENERALIZATION

2.1 Main and Subsidiary Eventlines

Every language has at least one storyline. English is a language where only one such storyline is marked—and even here it is not marked consistently since cognitive states are encoded also as the simple past tense and we must rely on adverbs or other contextual clues to distinguish cognitive events from cognitive states. Totonac, with its preterite; Aguacatec, with its uses of unmarked aspect ("completed definite"); Kickapoo, with its use of the conjunct conjunctive, second aorist; and Biblical Hebrew, with its regular use of the preterite (waw-consecutive imperfect), all mark quite consistently the main storyline of narrative text.

These same languages also have secondary storylines, the precise characteristics and functions of which vary from language to language. Thus, Totonac uses the imperfect as a secondary storyline. This tense, although basically an incompletive, can encode a background action/event as well as an activity. In "cyclic narrative" the imperfect represents a collapse of storyline and supportive material. Aguacatec uses its so-called participle as a secondary storyline; the participle seems clearly to refer to actions/events that are in some sense subsidiary. Kickapoo uses the conjunct conjunctive, second aorist as a secondary storyline but this mode and tense may encode *promoted* background materials as well as *demoted* actions/events. Biblical Hebrew uses the perfect (basically a completive but only weakly sequential) to background actions/events, or to make an action/event relative to a participant, to paraphrase an action/event, to negate what would otherwise have been a preterite, or even to encode a flashback (cf. English and Totonac pluperfects). In all these cases we see that the precise functioning of what appears to be a secondary storyline tense/aspect must be evaluated in each language, since other functions besides that of marking the secondary storyline (strictly speaking) can be assumed by the same verb form.[13] Halbi splits the storyline three ways with distinct tense aspect forms marking the first two and the third level marked by action verbs with depictive endings. The latter, when not used on action verbs, are depictive and marks setting. Woods describes the main storyline as action verbs which are sequenced temporally; the secondary storyline as actions/events which also are sequenced temporally but which refer to less important happenings or participants (and which add detail to the main storyline); and the tertiary storyline as only weakly sequential and often referring to routine or habitual (script-predictable) actions/events. As for Gujarati, the other Indic language summarized above, it seems best to me to consider that this language has but one storyline; I consider Christian's "secondary

---

[13]We again are forced back to the necessity of a consideration of *etic* versus *emic* distinctions. To the nonnative speaker, that is, an outsider to the language community, a language may seem to combine several more or less distinct verb functions which to the native speaker may be intuitively unified simply by virtue of being signalled by the same form of the verb.

eventline" to pattern as primary and his "primary" storyline as essentially a kind of promotion to mark pivotal actions/events as described below.

Ténhé, however, can be described as having a main storyline and a secondary storyline. The secondary line is more like the tertiary storyline in Halbi, that is, we find here the encoding of habitual/routine (script predictable) activities. The secondary storyline, as I interpret Leenhouts' data, can be either a simple verb clause with habitual aspect, or serial clauses connected with *1E* "and" and with the habitual aspect in the first clause.

2.2 Pivotal Events

Many languages mark pivotal storyline status by *augmenting* in some way the main storyline. In some languages the clauses marked as referring to such pivotal actions/events constitute a tolerable abstract of the story; but in some (e.g., in Ténhé) the tense aspect in question apparently is too rare for instances of its use to constitute such an abstract. I first mention clear cases of languages which augment the storyline to pivotal, then speculate as to similar possibilities in other languages.

Totonac augments the main storyline to pivotal by adding *tuncan* "then" or *la' tuncan* "and then" in clause initial. Aguacatec augments by adding *-tz* to the VSO/VS/V nucleus of the clause. Gujarati augments the simple punctiliar to a compound verb where both the main and the auxiliary are punctiliar. In Rabinal Achi and Kickapoo, a pivotal action/event is encoded by augmenting the main line clause to a construction in which that clause is accompanied by a second paraphrasing clause, that is, the single clause goes to a paraphrastic doublet. In Ténhé the simple past is replaced by a serial verb construction in which no tense aspect is marked and the pronoun is repeated before each verb; I regard this as again a kind of augmentation of the main storyline.

As to the nonhomogeneity of meaning in the "pivotal storylines" in various languages, I note especially Gujarati and Ténhé. In the former, Christian remarks that the action/event is not simply punctiliar but is somewhat surprising and unexpected. As far as Ténhé, I have already remarked that the "dynamic past" (as Leenhouts terms it) does not in and of itself make a good abstract of the story; rather the dynamic past plus the simple past yields such an abstract.

But what of English and Biblical Hebrew? Burgen (oral communication) has suggested that Biblical Hebrew has a pivotal eventline or something of the sort formed by augmenting the preterite clause to a paraphrastic doublet (with a perfect in the second clause). I do not believe, however, that paraphrastic doublets occur with sufficient frequency to assume this function. They occur, rather, in the peak region of stories. I suspect that Biblical Hebrew marks pivotal actions/events in a more oblique way, that is, by preposing a back reference as described above.

As far as English is concerned, there is no simple and regular way of marking pivotal events as such in narrative; I suspect, rather, a conspiracy of means. What

English does do is mark the climax of a narrative sequence paragraph by *finally* or some such adverb, or by a recapitulatory back reference from the preceding sentence(s) as suggested for Biblical Hebrew. Climactic events of this sort probably are broadly comparable to "pivotal" events in other languages.

The clauses marked for pivotal storyline status in Totonac, Aguacatec, and Kickapoo can be assembled so as to yield an abstract of the story in which they occur.

2.3 Actions/Events in Subordinate or Medial Clauses

Here we encounter various problems—as already discussed. To begin with, relative clauses, whatever form of verb they have, seem to be demoted to the setting band or lower. In many languages adverbial clauses seem to divide as to whether they precede or follow the main clause. Adverbial "when" clauses, for example, when preposed, very frequently are a recapitulatory back reference to previous context and fall therefore into the cohesion band at the bottom of the salience schemes. There remain, however, some cases of postposed clauses that clearly report new events in the narrative. Furthermore, such clauses can sometimes be grammatically subordinated to independent clauses whose verbs are *lower* in salience. Thus, in the example already quoted: "He was up in the tree *when he saw the wolf coming.*" As already suggested, I feel that such clauses are promoted to Band 1 by a kind of grammatical inversion of setting and storyline, motivated by considerations of participant reference (thematicity).

In Biblical Hebrew preterites cannot occur in any sort of subordinate (relative or adverbial) clause; rather, the perfect (or some other form) must occur. Similarly in Aguacatec, the simple unmarked past cannot occur in a subordinate clause; rather, the participle. In both these languages the forms that report actions/events in subordinate clauses are those of the secondary storyline.

In Totonac, which in this respect is like English, preterites can occur in both relative and adverbial clauses. They probably pattern much as in English, involve us in the same range of problems and suggest the same sorts of solutions.

Gujarati and Halbi both have a medial-final verb distinction according to which medials sometimes correspond to adverbial clauses in English and Totonac. Such clauses which express back reference belong to the cohesive band; otherwise medial clauses express backgrounded, suppressed, and minor events, as suggested in the two rank schemes[14] (Tables 5 and 6), cf. Korean (Hwang, 1987).

---

[14]In this respect, Gujarati and Halbi cannot, however, be taken to be representative of SOV chaining languages in general. In Ethiopian language of this typology, we find a type of medial verb (called "gerund or *co-verb* by many students of these languages) which is of coequal rank with the independent final verb on which it depends. Thus in Gimira (Omotic), Haddiyyah (Cushitic), Kambatta (Cushitic), and Amharic (Semitic) an unmarked medial in a clause which depends on the final verb in its clause is storyline status if the final is also storyline. In any chaining language medial verbs must be evaluated as to storyline status relative to the storyline status of the final verb.

2.4 Backgrounded Activity

We can be confident regarding the universality of backgrounded activity. If temporal succession is a linguistic universal, it seems equally plausible that temporal overlap has the same status. Indeed, in reference to the chaining and switch-reference languages of Papua New Guinea and northern South America, very regular morphological devices exist (usually within the framework of the sentence) to distinguish *succession* from *overlap*. While in such languages any sort of a chronological flashback is difficult to document, backgrounded activity is regularly encoded.

For the languages which are referred to in section 1, we do not, however, have complete information. English, it is clear, encodes backgrounded activity with verbs in the past progressive; in somewhat similar function are backgrounded cognitive states (past tense often explicitly marked by means of durative adverbs). Totonac also has a past progressive verb which is explicitly durative, while some uses of the Totonac imperfect (cf. French and Spanish) are implicitly durative as well. The Aguacatec participle, actually a secondary storyline, is sometimes, like the Totonac imperfect, durative. Biblical Hebrew has two ways of indicating backgrounded activity: by the (comparatively rare) use of the imperfect and by the use of the Hebrew participle which is explicitly durative, whether as a main verb in its clause or as a modifier within the noun phrase. Gujarati and Halbi are chaining languages without morphological switch-reference. Medial verbs in such languages can report overlap, that is, backgrounded and simultaneous activity. Woods especially mentions certain medial affixal combinations that mark overlap. Christian reports for Gujarati a special progressive verb inflection which can occur on the final verb, thus marking the sentence which ends in that verb as one that encodes backgrounded activity (his category six in Table 5). In Kickapoo and Ténhé we apparently have no data on this category of information. In the former, presumably backgrounded activity would encode under Band 2 or 3 of the rank scheme (Table 4).

2.5 Flashbacks

By no means is a special flashback tense—such as the English and Totonac pluperfect—universal among the world's languages. In Biblical Hebrew, flashback is one of the functions of the perfect in narrative but by no means either the primary or most frequent use of that form. By contrast, the English and Totonac pluperfects are (1) specific as to flashback functions and (2) limited therefore to narrative discourse (including, of course, embedded narrative in other discourse types). Even here, however, there are subsidiary functions of the pluperfect which differ from language to language. See, for example, the use of the English pluperfect in paragraph climax and the use of the Totonac pluperfect to signal a greater time interval between the adverbial clause and the main clause than when the adverbial clause contains a preterite.

Halbi has a special compound verb (verb + -*u*- "and" + auxiliary *ro* "be" +

depictive endings) to signal "to be in a state of having done." This compound verb apparently is used mainly to encode flashback.

As for the other languages mentioned in section 1, we simply do not now have published information regarding the encoding of flashback. Indeed, it may be fallacious to assume that all languages tolerate flashback in narrative text. Some languages (noticeably those of Papua New Guinea) seem rather to have a strong predilection for telling events in straightforward sequence uncluttered by reference to events that are prior and out of the sequence. In languages where there is no distinctive flashback form but where flashback is tolerated, this function coalesces with one or more other functions to constitute a rank within a rank scheme.

2.6 Setting

Setting is essentially expository. Here we find existential, equative, and descriptive clauses. Verbs such as "be" and "have" and adjectives (a class of verbs in some languages) figure prominently here as well as some sentences which employ topicalization shifts and transformations (but see 2.8 below). Thus, in English, we have such statements as: "There was a crippled man who lived next door" (existential, with "there" topicalization). "His father was a lawyer" (equative with "be"). "He had three children" (stative-relational with "have"). "His house was well kept" (stative-descriptive).

In Biblical Hebrew verbless clauses occur here as well as nominal clauses +/− the verb $hāyâ$ "be," or certain predicates which either are adjectives or are which are adjectival in thrust. Thus: $habbôr\ rēq$ "the pit (was) empty," $en\ bô\ mayîm$ "nothing was in it of water," $ha'āres\ hāyĕtâ\ tohû\ wĕvohû$ "the earth was formless and empty," and $harā'āb\ kābēd$ "the famine was heavy (severe)," where $kābēd$ is an adjectival verb.

For Totonac, our source does not explicitly identify setting, but the general parallelism of the Totonac imperfect to, for example, the imperfect of Spanish and French, may well lead us to believe that setting is often encoded by resort to this tense.[15] For Aguacatec, H. McArthur explicitly mentions the use of existential clauses (with the verb at) and nominal clauses in setting.

In Kickapoo, the first aorist independent indicative (cf. Band 3 in Table 4) certainly encodes setting as part of a broad category which also includes description of mental and emotional states and other participant-centered information.

In Halbi, Woods set up a particular category which she labeled depictive; I have grouped this with "Background static activity" into a setting band. Perhaps the category 5.1 "Identification" should go here also. In Gujarati, the other Indic

---

[15]Thus on picking up any short story of a more-or-less traditional sort in Spanish or French we are struck by the often unbroken use of the imperfect in the staging of the story—until the first preterite signifies the onset of the storyline.

language considered here, information as to the encoding of setting is lacking; setting presumably falls somewhere in category 4 or below of Table 6.

For Ténhé, Leenhouts specifically refers to stative and nonverbal clauses in which I make category 4 of Table 7 and label *setting*.

2.7 Irrealis

Here our information is especially spotty with no relevant data from Aguacatec, Kickapoo, or Gujarati and often scant information elsewhere.

In English negation, modals, and some uses of the future seem to be relevant here and are grouped together in Band 5 of Table 1. In Biblical Hebrew, after having for several years treated negated clauses as elements shunted off to the side in each band (Longacre, 1981, 1982), I have now decided to let all of them constitute an irrealis band such as is posited in other languages. Modal uses of the Biblical Hebrew imperfect could also go here—were this construction to turn up in the narrative framework of a story as opposed to within reported speech. In both English and Biblical Hebrew it seems obvious that there are *momentous negations* that critically affect the course of a story and must therefore be considered to be promoted to storyline status.

In Totonac (contrary to Longacre, 1981) I now posit a special band (Band 5 in Table 2) for verbs (often preterite) that are marked with *ti-* "in vain," "to no avail," and *tu-* "negative." Here also could fit the Totonac special contrafactual tense aspect. Again, however, the latter is more likely to occur in quotations within a story than in the framework of the story.

In Halbi, Woods reports that items which would otherwise occur in category 1.2 (secondary storyline), when negated, take only depictive endings (category 4.2 in Table 5). This forms an interesting comparison with Hebrew where preterites cannot be negated without being replaced by perfects. Here negation patterns as a demoter.

In Ténhé, I have put together various constructions that appear to me to be irrealis: the potential (a serial-verb construction), the future, the conditional, and the subjunctive.

2.8 Discourse-Cohesive Functions

Here there are two broad functions to be distinguished: (1) back reference, which is a somewhat low level device for connecting sentence with sentence or paragraph with paragraph; and (2) thematic statements which preview or summarize. The latter are in fact mentioned explicitly only in reference to Kickapoo where Jones and Coleman report that the conjunct conjunctive, third aorist is used in this function. Here presumably the use of a distinctive tense-aspect-modal form in Kickapoo forced attention on this feature. Linda Jones, however, in her work on English expository prose (1977) reports on the use of various left shifts and cleft structures in English to indicate preview/summary function in English exposition. This suggests the possibility that something parallel to these construc-

TABLE 9
Etic Bands of Salience in Narrative

1'. Pivotal storyline (augmentation of 1)
  1. Primary storyline (S/Agent > S/Experience > S/Patient)
    2. Secondary storyline
      3. Routine (script-predictable action sequences)
        4. Backgrounded actions/events
          5. Backgrounded activity (durative)
            6. Setting (exposition)
              7. Irrealis (negatives & modals)
                8. Evaluations (author intrusions)
                  9. Cohesive & thematic

Note. 1. Flashback: as an ill-defined category, it can group with (2) or (4); as a well-defined morphosyntactic category it can be added after (5).

tions can occur in English narrative as well: "The next thing that McDugall did was to set out on a collision course with his employer."

In cohesive back reference, some sort of adverbial clause (in a coranking language like English) or a medial clause (in chaining languages whether or not characterized by switch-reference morphemes) is the quasi-universal device. Biblical Hebrew is peculiar in avoiding extensive use of this device (cf. Band 5 in Table 8 and accompanying notes). The situation in Biblical Hebrew is: (1) restriction of explicit back reference to very rare and pivotal storyline marking functions (as in Gen. 39:6–7: "And his master bestowed upon Joseph the total responsibility for all his house and all that he had. *And from the day that he bestowed upon Joseph responsibility for all his house and all that he had,* the Lord blessed the Egyptian on account of Joseph" (free translation). (2) More frequent use of a general reference instead of a specific back reference, for example, *'aḥar haddĕbbārîm hā'ēlê* "after these matters/happenings." (3) Use of recapitulation of part of a story via planes of overlay (cf. Longacre, 1979a). As already explained, preterites cannot be used in any adverbial (or relative) clause.

In coranking languages such as English and Totonac or chaining languages such as Gujarati and Halbi, we must distinguish *pure* back references and *script-dictated* backreferences. As described above, the latter introduces a further, but highly predictable, action at the onset of the new sentence. For Ténhé, statements regarding cohesive features of this sort are not available at present.

2.9 Summary

In an attempt to summarize the above, I submit the scheme given in Table 9. Here I summarize some of the overt distinctions that a language may mark by employing various tense/aspect/mode or clause types and relate these distinctions to distinct text functions. I do not include here subclassification by further marking of transitivity types—whether intransitive, transitive, ditransitive; or state, process, action, and action-process. I will have more to say about the latter in a subsequent section.

I start the scheme with what I label (1) storyline events, with (1') pivotal storyline, essentially an augmentation and elaboration of (1), whether by use of a conjunction, by verb compounding, by serial verbs, or by paraphrase in a doublet of clauses. The need for (2), a secondary storyline, is well documented above. While (3) is rare, it nevertheless is documentable, for script-predictable action sequences that employ a distinctive verb form are found in Halbi, Ténhé, and several languages which are not covered in this study. Most of the other categories are sufficiently discussed above. Notice that I omit flashback as not constituting a linguistic universal even on the notional level; where it occurs as a well-defined category it ranks between (5) and (6). On the other hand, while (8) is illustrated only for English in section 1 above, it is documentable in texts in many languages around the world, and is probably a linguistic universal.

This chart is at the same time an empirical generalization from attempts to rank verbs/clauses in many languages (only a few of which are sampled here) and a scheme with a certain inherent *a priori* plausibility. I offer it therefore as an (informal) theory regarding the structure of narrative discourse. It is an expansion of Hypothesis I into an instrument for generating a discourse from its abstract by progressive and orderly addition of further textual elements in addition to the storyline.

Primarily the scheme expressed in Table 9 classifies independent clauses—including coordinated clauses in languages such as English and medial-final clauses in a chaining language whenever the clauses thus related are essentially coordinating in spite of the medial-final verb clause distinction. Dependent/subordinate clauses represent a kind of *demotion*—either as, in effect, the lowest level of storyline (3) or as cohesive elements (9). Various types of *promotion* exist, whereby an element from a band of lower status can be made to function in a higher band. At present these promotion devices have to be described in a somewhat *ad hoc* way pending further research into various languages around the world.

There is a relationship between the etic scheme formulated here and macrostructure theory, including such formulations as van Dijk's rules for reducing a text to its macrostructure, that is, obtaining an abstract of the text (van Dijk, 1977:143ff). Storyline forms are the main stuff from which abstracts are made. But abstracts can be posited on various descending levels of generality as we add further elements to the storyline. We can expect, therefore, to encounter such distinctions as are embodied in the etic scheme, especially in its upper bands, as we progress from the more general to the more specific in generating a story.

There is necessarily a primary storyline in which the *actions* of the story are expressed. A language may also formally distinguish a level of pivotal storyline status—which yields in many cases a more *concise abstract* of the story, or at least labels some storyline events as more crucial to the abstract. A language may also mark as a secondary storyline actions/events that are presupposed, preliminary, or resultant from those on the primary storyline; or it may distinguish as secondary actions/events those which are related to less important participants. Some action sequences fall into the category of routine, script-predictable actions that are marked in special ways in certain languages. The latter seem even less crucial to the storyline than those which are summarized in the secondary storyline. Finally, some actions/events can be, by grammatical subordination, shunted to even further distance from the storyline; these are the background actions/events.

In obtaining an abstract of a story we sometimes get the most concise abstract at the level of the pivotal storyline (if such is marked in the language and is not overly specialized in function as in Gujarati and Ténhé). At any rate, the primary storyline either rounds out the pivotal storyline, itself indicates the most readily available abstract, or combines with the pivotal storyline to yield such an abstract. Bands 2, 3, and 4 progressively add detail to the abstract and yield ever more complete versions of the story.

Background activities (Band 5) overlap with one or more events of the storyline and are therefore a dynamic feature related to the storyline and further incrementing the abstract as it grows in the direction of the unrestricted text. Flashbacks, which can relate actions/events or activities, fill in some further lacunae in generating the text.

Bands 6–10 are static rather than dynamic elements of the story. Of these, setting is the nearest to the storyline. Here participants are introduced and described along with considerations of space and time. At the more abstract levels of text generation a certain deficiency is felt which is met by adding elements from the setting band.

Irrealis constructions—when not momentous, story-forwarding negations—present alternative reconstructions of the text world to which all the above bands belong. As such, they are necessarily lower in status than the setting, which clearly belongs to the text world. They are clearly a late addition in the generative process.

Evaluations, that is, author instructions, are clearly one of the most peripheral and optional elements in any narrative text. The story proper could proceed without them. They introduce familiar essay-like elements into a story and permit value judgments. Often, however, they betray that a story is not being told solely as entertainment but for some sort of instruction. They are important to the thematic/didactic thrust of a text even though they are not important to the story proper. Whatever their weight and cultural/didactic function, they nevertheless are a late and loose addition in the generating of the text.

Cohesive and thematic elements are the mortar which binds together the bricks of the textual edifice, and the framing which articulates the structure of the whole. They are more on the grammatical side of the text than on the side of its content.

Thus, beginning with the higher dynamic bands of text organization, and beginning with abstracts appropriate to those levels, we proceed on down to ever lower levels, generating the detail of the text as we go until we arrive at the actual text in unrestricted form.

3. SALIENCE SCHEMES AND LOCAL RANKINGS

The two hypotheses stated at the beginning of this paper made a two-fold claim: (1) that the verb forms/clause types of a language can be hierarchically ranked in a manner relevant to the main line of development in a given text type, and (2) that this ranking proves relevant to the analysis of constituent structure of local spans of text.

Sections 1 and 2 offer evidence that the verb forms/clause types of languages of very different structures can nevertheless be arranged in rank schemes that are broadly parallel with each other. In effect, these sections together offer partial validation of the claim that story building around the world has a certain universality which is expressed in the particulars of the storyline rank scheme in a given language. The fact that storyline rank schemes are broadly parallel in all languages further strengthens the plausibility of such a scheme in any language. So much for Hypothesis I.

The second claim advanced (in Hypothesis II) is that there is a correlativity of verb rank/clause type—especially in independent clauses—so that the rank scheme of a given language can serve as a set of guidelines for constituent analysis in local spans of text. In this section our task is to give evidence that this second claim can be validated in constituent analysis. We will have to be content here—because of limitations of space—with a token validation of this claim, that is, with the analysis of a paragraph each in three languages: English, Totonac, and Biblical Hebrew.

First of all, a clarification is needed regarding *local spans* of text. It is evident that a text (1) is not a simple unilinear sequence of sentences, but (2) sentences form groupings of various sorts within a text; and (3) groups of sentences form still larger groupings. My contention for several years has been that a unit intermediate between sentence and text needs to be posited, and if we make that unit recursive in structure and also make the text itself recursive in structure, only *one* intermediate unit is needed. We might as well call this unit by the traditional name *paragraph*, even while we realize that the traditional orthographic paragraph will often not correspond with the structural unit of the same name.

I believe that a consistent view of the constituency structure of the higher levels of text can be framed by positing that (1) texts are composed of paragraphs; (2) paragraphs are composed of sentences; (3) text, paragraph, and sentence are recursive, that is, shorter texts embed within longer texts, paragraphs within paragraphs, and sentences within sentences. In this view there are no loose ends: Every group of two or more sentences that belong together in a monologue text constitutes a text—much like the manner in which clusters of clauses constitute sentences. A finite inventory of paragraph and text types (and, of course, sentence types) plus recursion is adequate to describe the constituency structure of any text in any language.

Thus, I conceive of a monologue text as consisting of an intricate nesting of constituents involving embedded texts (e.g., where each point of a text is itself a text which narrates/discusses a given subject), paragraphs, embedded paragraphs, and sentences. The latter break down into the familiar constituents of traditional grammar.

But what of the internal structure of paragraphs? I have posited schemes of paragraph analysis for quite a few years (Longacre, 1968, 1972, 1979b, 1980). Is there any way in which the arbitrariness of some of the analyses of past years can be constrained? I believe that there is and that the answer lies in taking seriously such rank schemes as those constructed here. The careful application of such salience schemes should (1) tell us which parts of paragraphs should be considered to be structurally *dominant* and which are structurally *ancillary;* and (2) in turn, provide a corrective for preliminary rank schemes when following such a scheme gives us intuitively unsatisfactory results in analyzing paragraphs within a given language. Or to put it differently: Better rank schemes and better paragraph analyses must develop in reciprocal corrective action with each other.

Let us begin with taking the sentence seriously as a structural unit: not the clause but the *sentence* which has one or more independent clauses and may be accompanied by adverbial and relative clauses (Longacre, 1985). Focusing on the sentence units of a paragraph, let us rank the verbs of the independent clauses according to the salience scheme appropriate to that text type in that language. Let us then attempt to take account of features such as overt sequence signals, lexical repetitions, cross-reference, paraphrase, and parallelism, anaphora, and deixis, which relate sentences to each other.

Serious work at this stage inevitably forces the realization that at this level of sentence-to-sentence cohesion (or sentence-to-subparagraph, or subparagraph-to-subparagraph), (1) a number—very probably a finite set—of relations are involved and (2) these relations may or may not be explicitly marked by surface structure sequence signals or morphosyntactic devices of a language but are often left implicit in the text. When unmarked, the relations are sometimes signaled by repetition, paraphrase, parallelism, commonality of thematic reference (by noun, pronoun, affix, or zero anaphora)—or simply by our general knowledge of frames and scripts (our cognitive encyclopedia/dictionary storage).

That such a set of relations exists and that it very probably is a finite set is being realized increasingly by many students of discourse. But whether we will all be able to agree on a common catalogue of these relations is another question;

a fragmentation of statement comparable to what has happened in "case grammar" seems, rather, to be the order of the day.

Most of the relations that occur between sentences can also occur within the (nonsimple) sentence in many languages as well. Within the sentence we speak of independent and subordinate clauses (or final and medial clauses in chaining languages). Between sentences, however, we feel a certain awkwardness in speaking of one sentence as subordinate to another. I suggest, therefore, that we speak of *dominance* and *ancillariness* between sentences. Within the following sentence we find an independent clause followed by a subordinate clause: *He went to the party because his boss told him to go*. But in the following paragraph we can consider sentence 1 to be dominant and the following sentence to be ancillary: *Yeah, he went to the party. His boss simply told him to go—that's why he went*. The second sentence could be variously phrased, for example, *The reason he went was his boss told him to go;* or can be left completely unmarked: *His boss simply told him to go* or *His boss had told him to go*. On the other hand, clauses can be coordinated within the sentence and sentences can be coordinated (whether marked or unmarked) within the paragraph: *John is a model airplane enthusiast and works at a museum of aviation history*. Compare the more fulsome paragraph level development: *John is a model airplane enthusiast of a most devoted sort. Moreover, he works at the Wright Museum of Aviation History where his vocation overlaps with his avocation*.

Various catalogues of such interclausal and intersentence relations are available. The Beekman-Callow catalogue (1974 and more recent recensions) is one of the oldest. Halliday and Hasan's (1976) catalogue is specific to the structure of surface connectives in English. Grimes' (1975) catalogue of rhetorical predicates has also been around for a while. Partial catalogues by van Dijk (1976) and de Beaugrande and Dressler (1981) are also on hand, as well as that found in the work of Mann and Thompson (1986).

My own catalogue was originally elaborated as a pair of joint papers with D. L. Ballard and R. Conrad (1971a, 1971b). It has gone through various elaborations and recensions (1972, 1976a, 1983a). One thing that I attempt to do in cataloguing such relations is to define, as well as I can, the lexical characteristics of the relations by characterizing their component predications in terms of synonyms, antonyms, and terms from the same semantic domain as well as by resort to an elaborated form of the statement (propositional) calculus.

I apply this catalogue directly to give one parameter of a system of paragraph types: conjoining, temporal relations, logical relations, elaborative devices, reportative devices. Further parameters of the system consist of (1) binary versus n-ary paragraphs and (2) fore-weighted, equi-weighted, and end-weighted paragraphs. Paragraphs take on the characteristics of the text types in which they occur, so that an antithetical paragraph will have narrative, procedural, hortatory, and expository variants. A paragraph may also have stylistic variants such as (1) cyclic or chiastic structure, (2) rhetorical question-and-answer structure, and (3) running quotation (Longacre, 1979b).

3.1 Relative Salience Within an English Paragraph

The paragraph which follows is from Stevenson's *Dr. Jekyll and Mr. Hyde*. I have, for convenience of reference, numbered the sentences. I have considered the orthographic sentence unit (4–5) to be two sentences which constitute an embedded paragraph—since apparently a function of the semicolon in English is to join the sentences of a low-level embedded paragraph.

> Thereupon, I arranged my clothes as best I could and, summoning a passing hansom, drove to an hotel in Portland Street, the name of which I chanced to remember. (2) At my appearance (which was indeed comical enough, however a tragic a fate those garments covered), the driver could not conceal his mirth. (3) I gnashed my teeth upon him with a gust of devilish fury; and the smile withered from his face—happily for him—yet more happily for myself, for in another instant I had certainly dragged him from his perch. (4) At the inn, as I entered, I looked about me with so black a countenance as made the attendants tremble; (5) not a look did they exchange in my presence, but obsequiously took my orders, led me to a private room, and brought me wherewithal to write. (6) Hyde in danger of his life was a creature new to me: shaken with inordinate anger, strung to the pitch of murder, lusting to inflict pain. (7) Yet the creature was astute: mastered his fury with a great effort of the will, composed his two important letters—one to Lanyon and one to Pool—and, that he might receive actual evidence of their being posted, sent them out with directions that they should be registered. (By permission, Scholastic Book Services, New York, copyright 1966.)

Consider now FIG. 1: a constituent structure tree graph of the paragraph from Stevenson. I have underlined here in the abbreviated text in the left-hand side the foregrounded (Band one) verbs (in terms of Table 1). These verbs and their clauses are:

(1) I *arranged* my clothes.
   I *drove* to an hotel in Portland Street. . .
(3) I *gnashed* my teeth upon him. . .
   the smile *withered* from his face.
(4) I *looked* about me. . .
(5) [they] obsequiously *took* my orders,
   [they] *led* me to a private room
   [they] *brought* me the wherewithal to write
(7) [he] *mastered* his fury. . .
   [he] *composed* his two important letters.
   [he] *sent* them out. . .

Notice that (according to my internal classification within Band 1 of Table 1) in all the above clauses the subject is agent—except in 3b where presumably the subject (the cab driver's smile) is patient, and has to do with a minor participant. Within sentence 3, although the independent clauses are coordinated, the second is notionally the result of the first where Dr. Jekyll/Mr. Hyde is agent. Minor

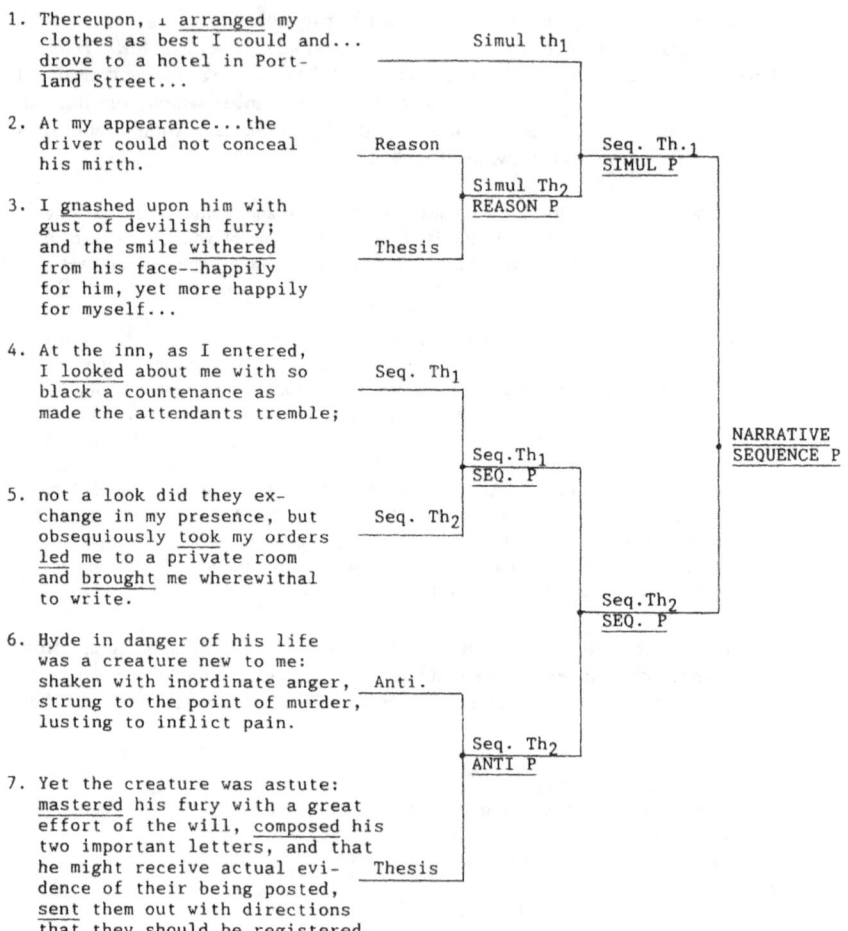

1. Thereupon, I arranged my clothes as best I could and... drove to a hotel in Portland Street...

2. At my appearance...the driver could not conceal his mirth.

3. I gnashed upon him with gust of devilish fury; and the smile withered from his face--happily for him, yet more happily for myself...

4. At the inn, as I entered, I looked about me with so black a countenance as made the attendants tremble;

5. not a look did they exchange in my presence, but obsequiously took my orders led me to a private room and brought me wherewithal to write.

6. Hyde in danger of his life was a creature new to me: shaken with inordinate anger, strung to the point of murder, lusting to inflict pain.

7. Yet the creature was astute: mastered his fury with a great effort of the will, composed his two important letters, and that he might receive actual evidence of their being posted, sent them out with directions that they should be registered.

Note: P = PARAGRAPH
　　Nodes are indicated in CAPITALS and underlined; branches are indicated in lower case.

FIG. 1.

participants are agents in 5; their actions are consequent upon the baleful look Dr. Jekyll/Mr. Hyde presented on arrival at the inn. Dr. Jekyll/Mr. Hyde is clearly in control throughout the paragraph.

The paragraph divides into two main parts, sentences 1–3, "in the hansom/on the road," and sentences 4–7, "at the inn"; in the former Jekyll/Hyde is interacting with the hansom driver while in the latter he interacts with the attendants at the inn and writes letter. I call the whole a narrative sequence paragraph and consider that all the embedded paragraphs are also narrative paragraphs (without repeating the label narrative each time). The main sequence paragraph consists of two slots: a Sequential Thesis$_1$ expounded by a Simultaneous Paragraph and a Sequential Thesis$_2$ expounded by a Sequence Paragraph. Within the Simultaneous Paragraph (sentences 1–3) there are two slots: Simul Thesis$_1$ and Simul Thesis$_2$; the two halves appear to be of equal weight since the salient verbs in 1 and 3 are of the same rank. But what of sentence 2? Here we find resort to a verb of different rank: *The driver could not conceal his mirth*. The resort to a negative modal (Band 5) pushes this sentence down in the scale of salience. The author *could* have said *the driver laughed openly at me* or something to that effect—but he did not. Therefore, sentence 2 must be made ancillary to some dominant sentence in the context. It seems to me to be plausible to relate it to sentence 3 as the dominant member (since 2 and 3 have to do with the interaction of the driver with the major participant). Sentences 2 and 3 are considered to constitute a Reason Paragraph (in which 2 is the reason for 3).

In the second main part of the paragraph which itself structures as a Sequence Paragraph, I posit two slots, a Sequential Thesis$_1$ and a Sequential Thesis$_2$. Furthermore, it seems to have been the author's intent to recognize a close bonding of 4 and 5 which he punctuates as one orthographic sentence and which I interpret to be an embedded paragraph. Sentences 4 and 5 have verbs of equal rank; both are Band 1 and have agential subjects. I therefore take these two sentences to be a further embedded Sequence Paragraph with its own Sequential Thesis$_1$ and Sequential Thesis$_2$. As in some binary sequence units there is an implied reciprocity; Jekyll/Hyde looked blackly at them, and they obsequiously served him (Pab $\wedge$ Pba).

Finally, sentences 6 and 7 also belong together; I construe them as an embedded Antithetical Paragraph—as witnessed by the surface structure connective *yet* (in 7). Here, however, it is very clear that 7 is more salient than 6 which contains only elements of Band 4. Sentence 7 begins in the same fashion (*Yet the creature was astute*) but shifts to verbs with Band 1, subject-as-agent forms. I consider, therefore, that sentences 6 and 7 constitute an *end-weighted* Antithetical Paragraph and consider sentence 7 to be the The .

It is a convention of the labeling in tree tables of the sort here given that by beginning at the right hand side of the table and proceeding to the left *via branches marked Thesis* we arrive at sentences whose independent verbs are *storyline*.

452   LONGACRE

1. Lā'$_1$ a'xni'ca'(tza')$_2$ i'xa'ni't(za')$_3$, [tuncan]$_4$ nā$_5$ xla'$_6$ macacā'tēlh$_7$ nā$_8$ lakating cahuayuj$_{10}$. 2. [Lā'$_1$ tuncan]$_2$ tzuculh$_3$ sta'jni'$_4$ i'xka'lhni'$_5$. 3. Lā'$_1$ como$_2$ laktzī'li$_3$ que lēj ī'sta'jmā'$_6$ i'xka'lhni'$_7$, lēj$_8$ lacapali$_9$ hui'līni'ko'lh$_{10}$ i'xmacalīcā'n$_{11}$ huan$_{12}$ cahuayuj$_{13}$. 4. [Lā'$_1$ tuncan]$_2$ tiyāhuani'cu'tulh$_3$ i'xmacan$_4$; tūlalh(tza')$_5$ yāhuani'lh$_6$. 5. Lā'$_1$ tantu$_2$ tilali$_3$ tiyāhuani'cu'tulh$_4$ i'xmacan$_5$ lā'$_6$ tūlalh(tza')$_7$ yāhuani'lh$_8$ i'xmacanī'n$_9$ huan$_{10}$ cahuayuj$_{11}$. 6. Lā'$_1$ tantu$_2$ tilali$_3$, pero$_4$ por$_5$ masqui$_6$ i'xpuhuan$_7$ a'nchī$_8$ i'xlīcāyāhuani'lh$_9$ i'xmacanī'n$_{10}$ lā'$_{11}$ tūlalh(tza')$_{12}$ cāyāhuani'lh$_{13}$. 7. [Tuncan]$_1$ a'lh$_2$ māputzanīni'n$_3$ huan$_4$ chi'xcu'$_5$ a'ntī$_6$ temasu'ni'lh$_7$ a'nchī$_8$ i'xmacāca'te$_9$ huan$_{10}$ cahuayuj$_{11}$, lā'$_{12}$ como$_{13}$ xla'$_{14}$ a'xni'ca'$_{15}$ i'xmacacā'tē$_{16}$ lā'$_{17}$ como$_{18}$ xla'$_{19}$ tū'$_{20}$ ī'sta'ja$_{21}$ i'xka'lhni'$_{22}$ huan$_{23}$ cahuayuj$_{24}$.

FIG. 2.

3.2 Relative Salience Within a Totonac Paragraph

I first give the following Totonac paragraph (Reid et al., 1968) en bloque with English translation (FIG. 2). Sentences and words are correspondingly numbered in the Totonac and in the English translation. All preterites are underlined on the Totonac side; all tenses are identified with abbreviations after the verb (PLUP = pluperfect; IMPF = imperfect; PPRO = past progressive) on the English side. On the Totonac side, *tuncan* and *lā' tuncan* ("then" and "and then") are boxed, while *-tza'* ("important background") is encircled.

In FIG. 3 I give a tree structure of the Totonac paragraph in English gloss with indications of the relevant Totonac features which determine the tree structure. Again, an underlined English gloss indicates a Totonac preterite; other Totonac tenses are indicated by the abbreviations mentioned above and used in the presentation of the excerpt from the Totonac story. *Tuncan/la' tuncan* are underlined; other Totonac morphemes are indicated in parentheses.

While in general the storyline of a Totonac paragraph turns on the use of independent noncollateral preterites (cf. Table 2), there are some special things going on in this paragraph—which represents a dramatic climax of an embedded narrative. In brief, the distribution of *tuncan* is such as to promote onto the storyline elements that would otherwise not so structure.

Notice the first three sentences. Sentence 1 begins with a backreference in the pluperfect and with a two-fold use of *tza'*, important background marker in the back-referential adverbial clause. The implication is: Now that the blacksmith's temporary (but methodologically astounding) assistant is gone, watch, for things will begin to happen! The pluperfect instead of the preterite in the back-reference functions here as an interval marker; it probably signifies that no matter how

1. And$_1$ when$_2$ he had gone-PAPF$_3$, then$_4$ he$_6$ also$_5$ cut off the forefoot of PRET$_7$ a$_9$ horse$_{10}$ also$_8$. 2. And$_1$ then$_2$ his blood$_5$ began-PRET$_3$ to flow-PRES$_4$. 3. And$_1$ since$_2$ he saw-PRET$_3$ that$_4$ his blood$_7$ was flowing-PAPR$_6$ very much$_5$, very$_8$ quickly$_9$ he finished putting on-PRET$_{10}$ the shoe of$_{11}$ the$_{12}$ horse$_{13}$. 4. And$_1$ then$_2$ he tried to put on-PRET$_3$ his forefoot$_4$; he could not-PRET$_7$ put it on-PRET$_6$. 5. And$_1$ so much$_2$ he tried-PRET$_3$ to put on-PRET$_4$ his forefoot$_5$ and$_6$ he could not-PRET$_7$ put on-PRET$_8$ the forefeet of$_9$ the horse$_{10}$. 6. And$_1$ so much$_2$ he tried-PRET$_3$, but$_4$ although$_5$,$_6$ IMPF-he thought about$_7$ how$_8$ he would put on-CONT$_9$ its forefeet$_{10}$ (and) yet$_{11}$ he could not-PRET$_{12}$ put them on-PRET$_{13}$. 7. Then$_1$ he went-PRET$_2$ to look for-PRES$_3$ the$_4$ man$_5$ who$_6$ had passed by to show him-PRET$_7$ how$_8$ IMPF-he cut the feet off$_9$ the$_{10}$ horse$_{11}$, and$_{12}$ how$_{13}$ he$_{14}$ when$_{15}$ IMPF-he cut off the feet$_{16}$ and$_{17}$ as for$_{18}$ him$_{19}$ the blood of$_{22}$ the$_{23}$ horse$_{24}$ IMPF-did not flow$_{20,21}$.

FIG. 2. (*continued*)

impatient the blacksmith was to get on with the new technology he let the temporary assistant get a decent interval down the road before implementing it. After the back-referential adverbial clause a *tuncan* marks what follows as pivotal.

Likewise in sentence 2 *la' tuncan* "and then" marks its event as pivotal. So far there have been two events in succession: the cutting off of a forefoot of the horse and blood beginning to flow. The first is clearly the cause of the second and is a preterite clause whose subject is agent. We might expect that sentence 2, whose verb is a preterite and whose subject is patient, might be simply the result of 1. But—the narrator by his use of *la' tuncan* has chosen not to signal causality and presumably encodes what happens as a sequence of *two* pivotal events.

Sentence 3, however, lacks a *tuncan* and has a long back-referential predicate ("since the blacksmith saw that the blood was flowing heavily") before a preterite clause with a subject as agent. Here, apparently sentence 3 is outranked by both 1 and 2. While sentence 3 contains a preterite, the first two sentences are marked as pivotal not just mainline. Furthermore, the type of back reference found initially in this sentence is typical of sentences which express result (cf. Longacre, 1968, 1979b). I therefore relate sentences 1 and 2 to each other as Sequential Thesis in a Sequence Paragraph and unite this Sequence Paragraph to sentence 3 in a Result Paragraph as diagrammed. This Result Paragraph in turn expounds Sequential Thesis$_1$ of the main Narrative Sequence Paragraph.

Sentences 4, 5, and 6 belong together because all have *ti-/tu-* compromised preterites reinforced with *-tza'* "important background information" on the *tu-*

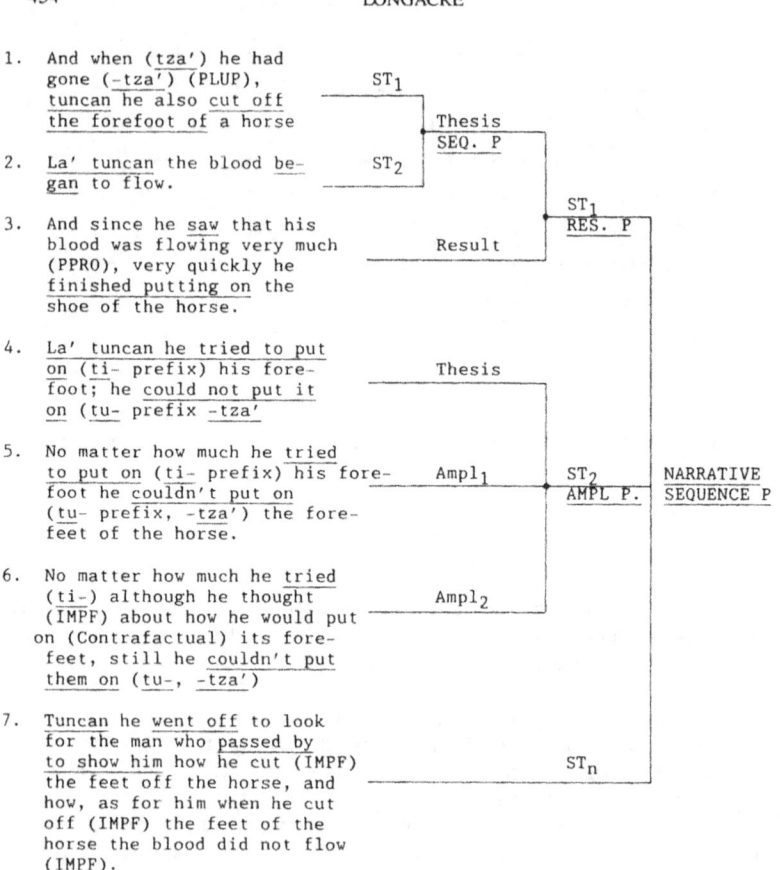

FIG. 3.

preterites. This group of sentences plausibly forms an Amplification Paragraph which adds progressive detail to the portraiture of the blacksmith's frustration, with each sentence a bit longer and more detailed than the preceding. Normally this paragraph would be considered to be ancillary to some other sentence/embedded paragraph, for example, in antithetical relationship with sentences 1–3 in a foreweighted antithetical paragraph. The narrator, however, has used an initial *la' tuncan* "and then" in sentence 4 so that material from Band 5 (irrealis) is promoted here to first rank. This is not routine narration, but is rather a special feature of a great moment of a story in Totonac, that is, a slowing down of the storyline by incorporating into that line material which is not normally found there. Perhaps it is simplest to take *la' tuncan* as simply elevating the whole Amplification Paragraph to the status of an exponent of a Sequential Thesis; in this case, Sequential Thesis$_2$. Within this unit, sentences 5 and 6, which are unmarked with *tuncan*, are considered to be ancillary to sentence 4, which is so marked; the three sentences are considered to constitute an Amplification Paragraph with sentence 4 as Thesis and sentences 5 and 6 as two amplifications of the thesis.

Note in passing the special fullness in sentence 6 where imperfect and a contrafactual tense forms are found in the second amplification of the thesis.

Finally, sentence 7 is climactic; or rather, it has almost the force of a denouement after the climax of frustration in sentences 4–6. It is the longest and most involved of the sentences in the paragraph, and has a preterite as its main verb. It begins abruptly with *tuncan* instead of *la' tuncan*.[16] It uses several imperfects in clauses at the end as the blacksmith presumably recollects how his temporary assistant has so easily and bloodlessly employed surgery in the horseshoeing process.

An interesting touch in this paragraph is the third person *xla'* "he" as used in the first and last lines. Pronouns are used very sparingly in Totonac; often their use is mildly or pointedly contrastive. In sentence one the *xla'* after the *tuncan* represents the blacksmith (he, of all people!) embarking on an attempt to shoe horses as he had seen his assistant do. In the last sentence the pronoun occurs twice as the blacksmith recalls how *xla'* "he" (the assistant) had managed to do the horseshoeing so quickly and bloodlessly. In both sentences 1 and 7 the use of *xla'* "he" throws into tacit contrast—from one side or the other—the two men: "our God" in human form wandering about as a laborer, and the arrogant and rash blacksmith.

3.3 Relative Salience Within a Biblical Hebrew Paragraph

I choose here a paragraph from Genesis 39:2–6. To avoid presenting this material twice I present the paragraph conjointly with its analysis in a step-wise indentation diagram (FIG. 4) with accompanying English translation. I do not draw a tree; rather I present an indentation diagram which is essentially equivalent to a tree representation.

---

[16]Notice that *tuncan* "then" in sentence 6 is simply indicating pivotal storyline status for its sentence. In contrast, the longer connective *la' tuncan* "and then" in sentence 4 promotes non-storyline ranking material to storyline while the *la' tuncan* in sentence 2 signals sequence where we might rather expect result. Perhaps *la' tuncan* is more strongly sequential and promotional than *tuncan* as indicated in this sample. This possibility needs to be crosschecked on a broader scale.

```
              SETTING:  E COORDINATE ¶

39:2          ITEM₁:  wayhî₁   yhwh₂   ʾet yôsēp₃.
              ITEM₂:  wayhî₁   ʾîš₂    maṣlîaḥ₃
              ITEM₃:  wayhî₁   bĕbêt₂  ʾădōnāyw₃   hammiṣrî₄

          ST₁:  AW Q WHOSE QUOTE = E AMPL ¶

39:3      vayyarʾ₁   ʾădōnāyw₂   kî₃
              THESIS·  yhwh₁  ʾittô₂
              AMPL:  vĕkōl₁  ʾăšer-hûʾ₃  ʿōśeh₄  yhwh₅  maṣlîaḥ₆  bĕyādô₇.
39:4      ST₂:  wayyimṣaʾ₁  yôsēp₂  ḥēn₃  bĕʿênāyw₄.
          ST₃:  wayšāret₁  ʾōtô₂.
          ST₄:  N AMPL ¶
              THESIS:  wayyapqidēhû₁  ʿal-bêtô₂.
              AMPL:  vĕkōl₁-yeš₂-lô₃  nātan₄  bĕyādô₅.
          STₙ (CLIMAX):  N AMPLIFICATION ¶
39:5          THESIS:  wayhî₁  mēʾāz₂  hipqîd₃  ʾōtô₄  bĕbêtô₅  vĕʿal₆  kōl₇
              -ʾăšer₈  yeš₉-lô₁₀  (BACK REFERENCE)  waybārek₁₁  yhwh₁₂
              ʾet-bêt₁₃  hammiṣrî₁₄  biglal₁₅  yôsēp₁₆.
              AMPL:  wayhî₁  birkat₂   yhwh₃  bĕkol₄  ʾăšer₅  yeš₆-lô₇
              babbayit₈  ûbaśśādeh₉.
          STₙ₊₁:  N NEGATED ANTONYM PARAPHRASE ¶
39:6          THESIS:  wayyaʿăzōb₁  kol₂-ʾăšer₃-lô₄  bĕyad₅  yôsēp₆.
              PARA:  vĕlōʾ₁-yāda₂  ʾittô₃  mĕʾûmâ₄  kî₅  ʾim₆  hallehem₇
              ʾăšer₈-hû₉  ʾôkēl₁₀.
              TERMINUS:  wayhî₁  yôsēp₂  yĕpēh₃  tōʾar₄  vîpeh₅  marʾeh₆.
```

FIG. 4.

This paragraph consists of an initial setting and a final terminus. In between is a chain of Sequential Theses (ST's). The ST_n is climactic as seen by its elaborate back-reference and verbal-nominal paraphrase (between Thesis and Ampl in v. 5): it is followed by ST_{n+1}, a postclimactic ST.

The verbs of the setting and terminus are from band 3 ("be" verb) and are clearly outranked by the preterite verbs which are found in the ST's. Setting and terminus are ancillary to the ST's of the paragraph. The setting coordinates three "be" clauses into an expository coordinate paragraph.

The first ST (39:3) is an awareness quotation sentence whose main verb "and-

And YHWH$_2$ was$_1$ with Joseph$_3$.

And-he-was/became$_1$ a man$_2$ (who) prospers$_3$.

And-he-was$_1$ in the house-of$_2$ his master$_3$ the Egyptian$_4$.

And-he-saw$_1$ his master$_2$ that$_3$

YHWH$_1$ (was) with him$_2$

And everything$_1$ which he$_2$ was-doing$_4$ YHWH$_3$ caused to prosper$_4$ in his hand$_7$

And-he-found$_1$ Joseph$_2$ grace$_3$ in his eyes$_4$.

And-he-served$_1$ him$_2$ (=became his personal attendant).

And-he-appointed-him$_1$ over all his house$_2$.

And everything$_1$ (that) was$_2$ to-him$_3$ he-gave$_4$ in his hand$_5$.

And-it-happened that$_1$ from when$_2$ he-appointed$_3$ him$_4$ over his house$_5$ and over$_6$ all$_7$ that was$_9$ to him$_{10}$

he-blessed$_{11}$ YHWH$_{12}$ the house$_{13}$ of the Egyptian$_{14}$ on account of$_{15}$ Joseph$_{16}$

And-it-was$_1$ the blessing of$_2$ YHWH$_3$ on all$_4$ which$_5$ was$_6$ to him$_7$ in-the house$_8$ and in the field$_9$.

And-he-abandoned$_1$ all$_2$ which$_3$ (was) to him$_4$ in the hand$_5$ of Joseph$_6$.

And not$_1$ he-kept-account$_2$ with him$_3$ anything$_4$ except$_{5,6}$ the bread$_7$ which$_8$ he$_9$ ate$_{10}$.

And-he-was$_1$ Joseph$_2$ shapely$_3$ of form$_4$ and-fair$_5$ of face$_6$.

FIG. 4. (*continued*)

he-saw" represents a cognitive event (subject as experiencer). The awareness quotation itself (the part that follows "and-he-saw-that. . .") is an embedded expository amplification paragraph whose parts are ranked according to a salience scheme appropriate to expository discourse.[17]

---

[17]According to this scheme the *most static* elements are dominant; the whole salience scheme is the inverse of that used in narration (cf. Longacre, 1982:198–201). Thus, a verbless (nominal) clause ranks as thesis, while the participial clause ranks as amplification of the thesis with the latter ancillary to the former. In the expository paragraph found in Gen. 39:2, all the sentences have verbs of the same rank, that is, mainline with "be" verbs.

In the second ST unit Joseph is presumably subject as patient and in the third such unit, he is subject as agent (but perhaps emphasizing Joseph's role as personal attendant of his master). At any rate, I have not further complicated Biblical Hebrew paragraphs at this time with transitivity subclassifications according to case.

The fourth ST, which is just prior to the paragraph climax, has an embedded narrative amplification paragraph. Its thesis contains the strongly agentive predicate: "and-he-appointed-him over-all-his-house," and has a primary storyline verb (1.1). The following clause contains the noun + perfect construction of 1.3 (secondary storyline with noun focus), and amplifies the previous statement. Here the second sentence is ancillary to the first.

The ST_n likewise contains a strongly agentive element from Band 1 *waybārek yhwh* "and-he-blessed Yahweh", that is, "and Yahweh blessed (the house of the Egyptian on account of Joseph)." It, in turn, is amplified by a nominal clause from Band 3, in which the verb "bless" is nominalized to "blessing" *birkat yhwh* "the blessing of Yahweh." Again the latter is considered to be ancillary to the former.

The ST_{n+1}, which is postclimactic, is a negated antonym paraphrase paragraph. Its thesis is again a strongly agentive preterite ("he turned all that he had over to Joseph") whose paraphrase is a negated perfect from Band 4 ("and he didn't concern himself with anything that he had except for the food that he ate"). The paraphrase is ancillary to the thesis.

3.3.1 In attempting to partially validate Hypothesis II, which is concerned with verb/clause ranking and constituent structure in the local span, I have had resort to examples from English, Totonac, and Biblical Hebrew. In every case the rank scheme which has been outlined for narrative in the language in question has been seen to guide decisions of dominance and ancillariness in analyzing constituent structure in local spans of text. Actually, the type of constituent analysis which is exemplified here has been applied to some rather extensive bodies of text in three languages: (1) to chapter 3 of A. Hailey's novel, *The Final Diagnosis* (analysis unpublished); (2) to most of the Hebrew text of Genesis 37–45 (Longacre, 1989); and (3) to the Greek text of the first epistle of John (Longacre, 1983b). It is in the light of these more extensive analyses that the feasibility of such an analysis as that exemplified here can be evaluated best.

REFERENCES

Bailey, A. (1983). *A tense-aspect-discourse study of the Hebrew perfect verb in the Genesis narrative.* Master's thesis, University of Texas at Arlington.

Ballard, D. L., Conrad, R., & Longacre, R. E. (1971a). The deep and surface structure of interclausal relations. *Foundations of Language, 7,* 70–118.

Ballard, D. L., Conrad, R., & Longacre, R. E. (1971b). *More on the deep and surface relations of interclausal relations* (Language Data Asian Pacific Series, No. 1). Ukarumpa (Papua New Guinea): Summer Institute of Linguistics.

de Beaugrande, R., & Dressler, J. W. (1981). *An introduction to text linguistics.* London: Longmans.
Beekman, J., & Callow, J. (1974). *Translating the Word of God.* Grand Rapids, MI: Eerdman's.
Bishop, R. (1979). Tense-aspect in Totonac narrative discourse. In L. Jones (Ed.), *Discourse studies in Mesoamerican languages* (Vol. 1). Summer Institute of Linguistics Publications 58. Dallas: Summer Institute of Linguistics at the University of Texas at Arlington.
Christian, I. (1987). *Language as social behavior.* Language Data, Asian-Pacific Series, Number 7. Huntington Beach, CA: Summer Institute of Linguistics.
Grimes, J. (1975). *The thread of discourse.* The Hague: Mouton.
Halliday, M. A. K., & Hasan, R. (1976). *Cohesion in English.* London: Longmans.
Hopper, P. J., & Thompson, S. A. (1980). Transitivity in grammar and discourse. *Language, 56,* 251–299.
Howard, L. (1977). Camsa: Certain features of verb inflection as related to paragraph types. In R. E. Longacre & F. Woods (Eds.), *Discourse grammar: Studies in indigenous languages of Colombia, Panama, and Ecuador* (Vol. 2). Dallas: Summer Institute of Linguistics and the University of Texas at Arlington.
Hwang, S. J. J. (1987). *Discourse features of Korean narration.* Summer Institute of Linguistics Publications 77. Dallas: Summer Institute of Linguistics.
Jones, L. (1977). *Theme in English expository discourse.* Lake Bluff, IL: Jupiter Press.
Jones, L., & Coleman, R. N. (1979). In L. Jones, (Ed.), *Discourse studies in Mesoamerican languages* (Vol. 1). Summer Institute of Linguistics Publications 58. Dallas: Summer Institute of Linguistics at the University of Texas at Arlington.
Jones, L., & Jones, L. (1979). Multiple levels of information in discourse. In L. Jones (Ed.), *Discourse studies in Mesoamerican languages* (Vol. 1). Summer Institute of Linguistics Publications 58. Dallas: Summer Institute of Linguistics at the University of Texas at Arlington.
Labov, W., & Waletsky, J. (1967). Narrative analysis: 'Oral versions of personal experience'. In J. Helm (Ed.), *Essays on the verbal and visual arts.* Seattle: University of Washington Press.
Leenhouts, I. (1983). *Functions of the verb in Ténhé narrative discourse.* Master's thesis, The University of Texas at Arlington.
Longacre, R. E. (1968). *Discourse, paragraph, and sentence structure in selected Philippine languages.* Summer Institute of Linguistics Publications 11. Santa Ana, CA: Summer Institute of Linguistics.
Longacre, R. E. (1972). *Hierarchy and universality of discourse constituents in New Guinea languages.* Washington, DC: Georgetown University Press.
Longacre, R. E. (1976a). *An anatomy of speech notions.* Lisse, The Netherlands: Peter de Ridder Press.
Longacre, R. E. (1976b). 'Mystery' particles and affixes. In S. S. Mufwene, C. A. Walker, & S. B. Smith (Eds.), *Papers from the twelfth regional meeting,* Chicago Linguistic Society. Chicago: Chicago Linguistic Society.
Longacre, R. E. (1979a). The discourse structure of the flood narrative. *Journal of American Academy of Religion, 47.*1. Supplement (March 1979) B.89-133.
Longacre, R. E. (1979b). The paragraph as a grammatical unit. In T. Givon (Ed.), *Discourse and syntax.* (Syntax and semantics 12) New York: Academic.
Longacre, R. E. (1980). An apparatus for the identification of paragraph types. *Notes on Linguistics, 15,* 5–23. Dallas: Summer Institute of Linguistics.
Longacre, R. E. (1981). A spectrum and profile approach to discourse analysis. *Text, 1,* 332–59.
Longacre, R. E. (1982). Verb ranking and the constituency structure of discourse. *The Journal of the Linguistic Association of the Southwest, 5,* 77–202.
Longacre, R. E. (1983a). *The grammar of discourse.* New York: Plenum.
Longacre, R. E. (1983b). Exhortation and mitigation in the Greek text of the First Epistle of John. *Selected Technical Articles Related to Translation, 9.* Dallas: Summer Institute of Linguistics.
Longacre, R. E. (1985). Sentences as combinations of clauses. In T. Shopen (Ed.), *Language*

typology and syntactic description (Vol. 2). Cambridge, England: Cambridge University Press.

Longacre, R. E. (1989). *Joseph: A story of divine providence*. A Textlinguistic and Text Theoretical Analysis of the Hebrew text of Genesis 37; 39–48. Winona Lake, IN: Eisenbraum's.

Longacre, R. E. (1984). Discourse analysis and dejargonized tagmemics. In L. Polanyi (Ed.), *Discourse structure*. Unpublished manuscript.

McArthur, H. S. (1979). The role of aspect in distinguishing Aguacatec discourse types. In L. Jones (Ed.), *Discourse studies in Mesoamerican languages* (Vol. 1). Summer Institute of Linguistics Publications 58. Dallas: Summer Institute of Linguistics at the University of Texas at Arlington.

McArthur, L. (1979). Highlighting in Aguacatec discourse. In L. Jones (Ed.), *Discourse studies in Mesoamerican languages* (Vol. 1).

Mann, W. C., & Thompson, S. A. (1986). Relational propositions in discourse. *Discourse Processes, 9*, 57–90.

Reid, A., Bishop, R., Button, E., & Longacre, R. (1968). *Totonac: From clause to discourse* (Summer Institute of Linguistics Publications No. 1). Norman, OK: Summer Institute of Linguistics of the University of Oklahoma.

Thompson, S., & Longacre, R. (1985). Adverbial clauses. In T. Shopen (Ed.), *Language typology and syntactic description* (Vol. 2). Cambridge, England: Cambridge University Press.

Van Dijk, T. A. (1977). *Text and context*. London: Longmans.

Voorhis, P. H. (1974). *Kickapoo grammar*. Doctoral dissertation, Yale University.

Woods, F. (1980). *The interrelationship of cultural information, linguistic structure, and symbolic representations in a Halbi myth*. Doctoral dissertation, University of Texas at Arlington.

4

Some Interlocking Concerns which Govern Participant Reference in Narrative

Robert E. Longacre

1. Introduction

My excuse for adding another article on participant reference in narrative to the arleady excellent and extensive literature on the subject (Grimes 1995, Givón 1983, Kim 1994, and others) is to suggest that there are some interiocking concerns which have not adequately been disentangled, described, and correlated in this ongoing discussion. One such set of correlations has to do with three variables: the resources of a given language which are available for participant reference: the ranking of participants so referenced in given stories: and the *particular* operations all lumped together under the general rubric participant reference. The interlocking of these three factors characterizes any and all participant references within a narrative so that each variable, actualized in a given value is found jointly with values of the other two variables. Any given instance of participant reference in any story within any language can be described in terms of values of the three variables. The data thus marshalled and organized can then make possible generalizations regarding participant reference in a given text in a given language. With the additions of further texts in the language a theory of participant reference for narrative text can be formulated for that language-subject to correction or expansion in the light of further texts which can be more quickly scanned than the texts used for the original theory building.

But a second concern to be further correlated with participant reference according to the three variables posited, is the presence of word order variation within the clause and sentence-those matters in the general area of highlighting, topicalizing, and focus. It is by no means clear what these various terms mean but they are relevant here as attempts to verbalize ways in which word-order shifts and associated modifications further affect participant reference and thematicity. These latter concerns lead into a still more comprehensive correlation, that of relating storyline salience and dominance (mainly verb-related, Longacre 1989b) to the essentially nominal concerns which occupy us in this paper.

2. Three Variables in Participant Reference

2.1. Participant Reference Resources

The first such variable compels us to set out the resources of a given language for participant identification, to recognize a possible hierarchical arrangement among them, and to recognize that this arrangement gives us a set of values which can be used. While ultimately such an inventory of language resources must be carried out in reference to narrative text in individual text languages, I attempt here to set down some broad categories which have been suggested and say what can be said in terms of universals and tendencies. I suggest the following hierarchy arranged according to decreasing explicitness of reference:

(1) Nouns (including proper names) accompanied by qualifiers which range all the way from indefinite/definite articles, adjectives, and relative clauses-all within the noun phrase-to further information ranging beyond the noun phrase and found in separate ensuing sentences

(2) Nouns (including proper names) without any such qualifiers beyond the definite article (which represents a special concern, e.g., in English and Greek)

(3) Surrogate nouns, especially kinship, occupation, and role
  (a) as substitutes for (1) and (2)
  (b) as the highest level of participant reference within a given narrative

(4) Pronominal elements
  (a) Pronouns proper
  (b) Deictics

(5) Affixal elements
  (a) Subject affixes on verbs

(b) Object affixes (or subject-object combinations) on verbs
(c) Switch reference affixes on verbs
(d) Possessor affixes on nouns
(6) Null reference, where conventions of usage make such reference unambiguous

An attempt to compile such a list can be relatively universal in regard to levels 1-3 above. Considerable language specific variation is encountered, however, on levels 4 and 5. On level 4 systems of pronouns and deictics may differ greatly from language to language. To begin with, pronouns may mark person only, or person and number, or person, number and gender. Even person categories can differ, e.g., in regard to inclusive and exclusive first person plural and in regard to the possible marking of an obviative or fourth person. There is the further complication encountered when a lagnuage apparently has several parallel sets of pronouns whose usage cannot be readily explained and where an adequate explanation must take account of such discourse-pragmatic concerns as agency hierarchy (Silverstein 1976), honorifics, and the like. In a typical Philippine language there are three sets of pronouns to mark person number agentive categories according to (a) what is focused in the verb morphology, (b) what is out of focus, and (c) what is made local topic (Barlaan 1986). In some West African languages there is a distinction between logophoric and nonlogophoric pronouns according to whether the subject within a quoted sentence has the same or different subject from the framing sentence found outside the quoted material (Weisemann 1985).

The parameters involved in deictic systems typically are based on proximity to the speaker (or speaker-hearer), but other very specific categories may enter in such as up-river versus down-river, towards the ocean versus away from the ocean, and up-hill versus down-hill. In these further categories we see a reflection of the geographic environment of the speakers of the language, whether a river people, an ocean-side of island people, or a hill-country people. The use of deictic categories in connected context is often characterized by the selection of one category to function anaphorically.

Affixal elements, level 5, can mark subject and object in a straightforward way or may simply indicate a person number category involved in the action represented in the verb. In the latter case, the precise reference of the indicated person, etc., category may have to do with the function of further affixes in the word string. Sometimes, as in Algonquian and Mixe (Lyon 1967), agency hierarchy is involved. Furthermore, a given affix may indicate an interplay of two persons, e.g., first person acting on second person, as in Totonac (Reid et al. 1968) and Zoquean (Wonderly, 1951) of Mesoamerica. When the verbs of a language are marked for switch reference, i.e., for same of different subject in a sequence of clauses, a narrative can proceed without an explicit subject for an indeterminate stretch in the case of the former and can use the latter simply to indicate the other participant involved in the context-again, without the use of an explicit subject (Longacre 1972, 1983). Possessive affixes on nouns, provide, of course, a further marking in regard to a participant even if the latter is off-stage when an item possessed by him/her is indicated.

Null or zero anaphora, level 6, is typical of such languages as Japanese and Korean where, once a participant is established as subject in a local span of text, e.g., a paragraph, he/she continues as the unnamed subject participant until a new participant is established by the overt use of a noun.

As a summary comment, it needs to be noted that pronouns used for running anaphoric reference in text constitute a trait which is especially characteristic of Indo-European languages. As already stated, certain languages of Asia employ null reference while chaining languages such as are found on the island of New Guinea and much of South America rely heavily on switch-reference affixes for routine participant tracking-operation T in 2.3. below. So characteristically Indo-European is the very notion of *pronoun* as a stand-in or place-holder for a noun that we could wish for a more neutral term such a *generic noun* to use in preference to *pronoun*, but the latter term with all its institutionalized Indo-European bias is apparently here to stay and is enshrined in certain contemporary theories of grammar.

2.2. Ranking of Participants

The important distinction here is between major participants, minor participants, and props.

   A. Major participants are relevant, for the most part, to the entire story. Here we can customarily distinguish a central versus non-central

major participant.
1. Central (protagonist)
2. Non-central
   a. Antagonist
   b. Helpers of 1 or 2 above that figure prominently in the whole story; otherwise they are best considered under the next main category
B. Minor participants, whose role is restricted and do not act throughout the story
C. Props
1. Human
2. Animate non-human
3. Inanimate
4. Natural forces

In implementing the above classification, care must be exercised in several regards. One problem arises from the presence of embedded narratives where a minor participant in the embedding, i.e., the matrix story is nevertheless central in the embedded discourse which expounds a given episode of the matrix story. In such circumstances, major and minor participants are defined according to the level of embedding. The problems encountered in defining props is similar to the problems involved in defining the category of instrument in defining notional case or role relations. Props are typically things which are used by agents in the carrying out of actions (Longacre 1983b, especially chapter 4). Here the inanimate prop, category 3 above, is prototypical. But people can use other people for their own ends, thus subverting their humanity and reducing them to tools (e.g., slaves or prostitutes), hence category 1 above is needed. Animals, e.g., horses and cattle, figure as props in category 2. What all three categories have in common is that those so classified do not act as voluntary agents in their own right. Category 4 is more problematic. Natural forces may be helpful or unhelpful, or may be simply a foil against which actions are carried out. On the other hand, a natural force often patterns as the antagonist of a story: cold, flood, or fire and a person's struggle in such circumstances: a woman abandoned and facing childbirth alone: a man or woman's struggle against disease: or against the results of an impairing accident.

A further difficulty lies in the attempt to use the often useful terms **protagonist** and **antagonist**. The former is typically used when the central participant is dominant or struggling against odds to become dominant, and when he/she is respectable or at least imitable in certain respects, so that in some contexts the protagonist may be the champion. But what of the anti-hero or complete idiot? The former may come out on top in a story which denies the values of a culture: from this point of view it has an "immoral" ending. The latter may end up as foolish as he began with everyone tricking him and outwitting him (J. and S. George 1990). Three separate parameters are involved here: centrality versus non-centrality, dominance versus non-dominance, and embodiment of cultural values versus a denial of them. Probably, therefore, the three main categories A, B, and C, indicated here, are the most useful in narrative analysis, but the use of protagonist versus antagonist is often justified provided that one uses them knowledgeably.

2.3. The Operations of Participant Reference

The *particular* operations involved under the general rubric "participant reference" can be represented summarily as follows: the indexing letters are chosen for their memnomic value.

M : first Mention within a story
I : Integration into the story as central to the whole narrative or to some embedded narrative
T : routine Tracking (characteristic of the storyline but not confined to it)
R : Reinstatement/restaging of a participant that has been offstage
C : Confrontation and/or role change (i.e., a flip in dominance patterns)
L : marking of Locally contrastive/thematic status
E : an intrusive narrator Evaluation or comment

[Texts in some languages may employ X, Exit of participant from the story]

In commenting on the above: M applies to either a central or non-central participant. In the case of central participant, M characteristically merges into I, the integration of the participant as central to the narrative. A story may, however, not especially mark the central participant as such in the earlier parts of the story and leave the reader to find out who is central as the story progresses towards its climax (e.g., Crane 1957). With a non-central participant the first mention is followed by T, routine tracking, when the participant is major but not central. In the case of a minor participant, the first mention may sometimes be the last mention or T may follow. Storyline clauses commonly reflect T routine tracking. The participant operations R, C, L and E either characterize the storyline at peak or are non-storyline. Thus, R as staging, albeit restaging, and L typically occur in the paragraph setting. E, as author evaluation, is at considerable distance from the storyline. Operation C, the portrayal of a confrontation, most characteristically emerges as a modification of participant reference from that found in routine tracking in storyline clauses. The portrayal of a confrontation may resort to a conspiracy of means in which modification of participant reference is only one factor among several. These concerns lead into the high-level correlation of storyline schemes and participant reference referred to at the beginning of this article.

3. Ordered Triplets as a Descriptive Device

In the above section, three variables were posited. A description of the precise function of any given reference to a participant or prop within a story may be given as an **ordered triplet** in which the first position gives the symbol which represents the participant reference resource used in making the reference: the second position gives the symbol which represents rank of the participant/prop which is indicated in the reference: and the third position gives the symbol for the particular participant reference operation which is invloved at that point. In this section I give ten such ordered triplets with explanation and illustration.

(1) {1.A1.M}
(2) {3.B.M}
(3) {2.A1.I}
(4) {4a.A1.T}
(5) {3.A2a.T}
(6) {6.A1.T}
(7) {2.A1.C}
(8) {3.A2.C}
(9) {4b.C3.L}
(10) {2.A1.E}

The ordered triplet {1.A1.M} indicates a noun (or proper noun) with qualifiers used in reference to the central participant on first mention in the story. This is a quite regular way of introducing central participants on first mention in stories in many languages and cultures around the world. Thus, a story with "Dan" as central participant could typically introduce him in some such fashion as follows.

Example 1

Dan Wiggins, a man of 45 years when I first met him, had worked for my great uncle for some twenty years. He was respectability and responsibility personified.

The ordered triplet {3.B.M} indicates a surrogate noun (typically kinship, occupation, or role) used in reference to a minor participant on first mention within a story.

Example 2

On getting to the motel, the night clerk had us register and insisted that we pay for the room in advance.

Somewhat characteristic of minor participants referred to by surrogate nouns is the presence of the definite article in English. Considerations of script predictability lead us to expect a night clerk at a hotel when someone arrives late at night. His presence is assumed even on first mention and he is never formally introduced into the text (cf. Larry Jones 1983)

The ordered triplet {2.A1.I} indicates the use of a noun referring to the central participant when integrating him as central into the story. This is standard usage in Biblical Hebrew. The central participant is first mentioned at level one of participant reference resources: then he/she is referred to by noun once or twice more to establish that participant unambiguously as central. This is illustrated at several places in the Joseph story (Gen 37 and 39-46) where various participants are thus established as central in the main story and in the embedded narratives that constitute episodes of the main story (Longacre 1989, chap. 6). For a possible similar structuring in Korean, see Hwang 1987.

Both the ordered triplets {4a.A1.T} and {3.A2a.T} reflect usage in Guambiano, a Chibchan language of Columbia (data from Thomas Branks). In a two participant story with protagonist and antogonist, the protagonist is routinely tracked by the third person pronoun as indicated in the first ordered triplet above while the antagonist is tracked by a noun, typically a surrogate noun, as indicated in the second ordered triplet above. Thus, in a story of cattle rustling in the Andean highlands, the central participant and protagonist, the owner of the animals, is 'he', while the other major participant, the antagonist, is regularly referred by a role noun, 'the thief'. On obtaining an alternate version of the story which changes the viewpoint by making the thief the protagonist and the cattle owner the antagonist-a version of the story such as we might get from a sympathetic relative of the cattle thief-the thief is now referred to as 'he' and the antagonist from this point of view is now 'the owner of the cattle' or simply 'the owner'. The Guambiano usage, according to which the central participant and he only is tracked by pronoun, is quite distinct from that of a language where the central participant is routinely tracked by verb affix or by zero anaphora.

The ordered triplet {6.A1.T} indicates routine tracking of a central participant by zero anaphora as in Korean and Japanese. While this is not standard usage in English, it does occur in what we might call American English postcard style. Note Example 3:

Example 3
Arrived here yesterday. Am having a grand time. Slept in until 11:00 A.M. this morning and had breakfast in bed. Caught a sword-fish yesterday.
Love, Harry.

The ordered triplet {2.A1.C} indicates a noun (without qualifiers) used in reference to the central participant (protagonist) at a point of role change, or any sort of fateful confrontation. In depicting such a confrontation the other central participant (antagonist) is characteristically also referred to by noun in many languages. The noun is often a surrogate noun as indicated in the ordered triplet {3.A2a.C}. This pattern of participant reference for protagonist and antagonist in confrontation is well illustrated in the Hebrew text of the story of David and Goliath (Samuel 17:41-50). In this account, the protagonist is consistently called by his proper name David, and the antagonist is consistently termed 'the Philistine' (surrogate noun of role) all through the struggle. Neither is referred to only by the agreemant affix on the verb or by pronoun-until verse 51 where the Philistine champion is "reduced" to a pronoun by having his head chopped off! So runs the report of the military exploit which brought David much fame and eventually led to his becoming king. The fateful interview of Joseph and Pharaoh in Genesis 41:15-36 has the identical structure: the protagonist is referred to by his name Joseph and the antagonist (or at least the second central participant of this part of the story) is referred to by his title 'Pharaoh'. So runs the account of the interview which resulted in Joseph's meteoric rise from prison to grand vizier of Egypt. Example 4 below for English is not essentially different.

Example 4

This time, however, John stood his ground. The school bully walked warily about him for ten long seconds. Suddenly, John gave him a shove. The bully fell down but was soon back on his feet in a flash. John was clearly in trouble!

The ordered triplet {4b.C3.L} indicates a pronominal element (in this case deictic) used in a section of text where a prop has locally contrastive status.

Example 5

The first gladiator had the conventional arms of a Roman soldier. The second, however, was armed with a net and a trident. But these were all he needed to confront, stalk, ensnare, and kill his adversary.

The ordered triplet {2.A1.E} indicates the use of a noun in referring to the central participant in a narrator evaluation.

Example 6

But Rudolph was too clever to be deceived by such a transparent strategem.

Thus, in a language where routine tracking (operation T) proceeds by any level of participant reference resources from level 4 to 6, it is typical that an intrusive narrator evaluation will revert to 2 or 3. Example 6 illustrated this for reversion to level 2: example 7 illustrates this for level 3.

Example 7

But, as I recall it, a typical Maine farmer is not that easily deceived!

4. Generalizing from Ordered Triplets to Systematic Statements

Characterizing every participant reference in a text as an ordered triplet provides a bank of data which facilitates generalizations regarding participant reference in that text-with possible extension to other texts with a view towards formulating a theory of participant reference in narrative text in that language.

Thus, on the basis of four Konda (Dravidian) narratives, Jacob and Susan George (Longacre 1990, 111-113) made a preliminary statement of participant reference in Konda narrative. The first paragraph of their summary runs as follows:

In all four narratives we see that minor participants and the props are referred to by nouns after the first mention of them occurs in the stories. Among the major participants the protagonists are mentioned the first time by nouns (or noun phrases) with or without qualifiers. Routine trackings proceed via verb suffixes. Once a major participant is established as the hero of the story or as the dominant participant ⋯ he requires a pronoun to reference him. In the case of antagonists, they are referred to by nouns throughout. If the antagonist undergoes a role change ⋯ he/she merits a pronoun. If the antagonist is a natural force, it will be referred to by a noun.

This introductory paragraph gives general observations regarding the use of noun, pronoun, and verb suffixes in reference to major participants, minor participants, and props as far as the operations M, I, and T are concerned. Further paragraphs give additional detail concerning the first two operations and the use of indefinite numerals and deictics. The social status of a participant, king or commoner, is cited as a further complication. Operations R and C are systematically covered in regard to the use of surrogate nouns ('the king') and pronouns-as mentioned in in the paragraph quoted above. Finally, the reader is offered a tabulation (p. 112) in which references to major participants in the four tales are plotted in regard to the various operations and the lagnuage resources employed. Special attention is given to the peculiar use of pronouns in Konda as sort of reward for the participants achievement (making this almost a subtle kind of author evaluation [REL]).

Such initial sketches need, of course, to be rounded out, and even corrected at specific points wherever a broader data base makes possible more effective generalizations.

5. Word Order Shifts which Involve Participant Reference

In describing narrative structure in any language, the analyst customarily encounters word order shifts, or to put it more carefully, variation in the order of the main constituents of the clause. To speak of *shifts* in constituent ordering implies the *assumption of a basic order*. If a language employs word order as a grammatical device, then departures from grammatical word order are easily detectable and cannot fail but to have communicative importance. This holds true for such subject-verb-object languages as English, or certain verb-subject-object languages of Mesoamerica such as Trique, and some Asian languages of subject-object-verb structure. If, on the other hand, word order is primarily a matter of pragmatic strategies (witness the **Functional Sentence Perspective** of the Prague school as applied to certain Slavic languages), then we do well not to speak of word order shifts so much as word order variations which we proceed to study, classify, and functionally analyze. In this article I do not consider languages with only pragmatic ordering of constituents: rather I discuss here narrative structures in languages where word order is at least partially relevant to grammar.

Before discussing these narrative word-order shifts as such, I first mention below certain order-preserving transformations in English which have no place in narrative structure proper but which pragmatically adapt a proposition to fit the needs of certain non-narrative contexts. When such transformations do occur in narrative they occur not in the framework of the narrative but in non-narrative material embedded within the narrative framework. All these modifications of simple proposition-asserting clauses can be termed clause extensions. I present these structures to demonstrate that there are sizeable areas of English structure that are not much used in narrative. I also want to open the question as to whether languages that do not have such transformations may in effect be using word order variation to accomplish some of the same non-narrative ends. It would therefore follow that certain word-order shifts in such languages have limited or null function in narrative. Consider the following set of sentences:

(1) John stole the automobile.
(2) Now, did John steal the automobile?
(3) (a) What John stole was an automobile.
   (b) John was the one who stole the automobile.
(4) It was John who stole the automobile.
(5) There was, e.g., John's theft of an automobile.
(6) As for John, he stole an automobile.

Of these six sentences, only sentence (1) patterns in a straightforward way as a "narrative" sentence, i.e., as a sentence on the storyline of some narrative: it simply reports a happening. All the other sentences essentially are explanatory-expository (Linda Jones 1971, chapter 6). Sentence (2) might raise the question of John's having committed the theft in, e.g., a judicial inquiry. Sentence (3a) assumes as a common speaker-hearer assumption that John committed a theft and identifies the thing stolen as an automobile. Sentence (3b) assumes as a speaker-hearer assumption that an automobile-theft has been committed and puts the finger on John. Sentence (4) is similar and can involve *contrastive* pointing: "It was John (not Tom or Edward)". Sentence (5) cites John's theft in what is probably a catalogue of his misdeeds. Sentence (6), cataloguing perhaps the misdeeds of a gang, identifies John's part as consisting in the theft of an automobile. Of all these sentences, only the first simply answers the question "What happened?" This is not to deny that any and all the sentences (2) to (6) above can occur within the bounds of a story, if they occur, however, they are at some distance from the storyline itself and are found in non-narrative embedded material, i.e., in explanation, evaluation, or in reported speech.

5.1. Word Order Shifts in an SVO (subject-verb-object) Language

S. Thompson (1978) describes English as a strongly SVO language where word order has mainly a grammatical function. As evidence of this, she cites how even in such transformations as those cited in the six sentences above, the SVO order is kept, thus enabling us to characterize these transformations as "structure preserving". Even meteorological clauses such as "it's raining" insert a dummy "it" to fill the expected subject slot even though the real-world correlate of "it" is problematical. Thompson mentions three departures from the SVO order as typical of English:

topicalizaiton, directional verb preposing, and right dislocation.

Topicalization (and the sometimes distinguished left dislocation) name a participant or prop which is singled out for special mention in limited context-in its own sentence or as well as in a sentence or two following. It could almost be characterized as a "sentence topic" (Longacre 1968, 2). A sentence such as Tompson cites "Scrambled eggs I can't stand to look at in the morning" is very similar to sentence (6) above. The sentence that Thompson cites is obviously non-narrative. But what about such examples as "The murderer he pardoned: the pick-pocket he summarily sentenced to death". Assuming that this sentence is part of an ongoing story and without information as to the participant ranking of the two criminals who are mentioned, there is something in the nature of a summary disposal in the mention of the two. Probably here we have operation L, **marking of locally contrastive status**, rather than T, **routine tracking** in storyline clauses.

Directional verb preposing is often found at a great moment of a story, i.e., a climax or a denouement. Such departure from normal order to location-verb-subject is illustrated by the denouement of the English folktale, The Three Little Pigs: "Into the pot fell the wolf with a big splash". This construction is pragmatically fitting when an unexpected development takes place-the wolf had expected to kill the pig but instead the pig brings about the death of the wolf. Consider also the further example: "Into the room walked the man that we all supposed to be dead". Here we find operation C, **confrontation of role change**.

Right dislocation can be effectively used to append an author evaluation to a storyline clause: indeed this seems to fit Thompson's example: "He nearly ran over me, that crazy bum". Here operation E, **an intrusive author evaluation,** is exemplified in the right dislocated phrase (if the context should prove to be narrative, e.g., an informal account of an experience).

5.2. Word Order Shifts in VSO Languages

Doris Payne (1990) and Longacre (1995) have considered departures from canonical order verb-subject-object in strongly VSO languages. Somewhat earlier (1978) Simon Dik had noted the fact, immediately evident to anyone who studies such a language, that a formula (X)VSO can be posited to summarize left shifts of any normally post-verb constituent. This formula captures the generalization that any one- and customarily only one-constituent can be rotated to the fore for special purposes. Payne calls Dik's X the Pragmatically Marked Constituent, PMC for short. In some 50 carefully written and lucid pages (189-238) she describes the functions of the PMC in Yagua, an indigenous language of Peru. Some of the uses refer to the interplay of dialogue relations. Uses that occur in the narrative framework are contrast, counterexpectation, restatement, and added detail restatement. The first two possibly reflect what 1 term operation L, marking of locally contrastive/thematic status. The latter two belong to what Payne herself calls "a communicatively marked event" which, judging by certain of her examples, I interpret as being similar to my operation C, confrontation and/or role change.

My study (Longacre 1995) was directed at three languages, Trique (Mesoamerica), Biblical Hebrew (ancient Near East), and Jur-Luwo (Sudan), all of which are strongly VSO. My results are not startingly different from Payne's for Yagua.

5.3. Word Order Shifts in SOV Languages

On superficial examination it could be posited that just as we have an (X)VSO structure in verb-initial languages we can expect to find an SOV (X) structure in verb-final languages. We could label the X in the latter a pragmatically marked constituent just as we so labelled the X in the former. But the structures are not simply mirror-image reversals. Most SOV languages are more conservative about shifting to post-verb position than are VSO languages about shifting to pre-verb. But current research is beginning to document pragmatic uses of post-verb position in some languages of this typology. To be sure, in some SOV languages any element beyond the verb is simply an "afterthought" to be edited out in the next printout by putting it into its correct pre-verb position. But other such languages have systematic uses for a noun phrase in post-verb position, thus making it a pragmatically significant position. Thus S. Herring (1994) reports uses of post-verb position as **antitopic** and for **emphasis** in Tamil. I have yet to look at her results in the light of the apparatus contained in Sec. 2 above.

I close this paper with reference to a South American language, Cayapa, for which Neil Weibe supplied me data in 1975. In Cayapa, a folktale frequently presents two major participants, a protagonist and an antagonist: the former is smaller and apparently powerless while the latter is large and powerful. One such story features the snail versus the jaguar. The latter challenges the former to a combat. In the early part of the story the snail is regularly tracked by the noun 'snail' in post-verb position, while the jaguar is tracked by the noun 'jaguar' in normal pre-verb position. Towards the end of the story the roles are reversed- and so are the positions within the sentence, i.e., 'jaguar' now appears in post-verb position and 'snail' occurs in the normal pre-verb position. All this can be tracked well in terms of my three coordinates in Sec. 2. In particular it is the crucial operation of C, **confrontation and role reversal,** that is in evidence here. In depicting a conflict, it is the non-dominant participant that is right-shifted to the post-verb position in a given part of the story.

References

Barlaan, Rodolfo (1986) *Some Major Aspects of the Focus System in Isnag,* Doctoral Dissertation, University of Texas at Arlington, Arlington, TX.

Crane, Stephen (1957) 'The Open Boat' in Wallace and Mary Stegner eds., *Great American Short Stories,* 257-286, New York: Dell Publishing Co.

Dik, Simon (1978) *Functional Grammar,* Amsterdam: Elsiever.

George, Jacob and Susan (1990) 'Participant Reference in Konda,' in R. Longacre and D. Shaler eds., *Indian Textlinguistic Sketches, Occasional Papers in Translation and Textlinguistcis* 4:95-113.

Givón, Talmy (1983) 'Topic Continuity in Discourse: an Introduction' in T. Givón ed., *Topic Continuity in Discourse: a Quantitative Cross-Linguistic Study,* Amsterdam: Benjamins.

Grimes, Joseph (1975) *The Thread of Discourse,* The Hague: Mouton.

Herring, Susan (1994) 'Afterthoughts, Antitopics, and Emphasis: the Syntacticization of Postverbal Position in Tamil,' in M. Butt, T.H. King and G. Ramchand eds., *Theoretical Perspectives on Word-Order in South Asiasn Languages,* 119-152, Stanford: CSLI Publications.

Hwang, Shin Ja (1987) *Discourse Features of Korean Narration,* Summer Institute of Linguistics Publications 77, Dallas: Summer Institute of Linguistics and the University of Texas at Arlington.

Jones, Larry (1983) *Pragmetic Aspects of English Text Structure,* Summer Institute of Linguistics Publications 67, Dallas: Summer Institute of Linguistics and the University of Texas at Arlington.

Jones, Linda (1977) *Theme in English Expository Discourse,* Lake Bluff, IL: Jupiter Press.

Kim, Kyu-Hyun (1994) 'An Analysis of Normal Reference in English Conversational Stories,' *Language Reseach* 30, 449-471

Longacre, Robert (1968) *Philippine Languages: Discourse, Paragraph, and Sentence Structure,* Summer Institute of Lingustics Publications in Lingustics and Related Field 21 (two volumes bound in one), Santa Ana, CA: Summer Institute of Linguistics.

Longacre, Robert (1972) *Hierarchy and Universality of Discourse Constituents in New Guinea Languages,* Two volumes: Discussion and Texts, Washington: Georgetown University Press.

Longacre, Robert (1983a) 'Switch Reference from Two Distinct Linguistic Areas: Wojokeso (Papua New Guinea) and Guanano (Northern South America),' in John Haiman and Pamela Munro eds., *Typological Studies in Language* 2: *Switch Reference and Universal Grammar,* 185-207, Amsterdam: Benjamins.

Longacre, Robert (1983b) *The Grammar of Discourse,* New York: Plenum.

Langacre, Robert (1989a) 'Two Hypotheses Regarding Text Generation and Analysis,' *Discourse Processes* 12, 413-460

Longacre, Robert (1989b) *Joseph, a Story of Divine Providence: a Text Theoretical and Textlinguistic Analysis of Genesis* 37 and 39-48, Winona Lake, IN: Eisenbraums.

Longacre, Robert (1993) 'Review of *the Pragmatics of Word Order: Typological Dimensions of Verb Initial Languages* by Doris Payne 1990,' *International Journal of American Linguistics* 59, 102-107.

Longacre, Robert (1995) 'Left Shifts in Strongly VSO Languages' in Pamela Downing and Michael Noonan eds., *Word Order and Discourse,* Amsterdam: Benjamins.

Lyon, Shirley (1967) 'Tlahuitoltepec Mixe Clause Structure,' *International Journal of American Linguistics* 33, 25-33.

Payne, Doris (1990) *The Pragmatics of Word Order: Typological Dimensions of Verb Initial Languages,* Berlin: Mouton de Gruyter.

Reid, Aileen, R. Bishop, E. Buttons, and R. Longacre (1968) *Totonac from Clause to Discourse,* Summer Institute of Lingustics Publications in Linguistics 17, Santa Ana, CA: Summer Institute of Linguistics.

Silverstein, Michael (1976) 'Hierarchy of Features and Ergativity,' in R. M. W. Dixon ed., *Grammatical Categories in Australian Languages* 112-171, Canberra: Australian National Institute of Aboriginal Studies.

Thompson, Sandra (1978) 'Modern English from a Typological Point of View: Some Implications of the Function of Word Order,' *Linguistiche Berichte* 54, 19-35.

Weisemann, Ursula, C. Nsémé, R. Vallette (1985) *Manual d'Analyse de Discourse,* Yaounde: Propelca 26.

Wonderly, William (1951) 'Zoque III: Morphological Classes, Affix List, and Verbs,' *International Journal of American Linguistics* 17, 137-162.

University of Texas at Arlington
and the Summer Institute of Linguistics
Texas, U. S. A.

ROBERT E. LONGACRE

The dynamics of reported dialogue in narrative

Abstract. The storyline of a narrative may be advanced as much by reported dialogue as by the recital of other sorts of interaction. In reported dialogue the main functions of the formula of quotation (QF) is to tie the speech acts which consitute dialogue explicitly into the storyline, and to identify the speakers and addressees as participants within the slate of participants which characterizes the story. There is a bewildering variety of ways in which the speaker and/or addressee may be related to the speech act; these are briefly indicated. But the formal variety which is encountered is not entirely explained by the sheer need of participant identification and tracking, i.e. by simply identifying who-said-what-to-whom. Further functions are indicated. The claim is made here that mention/non-mention of speech act participants—over and beyond the textual needs of participant identification and tracking—is indexical of the intensity of participant interaction in dialogue. I attempt to substantiate this claim in reference to English, Totonac (Mesoamerica), Kagan-Kalagan (Philippines) and Biblical Hebrew (ancient Near East).

1. Introduction. A crucial feature of the definition of narrative is the reporting of a chain of sequential punctiliar happenings (which are, for the most part, casually connected): actions, motions, cognitive events, contingencies, and last but not least *speech acts*. A storyline may be advanced as much, if not more, by reported speech acts as by the recital of other sorts of happenings (Larson 1978: 26–36). Reported speech acts (ibid.) are tied to the storyline by means of formulas of citation, which in the balance of this paper I refer to as QF, i.e. *Quotation Formula*. The tenses of the verbs in the QF's are regular enough, but the QF simply tells us that a speech act took place and who the speaker and (overt or inferred) addressee is. On the other hand the content of the *Quotation, Q*, tells us the nature of the speech act, i.e. flattery, compliance, suggestion, etc. Therefore, in advancing the storyline the verbs of the QF's may be expected to have the requisite storyline status (simple past in English), but not the verbs internal to the Quotation itself (which may be any verb tense or mood appropriate to that point in the dialogue). Rather, the Q's, which are in essence embedded Discourses, give the nature of the speech act by which the storyline is advanced. Furthermore, the QF's tie the Speech Acts to one or more of the participants of the story.

Before coming to the main thesis of this paper, I cite two fragments of English narrative—one traditional and one contemporary—to reinforce the above observations and to lay the groundwork for the balance of this paper.

1.1 Example 1 (from a traditional English folktale "The Three Little Pigs" (TTLP))

(1) Once upon a time there was a mother pig who had three little pigs.

(2) The three little pigs grew so big that their mother said to them: "You are too big to live here any longer. You must go and build houses for yourselves. But take care that the wolf does not catch you."

(3) The three little pigs set off.

(4) "We will take care that the wolf does not catch us," they said.

(5) Soon they met a man who was carrying some straw.

(6) "Please, will you give me some straw?" asked the first little pig. "I want to build a house for myself."

(7) "Yes," said the man, and he gave the first little pig some straw.

(8) Then the first little pig built himself a house of straw.

(9) He said, "Now the wolf won't catch me and eat me."

(10) "I shall build a house stronger than yours," said the second little pig.

(11) "I shall build a house stronger than yours, too," said the third little pig.

This opening portion of the folktale has reported speech in most of its sentences (excluding 1,3,5, & 8). Sentence (1) describes a static initial situation; (2) reports the inciting incident and includes a speech of the mother; (3) reports an action; (4) reports a speech act which accompanies that action; (5) reports a contingency (i.e., they happened to meet a man carrying straw); (6) and (7) report speech acts which are proposal & response respectively; (8) reports an action; (9) reports a speech act which is a remark (actually a claim of sorts); (10) and (11) report speech acts which are counter-remarks. From the static situation reported in (1), the storyline moves forward via *action*, *contingencies* (only one in this sample) and *speech acts*—as indeed is typical of narration.

The quotation formulas (QF's) vary as to their placement relative to the quote (Q) and as to specification of only the speaker versus the specification of both the speaker and the addressee.

Preposed QF's occur in sentences (2) and (9). Postposed QF's occur in sentences (4), (7), (10), and (11). In sentence (6) an interlarded QF splits the quotation (Q) into two parts.

Between the preposed QF and the postposed QF, the usual convention in English has been: while the preposed QF conforms to the normal Subject Verb constituent order of English with the Q analogous to an object, the postposed QF is typically of Verb Subject order. The postposed QF's in (7), (10), and (11) illustrate the expected order of constituents in this construction. Sentence (4), while postposed, has SV order.

Of relevance here to the dialogue structure is the thematic importance of *avoiding the wolf*, as originally warned by the mother pig in (2), with the answering assurance on the part of the pigs in (4), and the confident assertion of the first little pig, on the building of his house, that the wolf would not catch him (9); in all these sentences the QF's are of SV structure. The only preposed QF's in this part of the story are in (2) and (9), while even the postposed QF of (4) preserves the SV order. Other less thematic utterances are more casual—or at any rate routine—and conform to the postposed VS patterns. The mother's speech act in (2) provides the inciting incident of the story, while attempts to avoid the wolf make up the material of the various episodes.

A QF that is interlarded between the two parts of the Q occurs in (6). It is most similar to the postposed QF in terms of the order of constituents. Typically, material which precedes the postposed quote is brief—and the balance of the Q can be given in the next sentence. The split Q splits along some natural line—here the division between a request and its reason.

In terms of extent of specification in the QF, it is noteworthy that only in (2) do we find specification of the addressee as well as of the speaker: ". . . their mother said to them". In all the other QF's only the speaker is mentioned. This might lead us to suspect that, aside from dialogue initial, the normal form of continuing citation in English (i.e. citation subsequent to initiation of the dialogue) mentions only the speaker. Sentence (2) in this case initiates the dialogue and as such mentions both speaker and addressee. Also, as inciting incident of the whole story this speech act is plausibly accompanied by a rather full and explicit QF.

What of the rest of the story? Our suspicion is confirmed that the QF which specifies only the speaker is the normal form of continuing citation in English. This is, however, only half of the matter. Within the Q itself vocatives may serve to specify the addressee. This convention comes into play when the wolf arrives and begins to menace the pigs. Thus: "The wolf knocked on the door and said, 'Little pig, little pig, let me come in'." The convention of identifying each little pig by ordinal reference (whether the first, second, or third one) is maintained by the narrator throughout the story whenever the wolf initiates a conversation. In the one case where the third little pig (up in a tree at that point in the story) initiates a conversation, he addresses the wolf as "Mr. Wolf".

The cross play between the QF and the vocatives in the Q has two discourse functions in this story: (a) By mentioning both participants the confrontational nature of these episodes is emphasized; (b) at the same time, by the polite tone of the vocatives a *fiction of civility* is created between the wolf (posing as a somewhat benign and avuncular character) and his intended victim (who does not admit openly the deadly character of the game).

1.2. Our second example is from a story (Blank 1988:95–100)[1] concerning the plight of an injured skier; the selection below picks up the denouement of the story (98–99).

Example 2 ("Ordeal in the Winter Woods" (OWW))

(1) Early in the afternoon of the tenth day, a Friday, Robin suddenly heard the swish of skis.

(2) He saw a cross-country skier on a course that would bring him about 100 feet away.

(3) Robin shrieked, "Hello".

(4) The skier was a 22-year old, John Steinmetz, a state parks lifeguard in Sta. Cruz.

(5) Also a lone skier he was trying to come to grips with a problem of his own.

(6) A few weeks earlier, he and others had failed to resuscitate a drowned swimmer.

(7) He was ridden with remorse.

(8) Some quality in Robin's shout made John swerve to a halt and pole his way back.

(9) "How's it going?" he asked the injured skier.

(10) "I have a broken leg and ankle."

(11) "How long have you been out here?"

(12) "Ten days."

(13) "It took me about 45 minutes to get here from McCabe Lake," John said.

(14) "Well," Robin answered, "it took me six days."

Reported speech occurs in sentences (9)–(14) (aside from (3) where "Robin shrieked 'Hello'"). The dialogue is initiated with a sentence (9) in which both speaker and addressee are specified. This seems to be much the normal way to initiate dialogue in many languages. The QF is postposed and is in the normal SVO order. While postposed QF's are commonly in VS order when only speaker is specified, this text has no preposed QF's and all QF's occur in the normative word order of English. This is perhaps a feature of Reader's Digest, keep-it-simple English.

What is of special interest in this dialogue paragraph is the complete absence of QF's of any sort in sentences (10)–(12), along with the reintroduction of QF's which specify the speaker in sentences (13)–(14). While what we might term the nul QF was not illustrated in the preceding dialogue sample (TTLP), it is by no means uncommon in English. All that is required to prevent ambiguity is: (a) regular alternation of speakers, and (b) content appropriate to a given speaker. Alternation of speakers is carefully observed here in Sentences (9)–(12). In sentence (10) it is obvious that the injured skier is the one who says, "I have a broken leg" and it is equally obvious that it is the newcomer who asks, "How long have you been out here?" (11). Again, the sentence fragment in (12) is clearly the answer of the injured skier.

Nul QF functions here mark a high point of the story—a denouement in which rescue comes to the injured man.

But why the reintroduction of QF's in (13) and (14)? Here, contrary to the question-answer nature of the two previous exchanges ((9) and (10), (11) and (12)), where the newcomer has the initiative and Robin simply answers his questions, we have in (13) and (14) an exchange which consists of remark and counter-remark. The newcomer, John Steinmetz, and the injured skier, Robin, are contrastively presented in what amounts to a polite confrontation. In such a situation the names are thrown into explicit contrast by the QF's ". . . John said", ". . . Robin answered . . ."

2. Variations in the QF's. The above excerpts from English stories (of a rather straightforward sort) illustrate that QF's can vary, but the range of variety is only weakly illustrated in these excerpts. I summarize here some features which we observed in the two excerpts with indication of the possible further range of variety of each feature.

2.1 Verbs of the QF's. Thus, most of the QF's employ the verb 'say' in the two excerpts. This is the only citation verb in TTLP, but varies to 'shriek', 'ask', and 'answer' in OWW. English has, of course, a great variety of speech act verbs available for use in QF's as well as paralinguistic verbs ["He smiled, 'Don't thank me'"], verbs of head movement ["He nodded, 'That's O.K. with me'"], verbs expressing movements of other parts of the body ['nudge', 'point',]; and verbs which simply express actions but which are juxtaposed to a stretch of reported speech with the implication that the actor and the speaker are the same ["he pressed down angrily on the starter, 'Who are you trying to fool?'"]. Several of the latter varieties of attributing speech to a speaker could be termed quasi-QF's (see Ware 1993).

Other languages may be much more limited in devices of attributing speech to a participant. They may, for example limit a QF to the use of the verb 'say' or to a small handful of such verbs, and may not use any of the quasi-QF's characteristic of English.

2.2 Position of the QF. The two excerpts illustrate how the QF can vary relative to the Q from preposed to postposed to interlarded. Some languages (cf. Totonac below) permit a variety of placement of the QF that is similar to English; others do not (Biblical Hebrew, see below). Typological differences (SVO, VSO, SOV) are relevant here as well. In the discussion which accompanies the presentation of the two excerpts above there is suggestion of some factors which partially govern this positional variation in placement of the QF relative to the Q.

2.3 Nul QF. Excerpt OWW illustrates the use of the nul QF, i.e. no quotation formula at all. This was seen to correlate with the onset of a high point (climax or denouement) in a story. Nul QF is certainly used for this purpose in English and in many other languages; but we can hardly claim that this is its only function.

2.4 Portrayal of Confrontation. The same excerpt OWW also illustrates something of the textlinguistics of confrontation in a narrative. This is seen in the reintroduction of QF's after their being phased out. This is one example of how the language of a story can give the set-piece portrayal of a confrontation. See Biblical Hebrew below for such a device used in that language.

2.5 Mention of speaker and/or addressee. Somewhat related to some of the above concerns is the variation within QF's in regard to the mentioning of the speaker versus the mentioning of the addressee. It was suggested that for English the unmarked form of continuing citation (after dialogue initiation) requires the mention of the speaker only, i.e. once we know the parties involved in a dialogue, the dialogue can continue with QF's which reference the speaker but not the addressee. This convention is not necessarily true in other languages, e.g. in Biblical Hebrew the unmarked form of citation mentions only the addressee by noun or pronoun (in addition, of course, to subject agreement in the verb). In both Totonac and Biblical Hebrew the presence of a person-inflected verb makes their norms different from English.

2.6 Some un-English expedients. Some factors characteristic of other languages but not so easy to illustrate (or even found at all) in English are: (a) use of an uninflected verb of speech (cf., however, English 'saying'), or even of a noun ('the word was . . . '); (b) use of nominalized forms often with cleft ('his word was . . . '); and (c) double QF's ['he answered and said'] which, for the most part are translationisms in English.

3. Variation in QF's as indicative of dialogue dynamics. In keeping with such considerations as those discussed above. *I here make the claim that variations in QF in regard to mention/non-mention of Speaker and/or Addressee—beyond the basic need of participant identification and reference—are indexical of the intensity of participant interaction in reported dialogue.* Several things need to be said here: (a) Basic needs of participant identification and reference can be assumed to constrain surface structure devices of participant reference throughout the discourse, especially in regard to usage with non-speech verbs. (b) In opening a reported dialogue the QF of the first reported speech is especially regulated by needs of participant identification and reference and is not so likely to be indexical of the further concerns which are treated here. (c) While the nature of the Q itself is the ultimate index of the nature of a reported speech act, the mention/non-mention of Speaker and/or Addressee in excess of the need to know who-said-what-to-whom is here demonstrated to be indexical of the intensity of interchange. (d) Indexing the intensity of participant interchange can be in regard to changes in the level of emotional tension as well as in regard to dominance or attempted dominance of one participant over the other. (e) In regard to the preceding concerns, reported dialogue may manifest differing *keys* in narratives or dialogues of different genre. The key consists of a QF variant which is normal for that genre with departures from the key in response to changing contextual conditions.

In discussing the indexical functions of QF's in various languages I present, in order, data from Totonac (a Macro-Mayan language of Mexico); Kagan-Kalagan (an Eastern Mindanao language of the Philippines); and Biblical Hebrew[2]. The Totonac texts illustrate dominance and bids for dominance as reflected in variations in QF's; Kagan-Kalagan marks the general intensity level by means of QF variations but illustrates three genre of narrative discourse in distinct keys; Biblical Hebrew, in its variations of QF's reflects both dominance and bids for dominance and also the marking of the general level of intensity. Biblical Hebrew also illustrates reported dialogue in three keys.

3.1 Totonac (Mexico). Reid (1979) attempts "to formulate a set of rules to account for the dynamic interaction of two participants in reported dialogue" in Totonac (293). The problem is two-fold: to account for variations in the *position* of the QF; and to account for variation in the *form* of the QF. I will not discuss the former concern here. Briefly, however, postposed QF marks closure of some unit, while, interlarded QF frequently indicates a topic change.

Variation in the form of the QF has to do with the noun phrases which can occur in conjunction with the inflected transitive verb that constitutes the core of the QF and which indicates in its morphology the person and number of both the subject and the object. This verb may simply occur by itself: V (verb only). Or it may occur along with a NP which expresses the speaker: V + Sp. Alternatively, it may occur with a NP which expresses the addressee: V + Ad. It may overtly express both the speaker and the addressee by noun phrases: V + Sp + Ad (the language is SVO; the formulae are framed to highlight the verb). Finally, the verb may occur with a suffix *-can/ca* which suppresses the identity of the subject and makes the use of a subject noun phrase impossible in the QF. This suffix marks a reflexive verb, or a "verb whose subject is unknown or irrelevant" (Reid 1979:301), or suppression of the subject in the interest of highlighting the object (which with speech verbs is the addressee). Thus, a QF may be V-*can/ca*, or V- *can/ca* + Ad.

To plot the distribution of these variants in the QF, Reid formulates three varieties of rules: (a) *thematicity* rules; (b) *thematicity projection* rules (how thematicity carries over across a paragraph boundary) and (c) *dominance* rules. She argues that thematicity and dominance are separate concerns as "seen in the fact that while A may dominate B (order him about, reprove him, or subject him to searching interrogation), nevertheless the paragraph may be about B" (1979:303). It is impossible in the scope of this article to fully summarize and illustrate all the Reid rules. She first discusses thematicity in general, then thematicity-dominance when the two are in phase (the thematic participant is in control), then thematicity-dominance when the thematic participant (who is also global theme) is not in control; and finally thematicity-dominance when the dominant participant (who is also the global theme) is *not* locally thematic. These varying situations affect the form of the QF, or the way in which Speaker or Addressee is referred to in the QF. The additional 'thematicity projection' rules do not greatly affect the form of the QF, but state under what conditions the theme of one paragraph carries over into the following paragraph.

The dominance rules (rather than the thematicity rules) are determinative of the form of the QF. It is these rules that are of peculiar interest to us here. Reid posits three situations which require the terms 'initiator' (starter of the whole dialogue) and 'responder' (initial addressee): "dialogue with initiator and responder on equal footing"; "dialogue with initiator dominance"; and "dialogue with responder dominance."

In respect to dialogue in which initiator and responder are on equal footing the QF's are neutral as to dominance and the content of the QF is determined by relatively straightforward concerns of participant identification. Thus QF:V can occur if both participants are well identified in previous content; QF:V + Sp + Ad can occur if the QF must introduce both participants, while QF: V-*can/ca* + Ad can occur if the speaker has been introduced but not the addressee—plus a few further complications.

Where, however, the initiator dominates in the QF and in the immediately preceding context (defined as no more than three preceding clauses) the initiator is named to the exclusion of the responder. Here, with few exceptions the initial QF is V + Sp.

One variation of this rule is when the opening QF is immediately preceded by a directional verb with which the speaker is identified; in such circumstances the speaker is identified in connection with the directional verb. Nevertheless, it is the speaker which is identified by a noun phrase rather than the addressee.

Example 3 (Totonac (Reid 1979:313))
La' milh   lakatin chi'chini' la' lakmilh   kalhatin to'kotzin   la' huani, . . .
and it came a   day   and she came to her an   old woman and she says to her
'One day an old woman came to her and said to her, . . . '

Where the responder dominates in a dialogue, then in the QF and in the immediately preceding context the responder is named to the exclusion of the initiator. Here the opening QF is V-*can*/*ca* + Ad unless the speaker is the global theme (central participant of the narrative) in which case V + Ad is more appropriate.

When the QF is preceded by a directional verb (Vcan) with which the addressee is identified, in which case an opening QF:Vcan may occur. Be this as it may, it is the addressee which is identified rather than the speaker.

Example 4 (Totonac (Reid 1979:314))
Lakcha'nca   Xihuan la' huanica, . . .
he was approached John   and he was told
'John was approached and was told . . . '

Reid has a further section concerning shifting of dominance *within* a dialogue, and a number of valuable appendices. Nevertheless, her main contribution is pointing out that the dominating participant in a dialogue is named in the QF to the exclusion of the other participant.

3.2 Kagan-Kalagan (Philippines). Wendell (1986) posits for Kagan-Kalagan a variety of QF's that is indexical of the intensity of participant interchange[3]. But there are further complications occasioned by (a) variation in the position of the QF; (b) simple vs. "double-barrelled" QF; (c) whether the quote itself is in focus or the speaker; and (d) the existence of narrative texts of different types that have differing preferred norms for the formula of quotation (with stateable departures from the norm).

Wendell reports that an unaffixed speech verb (*lawung* 'said') regardless of the position of the QF in which it is used, indicates focus on the quotation itself. Three variants of this occur as to whether the QF is preposed, interlarded, or post-posed relative to the quotation; however, he assumes that it is the quotation that is left-shifted, not the QF that is right-shifted[4]. Within these QF variants the speaker is regularly specified in the usual post-verbal subject slot, while the inclusion of the addressee (only in the preposed QF) is indicative of initiating or terminating a dialogue paragraph. Here, in contrast to usage in many languages, the mentioning of the addressee is a boundary feature and has nothing to do with questions of thematicity or dominance.

The use of an affixed verb in the quote formula indicates regular speaker focus (a semantic specialization of subject or agent focus). Two variants of this occur: with the order, Verb + Speaker ± Addressee + Quotation; and Speaker + Verb ± Addressee + Quotation. While both are speaker focus, the use of the second formula especially highlights the speaker by putting him in the (X)VSO slot possible in a language of this typology. In both these variants, presumably, specification of the addressee has a closure function as mentioned above.

Besides these variants, double QF's exist (actually a combination of two QF's) and QF deletion. The former can serve, e.g. "to intensify a proposal or highlight an important piece of information. The latter occurs only at the peak of a discourse and increases vividness and tension (as do other peak-marking devices)."

Wendell cites in some detail three stories which can be considered to have differing norms for their formulas of quotation (perhaps similar to different key signatures in music).

Calling the QF with the *unaffixed* speech verb preposed to the Quotation (Verb + Speaker + Q) "regular quote focus", Wendell sets this up as the norm for the Tilanduk story (the story of a hero who has several encounters with an evil spirit whom he deceives and finally kills). Wendell says (1986:5–6):

"QF **-la** (regular quote focus) without addressee is the norm for all the dialogues [of this text, REL] and may occur at any stage but it is most typically used for continuing utterances[5]. The split quote (with interlarded QF) QF **-lb** is used for vividness in some initiating and resolving utterances and in the final rhetorical quote of Episode 3. The double QF (QF 3) is used with a verb of motion for dialogue initiation . . . It is also used with a speech verb to intensify a proposal."

Dialogue is phased out entirely at the peak of this story.

Example 5 (from "Tilanduk" (Kagan-Kalagan) (Wendell 1986:54))

(1) Lawung na busaw, 'Kanak da ya agong yan.'
    said the busaw mine already the gong.F that

(2) Lawung ni Tilanduk 'Di ku iyatag yan, kay pusaka yan ni Ama.'
    said PM tilanduk not I will.give that because inheritance.F that PM father

(3) Lawung na busaw, 'Atagan da yan kanak, kay aku ra ya
    said the busaw give just that.F to.me because I.F just the

magdayaw   san.'
take.care.of.F that

(4) Lawung ni Tilanduk, 'Ee, iyatag ku kanmu aw silang mu tingkuun yan
    said PM tilanduk yes will.give I to.you and if you will.beat that.F

na di dumengeg kay magkaani-anit ya ginawa ku.'
when not will.hear because will.become.sad the breath.F my

(1) The busaw said, '(I want) that gong to be mine.' (2) Tilanduk said, 'I will not give it (to you) because it is inherited from my father.' (3) The busaw said, 'Just give that to me, because I will be the one to take care of it.' (4) Tilanduk said, 'Yes, I will give it to you if you will beat it only when I cannot hear it, because (if I will hear it) I will become unhappy.'

Wendell goes on to describe a further text in which the *affixed* speech verb, what he calls "regular speaker focus" is the norm, i.e. (Verb + speaker + Q). He comments that this narration "is more participant oriented" (25). While the Tilanduk story has an unchanging cast of characters (Tilanduk and the evil spirit) and the dialogue is somewhat repetitious and predictable from episode to episode, in this second story, which is about a chieftain (Mag-Agong) who sets out to win a princess to be his wife, the participant slate varies as the chieftain confronts in turn an evil spirit, a crocodile, an old man, and the princess herself. The speaker focused formula of quotation serves as the norm for much of the story, but other QF variants occur: (a) The QF with affixed verb and *preposed speaker* becomes the norm at peak (like a key-change in a musical composition). (b) Preposed speaker plus specification of the addressee is used once—for an initiating utterance (directed to the old man) where, no response is given (cf. specification of addressee in closure) and the chieftain's utterance is a conclusion (his resolve to go on at great hazard to win the princess). (c) Regular quote focus (as described above) is used for an utterance which involves a flashback—where the chieftain recalls a highly relevant piece of advice from his father. Double QF's and split quotes also occur a time or two in special functions.

Example 6 (from "Mag-Agong" (Kagan-Kalagan) (Wendell 1986))

(1) Mingusip ya datu   'Ayin kaw tepad?'
    asked   det datu.F where you place

(2) Miglawung ya tingeg 'Ari aku ay tas na buntud.'
    said   the voice   here I at top of mountain

(3) Miyanik ya datu   aw kinita nan ya busaw na   piglagketan na kadina.
    went.up the datu.F and saw   he   the busaw who bound   by chain

(4) Mig -usip ya datu, 'Nanga aw   piglagketan asiri?
    . . . -asked the datu.F why   you.F bound   here

(5) Wan ya se   mu?'
    what det sin.F your

(6) Timubag ya busaw, 'Mikase aku sa   eped   nami,   sagaw
    answered the busaw sinned I.F against companion our.ex that.is.why

piglagket aku asiri.'
bound   I.F here

    (1) The datu asked, 'Where are you?' (2) The voice said, 'I am here, at the top of the hill.' (3) The datu went up and saw the busaw who was bound by a chain. (4) The datu asked, 'Why are you bound here? (5) What is your sin?' (6) The busaw answered, 'I have sinned against our companion, that is why I am bound here.'

    Wendell describes still a third text which has highlighted speaker focus, i.e. with the speaker regularly preceding the affixed verb (Speaker + Verb + Q). Wendell comments concerning this story ("The Monkey and the Butterfly"): "The whole story is confrontational and highly vivid in style, and the use of preposed speaker effectively contributes to express this" (37). Other quotation formulas figure in this text as well, e.g. quote focus with addressee (unaffixed Verb + Speaker + Addressee + Q) at the borders of paragraphs and episodes, and regular quote focus (unaffixed Verb + Speaker + Q) in post-peak—i.e. after tension and confrontation have been resolved.

Example 7 (from "The Monkey and the Butterfly" (Kagan-Kalagan) (Wendell 1986))

(1) Ya ube   miglawung, 'Tey   sa kataw   mo   bila   ming kaw
     the monkey.F said   shucks at cowardice your friend like you

na beke na eseg.'
of not of man

(2) Mikaike ya lahat na ube,   untu nilan pigtampeyes ya kalibangbang.
     laughed the all.F of monkey very they criticized   the butterfly.F

(3) Ya kalibangbang miglawung, 'Bila   kun pigdablek kaw   na
     the butterfly.F said   friend if desire   you.F of

tanam tagad kaw   arun na katibuk na buwan kay   atuwan   ko kamu.'
fight wait you.F now at full   of moon   because will.fight I you.F

(4) Ya ube   timubag, 'Yan ya paganapen   nami eseg, dili magdumili sa tanam.'
     the monkey answered that the looking.for.F we man not reject   a fight

(1) The monkey said, 'Shucks, friends, you are a coward, you are not like a man.' (2) All the monkeys laughed; they really ridiculed the butterfly. (3) The butterfly said, 'Friend, if you want to fight, you wait till the full moon, because I will fight against you.' (4) The monkey answered, 'That is the man we are looking for who will not refuse to fight.'

Wendell's (1986) three texts with three differing norms for the QF match up plausibly with his characterizations of the three texts themselves. Text One, the Tilanduk text, is a somewhat routine story with parallel episodes and parallel dialogue within the episodes. It has the same protagonist and the same antagonist throughout. Its norm is the quotation-focus QF. Text Two (Mag-Agong) has non-parallel episodes and has the protagonist confronting several antagonists serially; its norm is the speaker-focus QF. Text Three, "The Monkey and the Butterfly", is described by Wendell as "highly confrontational"; its norm is highlighted speaker focus. Wendell also mentions that in the Mag-Agong story, preposed speaker QF's are used in the last two pre-peak sentences that in a sense "trigger" the peak while in "The Monkey and the Butterfly" story, regular quote focus is the norm in post peak. As already suggested, these changes in norms within a story can be likened to key changes within a musical composition.

3.3 Biblical Hebrew. This language, (Longacre 1989, chap. 7) uses neither postposed formula of quotation nor the nul formula within reported speech in narrative. In this respect it is simpler than the languages referred to above in this section. The storyline speech act verbs indicate person/gender/number of the speaker: **wayyo?mer** "and-he-said"; **watto?mer** "and-she-said"; **wayyo?meru** "and-they [masc]-said", etc. Formulas of quotation vary, however, in regard to further specification of the speaker or addressee by noun or pronoun.

A dialogue is regularly initiated by a formula of quotation which indicates the speaker and the addressee by nouns which establish at the outset the participants in the dialogue; this is a rather routine piece of participant identification. Use of nouns for both speaker and addressee throughout the quotation formulas of a dialogue indicates a confrontation or at least a momentous interview of two important people (cf. Joseph's Interview with Pharaoh in Gen. 41). On the other hand the use of QF's with verbs of speech without accompanying nouns through the remainder of a dialogue (once participants have been established) is indicative of lack of tension and lack of confrontation in what can be described as routine interchanges. Gen. 33.5–8 is indicative of such a dialogue between Esau and Jacob, where Sp:$\emptyset$ + Ad:$\emptyset$ corresponds to the atmosphere of forced civility that characterizes the passage. These are two polar extremes which correspond to two genres of (marked) reported dialogue (confrontational dialogue versus routine exchange).

V + Ad (pronoun) is a basic form for continuing dialogue in what may be regarded as a third genre of (unmarked) reported dialogue; any promotions or demotions from this norm are significant; V + Sp (N) + Ad (pr) signals speaker dominance or an attempt on his part to pull rank; V + Sp (N) without mention of the Ad equals speaker preoccupation with himself (or a speech spoken to no one in particular); while V + Ad (N) signals the dominance of the addressee (cf. Totonac above).

Further key changes in this third type of dialogue involve resort to devices from the polar extremes, i.e. the other two types of dialogue. Thus, use of an isolated V + Sp (N) + Ad (N) in dialogue medial indicates a speech act which signals a fresh beginning or a redirection of a dialogue—especially after a stalemate in the argument. Likewise, use of an unaccompanied speech verb (-Sp, -Ad) in dialogue medial can indicate a stalemate (i.e. no one is saying anything decisive), while the same formula at dialogue end indicates speaker compliance. The long dialogue between Jacob and his sons in Gen. 48:1–14 is of this third type and illustrates several of the key changes mentioned here.

The relevant parameters governing dialogue in Biblical Hebrew are, in summary:

(1) Key choice: (a) high tension dialogue; (b) low tension dialogue; and (c) normal dialogue pitched between the two extremes—with the possibility of key changes.

(2) Linear placement in the dialogue: dialogue initiation, dialogue continuance, stalemate, redirection, final compliance.

(3) Dominance patterns: (a) nothing implied; (b) speaker dominance (or speaker-centered); (c) addressee dominance.

4. Conclusion. The purpose of this paper has been to study the dynamics of reported dialogue in narrative; the thesis has been presented that in at least some languages variations in the QF's can be indexical of the intensity of participant interaction. QF's can vary all the way from very full structures with an inflected speech verb and mention of both speaker and addressee, to more rudimentary structures, to nul (absence of any QF). Positionally, in many languages the QF can vary as to preposed, postposed, and interlarded.

The two brief English narrative passages illustrate in a limited way these types of variation. In English, for example, specification of only the speaker is normal in continuing QF (after dialogue initiation); nul QF's are often reserved for great moments of the story; and specification of both speaker and addressee in the QF's in the interior of a dialogue—or of the speakers only in successive QF's after nul QF's—can be a way of signalling a confrontation.

Data from three additional languages, widely separated in time and space, were also cited: Totonac, a contemporary language of Mesoamerica; Kagan-Kalagan, a contemporary language of the southern Philippines; and Biblical Hebrew, a classical language of more than 2000 years ago. Data from these three languages form a fruitful comparison in respect to several parameters: positional variation of the QF; indication of speaker or addressee dominance; marking a confrontation between speaker and addressee; variation in the context of the QF's according to different norms or keys, which signal subgenres of narrative—as well as key changes (cf. musical accidentals) in the same overall key. In this indexing of the intensity of participant interaction, Totonac and Hebrew are similar in regard to their mention/non-mention of the speaker/addressee as a means of indicating participant dominance, while Kagan-Kalagan and Biblical Hebrew are similar in respect to casting dialogue into various keys. To illustrate these and other points of comparison or contrast among the three languages I submit a summary table:

	TOTONAC	KAGAN-KALAGAN	BIBLICAL HEBREW
+/- Positional Variation	+	+	-
Speaker Dominance	- addressee	fronting of speaker	- addressee/ Sp:N + Ad: Pr
Addressee Dominance	- speaker		- speaker
Confrontation		highlighted speaker focus	Sp:N + Ad:N
Key Changes		(3 keys)	(3 keys)
Quote Focus	?	+	?
Dialogue Closure	postposed QF	+ addressee	V only (in final compliance)

Institute of Linguistics
7500 Camp Wisdom Road
Dallas, Tx. 75236

ENDNOTES

[1] Excerpted with permission from "Ordeal in the Winter Woods" by Joseph P. Blank, Reader's Digest, January 1988. Copyright 1987 by the Reader's Digest Assn., Inc.

[2] An earlier version of this paper also presented data from Forster (1983), Koontz (1977), and Waltz (1977), but this proved to be too much material to handle well in the confines of one paper.

[3] I take this occasion to mention the lamentable loss of our colleague Dag Wendell only a few years ago.

[4] This seems sensible in a (weakly) VSO language where left-shifts are a regular feature and the quotation bears a certain analogy to the object.

[5] Continuing utterances do not initiate or resolve a dialogue but keep up a contest for control within it.

REFERENCES

Blank, Joseph P. Ordeal in the Winter Woods. In Reader's Digest, January 1988. Copyright 1987 by the Reader's Digest Assn., Inc.

Clendenen, Ray. 1990. *The interpretation of Biblical Hebrew hortatory text: A textlinguistic approach to the book of Malachi*. Unpublished doctoral dissertation. University of Texas at Arlington.

Forster, Jannette. 1983. Use of dialogue in a Dibabawon narrative discourse. *Philippine Journal of Linguistics* 14.1.

Koontz, Carol. 1977. Features of dialogue within narrative discourse of Teribe. In *Discourse grammar: Studies in indigenous languages of Colombia, Panama, and Ecuador*, Part 3, R. Longacre & F. Woods. (eds) (SIL publication 52). Dallas: Summer Institute of Linguistics and the University of Texas at Arlington, pp 111–132.

Larson, Mildred. 1978. *The functions of reported speech in discourse*. Dallas: Summer Institute of Linguistics and the University of Texas at Arlington (SIL publication 59).

Longacre, Robert E. 1984. *The grammar of discourse*. New York: Plenum.

———. 1986. *Discourse, paragraph, and sentence structure in selected Philippine languages*. Dallas: Summer Institute of Linguistics Publications in Linguistics and Related Fields #21. Santa Ana (California): Summer Institute of Linguistics.

———. 1989. *Joseph: A story of divine providence: a text linguistic and text theoretical analysis of the Hebrew text of Gen 37: 39–45*. Winona Lake (Indiana): Eisenbraun's.

———. 1990. *Storyline concerns and word-order typology in East and West Africa*. Supplement 10, *Studies in African Linguistics*. Los Angeles: UCLA.

Longacre, Robert E. and Frances Woods (eds). 1979. *Discourse grammar: Studies in indigenous languages of Colombia, Panama, and Ecuador* (SIL publication 52). Dallas: Summer Institute of Linguistics and the University of Texas at Arlington.

Reid, Aileen. 1979. The dynamics of reported speech in Totonac. In *Discourse studies in Mesoamerican language*. L. Jones, (ed) (SIL publication 58). Dallas: Summer Institute of Linguistics and the University of Texas at Arlington, pp 293–328.

Waltz, Carolyn. 1977. Some observations on Guanano dialogue. In *Discourse grammar: Studies in indigenous languages of Colombia, Panama, and Ecuador*, Part 3, R. Longacre & F. Woods. (eds) (SIL publication 52). Dallas: Summer Institute of Linguistics and the University of Texas at Arlington, pp 67–110.

Ware, Jan. 1993. Quote formulae in *The Final Diagnosis*. *Journal of translation and text linguistics* 6.161–78.

Wendell, Dag. 1986. The use of reported speech and quote formula selection in Kagan-Kalagan. *Studies in Philippine Linguistics* 6.1.1–79. Manila: Linguistic Society of the Philippines and the Summer Institute of Linguistics.

6

THE PARAGRAPH AS A GRAMMATICAL UNIT

R. E. LONGACRE
The University of Texas at Arlington
and the
Summer Institute of Linguistics

1. INTRODUCTION

In this paper, it is assumed (*a*) that discourse has GRAMMATICAL STRUCTURE; and (*b*) that this structure is partially expressed in the hierarchical breakdown of discourses into constituent embedded discourses and paragraphs and in the breakdown of paragraphs into constituent embedded paragraphs and sentences—not to speak of further hierarchical parcelling out into clauses, phrases, and word structures. It is a special thrust of this paper to marshal whatever arguments may be marshaled for the grammatical structure of the paragraph.[1]

"Paragraph" is taken here to designate a structural rather than an orthographic unit. The paragraph indentations of a given writer are often partially

---

[1] I acknowledge here my indebtedness to an unpublished paper (1970) of Alan Healey: "Are there grammatical paragraphs in English?" An abbreviated version of his paper was used over a 5-year period in grammar classes at the University of Texas at Arlington and in classes of the Dallas Summer Institute of Linguistics. The general stimulus of this paper and its many specific germinal thoughts have so entered into the present paper that detailed acknowledgment is quite impossible.

dictated by eye appeal; that is, it may be deemed inelegant or heavy to go along too far on a page or a series of pages without an indentation or section break. A writer may, therefore, indent at the beginning of a subparagraph to provide such a break. Conversely, a writer may put together several paragraphs as an indentation unit in order to show the unity of a comparatively short embedded discourse. Finally, the orthographic rule in English composition that we must indent for each change of speaker in a dialogue obscures the unity of dialogue paragraphs (where, e.g., assuredly a question and its answer constitute a unit).

As far as the status of the paragraph at the present time in linguistic thinking is concerned, van Dijk (1972:125–126), although scarcely using the term PARAGRAPH as such, tells us emphatically that we cannot consider that a discourse is composed directly of a concatenation of sentences; rather, we must consider it to be composed of sequences of sentences. I do not see why the traditional term PARAGRAPH should not be applied to at least some of the sequences of sentences that van Dijk finds essential to the analysis of a discourse. Furthermore, explicit research on the structure of the paragraph is currently being carried out by Hinds (this volume) and Winter (1977).

I argue in this paper that we have good evidence in many languages of the world for paragraph closure (i.e., features of beginning and end) and paragraph unity and that we are able to construct a system of paragraphs that does not compare unfavorably with constructing, for example, a system of clauses in a given language.

Some assumptions of this paper are:

1. Monologue discourse in any language has a hierarchical constituent structure that runs somewhat as follows (the scheme can vary a bit from language area to language area): morpheme, stem, word, phrase, clause, sentence, paragraph, discourse.

2. In this scheme, since paragraph is spaced between sentence and discourse, it resembles in certain ways the two contiguous levels. Thus, in certain respects, a paragraph resembles a long sentence on the one hand and a short discourse on the other hand.

3. The best way to describe this constituent structure is to distinguish the functional slot from the set of items that may fill the slot. In particular, a functional slot within a paragraph (e.g., its setting, or its culmination) need not be expressed by just a sentence but can be expressed by a group of sentences that constitute an embedded paragraph. This assumption is very important throughout this chapter in that, although many of the examples involve only one sentence per functional slot, they are, in principle, recursively expandable to examples in which a group of sentences (embedded paragraphs) fill one or more such slots.

The Paragraph as a Grammatical Unit   117

4. The functional parts of a paragraph (whether consisting of a sentence or of an embedded paragraph) are often marked by overt sequence signals (conjunctions, sentence adverbs, back reference to a previous sentence, or deictics). But, even when unmarked (in a given example in a given language), the notional parallelism with marked structures justifies grammatical analysis. Thus, in languages such as Mandarin, Vietnamese, Cambodian, and Laotian, we still find "subject" (or topic), "object," and "verb" even when formal marking is almost nonexistent.

2. ARGUMENTS FOR THE GRAMMAR OF THE PARAGRAPH

Closure

Many languages have particles that indicate either the beginning or the end of a paragraph.[2] Thus, "paragraph introducers" in Huichol (Mexico) include *mérikʌ* 'well' and *hiikÁʌ* 'then'—which occur on the first or second word of a main or of a dependent clause (Grimes 1964:73–74). In Shipibo (Peru), *jainoasr* and *jainsron*, both roughly translatable as 'thereupon', serve a similar function. In fact, we are told that these words occur only as the first word of a paragraph (Loriot and Hollenbach 1970). In Capanahua, a form of the verb *ha-* 'do, be, have' serves a similar function as in: *ha-ska-ʔi-ya* 'and so then . . .' and *ha-ska-ska-há-ʔi-ya* 'So that is the way it was when . . .' (Loos 1973:701–702).

Another similar (and often interlocked) feature is back reference between paragraphs. Back reference occurs in many languages in various distributions between successive sentences of a discourse. It is not, as such, limited to the onset of a new paragraph. Thus, we can have such sequences as *Jim went downtown to see the parade. After watching it go by, he jumped in his car and came home*, where *after watching it go by* is a back reference to *to see the parade* in the preceding sentence.

Schulze and Bieri (1973:390), however, describe for Sunwar some peculiar kinds of back reference that are characteristic of paragraph initial. One, which consists of "chaining with identical verb phrases," apparently has no temporal or sequential function but functions merely to mark the end of one paragraph and the beginning of another. Thus, we may have at the end of the paragraph *I will buy a cow*, and the next paragraph will begin *I will buy a cow and . . . .* Paragraph onset can also be marked by chaining with temporal reference of the sort illustrated in my own example of back reference given above.

---

[2] Gary Singleton marshaled these data for me in a term paper at the University of Texas at Arlington.

In other languages (e.g., Gurung of Nepal and Sanio-Hiowe of New Guinea) we find back reference exclusively within the paragraph and not between paragraphs. Lack of back reference is indicative, therefore, of a paragraph boundary.

Another feature that often serves to mark off paragraphs from each other is the occurrence of characteristic constituents either at the beginning or at the end of such a unit. I have become accustomed to refer to sentences that introduce a paragraph as either SETTING or INTRODUCTION (depending on the discourse genre involved), whereas those that close a paragraph I refer to as TERMINUS. In regard to setting (with narrative) and introduction (with explanatory or hortatory material), I think we are faced with the psychological need for an "ice breaker." There is a certain reluctance on the part of the speaker to plunge immediately into a topic. He wants to spend a sentence orienting himself and the audience to what he is going to talk about. I do not mean here something as explicit as a topic sentence. I mean, rather, something that indicates time, place, or circumstances or gives a broad hint of what is to come in the body of the paragraph. Such a unit may be followed by a topic sentence proper in the explanatory paragraph or by the first sentence with the onset of action in a narrative paragraph.

Whereas in narrative discourse the setting is often used to reset the time or the place of a new paragraph, the terminus is often used to take one main participant off the stage or to indicate a lapse of time. The terminus often contains verbs of motion such as *he went away* or *he went off and slept* or *he waited until the next day* or something on that order.

Thematic Unity

Possibly of considerably more importance than the incidental occurrence of particles, back reference, setting, terminus, and other surface structure features to mark the onset or end of a paragraph is the fact of the thematic unity of a paragraph. Again, we do not simply allege thematic unity; rather, we find it reflected in the surface structure features of the paragraph itself. In narrative discourse, a narrative paragraph is built around a thematic participant, occasionally a small set of thematic participants. In other types of discourse, we find the paragraph built around a theme that is not different in kind from a thematic participant. I illustrate briefly.

In Paez (Colombia), Gerdel posits a paragraph topic that, presumably, would include both the thematic participant of a narrative paragraph and the theme of a non-narrative paragraph. She describes it as follows:

> Paragraph Topic is a paragraph-level feature which gives cohesion to a paragraph by indicating what topic is being developed in the paragraph as a whole. Paragraph topic may consist of a noun or locative phrase, or include a clause, or a certain type of

The Paragraph as a Grammatical Unit

sentence. It is marked in the same way as Sentence Topic, i.e., by a clitic *-a'/-'* occurring phrase-final or clause-final. It differs from Sentence Topic in the following respects: 1) Paragraph Topic must be referred to at least twice in the paragraph, as marked topic at least once; re-referal may be by a lexical surrogate occurring one or more times within the paragraph; 2) paragraph topic occurs initially in the paragraph and often finally in the paragraph, thus indicating the beginning and end of a topic and incidentally indicating the bounds of a paragraph; 3) paragraph topic occurs initially in linear order in the sentence and is grammatically independent of the rest of the sentence, although it may be cross referenced to by some other word in the sentence such as a demonstrative pronoun or verb; 4) a whole sentence, occurring initially in the paragraph, may function as paragraph topic [Gerdel and Slocum 1976:275].

In the following example of a Paez paragraph, *mestlu cyã'* 'that shaman' is the paragraph topic. The paragraph topic is cross-referred to by *cyã* in the same sentence. He is also referred to again as *mestlu* 'shaman' in the last sentence. All the activities reported in the paragraph are, moreover, activities of the shaman (SS-"same subject marker").

Mestlu cyã'   *"yu'tse'j ya'vatf"*   *jĩrra',*   *cyã'* wallinde
Shaman that-one cure   I-am-going-to saying-SS, **he**   liquor
(Paragraph Topic)   (cross-ref.)

wẽjy   *ẽsh*   *cyã'wẽ uty*   *pẽyi.*   *Vite*   *yu'*   *"cyã' cytũus*
tobacco coca thus   they demand. Others (theme)   that rainbow

yafyte acjwa'j" jĩna   *viyu*   *pẽjyna*   *ẽsh*   *ya'ja cshavyte ãshna*
eyes-in to-put   saying money demanding coca bag into   putting

uty yũ'. Cjĩrra cyajũ' ãtsã'saty cusa'   *eca*   *cutyi'jrra'*
they do. Doing then   sick-ones at-night outside making-go-SS

yu'cjte   *caachi'jrra'*   *"ipy-cjũch uweya'*   *spayuutstja'u"*   *jĩna*
woods-in making-set-SS   firefly   to-catch we-are-looking saying

ipy-cjũch teerrãava   *uwerra'*   *wala-yuj wechana neeyũ'uty.*
firefly   even-just-one catching-SS very   happy   they-remain.

"Na' aca ũssa's uwetja'u" jĩna   *"na' ptjãawesa*   *caajnita'"*
This pain giver   we-caught saying   this harmful-one sent-by

jĩna   *ẽjya etste jyũtf*   *yacj yaprra'*   *uty cjicje'. Manz*
saying bush leaf-in with   with wrapping-SS they place. Many

cus   **mestlurráa**   *e'su-yã'ja' case'je'uc*   *ipy-cjũch yupya'*
nights **shaman-only** afterwards he-goes-out firefly   to-intercept
         (cross-ref.)

sa'   *cuj*   *uwerra'*   *"ãtsã'a'*   *catyjina"*   *jĩ'c.*
and-SS several catching-SS   sick-one will-recover he-says.

The shaman demands liquor, tobacco, and *coca*, saying: "I am going to perform a cure." Others, saying: "that is for throwing in the eyes of the rainbow," demanding money, they put it into the *coca*-bags. They, taking the sick persons outside at night and making them sit in the woods, they say: "we are going to watch for fireflies to catch," and catching even one firefly, they are very happy, saying: "we have caught this one that gave the sickness; this was sent by someone as a curse" and, wrapping them in a leaf with the remedy, they put them there. Afterwards, the shaman alone goes out several nights to intercept fireflies and, catching several, he says: "the sick person will recover."

For Ica (Colombia), the identification of the thematic participant is of peculiar importance. Thus, a colleague of mine who has studied Ica for several years was puzzled for some time as to the formal means to distinguish subject from object within an Ica clause in connected discourse. He had to go mainly by such lexical probabilities as the fact that it is more probable that *the dog bit the man* than that *the man bit the dog*. Otherwise, he simply had no clue as to who was meant to be subject of a given clause. A study of paragraph structure, however, resolved the difficulty in the following manner. Ica paragraphs have a thematic participant who is referred to in the first sentence or two and is marked by the suffix *-ri*. He is assumed to be the subject of all clauses in the paragraph unless something is marked to the contrary. The latter is accomplished by adding the suffix *-se?* to any noun that is indicated as subject of a clause when that noun is not the thematic participant of the paragraph. There is even a means of switching the thematic participant of the paragraph halfway through it (so as to yield a compound paragraph with one thematic participant in the first part and another in the second part). To accomplish this, the noun that comes on not only as subject but also as new thematic participant is suffixed by both suffixes, namely, *-se?ri*. Here, an understanding of the paragraph is crucial to an understanding of the constituent structure of individual clauses within it, so that we are inevitably carried to the grammar of the paragraph from the grammar of the clause (Tracy and Levinsohn 1977).

To these examples could be added illustrative material from the Philippines, Southeast Asia, and Biblical Hebrew—to cite only a few possibilities.

3. A SYSTEM OF PARAGRAPHS WITH STRUCTURAL PARAMETERS

In the preceding section, I have argued that a paragraph unit exists, that with various degrees of clarity its boundaries are indicated in the languages of the world—both in spoken and written discourse—and that such a unit has thematic unity. There are, however, other considerations that are possibly more conclusive.

Thus, from the standpoint of Halliday and Hasan (1976:10), the sine qua non of grammatical structure in regard to such a unit as the paragraph is the ability to demonstrate system, that is, systematic parameters and choice among them. It is to this task that I address myself in this section. In outlining a system of paragraph types, I posit in the first subsection three basic parameters. I suggest, then, in the next subsection, how paragraph types produced by the intersection of these parameters are in turn realized as genre-conditioned variants. Thus, we may have, for example, a sequence paragraph that must occur either as a narrative paragraph in narrative genre or as a procedural paragraph in procedural genre. Genre imposes on the paragraph certain characteristics of itself. In the third subsection, I posit further context-conditioned variants of the sort frequently called STYLISTIC. Finally, this whole main section is followed by another section in which I claim that such a system of basic uncomplex paragraph types as are here described is sufficient to account for the wild and woolly variety of paragraphs in the real world of discourse. This is demonstrable by showing that paragraph structure is recursive, that is, that paragraphs may occur within paragraphs in an open-ended way that is sufficient to account for whatever variety of paragraph structure is encountered anywhere.

Because of limitations of space, the system of paragraph types here suggested will have to be presented in summary form, with only partial illustration.

The Basic Parameters

I posit here as basic parameters to a system of paragraphs in any language the following: (*a*) binary versus *n*-ary constructions; (*b*) movement along a parameter with the following values: conjoining, temporal relations, logical relations, elaborative devices, reportative devices; and (*c*) weighting considerations. The first parameter is essentially a matter of division of all possible paragraphs into closed versus open structures. Closed structures are typically binary; that is, the paragraph has two constituents. Occasionally, claims are made that we encounter trinary paragraphs. Although these are somewhat doubtful, if such structures exist they are also essentially closed structures—versus the open structures, which have *n*-ary constituents.

The second parameter is essentially a parameter involved with notional relations. These relations are not semantic in the referential sense of *dog* versus *cow* or *hit* versus *slap* but, rather, have to do with the underlying notions whereby clauses or sentences combine into larger units (Longacre 1972, 1976).

As for the third parameter, it is a matter somewhat similar to the metrical distinction between spondaic, iambic, and trochaic meters. In reference to binary paragraphs, we find that the two constituents may have equal weight or that the second may outweigh the first or that the first may outweigh the second. We can then proceed to marshal *n*-ary paragraphs under essentially the same heads. *N*-ary paragraphs may likewise consist of nuclear constituents all of which are of the same weight or of constituents with greater weight on the last (nuclear) constituent or of constituents with greater weight on the first (nuclear) constituent. Positing weighted variants brings together as essentially the same some paragraphs that at first blush appear to be different.

THE BINARY VERSUS *n*-ARY AND NOTIONAL
STRUCTURE PARAMETERS

I handle here together the first two parameters by taking the second as basic to my argument and dividing it according to the binary versus n-ary parameter. In regard to the notional structure, we progress along a parameter consisting of the following values: conjoining, temporal relations, logical relations, elaborative devices, reportative devices. Conjoining has to do with grouping considerations; that is, items are grouped, contrasted, or given as a field of choice. In temporal relations, items are ordered temporally. In logical relations, they are ordered logically. In the elaborative devices, detail of various sorts is added. In reportative devices, detail is also added, but more from the standpoint of the discourse as a whole; that is, quotations are introduced into the discourse; introduction and identification paragraphs are used to bring on to stage new participants or props; and comment paragraphs are used to make possible evaluative observations by the composer of the discourse. Reportative devices are found only among binary paragraphs, and temporal relations are found only among open-ended paragraphs.

As for the conjoined binary structures, we find contrast, exception, and frustration encoded under the antithetical paragraph, as well as alternative paragraphs with only two logically possible alternatives. I use here conjoining in a more loose and inclusive sense than I have used it in former editions of my notional apparatus (such as is found in Longacre 1976: Chapter 3).

The antithetical paragraph exists, I assume, primarily to encode contrast, as in the following example: *I got on a bus, traveled around an hour or two, got off, went through the museum, and altogether had a delightful time. Tom, on the contrary, stayed home and felt sorry for himself*. Here *I* and *Tom* are contrasted as to differing courses of activity.

I handle exception as a variety of contrast in which one member of a set is contrasted with all the other members of the set. This is seen in such an example as the following: *Everybody got drowsy and eventually fell sound asleep. Only grandfather kept awake and watched for his chance.*

The antithetical paragraph also has come (in many languages) to include frustration, which is not, properly speaking, a conjoining notion but is subsumed here because it typically encodes in the same surface structure or in a very similar surface structure to those used to express contrast and exception. Thus: *He drives down crowded streets where there are children at play and adults wandering leisurely over the pavements. He never, however, seems to be on the lookout for pedestrians.* This illustrates frustrated overlap, that is, we do not get in the second sentence the expected concomitant activity indicated by the first sentence, but quite the contrary. Note also the following paragraph: *They started out for Paris promptly at seven o'clock, as planned. They never, however, got there.* Notice that it is not appropriate to these sentences to use a sequence signal such as *on the contrary*, which would be appropriate to an antithetical paragraph of the contrast variety. *But, however*, or some such conjunction is the appropriate sequence signal for a frustration paragraph. This paragraph just given is an example of frustrated succession; that is, we do not get the anticipated sequel indicated by the first sentence.

A further type of conjoined binary structure, one that encodes two alternative choices or possibilities, can fittingly be termed the ALTERNATIVE PARAGRAPH. An example follows of such a paragraph in which only two possibilities are envisioned: *John was possibly the one who turned the air conditioner on over the weekend. If he didn't, then it must have been Titus.*

Still other types of binary paragraphs encode logical relations. Exemplification of certain types of implicational paragraphs follows. Take, for example: *It may be that he'll come and call for me between six o'clock and seven o'clock tonight. If he comes, I'll be glad to spend the evening with him in whatever place he chooses.* Notice that in this paragraph the *if he comes* in sentence two is a recapitulation, contraction, and back reference to the first sentence. Or, viewed somewhat differently, the first sentence may be thought of as the full statement of the antecedent, whereas the initial stretch of the second sentence constitutes an abbreviated statement of that antecedent. At any rate, we can see that the conditional paragraph that expresses hypotheticality is essentially an expansion of a one-sentence unit that expresses the condition within itself. The following paragraph is not dissimilar; it illustrates a conditional paragraph with a universal quantifier: *First we sent Bill, then James, then Arthur, then Meredith. Whomever we sent got lost every time.* Here we see that the first sentence is essentially an expansion and elaboration of the abbreviated structure *whomever we sent* that occurs in the second sentence. Again, the conditional paragraph with universal quantifier is a rather obvious elaboration of the corresponding sentence type. Note, finally, the contrafactual paragraph that follows: *He almost came over to get me last night. Had he come, I would have gone out with him.*

Notice again that *had he come* is an echo and summary of the first sentence. So, the contrafactual paragraph, like the preceding types just mentioned, is essentially an extrapolation from the corresponding sentence type by virtue of expansion of the first member of the conditional sentence.

Result and reason paragraphs will have to be discussed more at length in that they present a more varied picture. Result and reason paragraphs may both use recapitulation via sentence margins to show the relationship of the two parts of the paragraph. Thus, a result paragraph such as the following is translated from a language of the Philippines (Dibabawon): *It's really a beautiful place there at Nasuli. That's why they choose to live there, because it's really beautiful there at Nasuli.* We note in this paragraph that the cause margin of the second sentence is a recapitulation of the entire first sentence. Again, notice that the whole relation, result and reason, is given in the second sentence, so that we can think of the first sentence as an extrapolation and prior statement of the cause margin of the second sentence. This is one way to mark the result. Notice also how easily the cause margin can be omitted: *It's really a beautiful place there at Nasuli. That's why they choose to live there.* Here, *that's why* acts as a sequence signal expressing result without further reinforcement.

Similarly, in a reason paragraph we have such examples as the following: *He came because his boss forced him to come. McDougal simply told him that he was to go to the party.* Here note that there is a cause margin in the first sentence that is expanded and stated more fully in the paraphrase element that composes the entire second sentence. This is the inverse of the function of the cause margin in the result paragraph.

Rather than a cause margin in sentence one of such a paragraph, we could have a purpose margin. *Jim dropped in on us to get another free meal. He hoped that we would continue to be generous.* Note that *to get another free meal* is somewhat freely paraphrased as *he hoped that we would continue to be generous*, that is, defining generosity as giving another free meal, in which *free meal* is the specific and *generosity* is the generic term. Again, the purpose margin of the first sentence is brought down and expanded and paraphrased in the second sentence, and we are in the structure of a reason paragraph.

Further varieties of both result and reason paragraph involve either other explicit sequence signals or juxtaposition. Space forbids their exemplification here.

I now turn to illustrations of elaborative devices of binary structure. Two varieties of binary paraphrase remain to be illustrated: *He's one of the most reliable men that we have ever had on the job. He's not always trying to evade responsibility, like so many of our employees.* This paragraph is really a roundabout way of saying *He's one of the most reliable; he's not unreliable.*

and thus is clearly seen to be negated antonym paraphrase. For an example of contraction paraphrase, take the following: *All I know is that he has taken off for the fresh air, the fields, the open country where he can feel like himself again. All I know is that he has taken off.*

A further elaborative device is illustration. The illustration paragraph (simile) is also an expansion of a one sentence unit. Thus, we could have a sentence like *Getting money out of that old miser was like a dentist extracting a wisdom tooth*. But this can be expressed as a two-sentence unit in such a paragraph as follows: *It was like watching a dentist extract a wisdom tooth. That's how it was getting some money out of the old miser.* Here *that's how* is the crucial sequence signal in the second half of the paragraph.

As elaborative devices, both introduction and identification paragraphs have important discourse functions in terms of introducing new characters. For introduction paragraph, note the following: *There was a man who lived on our street 25 years ago. Soon after my Dad opened the grocery store, he came to ask for employment and was hired on the spot.* In such a paragraph as that just given, there is no overt sequence signal. Very commonly, however, such paragraphs have a deictic element in the second sentence. Thus, we could have *There was a man who lived on our street 25 years ago. That man was one of the first men ever employed by my father in his new business.* For identification paragraph, note the following: *They found an old house with weeds growing around it, a leaking roof, and a treacherous floor. That's what they eventually made into their home.* This could, of course, have been expressed without the deictic element in the second part, in such a paragraph as the following: *They found an old house with weeds growing around it, a leaking roof, and a treacherous floor. They eventually made it into their home.* So close are illustration and identification paragraphs in surface structure that they are often taxonomically grouped together (as deictic paragraphs) with other paragraphs that involve a deictic element in the second part.

There are also reportative devices of binary structure. One such structure, the quote paragraph, exists in English (alongside the more usual quotation sentence; see Longacre 1978). This structure is the standard device of quotation in certain languages, such as Guanano and other South American languages. An English example might run something as follows: *"I saw her downstairs at two o'clock a.m. reading a book." Those were his words the next morning.* Note, however, the deictic element in the second clause of this example, which probably means that this and the two preceding examples could all be grouped together in a common deictic paragraph in English.

Another reportative device is the comment paragraph. For a comment paragraph, note the following: *She began to pick her way through the mud. That road was always pretty muddy, I recall.* We have here a comment by the narrator in the second part of the paragraph. Note, however, the deictic element. Again, this might lead us to combine this paragraph in English with others as a deictic paragraph. In Guanano, however, there is a very important difference in tense forms in such paragraphs as that just given. The verb *began to pick her way* would be in the regular uninvolved narrative tense, but the comment by the narrator would be in the involved tense. It is his own comment that involves him as an observer. This difference in tense forms would not characterize other paragraphs that are called deictic in Guanano. Therefore, in Guanano the comment paragraph is clearly distinct from the deictic paragraph. This distinction may run through quite a few South American languages, in that the involved–uninvolved or witnessed–unwitnessed distinction is very common through a large area of South America (cf. Waltz 1976).

I now turn my attention to *n*-ary paragraphs. Conjoining paragraphs of *n*-ary structure include the coordinate paragraph and alternative paragraphs that express more than two alternatives and are, presumably, open in structure.

For the coordinate paragraph, consider the following (in which, however, the first sentence is introductory): *Here is a bit about our family. My brother John is a sculptor. My sister Jane is a portrait painter. I myself do pen sketching.* This paragraph is essentially a list with one sentence each devoted to *John, Jane,* and *I.*

An alternative paragraph of *n*-ary structure follows: *A passing motorist might have seen and reported the accident. Alternatively, it could have been someone who lived nearby. It might even have been noticed by a traffic helicopter.* Further possibilities could be listed and probably exist in the reported situation.

Temporal relations that are, I believe, in principle always *n*-ary and never binary—whatever the stringencies of surface structure in a given language—are of two main varieties: overlap and succession.

Temporal overlap is illustrated in the following paragraph, where it is marked by the presence of *meanwhile*: *My wife did the town that morning—especially the tourist market and the popular bazaar. Meanwhile, I spent the time in a leisurely inspection of the municipal museum.* Notice, however, that temporal overlap need not be exclusively of the coterminous activities variety illustrated above. We can have a period of time indicated during which something happens, as in the following paragraph: *She was nursing the baby in a drowsy, contented sort of way. She fell asleep, and the baby nursed on.* This paragraph could be recast as *She was nursing the baby in a drowsy, contented sort of way. As she was nursing, she fell asleep.* In the first instance, the second part of the coordinate sentence is a back reference to the first sentence. In the second recasting of the paragraph, we find an adverbial clause initial in the second sentence, which is a back reference to the first sentence.

The following example of temporal overlap involves punctiliar–punctiliar; that is, the two actions represented are not time spans but are simple events that are conceived of as simultaneous. *Standing there, I brought my head up to steal a look at her. As I brought my head up, she threw the knife in one deft, sweeping motion.*

To show that paragraphs expressing various varieties of temporal overlap are not necessarily binary, note the following example, which is an expansion of a paragraph already given: *My wife did the town that morning—especially the tourist market and the popular bazaar. Meanwhile, I spent the time in a leisurely inspection of the municipal museum. At the same time, my daughter, escorted by a Mexican friend, attended a bullfight. As for my teenage boys, they slept through the whole morning.*

Temporal sequence of the event–event variety is illustrated in the following: *John was at no loss as to how to proceed. He went back quickly to get an ax. Returning to the fallen tree, he lopped off all the branches. Cutting them up, he threw them on to the sled and set off. On getting to the cabin, he carefully stored away his hoard of firewood.* We can just as easily have temporal sequences that involve spans rather than events, as in: *They played tennis for 2 hours under the vertical tropical sun. After that, they swam for another 2 hours in the warm ocean by the coral reef. Then they stretched out on the sand and slept the rest of the day.*

Induction, attestation, and syllogism paragraphs are all types of logical relations of the argumentative variety. They are as open-ended as the necessary links in the argument or the necessary bolstering evidence requires. In the induction paragraph, the conclusion is given at the end, as in: *She looked haunted and tired, and her voice was absolutely colorless. I saw immediately that something was wrong.* Here, *I saw that* is a sequence signal that marks the conclusion of the paragraph. This paragraph could have run through several sentences before the conclusion was stated at the end. For an example of attestation paragraph, I use the preceding paragraph, invert the order of conclusion and evidence, and add on a few more bolstering arguments: *I saw right off that something was wrong. She looked haunted, tired, and old. Her voice came out devoid of any inflection and absolutely colorless. There was a big purple bruise on the side of her face.* The similarity of these two paragraphs is such that they probably prove to be weighted variants (cf. below) of each other, much like the variants of the antithetical or alternative paragraphs.

An example of a syllogism paragraph follows: *Socrates is a man. All men are mortal. Therefore, Socrates is mortal.*

Elaborative *n*-ary structures exist as well. Equivalence paraphrase is, I believe, not essentially a binary structure—although it often emerges as binary due to the paucity of near synonyms. Note the following example: *I've never met such a prejudiced man. I've never known such a complete bigot.* Amplification paraphrase can be described as a circling-in-on-the-target sort of structure. This is evident in such a paragraph as the following: *He took off yesterday. He took off for the country. He took off for the open fields, the woods, the mountainsides, where he could feel like himself again.* Here the third sentence embodies the most adequate and full expression of the content of the paragraph.

As for the other elaborative devices, two other varieties of paraphrase, generic–specific and specific–generic, have been mentioned as encoding into paragraphs. Note the following example of generic–specific: *They took care of his needs. They sobered him up, fed him, clothed him, and gave him a place to stay.* This is a two-sentence paragraph in which a generic expression *took care of* occurs in the first sentence and details are given in the second sentence. Obviously, this could be expanded into a paragraph in which there is a series of sentences rather than just one describing what they did for him or how they took care of him. With no difficulty at all, this paragraph could be permuted as follows: *They sobered him up, fed him, clothed him, and gave him a place to stay. They took care of his needs.* Now the paragraph is specific–generic, and the last sentence comes across as some kind of summary.

For exemplification, a further elaborative device, note the following: *There is a lot that could be done to ease the situation. For example, you could try taking her problems as real instead of as imaginary. You might also try listening to her once in a while.* Notice that the sequence signal *for example* occurs in sentence two. The further example in sentence three is indicated by the sequence signal *also* in that sentence.

WEIGHTING CONSIDERATIONS

Because of space limitations, nothing like a complete treatment of this parameter is possible. I give only a few examples of how attention to weighting considerations can (*a*) bring together similar but differing types; and (*b*) explain certain variations within a given type.

In English, the result paragraph has efficient cause in the first member and result in the second member, whereas the reason paragraph has efficient cause in the second member and the event or happening in the first member. I therefore classify the result paragraph as IAMBIC and the reason paragraph as TROCHAIC. The two are seen, therefore, to be related as weighted variants.

Induction and attestation paragraphs are types of argumentation. In the induction paragraph there is a final conclusion, and in the attestation paragraph there is an initial thesis. In both cases, other sentences in the paragraph support the conclusion or the thesis. I call the induction paragraph IAMBIC and the attestation paragraph TROCHAIC. On this basis, the two paragraph types are seen to be related (as illustrated). Finally, generic–specific paraphrase and specific–generic paraphrase paragraphs likewise emerge as weighted variants (see above).

As far as the consideration of n-ary paragraphs, it would seem at first blush that coordinate paragraphs of all descriptions would be essentially SPONDIAC because they are a list. Take again the following paragraph (in which the first sentence is part of the periphery of the paragraph): *Here is a bit about our family. My brother John is a sculptor, My sister Jane is a portrait painter, I myself do pen sketching.* It appears that no part of this paragraph is meant to be more prominent than the other but that the three nuclear sentences simply deal with three different members of a family and with their artistic interests. What about, however, such a paragraph as the following: *Here is a bit about our family. My brother John is a sculptor. My sister Jane is a portrait painter. I myself do pen sketching. Best of all, my youngest brother Charles is a capable young pastor–counselor—whose artistry is human lives.* Here, it appears that the paragraph is definitely weighted toward the last sentence, as is seen in the use of the introductory sequence signal *best of all*. I therefore consider that this is an iambic paragraph—and use the term IAMBIC here to indicate a structure that is not strictly iambic in the sense of unweighted plus weighted but consists of a sequence of three unweighted followed by a weighted.

With sequence paragraphs, wherein we express a series of spans or events or a mixture of spans and events in the same series, we can likewise expect to find weighted variants. If there is no climax to the paragraph, it is spondaic. If there is a climax, the paragraph is iambic in that, presumably, the climax comes at the end of the paragraph and the rest of the paragraph builds up to that climax. Take, for instance, the difference between the following two paragraphs (again, the first sentence of the paragraph is setting): *John was at no loss as to how to proceed. He went back quickly to get an ax. Returning to the fallen tree, he lopped off all the branches. Cutting them up, he threw them on to the sled and set off. On getting to the cabin, he carefully stored away his hoard of firewood.* Expressed in this fashion, the paragraph simply records a series of events, although no doubt getting to the cabin and storing away the wood is what the action is all about. Still, there is no surface structure marking of climax, and very probably we are in a spondaic paragraph. It is possible, however, to reinforce the final sentence in various ways so as to make clear that this is the climax of the whole paragraph. A frequent marker of such climax is simply the addition of the term *finally*, as in *Finally on getting to the cabin, he carefully stored away his hoard of firewood.*

Further Parameters

Genre-Conditioned Variants

It is important to note here that each of the preceding examples of paragraphs has inevitably been of a basic paragraph type in a genre-conditioned variant. It now remains to show how the genre choice conditions variants and to show something of the range and variety of genre conditioning.

I will attempt to show for one of the paragraph types already given how genre choice necessarily influences the structure of the paragraph. Thus, the antithetical paragraph can occur in any discourse genre. The examples given were those of the antithetical paragraph in narrative discourse. In accordance with the fact that it was narrative discourse, the main-line verbs were past tense and, obviously, here we seemed to be dealing with a segment of a continued story. But the antithetical paragraph need not be narrative. We can, for example, have a procedural antithetical paragraph. The following has to do with burial customs among the Tboli, where at one stage of the rites the pallbearers engage in a tug-of-war with the family of the deceased: *Here, the ones who are trying to bear the coffin off to burial take it up and try to get out of the front yard of the house with it. The relatives of the dead one try, however, to hold it back and keep it from going to the burial place.* Notice that we do not deal here with past-tense verbs but with the present-tense forms that are typical of procedural discourse. Furthermore, we do not deal here with specific agents, as in a narrative, but rather with the activities of typical people involved in such a situation. We are here in a discourse that is essentially activity-oriented instead of agent-oriented. Again, the antithetical paragraph may occur in a behavioral discourse, such as the following: *Concerned citizens of Dallas, get out and vote in the next election and choose responsible men for county commissioners. Those of you, however, who are unconcerned with the quality of county government can stay home (for all I care)—and complain about how things go.* Here, we are still in an antithetical paragraph of the contrast variety. The contrast is between getting out to vote and staying home and not voting, between the concerned and the unconcerned. As befits a hortatory discourse, the main verbs are imperative. Finally, we can have within expository discourse an antithetical paragraph of the contrast variety. *We submit, with varying degrees of passivity, to a great burden of federal, state, and local taxes. Our forebears of 200 years ago rose up, however, in active resistance to throw off a tax levy that was not even a tithe of our present burden.* Let's assume that the preceding is from an essay on taxation past and present. The contrast here is between *we* and *our forebears*, between *passivity* and *resistance*, between *a great tax burden* and *a relatively small tax burden*.

OTHER CONTEXT-CONDITIONED VARIANTS

Here we get into the realm of things that are often referred to as *stylistic*. We can consider the parameters described here as multipliers of the basic system that consists of Basic Parameters × Discourse Genre Specifications.

Many, if not all, paragraph types can be made cyclic by repeating at the end an element found at their beginning. In some paragraph types, the cyclic element must be done through a setting or introductory element that is not part of the nucleus proper. In other cases, an element of the nucleus may be reechoed at the end in order to give cyclic structure. In a few cases, the cyclic structure is expounded to a full-blown chaismus. We get, for example, paragraphs structured a,b,c,c',b',a' as the paragraph winds itself up and then unwinds itself in reverse order.

It is also possible to give a paragraph a rhetorical question-and-answer structure, which gives it special poignancy as a teaching device or, perhaps, as effective scolding.

Then, a whole paragraph may be quoted, not in the sense that we say *John said* . . . and then give a whole paragraph, but with multiple indication of quotation all through it. This interrupts the sequence of the paragraph so that sometimes one has to ignore the interspersed quotation formulas if he is to get at the structure of the paragraph itself. Then he finds that it conforms to one of the Basic Types + Genre Specifications as already described.

It must also be mentioned that in some parts of the world there is a special predilection for some of these devices or for a special avoidance of some of them. Thus, cyclic paragraphs are extremely common in Australian Aborigines languages, but rhetorical question-and-answer paragraphs are extremely rare in the typical Mesoamerican language.

4. THE STRUCTURE OF UNRESTRICTED PARAGRAPHS

The great majority of the examples given in the previous sections of this paper have been simple examples with no layers of embedding, that is, have not contained two or more sentences that constitute a paragraph within a paragraph. Actually, of course, in the world of real discourse such examples are comparatively rare—although they have illustrative value in a paper of this sort. Actually, here we must face the fact that a theory of a finite number of paragraph types must have as its corollary the proviso that there is recursive embedding of paragraph within paragraph. We can have a theory of a finite number of paragraph types for language in general or for one language in particular if and only if we admit the possibility of recursion within the paragraph unit. Otherwise, every new embedding situation we encounter would be a new paragraph type, and, ultimately, the number of paragraph types would be infinite. It is the purpose of this section to give an analyzed example of such unrestricted paragraph structure.

The following example is from a travelogue book concerning Mexico (Castillo 1939). The paragraph here reproduced conforms to the general structure of the discourse, which is procedural. That is, the whole discourse may be paraphrased as *If you were to come to Mexico, these are some things which you would see in a typical itinerary.*

> (1) *By the light of the electric bulbs which have been placed inside the caves, you look about in amazement.* (2) *Turning your eyes upward, you get a wonderful view of the great, long stalactites that hang from the ceiling.* (3) *These, as you know, have been formed by the limestone-containing water that has seeped down through the roof of the caves.* (4) *Then, looking down, you see the enormous stalagmites that seem to grow upward out of the floor, where they have been formed by the water that has dripped from the ceiling.* (5) *As you look at these strange formations, you get the idea that each is reaching for the other, that the two are trying to meet.* (6) *Then, on going farther, you see that some of them have succeeded, for here and there you find a huge, glistening column which has been formed by the meeting of a stalactite and a stalagmite* [p. 175].

In looking at the above example, I think it may be rationally held that sentence (1) is an introduction to the whole unit. It has preview value in that it says *you look about in amazement* and that the rest of the paragraph tells what you see as you look about. Whatever the notional structure of this unit, I think that the function of the sentence in the surface structure is clearly simply to break the ice and to get the paragraph going by providing a preview of what is going to happen. The body of the paragraph is a sequence paragraph in which sentences 2–5 form an embedded simultaneous paragraph that expounds the antecedent, and sentence 6 is a single sentence that expounds the consequent. Within the embedded simultaneous paragraph (sentences 2–5), $Simul_1$ is expounded by a sequence paragraph (sentences 2–4) and $Simul_2$ is expounded by sentence 5. The embedded sequence paragraph has as its antecedent an embedded deictic paragraph (sentences 2 and 3) whose topic is sentence 2 and whose comment is sentence 3, and the consequent of the embedded sequence paragraph is sentence 4. For the formal justification of this structure, note that sentence 6 is marked as consequent by the phrase *then, on going farther*, which is a typical sequence marker and describes the trajectory of the trip within the cave. Sentence 5 is marked as $Simul_2$ versus sentences 2, 3, and 4 by virtue of the initial stretch *as you look at these strange formations* in sentence 5. Sentence 4 is marked as a consequent in reference to sentences 2 and 3 by the initial conjunction *then*. Sentence 3 is marked as a comment in reference to sentence 2 by virtue of the occurrence of the word *these* (cross-reference to *stalactites* in sentence 2). See the accompanying indented analysis diagram.

        Sequence ℙ
        PREVIEW (S_1)
        ANTECEDENT: SIMULTANEOUS ℙ
          $SIMUL_1$: SEQUENCE ℙ
            ANTECEDENT: DEICTIC ℙ
              TOPIC: S_2
              COMMENT: S_3
            CONSEQUENT: S_4
          $SIMUL_2$: S_5
        CONSEQUENT: S_6

Space forbids presenting the analysis of more examples of unrestricted paragraphs. There seems to be good reason to believe, however, that the system of basic types in genre variants, with further possible stylistic variants, is able in principle to describe the wild and woolly world of "real" paragraphs—provided we admit recursive embedding of type within type.

REFERENCES

Castillo, C. (1939) *Mexico* (ed. by Burton Holmes), Wheeler Publishing Co., Chicago.
Gerdel, F. and M. C. Slocum, (1976) "Paez Discourse, Paragraph and Sentence Structure," in R. E. Longacre ed., *Discourse Grammar, Part I*, The Summer Institute of Linguistics, Dallas.
Grimes, J. E. (1964) "Huichol Syntax," *Janua Linguarum, Series practica* 11. The Hague: Mouton.
Grimes, Joseph E. (1975) "The Thread of Discourse," *Janua Linguarum 207*. The Hague: Mouton.
Halliday, M. A. K. and Ruqaiya Hasan. (1976) "Cohesion in English," in R. Quirk, ed., *English Language Series, No. 9.*, Longman, London.
Healey, A. (1970) "Are there grammatical paragraphs in English?," unpublished paper.
Longacre, Robert E. (1972) Hierarchy and Universality of Discourse Constituents in New Guinea languages: discussion. Washington: Georgetown University Press.
Longacre, Robert E. (1976) *An Anatomy of Speech Notions*, The Peter de Ridder Press, Lisse.
Longacre, Robert E. and F. Woods, eds. (1976–77) "Discourse Grammar: Studies in Indigenous Languages of Colombia, Panama, and Ecuador, Parts I–III," *Summer Institute of Linguistics Publications in Linguistics and Related Fields*, No. 52, The Summer Institute of Linguistics, Dallas.
Longacre, Robert E. (1977) "Discourse Genre," paper read at the XII International Congress of Linguists in Vienna.

Longacre, Robert E. (1978) "Sentences as Combinations of Clauses," paper to appear in Stephen Anderson et al., eds., *Language Typology and Linguistic Field Work*, Center for Applied Linguistics, Washington.

Loos, E. (1963) "Capanahua Narrative Structure," *Texas Studies in Literature and Language* 4 (supplement), 697–742.

Loriot, J. and B. Hollenbach. (1970) "Shipibo Paragraph Structure," *Foundations of Language* 6(1), 43–66.

Schulze, M. and D. Bieri. (1973) "Chaining and Spotlighting: Two Types of Paragraph boundaries in Sunwar," in A. Hale, ed., *Clause, Sentence and Discourse Patterns in Selected Languages of Nepal, Part I*, The Summer Institute of Linguistics of the University of Oklahoma, Norman.

Tracy, H. P. and S. H. Levinsohn. (1977) "Participant Reference in Ica Expository Discourse," in R. E. Longacre, ed., *Discourse Grammar, Part III*, The Summer Institute of Linguistics, Dallas.

van Dijk, Teun A. (1972) *Some Aspects of Text Grammars*, The Hague: Mouton.

Waltz, N. E. (1976) "Discourse Functions of Guanano Sentence and Paragraph," in R. E. Longacre, ed., *Discourse Grammar, Part I*, The Summer Institute of Linguistics, Dallas.

Winter, E. (1977) *Replacement as a Function of Repetition: A Study of Some of Its Principal Features in the Clause Relations of Contemporary English*, University Microfilms International, London.

7

The Discourse Structure of the Flood Narrative

Robert E. Longacre

ABSTRACT

This paper approaches the Genesis Flood Narrative from the standpoint of contemporary discourse analysis. As a developing discipline within linguistics, discourse analysis is currently being applied to a variety of texts in many languages—from Western Europe to folk cultures. The aim has been to apply the techniques of discourse analysis in a somewhat routine way to the Flood Narrative without resort to *ad hoc* procedures.

Discourse analysis anticipates a certain range of style within any text. Thus, material which is on the BACKBONE (event-line of a narrative) will inevitably differ from material of a supportive and depictive nature. Likewise, material at the peak (high point) of a story will almost always differ from routine narration. Finally, quoted material will differ stylistically from the surrounding narrative framework.

All these insights contribute to the understanding of the Flood Narrative and the appreciation of its unity. Thus, the material on this event-line of this and other narratives in Biblical Hebrew consists of verb-initial clauses with verbs in the *waw* plus prefixal tense—exclusive of wayĕhîy (from hāyâh 'be') which is usually depictive and functions in the paragraph setting to initiate a chain of backbone verbs. Clauses off the backbone have verbs in other tenses—often preceded by an initial noun—or are verbless. At the peak of the Flood Narrative (Gen. 7:17-24), however, a special feature of event-line paraphrase sets in, so that explanatory and depictive material, instead of being off the line, is expressed in the *waw* plus prefixal verbs which are elsewhere restricted to the event-line. The effect is like that of slowing down the camera at the high point of a movie.

Quoted material in the Flood Narrative differs considerably from that found in the surrounding context; e.g., the speeches of God are not themselves narrative but procedural (how to build the ark), instructional (what to do when the ark is built), and predictive-promissory (the convenant after the Flood). Since different genres have different features which have radical effects on the details of a discourse, considerable stylistic variety ensues within the overall unity.

The slow-moving and redundant nature of the pre-peak episodes is explained as OVERLAY—a rhetorical device in which the same ground is gone over repeatedly in a way which highlights important motifs. This device is well attested in non-Western literatures. Such repetitions need not be attributed to divergent sources.

Robert E. Longacre is Professor of Linguistics in the Department of Foreign Languages and Linguistics of the University of Texas at Arlington, and International Linguistic Consultant for the Summer Institute of Linguistics. He has translated the New Testament into Trique (Mexico) and directed workshops in discourse grammar in the Philippines, Papua New Guinea, Colombia, and Mexico. A recent book of his is *The Anatomy of Speech Notions*.

Copyright © 1979 American Academy of Religion

90   Robert E. Longacre

Introduction

The purpose of this paper is to approach the biblical flood narrative from the standpoint of its discourse structure, as the latter is currently being studied in contemporary linguistics /1/. The author's credentials are those of a linguist rather than those of a Semitist.

The general goals and methodology of discourse analysis as here applied have been stated elsewhere (Longacre and Levinsohn, 1977; Longacre, 1976; Grimes, 1976). To summarize here briefly, however: contemporary discourse analysis is interested in questions of the classification of discourse genre, e.g., the matter of distinguishing a narrative discourse from other sorts of discourse such as procedural, behavioral, expository, and the further matter of distinguishing specific genre within these types; the articulation of parts of a discourse such as formulaic beginnings and endings, episodes, and high points in the story (called peaks); the status of discourse constituents such as sentences, paragraphs, and embedded discourses; the cast of participants in a given discourse, and the thematic participant(s) of a given paragraph; author viewpoint and author sympathy as indicated in the text; the relation of the abstract plan of the discourse to its full, unrestricted text; the main-line development of a discourse as opposed to subsidiary and supportive materials; the role of tense, aspect, particles, affixes, pronominalization chains, definitivization, paraphrase, and conjunctions in providing cohesion and prominence in a discourse; ways of marking peak in a narrative; and the function of dialogue in a discourse. In accordance with the charting technique described in Longacre and Levinsohn and adapted here to Hebrew, the Hebrew text of the flood story has been plotted out word for word in multi-columnar arrangement. This charting facilitates separation of mainline from subsidiary developments and tracking of participants through the discourse.

Discourse analysis of this sort may well revolutionize the contemporary scene in linguistics. It is being increasingly realized that the study of isolated sentences out of context is scarcely worth being called the study of language. Many facets of language from verb and noun morphology on up remain opaque to analysis in terms of isolated sentences. Discourse analysis of this sort is being applied extensively to the study of many aboriginal languages throughout the world. The author of this paper was involved a few years ago in directing a discourse oriented

The Structure of the Flood Narrative   91

research project which embraced some thirty languages of Colombia, Ecuador, and Panama /2/. Earlier projects, in which some of the fundamental concerns of discourse analysis were not as well pinpointed as in the more recent project, embraced some seventy-five languages of the Philippines, Papua New Guinea, Australia, and Mexico (Longacre, 1968, 1972). My colleague, Joe Grimes, has had similarly extensive experience in applying discourse analysis techniques in various areas throughout the world (Grimes, 1976, and bibliography in that volume).

Discourse analysis expects and tolerates a considerable range of stylistic variety within the same discourse. Specifically, in regard to narrative itself, we should expect different parts of a story to differ stylistically. We should not expect the style at the peak of a narrative to resemble that of more routine narration in other parts of the story. We should not expect long quotations (which are often embedded discourses of a different genre) to have the same style or syntax as the more frankly narrative portions, nor should we expect background information of various sorts to sound like backbone narration. We can expect to find tenses and aspects used carefully and differently in separate parts of the story.

I. Some Overall Observations

An immediate problem is the delineation of the flood story from the surrounding context. The flood story is part of the continuous ongoing structure of Genesis, and as such, of course, has certain characteristics of embedded narrative--characteristics which betray that it belongs to something larger. As to the main peak of the flood story, there can be no doubt that in Gen 7:17-24 we are at the high point of the narrative itself. Somewhat more difficult to decide, however, is the precise place that the flood narrative begins and ends. Take the problem of the beginning. The birth of Noah himself is given in Gen 5:28-32 which seems, however, very definitely not to be a part of the flood story proper. Gen 6:1-4 recounts an incident (the "sons of God" going into the "daughters of men") which likewise does not seem to be part of the flood story proper; but which may, on the other hand, pattern as the inciting incident which leads to God's decision to bring the flood. Gen 6:1-4 is followed, however, by section 6:5-8 (God's decision to destroy humanity) which apparently brings us up to the very onset of the flood story, with reintroduction of Noah as the main (human) participant in verse 8.

We are confronted in 6:9 with the phrase "these are the generations tōlĕdōt of Noah." That this phrase is some kind of section marker of important chunks of Genesis seems obvious from inspection of the whole book. In that Genesis is divided into tōlĕdōt sections, there is a sense in which the flood story as such is not a natural division of the book, which is largely concerned with the remoter origins of Israel and therefore is a sort of genealogical chronicle with long sections on the life, times, and descendants of various individuals mentioned within it. A few things stand out about the tōlĕdōt sections of Genesis. (1) Commonly, the participant for whom a tōlĕdōt section is named is born and on stage before his section begins. When he is firmly established as clan head, then his "life and times" are described.
(2) Therefore, much of the "tōlĕdōt of X" may be about the son of X, e.g., the tōlĕdōt Isaac is largely about Jacob, and the tōlĕdōt Jacob is largely about Joseph (with one chapter on Judah). (3) The tōlĕdōt typically concludes with the death of the person for whom it is named and a preview of what is to come in the following section (or at least a mention of its main character). Thus, in Gen 25:9 it is mentioned that Isaac and Ishmael buried Abraham; in in 25:12-18 follows the tōlĕdōt Ishmael; and in 25:19 begins tōlĕdōt Isaac. In Gen 35:29 Isaac dies, Esau and Jacob bury him, and this is followed by two short tōlĕdōt sections for Esau (36: 9-43). Then follows one of the more striking instances of a tōlĕdōt ending with a preview of the next section, viz. Gen 37:1, "And Jacob dwelt in the land wherein his father was a stranger, in the land of Canaan." This preview is completely unrelated to the subject matter of the section which it concludes and is followed immediately by ēlleh tōlĕdōt ya'aqōb.

To return now to the relevance of the above observations to the flood narrative. (1) The birth of Noah and his sons (Gen 5: 28-32) occurs towards the end of the tōlĕdōt Adam (Gen 5:1-6:8). (2) This tōlĕdōt ends, however, on a note of rising tension and gives a preview of what is to come. Thus, Gen 6:1-4 reports an incident which presumably was a climax of man's rebellion against God, while 6:5-8 tells of God's decision to destroy life from off the earth but to spare Noah who is abruptly reintroduced by name in 6:8. (3) The tōlĕdōt Noah begins with a repetition of some of this material merged into God's instructions to Noah to build an ark. (4) The tōlĕdōt Noah ends with the incident of incest reported in Gen 9:18-27 and the death of Noah (9:28-29). This

The Structure of the Flood Narrative 93

concluding section is clearly set off from all the previous material by the explicit new beginning in 9:18-19, "And the sons of Noah, that went forth of the ark, were Shem, Ham, and Jephath; and Ham was the father of Canaan. These are the three sons of Noah, and by them the earth was repopulated." Thus, this section--while a concluding incident from the times of Noah--admirably serves as preview for the table of nations in chapter 10 under the caption: *wĕ'ēlleh tōlĕdōt bĕnĕy nōaḥ*.

On these grounds, I believe it possible in a non-arbitrary fashion to set the boundaries of the flood story as structurally established in Genesis. The flood story, I believe, should be considered to consist of Gen 6:9b through 9:17. We cannot consider that the phrase *ēlleh tōlĕdōt nōaḥ* is aperture of the flood story itself. It is simply the title of its *tōlĕdōt* section and happens to coincide with the beginning of the flood story which follows. On the other hand, I am reluctant to assemble a story which crosses *tōlĕdōt* boundaries and disregards them. Nor does this make good sense in terms of the structure of the flood narrative itself. Thus, while Gen 6:1-4 and God's reaction in Gen 6:5-8 could be regarded as the inciting incident of the flood narrative, I find it awkward to have all this occurring before what looks like the stage of the story in 6:9b-12. Stage normally precedes inciting incident, not vice versa. Likewise, while I appreciate Frank Andersen's perceptive suggestion (private correspondence) that 9:20-27 balances with 6:1-4 in a kind of incest, judgment and salvation, incest pattern (or: "here we are right back where we started from"), I believe that this is a subtler connection which overrides the primary structure of this part of Genesis (as chiasmus often does). Only by taking seriously the articulation of Genesis into *tōlĕdōt* sections can we make sense of the book as a discourse. Once we see that the end of a *tōlĕdōt* can heavily anticipate the following section, there are no great problems.

Bounding the flood narrative in this fashion I proceed to recognize a stage, a peak (Gen 7:17-24), and episodes which are numbered according to their proximity and placement relative to the peak, so that episode P-1 labels the episode which immediately precedes the peak and episode P+1 is the episode which immediately follows the peak. In all this, the labeling of 7:17-24 as peak is crucial; I present the evidence for this below (section III). Specifically: Gen 6:9-12 is stage (Noah and world conditions in his day); 6:13-22 is episode P-3 (God gives Noah detailed

instructions for building the ark, embarking animals, and taking
on food; Noah obeys); 7:1-10 is episode P-2 (God commands Noah to
enter the ark along with the animals; Noah obeys, enters the ark,
and the animals come to him); 7:11-16 is episode P-1 (natural
causes of the flood are given with the word that Noah embarked
with the animals on the very day that everything broke loose; ends
with "and Yahweh shut the door"); 7:17-24 is peak (remorseless
mechanism of judgment; waters rise, mountains are covered, everything dies except those in the ark); 8:1-5 is episode P+1 (the
flood recedes and the ark comes to rest); 8:6-12 is episode P+2
(Noah sends out birds); 8:13-19 is episode P+3 (earth dries out
and Noah leaves the ark); 8:20-22 is episode P+4 (Noah's sacrifice
and Yahweh's response); 9:1-17 can be labeled episode P+5 but is
really a kind of secondary peak (God blesses, makes a covenant,
and gives a covenant sign). The evidence for considering this
last section to be a kind of secondary peak is also given below.
For a schematic representation of all this, see Diagram 1 (following page).

   As we shall see in section II below, while there is nothing
especially problematical about the post-peak episodes, there is a
problem area (first pointed out to me by Hendrikus Boers) in the
pre-peak episodes. My central thesis (to be sketched below) here
is: episode P-3 and episode P-2 are approximations to peak, the
onset of which is artistically delayed until the end of episode
P-1. There is extensive overlay in the content of episodes P-3
to P-1 as opposed to the structure of the post-peak episode where
such overlay is not found. This will be examined in detail below.

   As far as the slate of participants in this discourse, apparently they are: God, Noah, the flood (variously referred to as "the
flood," "the waters," etc.), and the ark. God is the central participant in that we are told his feelings and no one else's, not
even Noah's. We are also told God's inner thoughts (but we are
not told the thoughts and purposes of Noah, although his actions
are reported). In rank, Noah is the next most important participant. Much of the story turns on Noah versus the flood waters.
The flood, although inanimate, must be construed as a major participant. That the ark is a major participant is evidenced from
its general importance throughout the story and its special prominence in episode P-3 and at peak. Noah's wife, his sons, and his
sons' wives are mentioned at several places but nowhere assume an
active role in the story. The animals which are brought into the

The Structure of the Flood Narrative

Discourse features	Episode	Plot	Content	Reference
(character introduced before his tôlĕdōt) / (run-down of previous paragraph)	Preview		Yhwh as thematic	6:5-8
tôlĕdōt (goes with whole unit → 9:20)	STAGE		Noah and world conditions	6:9-12
(God said / Noah did) / And God said to Noah	Ep(P-3)	RISING TENSION	Command to build the ark; further instructions to Noah	6:13-22
(Yhwh said / Noah did) / And Yhwh said to Noah	Ep(P-2)		Noah enters ark. Yhwh and Noah thematic in 7:1-5; Noah in 7:6-10	7:1-10
Yhwh shuts the door / long date	Ep(P-1)		Flood begins. Flood; animals are thematic	7:11-16
terminus (time-span) / wayĕhî hammabbûl		CLIMAX / Peak	The Flood (thematic) prevails. Remorseless mechanism of judgment. God is not mentioned. Noah mentioned only at the end	7:17-24
terminus (date) / And God remembered Noah	Ep(P+1)	DE- LOOSENING	Receding waters	8:1-5
wayĕhî and date / (dove doesn't return)	Ep(P+2)		Noah sends birds (assumes active role)	8:6-12
wayĕhî and long setting (double dating)	Ep(P+3)		Leaving the ark	8:13-19
poetic climax (Noah → Yhwh / Yhwh → Noah) / weak onset, but a distinct section	Ep(P+4)	WRAP-UP	Yhwh receives sacrifices. Yhwh is thematic	8:20-22
ends with quote / And God said to Noah	Secondary Peak Ep(P+5)		God's discourse to Noah: blessing, covenant, covenant sign	9:1-17

Diagram 1: General Profile of the Flood Narrative (Gen 6:5–9:17)

ark are minor participants. They, like Noah's family, are passively mentioned at most points in the story except where the raven and the dove assume importance in episode P+2. Various other entities are mentioned in the course of the story such as the parts of the ark, the fountains of the great deep, the windows of heaven, the rain, the earth, Noah's altar, the clouds, and the rainbow. Although these are for the most part minor participants (even props), on occasion certain of them, the animals and the earth, become thematic participants of a given paragraph or subparagraph. Furthermore, most of the above are associated with major participants, e.g., the "fountains of the great deep," the "windows of heaven," and the "rain" are associated closely with the "flood" and the rising "waters"--which indicate a major participant. Likewise the parts of the ark are associated with the ark itself as a major participant. The covenant is a main theme of the secondary peak at the end of the discourse and is in fact a major concern of the entire discourse. The clouds and the rainbow are associated with the covenant.

The backbone of this narrative is carried here as in Hebrew prose narrative in general by $w\bar{a}w$ plus prefixal verb--which has been recognized for some time (cf. Kautzsch/Cowley, 1910:326) as a special narrative tense for Hebrew. It is important to recognize, however, that Hebrew is not peculiar in having a special narrative tense. Such a function is indeed the commonest use for the past tense in English itself. A recent germinal paper by Paul Hopper (1977) shows that simple past tenses have a special narrative function (as opposed to some sort of imperfect or imperfective) in Romance and Slavic (to which we can certainly add the aorist-imperfect distinction in Koiné Greek). Hopper goes on to mention that in some languages a similar effect is achieved by restrictions in word order. For example, in Old English a clause with an initial noun is background material in which we are told something about a prop or participant, while a clause with an initial or final verb is featuring the action and is on the event-line. While the above observations are primarily applicable to narrative, it isn't hard to demonstrate that in fact all discourse genre have characteristic thematic lines carried by a given tense aspect or restricted set of tense aspects. Eventually we should be able to characterize the meaning and function of tenses and aspects in any language in terms of their roles in connected discourse.

The Structure of the Flood Narrative 97

The backbone of narrative in classical Hebrew is indicated then by *wāw* + prefixal verb. One of the special characteristics of this construction is that it does not tolerate any preposed element, not even the word *lō'* "not". Any clause that has a preposed noun or the word "not" must perforce have other than *wāw* + prefixal verb as its verb. The usual recourse in such circumstances is to the suffixal verb, but we may also have nominal clauses without any verb at all, or clauses with a medial verb *hāyāh* "to be," or clauses with a participle serving as verb. All such clauses (including those with suffixal verb) are CIRCUMSTANTIAL CLAUSES which add detail and background to the event line but which must be distinguished from the event-line itself. Very commonly such clauses serve to introduce paragraphs, but they occur paragraph medial as well /3/.

The status of negated verbs which sometimes appear to be on the event-line semantically (but which cannot employ *wāw* + prefixal verb) is somewhat problematical. Very often, as Grimes (1976) has observed for language in general, events which do not happen are not on the main-line of narrative discourse. It might, therefore, be argued that all such *lō'* verbs are per se off the event-line. However, this is overstating what is probably a statistical generalization for language. There undoubtedly are discourses in almost all languages where negated events are part of the event-line itself, i.e., it is important to the structure of the story that something did not happen. Therefore, I leave this question unresolved for a while. Maybe it will have to be resolved in each particular occurrence in the Hebrew narrative by resort to the structure of the narrative itself and semantic criteria.

It is, however, necessary to make one qualification regarding equating the event-line of Hebrew narrative discourse with *wāw* + prefixal verbs. This qualification has to do with the verb *hāyāh* "to be." The verb "to be" is in most languages a descriptive and equative device rather than an action verb. Thus, while English narration characteristically employs past tense forms to mark the event-line, "was" does not pattern on the line but frequently serves as paragraph setting. Similarly *wayĕhîy* fulfills such a function in Hebrew /4/.

Of some importance in understanding any bit of OT Hebrew narrative prose is taking account of the means by which the thematic participant (or participants) of a given paragraph is established. By taking note of these devices we can not only identify thematic participants, but establish paragraph boundaries as well.

98   Robert E. Longacre

Just as a story has a cast of participants organized around a central participant, so a paragraph has a dominating participant. The difference between a paragraph and a discourse is that while a discourse has a *slate* of major participants, a paragraph (which is a shorter structural unit) is usually dominated by one or at the most two participants, with the other participants pushed off to the side. Hebrew does this by introducing the thematic participant(s) early in a paragraph (usually in the first or second sentence), repeating him a time or two and (especially if he is not mentioned in intervening sentences of the paragraph) mentioning him afresh at the end of the paragraph. Furthermore, the thematic participant becomes the subject of at least one clause on the event-line, i.e., it is the subject of at least one $w\bar{a}w$ + prefixal verb.

This of course holds only for narrative discourse. For example, in an embedded procedural discourse as we have in episode P-3 (instructions for building the ark), the goal of the procedural discourse, i.e., the building of the ark, is thematic. In a discourse of this sort the thematic participants pattern as object of the verb instead of as subject. But this is simply a reminder that we must make our rules genre by genre and not mix genre in setting up rules for thematic participants.

A further consideration has to do with the overall abstract plan of the discourse before us. Professor van Dijk, one of the outstanding text grammarians on the European scene, suggests that we speak here of the *macrostructure* of a discourse. This is, according to van Dijk, its global plan, macro-plan or formalized abstract. It is, it seems to me, the germinal idea of a discourse expressed in prelexical terms. For the latter reason it is, almost necessarily, expressed in some kind of logical symbolism. The macrostructure is obtained by writing a summary or precis and then attempting to formalize the summary. The purpose of constructing such a macrostructure is not, however, simply an exercise in formalism, but has to do with the understanding of the nature of the whole. It explains, e.g., why certain parts are made more prominent than other parts. I attempt here to construct a macrostructure for the flood story and will show its relevance in section V below.

I obtained an abstract of the story by (1) writing down all the clauses which contain $w\bar{a}w$ + prefixal tense and omitting most of the remaining material. This reduced the narrative to something in the vicinity of forty clauses. (2) I then proceeded to delete repetitions (from episode to episode), consequent actions ("and Noah did accordingly"), presupposed actions (e.g., "and God remembered Noah"), and paraphrases (e.g., in Gen 7:17-24). (3) At a further stage I eliminated all direct quotations and reduced them to indirect summaries of what was said. Likewise, I replaced detail with summary so that e.g., the following is reduced to "The flood took place and everything died":

> and the waters prevailed,
> and the ark drifted on the waters,
> and all the high mountains were covered,
> and all flesh died from off the earth.
> Only Noah and those with him in the ark were left,
> and the waters prevailed at crest 150 days.

(4) This left the following shortened form of the story, which is a tolerably good abstract.

> God had Noah build an ark so that he, his family and animals wouldn't be destroyed in the flood. They all got in the ark. God shut them in. The flood took place, and everyone died. Then God caused the waters to recede and the ark came to rest. Noah opened the window of the ark and sent out birds. He removed the covering of the ark. Then God told them to go out. Noah offered a sacrifice and God was pleased. He promised never again to send such a flood. He blessed Noah and his sons and made a covenant with them.

(5) The above can then be further reduced to something like the following: "God destroyed all living things from the earth with a flood but saved Noah (and his party) by having them embark in an ark. Then God promised never to send another such flood." What is preserved in this summary is (1) God's having Noah embark in an ark to preserve his life, (2) God sending the flood, and (3) God's promise to never send another such flood. This can be formalized in the following abstract representation of the germinal idea of the narrative.

$$t_1 \; \{ \; Sa \; (Ebc) \; \wedge \; [Sa \; (Ebc) \; \supset \; Ebc] \; \} \; \wedge$$
$$t_2 \; \{ \; Da \; (U\text{-}b)d \; \wedge \; [\exists c \wedge \exists c \; \supset \; \overline{D}abd] \; \} \; \wedge$$
$$t_3 \quad Sa \; (t_\psi \overline{D} U d)$$

where S = say, E = embark, D = destroy, a = God, b = Noah, his family and animals, c = the ark and its parts, d = the flood and aspects of it; t_1, t_2 and t_3 = successive times in the narrative; t_ψ = any time. Also the following conventions are observed: $\exists$ = existential predicate "be", $P \wedge P \supset Q$ = representation of causation (where P is a given and P implies Q) /5/, U = universal set, $\overline{D}$ = negation of verb D.

100   Robert E. Longacre

   The germinal idea relates to the unrestricted text by virtue
of a series of addition transformations in which we add: (1) world
conditions which disposed God to send a flood; (2) detailed instructions about building the ark and what to embark on it; (3)
numerous chronological notes which tally up to a chronology of the
story and mark off parts within it; (4) information as to the
physical causes of the flood; (5) depiction of the course of the
catastrophe and of the receding waters; (6) depiction of measures
taken by Noah to see if the waters had receded and the earth was
dry; (7) record of leaving the ark; (8) record of Noah's offering
sacrifice and God's reception of it (with promise to never send
another flood); (9) God's blessing and covenant with the giving of
the covenant sign; (10) specific mention all through the story of
particular actions and responses such as (a) Noah obeyed what God
commanded; (b) Noah entered the ark; (c) God shut the door; and
(d) God ordered them to come out of the ark.

                    II. Preview and Prepeak Episodes

   While I do not believe that Gen 6:5-8 is a part of the flood
story proper, I will consider this passage briefly in view of the
peculiar way in which the end of one tōlĕdōt section anticipates
material in the following section. I will then proceed to describe
the prepeak episodes and the peculiar feature of overlay and delay
in reaching peak which characterizes these episodes.

                          Preview and Stage

   This passage may be considered to be a preview of the whole
story--much like scenes flashed on the cinema screen (scenes which
anticipate the substance of a story) while the names of the actors,
directors, costume designers, composers, etc., are being presented.
Structurally this constitutes one paragraph in Hebrew, beginning
with the wāw + prefixal verb, "and God saw." It is clear that this
is a new paragraph largely because of the marked run-down effect of
the previous paragraph which ends in a quotation plus a few remarks
which are almost parenthetical and are at least clearly background
in character. The thematic participant of this paragraph is Yhwh,
who is mentioned explicitly four times and is referred to in pronominal form once, plus three times as "I" in the contained quotation of the paragraph. He is subject of all the main event-line
verbs: "saw," "was sorry," "was pained in his heart," "said." The
final verb "said" is quote formula for a quotation in which Yhwh

The Structure of the Flood Narrative

speaks of His intention of wiping out man with other life from the earth. In the last sentence of this paragraph (6:8) Noah is abruptly introduced as one who found favor in the eyes of Yhwh. In that Noah is mentioned only once, he is clearly not the thematic participant of this paragraph. This is seen also by his late introduction in the ultimate sentence. Here the force of the *wāw* is probably antithetical; Noah found favor in the eyes of Yhwh as contrasted with Yhwh's negative evaluation of everyone else.

The stretch immediately following the *tōlĕdōt* title in 6:9a, i.e., 6:9b-12, is the stage of the flood story narrative. Of some interest here is the rather startling juxtaposition of Noah at the end of the title and at the beginning of stage, i.e., in the center of verse 9. Noah is described in three circumstantial clauses as "a righteous man," "perfect in his generation," and one who "walked with God." Noah occurrs in the first and third of the circumstantial clauses and is referred to by pronoun in the center clause. Next follows a *wāw* + prefixal verb on the event-line with Noah as subject: "and Noah begat three sons, Shem, Ham, and Japheth." Noah, then, is clearly established as thematic participant in this half of the paragraph. In the second half of the paragraph there is a new thematic participant, "the earth." There are no special transitional features between the former sentence and this one in 6:11. It therefore seems that we very probably have here but one surface structure, namely, a compound paragraph, the first half of which has a thematic participant, "Noah," and the second half of which has a thematic participant, "the earth": i.e., this paragraph treats of Noah and world conditions in his day.

In regard to establishing the thematic participant of verses 6:11-12, note that the "earth" is subject of two of the main event-line verbs: "And the earth was corrupted. And the earth was filled with violence." While God is subject of the last main event-line verb ("looked"), the "earth" is mentioned twice even in that sentence: "And God looked out on the earth and behold it was corrupt, for all flesh had corrupted its way upon the earth."

God apparently is not a thematic participant in either part of this paragraph. He comes in first in the third circumstantial clause of 6:9, "Noah walked with God." He is also mentioned in 6:11a, "All the earth was corrupted before God." While He becomes subject of a main event-line verb in 6:12, God does not seem to be as prominent here as either Noah or the earth.

102   Robert E. Longacre

                          Episode P-3 (Gen 6:13-22)

     The outer framework of this paragraph is what has been called
for many languages in various parts of the world an execution
paragraph, i.e., a command (suggestion, etc.) is given and the
command is followed out (Longacre, 1968, 1972). Thus, we have in
verse 6:13, "And God said to Noah" while in 6:22 we find, "And
Noah did according to all that God had commanded him." Verses
6:13-21 contain God's commands to Noah.
     The substance of the quote breaks apart into two subsidiary
paragraphs which have somewhat different characteristics. The
first paragraph is structured as a one paragraph procedural discourse which contains directions for building the ark. The second
paragraph, from verse 17 on, is a one-paragraph instructional
discourse, i.e., it has to do with what Noah is to do when the ark
is built. In procedural discourses we expect the object of the
procedures to be thematic; and consequently in the first paragraph
the ark proves to be thematic as is easily shown by an examination
of the structure of this paragraph. We expect an instructional
paragraph (implicitly behavioral) to be agent oriented and in
keeping with this expected orientation we find Noah thematic in
the second paragraph /6/.
     The part of the quote found in 6:13 consists of two circum-
stantial clauses which serve as setting for the first constituent
paragraph and probably constitute one sentence: "The end of all
flesh is coming before me, and lo, I am destroying them with the
earth." Note the chiasmic structure here with "before me" at the
end of the first clause and "lo I" at the onset of the next clause.
Verse 6:14 contains the imperative which dominates the paragraph:
"Make for yourself an ark of gopher wood." No more imperatives are
found in this paragraph. From here on the paragraph consists of
elaborative material, i.e., prefixal verbs with preposed nouns.
To be true, one $w\bar{a}w$ + suffixal verb occurs at 6:14b but it seems
to be dependent on the previous verb with which it forms a unit.
     The ark as thematic goal-participant is first mentioned in 14a,
"Make you an ark of gopher wood," and is repeated in the next clause
which is an elaboration of the first, "Rooms shalt thou make in the
ark." Reference to the ark is continued in the following $w\bar{a}w$ +
suffixal tense which constitutes a continuation of the same sentence: "and thou shalt pitch it within and without with pitch."
The details of making the ark continue with 6:15, "And this is how
you shall make it," with the ark referred to here (as in 6:14b) as

The Structure of the Flood Narrative

a suffix on the sign of the accusative. Verse 6:15 ends with three circumstantial clauses which evidently are conjoined into one sentence. In this unit, "ark" occurs in the first clause and pronouns referring to the ark occur at the end of the next two clauses: "Three hundred cubits (shall be) the length of the ark; fifty (shall be) its width; and thirty cubits (shall be) its height" /7/. The ark is referred to again in 6:16 where Noah is told to make a "window" in the ark, and in 6:16b where he is told, "The door of the ark thou shalt make in its side" (where the ark is referred to both by noun and by pronoun on the word "side"). Finally, the ark is referred to still once more at the end of 6:16 as "First, second, and third decks shalt thou make *it*." It may be further noted that the thematicity of the ark is seen in the fact that the various specific nouns mentioned, e.g., the "window," the "door," and the "decks," are all related to the thematic participant, i.e., to the ark, in a part-whole relationship.

The second paragraph of this quotation begins with a circumstantial clause which is in some ways reminiscent of the setting of the previous paragraph (6:13). Where verse 6:13 has, "And behold I am destroying the earth," in 17 we find, "And I, lo I, am bringing a flood of waters upon the earth to destroy it...." Here we find for the first time overt identification of the "flood" (*hammābbûl*) by name. The verse continues with a purpose clause, "To destroy all flesh which has in it the breath of life from under heaven" and adds on a second clause, "all which is in the earth shall die." (Note again here the chiastic arrangement within the last sentence.)

Before going on to describe the body of the paragraph which is so introduced, it's important to note that in both the circumstantial clause of 6:13 and of 6:17, although God is mentioned very emphatically and although in 17 the flood is mentioned, neither are thematic participants of their paragraphs in that these participants are mentioned in only the setting of each paragraph and are not found further on in the same paragraph. There is, to be sure, in 6:18 a *wāw* + suffixal verb which may be on the main line of this instructional discourse. It has as its subject "I" which, of course, is God. This, however, is the last reference to God within the quoted discourse. There is no further such reference until 6:22 where we revert to the framework of the execution paragraph and are out of the quoted material within it. Furthermore, the force of the *wāw* in 6:18 could conceivably be antithetical, i.e., "but I will establish my covenant with *you*" as contrasted with God's purposes to destroy the rest of mankind. Thus, it may be that 6:18 links in some way more to the setting than to the body of the paragraph.

In the body of this second paragraph, i.e., in verses 6:18-21, Noah (the addressee of the instructional discourse) is thematic. The second-person orientation of the paragraph is shown clearly in 6:18b: *ûbo'tā 'el-hattēbāh 'attāh ûbānêykā wě'ištěkā ûněšêy bānêykā 'ittāk*. Notice that not only does the main verb in this sentence (*wāw* + suffixal tense) have the second-person suffix, but we have the second-person pronoun, *'attāh* "you," occurring in the middle of the verse, as well as second persons on the various possessed nouns of the verse, and resumptive pronoun at the end, *'ittāk* "with you." In the balance of the paragraph a variety of devices serve to continue the second-person orientation. (1) In 6:19 where Noah is told to take all the animals with him into the ark, the verb is prefixed for second person, "You shall take" and the purpose clause also adds something very similar to a resumptive pronoun (*'ittāk* "with you") at the end, "to preserve alive with you." Again we may question whether there would be any real purpose for having *'ittāk* "with you" at the end except to further establish and continue Noah as the thematic participant of the paragraph. (2) In 6:20 the animals are recapitulated in a similar but in some ways differing list as object (as they were in the previous verse) and again there is a second-person reference, "They shall come *to you* to preserve life." (3) In 6:21a, in place of a simple imperative "take" we find that there are two devices used to continue the second-person orientation. First of all, the verse begins with an emphatic pronoun *wě'attāh* "and as for you." This is followed by *qaḥ-lěkā*... "take for you..." where we find the indirect object pronoun *lěkā* "for you" in the clause "take for you from all food which is (to be) eaten" and so forth. (4) In 21b, "and you shall gather (it) to you," we find a second-person suffix on a *wāw* + suffixal verb followed by *'ēlêykā* "to you." (5) And, finally, in 21c, *lěkā* "to you" occurs once more in "and it shall be to you and to them for food." The thematicity of the second-person reference is seen in the many references to the second-person singular: in the fact that second person is the subject of *wāw* + suffixal verbs (which may prove to be mainline in this genre); in the fact that in several cases resumptive pronouns are used which are otherwise unmotivated; and finally, in the fact that the emphatic pronoun "as for you" occurs as sentence topic in 6:21b.

The Structure of the Flood Narrative   105

Finally, we need to look at the overall framework and structure of an execution paragraph. In 6:22 we revert to this outer framework in the sentence "And Noah did according to all which God commanded him, thus he did," which corresponds to 6:13a, "And God said to Noah." Note in 6:22 the chiastic structure involving repetition of the verb "do"; this chiasmus serves to put the focus on Noah's activities rather than on God's command. The embedded discourses in the two quoted paragraphs steal the thematic spotlight from the paragraph framework itself, i.e., what is important in this episode P-3 is the command to build the ark and further instructions to Noah. The quoted discourses are procedural and instructional with emphasis first on the object of the proceedings (the ark) and then on the fact that further instructions are given to Noah. For these reasons God, referred to here as Elohim rather than Yhwh, does not appear to be a thematic participant in this unit.

Episode P-2 (Gen 7:1-10)

The general framework of this paragraph is in 7:1, "Yhwh said to Noah 'Enter the ark,'" and 7:5, "And Noah did as Yhwh had commanded him." This paragraph, too, has an execution structure. The reported quotation is much briefer and simpler than that given in the preceding episode. Furthermore, the balance of the paragraph (7:6-10) is an embedded subparagraph which further elaborates on what Noah did. The subparagraph has its own setting, its own conclusion, and its own thematic participant which is distinct from that of the paragraph in which it is found embedded. I consider below the main paragraph and the embedded paragraph which elaborates the material.

It can be rationally contended that both Noah and Yhwh are thematic in 7:1-5. First, the quoted discourse is much briefer and involves a mixture of first and second person references. While the sole imperative is $bō'-'attâh$ "come you (and yours) into the ark," and while this second-person orientation is maintained in a verb further on down, $tiqqaḥ-lĕkā$ "take for yourself," we also find first-person references in $kîy$ causal clauses as in 7:2, "for you have *I* found righteous before *me*" and in the structure found in verse 7:4, "for yet seven days, *I* am causing it to rain on the earth for forty days and forty nights, and I will destroy everything which I have made from off the face of the earth". In that the embedded instruction here is shorter than that found in the preceding episode and has no dominating goal participant such as "ark" or overriding second-person orientation such as "thou" /8/, it seems that we do not have here an embedded quoted discourse of the sort that would steal the thematic spotlight from the surrounding framework. Furthermore, in 7:5, "And Noah did as Yhwh commanded him," we do not find the chiastic repetition "thus he did" which serves to spotlight Noah in 6:22. Therefore we may, as stated above, fairly consider that both Yhwh and Noah are thematic in this paragraph. In keeping with the thematic status of deity, he is referred to as Yhwh in this paragraph.

This situation forms a clear contrast to the subparagraph embedded at the end--which elaborates "Noah did as Yhwh had commanded him" by explaining that this meant Noah's entering the ark. In the subparagraph it appears that Noah alone is thematic-- although the "flood" is prominent. Two circumstantial clauses constitute 7:6, "And Noah was 600 years old and the flood was upon the earth." It appears that the first clause modifies the second clause, i.e., the first is circumstantial to the second and then that entire unit is circumstantial to verse 7, "(All this being so) and went Noah and his sons into the ark and his wife and his sons' wives *with him*." Here Noah is subject of a main-line verb and the resumptive pronoun at the end of verse 7 also serves to mark him as thematic. Verse 7 adds an additional phrase, "from the face of the flood." Indeed, in both verse 6 and 7 there is balanced emphasis on both Noah and the flood. Nevertheless only Noah occurs as the subject of a main-line verb and only he is thematic. Noah's thematicity is further reinforced in verse 9. Thus, after verse 8, where there is an elaborate listing of all the forms of life which went into the ark, we are told in verse 9, "They came to *Noah* to the ark, male and female, as God had commanded *Noah*." Verse 10 (which is somewhat transitional) ends with a final reference to the flood /9/, "And it came to pass in seven days that the waters of the flood were on the earth." While the flood here is subject of a wāw + prefixal verb, the verb is hāyâh "be" and probably therefore not on the event-line. It appears then that only Noah is thematic, although the flood waters themselves are prominent. God is clearly not thematic in this subparagraph as he was thematic in the above paragraph. As nonthematic, he is referred to in the only reference to him as Elohīm (verse 9).

Episode P-1 (Gen 7:11-16)

This paragraph has three main-line verbs, "and (there) was," "and came," "and shut." We are initially suspicious of wayĕhîy "and there was/it came to pass" as a main-line verb. Very often it is introductory. It may, however, need to be construed as a main-line verb here because it seems to be the completion of the preceding suffixal verbs which occur in circumstantial clauses /10/. Indeed if *wayəhî* is not here a main-line verb, then this portion of the paragraph is entirely background and has no main-line verb at all (which is of course by no means impossible). The first part of this paragraph (7:11-12) is simultaneous with what is reported in a suffixal verb in the second part of the paragraph, "and that very day Noah went in" (7:13-14). There then follows in verse 14 a long reference (again) to the forms of life which went into the ark, followed in 7:15 by *wāw* with a prefixal verb (mainline) which tells us that they all came to Noah to the ark two-by-two from all forms of life /11/. This is, in turn, followed by further circumstantial elements one of which is participial, "and those going into the ark (were) male and female from all flesh"; and one of which has a suffixal verb, "they went in as God had commanded him." So far the paragraph has reported two simultaneous actions: on the day that the natural events took place which resulted in the catastrophe, on that very day Noah and the animals went into the ark. Then very suddenly all this is followed by one short staccato (main-line) verse, "and Yhwh shut him in." It appears that the entire structure of the paragraph is a sequence paragraph whose first event is an embedded simultaneous paragraph reporting the two events, the cosmic catastrophe and Noah's entering the ark, and whose final event is Yhwh's "shutting him in."

As stated above, either the entire passage 7:11-14 is meant to be background to what follows and entirely off the event-line or at the most we have but one narrative event-line verb in 7:12 *wayəhî*. If *wayəhî* is an event-line verb, then its subject *haggešem* "the (hard) rain" is thematic. In thematicity it is allied to the reference to "the fountains of the great deep" in 7:11 and "the windows of heaven"--all are aspects of the flood. Noah is prominent in this passage, but not thematic. He is mentioned in 7:11 in the impressive long date which begins this section: "In the 600th year, the year of the life of Noah, in the second month, on the 17th day of the month, on that very day...." We also have three references to Noah by name in verse 13 and one by pronoun: "On that very day went in Noah, and Shem, Ham, and Japheth, the sons of Noah, and the wife of Noah, and the three wives of his sons with them into the ark." Noah, however, here is not the subject of an event-line verb, but of a verb in the perfect.

In 7:15 we find the first nonsuspect main-line event verb in this paragraph, *wayyābō'û*. The animals are subject of this event-line verb. They are also mentioned before in 7:14 as subject of a (non-repeated) non-event-line verb. Verse 7:16 rounds out chiastically the construction of 7:15 with a further construction which involves a participle and a suffixal tense; again the reference is to the animals: "and the coming ones, male and female from all flesh went in as God had commanded him." The animals, then, are thematic in a subparagraph which consists of 7:15-16a.

All of which brings us up to the striking clause in 7:16b, "and Yhwh shut him in." This clause seems to be something special. It represents an event which is subsequent to the simultaneous events which are reported in the embedded simultaneous paragraph which precedes it. Although cryptic and short, this sentence patterns as one of the main events of the story. In brief, God who has threatened to judge mankind and encouraged Noah to make extensive preparations to save himself from the catastrophe, now here deliberately shuts the gates of mercy on mankind while shutting Noah securely within. Further, it pictures God in an active role such as is not usual in other references to the catastrophe. Thus in verses 7:11 and 12 the breaking up of the fountains of the great deep and the opening of the windows of heaven are reported as passives (suffixed niphal forms) and then rain ensues for forty days and forty nights. Neither here nor in the peak passage which follows is there any reference to deity. In the peak passage, God is not mentioned at all, but rather natural forces (initiated, of course, by God) are represented as taking over and destroying the earth. While the relevant conditions are not well understood at present, it appears that there are special stylistic reasons here for using Yhwh rather than Elohīm.

Overlay in Prepeak Episodes

It is evident here on even casual reading that the story is moving quite slowly. It is as if the author were deliberately delaying the onset of peak. All this requires some special consideration and explanation. My thesis here is that episodes P-3 and P-2 are approximations to peak, the onset of which is artistically delayed until the end of episode P-1. There is extensive overlay in the content of episode P-3 to episode P-1 as opposed to the structure of post-peak episodes. This overlay deserves to be examined in detail.

The Structure of the Flood Narrative

I use overlay here as (a) a technical linguistic term, which is (b) well documented in certain linguistic areas, but (c) not used in formal English. We are indebted to Joseph Grimes for description of this rhetorical device (1976:292-293).

> In working on several unrelated languages I became aware of a pattern of handling new information that does not fit Halliday's [1967] given-new paradigm too well. This pattern was first called to my attention by educators and others who found that speakers of some languages insisted on writing English in school in what the educators regarded as a prolix style that involved going around and around in multiple cycles, each of which said approximately the same thing.
>
> On looking further it became apparent that a tightly structured rhetorical pattern was involved, but one that was constructed on different lines than the patterns with which English speakers are familiar. One could say, in an approximation to Halliday's terms, that these structures (which I have labelled OVERLAYS) distinguish three kinds of information: given, new and HIGHLIGHTED....
>
> The overlay technique involves putting together two or more PLANES, each of which constitutes a narration of the same sequence of events. The first plane consists largely of new information. The second plane and others that follow it begin the sequence over again. Furthermore, they consist partly of new information that is being given for the first time in that plane, partly of given information such as that which is referred to anaphorically, and partly of information that is being repeated piecemeal from an earlier plane. This repeated information has a special status; it is the highlighted information that ties the whole overlay together. Informationally it is the backbone of the whole structure.

Grimes proceeds to illustrate overlay via a Bororo discourse and suggests a topological formalization.

Actually, on careful examination, the overlay phenomena in the prepeak episodes of the flood narrative are not as extreme as in the Bororo example that Grimes cites. Considering episode P-3, episode P-2, and episode P-1, it seems that episode P-2 is clearly consequential upon episode P-3, while episode P-2 and episode P-1 appear more like the planes of an overlay. It should not be forgotten, however, that even here the chronological framework of the story indicates succession. Episode P-3 is represented as an indefinite period of time preceding the flood and preceding the building of the ark. In this episode Noah is first told to build the ark. Episode P-2 is represented as seven days before the beginning of the catastrophe, while episode P-1 is represented as the very day in which the natural forces are set in motion which devastate the earth.

The first two episodes have in common commands of God to Noah. Specifically, in episode P-3 after an initial statement, "The end of all flesh is come before me, for behold the earth is filled with violence by them; I will destroy them with the earth," God gives the procedure for building the ark. This material is not repeated elsewhere. Furthermore, there is but one imperative in the set of building instructions: 'ăśēh-lĕkā tēbat 'ăṣêy gōper, "make for yourself an ark of gopher wood." As seen above in the examination of this paragraph, the balance of the procedural discourse which constitutes this paragraph is simply a matter of detail which elaborates the initial command to build the ark. In the instructional discourse which follows we note only one imperative, qaḥ-lĕkā. By means of other tenses Noah is told to enter into the ark (wāw + suffixal tense), to take on board animals (prefixal tense), and to further add the foodstuffs to the cargo (wāw + suffixal tense). A few uses of the verb hāyâh "be" round out the passage. It is noteworthy that in this extended discourse which consists of two paragraphs, one procedural and the other instructional, the only imperatives are "make an ark" and "take on foodstuffs."

This can now be compared with the shorter set of instructions which are found in episode P-2. We have here only one imperative, "come you and all your house into the ark." By means of a verb in the prefixal tense, tiqqaḥ-lĕkā "take for you," the instructions for taking on board animals are amplified and detailed. The new element here is that not only are animals to be taken on by pairs, as in the former set of instructions, but that there are to be seven pairs of clean animals and birds and only one pair of the other animals.

It is plain from comparing the imperatives in these two episodes that different activities are highlighted. Thus in the former set of instructions, building the ark is the main order of the day, although proper provisioning of the ark is also highlighted by the second imperative in that passage. In the second and briefer set of instructions the embarkation is especially highlighted, as is seen by its dominating imperative.

It is also of interest here to compare similar material in episode P-3 and episode P-2. Thus, the going into the ark and the taking on board animals is mentioned in both these episodes, but the embarkation is expressed as an imperative only in episode P-2. Other tributary and accompanying material can likewise be compared:

The Structure of the Flood Narrative   111

(1) "For you I have found righteous before me in this generation"
(7:1b) is comparable to "I'll make my covenant with you" in 6:18
of episode P-3; (2) "For yet seven days and I will cause it to rain
rain on the earth for forty days and forty nights, and I will kill
off every living thing that I have made from off the face of the
earth" in 7:4 is comparable with certain passages in episode P-3,
i.e., with 6:13 but more especially with 6:17: "I, even I, am
bringing a flood of water on the earth to destroy from under the
heavens all flesh in which is found the breath of life; all which
is in the earth shall die." Here the repetition in the planes of
the overlay highlights the *covenant* and the *destructiveness of the
flood*.

Equally insightful is a comparison of episode P-2 and episode
P-1 (7:11-16) in regard to the embarkation which again figures in
both episodes. In episode P-2, 7:5 has the words "and Noah did
all that Yhwh commanded him." These words are emplified and explained in 7:7-9 as the embarkation of Noah and the animals.
These verses are preceded, however, by a chronological note (7:6),
"and Noah was six hundred years old when the flood of waters was
on the earth," which patterns as the setting of the embedded paragraph which reports the embarkation. The report of the embarkation
is a chiastic sentence, "and went in (*wayyābō'*) Noah and his sons,
etc. into the ark from the presence of the flood; from unclean animals, from clean animals and from fowl, two by two they came (*bo'û*)
to Noah, to the ark, male and female as God had commanded them."
Noteworthy here is that the embarkation of Noah is recorded on the
event-line by means of a *wāw* + prefixal tense while that of the
animals is given off the line as supplementary information. A
chronological note, "Then, yet seven days and the flood of waters
was on the earth" (7:10), concludes the section.

In Episode P-1 (7:11-16) we likewise find a record of embarkation. The whole passage, however, begins with a long chronological note coupled with description of physical causes of the flood
(7:11-12). The embarkation of Noah and the animals is described
off the event-line and relative to the indicated time and events:
"On that very day, went into the ark, Noah, and Shem, and Ham, and
Japheth...they and every living thing after its kind..." (7:13-14).
Then the coming of the animals to Noah to the ark is expressly mentioned on the event-line: "and they came (*wayyabō'û*) to Noah to the
ark, two by two of all flesh which has in it the breath of life."
This is followed by further clarification off the event-line: "and

those going in, male and female from all flesh, came to Noah as God had commanded him." Here a participle wĕhabbō'îym and perfect (bō'û) figure.

What then? Clearly the mentioning both in episode P-2 and in episode P-1 of the embarkation of Noah and the animals is an overlay; the same ground is covered twice and in the process the embarkation is highlighted. But the repetition is subtly varied with the embarkation of Noah on the narrative line in 7:7, and off the line (related rather to the onset of the catastrophe) in 7:13. The embarkation of the animals is recorded off the event-line in both 7:8 and 7:14, but is featured on the event-line in 7:15 and 7:16. Clearly the embarkation of both man and beast is highlighted by the dual account, but in each account what is featured varies.

We have here a structure with evidence of a sophisticated and developed rhetorical pattern. Its unlikeness to rhetorical patterns of English (and possibly of other European languages) has probably led to a certain uneasiness with the narrative--an uneasiness which does not necessarily indicate any stylistic deficiencies of the narrative itself.

While I hope to show below that the postpeak episodes of the flood story go along nicely in chronological succession, the prepeak episodes present a somewhat different situation which can now be summarized as follows. (1) Prepeak episodes are arranged in a successive chronological framework: time of the original command to build and provision an ark, seven days before the flood begins, and the day on which the flood begins. (2) There is, however, considerable overlay between the successive prepeak episodes. (3) Thus, the whole plan is envisioned in the original instructions of episode P-3, although "make and provision an ark" is featured. (4) In the instructions of episode P-2 "going into the ark" is featured. (5) In both episode P-2 and episode P-1 the going into the ark is depicted with Noah and his family's embarkation featured in episode P-2 and the embarkation of animals featured in episode P-1. (6) The fact that the embarkation of Noah and the animals is mentioned (envisioned or depicted) in all three episodes highlights the importance of this to the story. (7) The fact of the destructiveness of the flood is mentioned in all three explicitly. (8) The skillful use of overlay not only highlights the embarkation and the destructiveness of the flood, but also creates dramatic delay and suspense relative to the onset of the peak.

III. Peak (Climax) (Gen 7:17-24)

The highpoint in a story is commonly either its climax, i.e., the point of confrontation, or its dénouement, i.e., a decisive event which makes resolution possible. Either may be marked for peak /12/. If both are so marked, then a story has both a peak and a peak´. It is clear in the narrative here under discussion that there are some very special stylistic characteristics which set apart 7:17-24 as a peak, while as we shall see later, episode P+5 qualifies as a secondary peak. There is no doubt that the passage here under consideration is the main peak of the story. The main peak coincides with the climax of the narrative. The climax here is the prevalence of the flood and its possible threat even to Noah and his family in the ark.

I now trace in detail the progress of this paragraph with a look at its unique features. Verse 7:17 starts out with a $wayěhîy$ "and there was a flood forty days upon the earth." This acts as setting for the entire paragraph. The events reported in the paragraph are not simple clauses, but are themselves embedded paragraphs. I will refer to these events as buildups (abbreviated BU) /13/. BU_1 is a slot filled by a sequence of three clauses found at the end of 7:17, "and abounded the waters. And lifted up (they) the ark. And (it) raised up from off the earth." Another such embedded unit of three clauses fills the BU_2 slot. Again, there is a beginning reference to the waters, "and prevailed the waters. And they abounded exceedingly upon the earth. And drifted the ark on the face of the water." Note here also that as in the first embedded unit, the concluding reference is to the ark.

From here on the paragraph develops a very striking structure. The third BU slot is filled by the material found in 7:19 and 7:20. While we could argue that in the above subunits, each $wāw$ + prefixal verb forwards the event-line of the paragraph, we come in 7:19 and 20 to a repetition of the $wāw$ + prefixal form of the verb "were covered." Each of these in turn is itself a bundle of clauses not unlike the structures which fill BU_1 and BU_2 above. In brief, BU_3 is a paraphrase paragraph consisting of two sentences which are very similar in overall structure. While we might have expected that the second element of the paraphrase would not be a $wāw$ + prefixal form, but rather a circumstantial clause (as in the following verse), we do not find that construction employed here. Rather we find a $wāw$ + prefixal form paraphrased and repeated as another $wāw$ + prefixal form. Presumably such repetition in which the repeated verb is given the same structure as a verb on the main event-line is a feature of the peak of a story--at least in epic style such as we have here.

It is also interesting that in both halves of this construction, i.e., the half found in 19 and the half found in 20, the verse begins with a reference to "the waters" even as BU_1 and BU_2 did above. This, however, by now is rather old information and the waters are demoted to a position of secondary importance (although they remain thematic). Thus, 19 begins with a circumstantial clause, "The waters prevailed more and more upon the earth." Likewise, 20 begins with a circumstantial clause, "15 cubits upward prevailed the waters." Then these in turn are followed in 19 and 20 respectively by "And were covered all the high mountains which are under the heaven" and, in abbreviated form, "And were covered all the mountains."

In verses 21, 22, and 23 a yet more elaborate paraphrase takes place which describes the destruction of life outside the ark. This whole unit fills BU_4. The first part of this paraphrase unit is itself a paraphrase unit in the form of a chiastic sentence. It begins with "and died" *wayyigĕwa'* and ends with *mĕtû* "they died." In between we find a long list of animals and forms of life, part of which goes with the first verb and part of which goes with the second. It is an extremely long and elaborate listing probably outdoing in complexity any previous list: "All flesh which moves upon the earth, with fowl, and with cattle, and with living things, and with every creeping thing which creepeth on the earth, and all men, all which stirs the breath of life in its nostrils, from all which is on the dry land." This whole unit, itself containing a paraphrase, is then in turn paraphrased in 23, "And was wiped out everything existing which is on the face of the earth from man to cattle to creeping things to birds of the heavens." This construction, which was introduced with a *wāw* + prefixal form, is now in turn paraphrased by another *wāw* + prefixal form involving the same verb with a shift from singular to plural, "And they were wiped out from the earth."

The whole paragraph thus far then confronts us with a structure somewhat as follows: the flood is mentioned early in the first sentence, which is setting. Then for the two following BUs we find references to the flood and its interaction with the ark. Following this, there is a third BU in which there is an elaborate paraphrase in which the flood is now referred to in circumstantial clauses and the covering of the mountains is referred to by the same verb repeated twice in $w\bar{a}w$ + prefixal form. This in turn is followed by an even more elaborate paraphrase involving the death of life outside the ark. The first member of this paraphrase is a chiastic sentence with two synonyms for "die," one occurring sentence initial and the other sentence final. The second member of this paraphrase is another paraphrastic unit in which the same verb occurs twice (with differing number) as $w\bar{a}w$ + prefixal form. There is an extremely extensive reference to varieties of animal life in the first main part of this overall paraphrase unit, and a more condensed reference to the forms of animal life that died in the last part of this unit.

The paragraph continues with the final BU (BU_n) where there is a reference again to Noah and those in the ark with him, "And was left only Noah and those with him in the ark." The paragraph terminates with another sentence which contains a final reference to flood waters, "Prevailed the waters [Speiser: "maintained their crest"] over the earth for 150 days" /14/.

What is striking in the passage under consideration is the stretching out or elongation of the event line by means of paraphrase reported as pseudo-events. Slowing down or "fleshing out" the event-line in some fashion is a common feature resorted to at the peak of narrative discourse in many languages; what is interesting here is the particular means by which it is accomplished. For a graphic representation of these features in the structure of this paragraph at peak, see Diagram 2a, which represents a transliteration of the Hebrew text, and Diagram 2b, which presents the same in a literal English translation (for ease in matching the two).

As far as the thematic participants of this paragraph, it is evident that the flood waters are thematic. They come in for repeated reference in the first three units, although they are eventually demoted to circumstantial clauses from their former position as subject of main-line verbs. After an intervening involved reference to the death of various forms of animal life, the flood waters as thematic participants are again referred to in the last verse, 7:24. Some of the embedded paragraphs found in the BU units have their own thematic participant as distinct from that of the paragraph as a whole. Thus the mountains are thematic in 7:19 and 20 in the embedded paragraph which expounds BU_3. Animal life of various sorts is mentioned as thematic in the embedded unit

	MAIN-LINE	CIRCUMSTANTIAL
SETTING: (7:17a)	wayĕhîy hammabûl 'arbā'îym yôm 'al-hā'āreṣ	
BU₁: Narr Paragraph (7:17b,c,d)	wayyirbû hammayim wayyiś'û 'et-hattēbāh wattārām mē'al hā'āreṣ	
BU₂: Narr Paragraph (7:18)	wayyigbĕrû hammayim wayyirbû mĕ'ōd 'al-hā'āreṣ wattēlek hattēbāh 'al-pĕnêy hammayim	
BU₃: Paraphrase Paragraph (7:19-20)	text { wayĕkussû kol-hehārîym haggĕbōhîym 'ăšer-taḥat kol-haššāmāyim paraph. { wayĕkussû hehārîym	wĕhammayim gābĕrû mĕ'ōd mē'ōd 'al-hā'āreṣ ḥămēš 'eśrēh 'ammāh milma'ĕlāh gābĕrû hammayim
BU₄: Paraphrase Paragraph (7:21-23a)	text { text { wayyigwa' kol-bāśār hārōmēś 'al-hā'āreṣ...wĕkōl hā'ādām paraph. { wayyimaḥ 'et-kol-hayĕqûm 'ăšer 'al-pĕnêy hā'ădāmāh... paraph. { wayyimāḥû min-hā'āreṣ	kōl 'ăšer nišmat-rûaḥ ḥayyîym bĕ'appāyw... mēṭû
BUₙ: (7:23b)	wayyiššā'er 'ak-nōaḥ wa'ăšer 'ittô battēbāh	
TERMINUS: (7:24)	wayyigbĕrû hammayim 'al-hā'āreṣ ḥămiššîym ûmĕ'at yôm	

Diagram 2a: Structure of Paragraph at Peak (Gen 7:17-24)

The Structure of the Flood Narrative

	MAIN-LINE	CIRCUMSTANTIAL
SETTING	And there was a flood forty days upon the earth	
BU_1:	And abounded the waters And they lifted up the ark And it raised up from the earth	
BU_2:	And prevailed the waters And they abounded exceedingly on the earth And drifted the ark on the face of the waters	
BU_3:	text { And were covered all the mountains the high ones which are under all the heavens paraph. { And were covered the mountains	And the waters prevailed exceedingly, exceedingly on the earth Fifteen cubits upward prevailed the waters
BU_4:	text { text { And perished all flesh moving on the earth...and all men; paraph. { paraph. { text { And was wiped out everything existing which was on the face of the earth paraph. { And they were wiped out from the earth	all which stirred the breath of life in its nostrils... died.
BU_n:	And was left only Noah and those with him in the ark.	
TERMINUS:	And prevailed the waters on the earth fifty and one hundred days.	

(Literal Translation into English)

Diagram 2b: Structure of Paragraph at Peak (Gen 7:17-24)

which expounds BU$_4$. Noah is mentioned only briefly at the end in the next to the last sentence where he is referred to once by name, once by pronoun; he is not thematic. The ark, however, is mentioned in 17 and 18 as raising up from the earth and drifting on the waters, and is mentioned again at the end of the entire passage, "And only was left Noah and those with him in the ark." It appears, therefore, that the ark is a secondary thematic participant in the paragraph as a whole.

IV. Postpeak Episodes (Gen 8:1-22)

Episode P+1 (Gen 8:1-5)

The onset of this new paragraph is signaled by a twofold reference to God, Elohīm, who was not mentioned at all in the peak of the narrative. This same passage, 8:1, also contains a direct reference to the living things that were with Noah in the ark--none of which are mentioned specifically at the peak of the narrative although there is a summary reference in 7:24 to those with Noah in the ark. Thus, 8:1 begins, "And God remembered Noah and all the living things and all the cattle which were with him in the ark" and continues with another reference to God, "And God caused a wind to blow across the earth." Thus, the first two main event-line verbs of the paragraph ($w\bar{a}w$ + prefixal verbs) mention God as subject. God is not mentioned, however, in the balance of the paragraph and, therefore, does not prove to be a thematic participant. The next main-line verb is, "And the waters abated" in which "waters" is the subject of the verb "abate" and proves to be a thematic participant of the paragraph. The main-line verbs, with reference to the waters or related phenomena, continue right through the remainder of a series of BUs in 8:2-3: "And were shut up the fountains of the deep and the windows of heaven. And ceased the rain from heaven. And receded the waters from off the earth going and returning. And diminished the waters at the end of 150 days." The BU$_n$ at the end of this series is apparently climactic (witness the date) and has the ark as its subject, "And came to rest the ark in the seventh month on the 17th day of the month on the mountains of Ararat." The ark, which is mentioned in verse 1 and rementioned here as subject of a main-line verb, probably qualifies, therefore, as a thematic participant. The paragraph ends with two circumstantial clauses, "And the waters were going and returning and diminishing until the 10th month. In the 10th month on the first day of the month became visible the mountains." Here the circumstantial clauses have preposed noun phrases and have suffixal verbs rather than the $w\bar{a}w$ + prefixal verb which characterizes the main-line of the paragraph. In accordance with their structure as circumstantial clauses, these clauses are found in postclimactic position within the paragraph (after the BU_n, "And rested the ark...") where they serve to terminate the paragraph.

The stylistic contrast between episode P+1 and the preceding peak is quite striking. Episode P+1 is a straightforward series of $w\bar{a}w$ + prefixal verbs which report successive events. This series culminates with the ark coming to rest on Mt. Ararat and then has some circumstantial clauses which terminate the paragraph. The clauses as a whole are short and almost no paraphrase is employed. In the peak, the successive stages in the growing vastness of the flood are reported not in clauses, but in embedded paragraphs with a large amount of paraphrase--often conveyed by main event-line verbs rather than by main event-line verb + circumstantial clause. In both the climax and in the episode P+1 we find, however, that "the waters" and "the ark" are thematic participants.

In regard to the story as a whole, this episode represents a decisive turn of events which makes resolution of the story possible; it is, therefore (Longacre, 1976:213-217), the deep structure dénouement (DE in Diagram 1). The peak ends with Noah, his family and the animals adrift on waters which, prevailing at crest for 150 days, show no sign of abating. Here, due to the intervention of God, the waters begin to subside, and the ark comes to rest.

Episode P+2 (Gen 8:6-12)

This passage starts off with a $way\check{e}h\hat{\imath}y$ plus date clause (8:6a), "And it came to pass at the end of 40 days." This clause can be regarded as setting. It is followed (8:6b) by the first of a string of verbs which are main-line ($w\bar{a}w$ + prefixal verb), "And Noah opened the window [Speiser: "hatch"] of the ark which he had made." This first main event of the paragraph (structuring as BU_1) is of considerable interest in that it shows Noah (as he is throughout this paragraph) in an active role. His role has been passive during the flood and even before the flood in that the actions which he performed were in response to God's direct commands. Now in this episode Noah assumes a more active role. He is certainly a thematic participant of this paragraph--but, the dove, prominent in the last three BUs is a secondary thematic participant.

There follow thirteen more $w\bar{a}w$ + prefixal verbs. They do not apparently, however, form a simple string of successive events. Although they are all chronologically consecutive, they seem to group into subparagraphs which continue the series of BUs which was inaugurated by Noah's opening the windows of the ark (BU_1). BU_2 (8:7) is filled by a subparagraph which is concerned with the sending out of the raven. BU_3 (8:8-9) is filled by a subparagraph which includes five clauses all with initial $w\bar{a}w$ + prefixal verbs-- as well as a purpose clause, a negative clause ($l\bar{o}$' + suffixal verb), and a cause clause. This passage, which treats of the first sending out of the dove has some graphic detail--which is somewhat of a relief after the preoccupation with the vastness of the disaster. Thus, we are told that "she [the dove] found no place to rest the sole of her foot," and that when she returned to the ark, "Noah put forth his hand, took her, and drew her to him into the ark." Verses 10 and 11 report (BU_4) the second sending out of the dove. This subparagraph is introduced by a temporal clause, "And he waited yet seven days more." Again, there is graphic, and highly relevant detail: "And the dove returned to him at evening, and behold she had a freshly-plucked olive leaf in her mouth." This, in turn, leads to a sentence that is probably climactic in this subparagraph: "And Noah knew that the waters had receded from the earth." It appears that the climactic sentence (in its subparagraph) is chosen as the natural place to repeat "Noah"--the name of the main thematic participant. Verse 12 constitutes another embedded unit (BU_n) which is also introduced by a temporal clause, "And he waited yet seven days more." This unit ends with the information that the dove came back to him no more--thus terminating the chain of events by removing one of the interacting participants from the story. In this episode, while the BUs are again complex (as in the peak), they do not involve the paraphrase through main-line verbs which so strikingly characterizes the peak of the narrative; rather, they are more like sub-episodes within an episode.

This episode is, like the former, on the downslope of the story. The tension, built to a maximum at peak, is loosening here. The several graphic details concerning Noah's interaction with the dove provide relief from the overwhelming disaster which is so effectively described earlier in the story.

Episode P+3 (Gen 8:13-19)

The most distinctive feature about this paragraph is its long setting expounded by an embedded paragraph. The embedded paragraph begins and ends with dates. Both dates are stages in the drying of the earth. The first date is given in a $wayěhîy$ clause: "In the 601st year on the first day of the month." The second date is found at the end of the embedded paragraph and at the onset of verse 8:14: "In the second month on the 22nd day of the month." Verse 8:13, after the introductory dateline continues, "dried out the waters from off the earth." "Dried out" here is a suffixal verb followed by a $wāw$ + prefixal verb, "And removed Noah the covering from the ark." This in turn is followed by another verb of the same construction, "And he saw that behold the face of the earth had dried." Finally, the date at the beginning of verse 8:14 precedes another suffixed verb, "was dry the earth."

It appears here that $hā'āreṣ$ "the earth" is the thematic participant of this subparagraph. To be true, Noah is mentioned once as subject of a verb of the sort which customarily is mainline in a narrative paragraph. There is a weak narrative line in this paragraph in the sequence "And Noah took off the covering from the ark. And he looked." Significantly, though, Noah is not repeated. The Septuagint translation supplies the word Noah in the long date beginning of 8:13. Possibly, however, the Masoretic text is to be preferred here. The supplying of Noah, i.e., "In the 601st year of the life of $Noah$" brings in a second reference to Noah which obscures the thematic structure of the paragraph as it stands in the Masoretic text—where Noah is mentioned only once and, therefore, cannot qualify as thematic participant, while $hā'āreṣ$ is mentioned three times and finally becomes subject of the last suffixal verb. Apparently the long dates fore and aft in this embedded paragraph and the repeated reference to the earth result in some kind of thematic inversion of the structure of this paragraph whereby the weak narrative line, consisting of two $wāw$ + prefixal verbs, proves not to be as important in the structure of the paragraph as the succession of perfects which refer to the earth. It can be argued that the line "And Noah removed the covering of the ark" is simply a necessary prelude to his perceiving that the earth was dry.

The setting paragraph which establishes the drying out of the earth in two stages is followed by the body of a paragraph in the familiar execution form, i.e., "God said to Noah, 'Go out'" (8:15) followed in verse 8:18 by, "And Noah went out." In the reported speech of God in this paragraph, "Go out" singular imperative occurs in 8:15, "Go out from the ark, you, your wife, and your sons and the wives of your sons with you." Verse 8:17 has a causative imperative, "Cause to go out with you" with a long preposed conjoined noun phrase referring to the animals. The rest of verse 17 has three imperatives which anticipate the words of the blessing in chapter 9 and presumably are directed here to both men and animals, "Increase in the earth. And be fruitful. And multiply on the earth." In verses 18 and 19, which belong to the outer framework of the paragraph, the verb "go out" is found again, "And went out Noah and his sons and his wife and the wives of his sons with him." Verse 19 continues with the other half of a chiastic construction, "Every living thing, all that creeps, and all fowl, everything that stirs on the earth according to their families went out from the ark."

It seems that in the second half of this paragraph, it is the "going out" that is thematic, i.e., there is a verbal theme. As for the participants, Noah, the animals, and the ark are all mentioned both early and late in the passage. It seems plausible to me that we do not have here three thematic participants as such, but that all these participants are subservient to the verbal theme of the paragraph, viz., the going out from the ark. The occurrence of the material at the end of verse 17--the anticipation of the blessing in 9--is a bit puzzling, but it makes possible a twofold repetition of the word "earth," thus, echoing the thematic participant of the first half of the paragraph, i.e., the paragraph which is embedded in the setting. Furthermore, anticipation of one section of a discourse in an earlier section is a cohesive device found in many discourses in many languages.

The place of this episode in the story is somewhat obvious. Loosening tension continues here; not only has the flood abated and the earth dried, but also the occupants of the ark are at last able to leave the craft in which they have been for so long confined.

Episode P+4 (Gen 8:20-22)

This paragraph has a string of five main-line, i.e., $w\bar{a}w$ + prefixal, verbs. "And built Noah an altar to Yhwh. And he took.... And he offered....And Yhwh smelled....And Yhwh said (in effect) 'Never again!'" Noah is not the thematic participant of this paragraph. He occurs as subject of the first verb and is implied as subject of the next two verbs, but is not as such referred by name or pronoun again in the paragraph (although he is referred to by the prefix on the two prefixal verbs). The altar is a prop which is referred to twice in verse 20. It appears that the real thematic participant of the paragraph is Yhwh. Noah "built an altar to Yhwh" in 20 and then we're told in 8:21 that "Yhwh smelled the soothing odor and Yhwh said in His heart...." This gives a total already of four references to Yhwh, three by the proper noun and one by pronoun. Furthermore, Yhwh is subject of the last mainline verb. In the quoted portion which follows in 8:21 and 22, we find further first-person affixal references to Yhwh. Two are prefixal in negative verbs, "I will never again curse" and, "I will never again destroy" (both in verse 21) and one is suffixal in the clause "which I have made."

The adverb '$\bar{o}d$ "yet, again" occurs twice in verse 21 and once more in verse 22. '$\bar{o}d$-kol-$y\breve{e}m\hat{e}y$ $h\bar{a}$'$\bar{a}re\d{s}$ "yet all the days of the earth," i.e., "as long as the earth continues." This repetition of the adverb gives the whole passage a strong "never again!" thrust. Taking off from the latter phrase, the verse ends with a quasi-poetic portion: "As long as the earth continues, seed time and harvest, cold and heat, summer and winter, and day and night shall not cease."

Although there are five main-line verbs in this paragraph, they probably do not structure as a simple sequence of five sentences. Three of these verbs have to do with the actions of Noah and two have to do with Yhwh's response. Consequently, this paragraph probably forms some kind of action-response unit with two embedded parts. The backbone of the embedded quote consists entirely of negated verbs, "I will never again curse the earth," "I will never again destroy every living thing that I have made," and "Seasonal variations shall not cease."

Again, it is instructive to note that deity is the thematic participant in this verse and as such He is referred to as Yhwh.

As to the place of this episode in the overall story, here the loosening tension proceeds to the point where assurance is given that such a judgment as the flood will never be repeated. This paragraph is, however, poorly delineated. It has no setting to signal the onset of a new unit; rather, the shift in thematic structure alone gives it its unity. It may well be, therefore, that this paragraph actually compounds with that found in Episode P+3. In effect, therefore, the offering of sacrifice and the divine response would be part of the complex of going out of the ark. I have not followed this alternative in that, to me, the resulting complexity of paragraph structure is implausible. But if we were to take this passage 8:20-22 as part of a long unit 8:13-22, we would (1) still note that 8:20-22 is an embedded paragraph in the larger unity, and (2) probably represent 8:20-22 as climactic in the larger paragraph. As evidence of the latter, note the poetic or quasi-poetic nature of 8:22--where something special seems to be afoot.

V. Secondary Peak (Episode P+5) (Gen 9:1-17)

There are several peak-like characteristics about this whole passage. First of all, it is the longest reported discourse in the entire story. Secondly, it is carefully articulated into sub-sections so that the recurrences of the formula of quotation mark the three main points of God's discourse to Noah and his sons. Thirdly, again we find special stylistic features of repetition and paraphrase. Thus the repetition of the blessing proper in 9:1 and 9:7 brackets the intervening instructional material. We further find reiteration of "establishing the covenant" in 9:9 and 9:11; of "this (is) the sign of the covenant" in 9:12 and 9:17; of the disavowal of intent to send a flood in 9:11b and 9:15b; and in regard to the covenant being not only with Noah and his descendants but with all living things in 9:10 and 9:16b. Furthermore, in one place at least this paraphrase takes the form of on-the-line paraphrase as we observed at the main peak of the story in chapter 7:19f.

Just as the main peak of the story emphasizes by special stylistic features the destructiveness and awesomeness of the flood, so the secondary peak of the story emphasizes the importance of the covenant to the story as a whole. As mentioned before, the discourse is broken into three parts by the recurrence of formulas of quotation in 9:9 and 9:12. The first section treats of the blessing, the second of the covenant, and the third of the covenant sign. Although the first section does not overtly use the word "covenant," nevertheless the central part of this section (bracketed by the repeated blessing which occurs in 9:1 and 9:7) is implicitly a set of terms such as are found in striking a covenant. Thus, while God's part of the covenant is given in 9:2-3, man's part is given in 9:4-6. The second section of the speech, 9:8-11, contains overt reference to the covenant in which God promises never again to send such a destructive flood. The third section, 9:12-16, has to do with the rainbow, the covenant sign. This is solemnly reiterated with quotation formula in the concluding verse, 9:17.

The importance of the covenant to the narrative as a whole was noticed--see pages 98-100--where it emerged as one of the main ideas in the macrostructure of the whole narrative. To reinforce this, note that early in the story (6:18) we find the words, "But with you I will establish my covenant," and that God's whole dealings with Noah have the characteristics of a covenant relation in which (a) God undertakes to save Noah from the flood and (b) Noah undertakes to obey God's instructions.

The first section of this three-point discourse to Noah can probably be considered to be (like 6:17-21) basically an instructional discourse. Its orientation is second-person plural. The way for this is prepared in the quotation formula of the framework of the paragraph by the summary plural $lāhem$ "to them." This is cross-referenced immediately by the second-person plural endings of the imperatives early in the paragraph. The second-person plural suffix (-kem on nouns and on l-) continues the second-person plural orientation through the following verses. About midway through 9:5 and in verse 6 the second-person plural component fades out, only to be reiterated with force in 9:7 where the blessing is recapitulated, "But as for you, be fruitful...." In keeping with these particular features and with the general characteristics of this discourse genre, it is clear that the addressees are thematic in this paragraph. The verbs are imperative in the clauses which bracket the passage and are largely imperfects elsewhere. These imperfects refer to the future while occasional use of perfects refer to either accomplished decisions or past events. In all these clauses there are preposed noun phrases which mark local topics from sentence to sentence.

In 9:8 the onset of the second portion of God's discourse to Noah and his family is signaled by the reintroduction of the quotation formula, "And God said to Noah and to his sons with him saying." The body of the paragraph starts off in 9:9 with the very solemn words, "I, lo I, am establishing my covenant with you." To what discourse genre does such a passage belong? It seems to me that it might well be considered to belong to a discourse which expresses plan or intention. It is like a procedural discourse in that the orientation of the discourse is on what is to be made or to be accomplished, in this case the covenant itself (which is therefore thematic). The first verb of the passage is a participle. The next is a *wāw* + suffixal verb followed by two *lō* + prefixal verbs. The participle and the *wāw* + suffixal tense constitute a paraphrase relation, i.e., "I am establishing my covenant with you" and "I will establish my covenant with you." The next two clauses with the negative verbs express the terms of the covenant to the effect that God will never send another flood. It is made clear that the "you" with whom the covenant is established includes not just Noah and his family, but also all living creatures which are with them. Thus a representative list of living creatures follows in 9:10. In that the covenant is thematic in this passage, this dominates the paragraph rather than the partners to the covenant (i.e., God on the one hand; Noah, his family, and all living creatures on the other)--although the two ideas are very close and difficult to extricate from each other.

The onset of the third point in God's discourse is likewise signaled by a quotation formula. This time the formula of quotation is briefer. It does not emphasize that God said so-and-so to Noah and his family, but just states, "And God said." The full quotation formula is certainly appropriate in 9:1 where it sets the stage for the repeated "you" plural which occurs as thematic in the quote itself. The full formula is likewise appropriate in 9:8 where it is followed by a quote in which God is one partner to the covenant and the addressees are the other partners. This bilaterality is anticipated in the quotation formula "And God said to Noah and to his sons with him, saying." But in 9:12 apparently the full formula of quotation is no longer necessary--partly because the speaker and addressees are already well identified and partly because the thematic participant of the quoted discourse is now different. In this portion, 9:12-17, it is apparently the covenant sign, i.e., the rainbow, which is thematic.

Since this paragraph has a preponderance of *wāw* + suffixal forms, in clauses without preposed nouns, it seems very likely that we have here a predictive discourse, i.e., a discourse which states a future course of action. Predictive discourse is the grammatical inverse of narrative discourse. Just as the event-line of a narrative discourse is *wāw* + prefixal verbs, so the event-line of a predictive discourse is *wāw* + suffixal verbs.

The covenant sign is first introduced in 9:12 in a non-verbal (nominal) clause, "This (is) the sign of the covenant I am giving between myself and between you and between all living things which are with you." Then, somewhat dramatically, in 9:13 the rainbow is introduced in preposed position before a suffixal verb, "My bow I have given (placed) in the cloud." This (circumstantial?) clause is followed by a *wāw* + suffixal verb, "And it shall be for a sign of the covenant between Me and between the earth," where "earth" here is used by metonomy for man and all other creatures on the earth. 9:14-15 and 9:16 constitute two sections which are in paraphrase relationship to each other. Again, however, as at the peak of the story in Genesis 7, the paraphrase itself is given the same on-the-line tense that characterizes the predicted event itself. Thus, verses 14-15 run: "And it shall be (*wĕhāyâh*) in the clouding over of clouds on the earth that shall be seen (*wĕnir'ătâh*) the bow in the cloud, and I shall remember (*wĕzākartîy*) the covenant...that never again shall be a flood...." This is rather closely paraphrased in verse 16 as: "And shall be (*wĕhāyĕtâh*) the bow in the cloud, and I shall see it (*ûrĕ'îtîyhā*) to remember (*lizkōr*) the everlasting covenant...." The *wāw* + suffixal forms of verse 14 are repeated with grammatical variation but still as *wāw* + suffixal verbs in 16: *wĕhāyâh-wĕhāyĕtâh*, and *wĕnir'ătâh-ûrĕ'îtîyhā*. The *wāw* + suffixal verb of verse 15, *wĕzākartîy*, is demoted, however, to an infinitive of purpose in 16: *lizkōr*.

Then all this is further reinforced by the reintroduction of the full form of the quotation formula in the concluding verse 9:17, "And God said to Noah, 'This (is) the sign of the covenant which I have made between myself and between all flesh which is on the earth.'" Notice how the final quotation sentence in verse 17 serves to bring to a close the entire quoted discourse. It is worth remarking here that the variations in the form and extensiveness of the formulas of quotation are not random and unmotivated; rather, all contribute to the unity and focus of the quoted discourse /15/.

VI. Macrostructure and Highlighting

It remains now to summarize how the three main ideas of the discourse as seen in its macrostructure are highlighted and given prominence throughout the story. The germinal idea in its stark simplicity has three main points: (1) God's having Noah embark on an ark to preserve his life and the lives of those with him; (2) God's sending a destructive flood; and (3) God's promise never to send another such flood. We have seen that the repetitive references to the embarkation in the prepeak episodes of the narrative highlight the importance of the embarkation as one of the main points of the story. The importance of the destructive judgment of the flood is emphasized in three ways: (a) by the peculiar rhetorical structure at peak (7:11-24)--where the remorseless mechanism of judgment is portrayed in a passage where God's name is not even mentioned; (b) by the suspense created by successive approximations to the peak in the slow-moving prepeak episodes, and (c) by repeated references to the destructive nature of the flood in the planes of the overlay within the prepeak episodes.

As for the importance of the covenant to the narrative as a whole, we have already noted this in the immediately preceding section. As stated there, it is mentioned early in the story in 6:18, and all the dealings of God's with Noah partake implicitly of the relations of a covenant. Note also the promise in episode P+4 (8:21-22) "...never again will I smite every living thing any more as I have done, but regular seasons and night and day will continue while the earth remains." Above all, the importance of the covenant is highlighted by the presence of the secondary peak is episode P+5 in which God's making a covenant with mankind is portrayed.

VII. Conclusion

I've attempted to show in this application of contemporary discourse structure to the flood account that the text of the flood story as it stands has a consistent and plausible discourse structure and that the variations in style found in certain parts of it are appropriate to the distinctions in the subject matter. Even small details of structure such as the presence or absence of resumptive pronouns and variations in the form of quotation formulas will probably be eventually explicable here and elsewhere in the Hebrew OT in terms of the demands of discourse structure.

I've also attempted to show that repetitive allusions to the same event--far from being evidence of more than one documentary source--are either (1) cohesive features (overlay) which contribute to the unity of the discourse, or (2) features of parallelism and paraphrase which mark the prominence associated with a peak.

I've also attempted to clarify the paragraph structure of the account, both in terms of the thematic participants which characterize the various paragraphs and subparagraphs and also in terms of the general progress and development within each paragraph. Thus, even the variation in divine names between Elohīm and Yhwh

The Structure of the Flood Narrative

need not be a matter of editorial patchwork, but seems to tie in to the matter of whether or not the deity is thematic in a given paragraph. I've attempted, also, to show that the various references to dates and chronology, far from being the hallmark of a special writer (P), are an integral part of the mechanism of introducing and closing paragraphs and maintaining discourse flow.

Apparent contradictions are actually minimal. Thus, when Noah is first told to build the ark, he is told to bring in the animals by pairs, but in a subsequent set of instructions he is told to take seven pairs of the clean animals and clean birds. Surely, if one allows the document to stand as it is, there is nothing implausible about a preliminary set of instructions being expanded and made more specific in a subsequent set of instructions--especially if a considerable time interval is implied (as seems plausible here). Likewise, the chronology of the flood as it stands in the present text is self-consistent and in fact has some nicely symmetric and chiastic features; it is only when the text is first cut apart into separate documents and subtexts are assembled from these pieces that different chronologies emerge. In brief, the problems in the chronology of the story are artifacts of documentary source criticism.

On anybody's theory of the origin of this story and of the book of Genesis as a whole, it is probable that the writer used sources. The sources, however, are from our point of view irrecoverable and probably bear no resemblance to the familiar documents of traditional source criticism. The application of contemporary discourse analysis to this portion of Genesis reveals a story elegantly structured with marked cohesion and highlighting in its various parts. It makes unnecessary the assumption of divergent documentary sources of the sort which have been assumed for the past century. In fact, the assumption of such sources obscures much of the truly elegant structure of the story.

NOTES

/1/ I acknowledge here the help of Sharon Bergstrom and Carolyn Kent in typing various drafts of this paper and the two preceding ones which are here summarized (Longacre, 1976b, 1977). I also acknowledge the criticisms and suggestions of Hendrikus Boers.

/2/ NSF grant 74-04763 and NEH grant RO-20280-75-5; results available in Longacre and Woods (1976-1977).

/3/ I am indebted here, as at many points, to Andersen (1974); I acknowledge this debt without imputing to him any of the failings of this present paper.

/4/ The peculiar way in which Hebrew carries the main line of a story, viz., by clauses beginning with $w\bar{a}w$ + prefixal verbs, may possibly shed some light on a further feature of the present narrative (and Hebrew narrative prose in general), i.e., the frequent repetitive references to the same event. Thus, e.g., the story contains several similar but differing lists of animals entering the ark, and tells us both in 7:6-9 and in 7:13-15 that Noah and the animals entered the ark. But that Hebrew uses such devices (discussed below as overlay) should not surprise us. Narrative structure in all languages demands some sort of recapitulation of old information while layering on new information—otherwise the pace at which the story proceeds will likely cause the listener/reader to loose the thread of the story. But—and this may prove important—the commonest and most standard method of recapitulation is not readily available in Hebrew along the main line of the story. To illustrate: (1) in many languages a story proceeds by some such device as the following: "He did A. Having A'd, he B'd. Having B'd, he C'd. Finally, he D'd." Here A, B, C, and D represent main-line activities in a story and the "having X'd" construction is a back-reference, initial in these sentences. This is a cohesive device of great importance and easily documentable in European languages, Philippine languages, Mesoamerica, Papua-New Guinea, and South America to name only areas where I have directly observed this device. But (2) biblical Hebrew does this only most infrequently and by means of rather roundabout syntactic devices. This is consequent on the restriction that any preposing of an element in the same clause with the $w\bar{a}w$ + prefixal verb results in throwing the clause off the event-line. Gen 15:1 is illustrative of the way in which summary back-reference is used in Genesis. *'aḥar haddĕbārîm hā'ēlleh hāyāh dĕbar yhwh 'el-'abrām...* "After these words/matters came the word of the Lord to Abraham." First of all we note that this clause introduces a wholly new story rather than simply a further episode in the same story. Furthermore, the entire clause is off the event-line and has as its main verb *hāyāh* "was." More frequently in such summary devices, we find something like what occurs in Gen 22:1 in which the $w\bar{a}w$ + the prefixal form of the verb, i.e., the special narrative tense, is used of the verb *hāyāh*. Here, however, in Hebrew as in so many other languages, the verb "was," even though occurring in the regular form of an event-line verb, reports background information. *wayĕhî 'aḥar haddĕbārîm hā'ēlleh wĕhā'ĕlōhîm nissāh 'et-'abrāhām.* "And it came to pass after these happenings that God put Abraham to the test." Here we have an initial use of the special narrative tense of *hāyāh* "to be" in an off-the-event-line use, followed by a second clause which is off the event-line by virtue of having an initial noun. Only in the third clause, starting with *wayyōmer*, do we get around to picking up the thread of the narrative once more. The moral of all the above is that in view of the rare and roundabout nature of Hebrew back-reference, is it to be wondered at that other devices such as overlay described in the section "Overlay in Prepeak Episodes" (see above, pp. 19ff.) serve to provide recapitulation of old information and supply discourse cohesion?

/5/   Thus, in the first line of the abstract representation, it is given that God told Noah to embark in the ark; this is symbolized as Sa(Ebc), which in turn implies (⊃) that Noah did this. The given (cause) plus its implication equals causation.

/6/   Taking two parameters + chronological linkage, and + agent orientation we can assign the following values to broad categories of discourse: Narrative (+c.l., +a.o.); procedural (+c.l., -a.o.); behavioral (-c.l., +a.o.); expository (-c.l., -a.o.) (cf. Longacre, 1977; Forster, 1977).

/7/   Hebrew here presents a usage similar to English, where with three conjoined clauses the "and" occurs only between the last two clauses.

/8/   Note also that the information here is not as a whole new but constitutes an overlay with quoted material in Episode P-3.

/9/   While this is material of the sort which is typically found in paragraph initial, it seems to be outranked by the imposing initiatory sentence found in 7:11. I therefore regard 7:10 as a terminating sentence with participation of the material in the next episode.

/10/   For a quite differing partitioning of this passage and construing of relations among clauses, see Andersen (1974:124-125).

/11/   I construe here the material found in 7:14 as an amplification of the subject of the verb *bā* "go in" in verse 13. It would be unlikely to construe it as subject of *wayyabo'ū* in 7:15 because of the restriction that subject nouns do not precede *wāw* + performative tense.

/12/   For a summary of some formal features which have been found to mark peak in a variety of languages, see Longacre (1976: 217-228).

/13/   This analysis is not ad hoc to the present paragraph. It has become a convention in the analysis of narrative paragraphs by myself and those working with me to analyze narrative paragraphs as consisting essentially of the following slots: an optional Setting, two or more Build-up's, and an optional Terminus (Longacre, 1968:1.56-68). While I have not felt it worthwhile to refer to this apparatus everywhere in this presentation, the apparatus seems useful here in explaining somewhat in detail the paragraph structure at peak. It is also invoked in a few subsequent episodes.

/14/   For an alternative analysis of this passage--but one which points out the same features of parallelism and paraphrase which are noticed here--see again Andersen (1974:124-125).

/15/   Presumably the focus of this three-point discourse is on the content not on the "God said to Noah." Here, as in 16:13-22, God is not thematic. By contrast, note 8:20-22 where deity is clearly thematic and 7:1-5 where such thematicity may also be inferred.

WORKS CONSULTED

Andersen, Francis I.
    1974   *The Sentence in Biblical Hebrew.* The Hague: Mouton.

Boers, Hendrikus
    1976   "Response to: Robert E. Longacre, 'The Discourse Structure of the Flood Narrative.'" Unpublished paper given at the SBL meeting, St. Louis (December).

Buth, Randy
    1976   *An Introductory Study of the Paragraph Structure of Biblical Hebrew Narrative.* Jerusalem: The American Institute of Holy Land Studies (unpublished thesis).

Davidson, Robert
    1973   *Genesis 1-11.* Cambridge: University Press.

Forster, Keith
    1977   "The Narrative Folklore Discourse in Border Cuna." Pp. 1-23 in Longacre and Woods, vol. 2. Dallas: Summer Institute of Linguistics.

Grimes, Joseph
    1976   *The Thread of Discourse.* The Hague: Mouton.

Halliday, M. A. K.
    1967   "Notes on Transitivity and Theme in English, Parts 1 and 2." *Journal of Linguistics* 3: 71-81, 199-244.

    1968   "Notes on Transitivity and Theme in English, Part 3." *Journal of Linguistics* 4: 179-215.

Hopper, Paul
    1979   "Aspect and Foregrounding in Discourse," in *Discourse and Syntax* (in press). New York: Academic Press.

Kautzsch, E. and Cowley, A. E.
    1910   Gesenius' *Hebrew Grammar.* 2nd English ed. Oxford: Clarendon.

Longacre, Robert E.
    1968   *Discourse, Paragraph & Sentence Structure in Selected Philippine Langauges.* Publication 21 of the SIL publications in linguistics and related fields. Santa Ana, CA: Summer Institute of Linguistics.

    1972   *Hierarchy and Universality of Discourse Constituents in New Guinea Langauges*: Vol. 1, *Discussion*; Vol. 2, *Texts.* Washington: Georgetown University.

    1976   *An Anatomy of Speech Notions.* Lisse: Peter de Ridder.

Longacre, Robert E.
1977 "Discourse Genre." In *Proceedings of the Twelfth International Congress of Linguists (Vienna)*. In press.

Longacre, Robert E. and Woods, Frances
1976-1977 *Discourse Grammar: Studies in Indigenous Languages of Colombia, Panama, and Ecuador.* 3 vols. Publication 52 of the SIL publications in linguistics and related fields. Dallas: Summer Institute of Linguistics.

Longacre, Robert E. and Levinsohn, Stephen
1978 "Field Analysis of Discourse." Pp. 103-122 in *Current Trends in Textlinguistics (Research in Text Theory* 2). Ed. W. U. Dressler. Berlin: Walter de Gruyter.

Speiser, E. A.
1964 *Genesis*. AB #1. Garden City: Doubleday.

Van Dijk, Teun A.
1972 *Some Aspects of Text Grammars*. The Hague: Mouton.

Von Rad, Gerhard
1961 *Genesis, A Commentary*. Trans. John H. Marks. Philadelphia: Westminster.

8

1

BUILDING FOR THE WORSHIP OF GOD
EXODUS 25:1–30:10

Robert E. Longacre

ABSTRACT

The Hebrew text of Exodus 25:1–30:10, i.e., the instructions for building the tabernacle in the wilderness, for making the clothing of the priests, and for instituting worship is examined. Contemporary textlinguistic methodology is brought to bear on these five and a half chapters, which are seen to constitute a unified discourse in their own right although they are embedded in the larger discourse context of Exodus. As an instructional discourse, these chapters are similar to but distinct from procedural discourse (e.g., the prescriptions for sacrifice in Leviticus) and predictive discourse—although in all three discourse types the *waw*-consecutive perfect (WQTL) forms the backbone structure. This instructional discourse, although replete with specifications, is not simply the textual equivalent of a set of blueprints; it shines with an inner glory, the prospect of God dwelling among His people and being their God. The texture of the discourse is analyzed so as to reveal this dual nature ("the spirit within the wheels"). To this end I employ macrosegmention ("gross chunking"), posit macrostructures as summary-control devices on various levels, set up a peculiar agency hierarchy (God–Moses–artisans/priests–artifacts), trace the cumulative progress of the discourse towards its peak (the active institution of worship), and mention a few microstructural details (how one sentence immediately relates to surrounding sentences).

0. A study of the discourse structure of Exodus 25:1–30:10, which contains instructions for building the Tabernacle, making clothing for the priests, ordaining them, and instituting the daily worship, can serve the following purposes: (1) afford perspective on a Biblical Hebrew (BH) discourse type other than narrative; (2) at the same time serve to distinguish instructional discourse from predictive and procedural, on the one hand, and hortatory and juridical, on the other; and (3) further clarify the role of the various forms of the Hebrew verb in connected discourse.

The set of assumptions that underlie not only this study but also my previous work on BH discourse includes: (A) Discourse structure cannot be understood without a classification into discourse types. (B) Each discourse type has a mainline structure that consists of Hebrew sentences whose main verb is of a specified form, along with other sentence structures whose main verbs (including verbless clauses) round out in various ways the structure of that type of discourse. (C) Other discourse characteristics, e.g., characteristic sentence length, typical paragraph structures, and systems of nominal/pronominal reference, will also differ from type to type. (D) Attention to the factors listed above will prove insightful into the overall meaning and conception of a text and lead to new exegetical insights.

1. Instructional Discourse as a Distinct Discourse Type

In Longacre (1989) I assume four broad discourse types for BH prose: Narrative, Predictive, Hortatory and Expository. These types are distinguished mainly by having different mainline structures. *Narrative discourse*, the story, takes the preterite (the so-called *waw*-consecutive with the imperfect) as its determining verb form. Clauses with this form (necessarily verb-initial) typically represent punctiliar sequential happenings with causal connections at least partially uniting the sequence. *Predictive discourse*, a story told in advance, (cf. 1 Sam 10:2-6), is the inverse of narration. Here the *waw*-consecutive with the perfect (in necessarily verb-initial clauses) represents punctiliar and sequential projected happenings with at least partial causal connection. *Hortatory discourse* has a mainline that consists of command forms, with imperative, cohortative, and jussive forms roughly sorting out according to person and according to affirmative-negative polarity. Hortatory discourse thus conceived of as interpersonal (not juridical) can be mitigated in certain ways or shifted into deferential court speech. *Expository discourse* is completely static and takes as its mainline verbless clauses and clauses with *hāyâ*, "be." If dynamic verbs occur, they are subservient as anecdotes or illustrative material. Thus, expository and narrative discourses are polar opposites in regard to the use of dynamic versus static constructions. *Predictive* discourse is distinguished from *procedural* discourse (Longacre, 1982) in that while the former has a slate of participants, much as in a story, and is still agent oriented, the latter is goal oriented and the procedures may be implemented by any qualified agent—for example, sacrificial procedures may be implemented by a priest. A predictive discourse is, in reality, simply a projected story; and, as observed above, the perfect and the imperfect flip grammatical functions between the two. Procedural discourse uses the *waw*-consecutive perfect (*WQTL*) in VSO clauses and the imperfect (*YQTL*) in NV clauses according to the encoding of major versus minor procedures.

Thus my previous work distinguished narrative, predictive, procedural, hortatory (with variants), and expository discourses for BH. Notwithstanding, my analysis of the flood narrative (Longacre 1979) dealt with a type of discourse, in speeches of God to Noah (Gen 6:13–21 and 7:1–4), which was characterized by sparse use of imperatives, liberal use of the *waw*-consecutive perfect, a certain amount of specification data (especially in nominal, i.e., verbless, clauses), a second person orientation (to Noah), and orientation of the speeches towards construction and implementation. While I spoke of these two stretches of reported speech as "instructional" (or even "instructional" paragraphs), I failed to see the full import of the data, viz., the desirability of positing an instructional discourse type distinct from both procedural and hortatory discourses.

All of which brings us back to the theme of this paper, "building for the worship of God," i.e., the analysis of the constructional discourse found in Exod 25:1–30:10 (and in some following parts of chapter 30).[1] The purpose of this paper is to delineate clearly instruction as a discourse type and to present in some detail the structure and discourse-effectiveness of this passage. The latter concern— the discourse-effectiveness of this passage—is of major importance. For although the surface texture is that of a set of rather detailed and involved instructions, the purpose of the construction, the institution of the regular worship of Yahweh at a central sanctuary—albeit a

---

[1] The original impetus for doing this analysis and writing this paper came from Nicolai Winter-Nielsen of the Danish Bible Institute of Copenhagen. He wrote the first draft of what we hoped to make a joint paper. Although the latter has not worked out, I acknowledge here my considerable debt to Mr. Winter-Nielsen for stimulating my interest in this part of the Hebrew Bible and for several initial insights regarding the structure of the passage.

24   *Discourse Analysis of Biblical Literature*

tent—is presented as something glorious and fraught with deep religious meaning.

Before plunging, however, into the macrosegmentation and microsegmentation of the text before us, it is necessary to mention still another discourse type that is contextually interwoven with the instructions, viz., the juridical discourse. The juridical component is prominent enough in the entire Pentateuch (but especially prominent in Exodus, Leviticus and Deuteronomy) to merit entitling the whole "The Law." In regard to the text under consideration: (1) juridical material both precedes our text (Exod 20-23) and follows it (30:11-16, 31:12-17); (2) furthermore, as we shall see in the internal analysis of our text, juridical paragraphs embed here and there within the instructional passages.

2.   Discourse Unity and Macrostructures

It seems plausible to treat all of Exod 25:1-30:10 as one unit. Although there are main sections marked off by 28:1-6, 29:1-9, and 29:38, yet the whole is introduced by one quotation formula in 25:1: "And Yahweh said to Moses. . . ." There are no further occurrences of such formulas of quotation until we reach 30:11. Here and in 30:17, 22, 34, and 31:1, 12 we again encounter "And Yahweh said to Moses. . . ." Although a single speech can be interrupted by reiterated formulas of quotation (as in Gen 9:1-17), which mark off main sections within it, it may be argued that a section uninterrupted by such reiterated formulas of quotation is even more evidently a unit.

What then of the materials in 30:11-31:17? The paragraphs, except for the last (31:12-17 on the Sabbath), seem to relate in a loose way to the main preceding discourse, while at the same time patterning somewhat like addenda to it. Thus, the first such paragraph—30:11-16—has to do with raising revenue to support the "service of the Tent of Meeting" (30:16); 30:17-21 has to do with the construction of the bronze laver and is juridical (as indeed are some sections in the main preceding discourse); 30:22-33 has to do with the compounding and use of the anointing oil; 30:34-38 has to do with the compounding and use of the incense for the Tent of Meeting; and 31:1-11 records Yahweh's instruction to Moses that Bezalel, Oholiab, and other craftsmen are equipped by God with the skills to carry out the work of construction and clothesmaking. In summary: following the main, unbroken discourse (25:1-30:10) there is then a string of six further

Building for the Worship of God

discourses (words of Yahweh to Moses), only three of which are plainly constructional, while others treat of raising revenue, compounding of oil and incense, finding the skilled craftsman, and the Sabbath. These "tacked on" pieces not only are set off by reiterated formulas of quotation but are somewhat disparate in subject matter when compared to 25:1–30:10.

What then is the macrostructure of the larger continuous unit? Let us begin by assuming three macrostructures corresponding to the three main sections. In 25:1–27:21 the macrostructure is indicated in 25:8, 9, which I will summarily give as "Have them make me a sanctuary—according to the pattern I'm showing you—so that I may dwell among them." The three elements here are: (1) Moses is commanded to have the people build the sanctuary; (2) it must be done according to the revealed pattern; and (3) the purpose is so that God may dwell among his people. We can, on the basis of this macrostructure, anticipate a discourse having to do with the construction of a sanctuary with cultic objects, furniture, and utensils. We can also expect to encounter a text heavy with clauses and sentences that give specifications of materials, dimensions, and the like. We can further expect overt references to the ultimate purpose, that God may dwell among his people, to crop up from place to place.

For chapter 28 in its entirety we find a macrostructure which is given with a certain amount of repetition and paraphrase in 28:1–5. I summarize: "Have them make sacred garments for Aaron and his sons that they may be clad with dignity and honor in serving me as priests." Perhaps mediatorial role and representative function are involved in the very concept of priest; if this is not granted, we would need to add to the above macrostructure a further clause that captures a motif that runs through chapter 28: "... and in representing the people before me."

A macrostructure for 29:1–38 can be given as: "Consecrate and ordain Aaron and his sons to serve as priests before me—with the privileges attendant on their office."

Since I regard 29:38–46 as a separate major section and as the peak (cf. 3.5) of the whole discourse (with 29:1–37 as prepeak and consequently sharing some peak features), I could also state its macrostructure as: "Institute the regular worship of God in the morning and evening sacrifices; thus I will dwell among my people."

26   *Discourse Analysis of Biblical Literature*

The making of the altar of incense is given in a postpeak section (30:1–10); its macrostructure may be succinctly given: "Make an incense altar for the priest to offer incense to me morning and night." This is similar to the macrostructure given for the peak section.

A somewhat succinct macrostructure of the whole can be posited as follows: *Make me a sanctuary according to the pattern I'm showing you so that I may dwell among my people. Make sacred garments for Aaron and his sons and ordain them to serve as priests before me. Institute the regular daily worship.* Here the following key concepts are included: the SANCTUARY, the PATTERN, God's DWELLING among his people, the SACRED GARMENTS, ORDINATION, PRIESTHOOD, and the daily WORSHIP. If our macrostructure is carefully construed, it should entail the contents of this discourse and the relative detail and elaboration of the parts. We will have resort again to the macrostructure below especially in reference to the ordering of various subsections within the text.

3.   Macrosegmentation (gross chunking)

Here I consider the articulation of the text into its various "chunks" with attention to features of opening, as well as attention to such privileged chunks as the "inciting incident" (cf. narrative), peak (cumulative development), and postpeak—and how the macrostructure controls the order of presentation. Although some features of paragraph structure are discussed in this section, most such features are not discussed here. These latter concerns of *microsegmentation* are discussed to some degree in section 4, but a full constituent structure of the discourse is not included in this paper.

The main divisions of the text have been referred to above in the consideration of the macrostructures. It now remains to justify this division of the text in terms of formal features. Analytically, of course, the procedure has gone in the opposite direction, i.e., it is the discovery of the formal features to be described below which led to the assumption of semantic unity within the sections thus marked. Evidence that our text has four main divisions is seen in the distribution of imperatives, cleft sentences, and, to some degree, in the distribution of explicit second person singular references. For the main sections (not counting the postpeak), onset of a new section is marked more clearly than closure.

3.1. The imperative as discourse opener

The incidence of the imperative is restricted in the text under consideration. In this section I consider all occurrences of the imperative in the MT as it stands—and dispose of one such occurrence as a textual corruption.

In 25:2, 28:1, and 29:1b a second person singular imperative occurs in the onset of new sections (embedded discourses).

25:2: "SPEAK to the sons of Israel and they will bring me an offering. . . ." The whole has the structure of an indirect command, "Tell the sons of Israel to bring me an offering," with a YQTL form serving at once as purpose and indirect quotation. Moses as mediator of the covenant passes on to the people of Israel God's command to take an offering and build a sanctuary. The second person imperative, directed to Moses as mediator, is the pattern for the imperative in this text.

28:1: "As for you, CAUSE Aaron your brother and his sons to COME near to you from among the sons of Israel to serve me in the priesthood." The imperative is a second person singular hiphil. The mediatorial work of Moses in hearing God's command and turning the priesthood over to his brother and his brother's sons is emphasized by $wə^ʾattâ$ ("now as for you") and by the use of the causative verb, "Now, as for you, cause X to do Q." The section thus introduced has to do with the making of sacred garments for the priests.

29:1b: TAKE a young bullock and two rams without defect . . . [various kinds of unleavened bread are specified in the balance of the sentence in v. 2]. Here the imperative is again directed at Moses who is to ordain his brother Aaron and Aaron's sons to the priesthood. The point of the imperative is that Moses is to gather the animals and breads necessary for the complex of ordination sacrifices in which Moses will turn over his implicitly priestly function to an explicit and duly instituted priesthood.

Besides the above imperatives, which contribute to the articulation of major sections (embedded discourses, i.e., distinctive sections couched within longer sections), there also occur imperatives in 25:40, and in 28:42.

The double imperative in 25:40, "SEE and MAKE [everything] according to the pattern which you see on the mountain," reminds us that the imperative need not be limited to the initiation of a new embedded discourse as illustrated above. Here the double imperative

28   *Discourse Analysis of Biblical Literature*

occurs at the end of the instructions (an embedded discourse) for building the Ark of Testimony, the Table of the Presence, and the Menorah. It can be taken as a sort of urgent but parenthetical reminder to Moses of his mediatorial responsibilities. It is probable, however, that it is not simply parenthetical but signals closure (see below, 3.2), since features of opening and closure often show resemblance—as in an overt *inclusio*. I therefore consider 25:10–40 to constitute a unit (i.e., an "embedded" discourse) on the making of the Ark, the Table, and the Menorah—with the double imperative marking closure of the unit.

The imperative in 28:42 is of special interest: "MAKE linen underwear to cover the flesh of their nakedness...." While every other garment of the priests is specified in the cleft structure in 28:4, the linen underwear is not specified. But the clothes specified in 28:4 were meant to be visible and to give the priest dignity and honor. The underwear is described here in a paragraph, the second half of which is clearly juridical, as a precaution against exposure of the priest's genitals in the course of his discharging his duties. Thus, the little section 28:42–43 is like an addendum to the major instructions given in chap. 28. Furthermore, 28:41 is clearly a cataphoric link to the next major section: "And you shall clothe them, Aaron and his sons with him, and you shall anoint them, and you shall ordain them that they may serve as priests to me."

In that the section 28:42–43 is not anticipated in 28:4 and is skipped over in the cataphoric linkage of 28:41, it can plausibly be construed as a (somewhat urgent) parenthesis. The use of the second person singular imperative 'MAKE' in 28:42 serves again to put the onus of responsibility on Moses to see that this "extra" instruction is carried out. In this respect the parenthetical section 28:42–43 is reminiscent of the structure of a major section.

I have yet, however, to consider the imperative in the MT of 25:19a. I refer here to the totality of verse 25:19: "And MAKE [*waʿăśeh*] a cherub on one end and a cherub on the other end; of one piece with the atonement cover, you (plural) shall make [*taʿăśû*] the cherubim on the two ends of it." Here, in 19a and 19b, we encounter textual variants involving other forms of ʿāśâ, "make." No such variants are witnessed for any other imperative found in this entire text. In contrast, both 19a and 19b have divergent readings witnessed to by both the Samaritan Pentateuch and the Septuagint translation—while in 19b the divergent reading is also witnessed to in the Syriac, in some Targums, and in some of the Hebrew manuscripts from the Cairo Geniza.

Let me line up the variants as follows:

	MT	Samaritan Pentateuch
19a	וְעָשָׂה	יֵעָשׂוּ
19b	תַּעֲשׂוּ	תַּעֲשֶׂה

In summary, the MT text has a 2m.sg. imperative in 19a, and a 2m.pl. YQTL form in 19b, while the Samaritan Pentatuech and the LXX witness to YQTL, 3m.pl. niphal in 19a and 2m.sg. YQTL (qal) in 19b. These variants can be plausibly explained as a confusion (interchange) of final *waw* and *he* in alternate lines of Hebrew text, plus a further problem involving *waw* and *yod* in the first consonant of the form in 19a. This gives a new translation for v. 19. I present here vv. 18 and 19 together to give adequate context:

> v. 18: And you shall make (WQTL) two cherubim of gold; from beaten work you shall make (YQTL) them at the two ends of the atonement cover.
>
> v. 19: They shall be made (YQTL, niphal) one cherub on this end and the other cherub on that end; from the atonement cover you (sg.) shall make (YQTL) the cherubim at the two ends of it.

Notice that the first mention of making the cherubim is in v. 18 in a paraphrastic sentence involving WQTL and YQTL forms of the verb "make." Verse 19 is specificatory and therefore has no initial *waw* conjunctival (cf. sec. 4.1 below). Verse 19 is also a paraphrastic sentence and has a niphal YQTL in 19b and a qal YQTL in 19b. The only thing that is unusual in the new reading and translation is the use of a YQTL form in specification (rather than just nominal clauses), but this need not be a great problem.[2]

3.2. The cleft sentence as discourse opener

A cleft sentence is found in the paragraph or sentence that initiates each main section (embedded discourse) of this instructional text.

---

[2] In narrative discourse, where WYQTL forms are mainline, not only are N-QTL forms found in the secondary line but also some QTL forms (perfects without a preposed noun phrase). While only a few such examples occur, nevertheless they do occur, and represent a crucial witness to the secondary role of the perfect per se, even without a preposed noun. It seems to me that instructional discourse is somewhat parallel, in that, while N-YQTL occurs in secondary roles and YQTL forms are usually found in purpose clauses, the occurrence of a YQTL form in specification is not implausible, although presumably rare.

Each cleft sentence has the structure "this/these Ø the X which you shall do,"[3] i.e.,

zeh/ ʾēlleh Ø X ʾăšer + Vb

In 25:2 the cleft sentence immediately follows the sentence that contains the imperative: "And this is the offering which you will take from them . . ." (materials to use in implementing the instructions). In 28:4, the cleft sentence is several sentences removed from the sentence (28:1) that contains the imperative, but is still in the stage paragraph: "And these are the garments which you shall make . . ." (enumerations of the garments to be made). In 29:1 the cleft sentence is initial in its section, and the sentence with an imperative follows: "And this is the procedure (haddābār) which you are to implement." In 29:38 there is no initiatory imperative; rather the cleft sentence initiates the section: "And this Ø what you are to do [= offer] on the altar: two lambs one year old each day continually."

In three of the major sections (embedded discourses) both an imperative and a cleft sentence serve to signal onset of the section; in the fourth a cleft sentence occurs, but no imperative.

3.3. Explicit pronominal references

As we have already observed, the whole text has a structure, "You tell them to do X," which gets shortened to "You do X." This 2nd p.sg. functioning as the causer of 3rd pl. actions is especially noticeable in the stage paragraphs of the first two major sections. There is, in fact, a special agency hierarchy in this text: God–Moses–others (includes artisans and priests)–artifacts. There will be reason to refer to this hierarchy later.

In 25:1–9 we have the following "You (sg.) tell them to bring me an offering." "You (pl., i.e., Moses and other leaders) are to receive their offerings." "They shall make me a sanctuary." "According to all I'm showing you (sg.) they shall make." This gets subsequently shortened to WQTL forms in 2 sg. "And you shall make" with only occasional resort to WQTL forms in 3 pl.

Likewise, in 28:1–5 we see a similar development in the second section:

"And you (wĕʾattâ) bring to you Aaron your brother and his sons. . . ."

"And you shall make holy clothes for Aaron your brother."

---

[3] Here Ø symbolizes a null verb in a nominal clause.

"And you (wĕʾattâ) shall speak to all that are wisehearted.... And they shall make holy garments ..." [verse 4 has only "They shall make ..." forms]. V. 5: "And they (wĕhēm) shall use gold and blue, purple and scarlet yarn and fine linen."

This passage is of special interest because of the 2nd person pronoun (ʾattâ) in vv. 1 and 3, and of the 3 pl. (hēm) in v. 5—thus making quite explicit the "you ... they" relationship of the agency hierarchy on which the whole text is built.

Overt wĕʾattâ, "and you," also occurs in the last instruction paragraph of the first main section, where in 27:20 it initiates the paragraph which closes that section.

3.4. Construction of a crucial item as parallel to the inciting incident in narrative

In reference again to the first two major sections, I note that each has as its first item to be constructed a crucial item that entails the rest of the construction. In the first section (25:1-22) it is the Ark of the Testimony and its atonement cover that provide initial excitement. In section 2 (chap. 28) it is the ephod and its breastplate of judgment that provide the initial excitement. I do not find such a feature in the third major section—where there is rather a steady crescendo building up from the bullock of the sin offering, through the ram of the fellowship offering, through the ordination lamb to the eating of the ordination lamb. Nor do I find such a feature in peak or in postpeak.

The two paragraphs 25:10-16 and 25:17-22 together constitute a short embedded discourse on a low level of embedding. There is no special indication of closure in 25:16. A new paragraph in indicated simply by the topic shift to the atonement cover in 25:17 and the parallelism of 25:10 to 25:17 in respect to "Make an X; and these (are) its dimensions." The whole sequence 25:10-22 builds up to a climax in its second paragraph, where the atonement cover and its two facing cherubim are treated in an instruction replete with paraphrase and amplification (vv. 18-20) and ending with a promissory passage (v. 22) regarding God making himself known there—"above the atonement-cover between the cherubim."

This crucial piece of furniture is, in a sense, the living heart of the whole tabernacle and entails the construction of all that accompanies and surrounds it.

In somewhat parallel fashion the construction of the ephod and its breastpiece of judgment is given in two paragraphs (28:6-14 and

32   *Discourse Analysis of Biblical Literature*

28:15-30). In the former, great emphasis is placed upon the engraving of the names of the twelve tribes of Israel on the two onyx stones that are to be mounted on the shoulder pieces of the ephod. In the latter—possibly the longest paragraph in our whole text—after a long and intricate section on the six rings and cords that will bind the breastpiece to the ephod (vv. 22-28), emphasis is put on the importance of the engraving of the names of the tribes of Israel on the twelve stones that are to be mounted on the breastplate (as in vv. 17-21). In v. 29 the names on the breastpiece are again mentioned, while in v. 30 the Urim and the Thummin (divination stones in the pocket of the breastpiece) figure in a joint reference to these pieces and to the stones on the breastpiece.

In both the first paragraph, referring to the names on the shoulder pieces of the ephod, and in the second paragraph, referring to the names on the twelve stones of the breastpiece, the work of Aaron as representative and mediator for the whole nation is emphasized with considerable paraphrase and amplification (28:12 and 28:29-30). Again, the ephod and its breastpiece are presented as the crucial pieces of clothing and as such are prescribed first.

In both the sections on the tabernacle construction and on the making of the garments of the high priest and his sons, an instruction regarding the crucial item immediately follows the stage (with its imperative and cleft sentence).

In various periods of Israelite history, as represented in Judges and the books of Samuel and Kings, the Ark of the Testimony is represented as the crucial item in the worship of God, while the priest is often referred to as "one wearing the ephod." In a very real sense the Ark symbolized worship and the presence of God, while the ephod symbolized the priesthood. Both, on occasion, were objects of superstitious veneration—with the Ark carried into battle on several occasions and an ephod set up as a cult object.[4]

3.5. Peak (cumulative development)

The Peak of the whole text can plausibly be considered to be 29:38-46. That this is clearly meant to be a major section—although

---

[4] If, indeed, "ephod" in such passages as Judges 17 and 18 is to be identified with part of the clothing of the priest. Possibly the reference is to divination stones associated with the ephod.

consisting of only one paragraph—is seen by the use of a cleft sentence in its introduction (29:38).

This is, in a sense, the "target" of the whole discourse: the institution of the daily worship. Furthermore, there is a certain sonority and solemnity achieved by resort to various devices which are noted below. The shift to first person singular (Yahweh speaking) in the center of v. 42 involves an unusual shift between the main clause and the relative clause and, of course, foregrounds God as the dominant agent in the peculiar agency hierarchy of this discourse.

The whole paragraph is juridical in tone and structure. The first part of the paragraph (vv. 38-42) is prescriptive of the daily ritual of the morning and evening sacrifice. The last verse, v. 42, is somewhat of a hinge between the two halves of the paragraph:

> Ø a continual offering for your generations at the door of the Tent of Meeting before YHWH—I who will be known to you (pl.) there to speak with you (pl.) there.

The first part of the verse is a solemn injunction: "It will be a continual offering for your generations...." The phrase "before YHWH" is followed by a relative ($'\check{a}\check{s}er$) clause with a verb in first person singular. The transition from a third person noun to a modifying relative clause in first person does not make for smooth translation and is somewhat unusual, but presents no grammatical problem. The relative clause in first person anticipates the second half of the paragraph, which involves a number of coordinated structures that are somewhat paraphrastic in function. There are several ekbalic relations (ranging semantically from result to purpose to promise) involved: (1) vv. 43-46 can be regarded as the result of the institution of the regular daily worship (= "Institute the daily worship, then I will sanctify the place and dwell among them"); (2) likewise, the last verse, v. 46 (= "I will sanctify the place and dwell there so that they will know that I am their God ..."), can be regarded as the result of vv. 43-45. However, we might better take the primary relation of vv. 38-42 to vv. 43-46 (i.e., to the whole paragraph) to be one of a conditional promise (as suggested in 4.3.1). The pronoun $'\check{a}n\hat{i}$ occurs twice in v. 46—while all the verbs from 42b on (except the third person singular niphal at the end of v. 43) are first person singular. Thus, the second half of this peak paragraph achieves a certain sonority by resorting to coordination and paraphrase, and develops in one grand crescendo the germinal idea found in the stage of the whole

34   *Discourse Analysis of Biblical Literature*

text: "They shall make me a sanctuary and I will dwell among them" (25:8). The whole ends on the grand chord: "I Ø YHWH their God."

3.6. The postpeak construction

Why is the construction of the altar of incense delayed until after the peak of the entire discourse rather than being given as part of the first embedded discourse, where construction of the furniture of the Tent of Meeting and of the Tent itself is given? The construction of the altar of burnt offering is given in 27:1–8, while the consecration of the altar for worship is given in 29:36–37; and the projected implementation of the altar in daily sacrifice is given in the peak (29:38–40). Here, in 30:1–10, the construction of the altar of incense and its projected implementation as a daily ritual, which is parallel to that of the daily sacrifices, are summarily given together. Both the peak and the postpeak have to do with the projected institution of daily worship.

Peak is not necessarily a discrete area, but rather a zone of turbulence and excitement. The target of all the procedures is the exciting prospect of the institution of daily worship of a God who dwells among his people. The consecration of the priests in prepeak and the construction and projected implementation of the incense altar in postpeak partake of some of the culminating tension that is expressed in the peak itself.

3.7. Order of projected construction as controlled by the macrostructure

Apparent irregularities in the order of construction procedures, e.g., the priority given to the construction of the Ark of Testimony, the Table of the Presence, and the Menorah, as well as the late positioning of the section regarding the incense altar, can now be reviewed again in the light of the macrostructure that is posited at the end of section 2 above.

In order to perceive clearly the controlling force of the macrostructure in ordering the construction procedures, it is of some interest to compare the order of projected construction in the text we are currently analyzing with the order of narrated construction as given in Exod 36:8–40:38, especially 36:8–39:31. The order of projected construction and that of narrated construction are given in parallel columns in Diagram I.

Building for the Worship of God 35

DIAGRAM I

Order of Narrated Construction Exod 36:8–39:31		Order of Projected Construction Exod 25:1–30:10
(1) The Tent Curtains	36:8–13	(6) The Ark of Testimony
(2) The Over-Tent	36:14–19	(7) The Atonement Cover
(3) The Tent Framework	36:20–34	(8) The Table of Presence
(4) The Veil	36:35–36	(9) The Menorah
(5) Entrance Curtain	36:37–38	(1) The Tent Curtains
(6) The Ark of Testimony	37:1–5	(2) The Over-Tent
(7) The Atonement Cover	37:6–9	(3) The Tent Framework
(8) The Table of the Presence	37:10–16	(4) The Veil (placement of furniture)
(9) The Menorah	37:17–24	
(10) The Altar of Incense	37:25–28	(5) Entrance Curtain
(11) Anointing Oil	37:29	(13) The Altar of Burnt Offering
(12) Incense		
(13) The Altar of Burnt Offering	38:1–7	(15) The Courtyard
(14) The Bronze Basin	38:8	(W) Oil for the Menorah (cf. 37:37)
(15) The Courtyard	38:9–17	
(16) Entrance Curtain	38:18–20	(17) The Ephod
(17) The Ephod	39:1–7	(18) The Breastpiece
(18) The Breastpiece	39:8–21	(19) The Robe of the Ephod
(19) The Robe of the Ephod	39:22–26	(21) The "Holiness" Tiara
(20) Tunics, turbans, sashes	39:27–29	(20) Tunics, turbans, sashes
(21) The "Holiness" Tiara	39:30–31	(X) Underpants for the priests
A. *Then*, Moses inspects	39:32–42	(Y) Long bloque on the ordination of priests (cf. 40:12–15)
B. God commands it to be assembled, etc.	40:1–15	
C. Moses assembles it, places furniture, etc.	40:16–33	(Z) Institution of worship (cf. 40:22, 20)
D. The glory of the Lord fills the Tent of Meeting	40:34–38	(10) Altar of incense
		Appended Discourses
		(14) The Basin
		(11) The Anointing Oil
		(12) The incense

36 Discourse Analysis of Biblical Literature

In the narrative which recounts the actual construction, first the tent curtains are made, then the over-tent, then the tent framework of staves, and the entrance curtains (bloques 1–5). Following this a number of cultic objects are constructed: the ark of testimony with its atonement cover, the table of the presence, the menorah, the altar of incense; the anointing oil and the incense; the altar of burnt offering, and the bronze basin (bloques 6–14). The surrounding courtyard with its entrance curtains (bloques 15–16) are constructed to enclose all the preceding.

The narrative of the construction of the above items is then followed by the narrative of the making of clothes for the priests (bloques 17–21). Finally, following the account of the construction of all these items, the narrative depicts Moses as inspecting the work for presumably both quality of workmanship and pattern-conformity (39:32–42), receiving God's command to erect the Tent of Meeting and its courtyard, placing its furnishings in the correct places, and ordaining the priests (40:1–15). Verses 40:16–33 resume the narrative, with a summary statement in v. 16: "Moses did everything just as the Lord commanded him." Verses 34–38 recount that the Lord took possession of His dwelling: "and the glory of the Lord filled the Tent."

In this narrative account of the construction, the institution of the regular worship—the morning and evening sacrifice and the offering of incense—is only summarily referred to at the end (40:27, 29). Nowhere in the narrative is the note clearly sounded that the various items were built so that God could dwell among His people—although this comes about in 40:34–38. Even the ordination of the priests is not recounted as such, although God enjoins this in summary fashion in Exod 40:12–15. Indeed, the whole account in chapters 36–40 is a rather routine recital to the effect that what was projected in chapters 25–30 was in fact carried out.

Turning again to the discourse with which this study is concerned, we are initially impressed that the order of the projected construction is less logical and harder to rationalize than the order of the narrated construction. Narrative bloques (6)–(9) precede bloques (1)–(5). Furthermore, the construction of the altar of incense (10), instead of being given after (6)–(9) is split off and forms the closure of the first long embedded discourse. Again, while in the narrated account the altar of burnt offering (13) and the bronze basin (14) (the furniture of the courtyard) appear before the construction of the courtyard (15) and

Building for the Worship of God 37

its entrance (16), in the projected construction the bronze basin (14) is postponed as one of the appended discourses (30:14–21). So neither the furnishings of the Tent nor of the courtyard are given in one continuous sequence, but one item in each set is dislocated and occurs elsewhere.

As far as the making of the garments for Aaron and his sons, the various pieces of apparel in bloques (17)–(21) occur in the same order in both discourses,[5] except that in the projected construction the "Holy to the Lord" tiara or plaque (21) is mentioned before the section on tunics, turbans, and sashes (20). Furthermore, bloque X of the projected constructions, which prescribes underpants for the priests in 28:42–43, is summarized in a noun phrase in 39:20 of the narrated construction.

Again, therefore, I refer to the macrostructure that is posited at the end of the section 2. The macrostructure, a distillation from the contents of chapters 25–30, does not merely mention making the Tent (and by implication, its furnishings) nor making things according to the revealed pattern; rather, integral parts of the macrostructure are: the purpose that God may dwell among his people, the ordination of the priesthood, and the institution of daily worship. These features make

---

[5] It may well be, however, that the projected order and the narrated order are both transposed in regard to the ephod and the robe of the ephod. While in both 28:6–35 and in 39:1–26 the making of the ephod and of the breastpiece is mentioned before the making of the robe of the ephod, the order of putting on these items of apparel was apparently the reverse, i.e., the robe of the ephod was first put on, then the ephod, then the breastpiece of the ephod. Several things point in this direction: (1) Why is the robe called the robe of the ephod unless the robe and the ephod were closely related? (2) It is hardly credible that the priest's insignia of office on the ephod would have been worn under and concealed by the robe. (3) At any rate, when Moses is told to clothe Aaron for the ordination rites (29:5), he is told to put on him "the tunic, and the robe of the ephod, and the ephod and the breastpiece," and this may well be the actual order of putting on the garments (cf. also Lev 8:7). See again sections 3.4 and 3.7 above.

As to the nature of the ephod, Levine in his beautiful coffee-table picture volume portrays the ephod as a kind of apron. With this substantially agree Wendland (1985:198), Pixley (1987:200), and Cassuto (1967:372–73), who describes it as "a kind of simple pinafore that covered the loins."

I believe that this mitigates somewhat Noth's complaint that "these pieces (of apparel) do not fit together into a convincing overall picture, but to some extent stand in the way of each other" (1962:220). It is his taking the ephod to be a loincloth that is a major source of his difficulties. A waist coat or a kilt could be worn over the robe of the ephod, but if the ephod were a loincloth this would not have been possible.

38 *Discourse Analysis of Biblical Literature*

these instructions quite distinct from the narrated account given in Exod 36–40. As an instructional text, the text is not only full of specifications, and thus heavily prescriptive, but is juridical in certain parts. Everything is to be done—and properly done "now and to all your generations"—with a glorious end in view. A certain atmosphere of religious excitement and awe enters the text at points where the end is envisioned (25:8; 25:22; 25:30; 27:21; 28:29–30 but especially 29:42–46 and to some degree in 30:6–10).

For this reason the apparent departures from logical order in the projected construction can be considered to be departures motivated by the need to highlight these elements of excitement and awe in the macrostructure. Thus, as already suggested, the permutation of the bloques (6)–(9) to the fore of the construction of the Tent and Overtent (1)–(3) can be likened to the presentation of an inciting incident in a story: building the Ark and its atonement cover where YHWH will dwell "between the cherubim" is an important enough step to entail everything else that is to be constructed. As far as the splitting off of the passage concerning construction of the Altar of Incense (10) and making it a postpeak procedure in the projected construction, here, as we have suggested, the incense altar with its morning and evening incense offering is effectively located after the peak, where the instruction of the morning and evening sacrifice of lambs is inculcated; both have to do with the institution of daily worship.

The dislocation of the construction of the bronze basin (14) to an appended discourse in 35:17–21, as well as that the anointing oil (11), given in 30:23–33, and of the incense itself (12), given in 30:34–38, at first blush seem not to be as well motivated. Even here, however, it is possible to conjecture that the overriding demands of the macrostructure has led to a brushing aside of certain details and their postponement to a later position. The discourse 25:1–30:10 is very evidently driving toward its culmination in the prepeak (ordination of the priesthood, 29:1–37), peak (institution of daily worship and God dwelling among His people, 29:38–46), and in the postpeak (more on the daily worship, 30:1–10). The framer of the discourse is, as it were, impatient to get on to his main objectives; and in the process certain items are set aside for later treatment lest they impede the progress of the whole.

From this perspective even the passage on underpants for the priest (28:42–43), which is not only prescriptive but juridical, needs to be considered. The worship of YHWH was to be in every way distinct from contemporary Canaanite worship, which was characterized by sexual motifs and activity. By contrast, there was not even to be accidental exposure of the genitals of an officiating priest—much less sexual activity around the Lord's altars. In the period of the judges the priests Hophni and Phineas were judged for, among other things, sexual activity with women attendants at the Tent of Meeting (1 Sam 2:22), while in the time of the reformer King Josiah it was necessary to expel sacred male prostitutes from their quarters in the Temple itself (2 Kings 23:7)

The passage of 28:42–43 constitutes, then, an urgent concern relative to the institutions of worship. Since the passage concerns the clothing of the priests, it properly finds its place at the close of the section on the priests' clothing. Nevertheless, the quasi-parenthetical nature lies in the fact that this bit of apparel concerns decency rather than dignity and is to this degree unlike the rest of the clothes-making prescriptions.

It is also of further interest here that the instructional discourse of chapters 25–30 is divided from its narrative implementation in chapters 36–40 by the interlude of the golden calf and the aftermath in chapters 32–34 (while 35 is mainly concerned with gathering materials for construction). Here the author of Exodus, in separating the projected construction from the narrated construction by means of this account of lapse into unauthorized worship and idolatry, has underscored the need for a worship according to the revealed pattern and has anticipated the struggle throughout Israel's history between such divinely instituted worship and the perennial invasions of Canaanite religious patterns.

4. A Beginning at Microsegmentation

The principles of microsegmentation that will be discussed and illustrated here are (1) the distribution and function of *waw*-conjunctival; (2) further considerations of thematicity and pronominal reference; and (3) the ranking of verb forms/clause types in a scheme of relative closeness to or departure from the main instructional line of the discourse. In respect to the latter consideration, height of ranking in the salience scheme correlates roughly with dominance within the local span (the paragraph).

40   *Discourse Analysis of Biblical Literature*

4.1. *Waw*-conjunctival in the sentence and the paragraph

In accordance with a theory of BH sentence structure which has been developed elsewhere (Longacre, 1989, chap. 4), the Hebrew sentence is, for the most part, a domain set off by *waw*, whether consecutive or conjunctival. Absence of *waw* is more likely to indicate the continuation of a sentence unit than its onset. Thus a BH sentence is basically of three sorts: (a) a main clause to which may be attached subordinate clauses and relative clauses; (b) complementation sentences with a *wayhî* or *wĕhāyâ* plus a temporal expression plus the main clause; and (c) paratactic sentences—without medial *waw*—and usually chiastic in structure: $V_1N_1 + N_2V_2$ where V_2 either repeats V_1 or is a synonym of V_1. The text type here under consideration uses (a) and (c) extensively with almost no use of (b)—which occurs mainly in narrative and predictive discourses.

Very frequently, then, a Hebrew sentence begins with a *waw*. A few exceptions occur, however. In some narrative discourses (possibly in some predictive as well) a temporal phrase can begin a clause without any preceding *waw* (cf. Gen 22:4 where this marks onset of an episode). In the text under analysis here, an instructional discourse, there occurs a specialized sort of comment paragraph whose thesis is accompanied by a specification structure. Thus, the thesis of such a paragraph can be "Build an X." It is typically accompanied by: "q cubits Ø its length. And r cubits Ø its width. And s cubits Ø its height." Here the whole complex of three sentences, which specify length, width, and height is a coordinate paragraph that is embedded in the specification slot. The *waw* is omitted in the first sentence of the embedded paragraph. If, however, more than one specification structure appears, then each initiating sentence is marked by the absence of the usual introductory *waw*.

Diagram II illustrates both the operation of minus *waw* in binding together clauses in paratactic (and chiastic) sentences, and the operation of minus *waw* in indicating a specification on the paragraph level. This diagram also serves to illustrate WQTL forms as mainline of this discourse type (sec. 4.3), and considerations of thematicity in setting up embedded paragraphs (sec. 4.2). I shall present the paragraph (Exod 25:10–17) in semiliteral translation from the Hebrew via an indentation diagram in which levels of indentation represent levels of embedding. The slot class assumption of dejargonized tagmemics (Longacre, 1983) is assumed throughout.

Building for the Worship of God 41

DIAGRAM II: TREE STRUCTURE OF EXOD 25:10–17,
AN INSTRUCTIONAL SEQUENCE PARAGRAPH

Sequential Thesis$_1$: (I) Comment Para.
   Thesis: And they shall make [WQTL] an ark of acacia wood.
   Spec: (E) Coord. Para.
     Thesis$_1$: $2^1/_2$ cubits Ø its L.
     Thesis$_2$: And $1^1/_2$ cubits Ø its W.
     Thesis$_3$: And $1^1/_2$ cubits Ø its H.
Sequential Thesis$_2$: And you shall overlay it [WQTL] with pure gold; inside and outside you shall overlay it [N-YQTL].
Sequential Thesis$_3$: And you shall make [WQTL] upon it a gold molding all around.
Sequential Thesis$_4$: (I) Seq. Para.
   Sequential Thesis$_1$: And you shall cast [WQTL] for it 4 rings of gold.
   Sequential Thesis$_2$: (I) Comment Para.
     Thesis: And you will attach [WQTL] them at it 4 feet.
     Spec: (E) Coord. Para.
        Thesis$_1$: 2 rings Ø on its one side
        Thesis$_2$: And 2 rings Ø on its second side.
Sequential Thesis$_5$: (I) Sequence Para.
   Sequential Thesis$_1$: And you shall make [WQTL] poles of acacia wood.
   Sequential Thesis$_2$: And you shall overlay [WQTL] them with gold.
   Sequential Thesis$_3$: (I) Comment Para.
     Thesis: And you shall insert [WQTL] the poles in the rings in the sides of the Ark to carry the Ark by means of them.
     Spec: (J) Paraphrase Para.
        Thesis: In the rings of the Ark shall be [N-YQTL] the poles.
        N.A.P.: You shall not [*lō^2*-TQTL] take them out of it.
Sequential Thesis$_n$: And you shall put [WQTL] into the Ark the testimony which I shall give you.

In Diagram II, Sequential Theses (abbreviated ST below) 1, 4, 5 are expounded by embedded paragraphs, while ST 2, 3, and n are expounded by sentence structures. ST$_2$ is expounded by a paratactic chiastic sentence without any internal *waw*. This sentence has an on-the-line WQTL form that initiates it and an off-the-line YQTL form of the same verb that closes it; intervening noun phrases are assigned either to the first or to the second clause.

ST$_1$ is expounded by an instructional comment paragraph whose thesis is a WQTL clause. The comment slot of an instructional paragraph is so semantically specialized that I call it specification slot here and everywhere in the paper. Here the specification is expounded by what is obviously a coordinate paragraph; I term it expository coordinate in that the sentence structures which occur in it characterize

42   *Discourse Analysis of Biblical Literature*

expository discourse. It has three component sentences in the coordinated theses; these sentences specify the dimensions of the Ark of Testimony. Theses 2 and 3 regularly begin with *waw*, the sentence marker. The *waw* does not occur in the sentence of Thesis$_1$, since this sentence initiates the specification unit and minus *waw* marks the initiation of this structure.

Similarly, in regard to specifying the location of the rings for the carrying poles (within the I Seq. paragraph embedded under main ST$_4$) under ST$_2$ of the embedded unit, there is an expository (E) comment paragraph in which the first sentence of the specification has no *waw*, while the second does.

A slight problem—between the somewhat conflicting functions of *waw* within the sentence and within the paragraph—is found in ST$_3$ embedded under main ST$_5$. I indicate here an embedded juridical paraphrase paragraph. Both the sentence in the Thesis slot and the one in the Negated Antonym Paraphrase (N.A.P.) slot lack initial *waw*. The language is typically juridical in the prescriptive use of the verb *hāyâ*, "be," and in regard to the prohibitive use of *lōʾ*-TQTL in the next sentence. That I do not join the two as one sentence is because of the typically juridical structure in both sentences. As for the absence of *waw* in the second sentence, an N.A.P. is, in a sense, a kind of specification of the previous injunction. Possibly the semantic category of specification occurs in more than one paragraph level slot. The absence of *waw* on the first sentence is, however, quite predictable as the initial sentence in a specification slot.

This paragraph illustrates nicely the mainline role of WQTL clauses in instructional discourse. It also illustrates the manner in which considerations of thematicity lead to the positing of embedded paragraphs. While all the WQTL sentences could be considered to constitute a simple linear string of nine sequential theses, it seems better to recognize as main ST$_4$ a stretch whose theme is the making of the rings and whose structure is that of an embedded instructional sequence paragraph with its own ST$_1$ and ST$_2$. Similarly, it seems plausible to posit in main ST$_5$ a stretch whose theme is the making of the carrying poles which are to go into the rings. This stretch is considered to consist of an embedded instructional sequence paragraph with its own ST$_1$, ST$_2$, and ST$_3$.

Building for the Worship of God 43

DIAGRAM III: TREE STRUCTURE OF EXOD 26:15–17

ST_1: (I) Comment Paragraph
   Thesis: And you shall make [WQTL] for the Tent staves of upright wood.
   $Spec_1$: (E) Coor. Paragraph
      $Thesis_1$: 10 cubits Ø the length of one stave.
      $Thesis_2$: And $1^1/_2$ cubits Ø the width of one stave.
   $Spec_2$: Two projections Ø on one stave, set woman against her sister.
   Summary: Thus shall you make [kēn TQTL] for all the staves of the Tent.

More complicated situations regarding the absence or presence of conjunctival *waw* occur where two or more specifications are attached to one thesis rather than where the specifications constitute a coordinate paragraph, which as a unit expounds specification. Such a situation is illustrated in the opening sentences of Exod 26:15–30, which as a whole is concerned with the making of the staves for the tabernacle framework (Diagram III).[6] In this embedded comment paragraph (26:15–17) there are two specifications and one summary, all of which are ancillary to the same thesis. The thesis itself has the usual WQTL verb that is characteristic of the mainline in the discourse type. Specification$_1$ is expounded by a coordinate paragraph. As seen above, no *waw* conjunctival occurs on the first sentence of such a unit, but *waw* regularly occurs on the second sentence. Specification$_2$ as the only sentence in this repeated slot also is minus *waw* conjunctival—as in the summary with *kēn*, "thus."

4.2. Thematicity and pronominal references

As we have seen, Diagram II illustrates subparagraphing determined by thematicity. Thus in a paragraph concerning making the ark there occur two embedded sequence paragraphs on the making of the

---

[6] While it is not within the scope of this article to discuss architectural details of the Tabernacle, the relation of the curtains (the tent proper) to the wooden staves, pillars, and what-have-you is a moot question that has evoked considerable comment. Were the wooden pieces solid pillars of wood, which would conceal the cherubim embroidered in the inside of the tent curtains and at the same time constitute very heavy pieces to carry around—or is there some other explanation? Noth eventually considers the text to present here an incongruous picture of a tent sanctuary and a portable wooden structure capable of being dismantled (1962:110–13). Kennedy, however, in his classic description of the Tabernacle (1902) supposes the wooden pieces not to be solid but to have consisted of two parallel pieces of wood with an opening between them and joined at top and bottom. While Hyatt (1971:271) and Pixley (1987:196) agree with Kennedy in this respect, Cassuto (1967) and Levine (1968) reject this view and argue for solid boards.

rings and of the carrying poles respectively. This is a typical situation. In fact, there are none of the 27 paragraphs that I have posited and diagrammed in this text that do not have at least one such embedded paragraph determined by thematicity shifts. One of the longest embedded sequence paragraphs found in the text is in 29:4–7, where, after a preliminary N-YQTL sentence, there occurs a succession of nine WQTL sentences. This is, however, an unusually long uninterrupted run of WQTL sentences. I mention here, somewhat at random, some further examples of subparagraphs determined by thematicity.

Exod 25:23–30 is an instructional sequence paragraph concerning the construction of the table on which was to be put the Bread of the Presence. ST_3 is a three-sentence paragraph (vv. 24b, 25) which has to do with the making of a molding around the table, a rim, and a further molding on the rim. ST_4 is a paragraph (vv. 26, 27) of three sentences concerning the rings which are to be attached to the table. ST_5 is likewise a three-sentence paragraph (v. 28) which provided for the making of the carrying poles. Other ST's are single sentences (ST_2 and ST_6 and ST_n) or an instructional comment paragraph of the sort already illustrated.

Exod 26:1–6 is an instructional sequence paragraph concerning the making of the Tabernacle curtains. ST_1 is an instructional comment paragraph (vv. 1–3) with one thesis and two specifications both of which are expounded by (E) coordinate paragraphs; it specifies the dimensions of the curtains as well as which are to be coupled. ST_2 is likewise an embedded instructional comment paragraph with both thesis and specification consisting of coordinated paragraphs; it treats of the making of loops in the curtains.

Exod 26:31–35, likewise an instructional sequence paragraph, is concerned with the construction of the Veil (to divide the Holy of Holies from the Holy Place), the hanging of it, and the placement of furniture relative to it. ST_1 instructs concerning the making of the veil and hanging it upon four wood pillars overlaid with gold and equipped with hooks and sockets (vv. 31–32). ST_2 instructs concerning the placement of the furniture relative to the veil (vv. 33–35), and ST_3 instructs concerning the curtain for the entrance to the Tent (vv. 36–37). Each ST unit is expounded by a paragraph of four or five sentences (and lower-level embedding).

Exod 27:9–19 is a rather unusual paragraph that hangs four specifications upon one thesis; the whole is concerned with the making of curtains for the courtyard. The thesis (v. 9) is: "And you shall make the courtyard of the Tent." The first specification unit (9b–16) specifies in a coordinate paragraph (with multiple layers of embedding) for the south side, the north side, the west side, the east side with hanging on each side of the entrance, and finally the entrance curtain itself. We have here five coordinated theses with only the first sentence of Th_1 lacking a *waw*, while further specifications within such a unit (charcteristically dimensions) show characteristic absence of *waw* in the first sentence. Further specifications 2, 3, 4 deal with in order: the staves (v. 17), the general dimensions of the courtyard (v. 18), and further utensils and tent pegs (v. 19)—all of which are to be of bronze. Initial sentences in these specifications are minus *waw*.

The instructions for making the breastpiece of judgment in Exod 28:15–30 is the longest paragraph in the text. Essentially it is an instructional result paragraph whose thesis is expounded by an instructional sequence paragraph with three ST's. ST_1 specifies the dimensions and spells out the job for the tailor (vv. 15–16). ST_2, expounded by an instructional comment paragraph, specifies the four rows of stones engraved with the names of the twelve sons of Israel (vv. 17–21). ST_3, expounded by an instructional sequence paragraph with multiple embedding, prescribes the making of wreathen gold chains, golden rings, and blue cords to bind the breastpiece of judgment securely on the ephod "so it won't swing out" (end of v. 28). Finally, a WQTL sentence with a subject switch to Aaron signals the onset of the result: (if everything is done as specified,) then Aaron shall bear continually on his heart the names of the children of Israel—as their mediatorial representative (vv. 29–30).

4.3. Verb ranking and relative salience within the paragraph

It is obvious from the above sections that WQTL sentences occupy a position of privilege in the instructional discourse and can be considered to carry the mainline of instruction. Sentences that have a noun phrase preceding a YQTL verb act in many ways like a secondary line of instruction. Sentences in which WQTL occurs with switch reference (SR) of subject commonly indicate a sort of ekbalic construction. Clauses with initial YQTL verbs occur in this text almost exclusively as (a) second member of indirect quote construction ("Speak to them and they shall bring" > "Speak to them that they bring ..."); and (b) purpose clauses. Participial clauses—characteristically accompanied by a form of *hāyâ*, "be"—nominal clauses, and cleft sentences occur in a specificatory, descriptive function. WQTL *hāyâ* sentences, N-YQTL *hāyâ* sentences, and *lōʾ*-YQTL sentences are more often than not prescriptive injunctive sentences in juridical discourse and are, properly speaking, not relevant to this scheme. Finally, we have also to account for the functions of the imperative and have a second look at the cleft sentence.

In the above section on the imperative (3.1.1), it was emphasized that all imperatives found in this text are 2 sg. and are addressed to Moses himself as mediator of the covenant. In this role he is the one who receives instructions and passes them on to the people. So much is he the causer of all that is built and done that very early in chapter 25, "You tell them that they do X" is replaced by, "And then you will do X." As already stated, there is an agency hierarchy assumed in the text: God, Moses, they (people, special artisans, and priests), artifacts. Imperatives are directed from God to Moses as causer/dispatcher. It is therefore necessary to realize that the use of the imperative is bound up with concerns that belong to the participant structure as formulated in the agency hierarchy.

But the same concerns also govern to some degree certain uses of WQTL that do not appear to be on the mainline of instruction. Any WQTL form characterized by switch reference from the previous subject (abbreviated WQTL-SR) has an ekbalic function. Switch reference which goes down the agency hierarchy expresses result; 26:16: "And you shall fasten the curtains to each other. And it shall be one tent." 29:21: "And you sprinkle [the blood] upon Aaron and his sons ... and he will be holy." On the other hand, switch reference which goes up the agency hierarchy expresses promise; 25:8: "And they shall make me a sanctuary. And I will dwell among them."

This is also partially true of YQTL forms in the text. YQTL forms in purpose clauses often display a SR relative to the main clause: "And you will make an X so that it may do/may not do Q."

Except for interference from the presence of embedded juridical paragraphs, participial clauses (usually with *hāyâ*), *hāyâ*-clauses, and nominal clauses function as forms of specification or closure in the instructions. Cleft sentences are very similar in function, but often seem to be amplifying instead of simply specifying.

A further function, portmanteau to the above, of both imperative and cleft sentences is that of marking the onset of a new section (3.1.1.).

These considerations have led to the formulation of the salience scheme found in Diagram IV.

DIAGRAM IV

Band 1 IMPV (2 sg.)
              command to causer/dispatcher/mediator
Band 2
   a. WQTL   primary line of instruction
   b. N-YQTL secondary line of instruction
Band 3
   a. WQTL (SR) ekbalic (result/promise)
   b. YQTL (±SR) purpose
Band 4
   a. participial (with *hāyâ*)
   b. *hāyâ* clauses
   c. nominal clauses
   d. cleft sentences
Band 5 (IMPV) portmanteau
        (cleft sentence) with above but articulating a new section

Promotion and demotion:
(1) 2b > 2a by explicit coordination and parallelism [non-periphrastic]
(2) clauses with WQTL forms deleted by gapping resemble nominal clauses but remain 2a.
(3) deletion of *waw* can demote 2b > 4
(4) when 3a ascends the Agency Hierarchy result > promise

A few residual problems (see notes at the bottom of Diagram IV) remain that will have to be discussed (along with full presentation of the tree structures) in a sequel to this paper. Thus, apparently some N-YQTL forms can, by explicit coordination and parallelism (non-paraphrastic), be promoted to the primary line of instruction (Exod 26:15–30, especially v. 22). This is quite exceptional to the usual use of N-YQTL clauses as preparatory or ancillary in the secondary line of instruction. In the same paragraph (v. 20) an apparent nominal clause is on the main line of instruction, but here a kind of verb gapping occurs and a WQTL can be supplied from what precedes. I also note that minus *waw* in a N-YQTL form demotes it to band 4 (specification).

Suffice it to say: secondary lines have a way of extending upward toward the primary line—whether in narrative (N-QTL) or in instruc-

48   *Discourse Analysis of Biblical Literature*

tional (N-YQTL). In general, however, any scheme of salience for any discourse type in any language has to permit some systematic promotions and demotions to make it work. A system without safety valves self-destructs.

5. Conclusion

In this paper we have moved from the larger concerns of the first two sections to more detailed concerns. In moving from the larger to the smaller concerns it is important to remember that the latter sort of analysis undergirds and supplements the former. Questions of macrostructure (textual meaning) in section 2 are seen to be interwoven with matters of macrosegmentation in section 3. But these concerns are themselves seen to be linked to the study of such linguistic features as the distribution of imperatives, cleft sentences, and pronominal references—although in regard to the ordering of subsegments of the text we resorted again at the end of section 3 to the concept of the macrostructure as a control. Everywhere broader concerns interlace with the narrower details of analysis. In section 4 the linguistic structure of the text, with WQTL forms as the mainline of instruction, is further rounded out with a few details that expedite local exegesis, e.g., the absence of initial *waw* in specification constructions, and the WQTL with switch reference as indicative of result/ promise.

Building for the Worship of God

WORKS CONSULTED

Cassuto, U.
    1967   *A Commentary on the Book of Exodus.* Trans. Israel Abrahams. Jerusalem: Magnes.

Childs, Brevard S.
    1974   *The Book of Exodus.* OTL. Philadelphia: Westminster.

Cole, R. Alan
    1973   *Exodus.* Tyndale Old Testament Commentaries. Downers Grove, Illinois: InterVarsity.

Hyatt, J. Philip
    1971   *Exodus.* New Century Bible. Grand Rapids: Eerdmans.

Kennedy, A. R. S.
    1902   "Tabernacle." Pp. 653–68 in *Hastings Dictionary of the Bible.* Vol. 4.

Knight, George A. F.
    1976   *Theology as Narration.* Grand Rapids: Eerdmans.

Levine, Moshe
    1968   *Mĕleket hammiškān.* Tel Aviv: Mlechet Hamishkan.

Longacre, R. E.
    1979   "The Discourse Structure of the Flood Narrative." *JAAR* 47 Sup. B:89–133.
    1982   "Discourse Typology in Relation to Language Typology." Pp. 457–486 in *Text Processing*, ed. Sture Allén. Stockholm: Almqvist and Wiksel.
    1983   *The Grammar of Discourse.* New York: Plenum.
    1989   *Joseph, A Story of Divine Providence: A Text Theoretical and Textlinguistic Analysis of Gen. 37 and 39–46.* Winona Lake, IN: Eisenbrauns.

Noth, Martin
    1962   *Exodus.* OTL. Trans. John Bowden. Philadelphia: Westminster.

Pixley, George V.
    1987   *Exodus: A Liberation Perspective.* Maryknoll, NY: Orbis.

Wendland, Ernst H.
    1985   *Exodus.* Milwaukee: Northwestern.

9

GENESIS AS SOAP OPERA:
SOME OBSERVATIONS ABOUT STORYTELLING
IN THE HEBREW BIBLE

Robert E. Longacre

ABSTRACT

The patriarchal narratives in Genesis contain some rather startling examples of discontinuity breaks in a story centered around one participant and the intrusion of material treating of others. Is this simply sloppy editing on the part of an editor obliged to piece together various materials into one narrative or is there some artistic-stylistic motivation? This article adopts the second alternative and compares the effect achieved to similar effects achieved in serial drama in contemporary media.

The thesis of this paper is that some apparent instances of editorial/compiler/author ineptness in the stories of Genesis might better be considered as artful devices of the storyteller's craft. I propose, in particular, to examine some discontinuities in the patriarch accounts with this thesis in mind. The relevant passages are (1) the discontinuity in the Joseph story which is occasioned by the intrusion of chapter 38, the story of Judah and Tamar; (2) the discontinuity in the Jacob story occasioned by the positioning of chapter 26 between 25:19-34 and chapters 27-35; and (3) chapters 14 and 18:16-19:38 as somewhat intrusive in the Abraham story. It is of possible relevance that the most outrageous intrusion is (1) above, with (2) a close second, and (3) less distressing; i.e., the use of the literary device which I describe here is more accentuated the farther we travel through Genesis from chapter 12 to the end of the book.

In saying that certain passages are apparently intrusive I am not arguing that the intrusive material is irrelevant to the author/compiler's purposes. All the material has to do with the patriarchal family and its extensions. The question simply put is: why does the farther material intrude into the main stories at the point that it does?

Before referring to the particular material and problems at hand, I locate the passages in their context in the relevant *tōlĕdôt* 'genealogy' sections of Genesis. The whole story of Joseph, e.g., is the most prominent thread in "the life and times of Jacob"—pursuant to the convention of naming a section of patriarchal history after an established clan head who is the father of the main participant in that portion of the story. So "the life and times of Jacob" includes the Joseph story and other material which has to do with Jacob's family. Likewise "the life and times of Isaac" (25:19), while almost entirely concerned with Jacob contains some further material on the life of Isaac himself. And, finally, "the life and times of Terah" (11:27), while largely concerned with his famous descendant Abraham, contains extensive material about another of Terah's descendants, Lot. The author/compiler's purposes are never narrowly confined to the chief participant who is the son of the clan head. Nevertheless, the query here is: why is certain material in each section positioned so as to break the continuity of the main story in each *tōlĕdôt* section.

1. Chapter 37 and the Joseph story. In chapter 37:2–36 the Joseph story begins by recounting the darkest happening in the patriarchal account: the hatred of Joseph's brothers for Joseph and the sale of him into Egypt as a slave. Deceit, incipient violence, and outright mayhem (cf. chapter 35) are by no means unknown in previous parts of patriarchal history—cf. Jacob as master trickster and Esau's hatred for him, but here in Genesis 37 hatred and violence rend the patriarchal family itself.

The account in chapter 37 is graphic and dramatic: Jacob's open favoritism of Joseph, Joseph's outrageous dreams of grandeur and power, Joseph's quest for his brothers at Dothan and at Shechem, the brothers' debate as to how to dispose of him, his seizure when arriving on the scene, the sighting of the caravan in the distance, the sale of Joseph at the arrival of the caravan, the attempted cover-up, and finally, Jacob's uncontrollable grief. The account is fast moving and graphic. There is, however, a strangely omitted scene about which we learn later in 42:21: Joseph's tears and protestations, as he is sold by his brothers.

A few extremely unusual devices occur: (1) the sighting of Joseph in the distance, the conspiratorial consultation regarding him, and his seizure when arriving on the scene (37:18–24) is paralleled by the sighting of the caravan in the distance, the discussion regarding selling Joseph, and the actual sale of Joseph when the caravan arrives (37:25–28); (2) the occurrence of the proper name Joseph three times in 37:28:—"they pulled Joseph out of the cistern, they sold Joseph for twenty pieces of silver, and the Ishmaelites carried Joseph away to Egypt." The use of the proper name three times in succeeding sentences is clearly beyond all sober needs of participant identification and tracking; clearly rhetorical emphasis of some sort is intended. In fact, in all but the more literal translations the threefold occurrence of the proper name is not found—whether in English or in translations in some thirty-five languages east to west across Africa (where I offered consultations in 1986). Here, in the Hebrew text the repetition of the proper name is used to underscore that it was to *Joseph*, Jacob's favorite son, that these things were being done. A loosely paraphrastic translation in English might capture the force of the Hebrew original somewhat as follows:

> And so the unbelievable happens:
> Joseph is pulled up out of the pit.
> Joseph is sold by his brothers for twenty pieces of silver;
> Joseph is carried away into Egypt
> —so much for Jacob's favorite son.

Why does the narrator pull out all the stops on the narrative organ in chapter 37? I refer here to the morphology of stories as given in Longacre (1983) (with roots going back to Aristotle). A story of a rather straightforward sort begins with a *stage*, followed by an *inciting incident, mounting tension, climax* (of difficulty and confrontation), and *denouement* (an incident which makes resolution possible), *final suspense/wind down* and *closure*. A story is a story if and only if it has a plot. But a plot inevitably turns on the occurrence of something out of the ordinary. To be sure, stories are made from the stuff of life, and large areas of life can be reduced to something as the order of predictable routine sequences or scripts. But a story requires the breaking of such a script. This is the inciting incident which is essential to plot structure. Furthermore, while a story customarily employs some special stylistic marking (peak) on its climax and/or denouement, it may also mark the inciting incident in some such way. And this is precisely what we find in chapter 37. Special resources as seen above are employed to mark the very unbrotherly action of Joseph's brothers (departure from accepted family norms), and the resulting trauma and grief—not only to Jacob but, as we see later, to the brothers themselves: grief on the one side and guilt on the other.

If we were capable of divesting ourselves of the knowledge of the outcome of the story, we as readers might well finish chapter 37 with many unanswered questions: What will happen to Joseph now? What of his dreams of lordship and grandeur? What will happen to the rest of the family with their grief and guilt? What will happen to the family chosen of God out of all the families of the earth? Is not all this a climactic anti-fulfillment of the promises given to Abraham? Will dismal failure and frustration be the final word?

Ah, gentle viewer of our drama, put your questions on hold and tune in at this same time, same channel, the day after tomorrow. Meanwhile our program for tomorrow runs the story of how Tamar managed to have children by her father-in-law, Judah; it's an intriguing two-act play.

It is precisely this device of breaking off a story at a highly suspenseful point and delaying for a while its resumption that leads me to the title chosen for this article. But is this not too sophisticated a device for *primitive* literature? The difficulty here is with the prejudice and disparagement represented in the word *primitive*. We need to lay aside the word and the prejudice that lies behind it and recognize that a superb story writer is at work. At any rate, the identical device is used in the Jacob story, to which I now turn.

2. Chapter 26 as discontinuity in the Jacob story. Genesis 25:19a contains the caption "This is the life and times of Abraham's son Isaac." This is followed in 19b–36 with a further brief account of Isaac's marriage to Rebekah (cf. the fuller account in chapter 24) as well as of the circumstances relating to the birth of Esau and Jacob (vv. 21–26), brief character sketches of the two as grown men (vv. 27–28), and finally the story of Esau's selling his birthright to Jacob (vv. 28–34). But the following section, chapter 26 (35 verses) is concerned not with Jacob but with Isaac's doings among the Philistines of Gerar and at Beersheba along with a footnote-like addition regarding Esau's marriages (vv. 34, 35).

Probably vv. 29–34 can be considered to be the inciting incident of the Jacob story. Although enmity and strife between Esau and Jacob was prophesied, and although the two grown men are presented as two very different sorts of individuals, and although the family was split down the center (with Isaac preferring Esau and Rebekah preferring Jacob), no match is put to the wood of this potential fire until Jacob maneuvers his brother into selling him the birthright. Later, after Jacob has also cheated his brother out of the paternal blessing, Esau is heard to complain (37:26): "First he took my birthright (*běkōratî*), and now he's taken my blessing (*běraktî*)."

But—much as in the Joseph story—the plot is scarcely put into motion before the Jacob story breaks off to give us a chapter on the doings of Isaac in Gerar and Beersheba. The latter is, of course, important material and revelatory of the character and personality of Isaac. Again, however, chapter 26 is intrusive as far as the continuity of the main story in this section. When the main story resumes in chapter 27, where Esau is further victimized by Jacob, we see that the Esau-Jacob trouble drives much of the continuing story, viz., Jacob's flight to Padan-Aram, his acquiring wives and children and possessions there, his return to Canaan, and his fearful anticipation of seeing Esau again—leading to the mysterious episode at Peniel and the changing of Jacob's name to Israel. Only with chapter 33, the peaceful meeting with Esau, are these matters resolved. Further episodes and subplots (including the rape of Dinah and the sacking of Shechem) carry the section forward to the death of Isaac and his burial by both his sons (35:28–29). The *tōlĕdôt* of Isaac, equivalent for the most part with the story of Jacob, is followed by skeletal but double *tōlĕdôt* of Esau (chapter 36) before the beginning of the *tōlĕdôt* of Jacob, which is, for the most part, equivalent to the Joseph story.

What then? In chapter 25:19b–34 the author/compiler stages the Jacob story, presents its inciting incident of Esau's sale of his birthright to Jacob, then promptly breaks off the story to resume it again in chapter 27. Again, is this authorial/editorial ineptness or is it the storyteller's art at work? I repeat, the material in chapter 26 is vital in that it gives us much of what we know about Isaac, that rather nondescript link between Abraham and Jacob; but why is this material positioned where it is?

Again, we are tempted to draw a parallel with the discontinuity and suspense of the radio programs of yesterday and the television programs of today. The message is, "Gentle hearer/viewer, tune in again at this same station/channel as scheduled in order to resolve further questions: Will the sale of the birthright stand up? Where will the budding rivalry and bad feeling between the brothers carry the story? Granted the prophecy before birth that 'the older will serve the younger' how will it be brought about? And how will a trickster like Jacob turn out in the end? Will his character develop so as to make him a worthy link in the succession of those who inherit the Abrahamic promises? Don't miss the ensuing broadcasts."

3. The story of Lot as a foil in the story of Abraham (Gen. 13:5–14:24; 18:16–19:38). The story of Abraham proceeds from the initial call and promise (12:1–3), through a series of anti-fulfillments (Abraham in Egypt and at Gerar, Abraham and Hagar), visions and covenants (15 and 17), specific promises regarding the birth of Isaac (18), the birth of the long-awaited heir (21), God's testing of Abraham (22), the death and burial of Sarah, the finding of a wife for Isaac (24), and Abraham's last days and burial. These episodes (including the contretemps) are certainly the main story and embody its thrust: Abram/Abraham's sojourn in Canaan, the land promise, and the miraculous provision of an heir. The accompanying spiritual development of Abraham in spite of certain ineffectual and non-productive actions on his part, moves forward to a climax with the sacrifice on Mount Moriah. Through the call and migration, the land promise motif, and the providing of a promised heir, there is the story of a spiritual pilgrimage as well.

But what of the subplot revolving around Lot? Abraham in bringing Lot along is pictured as a responsible clan head who cares for his nephew whose father has died. Almost from the start there are problems. The herdsmen of Lot begin to quarrel with the herdsmen of Abraham regarding pasture and waterholes. In chapter 13 Abraham suggests that Lot and he separate their households and herds. Given a choice of going in one direction or the other, Lot moves his tent toward the plain of the Jordan and toward the cities that were there. It is at once a selfish choice ("the land was well watered like the garden of the Lord, like the land of Egypt" 13:10) and a wrong choice ("the men of Sodom were wicked and were sinning greatly against the Lord" 13:13). Abraham's distress at Lot's choice was presumably assuaged by God's renewed promise, which says in effect, "Don't worry; your descendants are to have *all* this land someday" (13:14–17).

In chapter 14, however, Lot's selfish and unwise choice leads to his getting caught up in international developments that are much beyond his control. Strong forces from Mesopotamia sweep down on the Negev on a punitive expedition directed against people who live to the southwest of the Dead Sea. On swinging back north the invading forces defeat the forces of the Cities of the Plain, sacking them, and carrying off captives and spoil (including Lot and his household). On receiving word, Abraham and some allied chieftains set out in hot pursuit, catch up with the rear guard, which presumably travel slowly with the captives and spoils, launch a night attack, and recover everything. The chase takes Abraham far afield ("to Habah north of Damascus"). On returning he meets up with (to us) a mysterious figure, Melchisedek, king of Jerusalem, "priest of El Elyon", who blesses Abraham and receives tithes from him. The possessions and captives are returned to the newly rescued King of Sodom and to his people.

But is chapter 14 not a strange, Lawrence-of-Arabia-like, wide screen, Hollywood scenario? Nowhere is Abraham pictured as a warrior and organizer of military forces except here. Consequently, many have regarded chapter 14 as an intrusion which is somewhat uncomfortably spliced into the Abraham story. An intrusion it is, but not necessarily an uncomfortable one. Perhaps it is broadly resemblant to chapters 38 and 26, which are discussed above—although Abraham remains the central character even in the intrusion. At any rate, the story of Abraham's spiritual pilgrimage is scarcely begun ere it is broken off and he is away to the wars.

So, gentle viewer, bear with us as we watch Abraham waging war as a successful sheik; we'll come back next week to continue the main story.

The story of Lot, however, does not end with chapter 14. Having learned nothing from his terrifying experience, Lot settles in again at Sodom. Now, however, divine judgment is to fall on the Cities of the Plain. Here the story of Abraham's spiritual development and his obtaining an heir merges with the story of God's judgment on the Cities. The same angelic visit that notifies Abraham of the heir that Sarah is to bear him warns him of the coming destruction. So the end of chapter 18 pictures Abraham interceding for the Cities before God Almighty and finally ceasing his prayers on receiving God's assurance that if ten righteous men are found in Sodom, God will not destroy it.

It does not compute: Lot and his extended family do not tally up to "ten righteous people" that Abraham has envisioned. Consequently chapter 19 pictures the rescue of Lot and the fiery destruction of the Cities. But, alas! although Lot flees from Sodom, his wife falls under the ban for looking back. And the daughters on taking refuge in a cave with Lot subject their father to incest and bear children by him. And so runs the inglorious end of the inglorious story of Lot's degeneration—quite the converse of Abraham's development.

Gentle viewer, if you have borne with us this far, tune in again at this station as future programs return to the story of Abraham in its climactic developments: the birth of the Crown Prince, the Crown Prince's life required and spared, the death and burial of the Queen Mother, a Royal wedding, and finally the death of the King. You will get your fill of high drama!

Conclusion

Genesis has its own built-in devices of cliff-hanging suspense and involved scenarios. The author/compiler was not, however, an overworked editor hastily pasting stories together for the morning paper, but a superb storyteller. To the theist, Genesis pictures God everywhere at work against varied and often sordid scenarios of jealousy, violence, deceit, and threatened or actual disaster, and bringing to fulfillment his own plans in spite of all man does. And at the same time it does not make dull reading.

BIOGRAPHY

Robert Longacre has a Ph.D. from the University of Pennsylvania and is Professor Emeritus at the University of Texas at Arlington, where he taught for twenty-one years. As a field-worker under the Summer Institute of Linguistics he studied Chicahuaxtla Trique and translated the New Testament into that language (1968). He has also served under SIL as an international consultant in linguistics and translation. Biblical Hebrew has been one of his perennial interests over the past two decades (Cf. *Joseph, a Story of Divine Providence*. Winona Lake: Eisenbraums, 1989).

REFERENCES

Licht, Jacob, 1978. Storytelling in the Bible. Jerusalem: The Hebrew University, Magnes Press.

Ska, Jean Louis, S.J., 1990. "Our fathers have told us." Introduction to the analysis of Hebrew narratives. Rome: Studia Biblica 13: Editrice Pontificio Istituto Biblica.

EXHORTATION AND MITIGATION IN FIRST JOHN

Robert E. Longacre

During a recent linguistic workshop in the Philippines, we were exploring the structure of Hortatory Discourse in several languages. Using the concept of mitigation (Labov & Fanshel 1977:84-86), i.e. ways of toning down a command so as to make it more socially acceptable, we noticed that mitigation of a high order could, in effect, reduce a hortatory text to a structure which approaches that of expository discourse. At this point in our research, the tie-in of mitigated hortatory discourse with certain other elements of Philippine culture (avoidance of direct confrontation, the oblique approach to a problem, and "face saving") suggested itself. At the same time parallels with the Greek New Testament also claimed attention. Thus, it can fairly be argued, no New Testament epistle is basically expository—although many contain embedded expository discourses of varying length. Rather, in the New Testament "truth is in order to holiness", i.e. doctrine is not expounded simply to satisfy intellectual curiosity but the exposition is tied in to more or less overt exhortation to live differently from those who are not in possession of such truth. Leaving aside, therefore, tempting cultural comparisons (e.g. our blunt Anglo-Saxon culture vs. a more "gracious" Philippine or Latin culture vs. the cultural milieu implied by New Testament exhortations), I address here the question of exhortation and mitigation in one New Testament book, the first epistle of John.

In discussing exhortation and mitigation in the Greek text of 1 John, I will present my view of the overall structure of the book, assume (and at least partially justify) a segmentation into paragraphs, and present the structure of various paragraphs both in relation to notional and surface structure. A progress of sorts is seen in the book in that the commands are at first highly mitigated but surface and become more overt as the epistle develops.[1]

The basic schema in a hortatory discourse is: problem, command, motivation.[2] In 1 John, the schema is repetitive and recursive and runs through component sentences of the text instead of determining three major sections. The surface structure of the book is that of a long, somewhat overbalanced, and meandering Introduction (1:1—2:29), Body (3:1—5:12), and Closure (5:13-21). In turn, the individual sentences have a general surface structure ± preposed + main + postposed—where preposed elements are conditional adverbial clauses ("if" clauses) or articular participial phrases; and where postposed elements are adverbial cause clauses (hoti) or purpose clauses (hina)—plus a rare element or two to be described below. The sentences are bound to each other mainly by lexical cross-reference which often involves a parallelism of structure between successive sentences. Explicit connectives, kai 'and' and gar 'for', are occasionally employed to relate successive sentences. Vocatives serve mainly to delineate paragraphs; an occasional preposed subject (humeis) also occurs. The cataphoric en toutō which occurs initial in some sentences is cohesive within its own sentence; it anticipates and topicalizes some postposed element.

It would be tempting to try to correlate directly the tripartite structure of the sentence with the tripartite schema mentioned above. Thus we could have

4   S T A R T   NO. 9

the following in an English Hortatory discourse which tries to get people to give up smoking: "In that smoking causes all this physical damage, give it up for the sake of a longer and better life." Here the preposed element is circumstantial and mirrors the problem (smoking impairs health in many ways), the main clause "give it up" is the command element, and the postposed element, a purpose construction, is motivational. But we shall see in our examination of the text of 1 John that while this is a frequent arrangement, the tripartite surface structure grammar and the tripartite schema are only rarely thus neatly used in phase.

A word is in order here about "paragraph" and "sentence" as used in this study. Both are treated as structural rather than simply as orthographic units. Furthermore, both units are recursive in structure. While the paragraph is essentially a structured combination of sentences, a paragraph-level slot may be filled not only by a sentence but, alternatively, by an embedded paragraph. Similarly, while the sentence is essentially a combination of clauses, a sentence-level slot may be filled not only by a clause but, alternatively, by an embedded sentence. It is evident that the simple orthographic devices of indentation (to mark only primary paragraph divisions) and period, comma, and colon, to mark off sentences, and some of the relevant divisions within sentences, cannot prove at all adequate to represent intricate nestings of paragraph-within-paragraph and sentence-within-sentence. In fact, these two considerations are somewhat in conflict. Thus, while comma and colon could be fruitfully employed to distinguish two layers of complexity within the sentence, the colon (and sometimes the comma) is frequently employed to join two or more shorter sentences which constitute an embedded paragraph.

In the displays which are given for the various paragraphs within the epistle, I try, therefore, to do two things: (1) To take the sentence seriously as a structural unit—so that I do not carry my analysis as far as specifying the internal structure of the sentence. (2) On the other hand, I have to ignore at many points the editor's punctuation of the Greek text in our effort to cut down to the structural as opposed to merely orthographic sentences.

In cutting my analysis off at the sentence and not concerning myself with the further relations within the sentence, I do not mean to imply that the latter are unimportant. I simply mean to show that a great deal can be learned about this epistle by studying the inter-sentential and inter-paragraph relations. Traditional exegetical commentaries handle most of the intrasentential questions.

Before plunging into the book itself, a few statistical counts are in order. These counts catalogue the types of verbs which are found in independent clauses. The purpose of this classification and counting is to give an overall impression of the general cast of the surface structure of the book, i.e. does the Epistle have and overall expository cast or an overall hortatory cast?

An expository discourse should highlight the most static clauses of the language as its mainline, while a hortatory discourse should highlight command forms. Static clauses are relational rather than active. In 1 John there are 83 instances of main clauses that have "be", "have", or null in place of "be", or the verb "remain/stay". These main clauses are clearly static and relational. Twenty-four verbs of acquaintance or awareness ("know", etc.) also occur in main clauses; these likewise picture a static relation. Thirteen perfect verbs occur, some of which are clearly static in thrust. Twenty-five presents and futures occur. Eighteen performative verbs (testify, announce, write) occur, but mainly in chapters 1 and 2. Five narrative (aorist) verbs occur, each of which presumably could have begun an embedded narrative. Finally, sixteen command forms occur, i.e. imperatives, cohortatives ("let us love"), jussive ("let him love his brother also"), and 'ought' forms. Of the 184 verbs which were catalogued, the 83 "be", "have", or null clauses, and "remain/stay" clauses account for 45%. Acquaintance-awareness "know" verbs constitute an additional 13% which, if added to the above, gives a total of 58% of the main verbs that are decidedly relational and static. The overt command forms, by contrast, constitute only 9%. Obviously, the general cast of the surface structure of 1 John looks decidedly more expository than hortatory. Nevertheless, the matter is not to be settled so simply by appeal to verb classification and counting!

In the following exposition, I shall consider first the Introduction to the Epistle, then its Body and Closure—since, as we have said, the first section is quite extensive. I consider that the use of the verb "write" is diagnostic of both Introduction and Closure, but does not occur in the body of the book. Essentially, the writer of the Epistle starts off to explain in the Introduction why he is writing the epistle. He then proceeds in the Introduction itself to bring in many of the themes which are found in the Body. The argument proceeds mainly by overlay,[3] i.e. old material is repeated and some new material stirred in as the Introduction proceeds. The Introduction is a slot filled by an embedded discourse which has its own peak (cumulative development).

1. The Introduction (1:1—2:29)

I will not consider here in detail the paragraph constituted by verses 1:1-4. They seem to constitute an opening of both the whole epistle and of the discourse which embeds in the Introduction. This passage is, however, unique in several respects: (1) in its largely expository structure with behavioral implicates found only in the final purpose clauses of verses 3 and 4, (2) in its array of tense/aspect forms which are somewhat unique: (a) the only true imperfect tenses in the whole epistle are found here (ēn, 'was'); (b) there is a preponderance of perfects (akēkoamen, heōrakamen); (c) there is a sprinkling of aorists—enough to suggest a set of historical contingencies; and (d) there are some performative presents (marturoumen, apaggellomen, graphomen). The whole thing is of the following structure: "The Word of life was (impf.) from the beginning, but was manifested (aorist) in time. We have heard and seen it (perfects, i.e. past events, with continuing implications for the present), and we tell (present) you about it, so that you may have fellowship with us and so that your joy will be full."

I consider that the Introduction, itself an embedded discourse, contains three pre-peak points, a double peak (ethical and doctrinal) and a closure. In gross structure it resembles the body of the epistle, which has four pre-peak points, a double peak (doctrinal and ethical) and a post-peak point.

1.1 Point 1 (P-3) (i.e. Peak minus 3) 1:1-10

I consider that Point 1 is three removed from the Peak (2:12-27) of the Introduction.

6   S T A R T NO. 9

Before looking at the surface constituent structure of this paragraph, note that 1:5 is essentially introductory in its own paragraph; it contains a backreference to 1:1-4 ("and this is the message which we've heard from Him and announce to you") and then states a basic value (light vs. darkness) that is used in the motivational structure: "God is light and in Him is no darkness at all." The remaining sentences of the paragraph are conditional. Sentences six and seven involve an antithesis, and sentences 8-10 another (cyclical) antithesis. For this reason, I consider 6-7 to constitute the first Item of the coordinate paragraph of which sentences 8-10 are the second Item. Note the structure as displayed in Display I.

1 JOHN 1:5-10 (E) COORDINATE PARAGRAPH
(covert exhortations)
(performative in intro)

5.   INTRO: καὶ ἔστιν αὕτη ἡ ἀγγελία ἣν ἀκηκόαμεν ἀπ' αὐτοῦ καὶ ἀναγγέλλομεν

  ὑμῖν, ὅτι ὁ θεὸς φῶς ἐστιν καὶ σκοτία ἐν αὐτῷ οὐκ ἔστιν οὐδεμία.

  ITEM$_1$: ANTITHETICAL PARAGRAPH

6.   THESIS: ἐὰν εἴπωμεν ὅτι κοινωνίαν ἔχομεν μετ' αὐτοῦ καὶ ἐν τῷ σκότει

  περιπατῶμεν, ψευδόμεθα καὶ οὐ ποιοῦμεν τὴν ἀλήθειαν·

7.   ANTI: ἐὰν δὲ ἐν τῷ φωτὶ περιπατῶμεν ὡς αὐτός ἐστιν ἐν τῷ φωτί,

  κοινωνίαν ἔχομεν μετ' ἀλλήλων καὶ τὸ αἷμα

  Ἰησοῦ τοῦ υἱοῦ αὐτοῦ καθαρίζει ἡμᾶς ἀπὸ πάσης ἁμαρτίας.

8.   ITEM$_2$: CYCLIC ANTI. PARAGRAPH

  THESIS: ἐὰν εἴπωμεν ὅτι ἁμαρτίαν οὐκ ἔχομεν, ἑαυτοὺς πλανῶμεν καὶ ἡ

  ἀλήθεια οὐκ ἔστιν ἐν ἡμῖν.

9.   ANTI: ἐὰν ὁμολογῶμεν τὰς ἁμαρτίας ἡμῶν, πιστός ἐστιν καὶ δίκαιος ἵνα

  ἀφῇ ἡμῖν τὰς ἁμαρτίας καὶ καθαρίσῃ ἡμᾶς ἀπὸ πάσης ἀδικίας.

10.   THESIS: ἐὰν εἴπωμεν ὅτι οὐχ ἡμαρτήκαμεν, ψεύστην ποιοῦμεν αὐτὸν καὶ ὁ

  λόγος αὐτοῦ οὐκ ἔστιν ἐν ἡμῖν.

DISPLAY I

EXHORTATION AND MITIGATION IN FIRST JOHN

I consider this paragraph to be Expository. Note the verbs in the main clauses: pseudometha, ou poioumen (tēn alētheian) in 6; (koinōnian) echomen, katharizei in 7; estin in 8 and 9, (pseustēn) poioumen (auton) and estin in 10. Plainly echō and eimi are prominent here and several present tense verbs. Nothing approaches the level of a command form of any sort.

But this is not the whole story. Looking at the component sentences in more detail, we note that not only every sentence except that which is found in v. 5 is conditional, but that certain further features occur as well: (a) the main clauses inculcate a value system to which (b) the conditional clauses are related so that (c) correlations are set up between alternative behavioral choices and those values. Thus, we have "truth" in 6 and 8 as opposed to the verbal expressions "lie" (6), "deceive ourselves" (8), and "make God a liar" (10). Note also "have His word in us" (=truth in 10). We also have the positive values "fellowship" (7 and the conditional clause of 6), "cleansing from sin" (7 and 9), and "forgiveness" (9); the corresponding negative values are not stated.

Clearly, then, the main clauses express both the problem (a universe that is morally and spiritually polarized) and the motivation—which holds provided that one accepts the indicated positive values. What, then, of the preposed "if" clauses? They now emerge as covert commands. Thus, to say (6) "if we say that we have fellowship with him and walk in darkness, we lie and do not the truth" becomes equivalent to "don't say that you have fellowship with Him and walk in darkness—because you don't want to be on the side of the lie rather than on the side of truth". A supporting concern here is that "fellowship" is good (as presented in 7) and "darkness" is bad (as in vs. 5), therefore, to try to have fellowship with God and walk in darkness is to attempt a moral contradiction.

The passage proceeds on (7): "If we walk in the light as He is in the light (further echo of vs. 6) we have fellowship with each other and the blood of Jesus Christ His Son cleanses us from every sin." Here since the main clause encodes positive values, the covert command is "Walk in the light". Proceeding thus through the paragraph we obtain the following covert commands: "Don't say that you have no sin" (vs. 8); "Confess your sins" (vs. 9); and "Don't say that you've never sinned" (vs. 10). The positive values on which these covert commands hinge are truth, and cleansing from sin.

I believe, then, that this paragraph (1 John 1:5-10) is expository in surface structure but hortatory in its underlying or notional structure.

1.2. Point 2 (P-2) 2:1-6

It seems that a new paragraph is intended here because (a) a vocative begins the passage (2:1), and there is a renewed reference to "write". Thus tauta graphō humin can be compared to the reference to announcement (anaggellomen) which is in the first sentence of the preceding paragraph (1:5).

As for the internal structure of this paragraph, I group verses 1-2 over against 3-6. The former announces a Text whose Reason is expressed in the balance of the paragraph. The Text has an appended Concession which, in turn, has the structure of a comment paragraph. The Reason is developed as an amplification paragraph whose own Text is a cyclical antithetical paragraph. The Amplification of this Text is a single sentence. See Display II.

8   S T A R T   NO. 9

                 1 JOHN 2:1-6 (H) REASON PARAGRAPH
                 (overt commands, but buried in sentence margin and in complement)

      TEXT: CONCESSIVE PARAGRAPH

1.   TEXT: τεκνία μου, ταῦτα γράφω ὑμῖν ἵνα μὴ ἁμάρτητε.

      CONC: (E) COMMENT

             TEXT: καὶ ἐάν τις   ἁμάρτῃ, παράκλητον ἔχομεν πρὸς τὸν πατέρα,
             Ἰησοῦν   Χριστὸν δίκαιον·
2.   COMMENT: καὶ αὐτὸς ἱλασμός ἐστιν περὶ τῶν   ἁμαρτιῶν ἡμῶν, οὐ περὶ τῶν
             ἡμετέρων δὲ μόνον ἀλλὰ καὶ περὶ   ὅλου τοῦ κόσμου.

      REASON: AMPLIFICATION PARAGRAPH

      TEXT: ANTITHETICAL PARAGRAPH (CYCLIC)

3.   THESIS: καὶ ἐν τούτῳ γινώσκομεν ὅτι ἐγνώκαμεν αὐτόν, ἐὰν τὰς ἐντολὰς
      αὐτοῦ τηρῶμεν.
4.   ANTI: ὁ λέγων ὅτι Ἔγνωκα αὐτόν, καὶ τὰς ἐντολὰς αὐτοῦ μὴ τηρῶν, ψεύστης
      ἐστίν, καὶ ἐν τούτῳ ἡ   ἀλήθεια οὐκ ἔστιν·
5.   THESIS: ὃς δ' ἂν τηρῇ αὐτοῦ τὸν λόγον, ἀληθῶς ἐν τούτῳ ἡ   ἀγάπη τοῦ
      θεοῦ τετελείωται.

      AMPL: ἐν   τούτῳ   γινώσκομεν   ὅτι ἐν   αὐτῷ   ἐσμεν·
6.   ὁ   λέγων ἐν αὐτῷ μένειν ὀφείλει καθὼς ἐκεῖνος περιεπάτησεν καὶ αὐτὸς οὕτως
      [οὕτως] περιπατεῖν.

      [The reasons don't go with the "I write" but with the "Don't sin!"]

                              DISPLAY II

     In support of this analysis note the sequence signals which tag the
internal structure of this paragraph. The second main half of the paragraph,
the Reason unit, is introduced by kai en toutō, which is cataphoric within its
own sentence: the ean clause, which is normally preposed, is here postposed as
the cataphoric referent. The Antithesis of the embedded cyclical antithetical
paragraph is unmarked, but the Thesis' (repetition of the thesis) is marked by
de, which is weakly contrastive and often signals a change of participant
referent. This is followed by an amplification of all the above; the onset of

the Amplification employs the en toutō cataphoric phrase whose cataphoric referent is, in this case, a whole sentence: "He who says that he remains in Him, must walk even as that one walked." Here the second en toutō marks the sentence (vs. 6) as an enlargement/paraphrase/what-have-you of the unit (vss. 3-5) which likewise is marked with en toutō in verse 3.

Is this paragraph expository or hortatory? It has no overt command form as such. A subjunctive clause hina mē hamartēte occurs, however, as a postposed element in 2:1. Furthermore, the "reason" appended in vss. 3-6 clearly goes with the mē hamartēte in sense rather than with the tauta graphō. Thus the sense of the paragraph is "Don't sin, because in keeping God's commands (the opposite of sinning) we can be sure that we know God and we can have God's love perfected in us". The opposite course—saying we know God and not keeping His commands—makes us a liar. Or, to put it differently, in walking as he walked (i.e. in not sinning) we can be sure that we are in Him! The command element of this paragraph is, then, expressed in a postposed element of the first sentence, but semantically dominates the paragraph.

The appended Concession (1b, 2) simply recognizes that if we sin we have an advocate, while the accompanying Comment makes clear that this advocacy involves propitiation and is universal in scope. Note that the preposed clause in 2:1b is not a covert command either to sin or not to sin since the clause paraklēton echomen pros ton patera is more of a factual note than a value which is appealed to. It clearly cannot mean "Sin!" because 1a tells us that this sense is precisely what is not intended.

Because of the centrality of 2:1a to the structure of this paragraph, the decision as to whether this paragraph is hortatory or expository depends on our interpretation of this verse. In paragraph structure it is the most salient material that is most diagnostic of type. It seems, therefore, that since 2:1a is a command expressed via a performative, and is the Text of the Text unit ("I write these things to you so that you won't sin"), we must call this paragraph hortatory. Notice also how this is reinforced in the cataphoric complement of sentence 6 as a positive command: "Must walk as that one walked." Notice also the covert commands of verses 3-5. Here knowing God, truth (vs. being a liar), God's love perfected in us, and abiding in God are positive values (with truth repeated from the previous paragraph). This gives the preposed elements of clauses 3-5 the thrust of command elements, whether the element is a (transposed) conditional clause (vs. 3), a participial element (vs. 4), or an indefinite relative hos d' an (whosoever) clause (vs. 5). The thrust of these elements is: (a) "Keep His commandments"; (b) "Don't say you know Him when you don't keep His commands"; and (c) "Keep His word".

While the paragraph which is found in 1:5-10 seems to be expository in surface structure but hortatory in its notional structure, this paragraph 2:1-6 seems to qualify structurally as hortatory both in its surface and in its notional structure. It is of some interest, however, that the diagnostic command forms appear there only in postposed, nonnuclear elements in verses 1b and 6—so that it is only after considerable analysis and re-analysis that the decision to classify its surface structure as hortatory is reached.

1.3 Point 3 (P-1) 2:7-11

This paragraph is one of the most subtle pieces of argumentation in the whole epistle. It broaches indirectly one of the main themes of the

10   S T A R T   NO. 9

epistle—the inescapable obligation to love—but in a paragraph the surface
structure of which is clearly expository throughout. This paragraph, like the
previous, begins with a vocative, agapētoi, and the verb, graphō 'write', which
is repeated in vs. 8.

                1 JOHN 2:7-11 (E) CYCLIC ANTI. PARAGRAPH

   INTRO: ANTI PARAGRAPH

      THESIS: COMMENT PARAGRAPH

7.   TEXT: ἀγαπητοί, οὐκ ἐντολὴν καινὴν γράφω ὑμῖν, ἀλλ' ἐντολὴν παλαιὰν ἣν
                  εἴχετε ἀπ' ἀρχῆς·

         COMMENT: ἡ ἐντολὴ ἡ παλαιά ἐστιν ὁ   λόγος ὃν   ἠκούσατε.

8.   ANTI: πάλιν ἐντολὴν καινὴν γράφω ὑμῖν, ὅ   ἐστιν ἀληθὲς ἐν αὐτῷ καὶ ἐν
             ὑμῖν, ὅτι ἡ σκοτία παράγεται καὶ τὸ   φῶς τὸ ἀληθινὸν ἤδη φαίνει.

9.   THESIS: ὁ λέγων ἐν τῷ φωτὶ εἶναι καὶ τὸν ἀδελφὸν αὐτοῦ   μισῶν   ἐν τῇ
               σκοτίᾳ ἐστὶν ἕως ἄρτι.

10.   ANTI: ὁ ἀγαπῶν τὸν ἀδελφὸν αὐτοῦ ἐν τῷ φωτὶ μένει, καὶ σκάνδαλον ἐν
             αὐτῷ οὐκ ἔστιν·

11.   THESIS': ὁ δὲ   μισῶν τὸν ἀδελφὸν αὐτοῦ ἐν τῇ σκοτίᾳ ἐστὶν καὶ ἐν τῇ
                σκοτίᾳ περιπατεῖ, καὶ οὐκ οἶδεν ποῦ ὑπάγει, ὅτι ἡ σκοτία ἐτύφλωσεν τοὺς
                ὀφθαλμοὺς αὐτοῦ.

         [No overt commands.
          Connection between new/old command of Intro and
             mitigated commands of body is purely inferential.]

                            DISPLAY III

   I consider this paragraph to be (again) a cyclic antithetical paragraph.
Verses 7 and 8 function as a long introduction which features graphō as the
performative verb in both sentences. These two sentences together constitute an
embedded antithetical paragraph in which "I don't write a new command" (vs. 7)

and "I do write a new command" (vs. 8) are contrasted. Within the thesis of the embedded antithetical paragraph there is a comment paragraph in which 7b, appended to 7a, functions as a further explanation: "The old command is the word which you hear."

Verses 9-11 constitute the nucleus of the paragraph with the three verses identifiable respectively as Thesis, Antithesis, and Thesis'; "hate...darkness, love...light, and hate...darkness" are the crucial lexical pieces—with the metaphor of "darkness" especially well developed in vs. 11: "The one who hates his brother is in darkness, and walks in darkness, and does not know where he is going because the darkness has blinded his eyes."

Except where performatives are dominant in 7 and 8 of the Introduction, the dominating main verbs are static and typical of exposition: estin (in vs. 9), menei and estin (vs.10), estin (vs.11) with two present tense forms added in subsequent coordinate clauses: peripatei and ouk oiden. Even in verses 7 and 8, where the main verb is the performative verb graphō, the verb estin is prominent. Clearly the main paragraph and the embedded paragraphs which are found in the first two verses all conform to the surface structure of exposition.

Nevertheless, in the notional structure the hortatory thrust is evident. In verses 7-8 the author says that he is writing an old-new command to them—but the content of the command is not given. In verses 9-10, the nucleus of the paragraph, highly mitigated commands are given in a form which is by now familiar to us. Again the positive value "light" is contrasted with negative value "darkness". By linking imposed elements to these values, the following covert commands emerge: "Don't say you're in the light when you hate your brother" (vs. 11).

The mentioning of the new-old command in 7-8, and the covert commands "Don't hate, but rather love" in 9-11 make it extremely plausible that the latter supplies the otherwise unstated content of the former. The writer, however, is not willing yet to unveil the main hortatory thrust of the book as overt command forms. After the brief excursion into hortatory form (albeit highly mitigated) in 2:1-6, he drops back here to the expository surface form in which certain values are mentioned and desirable actions are linked with them.

1.4 Peak (ETHICAL) 2:12-17

The most characteristic feature of this passage is the prolonged Introduction in which the verb graphō figures six times in a repetitive pattern in which the first three uses are present tense and the last three uses are aorist. I take the whole unit in verses 12-14 to be an amplification paragraph both parts of which (Text and Amplification) are coordinate paragraphs.

As already observed, the verb graphō appears to be characteristic of introductory parts of the Epistle. It occurs in the prolonged Introduction to the whole book (1:1—2:28) and in its Closure (5:13-20). It occurs in the Introduction to the preceding paragraph. I, therefore, take verses 2:12-14 to be likewise introductory in spite of the elaboration and complexity found here. I do believe, however, that this elaboration and complexity is telling us something, that it is, in fact, signalling a peak of the discourse which embeds within the Introduction to the book.

12   S T A R T   NO. 9

                        1 JOHN 2:12-17 (H) SIMPLE PARAGRAPH
                        (Performatives in Peak/ tense shift in performative here
                              holds for whole book before and after)

       INTRO: AMPLIFICATION PARAGRAPH

         TEXT: COORDINATE PARAGRAPH

12.   ITEM₁: γράφω ὑμῖν, τεκνία, ὅτι ἀφέωνται ὑμῖν αἱ ἁμαρτίαι διὰ τὸ ὄνομα αὐτοῦ.

13.   ITEM₂: γράφω ὑμῖν, πατέρες, ὅτι ἐγνώκατε τὸν ἀπ' ἀρχῆς.

          ITEM₃: γράφω ὑμῖν, νεανίσκοι, ὅτι νενικήκατε τὸν πονηρόν.

         AMPL: COORDINATE PARAGRAPH

14.   ITEM₁: ἔγραψα ὑμῖν, παιδία, ὅτι ἐγνώκατε τὸν πατέρα.

          ITEM₂: ἔγραψα ὑμῖν, πατέρες, ὅτι ἐγνώκατε τὸν ἀπ' ἀρχῆς.

          ITEM₃: ἔγραψα ὑμῖν, νεανίσκοι, ὅτι ἰσχυροί ἐστε
                  καὶ ὁ   λόγος τοῦ θεοῦ ἐν ὑμῖν μένει καὶ νενικήκατε τὸν πονηρόν.

       TEXT: (H) REASON PARAGRAPH

15.   TEXT: μὴ ἀγαπᾶτε τὸν κόσμον μηδὲ τὰ ἐν τῷ κόσμῳ.

         REASON: (E) REASON PARAGRAPH

            TEXT: ἐάν τις   ἀγαπᾷ τὸν κόσμον, οὐκ ἔστιν ἡ   ἀγάπη τοῦ πατρὸς ἐν
            αὐτῷ·

            REASON: (E) ANTI PARAGRAPH

16.   INTRO: ὅτι πᾶν τὸ ἐν τῷ κόσμῳ, ἡ ἐπιθυμία τῆς σαρκὸς καὶ ἡ   ἐπιθυμία
               τῶν ὀφθαλμῶν καὶ ἡ   ἀλαζονεία τοῦ βίου, οὐκ ἔστιν ἐκ τοῦ πατρὸς ἀλλ'
               ἐκ τοῦ κόσμου ἐστίν.

17.   THESIS: καὶ ὁ κόσμος παράγεται καὶ ἡ ἐπιθυμία αὐτοῦ,
               ANTI: ὁ δὲ ποιῶν τὸ θέλημα τοῦ θεοῦ μένει εἰς τὸν αἰῶνα.

The tense switch in the six uses of graphō is not easy to rationalize. The first cycle is present; the second cycle is aorist. It is noteworthy, however, that this is not just a tense shift involving this passage. Rather, all uses of graphō up to and including 2:13 (cf. 1:4, 2:1, 2:7) are present tense in this epistle while all uses of graphō in 2:14 and following are aorist, i.e. egrapsa. Tense-wise, in reference to this performative verb, we are here at the watershed of the book. It is possible that we should think of 2:12-14 as a sort of performative peak even though the performative graphō occurs in 1 John 1 and 2 as ancillary to other main verbs (in paragraph introductions and in 2:1 as grammatically dominant but notionally subordinate to what follows).

Vocatives, which have heretofore been diagnostic of paragraph onset, here occur in each sentence: "children", "fathers", "young men" in 12-13 repeated in 14. The verses which are directed to the "young men" appear to be climactic both in 13b and in 14c. Since no further vocatives occur in 2:15-17, I take the latter three verses to be a continuation of the same paragraph—indeed, as the nucleus of that paragraph.

The whole paragraph 2:12-17 patterns as a simple paragraph in that it consists only of an Introduction and a Text. The Text is a unit which consists of a reason paragraph. The Text of this reason paragraph is clearly vs. 15a: "Don't love the world or the things which are in the world"—since here the highest ranking verb is an imperative. It is, again, a command which involves "love" but which is negative: "Don't love the wrong object (the world)."

All the balance of the paragraph expresses the reason for not "loving the world". The Text of this embedded reason paragraph is 15b. "If any man love the world, the love of the Father is not in him." The Reason is expressed in 16-17, which begin with a hoti 'because'; the internal structure of this further embedded paragraph is an antithetical paragraph. This antithetical paragraph has its own Introduction (vs. 16) which defines what is in the world; a Thesis "The world and its desires are passing away" (17a); and an Antithesis "But he who does the will of God remains forever" (17b).

So much for what I believe to be a plausible view of the surface structure of this paragraph. Note that while the whole paragraph is hortatory—because of the central nature of 16a—the Introductions and supportive material (Reason units) are expository.

Even in the expository sections we find, however, covert exhortation. Thus, in 15b, we have the by now familiar use of a conditional clause to express a covert command; here "if any man love the world" equals "don't love the world" and echoes in mitigated form the overt imperative of the preceding clause. Likewise, in 17b, the articular participle is similarly used so that "he who does the will of God" is equivalent to "do the will of God". The values to which these conditions are attached are "the love of the Father" in 15b and "remaining forever" (= "eternal life") in 17b.

What is the thrust of the six hoti clauses in 12-14? Probably, since they express causes or reasons within their respective sentences, they should best be regarded as expressing motivations. Alternatively they could be regarded as highly mitigated exhortations of the form: "Since X is your identity/norm, continue to act that way." The latter interpretation agrees with 15b and 17b, where "you've conquered the evil one" is perhaps a reminder to keep on conquering the evil one (13b, 14c).

14   S T A R T   NO. 9

Before leaving this paragraph, I note the strong motivational pitch in 16 and 17a where the nature of "the world" (= a system hostile to God) is set forth under three heads and the whole labelled as transient ("and the world passes away along with its desires").

Since this paragraph contains for the first time an imperative, it is considered to embody a Peak, in this case a peak of practical and ethical exhortation: "Don't love the wrong object (but rather God.)" Also the introduction to the paragraph embodies a sort of performative peak, marked by repetition, parallelism, and climax in the use of the verb "write". The semantic connection between the introduction and body of this paragraph seems to lie in the emphasis on "conquering the evil one" (13b and 14c) and "love not the world" as developed in the nucleus of the paragraph.

1.5 Peak (DOCTRINAL) 2:18-27

This paragraph begins with a vocative and shift of topic. Verses 18-23 are clearly expository (note the predominance of eimi and echō) while verses 24-27 are hortatory with the imperatives menetō 'let it remain' and menete 'remain' as the first and last verbs of the passage. How do the two parts of this paragraph relate to each other? I have again termed 18-23 Introduction and considered that 24-27 is the nucleus of the paragraph and embraces two coordinated structures (Items). Undoubtedly John is addicted to long introductions, whether in the epistle as a whole or in certain parts of it. On the other hand, the material in 18-23 is clearly motivational in regard to 24-27. We could consider, therefore, that the whole paragraph has a Reason (18-23)—Text (24-27) structure. I have not done this because: (1) Text-Reason sequences are common in this epistle but Reason-Text is much more poorly attested. (2) The encoding of motivation loosely into a long surface Introduction is, I suspect, quite typical of this writer.

The whole paragraph may be paraphrased and summarized: "It's the last hour, the hour of antichrist; you have an anointing from God; and there's a big lie on the loose—denying the Father and the Son—(so) let the teaching remain in you and be sure that you remain in Him."

I believe that the introductory/motivational material which is found in 18-23 is best construed as a coordinate paragraph. Coordination is a default relationship which is posited where other more specific relationships cannot be readily established. Thus, while kai humeis 'but you' in verse 20 is apparently contrastive with the schismatics and antichrists mentioned in 18-19, the passage does not seem to turn on this simple antithesis. Rather, in vs. 22 it goes off in a different direction with a rhetorical question signalling a new beginning. I have, therefore, simply considered 18-23 to contain three coordinated items as seen in the paraphrase above and in the accompanying display.

The first Item of the Introduction structures as a reason paragraph. The Text is "Little children, it is the last hour" while the rest of verse 18 and all of vs. 19 constitute the Reason. The Reason unit is itself an amplification paragraph whose Text is "and just as you have heard that the antichrist is coming, even now there are many antichrists—whereby we know that it is the last hour". Notice here the explicit final backreference to 18a (and hothen) which amounts to a way of telling us that the sentence in 18b is intended to supply a reason relative to 18a. This is a very regular device in Philippine languages

(Longacre 1968:792-793) and is also occasionally employed in English (Longacre 1970:1.115-120). Verse 19 amplifies this Text by explaining that the many "antichrists" are apostates and schismatics who have separated from the true Christian community. This is itself structured as a further embedded reason paragraph whose Text is "They went out from us but were not really part of us". The Reason (marked with gar) is "For if they had been part of us, they would have remained with us; but they went out from us to demonstrate that all of them (who visibly adhered to us) weren't really part of us." The ellipsis and the resort to a purpose construction further mark 19b as a Reason.

The second Item, or coordinated point, is, as we have said, implicitly contrastive with the first. It structures as a comment paragraph; Comments are typically only loosely associated with the preceding Text. This looseness of association of verse 20 and 21 is seen in the resort to the performative verb, egrapsa (typical of introductory material), in the latter.

The third coordinated Item begins, as we said, with a rhetorical question which could be paraphrased: "No lie can be worse than denying that Jesus is the Christ." This point is developed as an amplification paragraph of which the sentence just referred to (vs. 22) is the Text, and 22b and 23 are the Amplification. The Text of the embedded amplification paragraph is, in effect, an answer to the rhetorical question: "This one is indeed the antichrist, the one who denies the Father and the Son" with the initial houtos cataphorically anticipating the final participial phrase of the sentence. The Amplification of this text is a further embedded paragraph of the antithetical structure which contrasts denial and confession.

Turning down to the nucleus (or body) of the paragraph, we seek an analysis which gives proper weight to the imperatives of vs. 24—and 27 (last clause)—since these are the ranking verbs of the paragraph. I discuss here verses 24 and 25, which constitute Item$_1$ and then verses 26 and 27 which constitute Item$_2$. The whole paragraph (2:18-27) is considered to be a hortatory coordinate paragraph because these two Items constitute the body of the paragraph—and are in coordinate relation to each other—and because the sentences which dominate internally within each Item are unambiguously command forms (Longacre 1982:191-196).

Verses 24-26 constitute a comment paragraph whose Text is a reason paragraph. The Text of this reason paragraph is 24a: "As for you, let the word which you've heard from the beginning remain in you." The sentence which expounds Reason is conditional and echoes as a covert command what is overt in the Text: "If what you've heard from the beginning remains in you, then you will remain in the Father and the Son." Here "remaining in the Father and the Son" is assumed to be a positive value (but will be inculcated as a command in vs. 27) to which is attached a behavioral alternative. Thus, "if what you heard from the beginning remains in you" becomes a covert way of enjoining "let it remain in you"—making the conditional clause a backreference to and paraphrase of 24a.

Verses 26-27 comprise a nest of two embedded antithetical paragraphs, each of which is end-weighted, iambic, i.e. the antithesis in each case outranks the thesis. In the outer layer, the Thesis is verse 26: tauta egrapsa humin peri tōn planōntōn humas 'These things I've written to you concerning those who deceive you'. In keeping with the quite regular way in which sentences with the

16   S T A R T   NO. 9

performative "write" are not of the highest rank, I consider here that the
antithesis which is found in vs. 27 is more substantive and dominating. It
would be possible to label the whole unit 26-27 a concessive paragraph with
the Concessive and 27 the Text. This would more clearly highlight the initial
ranking of the two verses. However, this does not seem to be so applicable to
the internal structure of verse 27 where, again, the second half of the verse
outranks the first half. I have chosen, therefore, to consider both 26 and 27
as a whole and 27 in particular to be iambic antithetical paragraphs instead of
two different main types, concessive and antithetical. This is not as arbitrary
as it seems in this limited context. Rather, weighting (of one part of a
paragraph against the other) is one of the main parameters of a system of
paragraph types, such as I posit in Longacre 1979, especially pp. 129-131.

   Within verse 27, i.e. in the antithetical paragraph which is embedded
within the antithesis of the larger structure, the Thesis is an embedded
paragraph with two coordinated Items. The initial kai humeis 'but you' here
clearly marks the contrastive status of 27 relative to 26, i.e. "Although I've
written to you on these matters (28), you have an anointing from God and don't
really need any one to teach you on this subject".

   The structure within 27 continues, however, with the more weighty material
in 27b, which probably structures simply as one sentence. Here the Antithesis
is strongly marked with an initial alla, 'but'. Following this occurs a long
hōs construction which backloops a sentence with four clauses into an adverbial
circumstantial margin. This long and complex construction is a massive,
chiastic backreference which is quite unparalleled elsewhere in the book:

     A   all' hōs to autou chrisma didaskei humas,

         B   kai alēthes estin,

         B' kai ouk estin pseudos,

     A' kai kathōs edidaxen humas

This is followed by the command: menete en autō 'remain in Him'.

   Granted the presence of this massive chiastic backreference, there can be
no doubt that within 26-27 this last clause (which is introduced with such
flourish) is meant to be climactic. Just as the larger unit has an Antithesis
which outweighs its thesis, so within that Antithesis there is a unit whose
Antithesis outweighs its Thesis. Finally, within the sentence which expounds
the Antithesis of the embedded unit, the main clause—which contains the
command—outweighs the rest of the sentence, which may be considered to build up
to and anticipate the clause which comes crashing down at its end.

   I think that the above analysis is instructive in helping us understand the
way that hortatory paragraphs are built here in 1 John and, indeed, in many
discourses in many languages. Whenever there is an apparent mixture of verbs of
various forms, the analysis must give central place in the structure to main
clauses which contain command forms. An obvious exception here is when the
imperatives are performative, attention-catching devices, such as
"Note...consider...", etc., such as are found even in expository prose. These
may well be termed rhetorical commands as suggested by Linda Lloyd (verbal
communication).

Furthermore, exhortation does not stand alone—or, if it does, the exhortation is very aggravated and possibly even ineffective. Reasons, comments, and other material accompany the exhortations to make them effective. Imperatives are perhaps all the more effective for being sparingly used.

1 JOHN 2:18-27 (H) COORDINATE PARAGRAPH

INTRO: (E) COOR. PARAGRAPH

    ITEM$_1$: REASON PARAGRAPH (It's the last hour)

18.   TEXT: παιδία, ἐσχάτη ὥρα ἐστίν,

      REASON: AMPLI. PARAGRAPH

        TEXT: καὶ καθὼς ἠκούσατε ὅτι ἀντίχριστος ἔρχεται, καὶ νῦν ἀντίχριστοι πολλοὶ γεγόνασιν· ὅθεν γινώσκομεν ὅτι ἐσχάτη ὥρα ἐστίν.

      AMPL: REASON PARAGRAPH

19.   TEXT: ἐξ ἡμῶν ἐξῆλθαν, ἀλλ᾽ οὐκ ἦσαν ἐξ ἡμῶν·

        REASON: εἰ γὰρ ἐξ ἡμῶν ἦσαν, μεμενήκεισαν ἂν μεθ᾽ ἡμῶν· ἀλλ᾽ ἵνα φανερωθῶσιν ὅτι οὐκ εἰσὶν πάντες ἐξ ἡμῶν.

    ITEM$_2$: COMMENT PARAGRAPH (You have a chrisma)

20.   TEXT: καὶ ὑμεῖς χρῖσμα ἔχετε ἀπὸ τοῦ ἁγίου, καὶ οἴδατε πάντες.

21.   COMMENT: οὐκ ἔγραψα ὑμῖν ὅτι οὐκ οἴδατε τὴν ἀλήθειαν, ἀλλ᾽ ὅτι οἴδατε αὐτήν, καὶ ὅτι πᾶν ψεῦδος ἐκ τῆς ἀληθείας οὐκ ἔστιν.

    ITEM$_3$: AMPLIFICATION PARAGRAPH (There's a big lie on the loose!)

22.   TEXT: τίς ἐστιν ὁ ψεύστης εἰ μὴ ὁ ἀρνούμενος ὅτι Ἰησοῦς οὐκ ἔστιν ὁ Χριστός;

      AMPL: AMPLIFICATION PARAGRAPH

        TEXT: οὗτός ἐστιν ὁ ἀντίχριστος, ὁ ἀρνούμενος τὸν πατέρα καὶ τὸν υἱόν.

        AMPL: ANTI PARAGRAPH

23.   THESIS: πᾶς ὁ ἀρνούμενος τὸν υἱὸν οὐδὲ τὸν πατέρα ἔχει·

          ANTI: ὁ ὁμολογῶν τὸν υἱὸν καὶ τὸν πατέρα ἔχει.

18   S T A R T NO. 9

24. ITEM₁: (H) COMMENT PARAGRAPH

   TEXT: REASON PARAGRAPH

      TEXT: ὑμεῖς ὃ ἠκούσατε ἀπ' ἀρχῆς ἐν ὑμῖν μενέτω·

      REASON: ἐὰν ἐν ὑμῖν μείνῃ ὃ ἀπ' ἀρχῆς ἠκούσατε, καὶ ὑμεῖς ἐν τῷ υἱῷ

      καὶ ἐν τῷ πατρὶ μενεῖτε.

25.   COMMENT: καὶ αὕτη ἐστὶν ἡ ἐπαγγελία ἣν αὐτὸς ἐπηγγείλατο ἡμῖν, τὴν

      ζωὴν τὴν αἰώνιον.

   ITEM₂: (H) ANTI PARAGRAPH (iambic)

26.   THESIS: ταῦτα ἔγραψα ὑμῖν περὶ τῶν πλανώντων ὑμᾶς.

      ANTI: ANTI PARAGRAPH (iambic)

         THESIS: (E) COOR PARAGRAPH
27.   ITEM₁: καὶ ὑμεῖς τὸ χρῖσμα ὃ ἐλάβετε ἀπ' αὐτοῦ μένει ἐν ὑμῖν,

            ITEM₂: καὶ οὐ χρείαν ἔχετε ἵνα τις διδάσκῃ ὑμᾶς·

         ANTI: ἀλλ' ὡς τὸ αὐτοῦ χρῖσμα διδάσκει ὑμᾶς περὶ πάντων.

      καὶ ἀληθές ἐστιν καὶ οὐκ ἔστιν ψεῦδος,

      καὶ καθὼς ἐδίδαξεν ὑμᾶς.

      μένετε ἐν αὐτῷ.

                           DISPLAY V

1.6 Closure (of discourse which embeds in Introduction) 2:28-29

   The discourse which expounds the Introduction ends with a paragraph structure in which vs. 28 is the Text and vs. 29 is the Reason. The ranking verb of vs. 28 is an imperative and the whole paragraph is clearly a hortatory reason paragraph.

   I believe that the kai nun may well be taken to have summary force. This feature plus the vocative teknia signals onset of a new paragraph.

   Semantically, this paragraph seems to amount to: "In summary, remain in Him so you won't be ashamed before Him when He comes." A reason for remaining in Him is, "He is righteous, so every doer of righteousness is born of Him."

   As to surface structure, menete 'remain', an imperative, is clearly a form of the highest possible rank in a hortatory discourse. Verse 29, to be true, also contains an imperative but is essentially an attention-calling device rather than substantive: "know that...." A covert command is found, however, in 29b: "The one who does righteousness is born of Him", where "born of Him" is a positive value and where the participial phrase is equivalent to "Do righteousness".

Verse 29 frames the above covert command in a conditional sentence: "If you know that He is righteous, then know that...." Here, rather than the ean clause expressing a covert command, the whole is somewhat of a syllogism:

(a) "Granted that He is righteous,

(b) Therefore the conclusion is..."

I JOHN 2:28-29 (H) REASON PARAGRAPH
(Concludes INTRO of whole book)

(H) REASON PARAGRAPH

28. TEXT: καὶ νῦν, τεκνία, μένετε ἐν αὐτῷ, ἵνα ἐὰν φανερωθῇ σχῶμεν

παρρησίαν καὶ μὴ αἰσχυνθῶμεν ἀπ' αὐτοῦ ἐν τῇ παρουσίᾳ αὐτοῦ.

29. REASON: ἐὰν εἰδῆτε ὅτι δίκαιός ἐστιν, γινώσκετε ὅτι

καὶ πᾶς ὁ ποιῶν τὴν δικαιοσύνην ἐξ αὐτοῦ γεγέννηται.

DISPLAY VI

1.7 Concluding note on chapters one and two as Introduction

At this point we may well pause and ask ourselves: What does this Introduction accomplish and in what sense is it introductory? I have posited here a discourse with seven paragraphs:

1:1-4 (Introduces both the whole Epistle and this embedded discourse)
1:5-10 (P-1) Surface structure exposition; covert exhortation not to profess to be sinless but to "walk in the light", confess our sins and enjoy forgiveness.
2:1-6 (P-2) Surface structure probably classifiable as hortatory and emphasizing "Don't sin".
2:7-11 (P-1) A new/old command is announced and inferentially (and obliquely) connected with a covert command to love—one of the great themes of the body of the Epistle. The structure is expository.
2:12-17 Performative and ethical peak (hortatory). Here the writer develops more at length his reasons for writing the epistle and warns against loving the wrong object (the world).
2:18-27 Doctrinal peak (hortatory). Remain in Christ and in His teaching in spite of adverse teaching and practice. This will also be one of the main themes of the body of the epistle.
2:28-29 Closure (hortatory). Echoes previous paragraph: "Hold steady; don't get sidetracked."

20   S T A R T   NO. 9

This introductory discourse features the performative verb write in every paragraph but 1:5-10, where anaggellomen 'announce' is used instead. A pervasive purpose seems to be to explain why he is writing to them. At the same time, the typical value system of the epistle is introduced (truth, light, cleansing from sin, fellowship, etc.) and behavioral alternatives attached so as to form many covert commands.

Of what will prove to be the two main points of the body of the Epistle, the doctrinal point (Don't be sidetracked by false teaching) is developed in the next to the last paragraph—but will find even more climactic development in 4:1-6. The other emphasis, Christian love, is not developed well in the introduction; it is hinted at in 2:7-11 and stated somewhat negatively in 2:12-17. Its culminative expression awaits development in the body of the Epistle, where 4:7-19 is not only the culminating exhortation to Christian love compared to anything expressed elsewhere in the epistle but is perhaps the most eloquent and pointed such exhortation in the whole New Testament.

We will further see that in the body of the Epistle, the twin exhortations "believe in Christ" and "love each other" are brought together in ways which frame and bracket the peaks of the body of the Epistle.

The Introduction is for the writer a warm-up to his favorite topics. Earlier paragraphs have an expository tone which develops into overt exhortation as the (embedded) discourse develops.

2. The Body of the Book (3:1—5:12)

The body of the book, like the Introduction, is an embedded discourse. It contains four pre-peak points, a doctrinal peak, an ethical peak, and a post-peak point. The first two points (P-4 and P-3, i.e. Peak minus 4 and Peak minus 3) contain mitigated commands which consist of statements in the present tense, 3 p.s.: "Everyone who has this hope in him purifies himself..." (3:3); and "The one who is born of God does not practice sin..." (3:9). These are mitigated commands such as "a good American votes faithfully in every election" or "a responsible father keeps his children from running the streets late at night". In context, these commands are general ethical considerations such as are found in Peak-3 and Peak-2 (i.e. points 1 and 2) of the Introduction.

Peak-2 and Peak-1 reflect mounting tension. The former turns on "we ought to love another" (3:16), which is amplified as "Let's not just love in word or tongue but ´let us love, in deed and in truth" (3:18). Here the command to love is enjoined in relatively unmitigated form. By contrast, the framework of P-1 is expository, but the paragraph turns on (i.e. takes as its most salient point) the statement of the two-fold command which John represents as binding on the reader: "And this is his command that we should believe in the name of His Son Jesus Christ and love one another—even as He gave us the command." Here the two-fold peak, doctrinal, and ethical is anticipated.

In 4:1-6 the main doctrinal demand, that we accept the fact of the Incarnation, is developed. In 4:7-21, a long compound paragraph, the ethical demand of love (agapē) finds its classical development.

The post-peak point of the discourse which constitutes the body is a long run-on paragraph of concatenated structure—a rather unusual structure which it might be difficult to find a parallel to in the whole Greek New Testament. This paragraph echoes in its initial verse the twin demands, <u>believe</u> and <u>love</u>, that are found in the preceding peaks.

With the content of the two-fold command given in 3:23 and the echoing of this command in 5:1, we thus have the PEAK bracketed by thematic statements which summarize the peak.

2.1 Point 1 (P-4) 3:1-6

The onset of a new paragraph, indeed of the body of the book, is marked with the use of <u>idete</u> 'behold!'/'look!' The vocative, which is customarily associated with <u>paragraph</u> initial, is delayed until the next verse (3:2).

This paragraph, while hortatory, has a long introduction which is expository (3:1-2, an expository amplification paragraph). Here the verb <u>eimi</u> 'be' dominates most of the structure. The text of this embedded paragraph is constituted by an embedded result paragraph. Thus, the Text in verse 3:1a "behold what manner of love the Father has bestowed on us that we should be called the sons of God—and so <u>we are</u>", with its verbs "be called" and "be" is followed in 3:1b by the Result: "For this reason (<u>dia touto</u>) the world does not know us because it knew not Him", whose verb <u>ginōskei</u> 'know' is probably outranked by the more classic expository verbs of the preceding verse. Verse 3:2, which is the amplification of 3:1 in an expository coordinate paragraph whose two items feature the verb "be" in the present tense and in the future: "Beloved, now <u>we are</u> children of God. And it hasn't yet been manifested what <u>we shall be</u>...but <u>we shall be</u> like Him."

The body of the paragraph is a hortatory amplification paragraph. Its text embeds an antithetical paragraph whose Thesis is the mitigated command "he purifies himself" (<u>agnizei heauton</u>). The Antithesis is a comment paragraph. The Text of this comment paragraph is: "everyone who by contrast, practices sin practices lawlessness, for sin is lawlessness." The Comment is a reference to the sinless one who appeared in history to take away sin: "and you know that that one was manifested to take away sins and in Him is no sin." The above antithetical paragraph, which expounds the text, is followed by another antithetical paragraph which amplifies the amplification. The thesis is, again, a mitigated command-in-the-ideal-third person: "Everyone who abides in him does not sin." The antithesis is, "Everyone who sins has not seen Him nor known Him."

I JOHN 3:1-6 (H?) AMPL PARAGRAPH
(Commands: 3 p.s. present)

<u>INTRO</u>: (E) AMPLIFICATION PARAGRAPH

    <u>TEXT</u>: (E) RESULT PARAGRAPH

        TEXT: AMPLIFICATION PARAGRAPH

1.   <u>TEXT</u>: ἴδετε ποταπὴν ἀγάπην δέδωκεν ἡμῖν ὁ πατὴρ ἵνα τέκνα

               θεοῦ κληθῶμεν·

22   S T A R T NO. 9

       AMPL: καὶ ἐσμέν.

       RESULT: διὰ τοῦτο ὁ κόσμος οὐ γινώσκει ἡμᾶς ὅτι οὐκ ἔγνω αὐτόν.

    AMPLIFICATION: (E) COOR PARAGRAPH

2.   ITEM₁: ἀγαπητοί, νῦν τέκνα θεοῦ ἐσμεν,

       ITEM₂: AMPL PARAGRAPH

         TEXT: καὶ οὔπω ἐφανερώθη τί ἐσόμεθα.

         AMPL: οἴδαμεν ὅτι ἐὰν φανερωθῇ ὅμοιοι αὐτῷ ἐσόμεθα, ὅτι ὀψόμεθα αὐτὸν καθώς ἐστιν.

    TEXT: (H?) ANTI PARAGRAPH

3.   THESIS: καὶ πᾶς ὁ ἔχων τὴν ἐλπίδα ταύτην ἐπ' αὐτῷ ἁγνίζει ἑαυτὸν καθὼς ἐκεῖνος ἁγνός ἐστιν.

       ANTI: (H?) COMMENT PARAGRAPH

4.   TEXT: πᾶς ὁ ποιῶν τὴν ἁμαρτίαν καὶ τὴν ἀνομίαν ποιεῖ, καὶ ἡ ἁμαρτία ἐστὶν ἡ ἀνομία.

5.   COMMENT: καὶ οἴδατε ὅτι ἐκεῖνος ἐφανερώθη ἵνα τὰς ἁμαρτίας ἄρῃ, καὶ ἁμαρτία ἐν αὐτῷ οὐκ ἔστιν.

    AMPL: (H?) ANTI PARAGRAPH

6.   THESIS: πᾶς ὁ ἐν αὐτῷ μένων οὐχ ἁμαρτάνει·

       ANTI: πᾶς ὁ ἁμαρτάνων οὐχ ἑώρακεν αὐτὸν οὐδὲ ἔγνωκεν αὐτόν.

DISPLAY VII

2.2 Point 2 (P-3) 3:7-12

The onset of this paragraph is marked by a vocative (<u>teknia</u>) and an attention calling, perlocutionary, performative-like imperative: <u>mēdeis planatō humas</u> 'let no one deceive you'. This sentence patterns as introductory to a comment paragraph, the function of which is to introduce, in turn, the whole paragraph. The Text of this comment paragraph is, again, one of the writer's favorite paragraph types, the antithetical paragraph. Here Thesis and Antithesis contrast "doing righteousness" and "the righteous one" with "doing sin" and "the devil". The Comment on the preceding materials is another reference to the historical appearance of the Son of God in order to destroy the works of the devil.

The Text of the body of this paragraph is, again, a command mitigated to a third person singular present verb: "Everyone who is born of God does not practice sin because the seed of (child-of, descendant-of) God remains in God." This is paraphrased as, "He is not able to sin because he is born of God."

The body of the paragraph closes with a long Comment of rather involved structure (3:10-12). The Comment structures as a reason paragraph, and the Reason structures as a further embedded comment paragraph.

The Text of the reason paragraph is an involved sentence of internally cataphoric structure. This can be represented diagrammatically somewhat as follows:

"In this   is manifested the sons of God and the sons of the devil:

[he who does not practice righteousness is not of God
 neither he who does not love his brother."]

Verses 11 and 12 constitute the Reason which is appended to the above Text. Since these verses are introduced with hoti 'because', they could be construed as simply the sentence margin of the previous sentence (3:10). It is rare to have a paragraph backloop into a sentence margin, but by no means impossible. I follow the somewhat simpler course of breaking off verses 11 and 12 from verse 10. At any rate, however, verses 11 and 12 are subordinated structurally to 10, if not as cause margin to sentence nucleus, then at least as Reason to Text within the framework of a paragraph.

Internally within verses 11 and 12 there is considerable lexical density and grammatical ellipsis. The text announces one of the central themes of the book in this grammatically non-salient part of the paragraph. "For this is the message that we have heard from him, that we should love one another." Again the structure is internally cataphoric with the initial hautē 'this' cross-referencing to the final hina clause: "that we should love another." The sentence, a loose run-on structure, continues with "not as Cain was of the evil one and murdered his brother". Here there is ellipsis of at least three elements: "...(and that we should) not (do) as Cain (who) was of the evil one and murdered his brother."

The Comment (vs. 12) contains a rhetorical question and its answer—again with considerable ellipsis: "And why did he murder him? (He murdered him) because his own works were evil and those of his brother (were) righteous."

The reference to Christian love is a subdued and off-the-line reference to a major emphasis of the book, an emphasis which comes to classic expression in chapter 4:7ff. The reference to Cain occurs only here where it is considerably telescoped and not allowed to impede the progress of the main thematic stuff of the book. It is an allusion, a passing reference, which the readers are no doubt assumed to be familiar with.

24   S T A R T NO. 9

                1 JOHN 3:7-12 (H?) COMMENT PARAGRAPH
                     (Commands: 3 p.s. present)

       INTRO: (E) COMMENT PARAGRAPH
7.   INTRO: τεκνία, μηδεὶς πλανάτω ὑμᾶς·
         TEXT: (E) ANTI PARAGRAPH
            THESIS: ὁ ποιῶν τὴν δικαιοσύνην δίκαιός ἐστιν, καθὼς ἐκεῖνος δίκαιός
            ἐστιν·
8.   ANTI: ὁ ποιῶν τὴν ἁμαρτίαν ἐκ τοῦ διαβόλου ἐστίν, ὅτι ἀπ' ἀρχῆς ὁ
            διάβολος ἁμαρτάνει.
            COMMENT: εἰς τοῦτο ἐφανερώθη ὁ υἱὸς τοῦ θεοῦ, ἵνα λύσῃ τὰ ἔργα τοῦ
            διαβόλου.
         TEXT: (H) PARAPHRASE PARAGRAPH
9.   TEXT: πᾶς ὁ γεγεννημένος ἐκ τοῦ θεοῦ ἁμαρτίαν οὐ ποιεῖ, ὅτι σπέρμα
            αὐτοῦ ἐν αὐτῷ μένει·
            PARA: καὶ οὐ δύναται ἁμαρτάνειν, ὅτι ἐκ τοῦ θεοῦ γεγέννηται.
       COMMENT: (E) REASON PARAGRAPH
10.   TEXT: ἐν τούτῳ φανερά ἐστιν τὰ τέκνα τοῦ θεοῦ καὶ τὰ τέκνα τοῦ διαβόλου·
         πᾶς ὁ μὴ ποιῶν δικαιοσύνην οὐκ ἔστιν ἐκ τοῦ θεοῦ, καὶ ὁ μὴ ἀγαπῶν
         τὸν ἀδελφὸν αὐτοῦ.
         REASON: (maybe = CM of previous S) COMM PARAGRAPH
11.   TEXT: ὅτι αὕτη ἐστὶν ἡ ἀγγελία ἣν ἠκούσατε ἀπ' ἀρχῆς, ἵνα ἀγαπῶμεν ἀλλήλους·
12.   οὐ καθὼς Κάϊν ἐκ τοῦ πονηροῦ ἦν καὶ ἔσφαξεν τὸν ἀδελφὸν αὐτοῦ·
           COMMENT: (Rh-Q-A REASON PARAGRAPH)
              TEXT: (Rh-Q) καὶ χάριν τίνος ἔσφαξεν αὐτόν;
              REASON: ὅτι τὰ ἔργα αὐτοῦ πονηρὰ ἦν, τὰ δὲ τοῦ ἀδελφοῦ αὐτοῦ δίκαια.

                              DISPLAY VIII

2.3 Point 3 (P-2) 3:13-18

This paragraph again starts with a perlocutionary verb "Don't marvel", followed by a vocative, adelphoi. Again, I take this sentence (cf. 3:7) to be introductory within its own paragraph; and, again, we find a long Introduction which consists of an embedded paragraph. This unit, found in 3:13-15 is another antithetical paragraph. The Thesis (3:14a), "We know that we have passed from death to life because we love our brothers", is followed by an Antithesis which embeds a negated antonym paraphrase paragraph where "not loving" is paraphrased as "hating" and where "abiding in death" of the former is strengthened to "is a murderer" in the latter. The Paraphrase of the NAP paragraph is expounded by a comment paragraph whose Comment is 15b: "And you know that no murderer has eternal life abiding in him." So we see that the whole negated antonym paraphrase paragraph—taking account of the appended Comment—comes out somewhat as follows:

the one who doesn't love	abides in death
the one who hates	is a murderer and does not have eternal life abiding in him.

The body of this paragraph is an amplification paragraph whose Text is a reason paragraph with its elements in the inverted order: Reason, Text. The Reason is a sentence of internally cataphoric structure: "In this we've known (= 'come to know') love, in the fact that that one lay down his life for us." Here the initial en touto cross-references again to the final hoti clause. From this Reason springs the motivation for the Text, which is expounded by an antithetical paragraph. The Thesis most closely related to the preceding reason: "Also we must lay down our lives for our brothers" (3:16b). The Antithesis (3:17) contrasts with this the behaviour of someone who has possessions, sees a brother in need, and does not compassionately share with him. All this provokes the Amplification: "Little children, let us not love with words but with actions" (3:18). The latter sentence begins with a vocative, which typically initiates a paragraph but here apparently marks the closure of this one; it occurs in the vicinity of a paragraph boundary, although not precisely where we might expect it.

Notice that, according to the above analysis, 3:16b emerges as the central (most salient) sentence of the paragraph. Verses 13-15 are considered to be Introduction; 16a is considered to be a Reason relative to 16b; 17 is considered to be an Antithesis which is outranked by the preceding Thesis; and vs. 18 is simply an Amplification of what precedes.

1 JOHN 3:13-18 (H) AMPLIFICATION PARAGRAPH

INTRO: (E) ANTI PARAGRAPH

13.   INTRO: [καὶ] μὴ θαυμάζετε, ἀδελφοί, εἰ μισεῖ ὑμᾶς ὁ κόσμος.

14.   THESIS: ἡμεῖς οἴδαμεν ὅτι μεταβεβήκαμεν ἐκ τοῦ θανάτου εἰς τὴν ζωήν,

ὅτι ἀγαπῶμεν τοὺς ἀδελφούς·

```
26                      S T A R T  NO. 9
              ANTI:  NEGATED ANTONYM PARAPHRASE PARAGRAPH
                 TEXT:  ὁ μὴ ἀγαπῶν μένει ἐν τῷ θανάτῳ.
                 PARA:  COMMENT PARAGRAPH
15.              TEXT:   πᾶς ὁ  μισῶν τὸν ἀδελφὸν αὐτοῦ ἀνθρωποκτόνος ἐστίν.
                 COMMENT:  καὶ οἴδατε ὅτι πᾶς ἀνθρωποκτόνος οὐκ ἔχει ζωὴν αἰώνιον
                 ἐν αὐτῷ μένουσαν.
       TEXT:  AMPL PARAGRAPH
         TEXT:  REASON PARAGRAPH
16.        REASON:  ἐν τούτῳ ἐγνώκαμεν τὴν ἀγάπην, ὅτι ἐκεῖνος ὑπὲρ ἡμῶν τὴν
           ψυχὴν αὐτοῦ ἔθηκεν·
           TEXT:  ANTI PARAGRAPH
              THESIS:  καὶ ἡμεῖς ὀφείλομεν ὑπὲρ τῶν ἀδελφῶν τὰς  ψυχὰς θεῖναι.
17.           ANTI:  ὃς δ' ἂν ἔχῃ  τὸν βίον τοῦ κόσμου καὶ  θεωρῇ τὸν ἀδελφὸν αὐτοῦ
              χρείαν ἔχοντα καὶ κλείσῃ τὰ   σπλάγχνα αὐτοῦ ἀπ' αὐτοῦ, πῶς ἡ
              ἀγάπη τοῦ θεοῦ μένει ἐν   αὐτῷ;
18.           AMPL:  τεκνία, μὴ ἀγαπῶμεν λόγῳ μηδὲ τῇ γλώσσῃ ἀλλὰ ἐν  ἔργῳ καὶ ἀληθείᾳ.
```

DISPLAY IX

2.4 Point 4 (P-1) 3:19-24

This pre-peak point, which is expounded by the paragraph which is found in 3:19-24, contains several surprises for the analyst. One is, after the succession of hortatory paragraphs, we now come on one which is clearly expository in structure. Furthermore, it has a loose run-on form, which has no previous parallel in the book—but which also characterizes (in aggravated degree) the Peak +1 paragraph which is found in 5:1-12. The loose run-on surface structure contains, however, a lexical chiasmus at the key of which lies a summary of the central message of the book!

In considering these features we fall back on the conception of peak as zone of turbulence (Longacre 1983:25-38). In this epistle, both P-1 and P+1 have a peculiar, run-on, right branching structure in which extensive use is made of embedded comment paragraphs. By introducing into a paragraph a succession of comments—each only loosely connected with what precedes—a writer can achieve a certain lexical and thematic density which is not possible in more closely knit material. This density of thematic material around (and to some degree in) the Peak can be compared to the crowded stage (reference to many participants) in narration (Longacre 1983:27-28).

As to the passage being expository instead of hortatory, again both P-1 and P+1 have this feature. Maybe exposition in P-1 and P+1 is intended to frame the very explicitly hortatory material in the Peaks. The effect here in a hortatory discourse may be like a "suspension point" or "evaluation" point such as described by Labor and Waletsky. Just as in narrative, an event-line may be suspensefully interrupted, so here perhaps the line of exhorting is impeded and suspended.

Nevertheless, the central reason of the book, its hortatory essence, is summarized in verse 23 of this passage: "And this is His commandment, that we should believe on the name of His son Jesus Christ and love one another as He gave us commandment." Why is this summary buried down in a mass of right-branching comment paragraphs? Whatever the reason, as we have indicated, the summary is set off by making it the key of the lexical chiasmus. To begin with, there is a grand inclusio in verses 19-21 as compared with 24b; in both, the note which sounded is <u>assurance</u>, knowing that we are of God, having confidence before Him. Verse 21, where a fresh start of sorts is signaled by the vocative <u>agapētoi</u> (again in the second, rather than in the first sentence of its paragraph), is a Text which leads into its Result in verse 22 where the writer speaks of receiving things from God "because we keep His commandments and do those things that are pleasing in His sight". The words just quoted are echoed in 24a: "the one keeping his commands dwells in Him and He in him." Verse 23 has its own inclusio, beginning with "and this is His command" and ending with "as He gave us command". The key of the chiasmus is, therefore, the summary of the book: "believe in Jesus Christ and love one another." Note the accompanying diagram.

P-1 (3:19-24) (E) ANTITHETICAL (IAMBIC) PARAGRAPH

19. <u>THESIS</u>: [καὶ] ἐν τούτῳ γνωσόμεθα ὅτι ἐκ τῆς ἀληθείας ἐσμέν, καὶ ἔμπροσθεν αὐτοῦ πείσομεν τὴν καρδίαν ἡμῶν.

20. ὅτι ἐὰν καταγινώσκῃ ἡμῶν ἡ καρδία, ὅτι μείζων ἐστὶν ὁ θεὸς τῆς καρδίας ἡμῶν καὶ γινώσκει πάντα.

ANTI: RESULT PARAGRAPH

21. <u>TEXT</u>: ἀγαπητοί, ἐὰν ἡ καρδία [ἡμῶν] μὴ καταγινώσκῃ, παρρησίαν ἔχομεν πρὸς τὸν θεόν.

<u>RESULT</u>: COMMENT PARAGRAPH

22. <u>TEXT</u>: καὶ ὃ ἐὰν αἰτῶμεν λαμβάνομεν ἀπ' αὐτοῦ, ὅτι τὰς ἐντολὰς αὐτοῦ τηροῦμεν καὶ τὰ ἀρεστὰ ἐνώπιον αὐτοῦ ποιοῦμεν.

<u>COMMENT</u>: COMMENT PARAGRAPH

28   S T A R T   NO. 9
23.   TEXT: καὶ αὕτη ἐστὶν ἡ ἐντολὴ αὐτοῦ, ἵνα πιστεύσωμεν τῷ ὀνόματι
             τοῦ υἱοῦ αὐτοῦ Ἰησοῦ Χριστοῦ καὶ ἀγαπῶμεν ἀλλήλους, καθὼς
             ἔδωκεν ἐντολὴν ἡμῖν.
             COMMENT: COMMENT PARAGRAPH
24.   TEXT: καὶ ὁ τηρῶν τὰς ἐντολὰς αὐτοῦ ἐν αὐτῷ μένει καὶ αὐτὸς
             ἐν αὐτῷ·
             COMMENT: καὶ ἐν τούτῳ γινώσκομεν ὅτι μένει ἐν ἡμῖν,
             ἐκ τοῦ πνεύματος οὗ ἡμῖν ἔδωκεν.

                              DISPLAY X

                     Chiastic Structure of 3:19-24

A Verses 19-21--How to know that we are of the truth.
   B And whatsoever we ask we receive from Him <u>because we keep His</u>
      <u>commandments and do those things that are pleasing to Him</u>. (22)
      C And this is <u>His commandment</u>: (23)
         D That we should believe on the name of His son I.X,
         E And love one another,
      C' As <u>He gave us commandment</u>. (23)
   B' <u>The one keeping His commandments dwells in Him and He in him</u>. (24)
A' In this we know that He remains in us, by the Spirit which He has given us.

                              DISPLAY X.a

2.5 <u>Peak (DOCTRINAL) 4:1-6</u>

     The body of the book has two peaks which are doctrinal and ethical
respectively. The latter is much the longer of the two. Here (4:1-6), however,
the writer makes a plea for his readers/hearers to believe correctly regarding
Jesus Christ. The whole passage is a hortatory evidence paragraph—but since
the Text is hortatory the Text-Evidence sequence becomes in effect End-Means (or
Tests). An initial vocative <u>agapētoi</u> marks the onset of the new unit.

The Text is "Beloved, don't believe every spirit (teachings inspired by spirits) but test them out as to whether or not they are from God" (4:1). Evidence$_1$ (the first test) is expounded by an antithetical paragraph. The Thesis is, again, a sentence, with internal cataphora (topicalization): "In this you will know the Spirit of God; every spirit (teaching) which confesses that Jesus Christ is come in the flesh is of God." The Antithesis is a comment paragraph whose Text provides the contrastive element: "And every spirit (teaching) that does not confess Jesus Christ (incarnate) is not of God." The following Comment identifies this teaching as that of antichrist.

Evidence$_2$ (the second test) is elaborated in another antithetical paragraph. Verse 4 acts as Introduction to this embedded paragraph—and is echoed in vs. 6. A second vocative occurs in vs. 4 but it is not given prominent position but is delegated to clause-final; nevertheless, it may assist the articulation of the embedded paragraph 4:4-6. The paragraph Introduction simply says, "You are of God, little children, and you have conquered them (evil teachers)." The thrust of the embedded argument, the presentation of a second test for false teaching, is: "who listens to whom?" The Thesis presents false teachers as belonging to the world and gaining an audience with their own kind; this is expressed via a result paragraph. The Antithesis presents the writer and his audience/readers as belonging to God with the result that those who know God listen to them.

Verse 6b is probably the Conclusion of the whole paragraph. In this sentence, the initial ek toutou is anaphoric and has summary force: "In this we know the spirit of truth and spirit of error." It may, however, be simply the Conclusion of the embedded antithetical paragraph which is found in 4:4-6. If so, it has the force of a synthesis of the preceding Thesis and Antithesis.

IV. I JOHN 4:1-6 (H) EVIDENCE PARAGRAPH

[EVIDENCE, which is here dependent on TEXT (=EXHORTATION) is equivalent to MEANS or TEST]

1. TEXT (=EXHORTATION): ἀγαπητοί, μὴ παντὶ πνεύματι πιστεύετε, ἀλλὰ δοκιμάζετε

    τὰ πνεύματα εἰ ἐκ τοῦ θεοῦ ἐστιν, ὅτι πολλοὶ ψευδοπροφῆται ἐξεληλύθασιν

    εἰς τὸν κόσμον.

    EVIDENCE$_1$: (E) ANTI PARAGRAPH

2. THESIS: ἐν τούτῳ γινώσκετε τὸ πνεῦμα τοῦ θεοῦ· πᾶν πνεῦμα ὃ ὁμολογεῖ

    Ἰησοῦν Χριστὸν ἐν σαρκὶ ἐληλυθότα ἐκ τοῦ θεοῦ ἐστιν,

    ANTI: (E) COMMENT PARAGRAPH

3. TEXT: καὶ πᾶν πνεῦμα ὃ μὴ ὁμολογεῖ τὸν Ἰησοῦν ἐκ τοῦ θεοῦ οὐκ ἔστιν·

    COMMENT: καὶ τοῦτό ἐστιν τὸ τοῦ ἀντιχρίστου, ὃ ἀκηκόατε ὅτι ἔρχεται,

    καὶ νῦν ἐν τῷ κόσμῳ ἐστὶν ἤδη.

    EVIDENCE$_2$: (E) ANTI PARAGRAPH

30		S T A R T NO. 9
4.	INTRO:	ὑμεῖς ἐκ τοῦ θεοῦ ἐστε, τεκνία, καὶ νενικήκατε αὐτούς, ὅτι μείζων ἐστὶν ὁ ἐν ὑμῖν ἤ ὁ ἐν τῷ κόσμῳ.
	THESIS:	(E) RESULT PARAGRAPH
5.		TEXT: αὐτοὶ ἐκ τοῦ κόσμου εἰσίν·
		RESULT: διὰ τοῦτο ἐκ τοῦ κόσμου λαλοῦσιν καὶ ὁ κόσμος αὐτῶν ἀκούει.
	ANTI:	(E) RESULT PARAGRAPH
6.		TEXT: ἡμεῖς ἐκ τοῦ θεοῦ ἐσμεν·
		RESULT: ANTI PARAGRAPH
		THESIS: ὁ γινώσκων τὸν θεὸν ἀκούει ἡμῶν,
		ANTI: ὃς οὐκ ἔστιν ἐκ τοῦ θεοῦ οὐκ ἀκούει ἡμῶν.
	CONCLUSION:	ἐκ τούτου (anaphoric) γινώσκομεν τὸ πνεῦμα τῆς ἀληθείας καὶ τὸ πνεῦμα τῆς πλάνης.

DISPLAY XI

2.6 Peak (ETHICAL) 4:7-21

This long passage is clearly two surface structure paragraphs with vocatives in 4:7 and 4:11 to mark the initiation of both units. Just as clear, however, as the articulation into two paragraphs is the unity of the whole: verses 11-21 seem to amplify, i.e. dilate upon and add further material to, what is said in 4:7-10. This unity must be recognized on some level, either the level of the discourse or the level of the paragraph. It seems plausible that the latter is indicated. Proceeding in this fashion, I set up the first paragraph (4:7-10) as a Text which finds its Amplification in 4:11-21. The Texts of the two are very similar:

4:7— agapētoi, agapōmen allēlous...

4:11— agapētoi...opheilomen allēlous agapan...

In the first main constituent paragraph (4:7-10), the Text is supported by Reason units. In the second main constituent paragraph (4:11-21), we find an amplification paragraph whose Text is a further layer of embedding which is again of Text-Reason structure.

In this long passage the writer no longer uses mitigation or oblique ways of argumentation but confronts his readers with the stark necessity of loving, first as a cohortative form agapōmen 'let us love', then as a categorical obligation, opheilomen...agapan. Not only is the command to love more plainly enjoined here than elsewhere in the book, but the development of the motivation is much more elaborate. The motivation turns chiefly on the fact, recurrently expressed, that if God showed His love for us by sending His son to die for us, this places us under an obligation to reciprocate by loving each other (verses 9, 10, 14, and 16).

2.6.1 4:7-10

This paragraph is a hortatory reason paragraph. Its Text (verses 7-8) is a simple sentence whose Cause Margin (initial <u>hoti</u> 'because') backloops a result paragraph. Thus, this sentence contains both a command element (<u>agapōmen allēlous</u>) and motivation in the form of an extensive Cause Margin. The paragraph which backloops here into a sentence takes "love is of God" as its Text and traces out the Result in an embedded antithetical paragraph whose Thesis states "Everyone who loves is born of God and knows God" and whose Antithesis states, "The one who doesn't love doesn't know God because God is love." Note that the last sentence here has its own cause margin "because God is love" which together with the Text of the backlooped paragraph provides an inclusio (rudimentary chiastic structure):

A   Love is of God

    B   he who loves...knows God

    B'   he who doesn't love...doesn't know God

A'   God is love.

In verses 9 and 10 we have further motivational structure—but now on the level of the paragraph. The two Reason units are structurally quite parallel in that both have initial cataphoric <u>en toutō</u> phrases. Verse 9 has an <u>hoti</u> clause as the complement of <u>en toutō</u>; verse 10 has a more complex complement which, in effect, backloops an antithetical paragraph into the sentence as two successive <u>hoti</u> clauses:

<u>ouch</u> <u>hoti</u> <u>hēmeis</u> <u>ēgapēkamen</u> <u>ton</u> <u>theon</u>

<u>all'</u> <u>hoti</u> <u>autos</u> <u>ēgapēsen</u> <u>hēmas</u>

<u>kai apesteilen ton huion autou hilasmon peri tōn hamartiōn hēmōn</u>.

Verses 9 and 10 are, indeed, so similar that the two could conceivably be construed as an amplification paragraph. Both refer to God's sending his son into the world and both use the verb "send". While this verb is in the perfect tense in 9 (a past event with continuing results), it is in the aorist (along with the verb "love") in verse 10. The aorist tense is characteristic of narrative. Aside from the epistolary aorist, this tense is not too common in the epistle. Furthermore, most of the other occurrences of the aorist refer—as here—to the historical manifestation of Jesus Christ (1:1,2; 3:8; 4:19). Here in 4:9-11, there is a cluster of four aorist forms all of which refer to this manifestation. I make this point here because it will prove relevant below. Actually, the resort to the aorist in these contexts is a tacit appeal on the part of the writer to the facts—acknowledged by his believing readers—that are by this time or somewhat later assembled into the gospels. An aorist verb which refers to God's sending his son or Christ's appearing is, therefore, equal to a summary or macrostructure of a gospel and is implicitly narrative (cf. also 1 John 1:1-4).

32   S T A R T NO. 9

                I JOHN 4:7-10 (H) REASON PARAGRAPH

7.   TEXT: ἀγαπητοί, ἀγαπῶμεν ἀλλήλους, ὅτι

     [A (E) RESULT PARAGRAPH embeds in this Sentence Margin]

     TEXT: ἡ ἀγάπη ἐκ τοῦ θεοῦ ἐστιν.

     RESULT: ANTI PARAGRAPH

            THESIS: καὶ πᾶς ὁ ἀγαπῶν ἐκ τοῦ θεοῦ γεγέννηται καὶ γινώσκει τὸν θεόν.
8.   ANTI: ὁ μὴ ἀγαπῶν οὐκ ἔγνω τὸν θεόν, ὅτι ὁ θεὸς ἀγάπη ἐστίν.
9.   *REASON: ἐν τούτῳ ἐφανερώθη ἡ ἀγάπη τοῦ θεοῦ ἐν ἡμῖν, ὅτι τὸν υἱὸν

     αὐτοῦ τὸν μονογενῆ ἀπέσταλκεν ὁ θεὸς εἰς τὸν κόσμον ἵνα ζήσωμεν δι' αὐτοῦ.
10. *REASON: ἐν τούτῳ ἐστὶν ἡ ἀγάπη, οὐχ ὅτι ἡμεῖς ἠγαπήκαμεν τὸν θεόν, ἀλλ'

     ὅτι αὐτὸς ἠγάπησεν ἡμᾶς καὶ ἀπέστειλεν τὸν υἱὸν αὐτοῦ ἱλασμὸν περὶ τῶν

     ἁμαρτιῶν ἡμῶν.   (Here the Complement embeds an ANTI PARAGRAPH with οτι
     repeated.)

*or: an AMPLIFICATION PARAGRAPH of the ff. structure:

     REASON: AMPLIFICATION PARAGRAPH

        TEXT: (9)

        AMPL: (10)

                           DISPLAY XII
2.6.2 **4:11-21**

   This constituent paragraph, which amplifies the preceding, is by far the
lengthier and more complicated unit. It structures as an amplification
paragraph whose Text (4:11-18) is a hortatory reason paragraph and whose
Amplification is a hortatory antithetical paragraph. Embeddings run to several
layers. Embedded comment paragraphs introduce material that is not too tightly
integrated into the main thematic thrust of the paragraph.

   We turn now to the structure of the hortatory reason paragraph that
expounds the Text of the whole unit. The Text of this hortatory reason
paragraph is itself a hortatory reason paragraph, whose Text is verse 11:
"Beloved, if God so loved us we ought also to love one another." Here the "if"
clause functions both as a back reference to verses 9-10 and as motivational
element which is used as a backdrop for the strong reassertion of the obligation
to love.

By virtue of its dominating command form (<u>opheilomen allēlous agapan</u>) this reassertion of the obligation to love dominates all that follows in its paragraph. This is recognized structurally by making verse 11 the Text embedded three-deep (since Text dominates all use). While the Amplification in verses 19-21 has its own Text, the command to love is there mitigated to a present tense and does not have the ranking of the main clause of verse 11.

Returning now to the embedded reason paragraph which is found in 11-13, the Text (verse 11) is accompanied by a Reason unit which consists of a comment paragraph. While this paragraph is expository in form, it contains a covert command in its text. An Introduction initiates the comment paragraph: "No one has ever seen God"; a sentence which may be concessive in force. The Text is a conditional structure. "If we love one another, God dwells in us and his love is perfected in us." Here the familiar device first noticed in chapter 1 is employed: Since it is a positive value to have God dwelling in us and to have his love perfected in us, the accompanying conditional clause "if we love each other", becomes equivalent to "love each other". The comment (vs. 15), taking off on the word "dwell" which precedes (vs. 14), adds, "In this we know that we abide in him and he in us—in that he has given us his Spirit." Again, this sentence is cataphoric with an initial <u>en toutō</u> and a postposed complement.

Coming out to the second layer of embedding, we now turn to the examination of verses 14-18, where two Reason units provide motivation for the Text (verses 11-13). The first Reason unit in verses 14-15 is, again, a comment paragraph whose Text refers once more to the motivational value found in a consideration of God's sending His Son to us: "And we have seen and testify that God has sent His Son to be the Saviour of the world." The accompanying Comment (vs. 15) echoes the doctrinal peak (4:1-6) and takes off again on the word "dwell" (verses 12 and 13): "Whosoever confesses that Jesus is the Son of God, God dwells in him and he in God." Once more, however, the preposed element has the force of a mitigated command: "Confess that Jesus is the Son of God."

Verses 16-18 constitute a second Reason unit which again has the structure of a comment paragraph. As in such structures, it is the Text which is better integrated into the preceding context: "And we have known and believed the love that God has for us." Once more here, as with the two Reason units of 7-10, the two Reasons (cf. 14-16) are similar enough to possibly constitute an amplification paragraph which could together expound Reason. Looking again at the Texts of these two stretches (14, 16), we are struck again at the similarity of these passages to the introduction of the whole book, and the implicitly narrative nature of these references.

The Text in verse 16 is accompanied by a Comment (16b) on an inner layer of embedding—as opposed to the Comment found in 17 and 18, and going with the whole of vs. 16. This inner comment paragraph is an embedded expository result paragraph whose text is "God is love" and whose result is "The one dwelling in love dwells in God and God dwells in him".

The outer layer Comment (verses 17-18) is an amplification paragraph which deals with our love being made perfect—a topic only loosely connected with the preceding context. The Text, verse 17, is again characterized with an initial cataphoric <u>en toutō</u> whose postposed complement is an <u>hoti</u> clause: "In this love has been perfected with us so that we may have boldness in the day of judgment—in the fact that as he is so are we in this present world." The

34   S T A R T NO. 9

Amplification (vs. 18), itself an amplification paragraph, develops the idea of
"perfect love" as a love that has no fear.

   With verse 19, we return to the main thematic line of 7-21. Specifically,
19-21 is an amplification of 11-18 (its Text). This Amplification unit
structures as a hortatory antithetical paragraph—provided that we are able to
classify vs. 19 as hortatory: "We love because He first loved us"—where I
consider the present tense "we love" to be a mitigation of the cohortative
(which is incidentally, homophonous in the case of agapōmen). This verse also
neatly summarizes the previous motivational material in the clause "because He
first loved us" (with another summary aorist ēgapēsen). This Thesis finds its
Antithesis in verses 10-21, which structure internally as a reason paragraph.
The Text of this unit is, "If any one says 'I love God' and hates his brother he
is a liar." Again, there is a hidden command: "Don't claim to love God if you
hate your brother." The Reason unit is found in 20b and 21 which apparently
structure as a coordinate paragraph (in default of more specific relations). In
this coordinate paragraph Item$_1$ asserts that the one who doesn't love his
brother whom he has seen can't love God whom he has never seen. Item$_2$ reasserts
that we are under a command (tautēn tēn entolēn echomen ap' auton) that "he who
loves God is to love his brother also". So—here again at paragraph end and
deeply embedded in nested paragraphs and in a dependent clause within a
sentence, the command to love is reiterated.

   The whole passage 4:7-21 reinforces the main line exhortation "Love each
other" by multiple recurrent references to Christ's incarnation, mission to the
world, and death as our great motivation: "We have been loved, so we also must
love."

   Many side comments characterize the argument, especially from verse 11
onwards. The overall result is that of considerably lexical and thematic
density. We will notice this same tendency to use comment paragraphs and
multiple themes in 5:1-12 which is post-peak. In fact, granted that all chapter
4 is peak material, it should not surprise us if we find some peak features in
P-1 and in P+1 since peak is roughly a zone of turbulence. One feature found
all through 3:19—5:12 is development via comment paragraphs which, while
grammatically loose, is at the same time a way of achieving lexical
density—without losing the main thread of argumentation.

                I JOHN 4:11-21 (H) AMPL PARAGRAPH
            (This whole paragarph amplifies vs. 7-10 above.)

        TEXT: (H) REASON PARAGRAPH

           TEXT: (H) REASON PARAGRAPH

11.   TEXT: ἀγαπητοί, εἰ οὕτως ὁ θεὸς ἠγάπησεν ἡμᾶς, καὶ ἡμεῖς ὀφείλομεν

             ἀλλήλους ἀγαπᾶν.

           REASON: (E) COMMENT PARAGRAPH

12.   INTRO: θεὸν οὐδεὶς πώποτε τεθέαται·

13. TEXT: ἐὰν ἀγαπῶμεν ἀλλήλους, ὁ θεὸς ἐν ἡμῖν μένει καὶ ἡ ἀγάπη αὐτοῦ ἐν ἡμῖν τετελειωμένη ἐστιν

    COMMENT: ἐν τούτῳ γινώσκομεν ὅτι ἐν αὐτῷ μένομεν καὶ αὐτὸς ἐν ἡμῖν, ὅτι ἐκ τοῦ πνεύματος αὐτοῦ δέδωκεν ἡμῖν.

    REASON: (N) COMMENT PARAGRAPH

14. TEXT: καὶ ἡμεῖς τεθεάμεθα καὶ μαρτυροῦμεν ὅτι ὁ πατὴρ ἀπέσταλκεν τὸν υἱὸν σωτῆρα τοῦ κόσμου.

15. COMMENT: ὃς ἐὰν ὁμολογήσῃ ὅτι Ἰησοῦς ἐστιν ὁ υἱὸς τοῦ θεοῦ, ὁ θεὸς ἐν αὐτῷ μένει καὶ αὐτὸς ἐν τῷ θεῷ.

    REASON: (N) COMMENT PARAGRAPH

    TEXT: (N) COMMENT PARAGRAPH

16. TEXT: καὶ ἡμεῖς ἐγνώκαμεν καὶ πεπιστεύκαμεν τὴν ἀγάπην ἣν ἔχει ὁ θεὸς ἐν ἡμῖν.

    COMMENT: (E) RESULT PARAGRAPH

    TEXT: ὁ θεὸς ἀγάπη ἐστίν,

    RESULT: καὶ ὁ μένων ἐν τῇ ἀγάπῃ ἐν τῷ θεῷ μένει καὶ ὁ θεὸς ἐν αὐτῷ μένει.

    COMMENT: (E) AMPLIFICATION PARAGRAPH

17. TEXT: ἐν τούτῳ τετελείωται ἡ ἀγάπη μεθ' ἡμῶν, ἵνα παρρησίαν ἔχωμεν ἐν τῇ ἡμέρᾳ τῆς κρίσεως, ὅτι καθὼς ἐκεῖνός ἐστιν καὶ ἡμεῖς ἐσμεν ἐν τῷ κόσμῳ τούτῳ.

    AMPL: AMPL PARAGRAPH

18. TEXT: φόβος οὐκ ἔστιν ἐν τῇ ἀγάπῃ, ἀλλ' ἡ τελεία ἀγάπη ἔξω βάλλει τὸν φόβον, ὅτι ὁ φόβος κόλασιν ἔχει,

    AMPL: ὁ δὲ φοβούμενος οὐ τετελείωται ἐν τῇ ἀγάπῃ.

    AMPLIFICATION: (H) ANTI PARAGRAPH

19. THESIS: ἡμεῖς ἀγαπῶμεν, ὅτι αὐτὸς πρῶτος ἠγάπησεν ἡμᾶς.

    ANTI: (E) REASON PARAGRAPH

36   S T A R T NO. 9

20.   TEXT: ἐάν τις εἴπῃ ὅτι Ἀγαπῶ τὸν θεόν, καὶ τὸν ἀδελφὸν αὐτοῦ μισῇ,
       ψεύστης ἐστίν·

       REASON: COOR PARAGRAPH

       ITEM₁: ὁ γὰρ μὴ ἀγαπῶν τὸν ἀδελφὸν αὐτοῦ ὃν ἑώρακεν, τὸν θεὸν
       ὃν οὐχ ἑώρακεν οὐ δύναται ἀγαπᾶν·

21.   ITEM₂: καὶ ταύτην τὴν ἐντολὴν ἔχομεν ἀπ' αὐτοῦ, ἵνα ὁ ἀγαπῶν τὸν
       θεὸν ἀγαπᾷ καὶ τὸν ἀδελφὸν αὐτοῦ.

DISPLAY XIII

2.7 Peak +1 (5:1-12)

As we have stated before, this is a paragraph of very peculiar structure. In its outermost layer, it structures as an attestation paragraph, i.e. it presents a Text (5:1) and its Evidence (5:2-12). But the Evidence consists of a reason paragraph whose text is 5:2 and whose Reason is likewise the balance of the paragraph, i.e. 5:3-12. Similarly, the Reason is an embedded comment paragraph whose Text is 5:3 and whose Comment is 5:4-12. In this fashion the paragraph proceeds in right-branching fashion through a series of thirteen layers of embedding. Of the embedded structures, nine are comment paragraphs; one, a reason paragraph; two are antithetical; and one is amplification. In addition to these right branching structures, there is a coordinate paragraph embedded in the Text (at the highest node).

Much of the structure of this paragraph consists in what we call "going off at a word"—i.e. a word in one sentence (the Text) is commented on in the following material (the comment).

I will proceed in order through the structure of this passage in an attempt to elucidate its lexically-dense, grammatically run-on structure; then I will raise the question, "What do we make of it?"

As we have said, the highest node of this paragraph is Text-Evidence in structure. The Text, a coordinate paragraph, echoes the doctrinal and ethical obligations which the writer has been urging on his readers: They are to believe that Jesus is the Christ; and, as lovers of God (the one who has begotten so many children), they are to love the children of God (those begotten of him). But, these commands are given in the mitigated form that is common in the earlier part of the epistle: "Everyone who does X is an R, or everyone who does X does Y also." The question then arises: "What is the evidence/how does one know that he is an R or does Y?" In a sense, all 5:2-12 is an answer to this implied query, but the answer proceeds quickly from theme to theme in almost kaleidoscopic fashion.

In 5:2 a reason paragraph is initiated with 2 as the Text; "We can know that we are doing Y, i.e. loving the children of God, by loving God and keeping his commands." In verse 3, which, again, loosely dominates all that follows, a Reason structure is initiated: We can know that we love God because we keep his commandments, etc., (where "etc." applies to all that follows in 5:4-12).

With verse 4, we see that the Reason, referred to above, is really developed as a comment paragraph: the word "commands" (tas entolas autou) occurs in both the Text and the Reason of 5:2-3—and, siezing on this word, the writer comments concerning the commands that they are not "burdensome" (bareiai) because the one born of God overcomes/gets victory over the world. In turn, the introduction of the word "victory" leads to a Comment on that word—and this is developed as an amplification by a rhetorical question: "and this is the victory that overcomes the world; our faith. Who is the one who overcomes the world but the one who believes that Jesus is the Son of God?" The reference to Jesus as the Son of God—evoking the main doctrinal emphasis of the epistle—leads to several verses on Jesus and His work. So, again in 5:5-6, we have a run-on comment paragraph with the immediate Comment being "This is the one who came by water and blood—even Jesus Christ..." (being very probably a reference to Jesus' baptism and death). This in turn, however, is Text to which is appended a further Comment, evoked probably by the reference to Christ's baptism: "And the Spirit is the one who witnesses, for the Spirit is the truth." Again, this verse becomes a Text to which is appended a further Comment evoked by the word "witness": "For there are three who witness—the Spirit, the water, and the blood—and these three agree." Again, however, all this only evokes further Comment (perhaps by instantiating a courtroom frame: "witness" and "agreement"): "If we receive the witness of men (e.g. in law courts) the witness of God is greater, for this is the witness of God that He has witnessed concerning His Son." The immediate Comment on this matter—receiving the witness of God—is: "The one believing on the Son of God has the witness in Himself." Since this Comment is developed antithetically the converse is also given: "The one who doesn't believe God has made Him a liar because he hasn't believed the witness that God has witnessed concerning His Son." This in turn evokes a Comment as to the substance of God's witness, that "God has given to us eternal life and this life is in His Son". And finally all this provokes still one last Comment which is delivered in another typical Johannine antithesis: "He who has the Son has life. He who doesn't have the Son of God doesn't have life."

That these verses are only loosely joined is evident. I have presented the structure as a right-branching tree consisting mainly of a recursive nest of comment paragraphs. Perhaps some sort of concatenation diagram would be even better. At any rate, it is evident that there is considerable lexical/thematic density here, a sort of a whirlwind windup of the book. In some cases the coherence of the passage depends on positing of certain frames which are only obscurely instantiated (e.g. Christ's baptism and death; the courtroom). Thus, in succession, the following theses/frames are called up:

love of God and of God's children
keeping the commandments of God; their "sweet reasonableness"
victory over this world through faith
Faith in Jesus as God's Son
Jesus' baptism and death (water and blood)
the Spirit's witness of men and a fortiori, the witness of God concerning his Son; rejecting that witness; the content of that witness: eternal life.
eternal life in the Son; no life out of the Son

38 START NO. 9

I JOHN 5:1-12 POST-PEAK (E) EVIDENCE PARAGRAPH
(remarkable, run-on, right branching structure)

1. TEXT: (E) COORDINATE PARAGRAPH
   ITEM₁: πᾶς ὁ πιστεύων ὅτι Ἰησοῦς ἐστιν ὁ Χριστὸς ἐκ τοῦ θεοῦ γεγέννηται,
   ITEM₂: καὶ πᾶς ὁ ἀγαπῶν τὸν γεννήσαντα ἀγαπᾷ [καὶ] τὸν γεγεννημένον ἐξ αὐτοῦ.
2. EVIDENCE: (E) REASON PARAGRAPH
   TEXT: ἐν τούτῳ γινώσκομεν ὅτι ἀγαπῶμεν τὰ τέκνα τοῦ θεοῦ, ὅταν τὸν θεὸν ἀγαπῶμεν καὶ τὰς ἐντολὰς αὐτοῦ ποιῶμεν.
3. REASON: COMMENT PARAGRAPH
   TEXT: αὕτη γάρ ἐστιν ἡ ἀγάπη τοῦ θεοῦ, ἵνα τὰς ἐντολὰς αὐτοῦ τηρῶμεν·
   COMMENT: COMMENT PARAGRAPH
   TEXT: καὶ αἱ ἐντολαὶ αὐτοῦ βαρεῖαι οὐκ εἰσίν,
4. ὅτι πᾶν τὸ γεγεννημένον ἐκ τοῦ θεοῦ νικᾷ τὸν κόσμον·
   COMMENT: AMPL PARAGRAPH
   TEXT: καὶ αὕτη ἐστὶν ἡ νίκη ἡ νικήσασα τὸν κόσμον, ἡ πίστις ἡμῶν.
   AMPL: COMMENT PARAGRAPH
5. TEXT: τίς [δέ] ἐστιν ὁ νικῶν τὸν κόσμον εἰ μὴ ὁ πιστεύων ὅτι Ἰησοῦς ἐστιν ὁ υἱὸς τοῦ θεοῦ;
   COMMENT: COMMENT PARAGRAPH
6. TEXT: οὗτός ἐστιν ὁ ἐλθὼν δι' ὕδατος καὶ αἵματος, Ἰησοῦς Χριστός· οὐκ ἐν τῷ ὕδατι μόνον ἀλλ'
   ἐν τῷ ὕδατι καὶ ἐν τῷ αἵματι·
   COMMENT: COMMENT PARAGRAPH
   TEXT: καὶ τὸ πνεῦμά ἐστιν τὸ μαρτυροῦν, ὅτι τὸ πνεῦμά ἐστιν ἡ ἀλήθεια.
   COMMENT: COMMENT PARAGRAPH

7. TEXT: ὅτι τρεῖς εἰσιν οἱ μαρτυροῦντες,
8. τὸ πνεῦμα καὶ τὸ ὕδωρ καὶ τὸ αἷμα, καὶ οἱ τρεῖς εἰς τὸ ἓν εἰσιν.
9. COMMENT: COMMENT PARAGRAPH
    TEXT: εἰ τὴν μαρτυρίαν τῶν ἀνθρώπων λαμβάνομεν, ἡ μαρτυρία τοῦ θεοῦ μείζων ἐστίν.
    ὅτι αὕτη ἐστὶν ἡ μαρτυρία τοῦ θεοῦ, ὅτι μεμαρτύρηκεν περὶ τοῦ υἱοῦ αὐτοῦ.
10. COMMENT: ANTI PARAGRAPH
     THESIS: ὁ πιστεύων εἰς τὸν υἱὸν τοῦ θεοῦ ἔχει τὴν μαρτυρίαν ἐν ἑαυτῷ·
     ANTI: COMMENT PARAGRAPH
       TEXT: ὁ μὴ πιστεύων τῷ θεῷ ψεύστην πεποίηκεν αὐτόν, ὅτι οὐ πεπίστευκεν εἰς
       τὴν μαρτυρίαν ἣν μεμαρτύρηκεν ὁ θεὸς περὶ τοῦ υἱοῦ αὐτοῦ.
11. COMMENT: COMMENT PARAGRAPH
    TEXT: καὶ αὕτη ἐστὶν ἡ μαρτυρία, ὅτι ζωὴν αἰώνιον ἔδωκεν ἡμῖν ὁ θεός,
    καὶ αὕτη ἡ ζωὴ ἐν τῷ υἱῷ αὐτοῦ ἐστιν.
    COMMENT: ANTI PARAGRAPH
      THESIS: ὁ ἔχων τὸν υἱὸν ἔχει τὴν ζωήν·
12.   ANTI: ὁ μὴ ἔχων τὸν υἱὸν τοῦ θεοῦ τὴν ζωὴν οὐκ ἔχει

DISPLAY XIV

40   S T A R T   NO. 9

A key theme/recurrence theme, even in the above loose run-on string, is that of believing in Jesus: (5:1) "the one believing that Jesus is the Christ is born of God..."; (5:5—inverted) "the one who believes that Jesus is the Son of God is the one who overcomes the world"; (5:10) "the one believing on the Son of God has the witness in himself". The opposite course, not believing, is again represented (cf. 1:10) as making God a liar.

Thus, while the surface structure of this passage is clearly expository (note the predominance of <u>eimi</u> in main clauses), the underlying hortatory intent is clear: "Believe in Jesus—and enjoy all the benefits here enumerated, one crowding upon the other."

3. Closure of the Epistle (5:13-21)

It seems clear that the previous paragraph marks the end of the body of the epistle. With verse 13, the verb <u>graphō</u> 'write' is reintroduced into the epistle, after having not occurred since 2:26 at the close of the Introduction. The epistle closes on a note of <u>assurance</u>. While 5:13 can be considered to be introductory to this closing paragraph, it plainly announces the theme: <u>hina eidēte hoti zōēn echete aiōnion</u>. Assuming that his readers are believers (<u>tauta egrapsa humin...tois pisteuousin eis to onoma tou huiou tou theou</u>) he wants to reassure them that they have eternal life. In a grand inclusio, the paragraph also ends with a reference to eternal life in verse 20: <u>houtos estin ho alēthinos theos kai zōē aiōnios</u>. In between, there is another reference to "life" in verse 16.

The assurance then, which is basic to the paragraph, is echoed in each of its coordinated parts (Items). This is plain to see relative to $Item_2$, $Item_3$, and $Item_4$ (verses 18, 19, and 20 respectively) where "we know" is initial in each unit. The situation is somewhat more complex in regard to $Item_1$ (verses 14-17) which is a generic-specific paraphrase paragraph. Disregarding for the moment the paraphrase (vss. 16-17), we note the crucial placement of <u>parrēsia</u> 'assurance' in verse 14 and the two-fold occurrence of <u>oidamen</u> embedded in the complement (a reason paragraph) of the involved structure comprising verse 14 and 15. I will now look at all these structures in more detail.

The embedded paragraph which constitutes $Item_1$ can be considered to be a paraphrase paragraph of generic-specific structure, or verses 16-17 could be taken as an Example relative to the Text in 14-15. At any rate, it seems plausible that verses 14-15 are more on the main thematic line of the paragraph than verses 16-17. These four verses could be paraphrased: "We can be sure of answered prayer, i.e. if we ask anything according to his will we know that He hears and answers. If, e.g. a brother has fallen into sin, we can confidently pray for his restoration. This doesn't hold if the brother has 'sinned unto death'. While all sorts of unrighteousness are sin, there is a 'sin not unto death'."

$Item_2$ (verse 18) is an antithetical sentence which expresses assurance regarding the ability of the child of God to live (relatively speaking) above sin. The first part of the paragraph expressed this categorically with a perfect passive participle (emphasizing the current state of the child of God: "We know that the one who has been (and still is) born of God does not sin." The latter half of the sentence uses the aorist passive participle—turning our attention perhaps to the experiential reality of a past event: "but, he that has been born of God keeps himself and the wicked one does not touch him." There seems here good reason to believe that <u>auton</u> is used here as equivalent to <u>heauton</u>, the regular form of the reflexive pronoun.[4]

Item$_3$ (vs. 19) voices still another assurance: "We know that we are of God..." Probably here we find expression of a fundamental intellectual offense of Christianity: the confident claim to a privileged connection with the Creator and Sustainer of the universe. That offense is only deepened in reading the second half of the verse: "and the whole world lies in wickedness." Again (cf. 2:15-17), a polarity is affirmed: God on the one side, and the whole world system which has no room for God on the other side. There is no hint that the polarity can be transcended or the gulf bridged.

Item$_n$ (vs. 20) voices an assurance that is still more basic: "We know that the Son of God has come..." This echoes one of the central themes of the book, the Incarnation. A Christian is one who is quietly assured that in Jesus of Nazareth the eternal God was manifested in human form. The verse, however, does not stop here, but appends a second part to the (coordinate) sentence: "And has given us an understanding that we should know the truth/the true one." Here the Christian "understanding" is linked to God having come in human form. Consequently, the first century Christian was not a prey to the false claims of Gnosticism nor is the 20th century Christian a prey to the cults and Eastern religions to which many restless and spiritually disinherited moderns are increasingly turning. After all, if God really has appeared in human form to bring us a message directly from the other side, this Word is sufficient (St. John 1:1-14). But the verse does not stop even here. Rather a result is appended (possibly still part of the same sentence): "And we are in the true One, in His Son, Jesus Christ." As important as is the understanding that the Son of God has brought us, even more wonderful is our vital experiential connection with Him. No wonder the comment follows: "This is the true God and eternal life", i.e. the living reality of our experiences of God in Christ <u>is</u> eternal life. We want nothing more.

CLOSURE OF BOOK

I JOHN 5:13-21 (E) COORDINATE PARAGRAPH

13.   **INTRO:** ταῦτα ἔγραψα ὑμῖν ἵνα εἰδῆτε ὅτι ζωὴν ἔχετε αἰώνιον, τοῖς

              πιστεύουσιν εἰς τὸ ὄνομα τοῦ υἱοῦ τοῦ θεοῦ.

       ITEM$_1$: GEN-SP PARAPHRASE PARAGRAPH

14.   **TEXT (GEN):** καὶ αὕτη ἐστὶν ἡ παρρησία ἣν ἔχομεν πρὸς αὐτόν, ὅτι

            (COMPLIMENT EMBEDS A REASON PARAGRAPH)

               REASON: ἐάν τι αἰτώμεθα κατὰ τὸ θέλημα αὐτοῦ ἀκούει ἡμῶν.

15.   **TEXT:** καὶ ἐὰν οἴδαμεν ὅτι ἀκούει ἡμῶν ὃ ἐὰν αἰτώμεθα,

              οἴδαμεν ὅτι ἔχομεν τὰ αἰτήματα ἃ ᾐτήκαμεν ἀπ' αὐτοῦ.

       PARA (SP): COMMENT PARAGRAPH

42   S T A R T NO. 9

16.   TEXT: ἐάν τις ἴδῃ τὸν ἀδελφὸν αὐτοῦ ἁμαρτάνοντα ἁμαρτίαν
        μὴ πρὸς θάνατον, αἰτήσει, καὶ δώσει αὐτῷ ζωήν, τοῖς
        ἁμαρτάνουσιν μὴ πρὸς θάνατον.
        COMMENT: ANTITHETHICAL PARAGRAPH
            THESIS: COMMENT PARAGRAPH
                TEXT: ἔστιν ἁμαρτία πρὸς θάνατον·
                COMMENT: οὐ περὶ ἐκείνης λέγω ἵνα ἐρωτήσῃ.
17.   ANTI: πᾶσα ἀδικία ἁμαρτία ἐστίν, καὶ ἔστιν ἁμαρτία οὐ
                πρὸς θάνατον.
18. ITEM₂: οἴδαμεν ὅτι πᾶς ὁ γεγεννημένος ἐκ τοῦ θεοῦ οὐχ ἁμαρτάνει,
    ἀλλ' ὁ γεννηθεὶς ἐκ τοῦ θεοῦ τηρεῖ αὐτόν, (= ἑαυτον) καὶ ὁ πονηρὸς οὐχ
    ἅπτεται αὐτοῦ.
19. ITEM₃: οἴδαμεν ὅτι ἐκ τοῦ θεοῦ ἐσμεν, καὶ ὁ κόσμος ὅλος ἐν τῷ πονηρῷ
    κεῖται.
    ITEMₙ: COMMENT PARAGRAPH
        TEXT: RESULT PARAGRAPH
20.   TEXT: οἴδαμεν δὲ ὅτι ὁ υἱὸς τοῦ θεοῦ ἥκει, καὶ δέδωκεν
            ἡμῖν διάνοιαν ἵνα γινώσκωμεν τὸν ἀληθινόν·
                RESULT: καὶ ἐσμὲν ἐν τῷ ἀληθινῷ ἐν τῷ υἱῷ αὐτοῦ Ἰησοῦ
                Χριστῷ.
                COMMENT: οὗτός ἐστιν ὁ ἀληθινὸς θεὸς καὶ ζωὴ αἰώνιος.

                    FINES OF BOOK:
21. τεκνία, φυλάξατε ἑαυτὰ ἀπὸ τῶν εἰδώλων.

                    DISPLAY XV

4. Finis of the book

Somewhat puzzling is the apparent break between vs. 21 and all that has preceded. There is something in the nature of a routine warning, almost a slogan here: "Little children, keep yourselves from idols." One is reminded of the continuing use in Mexico of a formula above the signature in official correspondence: "Sufragio efectivo y que muera la reelección" ('effective elections and down with re-election'), the motto of the Madero Revolution (1911) when Porfirio Díaz, who had been reelected successively (in rigged elections) for 40 years, was finally overthrown. Since the issue of idolatry (and of whether one should eat food sacrificed to idols) was a very live one among first century Christians, it would not be strange if some such slogan or password were in vogue, at least in the circles around Ephesus where John was presbyter.

The warning, however, is never amiss. Everything in revealed religion (where there is word from the other side) is opposed to man-made religion and man-made systems all of which are violations of the second commandment.

Perhaps in a larger sense this warning—like the second commandment itself—is a warning against that type of subtle idolatry which recreates God in our own image and cuts Him down to dimensions that we can feel more comfortable with. God is not an Englishman, nor an American, nor a Catholic, nor an Episcopalian, a Lutheran, a Methodist, a Baptist, a Presbyterian, a charismatic, or an anticharismatic. Rather, He upsets all our definitions and comfortable packaging and boxing. Praises be to Him!

NOTES

[1] I trust that the analysis which is presented here will eventually profit from point-by-point comparison with the careful semantic analysis of the Greek text of this book as elaborated by my colleague, Helen Miehle (1981). Certainly, no one approach to such a culturally and religiously significant text as 1 John ever begins to exhaust its reality. Our various approaches and systems of analysis when applied to the same text are but pointers to the richness of reality which is the text itself. What I offer here as an analysis of 1 John embodies an approach which I have found useful in analyzing texts in a variety of languages (Longacre 1981, 1982, 1983).

[2] I believe that this way of looking at hortatory discourse eventually harks back to the work of Michael Walrod and Austin Hale in field workshops under the auspices of the Summer Institute of Linguistics in the Philippines.

[3] For a classic statement of the concept of overlay and its usefulness, see Joseph Grimes 1972 and 1975, 292-296.

[4] There is really no difficulty in accepting auton as a reflexive form especially if we give it the rough breathing (h-) as in St. John 2:24. Furthermore, there is good manuscript witness for heauton rather than (h)auton in this verse, 1 John 5:18. I am indebted to Wilbur Wallis of Covenant Theological Seminary for assistance on the exegesis of this verse via personal letter.

REFERENCES

Grimes, Joseph E. 1972. "Outlines and Overlays." *Language* 48(3):513-524.

Grimes, Joseph E. 1975. *The Thread of Discourse*. The Hague: Mouton.

Labov, William and David Fanshel. 1977. *Therapeutic Discourse: Psychotherapy as Conversation*. New York: Academic Press.

Longacre, Robert E. 1968. *Discourse, Paragraph, and Sentence Structure in Selected Philippine Languages*. Summer Institute of Linguistics Publications 21. Santa Ana: SIL.

Longacre, Robert E. 1970. "Sentence Structure as a Statement Calculus." *Language* 46(4):783-815.

Longacre, Robert E. 1979. "The Paragraph as a Grammatical Unit." *Syntax and Semantics* 12: *Discourse and Syntax*, ed. Talmy Givon 115-134.

Longacre, Robert E. 1981. "A Spectrum and Profile Approach to Discourse Analysis." *Text* 1(4):337-359.

Longacre, Robert E. 1982. "Verb Ranking and the Constituent Structure of Discourse." *Journal of the Linguistic Association of the Southwest* 5(3, 4):177-202.

Longacre, Robert E. 1983. *The Grammar of Discourse*. New York: Plenum Press.

Miehle, Helen L. 1981. *Theme in Hortatory Discourse: van Dijk and Beekman-Callow Approaches Applied in 1 John*. University of Texas at Arlington dissertation.

11

A TOP-DOWN, TEMPLATE-DRIVEN NARRATIVE ANALYSIS,
ILLUSTRATED BY APPLICATION TO MARK'S GOSPEL

Robert E. Longacre

1. *Theoretical Foundations*

Narrative analysis is necessarily dependent on the basic characteristics of narrative. What makes a story a story? A story is not an essay or a sermon, or a food recipe, or a set of procedures. It has a storyline, that is, a succession of happenings which are recounted. It involves a certain departure from the routine and expected. But nevertheless, it takes the stuff of life, sometimes with great detail and apparent arbitrariness, and weaves it into what Ricoeur calls an *emplotment*, or *plot*[1] for short. It necessarily has participants involved in some sort of struggle, however refined or crude. It has to bring such struggle to a head and resolve it someway, even if the resolution is not a happy one.

Obviously, there is some sort of narrative *template* according to which stories are made. Since classical times (beginning with Aristotle's writing on drama) such a template has been recognized, although various writers have expressed it differently. The schema I have held to for some time now[2] (but cf. Labov and Waletzky,[3] Rumelhart,[4] and others)

---

1. P. Ricoeur, *Time and Narrative* (3 vols.; trans. Kathleen McLaughlin and David Pellauer; Chicago: University of Chicago Press, 1984–88). The material of special interest to us here is vol. 1, Chapter 3.
2. Cf. R.E. Longacre, *An Anatomy of Speech Notions* (Lisse: Peter de Ridder, 1976), and *idem*, *The Grammar of Discourse* (New York: Plenum, 2nd edn, 1996). The particular form in which I have expressed the narrative schema is taken from W. Thrall, A. Hibbard and H. Holman, *A Handbook to Literature* (New York: The Odyssey Press, 1961).
3. W. Labov and J. Waletzky, 'Narrative Analysis: Oral Versions of Personal Experience', in J. Helm (ed.), *Essays on the Verbal and Visual Arts* (Seattle: University of Washington Press, 1967), pp. 12-44.
4. D.E. Rumelhart, 'Notes on a Schema for Stories', in D.G. Bobrow and A.M.

LONGACRE *A Top-Down, Template-Driven Narrative Analysis* 141

has the following elements: (1) *Stage*, (2) *Inciting Incident*, (3) *Mounting Tension*, (4) *Climax*, (5) *Denouement*, (6) *Closure*.

The purpose of (1) Stage is to lay the foundation for creating the storyworld, time, place, circumstances and participants (not necessarily the ones dominating the ensuing story). Element (2) brings in that which is unexpected and routine-breaking, so that 'thereby hangs a tale'. Element (3) typically involves a series of *episodes* which complicate the plot. Elements (4) Climax and (5) Denouement are further episodes which are somewhat correlative. The French terms *nouement* 'tying it up' and *denouement* 'untying it' capture this reciprocity quite well. The last element, Closure, brings the curtain down. It may, however, be preceded by one or more episodes of *Lessening Tension* or even *Final Suspense* which are consequent on the preceding denouement. The latter reports an event which makes resolution *possible*; it may leave many details to be worked out.

But while this is the underlying template, the actual story which is produced is like a theme with variations which it is the privilege of narrators to develop to their liking. Narrators elaborate the episodic *surface structure* of the story. They cannot tell all there is to tell at every stage of their narrative or the story would be both infinitely long and infinitely tiresome. They must be highly selective. They will, in fact, have portions of their story that they present summarily and other parts concerning which they give considerable detail. The latter are the great moments of the story, which I will call *action peaks*[5] in this essay. These great moments typically involve such sections of the underlying template as the Inciting Incident, the Climax and the Denouement. Narrators may also prepose a *Title* and/or *Aperture* to their story and may postpose a *Finis*. Aperture and Finis are characteristically formulaic and culture-determined.

A story of any length will typically have plots and subplots, that is, it may have story-within-story. Or narrators may find it necessary, if they are to guide the hearer/reader skillfully through the tale, to group the

---

Collins (eds.), *Representation and Understanding* (New York: Academic Press, 1975), pp. 211-36; *idem*, 'Understanding and Summarizing Brief Stories', in D. LaBerge and S.J. Samuels (eds.), *Basic Processes in Reading: Perception and Comprehension* (Hillsdale, NJ: Erlbaum, 1977), pp. 265-304.

5. Longacre, *Grammar*, Chapter 1; *idem*, 'Discourse Peak as Zone of Turblence', in J.R. Wirthe (ed.), *Beyond the Sentence* (Ann Arbor: Karoma Publishers, 1985), pp. 81-98.

happenings in wavelike successive units. In either case the template is applied recursively.[6] It is quite improbable to find a story of any length that is a simple linear string of happenings reported in successive episodes. Furthermore, narrators may group certain episodes of their story so as to suggest a special parallelism of one account with another account which consists of similar incidents. Narrators may even (especially if from a Semitic background) use a chiastic arrangement which suggests that there is a central episode which is pivotal. At all events the narrator is likely to echo at beginning and end—and maybe also in the center—certain themes.

The above brings us to the consideration that a story has not simply happenings and participants but *themes*. The latter can surface in various ways in a story: in background material which is not on the storyline, in the simple recurrence of certain 'key' words, and in reported speech. The latter is so important that a story may contain a *Didactic Peak*,[7] that is, an episode in which action ceases and themes are developed via monologue and/or dialogue. Thus every novel or story of Ayn Rand[8] contains a sermon, by its chief participant, on the virtue of self-reliance and the perniciousness of all forms of altruism and collectivism. In the book of Genesis the Flood Narrative[9] contains besides the action peak in ch. 7, a didactic peak in ch. 9 whose themes are covenant and promise. In the Joseph story[10] with which the book of Genesis terminates, Joseph's call to prepare himself for an audience with Pharaoh and his installation as grand vizier after the interview are elements of an action peak that bracket a didactic peak in which Joseph interprets Pharaoh's dreams and develops as theme the providence of God (total passage, Gen. 41.14-45). Thus, a didactic peak may occur in a distinct section of narrative from the action peak or it may occur in conjunction with the latter.

Analytically all this implies that a narrative analyst can proceed

---

6. Longacre, *Grammar*, Chapter 7.
7. Longacre, *Grammar*, Chapter 1.
8. For example, *Atlas Shrugged* (New York: The New American Library, 1943) and *Fountainhead* (New York: The New American Library, 1957).
9. R.E. Longacre, 'The Discourse Structure of the Flood Narrative', *JAAR* 47.1 (1979), pp. 89-133.
10. R.E. Longacre, *Joseph, a Story of Divine Providence* (Winona Lake, IN: Eisenbrauns, 1989).

LONGACRE *A Top-Down, Template-Driven Narrative Analysis* 143

somewhat as follows in the preliminary approach to a text.[11]

1. Search for natural fissures, joints or seams, in a narrative. This search requires both an intuitive following of 'hunches' and a sensitivity to formal marking by occurrence of conjunctions and other sequence signals, by cyclic recurrence of staging (time and locational expressions, change of participant slate, or radically changed circumstances), and by markers that an action sequence is slowing down or terminating.

2. Try to match underlying template segments with surface segments. In general the latter will be episodes of the story. A valid match between a template segment and a surface segment establishes the *function* of the surface segment.

3. Apply the template recursively as much as necessary so as to obtain a coherent picture of what is going on semantically and structurally. There is no point in trying to establish the moons of Jupiter in solar orbits, nor in viewing the hand as a direct appendage of the body instead of as an appendage of the arm which is attached to the body. Hierarchical structuring[12] must be recognized in astronomy, biology and in textlinguistics. We can expect, therefore, to find within a story *embedded discourses* up to several layers—as many layers as seem necessary to obtain a plausible grouping.

4. Watch for peak-marking whether in respect to actions or themes. Action peaks are marked by a variety of means[13] which I will summarize here as (a) augmentation of the storyline (verb forms, sentence lengthening or shortening, crowding the storyline with a rapid sequence of happenings, with minute components of actions, or even with para-

---

11. This top-down, template-driven analysis amounts to a beginning sketch; to be more adequate the analysis needs to be extended downward to include relations within the paragraph in which sentences and groups of sentences are related according to what I term 'interclausal relations' (*Grammar*, Chapters 3 and 4); or according to the system of 'rhetorical relations' formulated by W. Mann and S. Thompson, *Relational Propositions in Discourse* (Technical Report ISI/RR-83-115; Marina del Rey, CA: Information Sciences Institute, 1983); and by the same two authors, *Rhetorical Structure Theory: A Theory of Text Organization* (Technical Report ISI/RS-87-190; Marina del Rey, CA: Information Sciences Institute, 1987); 'Rhetorical Structure Theory: A Framework for Analysis of Texts' (International Pragmatics Association Papers in Pragmatics 1.79-105). For a narrative analysis that is both top-down and template-driven and also carried down through interclausal relations within component paragraphs, see Longacre, *Joseph*.

12. Longacre, *Grammar*, Chapter 9.

13. Longacre, *Grammar*, Chapter 2.

phrase of actions as pseudo-happenings); (b) immediacy (detail and dialogue); and (c) maximum interlacing of participants, that is, the 'crowded stage' effect.[14] As mentioned above we can expect to find peak-marking applied to surface units which correspond to the Inciting Incident, the Climax or the Denouement. Didactic peaks are large segments of reported speech in which thematic material is developed.

5. Watch for parallelism and chiasm in the development of the story. The former can determine a *compound discourse*, where successive events in two sections of a story are developed in a parallel fashion not generally characteristic of the rest of the story. While detailed use of chiasm is often best analyzed as an overlay over the successively episodic structure,[15] a looser chiasm can be employed so that one episode which cross-references both to the beginning and also to the end is developed as a *Pivot* in the episodic structure of the story. Such a pivot may take peak-marking.

---

14. R.E. Longacre, *Storyline Concerns and Word-Order Typology in East and West Africa* (Studies in African Linguistics Supplements, 10; Los Angeles: University of California, 1990), pp. 8-9.

15. Thus, my template-driven, linear-recursive analysis of the Genesis Flood Narrative ('Discourse Structure') can be fruitfully compared with Wenham's chiastic analysis of the same (G.J. Wenham, 'The Conference of the Flood Narrative', *VT* 28 [1978], pp. 336-48). Likewise my analysis of Mark in this article may be compared with M.P. Scott's masterful chiastic analysis in 'Chiastic Structure: A Key to the Interpretation of Mark's Gospel', *BTB*, pp. 17-26. I do not feel that a linear-recursive analysis and a chiastic analysis are ultimately incompatible; rather, they reflect different modes of linguistic structuring. The linear-recursive analysis is an extrapolation from the grammar of the clause and the sentence. Chiastic analysis addresses itself to the content and colligational characteristics of a text, what the Pikes call 'referential structure'. Cf. K. Pike and E. Pike, *Grammatical Analysis* (Summer Institute of Linguistics Publications in Linguistics, 53; Dallas: Summer Institute of Linguistics and the University of Texas at Arlington, 1977). I believe, therefore, that the type of analysis that is presented here and chiastic analyses such as those proposed by Wenham and Scott are *complementary* rather than contradictory. Ethel Wallis of the Summer Institute of Linguistics also has published a chiastic analysis of Mark: 'Mark's Goal-Oriented Plot Structure', *JOTT* 10 (1995), pp. 30-45. One matter of considerable interest is that even my linear-recursive analysis presented here by setting up EPISODE 3 as pivotal makes the Transfiguration account central and in this respects agrees with Scott's taking Mk 9.7 as central to his chiastic structuring. We have, in effect, a two-map problem with a central piece of topography common to the two maps and thus facilitating the relating of the two.

2. *Narrative Analysis of the Gospel According to Mark*

It is assumed here that Mark's Gospel can be analyzed as a narrative. The broad category 'narrative' embraces both fact and fiction. But even a story rooted and grounded in fact—as I believe this one to be—must be shaped according to narrative conventions if it is to be successful with its readers.[16] We could, of course, argue that the Gospel is a special genre developed in order to present the mighty words and works of Jesus. But even the recognition of a specifically Gospel genre—with, for example, approximately a quarter of its bulk devoted to the last week in Jesus' life—can hardly escape classification as narrative. At any rate, common to all four canonical Gospels is the plot that turns on the struggle between Jesus and the establishment of his day—a struggle that culminates in trial, crucifixion, death and resurrection. And the presence of plot is a diagnostic trait of narrative.

I have set about to develop a top-down, template-driven and functional analysis of Mark's Gospel with application of the assumptions of the previous section to the analysis of the text. The editors (Aland *et al.*) present us with a Greek text of Mark neatly divided into 91 pericopes but it may be regarded as a foregone conclusion that the Gospel is not a simple linear sequence of these pericopes. Most assuredly there is a higher organization into bigger blocks. Most of the pericopes have, however, an introductory element that may be temporal, locative, circumstantial or participant-presentative. Very frequently motion verbs with given participants as subject introduce a pericope. While in my organization of the text of the Gospel into a hierarchy of units I do not always mention the introductory elements of a pericope in the discussion below, they are carefully catalogued in the display that constitutes an appendix to this paper. I do not make much use of the term 'pericope' in this analysis; rather I recognize them as episodes, which are typically on the lowest level of discourse embedding.

In that the Gospels present both the works and words of Jesus, I frequently posit didactic peaks on various levels of organization in the text. Outstanding works (miracles) are frequently found marked as

---

16. Ricoeur's discussion (*Time*, III) of the mutual relationships of fact and fiction within the overall narrative genre is a good contribution to this contemporary issue. Cf. also R.E. Longacre, 'Paul Ricoeur's Philosophy and Textlinguistic Analysis', in *The Nineteenth LACUS Forum 1992* (Lake Bluff, IL: The Linguistic Association of Canada and the United States, 1993), pp. 47-55.

peaks in various ways; such a marked account of a miracle I posit as *climactic* on various levels of structure. While the Gospel of Mark as a whole has a climax with a matching denouement, most of the embedded discourses end in a climax without a corresponding denouement. Typically an embedded discourse ends with an outstanding work which is reported in vividness and detail; each such climax further complicates the overall plot and makes increasingly urgent the thematic question 'Who is he?'

The use of the historical present in this Gospel has long been considered to be a prime analytical concern.[17] No amount of local contextual explanation in terms, for example, of continuity and discontinuity, can answer the simple question as to why it is used at all and especially why *clusters* of historical presents characterize the text at certain points. In keeping with my assumptions regarding peak-marking, according to which tampering with the tense of the verb is a specially sensitive area in many languages, I take the historical present, when occurring other than pericope-initial, when not limited to speech verbs, and when clustering within a passage, to be a peak marker. This has sometimes turned my analysis in unexpected directions. For example, I tried at first to handle the episode of Christ's prayer in the garden of Gethsemane as simply another episode in the progress towards the cross, but the proliferation of historical presents in the passage, Mk 14.32-42, forced me to change my analysis at this point. Ralph Enos's suggestive article is of special relevance in this regard; he, however, discusses isolated uses of the historical present which I do not consider here.

---

17. A considerable bibliography could be cited at this point. Stephen Levinsohn's work of recent years attempts to go at the matter of the historical present in the Gospels and Acts largely in terms of local cohesion, in what I would characterize as a 'bottom-up' approach in contrast to my 'top-down' analysis as illustrated in this article. Cf. S.H. Levinsohn, 'The Historic Present and Speech Margins in Matthew', in S. Hwang and W. Merrifield (eds.), *Language in Context: Essays for Robert Longacre* (Dallas: Summer Institute of Linguistics and the University of Texas at Arlington, 1992), pp. 451-74, and the same material presented as Chapter 10 in S.H. Levinsohn, *Discourse Features of New Testament Greek: A Coursebook* (Dallas: Summer Institute of Linguistics, 1992). I also want to cite here an excellent but little-known work by R. Enos, 'The Use of the Historical Present in the Gospel According to Saint Mark', *The Journal of the Linguistic Association of the Southwest* 3.2 (1981), pp. 281-98. Enos's article is especially noteworthy for its extensive bibliography of work done on the historical present prior to the writing of his article, including some earlier work of Levinsohn.

LONGACRE *A Top-Down, Template-Driven Narrative Analysis* 147

A suggested gross segmentation of the Gospel follows immediately below with further discussion following and with a more detailed analysis displayed in the appendix to this essay. In both analyses, capital letters signify primary constituents, that is, constituents of the Gospel as a whole. Capitalization of only the first letter of a word indicates constituents on the first level of discourse embedding. Italics symbolize constituents on a lower level of discourse embedding.

TITLE/APERTURE of whole 1.1
STAGE: The ministry of John the Baptist 1.2-8
EPISODE 1 (INCITING INCIDENT): 1.9-13 (either a brief embedded discourse or a compound paragraph)
  The Spirit comes on Jesus and confirms his Sonship; the heavens are 'split' 1.9-11
  The Spirit 'drives' him out to be tempted by the Devil 1.12-13
EPISODE 2 The rise to prominence 1.14–5.43
EPISODE 3 At full tide; Jesus a power figure and nurturer 6.1–8.26
EPISODE 4 (PIVOTAL): 'Who is he?' 8.27–9.50
EPISODE 5 The last journey to Jerusalem 10.1-52
EPISODE 6 (PEAK): 11.1–16.8
Episode 1 (Inciting Incident): The Triumphal Entry 11.1-11
Episode 2 (The DIDACTIC PEAK of the whole book): Teaching amid controversy 11.12–13.37
Episode 3 (The ACTION PEAK of the whole book): Events which culminate in the crucifixion (CLIMAX) and resurrection (DENOUEMENT) 14.1–16.8

I will not comment on here nor attempt to justify the above segmentation but will reserve such comment for the sections below which discuss EPISODES 1–6 in order. I do, however, mention briefly here the way in which I have analytically disposed of the first 13 verses of Mark's Gospel. The ambiguity of v. 1 as to TITLE/APERTURE is discussed extensively by Cranfield.[18] It structures plausibly either way. John the Baptist's ministry as forerunner is cited by Mark as fulfillment of Mal. 3.1 and Isa. 40.3. This resort to Old Testament quotation is noteworthy in Mark since he is not given to as frequent a use of such quotations as is Matthew. The Baptist's own words in vv. 7 and 8 underline the preparatory nature of his own ministry: 'After me will

---

18. C.E.B. Cranfield, *The Gospel According to St Mark* (Cambridge: Cambridge University Press, 1959), pp. 34-35. I take occasion here to commend Cranfield's sensitivity to the flow and structure of Mark's Gospel; he is not as slavishly verse-by-verse in his approach as are many traditional commentaries.

come one more powerful than I...' In terms of narrative structure the presentation of the Baptist and his ministry qualify as STAGE for all that follows. Nothing of the main story happens in its stage but the groundwork is laid for what follows. Later in his Gospel Mark felt obliged to recount the imprisonment and death of John the Baptist in the flashback account which is found in Mk 6.14-29 even though the account does not integrate too well into the ongoing story.

a. *EPISODE 1 (INCITING INCIDENT): 1.9-13*
The passage 1.9-13 qualifies well as EPISODE 1, the INCITING INCIDENT of the whole Gospel. While the Greek text of Aland *et al.* makes vv. 12-13 a separate pericope, probably because of the parallelism with Mt. 4.1-11 and Lk. 4.1-12, Mark here abbreviates and makes vv. 12-13 one compound unit with vv. 9-11. The only transition particle is Mark's omnipresent εὐθύς. There is, however, a new locale, the wilderness. The Holy Spirit does not enter the scene as a new participant but is carried over from v. 10. Satan is the new participant in the new locale. It seems simpler neither to compromise the ongoing unity of vv. 9-11 with vv. 12-13 nor to disregard their differences. Whether to consider the whole one compound paragraph or a short embedded discourse is somewhat irrelevant; the two seem to go together as the INCITING INCIDENT of the Gospel. As the Spirit descends on him the heavenly voice declares him to be the Son of God, thus preparing us as readers for the works and words of power that follow. Furthermore, such an explicit word as to the identity of the man Jesus does not occur again until we hear it in the voice from the cloud Mk 9.7, and finally from Jesus' own mouth at the time of the trial in 14.61-62—although this is implied in Peter's confession in 8.29 as well. Indeed the passage before us sheds light on the whole central and theologically pivotal portion EPISODE 4 (8.27–9.50), which I have entitled 'Who is he?'

Similarly, the temptation of Jesus prepares us for the heavy emphasis on exorcism which characterizes Mark's Gospel as well as for the conflict with the establishment of his day. We are, as it were, taken behind the ensuing scenes along the lines indicated later by Paul: 'For our struggle is not against flesh and blood, but against the rulers, against the authorities, against the powers of this dark world, and against the spiritual forces of evil in the heavenly realms' (Eph. 6.12).

Therefore, in a fundamental sense 1.9-13 sets us up for all that fol-

LONGACRE *A Top-Down, Template-Driven Narrative Analysis* 149

lows and may plausibly be considered to have the characteristics of an inciting incident.

b. *EPISODE 2: The Rise to Prominence 1.14–5.43*
It is plausible to consider that the balance of ch. 1 and the entire four chapters that follow constitute an embedded discourse with 1.14-15 patterning as Stage, ch. 4 as Didactic Peak and ch. 5 as Action Peak. The latter recounts in great detail three miracles of Jesus, the exorcism of the demons in the Gadarene demoniac and the raising of Jairus's daughter, interrupted by the healing of the woman with a long-term disturbance of her menstrual cycle. The last is itself unique, no other recorded miracle has such a story interrupting and bracketed by another story. Moreover, the argument that ch. 5 is to be regarded as the Action Peak of the first part of the book is reinforced by the consideration that special peak-marking features are present as well. The second half of the chapter, the miracle-within-miracle, is well marked by special verb forms. To begin with, the case history of the afflicted woman is given in a long string of participles culminating in the verb ἥψατο, 'she touched' (v. 27). This is an unusually long chain of participles preceding the finite verb and is reminiscent of medial-final chaining in languages of Papua New Guinea.[19] Then there is a clustering of historical presents in the bracketing story, the raising of Jairus's daughter. It is noteworthy that Luke Johnson in his recent commentary on Luke[20] also considers that Luke's recounting of these miracles constitutes the end of a major section of Luke. With the performance of this exorcism, the healing, and a raising of one from the dead this part of Mark's Gospel comes to a climax and is given appropriate surface development as such.

Chapter 4, concerning Jesus' teaching in parables and giving a sample ensemble of the same, can be considered to be an embedded discourse which constitutes the didactic peak of this second main section of the Gospel. The internal structure of this one-chapter embedded

---

19. Among the various works that could be cited here I take my 1972 monograph as an introduction to languages of this type: Robert E. Longacre, *Hierarchy and Universality of Discourse Constitutents in New Guinea Languages* (Washington, DC: Georgetown University Press, 1972).

20. L.T. Johnson, *The Gospel According to Luke* (Collegeville, MN: Liturgical Press, 1993). Johnson makes tracing the discourse-structure and flow one of the main concerns in his commentary.

discourse ends with an action episode, the calming of the storm (4.35-41). It is closely spliced onto the teaching that precedes by the connective expression in v. 36 'And sending away the crowds they took him as he was in the boat [where he had been seated teaching]'.

Episodes one to three of the embedded discourse which manifests main EPISODE 2 likewise pattern as embedded discourses whose constituents are on a still lower level of embedding (represented with italic letters). Thus, within EPISODE 2, Episode 1 (1.16-45) is the story of Jesus' initial ministry in and around Capernaum; it is an embedded narrative with five *episodes*, the last of which may be its *action peak*. These *episodes* recount, presumably in chronological order, the calling of the four fishermen (1.16-20), an exorcism in the synagogue (1.21-28), healings and exorcisms at the house of Peter (1.29-34), a preaching tour which begins the next morning (1.35-39) and, finally, his healing of a leper which provoked such a large following of people that he could no longer openly enter a town (1.40-45). The latter is certainly climactic but may perhaps lack the specific marking which we expect to find in a peak. It is not implausible to suggest that this embedded narrative is of Petrine origin.[21]

Episode 2 of the embedded discourse which constitutes EPISODE 2 of the main story is considered by some to reflect a topical arrangement of stories[22] which are concerned with the beginnings of Jesus' conflict with the authorities of his day. This, of course, does not deny the possibility that whatever their principle of selection they could have occurred substantially in the order in which they are introduced. The Episode is set off locationally by indicating a return to Capernaum and temporally by δι' ἡμερῶν, 'after some days'. The lower level *episodes* of this embedded discourse which manifests Episode 2 are five of which the first may be the *inciting incident* and the last is at least the climax and may have some peak marking: *Episode 1*: Jesus heals a paralytic and presumes (?) to forgive his sins (2.1-12 with several historical presents serving as peak marking in an inciting incident); *Episode 2*: Jesus encounters criticism by calling Levi and attending a banquet with him and his friends (2.13-17); *Episode 3*: (unfriendly) questions about

---

21. So Cranfield, *Mark*, p. 61. In respect to the first four episodes he remarks that they are 'a closely articulated group of four narratives of Petrine origin'. What I consider the climax of this section he considers simply 'a link to what follows' (p. 90).

22. Cranfield, *Mark*, p. 61.

LONGACRE *A Top-Down, Template-Driven Narrative Analysis* 151

fasting (2.18-22); *Episode 4*: the disciples are criticized for plucking and eating grain on the Sabbath (2.23-27); *Episode 5*: Jesus heals a man with a withered hand on the Sabbath and there is first mention of a plot to kill him (3.1-6, plainly climactic; the fact that all speech verbs are in the historical present may be peak marking in this instance).

c. *EPISODE 3: Jesus a Power Figure and Nurturer 6.1–8.26*
This major episode, which pictures Jesus at full tide, has a compound structure with two parts each expounded by an embedded discourse. In each of the parallel discourses which constitute the compound structure, there is a feeding miracle. Furthermore, each embedded discourse ends with miracles of healing which are told in typically Markan (Petrine?) detail accompanied by scintillating dialogue and the use of the historical present for non-speech verbs. These similarly peak-marked endings of the parallel discourses make it awkward to attempt to account for all of 6.1–8.26 as one linear string of episodes on the same level. The first of the two embedded discourses also embeds some lower-level discourses in two of its episodes.

Part 1 (6.1–7.37) has four episodes, a didactic peak and an action peak. The first three Episodes are somewhat disparate but probably belong here to a new main EPISODE after the clearly marked and brilliant climax that constitutes ch. 5. Episodes 1 and 2 are the rejection at Nazareth ('his own country') 6.1-6 and the sending out of the Twelve 6.7-13. Episode 3 (6.14-29) reports Herod's conjecture that Jesus was John the Baptist come back from the dead; then gives in a flashback the death of the latter. It thus for the first time raises the question 'Who is he?' that is thematic in EPISODE 4. Episode 4 (6.30-56) of this embedded discourse appears to be an embedded discourse with three *episodes*; the whole could be entitled 'Miracles performed back and forth across the lake'. Two non-healing miracles are reported here; both emphasize Jesus' power over nature. In *Episode 1* (6.30-44), the disciples return from their mission and Jesus feeds the 5000. In *Episode 2* (6.45-52), Jesus walks on the water. These supremacy-over-nature miracles are told with great clarity and vividness, but do not otherwise have peak marking nor are they positioned in their discourses where we might expect a peak to be positioned. *Episode 3* (6.53-56), compared to what precedes, is more of a summary statement of healings in and around Gennesaret. Mark's Gospel is not characterized by large teaching blocks as is Matthew's, but 7.1-23 is a large section of teaching by

Markan standards. I consider this passage to be Episode 5, didactic peak of the whole embedded discourse which constitutes Part 1 of EPISODE 3. This stretch of teaching deals with Jesus' impatience with criticism of his disciples having eaten with unwashed hands and asserts that what comes out of a person's inner being defiles him, not what descends into one's stomach. Perhaps this is not inappropriately located here by Mark in a section where Jesus is pictured as one providing food.

I find it plausible in regard to 7.24-37 to believe that the two pericopes which are found here are meant to be taken together in that they have cross-referencing settings in 6.24, which refers to Jesus' going away to the environs of Tyre, and in 6.31, which refers to his leaving the environs of Tyre, coming through the environs of Sidon, and eventually proceeding towards the Sea of Galilee through the Decapolis. On this ballistic movement out of the land of Israel and returning around its northern fringe, two miracles of healing are performed: *Episode 1*, the healing of the Syrophoenician woman's daughter, and *Episode 2*, the healing of the deaf and dumb man. Both miracles are recounted in vivid detail with reported dialogue; in addition the account of the second miracle features the verbs 'bring' and 'beseech' in the historical present (v. 32) and reports the popular evaluation 'He's done all things well; he makes the deaf to hear and the dumb to speak'. I therefore label this whole passage 7.24-37 as action peak of the discourse which constitutes Part 1 of EPISODE 3. As we see from here and the conclusion of Part 2 of this compound discourse—as well as from the placement of ch. 5 at the end of EPISODE 2—a typically Markan way of bringing a discourse to a close is by giving its last pericope special peak marking, reserving the historical present of non-speech verbs for the second of two such accounts if two are found in the overall unit.

Part 2 of the compound unit that manifests EPISODE 3 has a somewhat simpler structure but is in certain ways parallel to the discourse found in Part 1. Its Episode 1 (8.1-9) recounts the feeding of the 4000; Episode 2 (8.10-12) depicts the Pharisees demanding a sign and getting Jesus' enigmatic answer; Episode 3 (8.13-21) records the disciples' confusion on receiving Jesus' warning against the 'leaven' of the Pharisees and the Herodians; again the food motif occurs reinforced with Jesus' explicit back reference to the two feeding miracles (vv. 19-20). Finally, Episode 4 (8.22-26) is an action peak in many ways marked like the action peak of the preceding part of this compound discourse:

both in respect to the detail, the dialogue, and the use of the historical presents of the verbs 'bring' and 'beseech'. Only in this account, among all of Mark's miracle accounts, do we find a man reported as being healed in two stages!

d. *EPISODE 4 (PIVOTAL): 8.27–9.50*
While there is no reason to believe that this block as a whole is not consecutive upon what precedes and anterior to what follows, it has certain unique properties which lead me to characterize it as in some sense central and pivotal in the narrative. The theme of the whole major EPISODE 4 seems to be 'Who is he?' first raised in effect by Herod in EPISODE 3, Part 1, Episode 1 (6.14). But here the matter of Jesus' identity is peculiarly foregrounded. The answer given is twofold: (1) he is the Messiah, the Christ; and (2) he is to be a suffering Messiah. In Episode 1 (8.27–9.1) of the embedded discourse found here, Peter understood the first point but resisted the second and was summarily rebuked by his Lord, who not only identified himself with suffering but extended 'cross-bearing' to be the lot of all his true disciples. Christ's rebuke of Peter is very severe. In addressing Peter as 'Satan' it is as if Jesus is recalling the temptation in the wilderness—although Mark gives none of the cross-avoiding nature of the temptations as do the parallels in Matthew and Luke.

But if we are in doubt as to whether there is an allusion here to the INCITING INCIDENT in respect to both the Baptism and the Temptation, the central episode of this embedded discourse, that is, Episode 2 (9.2-13), the transfiguration and the immediately following incident, removes this doubt. In the Transfiguration the voice from the cloud 'This is my beloved Son' echoes the baptismal voice 'You are my beloved Son'—and anticipates the trial scene where Jesus is forced to confess his identity as 'The Christ, the Son of the Blessed One' (14.61). Furthermore, just as the Baptism is followed by the Temptation in the INCITING INCIDENT, so the transfiguration is followed by a conflict with Satan in the exorcism of the evil spirit from the child in 9.14-29— which is represented as a difficult exorcism which the disciples could not perform in spite of their having been empowered to exorcise demons in 3.15.

Two further Episodes conclude this major EPISODE 4. In Episode 3 (9.30-32) of this embedded discourse, Jesus foretells his death and resurrection a second time, and Episode 4 (9.33-50) records further teaching arising out of the quarrel as to who would be the greatest. Episode 3 further reinforces the point that Jesus as Messiah will prove to be a suffering Messiah. Episode 4, probably a hortatory discourse with three points, may well qualify as a didactic peak. Only the motion verb and the new locality mentioned in 9.33 keep us from joining the two Episodes. But Episode 3 is relatively unelaborated and could perhaps be grouped with what follows. If we were to make such a grouping then the whole embedded discourse which constitutes EPISODE 4 could be reduced to three episodes with the transfiguration and its aftermath as central, that is, pivotal in the pivotal section of the Gospel. The didactic material at the end of ch. 9 brings in a new motif, speaking or acting 'in my name' (vv. 37-41) which is at this juncture quite congruent with the identification of who Jesus is as developed in the previous passages. Granted who he is, the Messiah, the suffering Messiah, and the beloved Son of God, then words and deeds performed 'in his name' are appropriate.

Taking EPISODE 4 as pivotal to the whole Gospel, we see that Mark has constructed it well with Peter's confession and the Transfiguration as the two main pieces but with congruent material combined with them. There is a backward look at the INCITING INCIDENT and an insistent forward look towards the momentous events, suffering, death and resurrection, the recounting of which constitutes the ACTION PEAK of the Gospel. Verse counting is revealing—in spite of the lateness and occasional arbitrariness of verse division. I count 316 verses preceding EPISODE 3, PIVOTAL, and 312 verses following it!

e. *EPISODE 5: The Last Journey to Jerusalem 10.1-52*
I take 10.1a to signify the beginning of the last journey: 'Jesus then again left that place and went into the region of Judea and across the Jordan'. Cranfield[23] chooses to consider that the last journey begins in 8.27 in the neighborhood of Caesarea Philippi but I do not see how the detour over to the Mount of the Transfiguration fits this too well. At all events, making 8.27–9.50 a pivotal portion distinct from what precedes and what follows makes it more convenient to believe that the fateful journey begins with 10.1. Note also 10.17, 'As Jesus started on his way', and the somewhat more explicit reference to their being on their way to Jerusalem in 10.32, and, of course, the arrival in Jericho in 10.46. The travelogue discourse which constitutes ch. 10 has a clear

23. Cranfield, *Mark*, p. 266.

LONGACRE *A Top-Down, Template-Driven Narrative Analysis* 155

Stage in 10.1, three Episodes, a further Episode 4 which is a complex Didactic Peak, and Episode 5, which is an Action Peak. The latter, exploiting a device previously noted in Mark, consists of a healing miracle told with vivid detail and dialogue and with a historical present in its interior.

In this embedded discourse, Episode 1 (10.2-12) recounts a question concerning divorce and Jesus' answer; Episode 2 (10.13-16) recounts his blessing the children; and Episode 3 (10.17-31) gives the story of the rich man who inquired concerning eternal life but found the price too high—along with ensuing teaching. Episode 4 patterns as Didactic Peak, 10.32-45; it is an embedded discourse with two subepisodes. *Episode 1* (10.32-34) pictures Jesus resolutely leading the way towards Jerusalem while the disciples follow in fear. The first part of v. 32 may be the stage for what follows. Jesus teaches them in vv. 32b-34 even more explicitly concerning his betrayal, rejection and death at the hand of the Gentiles, and resurrection. *Episode 2* (10.35-45) recounts the request of the sons of Zebedee that they be given pre-eminence in the coming glory along with Jesus' solemn answer that they will indeed drink from his cup and be baptized with his baptism. All this could possibly be regarded as a distinct episode from what follows in vv. 41-45. Notice however, that in trying to calm the indignation of the other disciples against James and John, Jesus utters a saying fraught with deep meaning concerning his coming death: 'For even the Son of Man did not come to be served, but to serve, *and to give his life as a ransom for many*' (10.45). It seems plausible that this final reference by Jesus to his death forms with vv. 33-34 an inclusio which unites all 10.32-45 into one unit, namely Episode 4 of the embedded discouse which constitutes EPISODE 5 in the larger context. The contrast is exquisite: Jesus is preoccupied with his coming death, while the two disciples are preoccupied with their possible coming prerogatives and pre-eminence; even Jesus' answer to them is couched in symbolic figures of grief and suffering!

Finally all the above is followed by a typically Markan action peak (10.46-52), the healing of blind Bartimaeus. Note the wealth of detail and the dialogue. Even the giving of the blind man's name is of itself noteworthy. His yelling for help in an attempt to gain Jesus' attention, his calling him 'Son of David', the attempts of the crowd to quiet him, his making all the more of a scene, and finally Jesus' stopping in his tracks and asking for the man to be brought to him—all this is high drama. But more is to come: they call to the blind man (historical present); he throws aside his rags and springs to his feet to have his royal audience; Jesus makes him state his need and then heals him on the spot. So Bartimaeus becomes one of the many in the crowd following Jesus. All this is first-rate storytelling and is delivered by Mark in a style reserved for great moments in his Gospel. If the many vivid details here and in other such passages are from Mark's having heard such incidents first hand from Peter—as many suggest—then we are bound to commend Mark's placement of the incidents which are told in this vivid storytelling style; his placement of them so as to close out structural sections of his story, reflects the skill of a major craftsman.[24] As already mentioned, each such vividly described miracle properly functions as a climax in terms of increasing the confusion and embarrassment of Jesus' adversaries—and thus making inevitable the final CLIMAX and DENOUEMENT.

f. *EPISODE 6 (DIDACTIC PEAK and ACTION PEAK): 11.1–16.8*

I assume that this extensive embedded discourse has three major Episodes, the first of which is Episode 1, the Triumphal Entry (11.1-11); the second of which is Episode 2, the DIDACTIC PEAK (11.12–13.37); and the third of which is Episode 3, the ACTION PEAK (14.1–16.8). An alternative analysis in which the two peaks would each be separate major structural EPISODES of the entire Gospel is precluded by the fact that the triumphal entry seems to be the Inciting Incident for *all* that follows while the embedded discourses which encode the two peaks each have their own inciting incidents. Nevertheless, while structural concerns of this sort must be given their proper weight the two peaks which are so introduced must be considered to be high points of the entire Gospel. Here structural and semantic concerns are somewhat askew, and it is best not to sacrifice one set of concerns to the

---

24. Cranfield (*Mark*, pp. 11-12) believes that 'there are four different kinds of narrative material': (1) narratives with vividness of detail which may be of Petrine origin, (2) narratives 'which give the impression of being units of oral tradition which have been worn smooth by frequent repetition', (3) narratives which although based on tradition were possibly constructed by Mark himself, and (4) 'brief summary statements indicating in general terms what was happening during a certain period'. I rather suggest that, whatever the variation in source, the narratives have been subtly shaped and adapted by Mark himself to fit the varying needs of particular contexts in which they are found.

LONGACRE *A Top-Down, Template-Driven Narrative Analysis* 157

other. I therefore accept the anomaly that the twin peaks of the entire Gospel are encoded as episodes of an embedded discourse. This necessitates a further layer of embedding than I have used earlier in the analysis. Thus, while I will continue to use EPISODE for a major section of the entire Gospel, Episode for the next lower level of embedding, and *Episode* for the layer below that, I will need to refer to a still deeper level of embedding as **Episode**.

Episode 1, The Triumphal Entry into Jerusalem (11.1-11). This is clearly the inaugural event of Passion week. Furthermore, the account is marked as a great moment of the story by the use of the historical present not only at the opening in v. 1: 'And when they draw near to Jerusalem...he sends two of his disciples' (v. 2 'and says to them'); but also in the interior of the account in vv. 4 and 7: 'And they loose it [the colt]...And they bring the colt to Jesus, and they throw their garments up onto it.' It is plausible to take 11.1-11 as the inciting incident of all that follows in the Gospel from 11.12 to the conclusion. The triumphal entry provoked the debates of the last week and its salvific events.

Episode 2, DIDACTIC PEAK (11.12–13.37). I have combined three pericopes into *Episode 1*, the Inciting Incident of the embedded discourse which constitutes Episode 2, in that they form an ABA chiastic sequence: the cursing of the fig tree **Episode** 1, the cleansing of the temple **Episode** 2, the withering of the fig tree **Episode** 3. The three pericopes are closely tied chronologically, with the cursing of the fig tree and its withering taking place on successive mornings, and the cleansing of the temple on arrival at Jerusalem the first of the two days. As a chiasm, presumably the center section dominates and may shed some light on the interpretation of the surrounding segments. Is the fig tree meant to symbolize the nation of Israel here? But, although Jesus ends this whole Episode 2 DIDACTIC PEAK with a prophecy of the desolation of Jerusalem and the nation, he never in any place curses the city and its people. Eliminating the curse from the metaphor as possibly not germane to the comparison, there may still be symbolism in the apparently flourishing but fruitless tree and its withering.[25] In terms of the narrative template I take this to be an inciting incident on the

---

25. For discussion concerning this incident and its possible symbolic value, see Cranfield, *Mark*, pp. 254-57, and W.L. Lane, *The Gospel According to Mark* (Grand Rapids: Eerdmans, 1974), pp. 398-402.

grounds that the chiastic structure, even in absence of historical presents except in v. 15, amounts to a kind of peak-marking, that is, the Inciting Incident of the discourse which constitutes Episode 2. A similar chiastic unit (14.1-11) patterns as the Inciting Incident of Episode 3, the ACTION PEAK. It is the parallel use of these two chiastic structures to mark inciting incidents, as well as the strongly marked account of the Triumphal Entry as also an inciting incident, that provides the clue that a complicated situation of discourse embedding is present here. We have various intertwined structures that need to be untangled so as to permit the assignment of the proper inciting incident to its appropriate structure.

Episode 2, the DIDACTIC PEAK, once past *Episode 1*, its inciting incident, unrolls as a series of controversial exchanges between Jesus and his opponents and culminates in the Olivet Discourse which is an answer to an inquiry on the part of the disciples. In some of the controversial exchanges the opponents of Jesus take the initiative in propounding questions, in other exchanges Jesus himself takes the initiative. In the latter case, here and in the accompanying display in the appendix, I mark with an asterisk * *Episodes* in which Jesus takes the initiative. Perhaps the shifting inititatives indicate a further dialogue-like structure of proposal and response between certain of the episodes, but I have not at present recognized any such groupings. I proceed now to present what follows in Part 1 as *Episodes 2-11* below.

Episode 2, 11.27-33:	Jesus silences a question regarding his authority by countering with a question regarding what authority lay behind the ministry of John the Baptist.
**Episode 3*, 12.1-12:	Jesus, taking the initiative, gives the parable of the Tenant Farmers which his opponents recognize as having been spoken against them and incites their desire to arrest him (v. 12).
Episode 4, 12.13-17:	Jesus answers the question about paying tribute to Caesar with, 'Render unto Caesar the things that are Caesar's and unto God the things that are God's'.
Episode 5, 12.18-27:	Jesus answers a *reductio ad absurdum* argument of the Sadducees regarding the resurrection by teaching that there is no sex in the afterlife while nevertheless stoutly affirming the resurrection and the life to come.
Episode 6, 12.28-34:	On being questioned regarding the greatest commandment Jesus reaffirms love to God and other humans and commends his interrogator.

LONGACRE *A Top-Down, Template-Driven Narrative Analysis* 159

Episode 7, 12.35-37:	Jesus, seizing the initiative, questions them as to how the Messiah can simply be called David's son when the latter addresses him as Lord in Ps. 110.1.
Episode 8, 12.38-40:	Jesus denounces the scribes.
Episode 9, 12.41-44:	Jesus commends the widow's offering.
Episode 10, 13.1-2:	In response to a remark of the disciples, Jesus foretells the destruction of the Temple.
Episode 11, 13.3-36:	Didactic peak of the whole discourse which is DIDACTIC PEAK. This is a hortatory discourse (the Olivet Discourse) given in response to further inquiry from the disciples. It has at least three or four points and is not analyzed here.
Episode 3, ACTION PEAK, chs. 14, 15 and 16.1-8:	a narrative discourse pivoting around *Episode 3*, 14.32-42 (see below).
Episode 1, Inciting Incident 14.1-11:	This is a chiastic structure ABA with the plot to kill Jesus as **Episode** 1, 14.1-2; the anointing at Bethany as **Episode** 2, 14.3-9; and Judas's agreeing to betray Jesus as **Episode** 3, 14.10-11. In this little embedded discourse Mary's anointing of Jesus, told with great detail and pictured as provoking considerable discussion and criticism, is clearly the central piece. It stands as an example of reckless, abandoned worship, even though surrounded by plotting and betrayal. In commending her Jesus said, 'She came beforehand to anoint my body for burial'—thus focusing even Mary's act of devotion on his coming suffering and death. Not once does the narrator break step in the remorseless march towards the finale.
Episode 2, 14.12-31:	The Last Passover. Here there are subepisodes marked by temporal expressions and verbs of motion; with the first two subepisodes, the introductory verbs of motion are historical presents.
Episode 1, 14.12-16:	Preparations.
Episode 2, 7-21:	Prophecy of betrayal.
Episode 3, 14.22-26:	Institution of the Lord's Supper.
Episode 4, 14.27-31:	Peter's denial foretold.

Episode 3, Pivotal 14.32-42: Jesus prays in Gethsemane. This episode cannot simply be treated as another in the ongoing string of successive episodes. It contains nine verbs in the historical present, three of which are speech verbs (and hence not very evidential of special marking) but six of which are motion verbs. These verbs occur scattered through the passage not merely at its head. We do not find a similar spate of historical presents until the portrayal of the mocking and crucifixion in *Episode 8* below—where again nine examples of this tense occur. The final spate of historical presents is in *Episode 11* below, the resurrection, where three such verbs occur. Taking *Episode 8* below as climax marked for Action Peak, and *Episode 11* as denouement marked for Peak, we raise the question as to the status of this episode, *Episode 3* (the ordeal in Gethsemane).

What is happening narrative-wise is not hard to explain: the narrator is, as it were, gathering his feet under him for the final sprint. But it occurs late in the total stretch of the discourse expounding the ACTION PEAK for an inciting incident, and besides we have already assigned this function to 14.1-11. We simply have to view Mark's narrative as marking, in addition to the Inciting Incident, three great moments in the Passion Narrative: Gethsemane, Calvary and the Empty Tomb. I label the first of the three *Pivotal* along with the Climax and Denouement, represented in the latter two. Mark pictures the sufferings of Christ as beginning in Gethsemane and properly underscores that point. The concept of pivotal has also been used in reference to the total structure of Mark's Gospel in our setting up of main EPISODE 3 in this function.

Episode 4, 14.43-52: The betrayal and arrest of Jesus. The verb tenses again merit comment here. Curiously enough, not only is there a verb in the historical present in the first verse of this passage, 'And immediately while he was still talking, up comes Judas', but also in its last vv. 51-52: 'And a young man, wearing nothing but a linen garment was following along, and they seize him. And he fled away naked.' While it is not unusual to have historical presents of verbs of motion and speech which initiate a section or which occur both initially and in the interior of a section, it is somewhat rare to find them closing out a passage. Two explanations are possible: (1) the verses in question are in reality not an addendum to what preceded but a separate section (as punctuated by Aland *et al.*), or (2) Mark writes of himself in these verses and

LONGACRE *A Top-Down, Template-Driven Narrative Analysis* 161

the historical present is resultant on his own vivid personal recollection of the incident.[26] It is also noteworthy that a perfect occurs in pluperfect sense in 14.44: 'The one who betrayed him had given a sign (δεδώκει)'.

Episode 5, 14.53-65: Jesus before the Council.

Episode 6, 14.66-72: Peter's denials.

Episode 7, 15.1-15: Jesus is sentenced by Pontius Pilate.

Episode 8 Peak, 15.16-32 (maybe two subepisodes): Jesus is mocked and crucified. Nine historical presents are found in this passage. No longer is the historical present simply limited to motion, transportation, and speech verbs. The verbs in the historical present here are συγκαλοῦσιν 'they call together' v. 16; ἐνδιδύσκουσιν 'they clothe [him] in' v. 17; περιτιθέασιν 'they place upon' v. 17; ἐξάγουσιν 'they lead [him] out' v. 20; ἀγγαρεύουσιν 'they commandeer' v. 21; φέρουσιν 'they take away' v. 22; σταυροῦσιν 'they crucify' v. 24; διαμερίζονται 'they divide' (in an Old Testament quotation) v. 24; σταυροῦσιν (two thieves) v. 27.

Thus, not only do we have an impressive number of historical presents but a more unrestricted domain of their occurrence. The crucial verb 'crucify' occurs twice in the historical present in the passage. Historical presents dominate the action part of the episode until the action merges into reporting of speech acts (mockeries and taunts) in vv. 29-32, where no more historical presents are found.

Episode 9, 15.33-41: The death of Jesus.

Episode 10, 15.42-47: The burial.

Episode 11, 16.1-8: The resurrection. There are three historical presents in this passage: ἔρχονται 'they come' v. 2; θεωροῦσιν 'they see' v. 4; λέγει 'he says' v. 6. Again these verbs characterize three out of the eight verses in this brief account.

In regard to the almost universally felt problem regarding the abrupt

26. Cranfield, *Mark*, pp. 438-39; and Lane, *Mark*, pp. 526-28.

162   *Discourse Analysis and the New Testament*

ending of the Gospel according to Mark—a problem felt from the earliest centuries when at least two attempts were made to 'finish' the Gospel—I adopt the suggestion that Mark himself terminated the Gospel in this abrupt manner. Just as the Gospel starts abruptly so it by his intention ends abruptly with denouement as peak—without further wind-down or closure.[27]

3. *Evaluation of the Exegetical Worth of Such an Analysis*

What then? Is the analysis offered here simply another tedious example of overstructuring on the part of the analyst? In sidestepping this accusation I point out here some theological implications of the analysis. To begin with, however, let us recognize that our bracketing and labeling is no more a part of the authorial intent of the author Mark than phonological and grammatical analytic conventions figure with us in our immediate intuitive use of language. All such analytical devices—including those invoked in this essay—are attempts to make the message of a text explicit. But in invoking the narrative template as the starting point we appeal to something rooted in our cognitve structure. We know, for example, from how people react, that pointless stories, plots without resolution and ceaseless rounds of events without prominence or progress are not tolerated by listeners or readers. Furthermore, in invoking recursion, story-within-story or simply pause-for-station-identification breaks we tread again on ground provided by basic facts of language structure. From these cognitive and linguistic concerns the present analysis has come about.[28]

I point out here as of special interest several analytical results of considerable exegetical import: (1) The setting up of a compound discourse in EPISODE 2 elevates the two feeding miracles of Jesus above the nagging doubt that we have here simply a source-motivated doublet.

---

27. For a brief bibliography of older authorities (prior to 1955) that accepted the view here suggested, see Cranfield, *Mark*, p. 471—although he himself rejects this explanation.

28. I also note here the appearance of Mark Wegener's book *Cruciformed: The Literary Impact of Mark's Story of Jesus and his Disciples* (Lanham, MD: University Press of America, 1995). Wegener's study and mine have in common a concern for wholistic analysis and discourse movement. His book is especially to be commended for its further concern with reader impact of the Gospel.

LONGACRE *A Top-Down, Template-Driven Narrative Analysis* 163

Each feeding miracle is in a separate but parallel embedded discourse with startlingly similar closures in 7.31-37 and 8.22-26. By thus twice presenting Jesus as nourisher/provider a strong theological point is implicitly made (cf. Gen. 41.32) which another Gospel writer, John, explicitly develops in ch. 6 of his Gospel: Christ the bread of life. (2) Miracles of healing told in detail with sparkling dialogue mark climaxes in several parts of the ongoing work, namely ch. 5, 7.31-37 along with 8.22-26, and finally 10.46-52. Each such climactic display of Jesus' supernatural power makes more acute and agonizing the challenge to the establishment of his day and makes more crucial the question 'Who is he?' (3) The putting together of 8.27–9.50 as central and pivotal to the whole work, connecting plausibly with the baptism and temptation in the Inciting Incident and with the trial scene at the end, foregrounds the question of the identity of Jesus: the claim is made that the historical Jesus is a supernatural figure, the Christ. All this is vindicated by the denouement of the Gospel, the resurrection. Even a linear/recursive analysis such as that here presented yields at this point to the presence of chiastic elements in Mark's composition. (4) The recognition of didactic peaks in Mark is a way of showing how larger blocks of teaching are deployed characteristically before action peaks, as in ch. 4, the parables; 7.1-23, clean and unclean foods; 10.32-45, servanthood in the light of Jesus' sufferings; and especially 11.12–13.37, the controversy-enveloped last teachings. (5) The manner in which Mark underscores the scene of Jesus' praying in the garden constrains us to recognize that the grand action finale has three great events: Gethsemane, Calvary and the empty tomb—with profound theological implications. (6) The recognition of local chiastic structures in 11.12-26 and in 14.1-11 has further import. With the former, the cleansing of the Temple is surely inciting and provocative of much of the following controversy, but it is wrapped up in the enacted parable of the cursed and withering figtree. In the latter passage, while conspiracy and betrayal lead to all that follows, Mark gives the story a wonderful twist by putting in, as the key of the chiasmus, the anointing of Jesus at Bethany—implying that devotion to the wonderful figure revealed in his Gospel will in the end outweigh conspiracy and dark betrayal.

Appendix

DISPLAY OF THE DISCOURSE STRUCTURE OF THE GOSPEL ACCORDING TO MARK

1. *Basic Assumptions*

A. Very probably Mark is not a simple linear sequence of pericopes—91 according to Aland *et al.*—such as we might obtain by attention to breaks based on all possible transition markers, e.g. time expressions (T), locative expressions (L), or introduction of new participants. Very probably a series of more inclusive blocks is present and these should have some relation to the typical narrative template.

B. Inciting incidents and peaks, both didactic and action, are very probably involved—as well as certain episodes which may be called *pivotal*.

C. Multiple occurrences of the historical present (HP), especially when not limited to verbs of speech or to verbs of speech and motion, may contribute to such marking as suggested in B above. Ralph Enos's suggestion (1981), that pericope-initial HP's may mark material of special theological importance, is of possible relevance. For this reason a pericope-initial HP is labelled below with the sign #. Typically these are motion verbs or verbs of speech.

APERTURE of whole book 1.1

STAGE of whole book (ministry of John) 1.2-8

EPISODE 1 (INCITING INCIDENT) 1.9-13. A brief embedded discourse or a compound paragraph:
    The Holy Spirit comes on Jesus and confirms his sonship; the heavens are 'split'
    The Holy Spirit drives# him out to be tempted by the Devil

EPISODE 2 The rise to prominence 1.14–5.43
    Stage: Time, place, circumstances, Jesus and his message 1.14-15
    Episode 1 An embedded discourse with five episodes, the last of which *may* constitute an action peak: 1.16-45.
        Episode 1 Calls four fishermen 1.16-20
        Episode 2 (motion verb#, place name) Exorcism in the synagogue 1.21-28
        Episode 3 Healings and exorcisms at the house of Peter 1.29-34
        Episode 4 (T, motion verb) Preaching tour begins next morning 1.35-39
        Episode 5 (action peak?) (motion verb#, participant) Heals a leper and great crowds follow so that he can no longer openly enter a city 1.40-45

LONGACRE *A Top-Down, Template-Driven Narrative Analysis* 165

Episode 2 (Capernaum, T 'after some days') Tangling with critics (embedded discourse with five episodes, the first of which is Inciting Incident and the last of which is Peak) 2.1–3.6:
  Episode 1 (Inciting Incident) (several HP's) Jesus heals a paralytic and presumes (?) to forgive his sins. (The latter is the big point according to Matthew who omits all the interesting details.) 2.1-12
  Episode 2 (motion verbs, L, and πάλιν) Jesus calls Levi and eats with sinners 2.13-17
  Episode 3 (motion verb#, speech verb#, participant switch) Questions about fasting 2.18-22
  Episode 4 (motion verb, L) Plucking and eating grain on the Sabbath 2.23-27
  Episode 5 Action Peak (πάλιν, all speech verbs are HP) Jesus heals a man with a withered hand on the Sabbath; first mentioning of a plot to kill him 3.1-6
Episode 3 Increasing confrontation and misunderstanding (embedded discourse with four episodes):
  Episode 1 (many place names, Jesus, motion verbs) Attempted withdrawal, great crowds, teaches from a boat 3.7-12
  Episode 2 (motion verb#, verb 'call'#, L) Choosing of the Twelve 3.13-19
  Episode 3 (2 motion verb#, L, and πάλιν) Great crowds; his family sets out to fetch him home; those who ascribe his power to Beelzebub receive a solemn warning 3.20-30
  Episode 4 (motion verb#, participant switch; all verbs of speech are HP) Arrival of his family; Jesus says that his disciples are his true family—is this a peak? 3.31-35
Episode 4 didactic peak (motion verb#, L, and πάλιν) Parables and aftermath 4.1-41. Internal structure? Two episodes, the second of which is an action peak which concludes a hortatory discourse:
  Episode 1 One long compound paragraph with clear aperture and closure—reinforced by a mid-paragraph reference in vv. 11-12; the theme is teaching in parables 4.1-34
  Episode 2 (action peak) This section is tightly connected to what precedes by 'evening of same day' and 'they take# him as he was in the boat' (L, internal HP's). Jesus stills a storm on the lake; for the first time the question is raised 'Who is he?' 4.35-40
Episode 5 action peak of whole embedded discourse (i.e. of 1.14–5.43) Great miracles in great detail. All of ch. 5 is an embedded discourse with two episodes the second of which has more explicit peak-marking:
  Episode 1 (L, motion verb) Healing of Gadarene demoniac 5.1-20
  Episode 2 (L, motion verb, proper names Jesus and Jairus; story within a story with woman's case history given in string of participles, HP's in the bracketing story) 5.21-43

EPISODE 3 compound narrative discourse with two somewhat parallel parts, Jesus at full tide as power figure and nurturer 6.1–8.26
Part 1 embedded discourse with four episodes, didactic peak and action peak.
　Episode 1 (2 motion verbs#, L) Rejection at Nazareth 6.1-6
　Episode 2 ('calls'#, new participants) Jesus sends out the Twelve 6.7-13
　Episode 3 (new participant, Herod raises question of Jesus' identity) flashback records death of John the Baptist 6.14-29
　Episode 4 embedded discourse with three episodes 6.30-56 (back and forth across the lake):
　　Episode 1 (motion verb#, participants, name Jesus) Disciples return and Jesus feeds the 5000 6.30-44
　　Episode 2 (motion verb, L) Jesus walks on water 6.45-52 (motion verb# in v. 48)
　　Episode 3 (motion verb, L) Healing in and around Gennesaret 6.53-56
　Episode 5 didactic peak (motion verb#, new participants) Disputation about the 'clean' and the 'unclean' 7.1-23
　Episode 6 action peak, Miracles performed on excursus through territory of Tyre and return; the two subepisodes have cross-referencing settings, dialogue and detail:
　　Episode 1 (motion verb, L, participant) The faith of Syrophoenician woman 7.24-30
　　Episode 2 (motion verb, L, participant, πάλιν) Healing of the deaf and dumb man 7.31-37 ('bring'# and 'beseech'# in v. 32; cf. 8.22-26 below)
Part 2 embedded discourse with three episodes and action peak:
　Episode 1 (time, participants, πάλιν) Feeding of the 4000 8.1-9
　Episode 2 (motion verb, L, participants) Pharisees demand a sign 8.10-12
　Episode 3 (motion verb, πάλιν) The 'leaven' of the Pharisees and Herod 8.13-21
　Episode 4 action peak (motion verb#, 'bring'#, 'beseech'# L, participant) Blind man healed in two stages! (unique in miracles of Jesus) 8.22-26

EPISODE 4 (CENTRAL AND PIVOTAL) 'Who is He?' 8.27–9.50 (316 verses precede this passage; 312 verses follow), embedded discourse with four episodes:
　Episode 1 (L—on the road to Caesarea Philippi, name Jesus) Peter's confession, Jesus predicts his death, rebukes Peter, and teaches on cross-bearing 8.27–9.1
　Episode 2 (time, L, 'takes'#, motion verb#, names of Jesus and three disciples) Transfiguration and aftermath, embedded discourse with two episodes:
　　Episode 1 Transfiguration 9.2-13 (the voice from the cloud, cf. 1.11)
　　Episode 2 (motion verb, L, participants) Jesus heals the boy with the evil spirit 9.14-29 (motion verb# in v. 25)
　Episode 3 (motion verb, L) Jesus foretells his death a second time 9.30-32

LONGACRE *A Top-Down, Template-Driven Narrative Analysis* 167

Episode 4 (motion verb, L) Teaching arising out of the quarrel as to who would be the greatest 9.33-50 (new theme 'in my name' vv. 36, 38, and 39-41)

EPISODE 5 The last journey to Jerusalem, embedded discourse with six episodes ch. 10:
Stage (2 motion verb#, πάλιν [2×]) 10.1
Episode 1 (participant?—textual variation) Questions on divorce 10.2-12
Episode 2 (motion verb, participants) Jesus blesses the children 10.13-16
Episode 3 (motion verb, participant) The rich young ruler; resultant teaching 10.17-31
Episode 4 didactic peak, compound discourse with two subepisodes 10.32-45:
Episode 1 (motion verb, L—in the road going up to Jerusalem, name Jesus) Jesus leads the way up to Jerusalem and for third time predicts his death 10.32-34
Episode 2 (motion verb#, proper names) Request of James and John provokes further teaching on servanthood, culminating with an insightful saying on the meaning of his death 10.35-45
Episode 5 action peak (motion verb#, participant) Healing of blind Bartimaeus. Story told with dramatic detail and dialogue ('call'# in v. 49) 10.46-52

EPISODE 6 DIDACTIC PEAK and ACTION PEAK 11.1–16.8:
Episode 1 Inciting Incident (motion verb#, 'send'#, 'say'# L, T, three more HP's occur internal) The triumphal entry 11.1-11
Episode 2 DIDACTIC PEAK 11.12–13.37, In the verbal dueling below * marks where Jesus takes the initiative:
Episode 1 Inciting Incident, a chiastic structure ABA
Episode 1 (motion verb, T, L) The cursing of the fig tree 11.12-14
Episode 2 (motion verb#, L) The cleansing of the Temple 11.15-19
Episode 3 (motion verb, T) The withering of the fig tree; lesson on faith 11.20-26
Episode 2 (2 motion verbs#, T, participants) The authority of Jesus is questioned 11.27-33
*Episode 3 Parable of the Tenants 12.1-12
Episode 4 (motion verb#, T, L, participants) Question regarding paying tribute to Caesar 12.13-17
Episode 5 (motion verb#, participants) Question regarding the resurrection 12.18-27
Episode 6 (motion verb, participants) Question regarding the greatest commandment 12.28-34
*Episode 7 (L) Jesus questions them about David's son 12.35-37
*Episode 8 Jesus denounces the scribes 12.38-40
*Episode 9 (L) Jesus commends the widow's offering 12.41-44

Episode 10 (motion verb, L, response to a remark of his disciples) Jesus foretells the destruction of the temple 13.1-2

Episode 11, didactic peak of this embedded discourse (motion verb, L, answer to a question put by three disciples) 'Olivet discourse' (hortatory, with at least three or four points; analysis not given here)

Episode 3 ACTION PEAK, chs. 14, 15 and 16.1-8:

Episode 1 (T) Inciting Incident in a chiastic structure ABA

Episode 1 (T, participants) The plot to kill Jesus 14.1-2

Episode 2 (motion verb, L, participants) The anointing at Bethany 14.3-9

Episode 3 (motion verb, participants) Judas agrees to betray Jesus 14.10-11

Episode 2 The Last Passover 14.12-31

Episode 1 ('send'#, long T) Preparations 14.12-16

Episode 2 (motion verb#, T) Prophecy of betrayal 14.17-21

Episode 3 Institution of the Lord's Supper 14.22-26

Episode 4 (Proper name Jesus) Peter's denial foretold 14.27-31

Episode 3 pivotal (motion verb#, L, eight HP's) Jesus prays in Gethsemane 14.32-42

Episode 4 (motion verb#, participants—Judas) Betrayal and seizure 14.43-52 (HP in the isolated incident mentioned at the close in v. 52)

Episode 5 (motion verb#, proper name Jesus, participants) Jesus before the council 14.53-65

Episode 6 (motion verb#, participants) Peter's denials 14.66-72

Episode 7 (motion verb, T, L, participants) Jesus is sentenced by Pontius Pilate 15.1-15

Episode 8 Action Peak (motion verbs, both initial and internal, new participants, nine HP's) (maybe two subepisodes) Jesus is mocked and crucified 15.16-32

Episode 9 (T marked twice, darkness, proper name Jesus) Jesus dies 15.33-41

Episode 10 (motion verb, T, participant) The burial 15.42-47

Episode 11 Peak (denouement) (motion verb, T marked twice, L, participants, three HP's) The resurrection 16.1-8

12

MARK 5.1-43: GENERATING THE COMPLEXITY OF
A NARRATIVE FROM ITS MOST BASIC ELEMENTS

Robert E. Longacre

1. *Introduction*

This essay is intended as a sequel to my overview of the Gospel of Mark.[1] As I say in n. 11 to that essay, 'This top-down, template-driven analysis amounts to a beginning sketch; to be more adequate the analysis needs to be extended downward to include relations within the paragraph in which sentences and groups of sentences are related according to what I term "interclausal relations" '.[2] But the analysis of such lower-level groupings turns on more than simply logical and rhetorical relations, as important as they are. The analysis necessarily must also take into account a hierarchy of information types, that is, the storyline and different sorts of relatively foregrounded and relatively backgrounded pieces of information, as reflected in the use of tense/aspect in the verbs of the component clauses.[3] In this regard, the priority of the Greek aorist has long been recognized as crucial to Greek narrative. But other forms in addition to the aorist have their place in building a Greek narrative and it is the intent of this essay to attempt a preliminary systematization of these functions and their semantic reflexes. I will try to demonstrate here the intimate tie-in between constituency structure and the functions of various forms of the Greek verb in reference to Mark 5.

In section 2 of this essay I consider Mk 5.1-20, the account of the healing of the Gadarene demoniac, present a stepped tree diagram of

---

1. See the previous essay in this volume, 'A Top-Down, Template-Driven Narrative Analysis, Illustrated by Application to Mark's Gospel'.

2. See R.E. Longacre, *The Grammar of Discourse* (New York: Plenum Press, 2nd edn, 1996), Chapters 3 and 4.

3. R.E. Longacre, 'Two Hypotheses Regarding Text Generation and Analysis', *Discourse Processes* 12 (1989), pp. 416-60.

this passage, and posit a saliency scheme for the various forms of the Greek verb that are used within it. In the course of doing this it is necessary to recognize a distinction between the function of the participle when preposed to the main clause and when postposed to the main clause, and to relate this distinction to the grammar of 'chaining' languages found around the world.

In section 3 of this essay I consider Mk 5.21-43, the account of the raising of Jairus's daughter along with the interrupting account of the healing of the woman with the issue of blood. I give stepped diagrams of these accounts with prose commentary on the same. In analyzing this part of the chapter the understanding of the role of the historical present becomes especially crucial.[4]

In section 4 I demonstrate the feasibility of generating Mk 5.21-43 by obtaining an abstract of the story as given in the clauses that have aorist verbs, and progressively fleshing out the abstract of the story by adding in order the following: clauses with the historical present, then clauses with preposed participles, then finally clauses with verbs in the imperfect—thus building up the text in four stages by a kind of lamination. This leads to a recognition of the peculiar elevated style used in the second half of Mark 5, a consideration of the thrust and import of this style, and the suggestion of a special salience scheme which could be posited to accommodate this passage and others.

Finally, in section 5 I compare Matthew's highly abbreviated, but parallel, account of this same passage with the Markan account. Without committing myself to any theory of literary dependency, I attempt to show that what is omitted in Matthew relates quite systematically to material found in certain information bands in Mark.

Mark 5 has been chosen as the testing ground for the theory of the interdependence of verb saliency and constituency structure because it occurs at a crucial spot in the structure of the Gospel, and for that reason has a certain fulness of structure and style. It concludes the first main section of the Gospel—which I entitle 'The Rise to Prominence' (1.14–5.43)—following the Stage (1.2-8), the Ministry of John the Baptist; and Episode 1, Inciting Incident (1.9-13), the Holy Spirit

---

4. For a little-known but careful piece of work I cite R. Enos, 'The Use of the Historical Present in the Gospel According to Saint Mark', *The Journal of the Linguistic Association of the Southwest* 3.2 (1981), pp. 281-98. See also S.H. Levinsohn's *Discourse Features of New Testament Greek: A Coursebook* (Dallas: Summer Institute of Linguistics, 1992), Chapter 10.

comes on Jesus at his baptism and confirms his Sonship, then drives him out to be tempted of the Devil. Chapter 5, with its three miracles—the healing of the Gadarene demoniac, the raising of Jairus's daughter, and the healing of the woman with the disorder in her menstrual cycle—marks the peak of the whole embedded discourse that treats of Jesus' rise to prominence.[5] Mark typically winds down major and some minor sections of his Gospel with miracle stories told very dramatically with great detail and with reported dialogue. Mark 5 illustrates these peak-marking features. The occurrence of one story interrupting another story occurs nowhere else in either Mark or the other synoptics than in this pericope. Therefore this feature is highly unusual. In addition, the accounts in this chapter are given with consummate narrative skill. While all the three miracles that occur in ch. 5 are marked with typically Markan detail and dialogue, the two interwoven stories of the second half of the chapter are especially marked by ringing the changes on the various possible forms of the Greek verb.

2. *Mark 5.1-20, the Healing of the Gadarene Demoniac*

In terms of the categories of the narrative template[6] we can distinguish sections of this story: Stage, 5.1-5; Inciting Incident, 5.6-8; Climax, 5.9-10; Denouement, 5.11-14, Closure, 5.15-20. Each of these sections has the structure of a recognizable paragraph type.

The Stage is expounded by a narrative comment paragraph. The Setting of this paragraph is a simple sentence with a motion verb in the aorist. Motion verbs are primarily verbs of orientation; here the verb ἦλθον, 'came', fulfills the narrative strategy of getting Jesus to the other side of the lake where he can interact with the Gadarene demoniac: 'And he came to the other side of the lake to the country of the Gerasenes'. The thesis of this sentence is a simple sentence with a preparatio and a relative clause. The preparatio (see next section), a genitive absolute, links the coming event with the previous sentence and signals an impending change of actor: 'And as he came up out of the boat...' The sentence base reveals the new actor: 'immediately there met him [aor.] out of the tombs a man with an unclean spirit who had [impf.] his dwelling in the tombs'. After this initial identification of

---

5. See Longacre, 'Top-Down, Template-Driven'.
6. See Longacre, *Grammar*, Chapter 2.

the man, the Comment part of the paragraph follows. The Comment is expounded by a chiastic observation paragraph consisting of evidence 1, conclusion, and evidence 2. The conclusion, the key of the chiasm, states briefly with a verb in the historical present (conclusion of v. 4): 'And no one is able to tame him'. The preposed evidence 1 is found in the second half of v. 3 and most of v. 4; the latter is an involved infinitival construction which does not translate smoothly into English: 'No one could bind him with a chain—though often having been bound with chains and foot-fetters, he burst the chains and pulled apart the foot-fetters'. The postposed evidence 2 in the second half of v. 5 further emphasizes the man's desperate condition with skillful parallel phrases: 'And all night and all day, in the tombs and on the mountains, he was crying out and cutting [periphrastic impfs.] himself with stones'.

The Inciting Incident can be taken to be vv. 6-8 which constitute a narrative sequence paragraph. Its first Sequential Thesis is expounded by a coordinate sentence with preparatio: 'And seeing Jesus from afar, he ran [aor.] and knelt [aor.] before him'. Sequential Thesis 2 is somewhat more involved in that it is expounded by a narrative reason paragraph. The Thesis of this embedded paragraph is a Quotation sentence with a preparatio and a speech verb in the historical present. 'And crying out with a loud voice, he says "What do we have in common, Jesus Son of the Most High God? I put you on oath before God that you don't torture me".' The Reason unit of the embedded paragraph gives the reason why the demoniac was so disturbed: 'For Jesus had been commanding [impf.] him, "Come out of the man, you unclean spirit"'.

I take the Climax to be vv. 9-10—although there is certain flow of the Inciting Incident into the Climax. The structure of the Climax is a resolved dialogue paragraph[7] with a terminus at its end. The semantic structure is that of question and answer. Jesus asks the man his name, and the demons reply, 'Legion is my name, for we are many'. As to speech verbs in the quotation formulas, the quotation formula of the question employs an imperfect verb and the quotation formula of the answer, a historical present. The terminus adds (with another impf. verb), 'And they kept beseeching him not to send them out of the country'. The Climax pictures the struggle as squarely joined, with Jesus intent on exorcising the demons and the demons unwilling to come out and be gone.

The Denouement is swift and dramatic (vv. 11-14) and is reported in

---

7. Cf. Longacre, *Grammar*, Chapter 5: 'Repartee: Dialogue Paragraphs'.

an Execution paragraph. The Setting of this paragraph is a simple sentence whose 'be' verb is in the imperfect: 'And there was near there a great herd of swine grazing on the mountainside'. The Plan element of the paragraph is given in a simple sentence with a consecutive (see next section), in this case the verb 'say' which introduces a quotation: 'And they beseeched him [aor.], saying, "Send us into the swine that we may enter into them".' The Execution is expounded by a narrative result paragraph whose Thesis is very terse: 'And he gave permission [aor.] unto them'. The Result is more complex: it consists of a narrative sequence paragraph with two Sequential Theses, each expounded by a coordinate sentence. The Sequential Thesis 1 is a coordinate sentence wth a preparatio and three coordinated bases: 'And the unclean spirits having come out of the man, entered [aor.] into the swine, and the herd rushed down [aor.] a cliff into the lake (around two thousand), and were drowned [aor.] in the lake'. Sequential Thesis 2 is expounded by a coordinate sentence which at first glance seems to have three coordinated bases but on closer look it appears that the first two coordinated bases are associated into a coordinate sentence against the third. Consequently we consider that the first base of the coordinate sentence is itself expounded by a coordinate sentence: 'And the ones who cared for them fled [aor.] and announced [aor.] to the town and countryside'. These two clauses group with the second base of the higher layer of sentence structure: 'And they came to see what had happened'.

The Closure, which treats of ensuing events (vv. 15-20), is one long narrative sequence paragraph with three sequential theses, the third of which is expounded by a simple dialogue paragraph which consists of a proposal, an answer and a correlate. The Setting of this narrative Sequence paragraph is expounded by a coordinate paragraph with three bases. The Setting is depictive and graphic, with the verbs of the first two bases historical presents and the verb of the last base an aorist: 'And they come, and they see the one who had been possessed sitting, clothed, and in his right mind, the one who had had the legion, and they feared [aor.]'. Sequential Theses 1 and 2: 'And those who had seen how it happened to the possessed one gave their account [aor.], and concerning the swine. And they began [aor.] to ask him to leave their country.' Sequential Thesis 3, as mentioned above, is expounded by a simple resolved dialogue paragraph. The Initiating Utterance (Proposal) of this dialogue is reported in a simple sentence with preparatio; it functions as an indirect quotation 'And as he was getting into the boat [gen. abs.],

174 *Discourse Analysis and the New Testament*

the one who had been possessed was begging [impf.] him that he might be with him'. The Resolving Utterance (Response) is expounded by a contrast sentence, the second base of which is adversative and embeds a quotation sentence: 'And Jesus did not permit [aor.] him, but says [historical present] to him, "Go back to your house and your family, and tell them how much the Lord has done for you and has had mercy on you".' The last sentence (v. 20) I label a Correlate.[8] A correlate reports activity which correlates with the Response of a Dialogue or Execution paragraph. Here the correlate is the coordinate sentence that reports the actions of the man in response to Jesus' injunction: 'And he went away [aor.], and he began [aor.] to proclaim in the Decapolis how much Jesus had done for him and had had mercy upon him'.

This is summarized and graphically illustrated in Diagram 1, which is a stepped (tree) diagram; abbreviations within the diagram correspond to the units set up discursively above. In constructing this diagram I have used my apparatus for describing paragraph types.[9]

Diagram 1. *Stepped (Tree) Diagram of Mark 5.1-20*

Stage: (N) Comment paragraph (5.1-5)
    Setting: and he came (aor.) to the other side of the lake to the country of the Gerasenes
    Thesis: Simple S with preparatio
        Preparatio: And as he came up out of the boat (gen. abs.)
        Base: immediately there met (aor.) him a man out of the tombs with an unclean spirit who had (impf.) his dwelling in the tombs.
    Comment: chiastic Observation paragraph:
        Evidence 1: And no one could (impf.) bind him with a chain—though often having been bound with chains and foot-fetters he burst the chains and pulled apart the foot-fetters (infinitival constructions)
        Conclusion: No one is able (HP) to tame him
        Evidence 2: By night and day among the tombs and on the mountainsides he was (impf.) crying out and cutting himself with rocks

---

8. Cf. R. Mansen and K. Mansen, 'The Structure of Sentence and Paragraph in Guajiro Narrative Discourse', in R.E. Longacre and F. Woods (eds.), *Discourse Grammar: Studies in Indigenous Languages of Colombia, Panama, and Ecuador, Part 1* (Dallas: Summer Institute of Linguistics/University of Texas at Arlington, 1976), pp. 147-258.

9. Longacre, *Grammar*, Chapter 4.

Inciting Incident: (N) Sequence paragraph (5.6-8)
    Seq. Thesis 1: Coord S with preparatio
        Preparatio: And seeing Jesus from afar
        Base 1: he ran (aor.)
        Base 2: and knelt before him (aor.)
    Seq. Thesis 2: (N) Reason paragraph
        Thesis: Quotation S with preparatio
            Preparatio: And crying out with a loud voice
            QF: he says (HP)
            Q: 'What do we have in common, Jesus, Son of the Most High God; I put you on oath before God that you don't torture me.'
        Reason: For Jesus had been (impf.) commanding him, 'Come out of the man you unclean spirit'.
Climax: Simple dialogue paragraph (5.9-10)
    IU (Q): and Jesus asked (impf.) him, 'What is your name?'
    RU (A): And he says (HP) to him, 'Legion is my name, for we are many'.
    Terminus: And they kept beseeching (impf.) him not to send them out of the country.

Denouement: Execution paragraph (5.11-14)
    Setting: And there was (impf.) near there a great herd of swine grazing on the mountainside
    Plan: Simple S with consecutive
        Base: And they beseeched (aor.) him,
        Consecutive: Quotation S
            QF saying
            Q: 'Send us into the swine that we may enter into them'.
    Execution: (N) Result paragraph
        Thesis: And he gave permission (aor.) to them
        Result: (N) Sequence paragraph
            Seq. Thesis 1: Coord S with preparatio
                Preparatio: and the unclean spirits having come out of the man
                Base 1: entered (aor.) into the swine,
                Base 2: And the herd rushed down (aor.) a cliff into the lake (around 2000),
                Base 3: and were drowned (aor.) in the lake.
            Seq. Thesis 2. Coord S
                Base 1. Coord S
                    Base 1: And the one who cared for them fled (aor)
                    Base 2: and announced (aor.) to the town and counryside;
                Base 2: and they came to see what had happened.

176   *Discourse Analysis and the New Testament*

Closure: (N) Sequence paragraph (5.15-20)
   Setting: Coord S
      Base 1: And they come (HP)
      Base 2: And they see (HP) the one who had been possessed sitting, clothed, and in his right mind, the one who had had the Legion.
      Base 3: and they feared (aor.).
   Seq. Thesis 1: And those who had seen how it happened to the possessed one gave their account (aor.), and concerning the swine.
   Seq. Thesis 2: And they began (aor.) to beg him to leave their country
   Seq. Thesis 3: Simple Dialogue paragraph
      IU (Prop): Simple S with preparatio (participle in gen. abs.)
         Preparatio: And as he was getting into the boat
         Base: the one who had been possessed was begging (impf.) him that he might be with him.
      RU (Response): Contrast S
         Base 1: And Jesus did not permit (aor.) him,
         Adversative Base: Quotation S
            QF: but he says (HP) to him
            Q: Coord S
               Base 1: 'Go back to your house and your family,
               Base 2: and tell them how much the Lord has done for you and has had mercy upon you.'
   Correlate: Coord S
      Base 1: And he went away (aor.)
      Base 2: and he began (aor.) to proclaim in the Decapolis how much Jesus had done for him and had mercy upon him,
      Base 3: and everyone marveled (aor.).[10]

In the above passage, the role of the aorist is crucial to the storyline and the imperfect fills in details. Note the depictive role of the imperfect in vv. 3-5 above, and in v. 11 where the grazing herd is introduced. In v. 8 the imperfect occurs in a reason slot which is ancillary to the preceding thesis and may indicate protracted activity rather than simple utterance: 'For Jesus had been commanding him...' Note also in v. 18 where the imperfect depicts the healed man as beseeching Jesus to let him go with him. Here too an ongoing activity, rather than a simple event, is depicted. Since Jesus' response to him uses a verb with the aorist this presumably makes the response outrank the original initiating utterance. The historical present occurs a few times where it

---

10. In this diagram, the following abbreviations are used: Coord = Coordinate; IU = Initiating Utterance; RU = Resolving Utterance; A = Answer; Prop = Proposal; (Q) = Question; Q = Quotation; QF = Quotation Formula; Inc Inc = Inciting Incident.

possibly dominates surrounding imperfects (vv. 3-5) but is outranked by the aorist.

For the most part, then, the storyline of koine Greek narrative is carried by clauses with verbs in the aorist. Topics which have not been discussed as yet are the function of the participle[11] and of the historical present. Preposed participles (whether nominative or genitive absolute) which are dependent on a clause with an aorist supply the immediate backup to the storyline by adding preliminary detail. When clauses with the historical present occur—especially when clustered and not simply limited to verbs of speech and motion—they constitute a kind of secondary storyline, which can be thought of as either a demotion from the primary storyline or a promotion of privileged background material. This is most clearly seen in the next section where the structure of the second half of the chapter is presented. Preposed participles which are dependent on a clause with a verb in the historical present provide back-up for the clause that they accompany. Clauses with the imperfect function as background and often encode something conceived of as an ongoing activity rather than as a punctiliar event. As with the aorist and the historical present, clauses with the imperfect can have as backup preposed participial clauses. In addition to these concerns, clauses with 'be' verbs in the imperfect and verbless clauses supply setting.

In the above paragraph, the postposed participle is not mentioned. It appears that the postposed participle is of the same semantic rank as the verb that it follows; that is, it is *consecutive* on the preceding main verb and continues its function. This applies not only to the indicative forms which are found in narrative but to the imperative forms which are found in hortatory discourse.

In terms of universal grammar koine Greek represents a curious union of two distinct chaining structures which are found in many parts of the world:[12] (1) Medial-final chaining structures where final verbs in

---

11. For a very careful and almost encyclopedic treatment of the preposed Greek participle, see A. Healey and P. Healey, 'Greek Circumstantial Participles: Tracking Participants with Participles in the Greek New Testament', *Occasional Papers in Translation and Textlinguistics* 4.3 (1990), pp. 177-259.

12. Longacre, *Grammar*, pp. 285-87. For more detail regarding chaining structures, see R.E. Longacre, *Hierarchy and Universality of Discourse Constituents in New Guinea Languages* (Washington, DC: Georgetown University Press, 1972); idem, *Storyline Concerns and Word-Order Typology in East and West Africa* (Studies in African Linguistics, 10; Los Angeles: University of California, 1990).

final clauses are preceded by clauses with verbs less fully inflected and variously called gerunds, participles and co-verbs, or simply 'medial' verbs; and (2) initial-consecutive chaining structures where an initial clause with a fully inflected verb is followed by clauses with less fully inflected verbs, variously called sequential or consecutive. In respect to medial-final chaining structures the (otherwise unmarked) medial verb may be of the same salience rank as the final, or of lesser salience, or of greater salience. Greek preposed participles apparently are like medial verbs in such a language as Koreete (Ethiopia) in respect to being of lesser salience than the main verb which they precede. On the other hand, the Greek postposed participle, which continues the sense and function of the main verb, is like many African initial-consecutive systems. This conflux of systems can be seen in such a passage as Mt. 28.19-20 where the preposed aorist participle πορευθέντες 'going' precedes the main aorist imperative μαθητεύσατε 'make disciples' and is followed by two consecutive participles, βαπτίζοντες 'baptizing' and διδάσκοντες 'teaching'. Here the preposed participle 'going' represents a preparatory action to what follows while the two postposed participles continue the action of the main verb and are semantically coordinate with it, issuing in a threefold command 'Make disciples... baptize... teach'.

I summarize these ranking concerns in Diagram 2. In this diagram the three ranks—aorist, historical present, and imperfect—are grouped along with indication of consecutive forms and preparatory forms. In the stepped diagrams of this paper I refer to preposed participles as 'preparatio' and to postposed participles as 'consecutives'. For the broader concerns reflected in the diagram, note the priority of the aorist over the imperfect with the occasional historical present as a construction of intermediate status. This is, in a sense, the primary dimension of the diagram. The participles in two broad functions are like an intersecting second dimension: the preposed ancillary function and the postposed co-ranking function.

The following salience scheme recognizes the primacy of the aorist over the imperfect and in addition assigns a place in the scheme of things to the historical present—even though it is present in force only in a few passages such as those being examined here (but cf. Mark's accounts of Gethsemane, the crucifixion and the resurrection). Isolated occurrences of the historical present with speech verbs and verbs of motion is a related problem not considered in this paper.

LONGACRE *Mark 5.1-43* 179

Diagram 2. *Cline of Dynamicity for the Greek Verbs Found in Mark 5*

1.1. Aorist and its consecutives (postposed participles)
    1.2. Preposed participles dependent on an aorist
        2.1. Historical present and its consecutives
            2.2. Preposed participles dependent on the historical present
                3.1. The imperfect and its consecutives
                      3.2. Preposed participles dependent on the imperfect
                          4. 'Setting': be verbs and verbless clauses.

Notes: 1.1, 2.1 and 3.1 are reminiscent of African chaining structures of the sort where the initial and the consecutive following it are of the same salience rank.[13] 1.2, 2.2 and 3.2 are reminiscent of Papua New Guinea, South America and Ethiopian Highlands in languages where the medial verb is one peg lower in salience than the final on which it depends.[14]

3. *Mark 5.21-43, Jairus's Daughter and the Woman with the Issue of Blood*

I now present in this section stepped (tree) diagrams of Mk 5.21-43. This presentation is somewhat more detailed than that found in regard to the account which is found in the first part of this chapter from Mark's Gospel. The increased detail of presentation is due to increased intricacy of the text itself at this point. I will also explain here in more detail the analytical apparatus assumed in the previous section.

Two interwoven structures are involved here: the bracketing story concerning the raising of Jairus's daughter, and the bracketed story of the woman with the issue of blood (disorder of the menstrual cycle). In presenting the constituent structure of these accounts, our first recourse is again to the narrative template, that is, the natural characteristics of a story which embody its semantic structure in Stage, Inciting Incident, Rising Tension, Climax, Denouement and Closure—even as we did

---

13. Longacre, *Storyline Concerns*, pp. 111-43, and 173-77.
14. Actually, there are three possible relationships of medial to final verbs: (1) the final verb outranks the medial, (2) the medial outranks the final, and (3) the medial and final are of equal rank. These concerns were not raised at the time of my New Guinea studies (Longacre, *Hierarchy*) but are presented as alternatives in Longacre, *Storyline Concerns*, where medial-final chaining languages of the Ethiopian highlands are seen to display all three possibilities.

180   *Discourse Analysis and the New Testament*

above in the story of the demoniac. But this does not access the constituent structure as such, since almost any size level unit may manifest one of these semantic functions, from an embedded discourse to a sentence. For this reason we again must also invoke models from paragraph and sentence structures. Here we have bundlings of clauses into looser and tighter structures which correspond respectively to the paragraph and sentence levels. A further complication is that a very short embedded discourse, such as a pericope which consists of a parable, realizes the whole semantic discourse structure within the domain of a single paragraph, that is, the narrative discourse structure collapses into the paragraph.

Specifically, I analyze the bracketing story, the raising of Jairus's daughter, into discourse-level constituents where elements of the narrative template correspond to paragraphs which can be isolated in the story. The bracketed discourse, the story of the woman with the flow of blood, seems to be best analyzed as a single paragraph in which the semantic elements of the narrative template are not distinguished in the surface constituent structure. Within the displays, when a sentence is posited, the constituents are labelled as appropriate to that level. Thus one or more sentence *bases* are posited as constituents of the sentence. Within paragraphs, paragraph level units such as *theses* and *sequential theses* are posited as appropriate for that level. Our sentence boundaries correspond as a whole to those indicated in the Greek New Testament as punctuated by Aland *et al.*, except that I take the colon (raised dot) as often indicating a new structural sentence.

a. *The Discontinuous Story of the Raising of Jairus's Daughter*
This narrative has four parts: the Stage (5.21; the Inciting Incident (5.22-24); the Climax (5.35-36); and the Denouement (5.37-43), which correspond respectively to the physical position and circumstances; the request by Jairus on behalf of his sick daughter, the persistence of Jesus in the face of being told that the little girl had died, and the raising of the girl from the dead. Between the Inciting Incident and the Climax occurs the intervening story of the woman with the issue of blood. If a story is to be discontinuous, a somewhat natural position for the intervening element is to follow the Inciting Incident—as in the stories of Joseph and Jacob in the Hebrew Bible.[15]

The Stage (v. 21) is expounded by a compound sentence with a

---

15. R.E. Longacre, 'Genesis as Soap Opera', *JOTT* 7.1 (1995), pp. 1-8.

preparatio which is a participle in the genitive absolute (cf. 5.2 and 18). The sentence is coordinate; its first base has a verb in the aorist and its second base has the verb 'be' in the imperfect. The motion verb of the preparatio gets Jesus to the other side of Lake Tiberias (cf. 5.1). The sentence bases report the gathering of a great crowd and Jesus' being with them by the lakeside. So far, business as usual!

The Inciting Incident (vv. 22-24a) is given in two sentences: a long coordinate sentence with three bases which reports the coming of Jairus with the request that Jesus come and heal his daughter; and a simple sentence reporting that Jesus went off with him as requested. The bases of the long coordinate sentence have verbs in the historical present: 'comes' in the first base, 'falls at his feet' in the second base, and 'greatly beseeches him' in the third base. The verb form 'falls' in the second base is preceded by a preparatio 'seeing him'. The verb 'beseeches' in the third base is accompanied by a consecutive 'saying' which introduces an embedded quotation sentence. Thus, the quotation formula has a consecutive verb which is equal in salience with the preceding verb 'beseeches'. The Quotation itself has a double purpose margin 'that you may put your hands on her that she might live', but the whole sentence is elliptical, in that the clause 'My daughter is dying' is not followed by some such element as 'I ask you'—which we might have expected. Perhaps the roughness of the grammar expresses the desperation of a father who is distracted and somewhat incoherent. The second sentence 'And he went away with him' has an aorist verb which reports the crucial fact that Jesus went off with Jairus towards the house where the sick child lay.

The Climax (vv. 35-36) is expounded by a Complex Dialogue paragraph which reports an initiating utterance, a proposal on the part of emissaries from Jairus's house that, since the daughter has died, he shouldn't trouble the teacher any further about coming to heal her; and a continuing utterance, a counter-proposal on the part of Jesus to Jairus that the latter should not despair but believe.

The proposal of the initiating utterance is given in a sentence that has both a preparatio and a consecutive. The preparatio (gen. abs.) 'and while he was yet talking' refers back to the embedded story which ends with Jesus telling the woman to go in peace; it thus serves to connect the bracketed material smoothly to the bracketing material. The sentence base reports the arrival of the emissaries: 'they come from the synagogue ruler's house'. The consecutive, with the participle 'saying', introduces another embedded quotation sentence 'Your daughter has died; why trouble the Teacher further?' Jesus' counter-proposal is given in a sentence with a preparatio and a base: 'And Jesus, having heard the word which was spoken, says to the synagogue ruler "Don't fear; only believe"'. All the main verbs found in the Climax are historical presents.

The Denouement (vv. 37-43) is the longest and most complex part of the narrative. The Climax left us with a tightly knotted situation: The daughter is dead but Jesus, far from turning back, persists in his purposes. The resolution of the dilemma is expressed in a long narrative sequence paragraph. The first Sequential Thesis of the sequence paragraph is expounded by another complex dialogue paragraph which after some preliminary moves ends up with Jesus insisting to the mourners that the child was not dead but merely sleeping, followed by the scornful response of the mourners. The preliminary moves of this complex dialogue paragraph include a setting reported in a negated aorist: 'And he didn't let anyone go with him except Peter, James and John, the brother of James'. Jesus' arrival at the house and what he saw on arrival are reported in a coordinate sentence whose verbs are, again, historical presents: 'He comes to the synagogue ruler's house and sees much commotion, crying and wailing'. The Initiating Utterance is given in a quotation sentence with a preparatio: 'And coming in [present participle], he says to them, "Why are you making this commotion and crying? The child is not dead but sleeping".' This remark of Jesus is followed by what is, in effect, the counter-remark of the mourners but given in a clause with an imperfect verb, probably implying 'They persisted in laughing at him'.

The second Sequential Thesis of this narrative sequence paragraph should probably be regarded as expounded by a reason paragraph. The verbs of the Reason (vv. 40-41) are in the historical present and report in sequence Jesus' actions in approaching the girl. The thesis, which expounds the consequences of this chain of actions, reports the resurrection of the child in a crucial aorist form followed by some imperfects: The clause with the aorist is further marked by the occurrence of εὐθύς, 'immediately'. Base 2 of the same sentence reports the child walking about a bit and a reason is appended 'for she was [impf.] twelve years old'. The structure of the Reason unit—the cause and explanation of the resurrection of the child—is that of an embedded narrative sequence paragraph (vv. 40b-41). The first Sequential Thesis of this embedded sequence paragraph is a coordinate sentence with a preparatio: 'And putting them all out [part.], he takes with him the father of the child and the mother and those with him and he enters where the child was'. Here again the main verbs are historical presents. The second Sequential Thesis is a quotation sentence with a preparatio. The structure of this quotation sentence is complicated by the narrator's parenthetical remark as to the meaning of the Aramaic phrase which Christ used. 'And taking the child by the hand [part.], he says to her [historical present] *"Talitha koum"*, which is, being interpreted, "Little Girl, I say unto you, Get up".' Finally, as already commented on above, the girl got up.

The last Sequential Thesis of the main sequence paragraph is expounded by another embedded narrative sequence paragraph; but now all the verbs are aorists—after the long spate of historical presents in the interior of the story: 'And they were astonished with great astonishment'. Then, in another coordinate sentence: 'And he commanded them not to tell anyone, and he told them to give her something to eat'. The structure of this narrative, as discussed above, is given in the stepped diagram which constitutes Diagram 3.

Diagram 3. *Stepped (Tree) Diagram of the Discontinuous Story of the Raising of Jairus's Daughter Mark 5.21-24, 35-43*

Stage (5.21): Coord S
    Preparatio (gen. abs. with aor. part.): And Jesus having passed over again to the other side,
    Base 1: a great crowd gathered (aor.) together unto him,
    Base 2: and he was by the sea (impf.).
Inc Inc (5.21-24a): (N) Sequence paragraph
    Thesis 1: Coord S
        Base 1: There comes (HP) one of the synagogue rulers named Jairus
        Base 2: Simple S
            Preparatio: and seeing him (part.)
            Base: falls (HP) at his feet
        Base 3: Simple S
            Base: greatly beseeches (HP) him
            Consecutive: (Q Sentence)
                QF: saying (postposed part.)
                Q: (Sentence with purpose margins and ellipsis): 'My daughter is dying; [I ask you] to come (prep.) put your hands on her that she may be healed and live.'

184   *Discourse Analysis and the New Testament*

Thesis 2: Simple S: And he went away (aor.) with him.

(This story is broken here by the insertion of the story of the healing of the woman with the issue of blood)

Climax (5.35-36): Complex Dialogue paragraph
    IU (Prop.): Simple S
        Preparatio ([gen. abs. with preposed part.] and backreference to the end of the interposed story): And while he was yet talking,
        Base: they come (HP) from the synagogue ruler's house
        Consecutive:
            QF: saying (postposed part.):
            Q: 'Your daughter has died; why trouble the Teacher further?'
    CU (C-Prop.): Simple S
        Preparatio (preposed part.): And Jesus having heard the word spoken
        Base: Quotation S.
            QF says (HP) to the synagogue ruler:
            Q: Coord S: 'Don't fear; only believe'.

Denouement (5.37-43): (N) Sequence paragraph
    Seq. Thesis 1: Complex Dialogue paragraph
        Setting: Simple S: And he didn't let (neg. aor.) anyone follow along with him except Peter, James and John the brother of James.
        Lead-in: Coord S
            Base 1: And he comes (HP) to the synagogue ruler's house,
            Base 2: and he sees (HP) commotion, crying and much wailing.
        IU (Rem.): Quotation S
            Preparatio: And coming in (pres. part.)
            QF: he says (HP) to them
            Q Coord. S
                Base 1: 'Why are you making this commotion and crying?
                Base 2: Contrast S
                      Base 1: The child has not died,
                      Base 2: but she is sleeping.'
        CU (non-speech verb; counts as c-Rem): Simple S: And they laughed (impf.) at him.
    Seq. Thesis 2: Reason paragraph
        Reason: (N) Sequence paragraph
            Seq. Thesis 1: Coord S
                Preparatio: And putting them all out (pres. part.)
                Base 1: he takes with him (HP) the father of the child and the mother, and those with him
                Base 2: And he enters (HP) where the child was (impf.)

```
        Seq. Thesis 2: Quotation S
            Preparatio: And taking the child by the hand,
            QF he says (HP) to her
            Q: 'Talitha koum' (which is interpreted)
                Q 'Little girl'
                QF I say to you,
                Q 'get up'.
    Thesis: Reason sentence
        Base: Coord S
            Base 1: And immediately the child stood up (aor.)
            Base 2: and she was walking about (impf.)
        Reason: for she was twelve years.
    Seq. Thesis n (N) Sequence paragraph
        Seq. Thesis 1: And they were astonished (aor.) with great
        astonishment
        Seq. Thesis 2: Coord S
            Base 1: And he commanded (aor.) them not to tell anyone
            Base 2: And he told (aor.) them to give her something to
                eat.[16]
```

In commenting on the structure thus conceptualized and diagrammed, I note: (1) It structures plausibly as a low level (embedded) narrative built on the narrative template even as is the entire Gospel of which it is a part. Breaking off after the Inciting Incident, it resumes after the interruption with a Climax and Denouement. In the course of the pericope, a lot of detail and liveliness is added by the use of the historical present while aorists occur at the most decisive points in the story.

b. *The Bracketed Story: The Healing of the Woman with the Issue of Blood (Mark 5.24b-34)*
This account probably can be considered to consist of one long narrative result paragraph. Semantically the functions of Stage, Inciting Incident, Climax and Denouement can be distinguished within the paragraph, but it hardly seems possible or necessary to break the paragraph into four subparagraphs which correspond to these functions.

The paragraph Setting is expounded by a coordinate sentence with two bases; both verbs are imperfects: 'A large crowd was following him and jostling him'.

---

16. Besides the abbreviations used in Diagram 1, the following further abbreviations are used in this diagram: CU = Continuing Utterance; c-Prop = counter Proposal; c-Rem = counter Remark; Rem = Remark; part. = participle.

186 *Discourse Analysis and the New Testament*

The Thesis of the Result paragraph is expounded by a reason sentence which has a long and complex structure. This sentence has an involved preparatio, followed by the sentence base, which is dominated by a verb in the aorist, and which is in turn followed by a reason margin. The preparatio which accompanies the base is a striking construction: it consists of a long chain of preposed participles organized as if it were an embedded coordinate sentence with all its verbs reduced to participles. The first five participles go together and give the woman's medical case history: 'A certain woman being in an issue of blood for twelve years, and having suffered many things from many physicians, and having spent all that she had, and having got none the better but rather coming out worse ...' (Notice how the last two participles are equivalent to a contrast sentence with its main verbs reduced to participles.) The embedded construction which gives the case history consists of participles that are connected with καί, 'and'. Two further participles occur without introducing conjunctions: 'having heard concerning Jesus, coming up behind him in the crowd'. The sentence base follows with its electrifying aorist verb: 'she touched his garment'. The appended reason is fittingly given in a clause with the imperfect; she must have been repeatedly reassuring herself as she pushed her way through the tightly packed and jostling crowd, 'If I but touch his clothing, I shall be healed'.

The Result part of the paragraph contains two theses which tell us, in effect, that she immediately realized that something had happened, and so did Jesus. Thesis 1, which reports to us the woman's point of view, is a coordinate sentence both clauses of which have aorist verbs: 'And immediately her bleeding ceased and she knew/sensed in her body that she was freed from her plague'. Thesis 2 reports the same event from Jesus' perspective. A simple sentence with a complex preparatio and a quotation verb in the imperfect reports Jesus' words 'Who touched my clothing?' The preparatio is an embedded coordinate sentence with its verbs reduced to participles: 'And Jesus immediately realizing that power had gone out of him, and having turned about in the crowd ...' The question of Jesus leads to a puzzled, if not impatient, counterquestion from the disciples: 'You see the people jostling you and you ask "Who touched me?"' The next sentence, a sort of indirect further question on Jesus' part is given with a verb in the imperfect; the sense might be 'But he persisted in looking around to see who had done it'. Here the interplay with the disciples ends and the very next sentence gives from a different quarter the resolving utterance which finally answers Jesus' question. This sentence, itself coordinate, has a preparatio which consists again of a coordinate sentence reduced to participles: 'And the woman fearing and shaking, and knowing what had happened to her...' Then follow the three coordinated sentence bases all with aorist verbs: 'came, and fell at his feet, and told him the whole truth'. Finally, Jesus terminates the interview by acquiescing in what has happened and blessing the happy but frightened woman: 'Daughter your faith has saved you; go in peace, and be healed of your plague'. See Diagram 4 for a summary presentation of this structure.

Diagram 4. *Stepped (Tree) Diagram of Mark 5.24b-34*

(N) Result paragraph
    Setting 5.24b Coord S
        Base 1: A large crowd was following (impf.)
        Base 2: and jostling him (impf.)
    Thesis: 5.25-28 Reason S
        Preparatio: (embedded) Coord S (preposed parts.)
            Base 1: (embedded) Coord S (preposed parts.)
                Base 1: A certain woman being in an issue of blood for 12 years:
                Base 2: and having suffered many things from many physicians
                Base 3: and having spent all she had
                Base 4: (embedded) Contrast S (preposed parts.)
                      Thesis: and having got none the better
                      Opp. Thesis: but coming out worse
            Base 2: having heard concerning Jesus
            Base 3: coming up in the crowd from behind
        Base: touched (aor.) his garment;
        Reason: for she was saying (impf.), 'If I but touch his clothing I shall be saved'.
    Result: (N) Coord paragraph 5.29-34
        Thesis 1: Coord S 29:
            Base 1: And immediately her (εὐθύς) bleeding ceased (aor.),
            Base 2: And she knew (aor.) in her body that she was freed from her plague.
        Thesis 2: Complex Resolved Dialogue paragraph 5.30-34
            IU (Q): Simple S v. 31
                Preparatio: (embedded) Coord S (preposed parts.)
                      Base 1: And Jesus immediately (εὐθύς) having known that power had gone out of him,
                      Base 2: having turned about in the crowd

>   Base: was saying (impf.), 'Who touched my clothing?'
>   CU (c-Q): And the disciples were saying (impf.) to him 'You see the people jostling you and you ask 'Who touched me?'.
>   CU (indirect; c-Q): And he was looking about (impf.) to see who had done it.
>   RU (A): Coord S
>   Preparatio: (embedded) Coord S (preposed parts.)
>   Base 1: And the woman fearing and shaking (parts.)
>   Base 2: and knowing what had happened to her (part.)
>   Base 1: came (aor.)
>   Base 2: and fell at his feet (aor.)
>   Base 3: and told (aor.) to him the whole truth
>   TU (Acq): And Jesus said (aor.) to her, 'Daughter, your faith has saved you; go in peace, and be healed of your plague'.[17]

Note especially in this paragraph the string of participles which encodes the woman's case history and her preparatory actions in approaching Jesus. Strings of participles of this length are uncommon in the Greek New Testament (cf. Mt. 14.19); where they do occur, they are reminiscent of chains of medial-final clauses in languages of Papua New Guinea. In the passage at hand the preposed participles serve to summarize neatly the woman's case history and preparatory actions while at the same time building up suspense relative to the aorist verb 'she touched his clothing' which follows. Imperfects also find their place in this narrative in representing the information that a large crowd was following and jostling Jesus, in reporting the woman's encouraging herself to take the action that she did, and in reporting Jesus' sideplay with the disciples regarding who touched him. While some compression is evident in the use of the preposed participles in the bracketed discourse, there is a certain expansion evident in the use of the imperfects.

In the two sections that follow I will demonstrate the generation of a story from the storyline downwards by progressively adding elements of less salience,[18] and will then compare Matthew's stripped down account of the same passage to show what elements he omits.

---

17. Besides the abbreviations used in the preceeding diagram, the following abbreviations are used here: c-Q = counter Question; TU = Terminating Utterance; Acq = Acquiescence.

18. Longacre, 'Two Hypotheses'.

4. *Generating the Stories from their Abstracts*

In performing this demonstration I handle the two stories together—the bracketing and the bracketed story as presented by Mark. I will refer to this composite account here simply as 'the story'.

A quite bare, unadorned abstract of the story can be obtained by putting down in order the clauses whose verbs are aorist; I note some of the deficiences of this abstract—especially in terms of participant reference in parenthesis at certain places. Sometimes, however, a noun phrase early in the sentence identifies the subject of the main clause before the string of preposed participles in the preparatio, so this is included in the abstract whenever the main verb is aorist. Jesus is the default participant (as central) who is often referred simply by third-person masculine pronoun or the corresponding verb affix.

Display 1 (clauses with verbs in the aorist)

A great crowd gathered together unto him.
And he went off with him (with whom?)
And she (a certain woman, as preposed topic of entire sentence) touched him.
And immediately her bleeding ceased.
And she knew in her body that she was free from her plague.
And she came, and fell before him, and told him the whole truth.
And he said to her, 'Daughter, your faith has saved you; go in peace, and be healed of your plague'.
And he didn't permit anyone except Peter, James and John to follow along with him.
And immediately the little girl got up.
And they were astonished with great astonishment.
And he commanded them strictly that they should tell no one about this.
And he said that they should give her something to eat.

The bare abstract of the story is fleshed out considerably by adding clauses which contain verbs in the historical present, thus making the latter appear somewhat as a surrogate for the aorist. I repeat all the clauses given under the above diagram and add the clauses which contain a historical present. More quotations occur here in this partially rounded out abstract of the story, because in this text there is more reported speech introduced by quotation formulas in the historical present than by speech verbs in the aorist. Also I count as equivalent to a historical present any consecutive participle that follows a historical

190 Discourse Analysis and the New Testament

present; just as above in one instance we counted as equivalent to an aorist a consecutive participle that followed an aorist.

Display 2 (abstract plus clauses with historical present)

A great crowd gathered together unto him.
> There comes to him a synagogue ruler named Jairus.
> He falls at his feet.
> And he greatly beseeches him, saying, 'My daughter is at the point of death. [I beseech you that] coming you put your hands upon her and she will be healed and live.'

And he went off with him.
And she touched him.
And immediately the flow of her blood stopped.
And she realized in her body that she had been healed of her plague.
And she came, and fell before him, and told him the whole truth.
> And they come from the rulers of the synagogue's house saying, 'Your daughter has died. Why trouble the Teacher further?'
> And Jesus says to the ruler of the synagogue, 'Don't fear; only believe'.

And he permitted no one to go with him except Peter, James and John, the brother of James.
> And he comes to the house.
> And he sees the confusion, crying and wailing.
> And he says to them, 'Why are you mourning and weeping? The child is not dead; she is only sleeping.'
> And he takes the father of the child and the mother and those with him and he goes in to where the child was.
> And he says to her *'Talitha koum,* which is being interpreted, Little girl, I say to you,
> Get up!'

And immediately the little girl got up.
And they were astonished with great astonishment.
And he commanded them strictly that they should tell no one about it.
And he told them to give her something to eat.

In the above, note that it is the bracketing story that is especially rounded out by the addition of clauses whose verbs are historical presents. This affords contrast with the bracketed story where the narrative is especially rounded out by participles and clauses with verbs in the imperfect.

I now enrich the above by adding preposed participles which I have called preparatio above.

Display 3

And Jesus having crossed over again to the other side,
a great crowd gathered together unto him;
> And there comes a ruler of the synagogue named Jairus,
> And he greatly beseeches him, saying, 'My daughter is at the point of death. [I beseech you that] coming you will put your hands on her that she may be healed and live.'

And he went off with him.
> And a woman being in an issue of blood for twelve years,
> And having suffered many things from many physicians,
> And having spent all that she had,
> And having got none the better,
> but rather coming out worse,
> having heard about Jesus,
> coming up in the crowd from behind,

she touched his clothing.
And immediately the flow of her blood ceased,
And she realized in her body that she was healed of her plague.
> And the woman frightened,
> and trembling,
> knowing what had happened to her,

came, and fell at his feet, and told him the whole truth.
> While he was yet talking (part. in gen. abs.)
> they come from the ruler of the synagogue's house, saying, 'Your daughter has died; why do you trouble the teacher further?'
> And Jesus, having heard the word that was spoken,
> says to the ruler of the synagogue, 'Don't fear; only believe.'

And he permitted no one to go with him except Peter, James and John the brother of James.
> And they come to the house of the ruler of the synagogue,
> And he sees confusion, crying and wailing.
> And coming in

he says to them, 'Why are you mourning and crying? The child hasn't died; she's only sleeping.'
> But he, putting them all out,

takes with him the father of the child and the mother and those with him, and goes into where the child was.
> And taking the child's hand,

he says to her, '*Talitha koum*', which is being interpreted, 'Little girl, I say to you, Get up'.
And immediately the little girl got up.
And they were astonished with great astonishment.

192 *Discourse Analysis and the New Testament*

And he commanded them strictly that they should tell no one about it.
And he said that they should give her something to eat.

To all the above we need to add clauses with verbs in the imperfect in order to generate the actual text of the story. Of course, a further parameter, that of participant identification and tracking, weaves itself in along with the concerns centering around the varying forms of the verbs.

As we have seen above, the subject is typically identified at sentence onset before the preparatio. Also we have taken note of Jesus' status as central participant and by default receiving minimal overt reference. The imperfect is especially used in rounding out the bracketing story, the raising of Jairus's daughter, but it is also relevant to the bracketed story. I now display the full text of the story with the clauses with the imperfect indented the furthest to the right.

Display 4

And Jesus having crossed over again to the other side,
A great crowd gathered together unto him.
    And he was beside the lake.
  And there comes a ruler of the synagogue named Jairus,
  And he greatly beseeches him, saying, 'My daughter is at the point of death,
  [I beseech you that] coming you will put your hands upon her that she may be healed and live'.
And he went off with him.
    And there followed him a great crowd,
    And they were jostling him.
  And a certain woman being in an issue of blood for twelve years,
  And having suffered many things from many physicians,
  And having spent all that she had,
  And having got none the better,
  but rather coming out worse,
  having heard concerning Jesus,
  coming up behind in the crowd,
she touched his clothing
    for she kept saying to herself, 'If I but touch his clothing, I will be healed'.
And immediately the flow of her blood ceased,
And she sensed in her body that she was healed of her plague.

And immediately Jesus realizing that power had gone out of
him having turned about in the crowd,
    said, 'Who touched my clothing?'
    But the disciples said, 'You see this crowd jostling you
and you say,
    "Who touched me?"
    But he kept looking around to see who had done this.
And the woman frightened,
and trembling,
and knowing what had happened to her,
came, and fell at his feet, and told him the whole truth.
    And while he was yet talking,
they come from the ruler of the synagogue's house saying, 'Your
daughter has died, why trouble the teacher further?'
    And Jesus having heard the word that was spoken,
says to the ruler of the synagogue, 'Don't fear, only believe'.
And he didn't let anyone follow along with him except Peter, James and
John the brother of James.
    And he comes to the house,
    And he sees confusion, crying and wailing,
    And coming in,
he says to them, 'Why are you mourning and crying? The child
hasn't died, she's only sleeping.'
    And they laughed at him.
    But he, putting them all out,
takes along with him the father of the child and the mother, and
    those that accompanied him,
he comes into the place where the child was.
    And taking the hand of the child,
he says to her, '*Talitha koum*', which is being interpreted, 'Little
girl, I say to you, Get up'.
And immediately the little girl got up.
    And she walked about.
    For she was twelve years.
And they were all astonished with great astonishment.
And he commanded them strictly that they should tell no one about it.
And he told them to give her something to eat.

In considering the progressively laminated text displayed above, several comments come to mind: (1) This is not a run-of-the-mill koine Greek New Testament narrative. The role of the historical present is such that in this passage it patterns as a secondary storyline in a manner reminiscent of certain languages of East Africa, for example, Avocaya.[19] The aorist clauses preserve the position of prominence but the historical presents add much to flesh out the story. The normal expectation would be that a koine Greek New Testament narrative would primarily be analyzable as an interplay between the aorist and the imperfect, but the intervention of the historical present is very striking in this account. (2) The role of the preposed participle is also especially heavy in this story with seven participles preceding the aorist 'she touched his clothing' and three participles preceding the coordinated aorist clauses 'She came, fell before him, and told the whole truth'. Clearly, if the majority of koine Greek New Testament stories were structured like this one, our views of both Greek grammar and of discourse structure would be quite different from those that we hold at present.

What then? I see no way of accounting for the distinct structure of this story but by positing that its peculiar elaboration correlates with its position in the context of the whole Gospel. Why does Mark pull out all the stops on his narrative organ at this point? I refer again here to the essay on which this one is built and to the analysis propounded in that essay.[20] All of Mark 5—including the story of the Gadarene demoniac in Mk 5.1-20—is the climax of the first grand wave of development in the Gospel. After the Aperture (1.1), Stage (1.2-8) and Inciting Incident (1.9-13), there occurs a section of the Gospel, beginning at 1.14 and terminating at the end of ch. 5, that describes the rise to prominence of Jesus as a teacher and miracle worker, and the beginnings of his controversy with the establishment of his day. This section, which is an embedded narrative discourse, contains a didactic peak in ch. 4 (the parables) followed by an action peak in ch. 5. Mark presents Jesus as one mighty in word and deed by this dual peak structuring in the first grand section. The action peaks of Mark are customarily miracle stories told with recourse to detail and dialogue. In Mark 5 the account of the healing of the demoniac exemplifies these features. But in the second part of the chapter, Mark outdoes himself. Not only do the features of detail and dialogue persist but the grammar and discourse structure are, as it were, reshaped by the unusual prevalence of the historical present

---

19. In an unpublished data paper of Lynne Callinan and Eileen Kilpatrick, whose main points are, with the permission of the authors, incorporated into Longacre, *Storyline Concerns*, pp. 91-99.
20. Longacre, 'Top-Down, Template-Driven'.

and the preposed participle. Even the overall effect of the story-within-story contributes to this effect. For anything at all similar to Mark's elevated style here we can look at the Gethsemane account in Mk 14.27-31 and the mocking and crucifixion in Mk 15.16-32. These portions of Mark occur in the action peak of the whole Gospel, where the Gethsemane episode is pivotal (the culmination of what precedes and the beginning of the culmination), the mocking and cruxifixion are Climax, and the resurrection account (16.1-8) patterns as Denouement. In the latter, however, there are only three historical presents compared to eight uses of this tense in the Gethsemane episode and nine such uses in the mocking and crucifixion. I believe that any attempt to analyze the role of these clusters of historical presents in Mark in terms of purely local constraints flies in the face of Gödel's theorem that the consistency of a system cannot be explained wholly within the system itself. Therefore, I ultimately have to explain the clusters of historical presents in Mark in terms of total context in the Gospel.

5. *Comparison with Matthew's Account in Matthew 9.18-26*

Matthew's account in comparison with Mark's seems to omit practically all the details which make Mark's account so vivid and appealing. Matthew collapses into one the two episodes in Mark where the ruler first comes and asks Jesus to heal his daughter and then receives word on the way to his house that his daughter is dead. The three historical presents which Mark uses to depict Jairus's coming to Jesus, falling before him, and beseeching him to heal his daughter are collapsed into a preparatio 'coming' and an imperfect 'he beseeched him'. The six historical presents found in Mk 5.38-40—'comes in', 'looks at/beholds', 'says', 'takes with him', 'goes in' and 'says' (to the little girl)—are variously reduced; the first two to preposed participles, the third to an imperfect, the fourth and sixth to zero and the fifth again to a participle. Matthew is much more summary: 'he took the girl by the hand and she got up'.

Mark's mention of the following and jostling crowd—depicted in imperfects—is omitted entirely with only the routine observation that the disciples accompanied him. The case history of the woman with the issue of blood, given in five participial clauses in Mark, is also omitted along with the mention that the woman had heard about Jesus (still another participle in Mark). Matthew settles for one participle 'having come up behind him' and the main aorist verb 'she touched [the edge of his cloak]'. The reason clause with the imperfect of the woman's inner speaking occurs, however, as in Mark, 'for she said to herself, "If I but touch his clothing I shall be healed"'. Along with the omission of reference to the jostling crowd is omitted the reference to Jesus' turning around, questioning the disciples, and making visual search to see who touched him—all Markan imperfects.

In all these ways the dramatic detail and dialogue of Mark are reduced to something approaching the macrostructure, that is, a bare summary, of the story.[21] It is interesting that the omitted material in Matthew's account corresponds to Mark's development via historical presents, participles and imperfects. This, in turn, emphasizes that Mark's extensive use of these three constructions is essentially embellishment. This throws us back again on the centrality of the aorist in koine Greek storytelling.

---

21. T. van Dijk, *Text and Context* (London: Longmans, 1977); *idem*, *Macrostructures: An Interdisciplinary Study of Global Structures, Interaction, and Cognition* (Hillsdale, NJ: Lawrence Erlbaum, 1980).

13

The Discourse Strategy of an Appeals Letter

Robert E. Longacre

0. As an appeal for funds, this letter[1] can be considered to be a variety of hortatory discourse, which is, in turn, a subtype of behavioral discourse (the latter can also include such discourses as eulogies and campaign speeches, Longacre 1983). Hortatory discourse aims at influencing conduct, that is, getting the receivers of the text to do something they are not currently doing, to discontinue doing something they are doing, to continue doing something they are already doing, to expend greater effort in an activity already embarked on, to modify the nature of their efforts, and so on. As an appeal for funds, this letter aims to elicit further contribution to a cause that the reader may already have given to and to solicit contributions from those who have not given previously.

A distinction needs to be made between hortatory discourse and persuasive discourse. Unlike hortatory discourse, whose goal is to influence conduct, persuasive discourse is primarily aimed at influencing beliefs and values. The text in hand is not a persuasive discourse as such. No attempt is made to give a careful statement of the goals of ZPG, to state the means whereby they could be attained, or to argue the worthwhileness of those goals. The worthwhileness of the cause is alluded to only obliquely, in terms of "population-related problems." Popular interest and hearty response to a press release is further assumed to vindicate the cause, as is also the imposing list of officers and sponsors on the left hand margin of the letterhead. Above all, it is assumed that the letter is directed to readers who are already friendly to the cause — "Dear Friend of ZPG" (segment 3). Assuming, then, that the writer and the reader have the same or very similar beliefs and values, the letter sets out to influence conduct in a very specific way, that is, to get the reader to send in a *contribution*.

In this article I shall discuss the schema/superstructure which characterizes this type of discourse and which is exemplified by this letter. I shall then attempt to match the schema to the surface structure by (1) inspecting the letter for natural seams which indicate groupings of the segments, and (2) looking for correspondences between moves of the schema and the natural groupings found within the discourse. This should yield a *macrosegmentation* of the discourse, i.e. a meaningful division into big 'chunks' — which can be recursive in more complicated discourses than the relatively simple one found in this letter.[2] Eventually *macrosegmentation* must lead into *microsegmentation*, i.e. the consideration of how the various segments (for the most part, sentences) within a large division of text relate to each other and what part each segment plays in the local and global context. In examining the microstructure of the discourse, attention will be paid to considerations of *dominance* (of one part of the discourse over near or more remote parts)[3] and *mitigation*[4] as a tactical device in composing the letter. *Macrostructures* of parts and of the whole will be formulated in the course of the analysis.

1. The schema/superstructure

A schema is discourse-type specific but it is not discourse specific in terms of the content of a particular text. Comparing the production of a discourse of a given type to a game, we can characterize the schema as a summary of the high-level moves of the game. Thus, a hortatory text, that is a text whose purpose is to modify the conduct of the receivers of the text, has four typical moves:[5] (1) establishment of the authority/credibility of the text producer; (2) presentation of a problem/situation; (3) issuing of one or more commands, which can be mitigated to suggestions of varying urgency; and (4) resort to motivation (essentially threats with predictions of undesirable results, and promises along with predictions of desirable results). In this schema, (3) is minimal and basic, i.e. a hortatory discourse cannot be such without commands/suggestion and it may consist wholely of commands/suggestions. Characteristically such a discourse is brusque and brief. But even in such a minimal hortatory text, the presence of (2) is implied (or present in the context of the situation), i.e. there is necessarily some problem/situation which evokes the command elements. Most hortatory discourse also includes (4), motivation — unless the power of the speaker/writer over the addressee is uncontestable. All of this in turn implies (1) even if not overtly stated.

Notice that this sets apart a hortatory discourse from a persuasive discourse which has essentially the following moves: (1) problem/question; (2) proposed solution/answer; (3) supporting argumentation (logic, experimentation, authority); (4) appeal (often very subtle) to give credence, or to adopt certain values. In this persuasive schema point (4) is minimal and basic. Point (3) includes among other things the authority of the speaker but this factor is perhaps not as prominent as in hortatory discourse. Notice, however, that persuasive and hortatory discourse can co-exist in one text, especially when the same text embeds persuasive discourse as a means of supplying motivation in the hortatory schema. Probably expository discourse is similar to persuasive but it does not have to have any move which corresponds to element 4 of persuasive discourse and is likely to have *evaluation* of the solution as one of its main points (Hoey 1983).

Narrative discourse and various kinds of procedural/instructional discourses are different still. Narrative discourse must have an *inciting incident* (something out of the ordinary has happened; otherwise how can there be a story?). A story also has *mounting tension* culminating in a *climax* of tension/confrontation followed by a *denouement* (Longacre, 1983). In a sense the inciting moment is parallel to the problem/situation of the other discourse types, but it is progressively developed to a climax (the problem is like a wave which comes to crest) in a way not characteristic of other discourse types. The denouement is like a solution in the other schemata. Elements of command and persuasion, if present, are characteristically expressed in a moral at the end. Above all, narrative discourse must have punctiliar sequential happenings — something not demanded in other discourse types, which have either a line of command (hortatory), of persuasion, or of exposition.

As for procedural discourse we expect: problem/need; preparatory procedures; the main, efficient procedures; and concluding (often utilization) procedures (Barnard and Forster 1968).

In applying the hortatory schema to the text at hand, segments 4-10 can be considered to constitute an effort to underscore the worthiness of the ZPG cause — although we observed above that this is also enhanced by the names on the left side of the letter, while the particular authority of the letter writer is established by her being executive director of the organization. Only at the end of the paragraph, in segment 10, are the background problems responsible for the existence of ZPG alluded to: "population-related problems that threaten health and well-being." So in the main, segments 4-10 correspond to move (1) of the hortatory schema with some passing allusion to (2). This paragraph, segments 4-10, is largely narrative in tone.

Segments 11-17 correspond to move (2) of the hortatory schema; here the problem/situation is presented as an opportunity occasioned by the results attained and attainable by ZPG's 1985 Urban Stress Text (henceforth UST). This paragraph, although superficially expository in tone, is covertly hortatory; without (yet!) making an appeal, segments 14-17 state a need.

Segments 18-24 contain a motivated appeal — and thus correspond to moves (3) and (4) of the hortatory schema. Segments 18-21 are largely motivation while segments 22-24 contain the overt appeal (to which the whole letter has led up).

What about segments 28-30, the postscript? Here the letter implements a familiar tactic of an appeal letter. In effect, the strategy is to get you — before you toss the letter into the waste basket — to at least take the letter seriously enough to do *something* with it, that is, fill out an enclosed simple questionnaire or response form. The P.S. contains a motivation (Segment 29) and an appeal (Segment 30).

2. The Macrosegmentation of the Text ('Chunking')

Chunking a text into its gross parts requires that we confront a discourse schema (such as those sketched above) with an examination of the text for surface structure indications of natural segmentation. In juxtaposing these two concerns we save ourselves from perpetrating a sterile dissection of the text; we are able, on the contrary, to immediately make a beginning at attributing *functions* to the various discourse parts. Attributing functions to the parts enables us to view it as a functioning whole rather than as a dissected cadaver.

Looking at the letter we find that we are not initially much helped in our gross segmentation. The writer has gone to an apparent excess of indentation which is of little help as far as discovering the structural paragraphs. Segment 15 is inset and underlined — presumably to point out something crucially significant. The letter, however, is framed and formatted so as to be an effective appeal. Accordingly, in an effort to make the contents more accessible to quick scanning by the average reader, an orthographic paragraph in this letter contains typically one or two sentences — although segments 4-6 containing three sentences in the first orthographic paragraph. The indentation and open lines between the orthographic paragraphs very probably make the letter more readable than could be achieved by more conservative paragraphing. In the balance of this article I will ignore the orthographic indentation and spacing, and will group the sentences which are contained in the body of the letter into the three parts noticed at the end of Section 1. above, i.e. segments 4-10: the worthiness of the ZPG cause (schema, move 1); segments 11-17, the UST presents an opportunity to be exploited (schema, move 2); and segments 18-24, the motivated appeal to send a contribution (schema, moves 3 and 4). I will refer to these three parts as *structural paragraphs* (Longacre 1979).

In justifying this three-fold gross chunking, I submit the following argument. Paragraph I (Segments 4-10) is largely narrative; it tells the story of the public reaction consequent on the release of the results of ZPG's 1985 UST. Paragraph II (Segments 11-17) takes as its topic ZPG's 1985 Urban Stress Test. The references to the topic in Segment 11 and 17 provide a nice *inclusio* for this paragraph (and the phrase is underlined in both sentences). Paragraph III, the motivated appeal, is similarly bracketed with references to the reader's making a contribution (Segment 18: "with your contribution" and Segment 22: "Please make a special contribution..."). This paragraph is overtly hortatory in tone; not only does it contain an imperative in Segment 22 but segments 18-20 contain modals and Segment 21 has "need" as its main verb. In Segment 19 the clause which contains the modal is underlined: "We can act to take positive action at the local level." Thus, in surface structure, we pass from narration (in Paragraph I), and mitigated (covert) exhortation (in Paragraph II) to overt exhortation ("we can do it"..."send in your contribution") in Paragraph III. Furthermore, the topic, i.e. what a stretch of text is about, is plainly marked in all three paragraphs: the story of the public reaction; the effectiveness of ZPG's 1985 UST; and the crucialness of your contribution. Again, as we say above, the segments function in the schema of the hortatory discourse so as to give respectively: the *authority* of the writer and her cause; the *problem* explained (ZPG's 1985 UST is a good instrument but our staff is overwhelmed in trying to get the message out); and the *motivated appeal*.

3. The microsegmentation of the text

No one who works for long and in detail with text analysis can avoid positing a set of relations to explain how the segments of the text relate to each other. This has been obvious for some time in Biblical studies and in translation theory. Beginning with the work of Fuller in 1959 ("Inductive Bible Study") a set of relations was elaborated by John Beekman and colleagues within the Summer Institute of Linguistics (culminating in Beekman and Kopesec 1981). My own somewhat parallel work has gone through a similar series of elaboration and revision (Ballard, Conrad, & Longacre 1971a, 1971b, and Longacre 1972, 1976, 1983b). De Beaugrande and Dressler (1981) give a catalogue, as do Grimes (1975), van Dijk (1977), and Mann and Thompson (1987, 1988). One could wish that all of us could agree on the number and labelling of the relations involved, but the underlying similarities among these lists are more significant than the disagreements.

Along with the elaboration of these interclausal relations (which can be found in both intrasentential and intersentential distribution) I have elaborated surface structure taxonomies for the sentence (Longacre 1970 and 1985) and paragraph (Longacre 1979 and 1980) both as recursive units. While the surface structure of the paragraph depends heavily on the relations which it encodes, I note the following differences and correlations between the encoding of such relations and the surface structure of the paragraph in which they are found.

(1) I take the sentence divisions (at least of written text) quite seriously as encoding options on the part of the text producer. Propositions that could have been represented seriatim as separate sentences are combined into sentences which display internal coordination and/or subordination. Presumably the text producer's discourse strategy is at work here in what he/she decides to 'bundle' together as one sentence as opposed to material encoded as separate bundles.

(2) I take, therefore, the task of paragraph-level microanalysis to be one of relating sentence to sentence with only an occasional excursion into the internal structure of sentences.

(3) A signal exception to the above is the need to account for the cohesive relations of adverbial clauses (Thompson and Longacre 1985, 178-234, Matthiessen and Thompson 1989).

(4) I believe that paragraphs sometimes have multi- functional surface slots such as setting/introduction, terminus/conclusion, and comment. Settings/introductions are like 'ice-breakers', necessary preliminary information which supersedes some of the other notional functions (for example introduction of a participant, a topic, a description of attendant circumstances). Likewise terminus/conclusion occurs to mark the end of the paragraph whatever further notional functions it may have. These openers and closers typically have elements that are off-the-line[6] in their discourse types and are morphosyntactically identifiable. Comment, likewise off-the-line and morphosyntactically identifiable, is often introduced by a word such as *it, this, that* which is deictic in function relative to the preceding sentence.

(5) I believe that a comparatively small inventory of paragraph types can be posited,[7] provided that we recognize that paragraphs take on chameleon-like the discourse features of the discourses that they occur in. For example, I set up a thesis- reason paragraph that has thesis as its dominant member (by virtue of being on the mainline of the discourse type and having the verb form that dominates its type) but which appends a *reason* as ancillary (i.e. a segment or segments which is not on the main-line of its discourse type and which semantically expresses cause or reason). I abbreviate the name of this paragraph type to *reason* paragraph; it is named for its distinctive ancillary member. This paragraph occurs in narrative to explain why someone acted in a certain way or suffered a given contingency. In such circumstances I call the paragraph type a *narrative reason paragraph*. In a hortatory text, however, the same paragraph type can occur with a thesis which is on-the-line of exhortation (some sort of command/suggestion) and an off-the-line reason unit which presents a motivation to implement the command/suggestion. One could set up here an exhortation- motivation paragraph peculiar to hortatory text. On the other hand, it avoids multiplying paragraph types if we simply say that we have here a hortatory reason paragraph with semantic modification of the reason paragraph occasioned by its occurring in hortatory discourse. We can likewise have other variants of this structure occasioned by other discourse types, for example, a procedural reason paragraph, or an expository reason paragraph (Longacre 1979).

All this means that we are left with the necessity of positing semantic variation in the surface structure slots of the paragraph: a kind of notional versus surface split-level structure. But this seems better than forever multiplying surface structure units occasioned by such semantic variations, or on the other hand ignoring the latter.

(6) The paragraph as thus envisioned is a highly recursive unit — but the recursive layering is resultant on the frequently complex nesting of relations which are implied or marked in the *surface* structure. All these relations must be identified and interrelated. Keeping track of this layering constitutes a reader-burden, whatever particular approach is followed in writing up the analysis. I suggest that the reader, in the balance of this paper, make frequent reference to the constituency display which is appended to this article. In an attempt to partially index the layering of recursive paragraph structure I will reserve the term *main* paragraph for the inclusive units which explain the three points of this letter, i.e. the three major chunks as described in Section 2.

3.1 *The Structure of Main Paragraph I (segments 4-10)*

As we have already stated, this paragraph is largely narrative in tone. What it tries to accomplish is to present ZPG as a worthy cause as judged by the public reaction to publishing the results of the 1985 UST. In this paragraph Segments 4-8 constitute the Thesis and Segments 9-10 the Comment; the whole unit (4-10) constitutes a narrative comment paragraph. Semantically the Thesis is a recountal (in the form of an embedded narrative sequence paragraph) while the Comment is a kind of analysis of what happened and can be considered to be a narrative contrast paragraph which turns on the contrast of "At first..." in Segment 9 and "Now..." in Segment 10.

In the first part of this paragraph, the Thesis (recountal) is structured as a narrative sequence paragraph which has four component slots: three Sequential Theses (ST's) and a Terminus. Segments 4,5, and 6 are on the line of this piece of embedded narrative; the verbs "started to ring," "jammed," and "stayed" portray sequential happenings which are either inherently punctiliar (Segment 4) or are viewed as simple happenings (Segments 5-6) in quite regular narrative fashion. In addition, time adverbs help the narrative movement: "At 7:00 A.M. on Oct. 25...all day....late into the night." The complex of related lexical items, "phones," "switchboards," and "staffers" provides thematic unity. The comparative length and detail which characterize Segment 6 (Sequential Thesis$_n$) in depicting the ZPG's staff working overtime to answer questions and to talk to reporters indicate a development which is locally climactic; by convention I label Segment$_6$

Sequential Thesis$_n$ (ST$_n$) instead of just Sequential Thesis$_3$ (ST$_3$) which would not indicate anything climactic.

Segments 7 and 8 constitute a Terminus which is summary in force; all the above is characterized as "an overwhelming response" (Segment 7) and a "reaction" which has been "nothing short of incredible" (Segment 8). The two sentences constitute a narrative concessive paragraph with Segment 7 as Concession and Segment 8 as Thesis. The initial adverbial clause "when we released the results of ZPG's 1985 UST", harks back to a time immediately preceding Oct. 25 and serves to introduce the 1985 UST which is made thematic further on in the second main paragraph of the whole discourse. Neither sentence 7 with its flashback in past tense (of "have") nor sentence 8 with its present perfect tense (of "be") has narrative verbs; the whole unit (7-8) — as a summary — is best considered to be off the main line of development of the narrative paragraph. Within the unit composed of Segments 7 and 8 the latter is dominant and is the thesis which outranks the irrealis negative structure in Segment 7 — which is ancillary and is labelled Concession.

The second half of this paragraph (Segments 9 and 10) is a comment (analysis) on the narrative presented in Segments 4-8. It represents a temporal contrast turning on the time adverbs "at first" and "now." It is, however, somewhat expository in tone and apparently Segment 10 should be considered to be the dominant member (and hence the Thesis) while Segment 9 can be considered to be ancillary and the *antithesis*. We can consider the paragraph (Segments 9-10) to be an expository contrast paragraph where time relations are used not to provide narrative movement but to explain and to analyze happenings which have been previously reported. It is important to note that, although the more inclusive unit, segments 4-10, is a narrative comment paragraph, the internal structure of the comment itself, Segments 9-10, is expository — and as exposition it is clearly off-the-line of the narrative paragraph to which it belongs.

In neither Segment 9 nor Segment 10 do the main verbs represent sequential punctiliar happenings; rather they represent spans of activity. The phrase "deluge of calls" in Segment 9 echoes the references to the unexpectedly large response as mentioned in Segments 7 and 8. The sentences in these segments could be schematized as: "At first...calls came (mostly) from X and Y; now we are hearing from Z", where X symbolizes "reporters"; Y symbolizes "outraged public officials" and Z symbolizes "concerned citizens." The contrastive adverb "now" — presumably referring to elapsed time from Oct. 25 and including the present — can be assumed to mark the more important segment of the paragraph. Here a study of the relative clauses in 9 and 10 is relevant. Thus, Segment 9 has "reporters [who were] eager to tell the public about UST results", and "outraged public officials who were furious that we had blown the whistle on conditions in their cities." Presumably the relevant additional information thus brought into Segment 9 gives a further opportunity to mention favorably the 1985 UST results (important in the rest of the letter), and the wretched conditions in certain U.S. cities. Segment 10 is a sentence which has a long relative clause with a further embedded complement of "know": "(concerned citizens) who want to know what they can do to hold local officials accountable for tackling population-related problems that threaten public health and well-being." Aside from the oblique reference to conditions in certain cities found in Segment 9, the deeply embedded phrase "population-related problems that threaten public health and well-being" is the first clear reference in the letter to the nature of the problems whose existence led to the formation of ZPG. Presumably the "friends of ZPG" referred to in the salutation (Segment 3) agree that conditions in many U.S. cities are deplorable and that unrestrained population growth is central in the development of these deplorable conditions.

The main verbs in Segments 9 and 10 occur in clauses which emphasize *source* and which contrast the calls from reporters and outraged public officials with the presumably more significant response now coming from concerned citizens. As we have already observed, this paragraph is essentially expository in tone even though it centers around a temporal contrast. Simplifying the sentences the contrast can be schematically represented as follows:

S.9   T past P_m $S_{x,y}$
S.10 T present P_m S_z

T represents time past and present; P_m represents verbs that can broadly be construed as motion, and $S_{x,y}$ represents earlier sources of calls versus S_z the latter and (more gratifying) source of calls. The paragraph (9-10) uses, then, a temporal contrast as a framework for presenting contrasting value judgements regarding earlier and later respondents.

The message is: ZPG is a worthy cause; not only has it had an overwhelming response to its promulgation of the 1985 UST results, but, in the last analysis, it is the more thoughtful and civic-minded portion of our citizenry who have answered — and they want to know what to do about it.

3.2 *The structure of Paragraph II (Segments 11-17)*

Having presented in paragraph I the story of the response to the promulgation of ZPG's 1985 UST results and having analyzed those results in a way to put ZPG in the best possible light, the writer of the letter goes on in main paragraph II to argue that the UST is an effective tool and that realizing its full impact will require the help of the readers of the letter. This paragraph is superficially expository in tone, but the references to "we need your help" (Segment 14) and to "your support...is crucial" (Segment 16) are probably typically pieces of mitigated exhortation which prepare us for the open appeal which is to follow in the last paragraph.

The superficially expository tone of the paragraph is evident from the main verbs which dominate it: "is" (copulative) in Segment 11, "ranks" (static-relational) in Segment 12; "translates" (static in the sense of "shows the equivalence of") in Segment 13; "need" (expression of a lack without a verb of pleading) in Segment 14; "is being swamped" (passive, represents an ongoing situation) in Segment 15a; "are being stretched" (similar) in Segment 15b; "is" (copulative) in Segment 16; and "may be" (modal of the copulative) in Segment 17. Nevertheless, Segment 14 can be interpreted as a mitigated appeal as can likewise Segment 16; this interpretation hinges on the use of the verb 'need.' In keeping with the mitigated hortatory tone of this part of the paragraph, I make Segments 14-17 dominant over the earlier Segments 11-13 in this paragraph, which are simply expository.

In keeping with the dominating role of the included (mitigated) hortatory paragraph (Segments 14-17), the whole paragraph (Segments 11-17) is likewise taken to be mitigated hortatory (symbolized as H?). Looking at the logical relation involved in the whole, we proceed to classify the structure as concessive with Segments 11-13 encoding the Concession and Segments 14-17 (which dominate) the Thesis. The whole paragraph (11-17) can therefore be called a (mitigated) hortatory concessive paragraph. The Concession consists of an expository coordinate paragraph with three Theses, Segments 11-13 respectively. The first Thesis explains that the 1985 UST is the nation's first survey of the effect of population-related pressures on our cities. The second Thesis gives some idea of the criteria used to rank the 184 urban areas thus surveyed. The third Thesis is that "complex technical data" is transformed by the survey into an "easy-to-use action tool for concerned citizens, elected officials and opinion leaders." I have labelled the three theses $Thesis_1$, $Thesis_2$, and $Thesis_n$ to recognize the climactic nature of the third thesis. Precisely because the survey's results translate into an action tool, a need has arisen as sketched in the last part of the paragraph.

The second part of this paragraph, the Thesis (Segments 14- 17) consists of a mitigated hortatory reason paragraph, which I will further characterize as cyclic.[8] I consider that it consists of a Thesis (Segment 14), a Reason (Segment 15), recapitulated Thesis (which I will label, Thesis', Segment 16) and a Terminus (Segment 17) which has an immediate function as closure relative to Segments 14-16, but which is somewhat multi- functional and will necessitate some further discussion. The bond between the Thesis and the Thesis' consists in the fact that Segment 16 is a paraphrase of Segment 14: "...we urgently need your help...Your support now is crucial." The opening words of Segment 14 are a backreference to sentence 13; thus the affirmation that the 1985 UST is an "easy-to-use action tool" is echoed in the next sentence: "But to use it well...". This backreference not only serves a cohesive function but leads into the statement of need[9] on which the overt appeal will eventually be based. In between Thesis and Thesis' comes the Reason (Segment 15), which is a coordinate sentence — the part which is orthographically set in. The staff is too small to answer all the inquiries and "our modest resources are being stretched to the limit." This adds some poignancy to the renewed statement of need in Thesis' (Segment 16) where the word "now" occurs.

But what does Segment 17 accomplish? I have construed it as Terminus of the paragraph which is found in Segments 14-16. It reiterates the phrase "ZPG's 1985 Urban Stress Test" which has not been mentioned since Segment 11; as such it provides a grand *inclusio* for the whole second main paragraph (Segments 11-17). On the other hand, the presentation of ZPG's 1985 UST as an opportunity to get "the population message heard" reaffirms the urgency mentioned in Segment 14 and this seems to more specifically relate Segment 17 to what *immediately* precedes in Segments 14-16. Finally, Segment 17 could well be taken as preliminary to the last main paragraph Segment 18-23. What then? Need any of these functions be ignored? Certainly not, whatever the limitations of tree diagrams in compelling us to make certain methodologically-induced choices. Let Segment 17 be primarily allocated to the paragraph consisting of Segment 14-16 but let us recognize that inclusio, chiasmus, and the like often override groupings based on other considerations, so that the first and last sentences of main paragraph II (with overt mention of ZPG's Urban Stress Test) have this feature regardless of their precise status within the parts of the paragraph. Let us go further and suggest that Segment 17 could be considered to be essentially transitional; i.e. it simultaneously concludes the second main paragraph and introduces the third main paragraph.

This whole paragraph (Segments 11-17) can be summarized as "Although ZPG's 1985 UST is a superb action tool it can't be effectively used without your help."

3.3 *The Structure of Main Paragraph III (Segments 18-23)*

This paragraph structures as a hortatory reason paragraph. The Reason (Motivation) is found in Segments 18-21; the Thesis (Appeal) is found in Segments 22 and 23. Since the latter is clearly hortatory (note "Please make a contribution" in Sentence 22), the whole paragraph is hortatory — since the dominating status of the thesis determines the paragraph's classification. *Moreover, since Paragraph III is overtly hortatory while Paragraph II is only covertly (mitigated) hortatory, and Paragraph I is narrative and expository, then Segment 22, which dominates the dominating paragraph (III) must be considered to dominate the entire discourse.* The reasoning here — as in earlier sections of the paper is simply: In any given discourse type the parts of the discourse that are nearer to the main line of that discourse type dominate over parts that are farther from the main line. In a narrative discourse, narrative elements dominant over non-narrative elements. In a hortatory discourse, hortatory elements dominate over non-hortatory elements. A corollary of the above is: overtly hortatory elements dominate over covertly hortatory elements (where exhortation is mitigated). I therefore in the body of this appeals letter rank main paragraph III, which is overtly hortatory (in segments 22 and 23) over main paragraph II, which is mitigated exhortation, and both over main paragraph I, which is narrative. This reasoning carried to its end makes Segment 22 dominant the entire discourse. And why not? Isn't the letter, stripped of all embellishment an *appeal for contributions*?

First of all, I examine the structure of the Reason (Motivation) in Segments 18-21. These sentences constitute a mitigated hortatory paragraph, in which three motivations are expressed as coordinated Theses. Theses one and two (Segments 18 and 19) have verbs of ability as their main verbs: "can arm", "can act"; while the verb "need" characterizes Segment 21 to which Segment 20 (with a passive present progressive) is attached as ancillary.

Segment 18, Thesis$_1$, begins with the phrase "with your contribution" — thus anticipating the appeal in Segment 22 and echoing the themes of "need" and "opportunity" from previous sentences. This thesis affirms that ZPG "can arm our growing network of local activists with the materials they need." A purpose clause is attached: "to warn community leaders about emerging population-linked stresses before they reach the crisis stage." Note here again the reference to the background problems that are the concern of ZPG (cf. Segment 10); again this reference is buried under several layers of constituent structure within the sentence — but achieves a certain prominence by being sentence final.

Segment 19, Thesis$_2$, is a concessive sentence whose initial concessive clause is critical of the national government's insensitivity to the problems that concern ZPG: "Even though our national government continues to ignore the consequences of uncontrolled population growth...". The main clause affirms that "we can act to take positive action at the local level." The nature of this positive action is not spelled out beyond what was suggested in the previous sentence, viz. seeing to it that "local activists" have the information that they need.[10]

Thesis$_n$ (which I consider the most specific and programmatic of the three) is expressed in an embedded paragraph. It is an Expository Circumstantial paragraph with Segment 20, the Circumstance, clearly ancillary to Segment 21, the Thesis. Segment 20 simply states that every day local officials make decisions "that could drastically affect the quality of our lives." Segment 21, the Thesis, states that such local officials and indeed the American public at large, need information regarding population-induced stresses, if "sound choices" are to be made in our community — and this needed information is precisely what ZPG's "study", that is, the ZPG 1985 UST, has revealed. So Segments 18 and 19 stress the *opportunity* suggested in Segment 17, while Segments 20, 21 revert to presenting a *need*. The presentation of opportunity and need (without overt appeal) is here a characteristic piece of mitigated exhortation.

All that is lacking is the overt appeal — to which the whole letter has been warming up — "Please make a special contribution to Zero Population Growth today" (Segment 22). While an imperative is used — the first in the whole letter — it is lightly mitigated with "please." Segments 22, and 23 together make up a hortatory reason paragraph in which the non-imperative Segment 23 is ancillary to the imperative Segment 22. Here the Reason is that type of motivation that can be called a promise; it also assumes in the opening clause that a contribution will be forthcoming: "Whatever you give — $25, $50, $100, or as much as you can will be used immediately to put the Urban Stress Test in the hands of those who need it most." Here the organization pledges itself to use the contributions sent in for the purpose intended — a necessary pledge in view of the non-too-rare abuse of contributions by such groups.

The whole paragraph (Segments 19-23) could be summarized as: "We have an unparalleled opportunity to use ZPG's 1985 UST to stimulate and guide action on the local level. Please send in your contribution today."

What of the postscript? Again we have a motivated appeal in a hortatory reason paragraph. The Reason (Motivation), Segment 29, reechoes Paragraph I in the body of the letter as to the worthiness of the ZPG cause as evidenced by the news coverage that is occasioned. The Thesis (Appeal) in Segment 30 is more carefully mitigated than the main appeal which is found in Segment 22. So instead of getting: "Please help us monitor this remarkable media coverage..." we read "we hope you'll help us monitor this remarkable media coverage...". The indicated activity desired on the part of the reader is "completing the enclosed reply form." [Any response is better than none; let us at least hear from you even in the absence of a contribution. We may get a contribution from you on the next round.]

4. Conclusion

The macrostructure (van Dijk 1977, and 1980) of this letter can be stated as follows (ignoring the gimmick in the P.S. at the end): "Public response to the promulgation of the results of ZPG's 1985 UST has proven ZPG to be a worthy cause. The 1985 UST is a superb action tool. With your help we can use it to stimulate and guide action on the local level. Please send in your contribution today."

Positing this macrostructure constitutes a hermeneutic of the text by accounting for: (a) what is included in the text and its reason for being included; (b) the relative elaboration of the parts of a text (e.g. the relative elaboration found within main paragraph I is both attention getting and authority establishing; and (c) the thrust, the semantic import of the whole.

Everywhere in the analysis I have been guided by the consideration that this is a hortatory text (not an essay, nor a story) in which commands/ suggestions necessarily dominate. The meaning of the letter is found in demonstrating the dominance of elements which express command/suggestion over other elements and in showing how all the other elements of the letter relate to the dominating element(s).

Thus, I have argued that Segment 22, the only one containing an imperative form, can be shown to dominate its own paragraph which in turn dominates the whole letter. This is, I believe, typical of discourses of this type (hortatory). What few command forms there are must be considered to be somehow central to the whole even if they are statistically in a minority. I have further argued that Points I and II (corresponding to the first two main paragraphs) are related to the command element with which Paragraph III terminates as establishing the credibility of the ZPG cause and warming up to the appeal by describing an opportunity and a need growing out of it. Our initial resort to a hortatory schema which includes certain moves considerably facilitated the beginning analysis. Schemata, properly used, have considerable analytic and hermeneutic value.

This appeal letter is a typical piece of hortatory discourse which starts out with narrative and expository material, warms up to an appeal via mitigated command elements, and finally graduates to an outright open appeal at its climax. A very different sort of hortatory discourse, the Greek text of the first epistle of John in Biblical literature, is developed along very similar lines (Longacre 1983a). It is significant that two different texts separated by some 2000 years and belonging to radically different cultural milieus exhibit very similar discourse strategies.

Appendix: Constituent Display of Appeal Letter of Noverber 22, 1985

Epistolary Conventions
S_1 (Identification)
S_2 (Date)
S_3 (Salutation)

Body of Letter (Hortatory Discourse)

$POINT_1$ (Credibility claim):(N) Comment Paragraph
    THESIS (Recountal): (N) Sequence Paragraph
S_4 ST_1: At 7:00 A.M. on October 25, our phones started to ring.
S_5 ST_2: Calls jammed our switchboard all day.
S_6 ST_n: Staffers stayed late into the night answering questions and talking with reporters from newspapers, radio stations, wire services, and TV stations in every part of the country.

TERMINUS (summary): (N) Concession Paragraph

S_7 CONCESSION: When we released the results of ZPG's 1985 UST, we had no idea we'd get such an overwhelming response.

S_8 THESIS: Media and public reaction has been nothing short of incredible!

S_9 COMMENT (Analysis): E (temporal) Contrast Paragraph
ANTITHESIS: At first the deluge of calls came mostly from reporters eager to tell the public about UST results and from outraged public officials who were furious that we had "blown the whistle" on conditions in their cities.

S_{10} THESIS: Now we are hearing from concerned citizens in all parts of the country who want to know what they can do to hold local officials accountable for tackling population-related problems that threaten public health and well-being.

POINT$_2$ (the Problem):(H?) Concession Paragraph
CONCESSION:(E) Coordinate Paragraph

S_{11} THESIS$_1$: ZPG's 1985 Urban Stress Test, created after months of persistent research, is the nation's first survey of how population-linked pressures affect U.S. cities.

S_{12} THESIS$_2$: It ranks 184 urban areas on 11 different criteria ranging from crowding and birth rates to air quality and toxic wastes.

S_{13} THESIS$_n$: The Urban Stress Test translates complex technical data into an easy-to-use action tool for concerned citizens, elected officials, and opinion leaders.

THESIS: Cyclic (H?) Reason Paragraph

S_{14} THESIS: But to use it well we urgently need your help.

S_{15} REASON: Our Small staff is being swamped with requests for more information and our modest resources are being stretched to the limit.

S_{16} THESIS': Your support now is crucial.

S_{17} TERMINUS: ZPG's 1985 Urban Stress Test may be our best opportunity ever to get the population message heard

POINT$_n$ (motivated appeal):(H) Reason Paragraph
REASON (Motivation):(H?) Coordinate Paragraph

S_{18} THESIS$_1$: With your contribution, ZPG can arm our growing network of local activists with the materials they need to warn community leaders about emerging population-linked stresses before they reach the crisis stage.

S_{19} THESIS$_2$: Even though our national government continues to ignore the consequence of uncontrolled population growth, we can act to take positive action at the local level.

THESISn: (E) Circumstantial Paragraph

S_{20} CIRCUMSTANCE: Every day decisions are being made by local officials in our communities that could drastically affect the quality of our lives.

S_{21} THESIS: To make sound choices in planning for people, both elected officials and the American public need the population stress data revealed by our study.

126   ROBERT E. LONGACRE

    THESIS (Appeal):(H) Reason Paragraph
S_{22} THESIS: Please make a special contribution to Zero Population Growth today.
S_{23} REASON (motivating promise): Whatever you give — $25, $50, $100 or as much as you can — will be used immediately to put the Urban Stress Test in the hands of those who need it most.
    EPISTOLARY CONVENTIONS
S_{24} Complimentary close
S_{25} Written signature
S_{26-27} Signature printed and title
S_{28} P.S.
    The POSTSCRIPT (Appended (mitigated) Hortatory discourse of one paragraph added according to a further epistolary convention): (H?) Reason Paragraph
S_{29} REASON (Motivation): The results of ZPG's 1985 Urban Stress Test were reported as a top news story by hundreds of newspapers and TV and radio stations from coast to coast.
S_{30} THESIS (Appeal): I hope you can help us monitor this remarkable news coverage by completing the enclosed reply form.

Notes

1. Because this is a letter, it is characterized by the customary epistolary conventions appropriate to its time and culture. Thus, the letterhead with the rubric ZPG and the Washington address at the bottom serves to identify the organization that has sent out the letter (Segment 1). The material in the left-hand margin — officers and sponsors of ZPG — serves further to identify the organization and put some substance to what might otherwise carry little weight. Segment 2, the date, Segment 3, the salutation, Segment 24, the complimentary close, Segment 25, the written signature, and Segments 26 and 27, the printed signature and title, as well as segment 28 (P.S.) are further epistolary conventions.

    These conventions primarily serve performative, that is, sender-receiver function, date the time of the appeal, and attempt by the letterhead conventions to identify ZPG and put it in a favorable light.

    That these conventions are used skillfully is seen in the wording of the salutation ['Dear Friends of ZPG'], begging the question of the reader's positive attitude to the cause represented; in the date [less than one month since the alleged storm of response broke on the heads of the ZPG staff]; and the signature wherein it is indicated (via letter head) that Susan Weber is Executive Director of the organization.

2. Recursion in macrosegmentation occurs when a major division of a discourse is itself a discourse, whose big 'chunks' must in turn be isolated and inspected to see if further such recursion must be postulated or if we can pass immediately to considerations of microsegmentation.

3. Dominance is here opposed to ancillary. The pair of terms *dominant* and *ancillary* are offered as the inter-sentential counterparts of the intra-sentential relations, independent

and subordinate. Thus, in "John went downtown because he was bored" we have the independent clause "John went downtown" and the subordinate clause "because he was bored". Notice, however, the following pair of sentences: "John went downtown. He was completely bored with sitting around the house all day". Here I term the first sentence "John went downtown", *dominant* and the second sentence *ancillary*.

4. The term has been used effectively by Labov and Fanshell (1977:84-86) in regard to making requests. An outright bald command may be disguised and softened to make it more socially acceptable to the hearer or reader. Thus, "Write this letter at once" can be mitigated to "Please write this letter as soon as possible" or to "Please give this letter top priority in your work this morning", or to "Would you mind getting this letter to me for my signature before coffee-break?" or even to "This letter should be mailed off this morning".

5. cf. Longacre 1983a. The hortatory schema employed here originated, however, in field workshops conducted in the Philippine branch of the Summer Institute of Linguistics by Austin Hale and Michael Walrod.

6. In any discourse type there is a main line of development and further elements which supplement/support the main line. In narrative text there is a storyline of punctiliar sequential happenings reported in sentences whose main verb(s) are some sort of past tense, completive aspect, or a special narrative tense (Biblical Hebrew, many African languages). In hortatory text there is a line of exhortation carried by imperative or modal forms which command, suggest, or urge some action. Everything else in the hortatory text supplements or support the line of exhortation. Other discourse types also have main line elements and additional elements. All of this can be tersely summarized as on-the-line versus off-the-line elements which are subject to morphosyntactic and/or lexical identification. On-the-line elements dominate off-the-line elements in local-span (paragraph analysis); cf. Longacre 1989b.

7. This is hardly the place to give a complete inventory and description of the paragraph types that are frequently encountered in languages around the world or even only in English (cf. Longacre 1979, 1980). I summarize briefly here; (1) a paragraph must have one or more *theses* which are characterized by having sentences whose main verb(s) is on the mainline in the discourse type in which that paragraph is found. Theses may be related to each other as coordinated (coordinate paragraph), contrasted (antithetical paragraph), or reflecting chronological succession (sequence paragraph). A single thesis may, on the other hand be accompanied by an ancillary segment whose main verb is off-the-line in the discourse type in which the paragraph is found. Besides setting/introduction, terminus/conclusion, and comment mentioned above under (4), further ancillary segments can relate to a thesis as reason, result, concession, paraphrase, amplification and the like. Longacre 1989b, 83-118, contains a more recent and more discursive presentation of paragraph types (relative to Biblical Hebrew) than are found in earlier articles cited above.

8. Paragraph types have (a) basic relational structures as indicated by such terms as coordinate, antithetical, reason, result, etc.; (b) variants determined by the discourse type which the paragraph represents, i.e. narrative, procedural, hortatory, expository, and the like; and (c) further stylistic variants of which *cyclic* (or chiastic) structure is the most common. A cyclic paragraph has a structure such as ABA, ABCBA, and the like — a sort of lexical rhyming. In the text above segments 14, 15, and 16 constitute a *cyclic hortatory reason paragraph* (of ABC structure); cf. Longacre 1979.

9. The placement of sentences which are an expression of need (and may use the actual verb 'need' as in segments 14 and 21), in the dominance pattern of hortatory discourse probably requires further consideration. I have at present decided that an explanation of need is a kind of mitigated exhortation — a covert solicitation for fulfillment of the need. While an expression of need is properly preliminary to an appeal, an appeal may be pragmatically carried out by going no further than expressing a need. Consequently, I have ranked 'need' as higher in dominance than (other) motivations such as threats/unpleasant consequences and promises/good consequences, cf:
    a. We need your help very much.
    b. If you help us, we'll be able to accomplish some significant results.
    c. If you don't help us, we may have to fold up our operation.

   Here, I think quite clearly that (a) outranks (b) and (c) which are given to support (a) and are ancillary to it.

   If, however, we say:
   a. Please help us this month;
   b. Our need is great and urgent.

   just as clearly (a) outranks (b) which is ancillary to (a).

10. The failure to specify ZPG's precise aims and the means proposed to accomplish them leaves the reader who has received no previous ZPG mailings wondering. Will zero population growth be accomplished by extensive use of birth control and sterilization, reducing teen-age pregnancies through a resurgence of continence in this segment of the population, or by extensive use of abortion?

References

Ballard, D. Lee, Robert J. Conrad, and R.E. Longacre
    1971a "The deep and surface grammar of interclausal relations." *Foundations of Language*. 7.70-118.
    1971b "More on the deep and surface grammar of interclausal relations." *Language Data*. Asian-Pacific Series, No. 1. Ukarumpa (Papua New Guinea): Summer Institute of Linguistics.

de Beaugrande, R., and W. Dressler
    1981 *An Introduction to Textlinguistics*. London: Longmans.

Beekman, J., J. Callow, and M. Kopesec
    1981 *The Semantic Structure of Written Communication* (private circulation).

Barnard, Myra Lou and Jannette Forster
    1968 The Dibabawon Texts in *Discourse, Paragraph, and Sentence Structure in Selected Philippine Languages*, volume III. Final Report Contract No. 0-8-062838-0391. Washington: Office of Education, Institute of International Studies, 269-301.

Dijk, T.A. van
    1977 *Text and Context: Explorations in the Semantics and Pragmatics of Discourse*. London: Longman.

1980   *Macrostructures: An Interdisciplinary Study of Global Structures in Discourse, Interaction, and Cognition.* Hillsdale, NJ: Lawrence Erlbaum Associates.

Fuller, Daniel P.
  1959   *The Inductive Method of Bible Study.* 3rd edition. Pasadena: Fuller Theological Seminary.

Grimes, J.E.
  1975   *The Thread of Discourse.* The Hague: Mouton.

Hoey, Michael
  1983   *On the Surface of Discourse.* London: George Allen & Unwin.

Labov, Willam and David Fanshel
  1977   *Therapeutic Discourse: Psychotherapy as Conversation.* New York: Academic Press.

Longacre, R.E.
  1970   "Sentence structure as a statement calculus." *Language* 46.783-815.

  1976   *An Anatomy of Speech Notions.* Lisse: Peter de Ridder Press.

  1979   "The paragraph as a grammatical unit." In T. Givón (ed.), *Discourse and Syntax.* New York: Academic Press, 115-134.

  1980   "An apparatus for the identification of paragraph types." *Notes on Linguistics.* 15.5-23. Dallas: Summer Institute of Linguistics.

  1983a "Exhortation and mitigation in the Greek text of the First Epistle of John." *Selected Technical Articles Related to Translation* 9. Dallas: Summer Institute of Linguistics.

  1983b *The Grammar of Discourse.* New York: Plenum Press.

  1985   "Sentences as combinations of clauses." In Timothy Shopen (ed.), *Language Typology and Syntactic Description:Complex Constructions.* Cambridge: Cambridge University Press, 235-286.

  1989a *Joseph, a Story of Divine Providence.* Winona Lake: Eisenbrauns.

  1989b "Two Hypotheses regarding text generation and text analysis." *Discourse Processes* 12.413-460.

Matthiesen, Christian and Sandra A. Thompson.
  1989   "The structure of discourse and 'subordination'." In John Haiman and Sandra A. Thompson (eds.), *Clause Combining in Grammar and Discourse.* Amsterdam/Philadelphia: John Benjamins.

Mann, W.C. and S.A. Thompson
  1987   *Rhetorical Structure Theory: A Theory of Text Organization.* Marina del Rey: University of Southern California, Information Sciences Institute. To appear in Livia Polanyi, ed. *Discourse Structures.*

Mann, W.C. and S.A. Thompson
    1987   "Rhetorical Structure Theory: toward a functional theory of text organization." *Text* 8:3.243-281.

Thompson, Sandra and Robert E. Longacre
    1985   "Adverbial clauses". In Timothy Shopen (ed.), *Language Typology and Syntactic Description: Complex Constructions.* Cambridge: Cambridge University Press.

14

Holistic Textlinguistics

Robert E. Longacre

SIL International
2003

Contents

Abstract	3
Introduction	3
1 Overarching concerns illustrated in *The Final Diagnosis*	6
2 Median range concerns	8
3 Overview with an example of a narrative paragraph	8
3.1 Dialogue paragraphs	10
3.2 Paragraphs that encode reflection	15
4 Verb/clause salience and dominance in the local span	17
5 Integration with a morphosyntax informed by textual concerns	18
Appendix	19
References	47

Abstract

This article is a rather full presentation of the author's approach to Textlinguistics with special emphasis upon the facts that a text is a *whole*—so that such matters as text types, profiles, macrostructures, text templates, and other high-level concerns are inextricably bound up with the morphosyntax. While it is a truism to say that everything expressed in a text much use the language of the text as its medium, it is not generally realized how the text not only is constrained by that language but skillfully exploits features of it by artistically distorting those features to convey what the text has to say. Passages from *The Final Diagnosis* by Arthur Hailey are used as illustrative material (by Hailey's permission).

Introduction

In this paper I present textlinguistics or discourse analysis as the completion and fulfillment of linguistics as generally conceived and bounded. Textlinguistics ties up the many loose ends left from the morphosyntax. There are many unanswered questions that remain after the analysis of words, clauses, and sentences (Longacre 1979). In regard to these unanswered questions, textlinguistics has considerable explanatory power. I have argued this for many years, and the field of linguistic studies has not been wholly unaffected by such argumentation on the part of myself and others. The point of this paper, however, is to argue that textlinguistic analysis itself must be considered to bend back upon itself so that the most general and holistic text concerns are interlaced with lower level and more specific concerns. The analysis is necessarily circular in a nonvicious and reinforcing sense. The strategy of this paper will be to present the concepts displayed on the accompanying chart, then to apply them to the analysis of a novel, *The Final Diagnosis* (TFD), by Arthur Hailey (1959).

I briefly touch here on certain background considerations: the relation of monologue to dialogue, of sentence to text, and structural paragraphs and relations within them.

The first consideration leads to the recognition that monologue can embed within monologue, and dialogue can embed within monologue. In dialogue a question such as "How did your trip to Denver turn out last week?" can lead to a lengthy answer, possibly to a story, complete with a rudimentary plot structure. Or someone may make a remark that a certain teacher at the university impresses her as "wholly incompetent" only to have her dialogue partner offer a spirited defense of the teacher in question with several main points and subpoints figuring in the defense. Or a request may be expressed which the dialogue partner feels oblidged to turn down while at the same time realizing that the situation is delicate and that the refusal must be very carefully worded and hedged.

Conversely, dialogue regularly embeds in monologue—even in informal situations. A dialogue partner may recount the gist of a conversation that he/she has heard or in which he participated. Of course, in more formal discourses, especially in a short story or novel, the story advances by means of interaction between participants and much of the interaction may be verbal. More properly put, the story may advance by complex interactions which have both verbal and nonverbal elements.

A second consideration is the relation of a sentence to its monologue or dialogue context. Here what we came to call "Functional Sentence Perspective" was exploring as early as a century and a half ago how sentences succeed each other in context. Dividing each sentence into theme and rheme, such analysis showed how the rheme of one sentence with considerable regularity becomes the theme of the following sentence—thus unifying the discourse in terms of what could broadly be described as the interweaving of older and newer information. Somewhat later, another idea—of which Harald Weinrich (1964) may be the most eloquent early voice, if not the founder—was making itself known. Essentially, this idea was that a text is also unified by a consistent use of the tense forms of the language in which the text is written. Weinrich and Beneviste (1974) and others developed this idea in Europe, and developments of the same idea were heard across the Atlantic in the writings of Gleason (1968), Grimes (1975), Hopper (1979), and Longacre (numerous articles). The system of tenses in a language selects one or two privileged tenses for use in sentences on the mainline of a discourse and uses other tense forms in supporting sentences. Paul Ricoeur (1985) has, in his brilliant summation of the work of his European predecessors in this regard, argued simply that tenses are used to facilitate the "followability" of a story. Unless we in some way distinguished the sentences which represent mainline events, how could a reader/hearer follow the story?

A third preliminary consideration has to do with the need for a level of structure intermediate between the sentence and the discourse. At the risk of confusion with concerns of practical formatting and indentation, I have for some years now called this unit the *paragraph*. Sentences only rarely occupy as such pivotal positions within a text. Or to put it differently, a text is almost never a simple sequence of sentences. Rather, the latter typically clump and cluster together into larger aggregates which eventually structure into the overall discourse. For practical conveniance, whenever two or more sentences belong together semantically and/or by virtue of surface signals, I have been calling the cluster a paragraph. Relations expressed in such clusters, whether small or large can be expressed in a finite inventory of relations (Longacre 1996 and earlier; Mann and Thompson 1983 and later).

Overarching concerns

My discussion here concerns which text types are grouped under A in the accompanying chart. The reason for insisting on text type and its corresponding template as a logical starting point in textual analysis is to insure that we are not barking up the proverbial wrong tree as we begin (Longacre 1996:7) A narrative, for example, has narrative movement and it is fruitless to analyze it as if it were a scientific paper, a food recipe, or a piece of logical argumentation. When we say that a text has narrative movement, we expect to find that it is built on a narrative template, a conceptual scheme which in broad outline is as old as Aristotle. More about this later. If we find a text to be a piece of exhortation, we expect to find it built on a hortatory template with cognitive components which are probably universal: Authority of the exhorter; Situation/Problem; Command element(s); Motivation (Longacre 1996:34). Explanation or descriptive discourse also involves, as a static discourse type that is quite the opposite of narrative, elements of universality. E. Winter and M. Hoey (1983) have successfully demonstrated in this regard a four-point template: Situation, Problem, Solution, Evaluation. This is not to deny that particular cultures or culture settings may not develop templates of applicability to discourses of a specialized nature, e.g., food recipes in current American culture, and, I suspect, a template underlying a typical piece of transformational-generative grammar (resemblant in some ways to the Winter-Hoey template mentioned above). Nor is it to claim that all discourse types necessarily have underlying templates; I do not, for example, think that we find them in lyric poetry.

Be all this as it may, it is particularly the narrative template that concerns us here because I have chosen to illustrate my general methodology via a novel. Certainly, an essential element of the narrative template (Longacre 1996:33–38) is the Inciting Incident—which is a way of saying that all stories must have a reason for being told. Something happens that breaks a normal expectancy chain and "thereby hangs a tale." Only in such circumstances as witnessing in a court of law are recitals without an inciting incident tolerated and relevant. After the Inciting Incident, the nascent story then proceeds by way of Mounting Tension to a Climax—and beyond Climax to a Denouement. The relation of the last two elements to each other is captured quite well in French where the former is called the Nouement. The metaphor is suggested: Knot it all up proper and then untie it. Commonly such concerns are referred to as plot.

The narrative template as just summarized is just the topological starting point which is subject to many skillful twistings and deformations in the hands of a competent story teller or novelist. Furthermore, a story may have episodes in which the narrative template is recursively applied—witness the series of episodes ending in cliffhangers in Victor Hugo's *Les Miserables*. And, as we shall see in looking at Hailey's novel, a longer sort of story may have several interweaving plot structures which are subservient to and which forward the main plot. The narrative template may be employed so as to intensively cultivate a small plot of ground as in Virginia Wolf's *Mrs. Dalloway* where much of the successive events of the day recounted by the novelist consist of ruminations and flashbacks on the part of its main character, so that even the "stream of consciousness" is not without a chronological framework.

Several points indicated in chart 1 under A "test type and its template" have already been commented on. Thus the last implicate, recursion, has been mentioned. The second implicate has only been hinted at. Portions of the constituency structure (paragraphs and embedded discourses) which correspond to naturally prominent points on the underlying template may be elaborated in some way to explicitly mark their prominence. Thus, while a Stage may inaugurate a narrative by sketching temporal and locational circumstances at the beginning of the story and by introducing one or more of the participants, and while various episodes may developing mounting tension, special surface structure marking may characterize the climax and/or the denouement, and occasionally the Inciting Incident. This special marking often has to do with augmenting in some way the verb structures that routinely mark the storyline, making that point in the narrative more immediate and vivid by a variety of devices, and maximum interlacing of participant reference (Longacre 1990:8–9; 1996:38–48). This surface structure marking gives the narrative its profile, which is built around one or more such peaks i.e., zones marked for special prominence in the surface structure.

Chart 1. Interrelationships of textual factors

A. Text type and its template*

    → macrostructure of given text

    → profile of its surface structure

    → recursion[1] of text type within same/different type

B. Constituents of text (domain of cognitive/rhetorical interclausal relations)

    (Structural) Paragraphs [also recursive]

    Constituents of paragraphs: sentences and clauses

    Intraparagraph relations [whether Longacre or Mann-Thompson]

C. Constraints on constituents (B ← A)

    Noninteractive vs. Interactive (e.g., dialogue) paragraphs

    Reflective paragraphs (often Flashback in Narrative.)

    Verb/Clause salience (Longacre 1989)

D. Exit to a morphosyntax informed by A, B, and C

*It cannot be assumed that all text types have templates; apparently lyric poems do not.

    What I have not as yet presented is the first implicate in point A, that a text has a macrostructure. This is true whether or not a text is built on a template. The macrostructure is peculiar to its text and not universal like the template. Developed and popularized by T. van Dijk (1997, 1980), this concept is of considerable importance to text analysis. For several years I've used the following working definition of macrostructure:

> The gist or abstract of a text which exercises a controlling function over the text in respect to (1) what is included or excluded from mention in the text; (2) what parts are developed in relatively more detail than others; and (3) departures in internal ordering of the parts of the text from the default ordering indicated in the template on which the text is built.

Obviously, the macrostructure is related to the theme, which is usually an attempt to capture in a noun phrase the gist of the story. These macrostructural concerns are basic in determining peak marking. Although the template per se indicates a certain natural prominence within the text, the macrostructure indicates at which point or points special surface structure marking may be encountered.

---

[1] By recursion I mean simply the occurrence of a construction on a given structural level within another construction on the same level, e.g., discourse within discourse, paragraph within paragraph, sentence within sentence, etc. (Longacre 1996:276–284).

1 Overarching concerns illustrated in *The Final Diagnosis*

The novel is, of course, built on a narrative template. Chapter 1, which functions as Stage for the whole novel, is a panoramic view of what is going on in various parts of Three Counties Hospital; it does not seem to foreground any particular participant but mentions several who will be of crucial importance in the following chapters. It does contain a hint of conflict in the efforts which had to be put forth by one of the ranking nurses to get Joseph Pearson. chief of pathology, to sign certain autopsy reports. Chapter 2 clearly foregrounds Dr. Kent O'Donnell by devoting the chapter to him with extensive flashback regarding him before he came to be the director of the hospital and how he came to be its director. It foreshadows coming conflicts by mentioning O'Donnell's sense of shock on coming to the hospital and finding things a bit careless and shoddy. The chapter closes with another reference to Pearson's dilatoriness in getting reports in on time and records O'Donnell's saying "I think we may have to go to war with Joe Pearson." Chapter 3 presents Joe Pearson performing an autopsy and displays him in his element and doing a superb job. Thus chapters 1–3 are largely staging in reference to time, location, and circumstances and introduce the reader to Kent O'Donnell and Joe Pearson who will head respectively the progressive and conservative factions who will be involved in the coming struggle. It smoothly works in the inciting incident or situation occasioned by Pearson's slowness in getting in pathology reports—without any special fanfare or surface marking. Before any further references to template elements, I first address myself to the delineation of the macrostructure of the novel along with its main plot and subplots

Adapting and revising a suggestion of Mary Williams (1978), I take the macrostructure of the novel to be:

> The struggle between progressives, headed up by Kent O'Donnell and conservatives, headed up by Joe Pearson, as to whether progressive medicine will prevail at Three Counties Hospital, or negligence and outdated procedures will force the hospital to shut down.

Williams in her brilliant paper points out that there are subtle clues that indicate that the struggle going on at the hospital is basically a bipartite struggle, in spite of the large cast of characters involved. Chief among these clues is the fact that while we as readers have access to the thoughts and feelings of the progressives through indirect speech which reports such thoughts and feelings, we are left to infer the thoughts and feelings of the conservatives from their facial expressions, body language, and overt utterances. Two observations are noteworthy at this point: (1) Essentially, it reduces the complexity of the participant slate to two parties, much like a two-party struggle, say, between a turtle and a monkey in a South American indigenous folktale (Longacre and Woods 1976–1977). (2) It links closely together the highest level concerns with low level phenomena such as use of reportive or reflective verbs in direct and indirect speech, and hence the structure of clauses and sentences. The latter is, of course, one of the main contentions of this paper. Even the noun phrases referring to various participants, involving the use of the adjectives "youthful" and "old" serve also to group the participants into the two factions.

Williams goes on to list the various subplots which tie into and forward the progress of the main plot. With some adaptation and expansion I take these subplots (macrostructures) from her:

(1) Will Joe Pearson be forced to retire?
(2) Will Vivian Lomburton, a nursing student who is having an affair with Dr. Seddons, a resident in Pathology, prove to have a malignancy in her leg, and how will her amputation affect the possible marriage of the two?
(3) Will Kent O'Donnell, the director of the hospital and the banner carrier of the Progressives, marry Denise Swayne, a wealthy socialite and leave Three Counties Hospital or will he marry the orthopedic surgeon Lucy Granger and stay on directing the hospital?
(4) Will old man Eustace Swayne, Denise's father and close friend of Joe Pearson come through with his anticipated donation to build a new wing of the hospital even if his friend Pearson is crowded out?
(5) Will a new lab worker in pathology, John Alexander, and his wife Elizabeth, have a healthy baby even though Pearson refused to authorize a further laboratory test regarding the possible presence of an RH negative factor?
(6) Will Dr. Dornberger, the Alexander's obstetrician, recognize it is time for him to retire?
(7) Will Mrs. Straughan, the chief dietician and director of the hospital kitchen, get the new dishwashers that she has requested on several occasions?

7

In regard to these various subplots, I notice that Joe Pearson is so colorful a figure in his own right that a colleague of mine suggested that the macrostructure of the whole novel should be centered on him, i.e., that it should be conceived to be "The sad story of the fall of Dr. Pearson." My answer to my colleague's suggestion was that too many parts of the novel would be left uncaptured in such a macrostructure for it to serve such a general purpose. I also note that the most colorful participant is not necessarily central—no more than Satan should be considered to be central, in Milton's *Paradise Lost* (cf. C. S Lewis 1961). Subplot 2 is of importance, aside from its human interest, in that it is Pearson in pathology who has to evaluate Vivian's biopsy and decide whether or not it is cancerous—but it comes out late in the novel (denouement of subplot 2) that his diagnosis is correct, when a younger colleague dissects the amputated leg. Subplot 3 is of obvious importance to the main plot in that removing O'Donnell from the hospital would be fatal to the progressive cause. Subplot 4, as to whether the Swayne donation will come through, also ties vitally into the plans to modernize the hospital. Subplot 5 culminates in the death of the Alexander's baby and the resignation of Pearson, and hence to the final resolution of the central tensions of the story. Subplot 6 is perhaps the most marginal of the subplots, but Dornberger is one of the progressives himself, although inclined at first to defend Pearson, and has enough vantage point on himself to know when the good of the hospital calls for his retirement. Subplot 7 ties into the final climax and denouement of the main plot. There is an outbreak of typhoid in the hospital—which threatens to close it down--and the new dishwashers desired by Mrs. Straughan should help prevent and control all such future emergencies.

Having sketched the main macrostructure and its subsidiary macrostructures as plot and subplots, I now note how the novel progresses to its climax and denouement. Helen Miehle (1978) rightly considers that pages 281–283 (halfway down the page) constitute a tight, well-marked climax for the entire novel. We have mentioned that the inner thoughts of the "good guys" are accessible to the reader, and in the passage here cited it is O'Donnell himself who is summarizing to himself the sorry predicament into which the hospital has come. Miehle rightly remarks on the sheer variety and rhetorical liveliness found in the nine component paragraphs of this section. She summarizes:

> Some of the rhetorical devices that Hailey uses to heighten tension in the scene to be examined here are (1) inner reflective monologue, (2) sequences of rhetorical questions, (3) flashbacks, and (4) frequent shifts in paragraph types which shift the time focus from past to present, and then to future.

Indeed the passage is replete with questions, self-recriminations, admission of failure—as well as resolution to better the situation. Especially telling is where O'Donnell watches from his office window the comings and goings of people below and meditates both on their trust in medicine and as to whether that trust is not sometimes misplaced. The whole passage is pitched in a high emotional key—but no higher than the circumstances warrant!

But if this passage is marked as climactic, no less marked is the denouement of the main plot some ten pages over in the novel (pp. 293–296). The health authorities have arrived at 5:00 P.M. as promised to shut down the kitchen of the hospital and hence the hospital itself. O'Donnell leads a doleful procession down to the pathology laboratory to show the city authorities how the overworked band of men down there have been doggedly analyzing fecal specimen after fecal specimen in order to track down the carrier of typhoid. In terms of participant cast, once the delegation arrives in pathology, we find indeed a crowded stage, that maximum interlacing of participants which so often marks a surface structure peak. On getting to pathology the dialogue is lively and those in the lab register shock at the imminent closing of the hospital. But precisely at this point, a releasing event takes place (Miehle, oral communication), and resolution of the plot is now possible. Just as the group of administrators and the health official are leaving, we are told: "They had reached the door when John Alexander announced, 'I have it.'" Pearson then bounds across the room and checks out Alexander's analysis of typhoid bacillus interactions as seen in diagnostic sugar tests. The presentation is very dramatic (dialogue registered in terse sentence fragments, p. 295) as the countdown proceeds suspensefully down a row of ten test tubes, and Pearson confirms Alexander's discovery of the carrier—one Mrs. Burgess who is even then working in the cafeteria's serving line where they have just begun to serve supper. She is quickly turned from worker into patient and the contaminated food disposed of. Time: 5:07 P.M. A real "hair's breath Harry" escape for the threatened hospital! Subsequent pages have denouements of various subplots listed above without the peak marking that characterizes the denouement of the main plot.

I note again here that the morphosyntactic surface structure is radically affected at the main denouement—thus demonstrating again the tie-in between the highest and most abstract concerns (template, macrostructure, profile, and peak) with the lower concerns of sentence, clause, and phrase structure.

2 Median range concerns

I illustrate here from TFD, chapter 3, the concerns which are grouped under B and C in chart 1.

Texts are composed of structural paragraphs (not always congruent with the orthographic paragraphing or indentation units of the author, Longacre 1779). But both text and paragraph are recursive units. Thus, while embedded texts/discourses may occur as constituents of a text, eventually texts on the lowest level of embedding are composed of paragraphs. And while ultimately paragraphs are composed of sentences, and while embedded paragraphs are the rule rather than the exception, nevertheless the latter ultimately break down into sentences on the lowest level of paragraph embedding. The assumption that embedding occurs on both text and paragraph levels is absolutely essential, if we are to posit a finite number of text types and paragraph types; otherwise, every new situation of embedding that we encounter would lead to positing a new type and the number of types on both levels would be infinite.

I will take here a few examples of paragraphs from chapter 3 of TFD and present them in indentation diagrams which are, in effect, trees turned on their sides. The entire chapter exists in this analyzed form (available on the internet: sil.org. by permission of A. Hailey). The intraparagraph relations here used are those found in Longacre (1996), but they could be expressed as the rhetorical relations catalogued by Mann and Thompson (1983, 1987a, 1987b).

3 Overview with an example of a narrative paragraph

I begin by giving an overview of TFD, chapter 3, giving the main captions down to the second layer of embedding:

Example 1

STAGE: EMBEDDED NARR. DISC. pp. 23–28 [Central participant, Pearson, off stage but his coming is anticipated]
    STAGE: (E) Coordinate Para.
    EP1 (Weidman and the janitor): NARR. DISC.
    EP2 (Rinne and Weidman): (N) Comment Para.
    EP3 (McNeil and Nurse Penfield): Compound Dial. Para.
    EP4 (Rinne and McNeil): Resolved Simple Dial. Para.
    EP5 (Seddons and McNeil): Compound Dial. Para.
    EPn (Mike meets Vivian): Embedded NARR. DISC.

EP1 (Entrance of Pearson): (N) Sequence Para.
    SETTING: (N) Simple Para.
    SEQ. THESIS1: Quote Para.
    SEQ. THESIS2: Sequence Para.
    SEQ. THESIS3: Sentence
    SEQ. THESISn: (N) Sequence Para.

EP2 (Greetings and preliminary remarks of Pearson): Compound Dial. Para.

EP3 (initial incisions) (N) DISC
    EP1 (inciting incident): Comment Para.
    EPn (Peak?): (N) Simultaneous Para.

EP4 (Further progress on the autopsy; Seddons evaluates): (N) Comment Para. [of discourse length]
    THESIS: (N) Sequence Para.
    COMMENT: Cyclic R-Q-A (N) comment Para. THESIS: (N) Comment Para.

EPn (Pearson finds something unexpected): NARR. DISC.
    EP1: Compound execution Para. for: (N) Sequence Para.?]
    EP2 [Vivian's reaction – simultaneous with EP1]: (E) Cyclic Reason Para.
    EP3 [Student nurses ask questions]: Compound Dialogue Para.
    EPn (PEAK) (The discovery): Compound Dial. Para.

CLOSURE: NARR. DISC.
FINIS

    Note in the above that we posit here an embedded discourse which constitutes the entire chapter, and which consists of Stage, five Episodes (of which the last is marked as Episode n and is climactic), Closure, and Finis. The Stage recounts getting the corpse to the autopsy room, preparations for the entrance of Pearson who is to perform the autopsy, and Mike's meeting Vivian. As indicated, Episode 1 recounts the entrance of Pearson, Episode 2, his preliminary remarks, and Episode 3, the initial incisions. Episode 4 is unique in its embedding of a discourse under the Comment of a Narrative Comment paragraph. This embedded discourse reports Seddons' musings as he watches the ongoing autopsy. It is a discourse with three points: (1) pathology was not for him (Seddons); (2) pathology deadens sensibilities; and (3) the doctor mustn't get insulated in a protective cocoon. In Ep n, which is climactic and the peak of the whole chapter, Pearson discovers what none of the doctors had suspected: although the man had died of a heart condition, he had an advanced case of fibrocaseous tuberculosis which would have killed him anyway, and which calls for precautions to be taken with his family and those who had had close contact with him. Pearson permits himself to gloat to Seddons: "Pathology has its victories too, Dr. Seddons." The Finis of the whole embedded discourse is puckish: "Then he was gone, leaving a cloud of cigar smoke behind him."

    We will now look at a paragraph found earlier in Episode 4 of the embedded discourse which expounds the Stage. As indicated in example 1, episode 4 is expounded by a Narrative Comment paragraph, the Comment of which contains the embedded discourse of Seddon's regarding pathology. The Thesis to which this Comment is appended is a Narrative Sequence paragraph of considerable length. Its first Sequential Thesis is a long embedded Simultaneous paragraph which reports what Pearson and Seddons were doing while McNeil applied himself to the head of the corpse. What the former two are doing is reported as simultaneous with what McNeil is doing, but each line of activity is reported in a Sequence paragraph. The degrees of embedding are complex, but it is the price we pay for endeavoring to account for the function of each sentence in its context.

    Example 2 consists of the first part of this Simultaneous paragraph, i.e., what Pearson and Seddons were doing.

Example 2 (TFD, p. 31)

PRELIMINARY:
    Now McNeil slipped on his own gloves and went to work with Pearson.

SIMUL1: (N) Sequence Para.
    SETTING:
        By this time, moving, swiftly, the older man had peeled back the chest flap and, hacking the flesh loose with a larger knife, exposed the ribs.

    SEQ. THESIS1: Simultaneous Para. [fore-weighted]
        SIMUL1:
            Next, using the sharp levered rib cutters, he cut his way into the rib cage, exposing pericardium and lungs.
        SIMUL2:
            The gloves, instruments, and table were now beginning to be covered with blood.

    SEQ. THESIS2: Simultaneous Para. [fore-weighted]
        SETTING:
            Seddons, gloved also, on his side of the table was cutting back the lower flaps of flesh and opening the abdomen.

SIMUL1:
He crossed the room for a pail and began to remove the stomach and intestines, which he put into the pail after studying them briefly.
SIMUL2:
The odor was beginning to be noticeable.
SEQ. THESISn: (N) Sequence Para.
SEQ. THESIS1:
Now Pearson and Seddons together tied off and cut the arteries so the undertaker would have no trouble when it came to embalming.
SEQ. THESISn:
Taking a small tube from a rack above the table, Seddons turned on a tap and began to siphon blood that had escaped into the abdomen and, after a nod from Pearson, did the same thing for the chest.

This example, among other things, illustrates nicely the use of the adverb "now" as a transition marker in narrative text (cf. H. Dry on "now" in *The Great Gatsby*). The previous paragraph terminates with a long passage on resident McNeil's concern for how the student nurses were handling what they were obligated to watch. The word "now" as the first word of the paragraph we are now examining serves to jerk us back to the business at hand. The whole sentence is preliminary and is labelled as such in the indentation diagram.

Simul 1 (as over against Simul 2 which is not given above) is expounded by a narrative sequence paragraph which consists of three Sequential Theses (actions/events reported in temporal sequence).

While the Setting has verbs in the pluperfect, "had peeled....(had) exposed"—and is thus off the main sequence by virtue of prior occurrence—the Seq. Theses have verbs in the simple past and in the past progressive. The former are considered to dominate over the latter and the two-sentence unit (Simultaneous paragraph) is considered to be foreweighted. Thus, in Seq. Thesis 1 the event is Pearson's cutting his way into the rib cage, while it is reported that as he was doing that: "The gloves, instruments, and table were now beginning to be covered with blood." In Seq. Thesis 2 there are two past progressive verbs and one simple past. Prominence is given to the simple past which occurs in the second sentence which reports a series of actions by Seddons. The first sentence, which I label Setting brings Seddons into the picture and tells what he was doing prior to his actions given in the second sentence. The third sentence, also with a past progressive verb, reports that simultaneous with the action complex reported in the previous sentence "The odor was beginning to be noticeable." Thus, in the first two Seq. Theses author Hailey by careful use of tense/aspect distinctions distinguishes punctiliar happenings from concomitant phenomena (sights and smells!). In the third Seq. Thesis Pearson and Seddons are reported as working together; the two sentences which report their joint activities are considered to constitute an embedded Sequence paragraph. Again, the adverb "now" occurs to mark the transition from what each man was doing separately to their embarking on a joint activity. Simple past tense verbs, "tied off," "cut," "turned on," "began," and "did" mark the main events which are reported in the two sentences. Grammatical subordination sets off a purpose clause and its related temporal clause —"so the undertaker would have no trouble when it came to embalming"— in the first sentence. In the second sentence grammatical subordination sets off the initial participial construction "taking a small tube from a rack above the table" and a relative clause with a pluperfect verb "that had escaped into the abdomen." Here grammatical subordination is seen to function as a further device—along with tense/aspect distinctions—for preserving dominant versus ancillary distinctions and thus forwarding discourse movement at this point. Here morphosyntactic concerns intermesh with textual concerns, so that the latter is seen to have explanatory power in regard to the former.

3.1 Dialogue paragraphs

Typically, the storyline of a narrative is moved forward not only by sequential punctiliar happenings as reported in narrative paragraphs such as sequence, simultaneous, reason, result, and the like (cf. Longacre 1996:101–122) but in interactional paragraphs (Longacre 1996:123–151). While such interactional paragraph types as execution and stimulus-response are not uncommon (Longacre 1996:136), by and large the commonest type of interactional paragraph is the dialogue paragraph (really a complex of paragraph types). Dialogue paragraphs move the storyline forward by reporting verbal interactions arranged sequentially. In thus moving the storyline forward not only is an answer considered to be subsequent to a question, but whole dialogues occur in the sequence of verbal and nonverbal activities. This is perhaps the most common texture of a novel. Reportative verbs, commonly storyline forms like other action verbs, serve to join the reported speech to the storyline, but even in cases of zero formulae of quotation, the reported speech and dialogue usually must be considered to be verbal events on the storyline (Longacre 1994).

Example 3

EP2 (Rinne and Weidman): (N) Comment Para.

INTR:
    The autopsy-room doors swung open.

THESIS: (N) Sequence Para.
  SEQ. THESIS1: Unresolved Complex Dial. Para.
    LI: (N) Comment Para.
      THESIS:
        George Rinne, the pathology department's Negro diener—keeper of the morgue—looked up as the stretcher rolled in.
      COMMENT: (N) Result Para.
        THESIS:
          He had been swabbing the autopsy table.
        RESULT:
          Now it shone spotlessly white.
    IU (Rem): Quote Para.
      QF:
        Weidman greeted him with the time-worn jest.
      Q:
        "Got a patient for you."
    CU (Prop): Quote Para.
      QF: (N) Seq. Para.
        SEQ. TH1:
          Politely, as if he hadn't heard the line a hundred times before, Rinne bared his teeth in a perfunctory smile.
        SEQ. THn:
          He indicated the white enameled table.
      Q:
        "Over there."
  SEQ. THESIS2: (N) Seq. Para.
    SEQ. THESIS1:
      Wiedman maneuvered the stretcher alongside, and Rinne removed the sheet covering the naked corpse of George Andrew Dunton.
    SEQ. THESIS2: (N) Reason Para.
      THESIS:
        He folded it neatly and handed it back to Weidman.
      REASON:
        Death notwithstanding, the sheet would have to be accounted for back in the ward.
    SEQ. THESISn:
      Now, with a second drawsheet under the torso, the two men slid the body unto the table.

12

```
SEQ. THESIS3: (N) Reason Para.
    THESIS:
                George Rinne grunted as he took the weight.
        REASON:
                This had been a heavy man, a six footer who had run to fat near the end of his
                life.
SEQ. THESISn: Unresolved Complex Dial. Para.
    IU (Rem): Quote Para.
        QF:
                As he wheeled the stretcher clear, Weidman grinned.
        Q: (P) Reason Para.
            REASON:
                "You're getting old George."
            THESIS:
                "Be your turn soon."
    CU (Rem): Quote Para.
        QF (or LI?):
                Rinne shook his head.
        Q:
                "I'll still be here to lift you onto the table."
COMMENT: (E) Coordinate Para.
    THESIS1: (E) Reason Para.
        THESIS:
                The scene ran smoothly.
        REASON:
                It had had many performances.
    THESIS2: (E) Antithetical Para.
        ANTI:
                Perhaps in the distant past the two had made their grim little jokes with an
                instinct to create some barrier between themselves and the death they lived
                with daily.
    THESIS: (E) Reason Para.
        PRELIMINARY:
                But if so, this was long forgotten.
        THESIS:
                Now it was a patter to be run through, a formality expected, nothing more.
        REASON:
                They had grown too used to death to feel uneasiness or fear.
```

This example illustrates how dialogue can be integrated with other elements in the presentation of an ongoing flow of events. Looking again at the overview given in Example 1, our present example is Episode 2 of the embedded narrative discourse that expounds Stage of the narrative that constitutes this chapter. The whole example is a Narrative Comment paragraph whose Thesis is expounded by a narrative Sequence paragraph and whose Comment might best be considered to be an expository Coordinate paragraph—since it contains no narrative movement as such but simply explains what precedes. The whole example has an Introduction consisting of the sentence "The autopsy-room door swung open." In this novel, whose scenes range for the most part through various departments of a hospital a frequent transition between scenes is a reference to the opening or shutting of doors.

The Thesis, expounded by a Narrative Sequence paragraph has a Lead-In (LI) and four Seq.Theses. The LI is expounded by a Narrative Seq. paragraph whose structure need not detain us; it introduces George Rinne and tells us what he was doing when the stretcher, its attendant, and the corpse rolled in. An Initiating Utterance by Weidman consists of a well-worn jest, "Got a patient for you." Rinne does not evaluate this Remark beyond a perfunctory smile, but points to the autopsy table and says, "Over there." I term this dialogue an unresolved complex dialogue paragraph. It is complex because it contains a countertoken instead of a true reply and it is unresolved because no resolving utterance occurs (Longacre 1996:129–131).

Seq. Thesis 2 is expounded by an embedded narrative Sequence paragraph whose own second Seq. Thesis is a narrative Reason paragraph—illustrating how the narrator of a story often attaches rationales and explanations to the actions of his characters. In this same embedded Sequence paragraph the third and climactic Seq. Thesis is introduced with that handy transitional adverb "now." The last Seq. Thesis of the higher level (Seq. Thesis n) is again a dialogue paragraph, again an unresolved complex dialogue paragraph, since as we are told in the following Comment that this is banter rather than serious exchange. Weidman proposes that he will be around to lift Rinne onto the autopsy table someday, but Rinne makes a counter remark "I'll be here to lift you onto the table." So far two of the Seq. Theses have been expounded by dialogue paragraphs, and two by paragraphs not consisting of dialogue. The Comment that follows has two theses: (1) that the scene ran smoothly because it had had many performances and (2) that although it might have had its rationale in the past (levity in face of death) now it was merely a patter to be run through. Thus the author combines dialogue, nondialogue, and narrator comment into one harmonious unit. I add two observations: (1) None of the quotations indicate the speaker by a formal formula of quotation, but attribute speech to speaker by more indirect ways (Ware 1993); and (2) The conversation runs to short sentences and sentence fragments as befits the nature of the dialogue. Again, lower level grammar waits upon higher level concerns.

Example 4

EP5 (Seddons & McNeil): Compound Dial. Para.
  INTRODUCTION: (N) Identification Para.
    THESIS:
        The autopsy room door swung open and Mike Seddons breezed in.

    IDENTIFICATION: (E) Coordinate Para.
      THESIS1:
        Mike Seddons was a surgical resident, temporarily assigned to Pathology and he always breezed.
      THESIS2:
        His red hair stood up in odd places as though a self-created wind would never leave it static.
      THESIS3:
        His boyish, open face seemed creased permanently in an amiable grin.
      TERM:
        McNeil considered Seddons an exhibitionist, though in his favor the kid had taken to pathology a lot more readily than some of the other surgical residents McNeil had seen.

  EXCHANGE1: Unresolved complex Dial. Para.
    IU (REM): Quote Para.
      LI:
        Seddons looked over at the body on the table.
      Quote:
        "Ah, more business."
    CU (Prop?):
        McNeil gestured to the case papers and Seddons picked them up.

  EXCHANGE2: Resolved simple Dial. Para.
    IU (Rem): Rh-Q-and-A (N) Sequence Para.
      SEQ. THESIS1 (Q):
        He asked: "What did he die of?"
      SEQ. THESIS2 (A):
        Then, as he read on "Coronary, eh?"
    RU (Eval):
        McNeil answered: "That's what it says."

  EXCHANGE3: Resolved simple Dial. Para.
    IU (Q):
        "You doing this one?"

                    RU (A): Quote Para.
                        LI:
                                    The resident shook his head,
                            Q:
                                    "Pearson's coming."

EXCHANGE4: Resolved simple Dial. Para.
    IU (Q): Quote Para.
        LI:
                    Seddons looked up quizzically.
            Q:
                    "The boss man himself? What's special about this case?"
    RU (A):
                    "Nothing special"

EXCHANGE5: Resolved simple Dial. Para.
    IU (Rem): Quote Para.
        LI:
                    McNeil snapped a four-page autopsy form into a clipboard.
            Q:
                    "Some of the student nurses are coming in to watch. I think he likes to impress them."
                    [Note: (E) Reason Para.: Reason-Thesis]
    RU (Eval):
                    "A command performance."

EXCHANGE6: Unresolved Complex Dial. Para.
    IU (Rem): Quote Para.
        QF:
                    Seddons grinned,
            Q:
                    "This I must see."
    CU (Prop):
                    "In that case you may as well work."

EXCHANGE7: Resolved Simple Dial. Para
    IU (Prop) Quote Para.
        LI:
                    McNeil passed over the clipboard
            Q:
                    "Fill in some of this stuff, will you?"
    RU (Res):
                    "Sure."
    SD: Quote Para.
        LI:
                    Seddons took the clipboard and began to make notes on the condition of the body.
        QF:
                    He talked to himself as he worked.
        Q: Coordinate Para.
            THESIS1: Coordinate Para.
                THESIS1:
                    "That's a nice clean appendix scar."
                THESIS2:
                    "Small mole on the left arm."
            THESIS2: Quote Para.
                LI:
                    He moved the arm to one side.

```
                Q:
                        "Excuse me, old man"
                THESIS3:
                        He made a note, "Slight rigor mortis."
                THESIS4:
                        Lifting the eyelids he wrote, "Pupils round, 0.3 cm. diameter."
                THESIS5:
                        He pried the already stiff jaw open, "Let's have a look at the teeth."
```

This example, which is even longer than the preceding comes from Episode 5 of the embedded narrative that expounds Stage of the chapter. It has a long introduction and a series of seven exchanges. The long introduction presents Dr. Mike Seddons for the first time; its length may be alerting us to expect the one so introduced to play an important part in the novel. The seven exchanges group together into a compoound dialogue paragraph between McNeil and Seddons. Only two of the dialogue paragraphs found in the exchanges are unresolved; in the other dialogue paragraphs there is real communication of information rather than just banter, although something of the latter occurs also.

The first exchange is unresolved; Seddon's attempt at banter ("Ah, more business.") excites no serious response from McNeil, rather an impatient gesture towards the case papers serves as a proposal that Seddon should get to work. The second exchange is a resolved simple dialogue paragraph. What Seddons says amounts to a remark since he answers his own question as to what the man died of. McNeil's reply is an evaluation that serves as the resolving utterance. The third exchange is a question regarding who is to perform the autopsy, and the answer is Pearson. Again, we have a question and answer exchange that constitutes a resolved simple dialogue paragraph. The fourth exchange consists of a query from Seddons as to why the bossman himself is doing it, and McNeil has no immediate answer except "Nothing special." Nevertheless the exchange has, again, a question-answer structure that makes it a resolved simple dialogue paragraph. The fifth exchange contains a remark followed by an evaluation, which like question and answer constitutes a resolved paragraph. Exchange 6 reflects McNeil's growing impatience with Seddons, so that when Seddon's says ironically, "This I must see," McNeil, equally ironic, says, "In that case you might as well work." The remark followed by a proposal as countertoken leaves the paragraph unresolved, and reflects the fact that little of moment characterizes the transaction. In Exchange 7, which may be climactic, McNeil passes a clipboard to Seddons with the request that he fill in some of the needed information. While Seddon's answer is "Sure"—thus matching the proposal with a response and securing resolution of the paragraph, a step-down unit follows in which Seddons talks to himself as he works. This is reported speech but not dialogue. In this episode of the embedded narrative, dialogue or at least reported speech prevails throughout and advances the storyline in its own right. Exchanges are tacitly assumed to be successive.

3.2 Paragraphs that encode reflection

Moving on down through the material marshalled under caption C in the chart, I now exemplify reflective paragraphs. All that is required in a reflective paragraph is thought (inner speech) without overt verbal activity. Often, but not necessarily, such units function as flashbacks. We have mentioned such a reflective passage in the embedded discourse on Pathology that shaped up in Seddons' mind as he watched the autopsy proceed. Another such reflective passage is McNeil's speculation regarding whether he could get Nurse Penfield into bed with him (in Episode 4 of the narrative embedded as Stage). In Episode n of the main discourse, there is an embedded narrative whose Episode 2 recounts how a recollection of an injury to her father in the forest in Oregon helps Vivian Lomburton steady herself. I give this, along with its immediate context, as Example 5.

Example 5

EP2 [Vivian's reaction – simultaneous with EP1]: (E) Cyclic Reason Para.

```
        THESIS: (E) Amplification Para.
                THESIS:
                        Vivian was steadier now.
```

16

```
AMPL:
            She believed she had herself in hand.
REASON: Awareness Quote Para.
  LI: (N) Seq. Para. (backset)
    SEQ. THESIS1:
            Near the beginning and when the saw had cut into the dead man's skull she
            had felt the blood drain from her head, her senses swim.
    SEQ. THESIS2:
            She knew then that she had been close to fainting and had determined not to.
AW QF:
            For no reason she had suddenly remembered an incident in her childhood.
  AW Q: (N) Result Para.
    THESIS: (N) Seq. Para. (backset)
      SEQ. THESIS1:
            On a holiday, deep in the Oregon forest, her father had fallen on an open
            hunting knife and cut his leg badly.
      SEQ. THESIS2:
            Surprisingly in so strong a man he had quailed at the sight of so much of his
            own blood and her mother, usually more at home in the drawing room than the
            woods, had become suddenly strong.
      SEQ. THESIS3:
            She had fashioned a tourniquet, stemmed the blood, and sent Vivian running
            for help.
      SEQ. THESISn:
            Then, with Vivian's father being carried through the woods on an improvised
            litter of branches, every half-hour she had released the tourniquet to keep
            circulation going, then tightened it to halt the bleeding again.
    RESULT:
            Afterwards the doctors had said she had saved the leg from amputation.

THESIS' (reiterated):
            After that, she knew that there would not be any problem about watching an
            autopsy again.
```

The paragraph is an expository cyclic reason paragraph; it is cyclic because the thesis to the effect that Vivian now "had herself in hand" brackets the paragraph. The reason given is a remembrance of an incident from her childhood. The Reason is expounded by a structure of the sort that I have found it fruitful to call an "awareness quotation" (abbreviated to "awareness quote"). This terminology suggests itself because of the similarity of constructions involving such verbs as the verb "know" and its complement to the structure of indirect quotations. This paragraph has a lead-in which explains that "Near the beginning and when the saw had cut into the dead man's skull she had felt the blood drain from her head, her senses swim" and she realized "that she had been close to fainting and had determined not to." The Awareness Quotation Formula involves the verb "remember": "For no reason she had suddenly remembered an incident in her childhood."

The Awareness Quotation itself is a Narrative Result Paragraph all of whose verbs are pluperfects, thus marking the shift into a flashback. The substance of the recollection, involves her father getting hurt "deep in the Oregon forest," his dismay, and her mother's resourcefulness in fashioning a tourniquet, getting her father carried out—and thus saving her father's leg from amputation.

While I will cite no further examples of such structures which encode reflection, I point again to the climax of the novel, as referred to above under section 2 where the string of nine paragraphs on pages 281–283 are all the inner recollections of O'Donnel concerning the impasse to which the Three Counties Hospital had come.

We can now summarize the material found in the novel as various strands of content; what the narrator reports is: (1) successive happenings, (2) exposition of happenings, participants, localities, etc., (3) reported speech and dialogue, and (4) reflection/comment on the part of participants or the narrator himself. Of these various content strands, the second has been only incidentally illustrated in the examples above.

These four strands make up the interwoven texture of the novel. Some elements are directly on the storyline; others relate to it indirectly. Thus when Mike Seddons reflects about Pathology and why he would never choose to specialize in it, his reflection is attached to the storyline as "whole, i.e., at a given juncture in the story, particularly in the progress of the autopsy which is reported in chapter 3, Mike Seddons has a prolonged reflection about Pathology. His having this reflection is reported as a happening within the story. But the particular points and content of his reflection are not on the story line as such; rather the embedded discourse is attached as a whole to the story, and may be opened up accordion-wise to display its content or be kept as simple attachment. The best analogy is perhaps to a computer program where additional information may be called up which is not necessarily relevant at every stage of the program.

4 Verb/clause salience and dominance in the local span

All the above brings us around to a discussion of what elements dominate a discourse of a given type and a possible ranking of other elements in terms of relative proximity to or distance from the dominating element. I have discussed this at great length in the past (Longacre 1989) with special reference to narrative and with data (initially) from eight languages. I will here simply summarize the scheme relative to English narrative discourse, with a side glance at a few other discourse types. The hypothesis proposed in the 1989 article was that proximity to the storyline—with the latter as of the highest salience—correlated with dominance in paragraph structures.

Simplified somewhat, the salience hierarchy for English narrative is:
1. Storyline: clauses with simple past tense>
    2. Background: clauses with past progressive tense/with past tense verbs of cognitive state>
        3. Flashbacks: clauses with pluperfects>
            4. Setting: clauses with stative/adjectival predicates; intr. verbs with inan subjects>
                5. Irrealis: clauses that are negatives and/or modal>
                    6. Intrusive author evaluations: clauses with past tense/gnomic present>
                        7. Cohesive materials: adverbial clauses, participials.

The above scheme is not meant to be an analytical straightjacket. In local context promotion and demotion can occur relative to the scheme. Thus, a punctiliar adverb such as "suddenly" can promote a clause of lower rank to higher. For example, an element of rank 2 can be thus promoted to rank 1: "Suddenly, he was hanging on as if his life depended on it." Similarly, for rank 3: "Suddenly he had realized his heart's desire." And the same for lower bands short of 6 and 7. Demotion can simply come about by grammatical subordination.

The normal storyline scheme is followed in Example 2, where in the hierarchical analysis of the paragraph the simple past tense is taken to outrank both the pluperfect (whose clauses are relegated to setting) and the past progressives (whose clauses are relegated to setting in one case, and to simul 2 in two other cases of foreweighted simultaneous paragraphs). We also noted in the same example demoting occasioned by grammatical subordination.

In Example 4 we did not look in detail at the clauses which preceded the onset of dialogue in that paragraph. We now look at them in more detail. The first sentence is "The autopsy-room doors swung open." This sentence has a verb of rank 4, i.e., an intransitive verb with an inanimate subject; as a comparatively low ranking element it is assigned to Introduction to the entire episode, where it clearly fits semantically as well. The three sentences found in the lead-in structure are mutually ranked. The first sentence with the verb "looked up" is storyline. The second "had been swabbing" is pluperfect past progressive which we probably can consider to be in rank 3. By making it Thesis of a Comment it is lower than the main Thesis on which the Comment depends but higher than the Result structure which follows: "Now it shone spotlessly white." The latter verb is again, an intransitive verb with an inanimate subject—as are many descriptives; as rank 4 it is outranked by the preceding sentence. This, course, also squares with the semantics where the practical result of swabbing should be a clean surface..

Example 5 is somewhat different. To begin with it is not narrative in its outermost layers but explanatory; it is describing Vivian's feelings. In this explanatory structure static elements outrank the dynamic—quite the opposite of narrative structure. So, the Thesis and the reiterated Thesis' at the end of the paragraph are dominative as static elements, but the Reason as a dynamic element is ancillary. It has the structure of a narrative sequence paragraph with two stages of backlooping. In the lead-in it is explained that Vivian had been close to fainting but had got herself in hand due to a recollection of an incident in her childhood. The content of the Awareness Quote gives a second stage flashback (recollection of an incident in Vivian's childhood) that has the structure of a narrative sequence paragraph whose verbs are pluperfect. There is a consistent verb dominance here (although the flip structure from narrative), with the pluperfects on the embedded storyline and the whole thing surrounded by the thematic static material. Again, I repeat, all this is the inverse of narrative salience ranking, i.e., the static outranks the dynamic. The sequence paragraph in the flashback does not link up with the main line of the story; rather it relates to it as a whole simply on the grounds that Vivian had a recollection which helped her steady herself.

Conclusion: Verb ranking and relative salience—as well other features noted here and there in this paper—tie up the analysis of the text so that lower level concerns are constrained by higher level concerns, and higher level concerns build on and are realized by the lower levels. From the template proper to a type and the macrostructure characteristic of a given text and from its particular profile, a variety of constraints influence the constituent structure—whose purpose is, of course, to develop the strategy and various ploys of the text. The text displays a movement in its structure, the movement of its main line, but attachments are possible here and there that enhance the main text and relate as wholes to it. Our goal is, therefore, a kind of holistic textlinguistics, which knits together a text in all its dimensions. Perhaps this is still somewhat more of a goal than a reality but traveling hopefully down this road we can discover many things we couldn't see if we were standing still!

5 Integration with a morphosyntax informed by textual concerns

Considerations such as we have developed and illustrated here suggest that textlinguistics should not be considered to be merely a supplement to the morphosyntax but that the study of the two should be integrated or at least considered to be closely related modules. Many elements in the morphosyntax can be and should be illuminated by resort to textual structures. While not every element in the structure of words, clauses, and sentences directly relates to such larger structures, a surprising amount of them do so relate. For example, the teaching of the verb structure of a language, its tense, aspect, tense, and mood, can be greatly enriched by recourse to discourse concerns. With the evidence that has continued to accumulate along these lines, it can now be said that attempts to teach the verb system of a language without resort to text is unnecessary obscurantism. Why should French teachers belabor the teaching of the meaning and function of the *imparfait*, when a few paragraphs of French narrative would illuminate most of the mystery? And why have we wrangled for close to two hundred years about the tense-aspects of Biblical Hebrew when a similar resort to text (as is now underway from certain quarters) could similarly shed light on the whole tangle? Why should whole schools of grammar continue to flourish and revise their elaborate and elegant frameworks at regular intervals and continue to ignore textual concerns?

My deep conviction is that textlinguistics should enter into fieldwork at an early stage, should form an integral part in the teaching of linguistics at our various institutions, and should be allowed to illumine old controversies and problems.

Appendix
The Final Diagnosis (Arthur Hailey © 1959; used by permission)
Constituent Display of Chapter 3[2]

STAGE: EMBEDDED NARR. DISC. pp. 23–28 (Central participant, Pearson, off stage but his coming is anticipated)

    STAGE: (E) Coordinate Para.
        INTR: (E) Coordinate Para.
            THESIS1:
> In contrast with the heat and activity of the floors above in the white-tiled corridor of the hospital's basement, it was quiet and cool

            THESIS2:
> Nor was the quietness disturbed by a small procession—Nurse Penfield and along side her a stretcher gliding silently on ball bearing casters and propelled by a male orderly wearing rubber-soled shoes below his hospital whites.

        THESIS1: Rhetorical Q & A (E) Amplification Para.
            THESIS:
> How many times had she made this journey, Nurse Penfield speculated, glancing down at the shrouded figure on the stretcher.

            AMPL: (E) Amplification Para.
                THESIS:
> Probably fifty times in the past eleven years.

                AMPL:
> Perhaps more because it was not something you kept score of—this final journey between the ward and the hospital's morgue, between the territory of the living and the dead.

        THESIS2: (E) Coordinate Para.
            THESIS1:
> A tradition [was] this last walk with a patient who had died, discreetly timed and routed through back corridors of the hospital, then downward in the freight elevator so that the living should take no darkness or depression from death so close at hand.

            THESIS2:
> It was the last service from nurse to her charge an acknowledgement that, though medicine had failed, it would not dismiss the patient summarily; the motions of care, service, healing, would continue for at least a token time beyond the end.

EP1 (Weidman and the janitor): NARR. DISC.
    STAGE: (E) Antithetical Para.
        INTR:
> The white corridor forked two ways here.

        THESIS: (E) Reason Para.
            THESIS:
> From a passage to the right came the hum of machinery.

            REASON:
> Down here were the hospital's mechanical departments—heating plant, hot-water systems, electrical shops, emergency generators.

        ANTITHESIS:
> Pointing the other way, a single sign read: "Pathology Department. Morgue."

    EP1: Simple Resolved Dial. Para.
        LI1:
> As Weidman, the male orderly, swung the stretcher left, a janitor—either on work break or stolen time—lowered the coke he had been drinking and moved aside.

---

[2] Formatted by Stephen Echerd; from Longacre, December 1986, slight changes 2002).

LI2:
        He wiped his lips on the back of his hand, then gestured to the shroud.
IU (Rem): Quote Para.
    Quote:
        "Didn't make it, eh?"
    QF:
        The remark was to Weidman; it was an amiable gambit, a game played many times.
RU (Eval): Quote Para.
    QF:
        Weidman, too had done this before.
    Quote:
        "I guess they pulled his number, Jack."
TU (Acq):
        The janitor nodded, then raised his coke bottle again and drank deeply.
EP2 [Simultaneous with EP1]: Cyclic, Quoted Resol. Simple Dial. Para.
    INTR: (E) Amplification Para.
        THESIS:
            How short a time, Nurse Penfield thought, between life and the autopsy room.
        AMPL: (E) Comment Para.
            THESIS:
                Less than an hour ago the body under the shroud had been George Andrew Dunton, living, age fifty-three, civil engineer.
            COMMENT:
                She remembered the details from the case history on the clip board under her arm.
LI: (N) Result Para.
    THESIS:
        The family had behaved as well after the death as they had before—solid, emotional but no hysterics.
    RESULT:
        It had made it easier for Dr. McMahon to ask for permission to autopsy.
IU (Prop): (N) Amplification Para.
    THESIS:
        "Mrs. Dunton," he had said quietly, "I know it's hard for you to talk and think about this now, but there is something I have to ask. It's about permission for an autopsy on your husband."
        [Note: Para. backlooped into Quote of Quotation Sentence].
    AMPL: Quoted (N) Antithetical Para.
        THESIS:
            He had gone on, using the routine words, how the hospital sought to safeguard its medical standards for the good of everyone, how a physician's diagnosis could be checked and medical learning advanced, how this was a precaution for the family and others who would use the hospital in time to come.
        ANTI:
            But none of this could be done without permission...
    RU (Res):
        The son had stopped him gently and said: "We understand. If you make out whatever is necessary, my mother will sign it."
        [Note: Para. backlooped into Quote].
    TERM/CORRELATE:
        So Nurse Penfield had made out the autopsy form, and here now was George Andrew Dunton, dead, age fifty three, and ready for the pathologist's knife.

EP2 (Rinne and Weidman): (N) Comment Para.
    INTR:
        The autopsy-room doors swung open.

21

THESIS: (N) Sequence Para.
  SEQ. THESIS1: Unresolved Complex Dial. Para.
    LI: (N) Comment Para.
      THESIS:
        George Rinne, the pathology department's Negro diener—keeper of the morgue—looked up as the stretcher rolled in.
      COMMENT: (N) Result Para.
        THESIS:
          He had been swabbing the autopsy table.
        RESULT:
          Now it shone spotlessly white.
    IU (Rem): Quote Para.
      QF:
        Weidman greeted him with the time-worn jest.
      Q:
        "Got a patient for you."
    CU (Prop): Quote Para.
      QF: (N) Seq. Para.
        SEQ. TH1:
          Politely, as if he hadn't heard the line a hundred times before, Rinne bared his teeth in a perfunctory smile.
        SEQ. THn:
          He indicated the white enameled table.
      Q:
        "Over there."
  SEQ. THESIS2: (N) Seq. Para.
    SEQ. THESIS1:
      Wiedman maneuvered the stretcher alongside, and Rinne removed the sheet covering the naked corpse of George Andrew Dunton.
    SEQ. THESIS2: (N) Reason Para.
      THESIS:
        He folded it neatly and handed it back to Weidman.
      REASON:
        Death notwithstanding, the sheet would have to be accounted for back in the ward.
    SEQ. THESISn:
      Now, with a second drawsheet under the torso, the two men slid the body unto the table.
  SEQ. THESIS3: (N) Reason Para.
    THESIS:
      George Rinne grunted as he took the weight.
    REASON:
      This had been a heavy man, a six footer who had run to fat near the end of his life.
  SEQ. THESISn: Unresolved Complex Dial. Para.
    IU (Rem): Quote Para.
      QF:
        As he wheeled the stretcher clear, Weidman grinned.
      Q: (P) Reason Para.
        REASON:
          "You're getting old George."
        THESIS:
          "Be your turn soon."
    CU (Rem): Quote Para.
      QF (or LI?):
        Rinne shook his head.
      Q:
        "I'll still be here to lift you onto the table."

COMMENT: (E) Coordinate Para.
   THESIS1: (E) Reason Para.
      THESIS:
         The scene ran smoothly.
      REASON:
         It had had many performances.
   THESIS2: (E) Antithetical Para.
      ANTI:
         Perhaps in the distant past the two had made their grim little jokes with an instinct to create some barrier between themselves and the death they lived with daily.
      THESIS: (E) Reason Para.
         PRELIMINARY:
            But if so, this was long forgotten.
         THESIS:
            Now it was a patter to be run through, a formality expected, nothing more.
         REASON:
            They had grown too used to death to feel uneasiness or fear.

EP3 (McNeil and Nurse Penfield): Compound Dial. Para.
   INTRO:
      On the far side of the autopsy room was the pathology resident, Dr. McNeil.
   LI: (E) Contrast Para. ("before/after")
      ANTI (before):
         He had been shrugging into a white coat when Nurse Penfield and her charge came in.
      THESIS (after): (E) Amplification Para.
         THESIS:
            Now, glancing through the case history and the other papers she had handed him, he was acutely conscious of Nurse Penfield's neatness and warmth.
         AMPL:
            He sensed the crisp starched uniform, a faint breath of perfume, a slight disarrangement of hair beneath her cap; it would be soft to run his fingers through.
   EXCHANGE1: Simple resolved DIAL. Para.
      IU (Rem): Simultaneous Para.
         Simul. Thesis1 Quote Para.
            QF:
               He snatched his thoughts back to the papers in hand
            Q:
               "Well, everything seems to be here."
         Simul. Thesis2: (H) Alternative Para.
            THESIS:
               Should he try for Nurse Penfield or not?
            OPTION (POS): (E) Coordinate Para.
               THESIS1:
                  It had been six weeks now, and at the age of twenty-seven six weeks was a long time to be celibate.
               THESIS2:
                  Penfield was more than averagely attractive, probably thirty-two, young enough to be interesting, old enough to have long since shed innocency.
               THESIS3:
                  She was intelligent, friendly, good figure, too.
               THESIS4:
                  He could see a slip beneath the white uniform; in the heat she probably was not wearing much else.
            OPTION (NEG): (E) Reason Para.
               INTRO:
                  Roger McNeil calculated.

23

REASON:
    He would probably have to take her out a couple of times before she came through.
THESIS:
    Then that settled it; it couldn't be this month – money was too short.
TERM (a suppressed Prop): (H) Reason Para.
  THESIS:
    Save it for me, la Penfield.
  REASON:
    You'll be back; other patients will die and bring you here.
RU (Eval): Quote Para.
  Q:
    "Thank you doctor."
  QF:
    She smiled and turned away.
  SD:
    It could be arranged; he was positive of that.
EXCHANGE2: Unresolved simple Dial. Para.
  IU (Prop): (N) Comment Para.
    THESIS: Quote Para.
      QF:
        He called after her.
      Q:
        "Keep 'em coming. We need the practice."
        [Note: =(H) Reason Para. : Thesis + Reason]
    COMMENT:
      Again the timeworn jest, the defensive levity in face of death.
  SD: (E) Antithetical Para.
    INTRO:
      Elaine Penfield followed the attendant out.
    THESIS: (E) Amplification Para.
      THESIS:
        Her journey was done, tradition honored, the extra unasked service given.
      AMPL:
        She had gone the second mile: now her duty lay with the sick, the living.
    ANTITHESIS: (E) Antithetical Para.
      THESIS:
        She had a feeling, though, that Dr. McNeil had come close to suggesting something.
      ANTI:
        But there would be another time.

EP4 (Rinne & McNeil): Resolved Simple Dial. Para.
  LI: (N) Amplification Para.
    THESIS:
      While George Rinne slipped a wooden headrest under the neck of the body, arranging the arms at the side, McNeil began to lay out the instruments they would need for the autopsy.
    AMPL: (E) Reason Para.
      THESIS:
        Knives, rib cutters, forceps. power saw for the skull…all of them clean—Rinne was a conscientious worker—but not sterile, as they would have to be in the operating room four floors above.
      REASON:
        No need here to worry about infection of a patient at the table; only the pathologists need take precautions for themselves.
  IU (Prop): Quote Para.
    QF:
      George Rinne looked at McNeil inquiringly, and the resident nodded.

Q: (H) Coor. Para.
    PRELIMINARY:
        "Better phone the nursing office, George."
    THESIS1:
        "Tell them the student nurses can come down now."
    THESIS2:
        "And let Dr. Pearson know we're setting up."
RU (Res): Quote Para.
    Q:
        "Yes, Doctor"
    QF/Coor:
        Rinne went out obediently.
CORR (McNeil's thoughts) (E) Antithetical Para.
    THESIS:
        McNeil as pathology resident, had authority even though his hospital pay was little more than the janitor's own.
    ANTHITHESIS: (P) Result Para.
        THESIS: (P) Paraphrase Para.
            THESIS:
                It would not be long, though, before the gap between them would widen.
            AMPL:
                With three and a half years of residency behind him only another six months separated McNeil from freedom to take a post as staff pathologist.
        RESULT: (P) Result Para.
            THESIS:
                Then he could start considering some of the twenty-thousand-a-year jobs, because fortunately the demand for pathologists continued to be greater than the supply.
        RESULT: (P) COMMENT Para.
            THESIS:
                He would not have to worry then about whether he could afford a pass at Nurse Penfield—or others.
            COMMENT: (N) Comment Para.
                THESIS:
                      McNeil smiled inward, at the thought, though he did not betray it on his face.
                COMMENT: (N) Antithetical
                    ANTI:
                        People who had to deal with McNeil thought he was dour, which he often was, and sometimes lacking in a sense of humor, which he was not.
                    THESIS: (E) Comment Para.
                        THESIS:
                            Actually he did not make friends easily with men but women found him attractive, a fact which he had discovered early and turned to advantage.
                        COMMENT: (E) Comment Para.
                            THESIS:
                                When he was an intern his colleagues had found this puzzling.
                        COMMENT:
                        McNeil the gloomy brooding figure of the common room, had had uncanny success in whisking a succession of student nurses into bed, frequently where others who fancied their ability as paramours had failed.

EP5 (Seddons & McNeil): Compound Dial. Para.
    INTRODUCTION: (N) Identification Para.
        THESIS:
            The autopsy room door swung open and Mike Seddons breezed in.
        IDENTIFICATION: (E) Coordinate Para.
            THESIS1:
                Mike Seddons was a surgical resident, temporarily assigned to Pathology and he always breezed.

25

THESIS2:
  His red hair stood up in odd places as though a self-created wind would never leave it static.
THESIS3:
  His boyish, open face seemed creased permanently in an amiable grin.
TERM:
  McNeil considered Seddons an exhibitionist, though in his favor the kid had taken to pathology a lot more readily than some of the other surgical residents McNeil had seen.
EXCHANGE1: Unresolved complex Dial. Para.
 IU (REM): Quote Para.
  LI:
   Seddons looked over at the body on the table.
  Quote:
   "Ah, more business."
 CU (Prop?):
  McNeil gestured to the case papers and Seddons picked them up.
EXCHANGE2: Resolved simple Dial. Para.
 IU (Rem): Rh-Q-and-A (N) Sequence Para.
  SEQ. THESIS1 (Q):
   He asked: "What did he die of?"
  SEQ. THESIS2 (A):
   Then, as he read on "Coronary, eh?"
 RU (Eval):
  McNeil answered: "That's what it says."
EXCHANGE3: Resolved simple Dial. Para.
 IU (Q):
  "You doing this one?"
 RU (A): Quote Para.
  LI:
   The resident shook his head.
  Q:
   "Pearson's coming."
EXCHANGE4: Resolved simple Dial. Para.
 IU (Q): Quote Para.
  LI:
   Seddons looked up quizzically.
  Q:
   "The boss man himself? What's special about this case?"
 RU (A):
  "Nothing special"
EXCHANGE5: Resolved simple Dial. Para.
 IU (Rem): Quote Para.
  LI:
   McNeil snapped a four-page autopsy form into a clipboard.
  Q:
   "Some of the student nurses are coming in to watch. I think he likes to impress them."
   [Note: (E) Reason Para.: Reason-Thesis]
 RU (Eval):
  "A command performance."
EXCHANGE6: Unresolved Complex Dial. Para.
 IU (Rem): Quote Para.
  QF:
   Seddons grinned,
  Q:
   "This I must see."
 CU (Prop):
  "In that case you may as well work."

EXCHANGE7: Resolved Simple Dial. Para
  IU (Prop) Quote Para.
    LI:
        McNeil passed over the clipboard
    Q:
        "Fill in some of this stuff, will you?"
  RU (Res):
        "Sure."
  SD: Quote Para.
    LI:
        Seddons took the clipboard and began to make notes on the condition of the body.
    QF:
        He talked to himself as he worked.
  Q: Coordinate Para.
    THESIS1: Coordinate Para.
      THESIS1:
        "That's a nice clean appendix scar."
      THESIS2:
        "Small mole on the left arm."
    THESIS2: Quote Para.
      LI:
        He moved the arm to one side.
      Q:
        "Excuse me, old man"
    THESIS3:
        He made a note, "Slight rigor mortis."
    THESIS4:
        Lifting the eyelids he wrote, "Pupils round, 0.3 cm. diameter."
    THESIS5:
        He pried the already stiff jaw open, "Let's have a look at the teeth."

EPn (Mike meets Vivian): Embedded NARR. DISC.
  STAGE: Compound Dial. Para.
    LI:
        From the corridor outside there was the sound of feet.
    EXCHANGE1: (Greetings) Resolved Simple Dial. Para.
      IU: Quote Para.
        LI:
            Then the autopsy-room door opened and a nurse, who McNeil recognized as a member of the nursing school's teaching staff, looked in.
        Q:
            She said, "Good morning, Dr. McNeil"
      SD:
        Behind her was a group of young student nurses.
      RU:
        "Good morning."
    EXCHANGE2: Execution Para.
      PLAN: Quote Para.
        LI:
            The resident beckoned.
        Q:
            "You can all come in."
      EXECUTION: Identification Para.
        THESIS:
            The students filed through the doorway.
        IDENT:
            There were six, and as they entered all glanced nervously at the body on the table.

EXCHANGE3: Unresolved Simple Dial. Para.
  IU (Prop): Quote Para.
    LI:
        Mike Seddons grinned.
    Q: (H) Reason Para.
      THESIS:
        "Hurry up, girls."
      REASON:
        "You want the best seats, we have 'em."
EP1: Compound Dial. Para.
  LI: (N) Sequence Para.
    SEQ. THESIS1: Awareness Quote Para.
      AW QF:
        Seddons ran his eye appraisingly over the group.
      AW Q:
        There were a couple of new ones here he had not seen previously including the brunette.
    SEQ. THESIS 2: Awareness Quote Para.
      AW QF:
        He took a second look.
      AW Q:
        Yes indeed; even camouflaged by the spartan student's uniform, it was obvious that here was something special.
    SEQ. THESISn:
      With apparent casualness he crossed the autopsy room, then, returning, managed to position himself between the girl he had noticed and the rest of the group.
  EXCHANGE1: Unresolved Complex Dial. Para.
    IU (Rem):
      He gave her a broad smile and said quietly, "I don't remember seeing you before."
    CU (Rem):
      "I've been around as long as the other girls."
  EXCHANGE2: Unresolved Complex Dial. Para.
    IU (Rem):
      She looked at him with a mixture of frankness and curiosity then added mockingly, "Besides, I've been told that doctors never notice first year nursing students."
    CU (Rem): Quote Para.
      LI:
        He appeared to consider
      Q: (E) Antithetical Para.
        ANTI:
          "Well, it's a general rule"
        THESIS:
          "But sometimes we make exceptions – depending on the student of course."
  EXCHANGEn: Resolved Simple Dial. Para. (Introductions).
    IU (Introduction):
      His eyes candidly admiring, he added: "By the way I'm Mike Seddons."
    RU (Introduction):
      She said, "I'm Vivian Loburton," and laughed.
  CLOSURE: (N) Sequence Para.
    SEQ. THESIS1: (N) Reason Para.
      THESIS:
        Then, catching a disapproving eye from the class instructor, she stopped abruptly.

REASON: Reason Para.
   THESIS:
      Vivian had liked the looks of this redheaded young doctor, but it did seem wrong somehow to be talking and joking in here.
   REASON: Amplification Para.
     THESIS:
      After all, the man on the table was dead.
     AMPL:
      He had just died, she had been told upstairs; that was the reason she and the other student nurses had been taken from their work to watch the autopsy.
SEQ. THESISn: (N?) Coordinate Para.
   PRELIMINARY:
      The thought of the word "autopsy" brought her back to what was to happen here.
   THESIS1:
      Vivian wondered how she was going to react; already she felt uneasy.
   THESIS2:
      She supposed, as a nurse, she would grow used to seeing death, but at the moment it was still new and rather frightening.
(END OF STAGE: embedded N. DISC)

EP1 (Entrance of Pearson): (N) Sequence Para.
   SETTING: (N) Simple Para.
     SETTING:
      There were footsteps coming down the corridor.
     THESIS:
      Seddons touched her arm and whispered, "We'll talk again—soon."
   SEQ. THESIS1: Quote Para.
     LI:
      Then the door was flung open and the student nurses moved back respectfully as Dr. Pearson strode inside.
     Q:
      He greeted them with a crisp "Good morning."
   SEQ. THESIS2: Sequence Para.
     SEQ. THESIS1:
      Then, without waiting for the murmured acknowledgments, he strode to a locker, slipped off his white coat and thrust his arms into a gown which he had taken from the shelf.
     SEQ. THESIS2:
      Pearson gestured to Seddons, who stepped over and tied the gown strings at the back.
     SEQ. THESIS3:
      Then, like a well-drilled team, the two moved over to a washbasin where Seddons shook powder from a can over Pearson's hand, afterward holding out a pair of rubber gloves into which the older man thrust his fingers.
   SEQ. THESISn: (N) Sequence Para.
     SETTING:
      All this had been accomplished in silence.
     SEQ. THESIS1:
      Now Pearson shifted his cigar slightly and murmured a "Thanks."
     SEQ. THESIS2: (N) Comment Para.
      THESIS: (N) Amplification Para.
        THESIS:
          He crossed to the table and, taking the clipboard which McNeil held out to him, began to read it, apparently oblivious of everything else.
        AMPL:
          So far Pearson had not even glanced at the body on the table.

29

  COMMENT: (N) COMMENT Para.
   THESIS:
    Watching the performance covertly, as he, too moved across it occurred to Seddons that it was like the entrance of a maestro before a symphony.
   COMMENT:
    All that was missing was the applause.

EP2 (Greetings and preliminary remarks of Pearson): Compound Dial. Para.
 LI:
  Now that Pearson had digested the case history, he too, inspected the body, comparing his findings with the notes Seddons had written.
 EXCHANGE1: Resolved Simple Dial. Para.
  IU (Rem): Quote Para.
   LI:
    Then he put the clip board down and, removing his cigar, faced the nurses across the table. "This is your first experience of an autopsy, I believe."
  RU (Eval):
   The girls murmured "Yes, sir," or "Yes, Doctor."
 EXCHANGE2: Unresolved Stepped Dial. Para.
  EXCHANGE (enveloping): Unresolved Simple Dial. Para.
   IU (Rem): Quote Para.
    LI:
     Pearson nodded.
   Q: (E) Coordinate Para.
    THESIS1:
     "Then I will explain that I am Dr. Pearson the pathologist of the hospital."
    THESIS2:
     "These gentlemen are Dr. McNeil, the resident in pathology, and Dr. Seddons, a resident in surgery in his third year..."
    EXCHANGE: (embedded): Resolved Simple Dial. Para.
     IU (Q): Quote Para.
      LI:
      He turned to Seddons.
      Q:
      "Am I right?"
     RU (A): Quote Para.
      LI:
      Seddons smiled.
      Q:
      "Quite right, Dr. Pearson"
  IU (Rem) [continuation of discontinuous construction]:
   "In his third year of residency, and who is favoring us with a spell of duty in Pathology."
EXCHANGE3: Resolved Simple Dial. Para.
 IU: Quote Para
  LI:
   He glanced at Seddons
  Q:
   "Dr. Seddons will shortly qualify to practice surgery and be released upon an unsuspecting public."
 RU: (N) Simultaneous Para.
  SIMUL1:
   Two of the girls giggled; the others smiled.
  SIMUL2: Comment Para
   THESIS:
    Seddons grinned; he enjoyed this.

COMMENT:
    Pearson never missed an opportunity to take a dig at surgeons probably with good reason—in forty years of pathology the old man must have uncovered a lot of surgical bloopers.
SIMUL3: Awareness Quote Para.
  AW QF:
    He glanced across at McNeil.
  AW Q: Comment Para.
    THESIS:
      The resident was frowning.
    COMMENT: Reason Para.
      THESIS:
        He doesn't approve, Seddons thought.
      REASON:
        Mac likes his pathology straight.
EXCHANGE4: Unresolved Simple Dial. Para.
  LI:
    Now Pearson was talking again.
  IU (Rem): Quoted (E) Amplification Para.
    PRELIMINARY: (E) Antithetical Para.
      THESIS:
        "The pathologist is often known as the doctor the patient never sees."
      ANTI:
        "Yet few departments of a hospital have more effect on a patient's welfare."
    THESIS: Quote Para.
      LI:
        Here comes the sales pitch. Seddons thought. and Pearson's next words proved him right.
      Q: (E) Coordinate Para.
        THESIS1:
          "It is pathology which tests a patient's blood, checks his excrements, tracks down his diseases, decides whether his tumor is malignant or benign."
        THESIS2:
          "It is pathology which advises the patient's physician on disease, and sometimes, when all else in medicine fails"
          [embedded CORR/LI: Pearson paused, looked down significantly at the body of George Andrew Dunton, and the eyes of the nurses, followed him.]
          "It is the pathologist who makes the final diagnosis."
      CORR [embedded in the Above sentence]
  AMPL: Comment Para.
    THESIS: Quote Para.
      LI1: (N) Comment Para.
        THESIS:
          Pearson paused again.
        COMMENT: Amplification Para.
          THESIS:
            What a superb actor the old man is, Seddons thought.
          AMPL:
            What an unabashed. natural ham.
      LI2:
        Now Pearson was pointing with his cigar.
      Q: Quote Para.
        LI: Execution Para.
          PLAN:
            "I draw your attention," he was saying to the nurses, "to some words you will find on the wall of many autopsy rooms."
          EXEC:
            Their eyes followed his finger to the framed maxim thoughtfully provided by a scientific supply house—*Mortui Vivas Docent.*

Q:
    Pearson read the Latin aloud, then translated "The dead teach the living."
COMMENT: Quote Para
LI:
    He looked down again at the body.
Q: Comment Para.
  PRELIMINARY:
    "That is what will happen now."
  THESIS:
    "This man apparently
    [embedded CORR: he emphasized the word "apparently"]
    died of coronary thrombosis."
  COMMENT:
    "By autopsy we shall discover if this is true."
  CORR [embedded in the above sentence].

EP3 (initial incisions) (N) DISC
  EP1 (inciting incident): Comment Para.
    THESIS: (N) Sequence Para.
      SEQ. THESIS1: Comment Para.
        THESIS:
          At this Pearson took a deep draw on his cigar, and Seddons, knowing what was coming moved nearer.
        COMMENT:
          He himself might be only a bit player in this scene, but he had no intention of missing a cue.
      SEQ. THESIS2:
        As Pearson exhaled a cloud of blue smoke he handed the cigar to Seddons who took it and placed it down, away from the table.
      SEQ. THESISn: (CLIMAX): (N) Sequence Para.
        SEQ. THESIS1:
          Now Pearson surveyed the instruments laid out before him and selected a knife.
        SEQ. THESISn:
          With his eye he calculated where he would cut, then swiftly, cleanly, deeply, applied the sharp steel blade.
  COMMENT: (E) Reason Para. (Running Quote)
    INTRO:
      McNeil was watching the student nurses covertly.
    THESIS:
      An autopsy, he reflected, would never be recommended viewing for the fainthearted, but even to the experienced the first incision is somewhat hard to take.
    REASON: (E) Antithetical Para.
      THESIS:
        Until this point the body on the table has at least borne physical resemblance to the living.
      ANTI: (E) Comment Para.
        THESIS:
          But after the knife, he thought no illusions are possible.
        COMMENT: Amplification paragraph (end-weighted)
          THESIS:
            This was not a man, a woman, a child, but merely flesh and bone, resembling life, yet not of life.
          AMPL: Amplification Para. (end-weighted)
            THESIS:
              This was the ultimate truth, the end to which all must come.

32

    AMPL:
        This was the fulfillment of the Old Testament: "For dust thou art, and unto dust shalt thou return."
EPn (Peak?): (N) Simultaneous Para.
  SIMUL1: (N) Simultaneous Para.
    SIMUL1: (N) Amplification Para.
      THESIS:
        Using the skill, ease, and speed of long experience, Pearson began the autopsy with a deep "Y" incision.
      AMPL: (N) Sequence Para
        SEQ. THESIS1:
          With three strong knife strokes he brought the top two branches of the "Y" from each shoulder of the body to meet near the bottom of the chest.
        SEQ. THESIS2:
          There from this point he cut downwards, opening the belly all the way from chest to genitals.
  SIMUL2:
      There was a hissing, almost a tearing sound, as the knife moved and the flesh parted, revealing a layer of yellow fat beneath the surface.
  SIMUL2: (N) Comment Para.
    THESIS: (N) Sequence Para.
      SEQ. THESIS1:
        Still watching the student nurses, McNeil saw that two were deathly white, a third had gasped and turned away; the other three were stoically watching.
      SEQ. THESIS2: (N) Antithetical Para.
        THESIS:
          The resident kept his eye on the pale ones; it was not unusual for a nurse to keel over at her first autopsy.
        ANTI:
          But these six looked as if they were going to be all right; the color was coming back to the two he had noticed and the other girl had turned back, though with a handkerchief to her mouth.
      SEQ. THESISn: Resolved simple Dial. Para.
        IU (Prop):
          McNeil told them quietly
          [Note: Q = (H) Reason Para.]
          THESIS:
            "If any of you want to go out for a few minutes, that's all right."
          REASON:
            "The first time's always a bit hard."
        RU (Res):
          They looked at him gratefully, though no one moved.
  COMMENT: (E) Antithetical Para.
    THESIS:
      McNeil knew that some pathologists would never admit nurses to an autopsy until the first incision has been made.
    ANTI: (E) Reason Para.
      THESIS:
        Pearson, though, did not believe in shielding anyone.
      REASON:
        A nurse had to witness a lot of things that were tough to take—sores, mangled limbs, putrification, surgery; the sooner she learned to accept the sights and smells of medicine, the better for everyone, including herself.

EP4 (Further progress on the autopsy; Seddons evaluates): (N) Comment Para. [of discourse length]
  THESIS: (N) Sequence Para.
    SEQ. THESIS1: (N) Simultaneous Para.
      PRELIMINARY:
> Now McNeil slipped on his own gloves and went to work with Pearson.

      SIMUL1: (N) Sequence Para.
        SETTING:
> By this time, moving, swiftly, the older man had peeled back the chest flap and, hacking the flesh loose with a larger knife, exposed the ribs.

        SEQ. THESIS1: Simultaneous Para. [fore-weighted]
          SIMUL1:
> Next, using the sharp levered rib cutters, he cut his way into the rib cage, exposing pericardium and lungs.

          SIMUL2:
> The gloves, instruments, and table were now beginning to be covered with blood.

      SEQ. THESIS2: Simultaneous Para. [fore-weighted]
        SETTING:
> Seddons, gloved also, on his side of the table was cutting back the lower flaps and flesh and opening the abdomen.

        SIMUL1:
> He crossed the room for a pail and began to remove the stomach and intestines, which he put into the pail after studying them briefly.

        SIMUL2:
> The odor was beginning to be noticeable.

      SEQ. THESISn: (N) Sequence Para.
        SEQ. THESIS1:
> Now Pearson and Seddons together tied off and cut the arteries so the undertaker would have no trouble when it came to embalming.

        SEQ. THESISn:
> Taking a small tube from a rack above the table, Seddons turned on a tap and began to siphon blood that had escaped into the abdomen and, after a nod from Pearson, did the same thing for the chest.

    SIMUL2: (N) Sequence Para.
      SETTING:
> Meanwhile, McNeil had applied himself to the head.

      SEQ. THESIS1:
> First, he made an incision along the vertex of the skull, starting slightly behind each ear and cutting above the hairline so that the mark would not be visible if the body were placed on view by the dead man's family.

      SEQ. THESIS2:
> Then, using all the strength in his fingers, he peeled the scalp forward in one piece, so that all the flesh from the head was bunched over the front of the face, covering the eyes.

      SEQ. THESIS3:
> The entire skull was now exposed and McNeil picked up the portable electric saw which was already plugged in.

      SEQ. THESISn: (N) Comment Para.
        THESIS:
> Before switching it on, he looked over at the student nurses to find them watching him with a mixture of incredulity and horror.

        COMMENT:
> Take it easy, girls, he thought; in a few minutes you'll have seen it all.

  SEQ. THESIS2: (N) Sequence Para.
    SETTING:
> Pearson was carefully removing the heart and lungs when McNeil applied the saw to bone.

SEQ. THESIS1:
>The metallic "Scrunch" of the oscillating steel teeth biting into the skull cut grimly across the quiet room.

SEQ. THESIS2:
>Glancing up he saw the girl with the handerchief flinch; if she was going to vomit he hoped it wouldn't be in here.

SEQ. THESIS3:
>He kept the blade cutting until the top of the skull was severed.

SEQ. THESIS4 : Comment Para.
  THESIS:
>>He put the saw down.

  COMMENT:
>>George Rinne would remove the blood from it when he cleaned all the instruments later.

SEQ. THESISn (Climax):
>Now, McNeil carefully pried loose the skull, exposing the soft membrane covering the brain beneath.

SEQ. THESISn+1: Awareness Quote Para.
  AW QF:
>>Again he glanced at the nurses.

  AW Q:
>>They were standing up to it well; if they could take this they could take anything.

SEQ. THESIS3 : (N) Sequence Para.
  SEQ. THESIS1: (N) Result Para.
    THESIS:
>>>With the bony portion of the skull removed, McNeil took sharp scissors and opened the large vein—the superior sagittal sinus—which ran from front to rear along the center of the membrane.

    RESULT: Comment Para,
      THESIS:
>>>>The blood poured out, spilling over the scissors and his fingers.

      COMMENT:
>>>>It was fluid blood, noted; there was no sign of thrombosis.

  SEQ. THESIS2:
>>He inspected the membrane carefully then cut and lifted it clear to expose the mass of the brain beneath.

  SEQ. THESIS3:
>>Using a knife, he carefully severed the brain from the spinal cord, and eased it out.

  SEQ. THESISn:
>>Seddons joined him, holding a glass jar half full of formalin, and McNeil gently lowered the brain into it.

COMMENT: Cyclic R-Q-A (N) comment Para. THESIS: (N) Comment Para.
  THESIS:
>>Watching McNeil's hands steady and competent, Seddons found himself wondering again what went on in the pathology resident's mind.

  COMMENT: (N) Comment Para.
    THESIS:
>>>He had known McNeil for two years, first as a fellow resident, though senior to himself in the hospital's pyramid system, and then more closely during his own months in Pathology.

    COMMENT: Embedded (backlooped) Expository DISC [with three points]
      PT1 [Pathology not for him]: (E) Reason Para.
        THESIS: (E) Amplification Para.
          THESIS:
>>>>>Pathology had interested Seddons; he was glad, though, it was not his own chosen specialty.

35

AMPL:
　　He had never had second thoughts about his personal choice of surgery, and would be glad when he went back to it in a few weeks time.
REASON: (E) Comment Para.
THESIS: (E) Amplification Para.
　　THESIS:
　　　　In contrast to this domain of the dead the operating room was a territory of the living.
　　AMPL:
　　　　It was pulsing and alive; there was a poetry of motion, a sense of achievement he knew he could never find here.
COMMENT:
　　Each to his own, he thought and pathology for the pathologists.
PT2: [Pathology deadens sensibilities]: (E) Exemplification Para.
　　PRELIMINARY:
　　　　There was something else about pathology.
　　THESIS:
　　　　You could lose your sense of reality, your awareness that medicine was of and for human beings.
　　EXAMPLE: (E) Contrast Para.
　　　　THESIS: (E) Amplification Para.
　　　　　　THESIS:
　　　　　　　　This brain now....Seddons found himself acutely aware that only a few hours ago it was the thinking center of a man.
　　　　　　AMPL: (E) Coordinate Para.
　　　　　　　　THESIS1:
　　　　　　　　　　It had been coordinator of the senses—touch, smell, sight, taste.
　　　　　　　　THESIS2:
　　　　　　　　　　It had held thoughts, known love, fear, triumph.
　　　　　　　　THESIS3:
　　　　　　　　　　Yesterday possibly even today, it could have told the eyes to cry, the mouth to drool.
　　　　　　　　THESISn (Climax): (E) Simple Para.
　　　　　　　　　　PRELIMINARY:
　　　　　　　　　　　　He had noticed the dead man was listed as a civil engineer.
　　　　　　　　　　THESIS:
　　　　　　　　　　　　This, then, was a brain that had used mathematics, understood stresses, devised construction methods, perhaps had built houses, a highway, a water works, a cathedral—legacies from this brain for other humans to live with and use.
　　　　ANTITHESIS:
　　　　　　But what was the brain now?—just a mass of tissue, beginning to be pickled and destined only to be sliced, examined, then incinerated.
PT3 [the doctor mustn't get insulated] (E) Amplification Para.
　　THESIS: (E) Antithetical Para. [end-weighted]
　　　　ANTI: (E) Reason Para.
　　　　　　THESIS:
　　　　　　　　Seddons did not believe in God, and he found it hard to understand how educated people could.
　　　　　　REASON:
　　　　　　　　Knowledge, science, thought, the more these advanced, the more improbable all religions became.
　　　　THESIS:
　　　　　　But he did believe in what for lack of better phrases, he thought of as "the spark of humanity, the credo of the individual."

AMPL1: (E) Antithetical Para. [end-weighted]
   ANTI:
      As a surgeon, of course, he would not always deal with individuals nor would he always know his patients, and even when he did he would lose awareness of them in concentrating on problems of technique.
   THESIS:
      But long ago he had resolved never to forget that beneath everything was a patient—an individual.
AMPL2: (E) Antithetical Para. [end-weighted]
   ANTI (E) Reason Para.
     THESIS:
      In his own training Seddons had seen the cocoon of personal isolation—a safeguard against close contact with individual patients—grow around others.
     REASON:
      Sometimes it was a defensive measure, a deliberate insulation of personal emotions and personal involvement.
   THESIS: (E) Coordinate Para.
     THESIS1:
      He felt strong enough himself, though, to get along without the insulation.
     THESIS2: (E) Comment Para.
       THESIS1:
        Moreover, to make sure it did not grow, he forced himself sometimes to think and soliloquize as he was doing now.
       COMMENT: (P) Alternative Para,
        THESIS:
         Perhaps it would surprise his friends who thought of Mike Seddons only as a buoyant extrovert to know some of the thoughts that went on inside him.
        ALTERNATIVE:
         Perhaps it wouldn't, though; the mind, brain, or whatever you called it, was an unpredictable machine.
THESIS (i.e. recapitulated): (E) Coordinate Para.
   THESIS1: R-Q-A (E) Comment Para.
     THESIS (Q):
      What of McNeil?
     COMMENT: Resolved simple Dial. Para.
      IU (Q):
       Did he feel anything, or was there a shell around the pathology resident also?
      RU (A):
       Seddons did not know but he suspected there was.
   THESIS2: R-Q-A (E) Comment Para.
     THESIS (Q):
      And Pearson?
     COMMENT: Aw. Quote Para.
      LI:
       He had no doubts there
      AW. Q: (E) Reason Para.
       THESIS:
        Joe Pearson was cold and clinical all the way through.
       REASON:
        Despite his showmanship the years of pathology had chilled him.

EPn (Pearson finds something unexpected): NARR. DISC.
   EP1: Compound execution Para. for: (N) Sequence Para.?]
     LI1: AW. Q: Para.
       LI:
        Seddons looked at the old man.
       Q:
        He had removed the heart from the body and was scrutinizing it carefully.

37

```
LI2:
                        Now he turned to the student nurses.
EXCHANGE1: Execution Para.
    PLAN: (H) Reason Para.
        REASON:
                        "The medical history of this man shows that three years ago he suffered a first
                        coronary attack and then a second attack earlier this week."
        THESIS:
                        "So first we'll examine the coronary arteries."
    EXEC:
                        As the nurses watched intently Pearson delicately opened the heart-muscle
                        arteries.
EXCHANGE2: Execution Para.
    PLAN:
                        "Somewhere here we should discover the area of thrombosis...yes, here it is."
    EXEC: Awareness Quote Para.
        LI:
                        He pointed with the tip of a metal probe.
        AW. Q:
                        In the main branch of the left coronary artery, an inch beyond its origin, he had
                        exposed a pale, half-inch clot.
        SD:
                        He held it out for the girls to see.
EXCHANGE3: Execution Para.
    PLAN:
                        "Now we'll examine the heart itself."
    EXEC: (N) Seq. Para.
        SEQ. THESIS1:
                        Pearson laid the organ on a dissecting board and sliced down the center with a
                        knife.
        SEQ. THESIS2:
                        He turned the two sections side by side, peered at them, then beckoned the
                        nurses closer.
        SEQ. THESIS3:
                        Hesitantly they moved in.
EXCHANGE4: Comment Para.
    THESIS: Execution Para.
        PLAN:
                        "Do you notice this area of scarring in the muscle?"
        EXEC:
                        Pearson indicated some streaks of white fibrous tissue in the heart and the
                        nurses craned over the gaping red body cavity to see more closely.
    COMMENT:
                        "There's the evidence of the coronary attack three years ago—an old infarct
                        which has healed."
EXCHANGE5: Execution Para.
    PLAN: Quote Para.
        LI:
                        Pearson paused, then went on.
        Q: (H) Simple Para.
            PRELIMINARY:
                        "We have signs of the latest attack here in the left ventricle"
            THESIS:
                        "Notice the central area of pallor surrounded by a zone of hemorrhage."
    EXEC:
                        He pointed to a small, dark-red stain with a light center, contrasting with the
                        rest of the heart muscle.
```

EXCHANGEn: Resolved Simple Dial. Para.
  IU (Q): Quote Para.
    LI:
      Pearson turned to the surgical resident.
    Q:
      "Would you agree with me, Dr. Seddons, that the diagnosis of death by coronary thrombosis seems fairly well established?"
  RU (A): (N) Comment Para.
    THESIS:
      "Yes. I would," Seddons answered politely.
    COMMENT: (E) Amplification Para.
      THESIS:
        No doubt about it, he thought.
      AMPL:
        A tiny blood clot, not much thicker than a piece of spaghetti, was all it took to cut you off for good.
TERM:
      He watched the older pathologist put the heart aside.

EP2 [Vivian's reaction – simultaneous with EP1]: (E) Cyclic Reason Para.
THESIS: (E) Amplification Para.
  THESIS:
    Vivian was steadier now.
  AMPL:
    She believed she had herself in hand.
REASON: Awareness Quote Para.
  LI: (N) Seq. Para. (backset)
    SEQ. THESIS1:
      Near the beginning and when the saw had cut into the dead man's skull she had felt the blood drain from her head, her senses swim.
    SEQ. THESIS2:
      She knew then that she had been close to fainting and had determined not to.
  AW QF:
    For no reason she had suddenly remembered an incident in her childhood.
  AW Q: (N) Result Para.
    THESIS: (N) Seq. Para. (backset)
      SEQ. THESIS1:
        On a holiday, deep in the Oregon forest, her father had fallen on an open hunting knife and cut his leg badly.
      SEQ. THESIS2:
        Surprisingly in so strong a man he had quailed at the sight of so much of his own blood and her mother, usually more at home in the drawing room than the woods, had become suddenly strong.
      SEQ. THESIS3:
        She had fashioned a tourniquet, stemmed the blood, and sent Vivian running for help.
      SEQ. THESISn:
        Then, with Vivian's father being carried through the woods on an improvised litter of branches, every half-hour she had released the tourniquet to keep circulation going, then tightened it to halt the bleeding again.
    RESULT:
      Afterwards the doctors had said she had saved the leg from amputation.
THESIS' (reiterated):
    After that. she knew that there would not be any problem about watching an autopsy again.

39

EP3 [Student nurses ask questions] Compound Dialogue Para.
  LI: Quote Para.
    Quote:
        "Any questions"
    QF:
        It was Dr. Pearson asking.
  EXCHANGE1: Resolved Simple Dial. Para.
    IU (Q): Quote Para.
      QF:
        Vivian had one.
      Q:
        "The organs—those that you take out of the body. What happens to them, please?"
        [Note: Although punctuated as two sentences I take the above to be one sentence with a long noun phrase as Sentence Topic].
    RU (A): (P) Sequence Para.
      SEQ. TH1:
        "We shall keep them probably for a week. That is the heart, lungs, stomach, kidney, liver, pancreas, spleen, and brain."
        [Note: although punctuated as two sentences I take the above to be one sentence with a long postposed sentence topic].
      SEQ. THn: Simultaneous Para. [foreweighted]
        SIMUL1:
          "Then we shall make a group examination which will be recorded in detail."
        SIMUL2:
          "At that time, also. we'll be studying organs removed at other autopsies probably six to a dozen cases altogether."
    CORRELATE: (N) SEQ. Para.
      SEQ. THESIS1: (N) Antithetical Para.
        THESIS:
          It sounded so cold and impersonal, Vivian thought.
        ANTITHESIS:
          But maybe you had to get that way if you did this all the time.
      SEQ. THESIS2:
        Involuntarily she shuddered.
      SEQ. THESISn: (N) Stimulus-Response Para.
        THESIS (Stimulus):
          Mike Seddons caught her eye and smiled slightly.
        THESIS (Response): (N) Paraphrase Para.
          THESIS:
            She wondered if he was amused or being sympathetic.
          PARAPHRASE:
            She could not be sure.
  EXCHANGE2: Resolved simple Dial. Para.
    IU (Q): Quote Para.
      LI: (N) Comment Para.
        THESIS:
          Now one of the other girls was putting a question.
        COMMENT:
          She sounded uneasy, almost afraid to ask.
      Q: (P) Comment Para.
        THESIS:
          "The body—is it buried, then...just by itself?"
        COMMENT:
          This was an old one.

RU (A): Comment Para.
   THESIS: (P) Coordinate Para.
      THESIS1: quote Para.
         QF:
            Pearson answered it.
         Q: Result Para.
            SETTING:
               "It varies."
            THESIS:
               "Teaching centers such as this usually do more study after autopsies than is done in non-teaching hospitals."
            RESULT:
               "In this hospital just the shell of the body goes on to the undertakers."
      THESIS2: quote Para.
         QF:
            He added as an afterthought.
         Q: Reason Para.
            THESIS:
               "They wouldn't thank us for putting the organs back, anyway."
            REASON:
               "Just be a nuisance when they're embalming."
   COMMENT: (E) Coordinate Para.
      THESIS1: (E) Paraphrase Para.
         THESIS:
            That was true, McNeil reflected.
         PARA:
            Maybe not the gentlest way of putting it, but true all the same.
      THESIS2:
         He had sometimes wondered himself if mourners and others who visited funeral parlors knew how little remained in a body that had been autopsied.
      THESIS3:
         After an autopsy like this one, and depending on how busy a pathology department was, it might be weeks before the body organs were disposed of finally, and even then small specimens from each were kept stored indefinitely.
EXCHANGE3: Compound Dial. Para.
   EXCHANGE1: Resolved simple Dial. Para. (with discontinuous RU)
      IU (Q): Quote Para.
         Q:
            "Are there never any exceptions?"
      STEP-DOWN/CORRELATE? (N) Antithetical Para.
         THESIS:
            The student nurse asking the questions seemed persistent.
         ANTITHESIS: (N) Reason Para.
            THESIS:
               Pearson did not appear to object though.
            REASON: (N) Comment Para.
               THESIS:
                  Maybe this is one of his patient days, McNeil thought.
               COMMENT:
                  The old men had them occasionally.
   RU (A): (N) Reason Para.
      THESIS:
         "Yes, there are," he was saying.
      REASON:(P) Amplification Para.
         THESIS:
            "Before we can do any autopsy we must have permission from the family of the deceased."

41

```
            AMPL: (P) Alternative Para.
                ALT. THESIS1:
                    "Sometimes that permission is unrestricted, as in this case, and then we can
                    examine the entire head and torso."
                ALT. THESIS2: (P) Exemplification Para.
                    THESIS:
                        "At other times we may get only limited permission."
                    EXAMPLE: (P) REASON PARA.
                        REASON:
                            "For example a family may ask specifically that the cranial contents be
                            undisturbed."
                        THESIS:
                            "When that happens in this hospital we respect their wishes."
    TU (Acq): Quote Para.
        Q:
            "Thank you, Doctor."
        SD:
            Apparently the girl was satisfied, whatever her reason had been for asking.
    RU [Cont]: Quote Para.
        LI:
            But Pearson had not finished.
        QUOTE: (P) Reason Para.
            REASON:
                "You do run into cases where for reasons of religious faith the organs are
                required for burial with the body."
            THESIS:
                "In that case, of course, we comply with the request."
EXCHANGE2: Resolved simple Dial. Para. (with long CORRELATE)
    IU(Q): Quote Para. (with discontinuous QUOTE)
        QUOTE:
            "How about Catholics?"
        LI/SD?:
            It was one of the other girls this time.
        QUOTE (Cont.)
            "Do they insist on that?"
    RU (A): quote para.
        QUOTE: (P) Result Para.
            THESIS:
                "Most of them don't, but there are some Catholic hospitals which do."
            RESULT: (E) Comment Para.
                THESIS:
                    "That makes the pathologist's work difficult."
                COMMENT:
                    "Usually."
    CORRELATE: (P) Comment Para.
        SETTING:
            As he added the last word Pearson glanced sardonically at McNeil.
        THESIS: (P) Amplification Para.
            THESIS: (P) Antithetical Para.
                THESIS:
                    Both of them knew what Pearson was thinking—one of the larger Catholic
                    hospitals across town had a standing order that the organs of all bodies
                    autopsied were to be returned to the body for burial.
                ANTI:
                    But sometimes a little sleight of hand was practiced.
```

```
         AMPL: (P) Comment Para.
            THESIS: (P) SEQ. Para.
               SETTING:
                  The busy pathology department of the other hospital kept a spare set of organs
                  on hand.
               SEQ. THESIS1:
                  Thus, when a new autopsy was done the organs removed were replaced by the
                  spare ones, so that the body could be released and the latest set of organs
                  examined at leisure.
               SEQ. THESIS2:
                  These organs, in turn, were then used for the next body.
            COMMENT:
                  Thus, the pathologists were, in effect, always one step ahead of the game.
            COMMENT: (P) Exemplification Para.
               SETTING:
                  McNeil knew that Pearson, though not a Catholic, disapproved of this.
               THESIS:
                  And whatever else you might say about the old man he always insisted on
                  following autopsy permissions both to the letter and the spirit.
               EXAMPLE: (P) Comment Para.
                  THESIS: (P) Anthithetical Para. [end=weighted]
                     ANTI:
                        There was one phrase sometimes used in completing the official form which
                        read "limited to abdominal incision."
                     THESIS: (P) Comment Para.
                        THESIS:
                           Some pathologists he knew did a full autopsy with this single incision.
                        COMMENT:
                           As he had heard one man put it, "With an abdominal incision, if you've a mind
                           to it, you can reach up inside and get everything including the tongue."
                  COMMENT:
                     Pearson—to his credit, McNeil thought—would never permit this and in Three
                     Counties an "abdominal incision" release meant examination of the abdomen
                     only.
EPn (PEAK) (The discovery): Compound Dial. Para.
   LI:
                  Pearson had turned his attention back to the body.
   EXCHANGE1: Execution Para.
      PLAN:
                  "We'll go on now to examine..."
      EXEC: (N) Seq. Para.
         SEQ. TH1:
                  Pearson stopped and peered down.
         SEQ. TH2:
                  He reached for a knife and probed gently.
         SEQ. THn:
                  Then he let out a grunt of interest.
   EXCHANGE2: Execution Para.
      PLAN:
                  "McNeil, Seddons, take a look at this."
      EXEC: Aw Quote Para.
         LI: (N) Seq. Para.
            SEQ. TH1:
                  Pearson moved aside and the pathology resident leaned over the area that
                  Pearson had been studying.
            SEQ. THn:
                  He nodded.
```

43

    AW QUOTE: Comment Para.
        THESIS:
            The pleura, normally a transparent, glittering membrane covering the lungs, had a thick coating of scarring—a dense, white, fibrous tissue.
        COMMENT:
            It was a sign of tuberculosis; whether old or new he would know in a minute.
    STED-DOWN:
        He moved aside for Seddons.
EXCHANGE3: Execution Para. (discontinuous)
    PLAN: Quote Para. (discontinuous)
        QUOTE: Reason Para. (discontinuous)
            THESIS:
                "Palpate the lungs, Seddons."
    QF:
        It was Pearson.
        QUOTE: (continued)
            REASON:
                "I imagine you'll find some evidence here."
    EXEC.: Aw. Quote Para.
        LI:
            The surgical resident grasped the lungs, probing with his fingers.
        QUOTE:
            The cavities below the surface were detectable at once.
        STEP-DOWN:
            He looked up at Pearson and nodded.
EXCHANGE4: Resolved simple Dial. Para.
    LI: (N) Simple Para.
        SETTING:
            McNeil had turned to the case history papers.
        THESIS:
            He used a clean knife to turn the pages so he would not stain them.
    IU (Q):
        "Was there a chest X-ray on admission?" Pearson asked.
    RU (A): Quote Para.
        LI:
            The resident shook his head.
        QUOTE: (N) Reason Para.
            REASON:
                "The patient was in shock."
            THESIS:
                "There's a note here it wasn't done."
EXCHANGE5: Execution Para.
    PLAN: Quote Para.
        Quote:
            "We'll take a vertical slice to see what's visible."
        QF:
            Pearson was talking to the nurses again as he moved back to the table.
    EXEC: Aw. Quote Para.
        LI:
            He removed the lungs and cut smoothly down the center of one.
        QUOTE: (E) Amplification Para.
            THESIS:
                It was there unmistakably—fibrocaseous tuberculosis, well advanced.
            AMPL:
                The lung had a honeycombed appearance, like ping-pong balls fastened together then cut through the center—a festering, evil growth that only the heart had beaten to the kill.

EXCHANGE6: Resolved complex dialogue Para.
    IU (Q):
        "Can you see it?"
    CU (A/Rem): Quote Para.
        QF:
            Seddons answered Pearson's question.
        QUOTE:
            "Yes. Looks like it was a toss-up whether this or the heart would get him first."
    RU (Eval):
        "It's always a toss-up what we die of."
EXCHANGE7: Unresolved simple dial. Para.
    LI:
        Pearson looked across at the nurses.
    Q: (E) Comment Para.
        THESIS: Result Para.
            THESIS:
                "This man had advanced tuberculosis."
            RESULT:
                "As Dr. Seddons observed it would have killed him very soon."
        COMMENT:
            "Presumably neither he nor his physician was aware of its presence."

CLOSURE (Final remarks of Pearson; Seddon's evaluation): NARR. DISC.
    STAGE: (N) Comment Para.
        THESIS:
            Now Pearson pulled off his gloves and began to remove his gown.
        COMMENT: (P) Amplification Para.
            SETTING:
                The performance is over, Seddons thought.
            THESIS:
                The bit players and stage-hands will do the cleaning up.
            AMPL: (P) Sequence Para.
                SEQ. THESIS1: Antithetical Para.
                    THESIS:
                        McNeil and the resident would put the essential organs into a pail and label it with the case number.
                    ANTI:
                        The remainder would be put back into the body with linen waste added if necessary to fill the cavities out.
                SEQ. THESISn:
                    Then they would stitch up roughly using a big baseball stitch—over and under—because the area they had been working on would be covered decorously with clothes in the coffin; and when they had finished the body would go into refrigeration to await the undertaker.
    EPn: Compound Dial. Para.
        EXCHANGE1: (N) Comment Para.
            THESIS: Unresolved simple dial. Para.
                LI: (N) Comment Para.
                    THESIS:
                        Pearson had put on the white lab coat with which he entered the autopsy room and was lighting a new cigar.
                  COMMENT:
                      It was a characteristic that he left behind him through the hospital a trail of half-smoked cigar butts, usually for someone else to deposit in an ash tray.
                IU (Prop): Quote Para.
                  QF:
                      He addressed himself to the nurses.

45

    QUOTE: (P) Sequence Para.
      SETTING:
        "There will be times in your careers," he said, "when you will have patients die."
      SEQ. THESIS1: (P) Amplification Para.
        THESIS:
        "It will be necessary, then, to obtain permission for an autopsy from next of kin."
        AMPL:
        "Sometimes this will fall to the physician, sometimes to you."
      SEQ. THESISn: (P) Reason Para.
        THESIS:
        "When that happens you will occasionally meet resistance."
        REASON: (P) Comment Para.
          THESIS:
          "It is hard for any person to sanction—even after death—the mutilation of someone they loved."
          COMMENT:
          "This is understandable."
STEP-DOWN
      Pearson paused.
COMMENT: (N) Amplification Para.
    THESIS:
      For a moment Seddons found himself having second thoughts about the old man.
    AMPL:
      Was there some warmth, some humanity, in him after all?
EXCHANGE2: Unresolved simple Dial. Para.
    IU:
      "When you need to muster arguments," Pearson said, "to convince some individual of the need for autopsy, I hope you will remember what you have seen today and use it as an example."
EXCHANGE3: Stimulus-Response Para.
    STIMULUS: Quote Para.
      LI:
        He had his cigar going now and waved it at the table.
      QUOTE: (Argumentative) Syllogism Para.
        PREMISE1:
        "This man has been tuberculous for many months."
        PREMISE2:
        "It is possible he may have infected others around him, his family, people he worked with, even some in this hospital."
        CONCLUSION:
        "If there had been no autopsy, some of these people might have developed tuberculosis. and it could have remained undetected, as it did here until too late."
    RESPONSE:
      Two of the student nurses moved back instinctively from the table.
EXCHANGE4: (Structured as Comment Para.)
    THESIS: Unresolved simple Dial. Para.
      IU (Rem): Quote Para.
        LI:
        Pearson shook his head.
        QUOTE: (P) Antithetical Para.
          ANTI: (E) Reason Para.
            THESIS:
            "Within reason there is no danger of infection here."
            REASON:
            "Tuberculosis is a respiratory disease."

46

THESIS:
"But because of what we have learned today, those who have been close to this man will be kept under observation and given periodic checks for several years to come."
COMMENT: (E) Reason Para.
THESIS:
To his own surprise Seddons found himself stirred by Pearson's words.
REASON: (E) Coordinate Para.
THESIS1:
He makes it sound good, he thought; what's more he believes in what he is saying.
THESIS2:
He discovered that at this moment he was liking the old man.
EXCHANGE5: Unresolved compound Dial. Para.
EXCHANGE1: Unresolved simple Dial. Para.
LI:
As if he had read Seddons' mind, Pearson looked over to the surgical resident.
IU: (Rem):
With a mocking smile: "Pathology has its victories too, Dr. Seddons."
EXCHANGE2: Unresolved simple Dial. Para. (?)
IU(?):
He nodded at the nurses.

FINIS:
Then he was gone, leaving a cloud of cigar smoke behind him.

References

Beneviste, E. 1974. *Problèmes de linguistique générale* Paris: Gallimard.

Dry, H. n.d. Deictic *Now: The Great Gatsby* as Case Study.

Gleason, H. 1968. Contrastive Analysis in Sentence Structure *Report of the Nineteenth Round Table,* 39–63. Georgetown Monograph Series 21.Washington, D.C.: Georgetown University Press.

Grimes, J. 1975. *The Thread of Discourse.* The Hague: Mouton.

Hoey, M. 1983. *On the Surface of Discourse.* London: Allen and Unwin.

Hailey, A. 1959. *The Final Diagnosis.* New York: Doubleday and Co.

Hopper, P. 1979. Aspect and Foregrounding in Discourse. In T. Givón (ed.), *Discourse and Syntax. Syntax and Semantics 12,* 212–242. New York: Academic Press.

Lewis, C. S. 1961. *A Preface to Paradise Lost.* Oxford: Oxford University Press.

Longacre, R. 1979a. Why we Need a Vertical Revolution in Linguistics. *The Fifth LACUS Forum 1978,* 427–270. Columbia, S.C.: Hornbeam Press.

Longacre, R. 1979b. The Paragraph as a Grammatical Unit. In T. Givón (ed.), *Discourse and Semantics: Syntax and Semantics 12,* 115–134. New York: Academic Press.

Longacre, R. 1989. "Two Hypotheses regarding Text Generation and Analysis" *Discourse Processes 12,* 413–460. Norwood, N.J.: Ablex.

Longacre, R. 1990. *Storyline Concerns and Word Order Typology in East and West Africa. Studies in African Linguistics* Supplement 10 Los Angeles: The James F. Coleman African Studies Center and the Dept. of Linguistics, University of California.

Longacre, R. 1996. *The Grammar of Discourse, second edition.* New York: Plenum Press.

Longacre, R. and Woods, F., eds. 1976-7 *Discourse Grammar: Studies in Indigenous Languages of Colombia, Panama, and Ecuador,* Parts 1–3. Summer Institute of Linguistics and the University of Texas at Arlington Publication 53. Dallas.

Mann, W. and Thompson, S. 1993. *Relational Propositions in Discourse*, Technical Report ISI/RR-83-115. Marina del Rey, Calif.: Information Sciences Institute.

Mann, W. and Thompson, S. 1987a. *Rhetorical Structure Theory: A Theory of Text Organization,* Technical Report ISI/RS 87-190. Marina del Rey Calif.: Information Sciences Institute.

Mann, W. and Thompson, S. 1987b. Rhetorical Structure Theory: a Framework for Analysis of Texts, IPrA. *Papers in Pragmatics* 1:79–105

Miehle, H. 1978. Linguistic Markers of Climax in *The Final Diagnosis.* University of Texas at Arlington. unpublished paper.

Ricoeur, P. 1985 *Time and Narrative, Vol 2 (The Configuration of Time in Fictional Narrative,* chapter 3, Games with Time). Chicago: University of Chicago Press.

van Dijk, T. 1977. *Text and Context: Explorations in the Semantics and Pragmatics of Discourse.* London: Longman.

van Dijk, T. 1980. *Macrostructures*. Hillsdale N.J.: Erlbaum.

Ware, J. 1993. Quote Formulae in *The Final Diagnosis*. *Journal of Translation and Textlinguistics* 161–178.

Weinrich, H. 1964. *Tempus: Besprochene und Erzählte Zeit*. Stuttgart: W. Kohlhammaer.

Williams, M. 1978. Cohesion Among the Plots in Arthur Hailey's *The Final Diagnosis*. University of Texas at Arlington. unpublished paper.

15

CHAPTER 11

Some Hermeneutic Observations on Textlinguistics and Text Theory in the Humanities

Robert E. Longacre
University of Texas at Arlington

1. Introduction

Homo Sapiens is an incessant creator of texts, both oral and written. Primarily, texts serve basic communication needs — as seen in any social milieu which is characterized by written exchanges as well as face-to-face relations, or for that matter as seen in the feverish interchange of memoranda which characterizes a modern corporation or a university. Casual *ad hoc* texts, rather than disappearing as a culture becomes technologically sophisticated, **proliferate** to a degree that is both amusing and alarming. We could perhaps voice a prophecy:

> This is the way the world ends,
> This is the way the world ends,
> This is the way the world ends,
> Drowned deep in paper.

Nevertheless, cultures of the past, and we hope our own as well, can produce **privileged** texts which are of more than ephemeral significance. In fact, the study of the humanities has traditionally revolved around the study of such texts, from the medieval student's preoccupation with Aristotle, to the University of Chicago's plan, which equated an adequate liberal arts education with the knowledge of the "great books of the Western world". Such texts presumably are a privileged few which survive as the embodiment of ideas and values that persist across time and outlive the cultures in which they originated.

But the study of the Humanities also perforce involves the study of more ephemeral texts — as, for example, the papers presented at a conference, class lectures, textbooks, and the like.[1]

The relevance of ephemeral texts to the Humanities can further be seen in text-theoretical studies of such ephemeral texts. This is exemplified in the sort of text studied by contributors to the journal *Text*: conversation between doctors, psychiatrists, and patients (Freeman and Heller [eds.] 1986), courtroom discourse and conversation between lawyers and clients, along with legal documents such as insurance policies and court decisions (Danet [ed.] 1984), the language of a church service (Borker 1986), the language of prejudice and discrimination (van Dijk & Wodak [eds.] 1988). Add to this a recent volume (Mann and Thompson 1992) on the textual structure of an appeals letter, and an article which studies the textual structure of a linguistic article (Farmer 1981).

2. Textlinguistics

Textlinguistics has developed in the last decades of this century as a way of getting at the meaning of a text through a study of its linguistic structure in the language in which it is written. While it is believed that certain text features are universal among the languages of the world, it is also believed that the particular working out of these strategies is language-specific. Thus, for example, while all languages have a way of indicating the storyline of a narrative, the specific verb system and clause structure of a language delimit the means by which this is done. The goal of the textlinguist is to confront the morphosyntax of a language with the structure of texts in that language to the mutual elucidation of both. This leads not only to a better understanding of the linguistic structure of a language, but also to a kind of text hermeneutic.

A textlinguistic analysis can fruitfully begin with an attempt to identify the framework of a discourse in terms of text type (Longacre 1983). Contingent temporal sequence in accomplished time and a slate of participants determine a narrative discourse — whether the EVENTS and the ACTORS are concrete and personal or abstract and impersonal (as in some historical writing — Ricoeur 1984, vol. I). Contingent temporal sequence in projected time with an appropriate

---

[1]. This article is a reworking of a paper which was read at the Tenth Annual Conference of the Association for Integrated Studies at Arlington, Texas, October 1986.

agent constitutes procedural how-to-do-it discourse; contingent temporal sequence in accomplished time constitutes, with appropriate agents, procedural how-it-was-done discourse. Various kinds of behavioral discourse exist: eulogy, promissory speech, exhortation, of which the latter is very common; in these, there is no contingent temporal sequence (except in limited context) and certain actions of an agent are praised, promised, or inculcated. Expository (including descriptive) discourse has neither temporal nor agentive orientation; rather it has some sort of logical/spatial development and heavy thematic structuring. Text typology is basic, not simply because humans are inveterate classifiers — although that is relevant — but because text analysis proceeds best by comparing **like** texts.

Having roughly isolated the text type which provides the framework of the discourse (which may contain many embedded texts of diverse types), the text analyst does well to raise the question of what a text is all about, i.e. its macrostructure. The macrostructure of a discourse (van Dijk 1977, 1980) provides a control as to what is included or excluded from mention in the text; what is developed in detail or merely summarily mentioned; and may affect the order of presentation in regard to big chunks of the discourse. It can also control some rather subtle details that we do not have time and space to develop here.

The textlinguist is now ready to focus on the linguistic structure of the text. Here a good beginning point is the examination of the verb forms and clause structures that characterize the text. Certain of these verb forms and clause types are highly relevant to the forward progress of the text. Each text type in a given language will have a way of encoding its main line of development. There will also be subsidiary lines of development. Thus, in a story in which action verbs dominate, explanation and description are subsidiary lines of development, while in an explanatory discourse where the main line is expository/descriptive, the action verbs that characterize the main line of a story come in only in subsidiary anecdotes and illustrations. Eventually the textlinguist should be able to make for any discourse type in any language a scalar arrangement of verb forms/clause types in terms of nearness (or degrees of departure from) the mainline of development (Longacre 1989).

The textlinguist must also be concerned with what nouns and pronouns do within a text. In a story nouns/pronouns/agreement references within the verb (as well as null reference) have to do with participant reference: first mention, integration into the story, routine tracking, reintroduction after absence from the story, narrator comments on a participant, local contrast between participants, and local thematicity. Themes as well as participants occur in stories, and participants occur as well as props. In a procedural discourse, the anyone-qualified agent acts on props to produce something (or to stage a ritual event). In a behavioral discourse, especially the hortatory type, the targeted audience is second person, and there may occur a proliferation of constructions to express mitigation of commands; noun phrases identify involvement with other participants or impingement on others, or occasional split of the target audience ("you men do x; you women do y"); or noun phrases may identify props used in implementing commands/suggestions. In explanatory/descriptive discourse, nouns provide characterization of the environment, whether human, non-human, props, or topological features. At any rate, whatever the discourse type, the use of noun versus pronoun versus reference in the verb (in an inflected language) versus null must be accounted for in terms of text structure and text semantics.

Particles and conjunctions must also be accounted for, as well as other prominence/cohesive features not included above, e.g. repetition/back reference (reprise) in adverbial clauses; and use of parallelism and paraphrase.

Certainly it is also part of the textlinguist's job to catalogue the ways in which a high point or cumulative development of a text is marked. I have written considerably about "peak marking" in other places (1983, 1985, 1990) and will not again elaborate this idea here.

Finally, a textlinguistic analysis can plug in all the above to come out with a presentation of the constituent structure of a text. An attempt is made in such a presentation to account for the function of every sentence, every part of a sentence, and every group of sentences in the plan of the whole. In regard to the functioning of parts of the constituent sentences, sentence-level grammar of any one of several varieties can be plugged in — but may need some restatement in the light of discourse perspective. The relation of sentence to sentence and of one group of sentences to another group of sentences requires some kind of logical calculus adapted to describing natural languages. Several such catalogues exist (Beekman, Callow, and Kopesec 1981; Longacre 1976, 1983, 1996; van Dijk 1977; de Beaugrande and Dressler 1981; Halliday and Hasan 1976; Mann and Thompson 1987). No linguist can do microanalysis without such a catalogue — although the macroanalysis into "big chunks" is more obvious and less problematic.

Especially valuable in microanalysis is the attention to verb forms/clauses in a scalar scheme such as that suggested above. In microanalysis the sentences whose main verbs/main clauses rank higher should predominate constituent-wise over those sentences whose main verbs/main clauses rank lower. Here, in the analysis of local spans (paragraphs), the concepts of DOMINANCE and ANCILLARINESS replace those of independent and subordinate on the sentence level.

The upshot of all this is a system of interrelated guidelines for the understanding of a text.[2] What is the author trying to make prominent or background, dominant or ancillary? What does he connect up well or decide to leave in implicit connection? What logical relations are implied? How do fine-grained details — use of one verb form rather than another, or of a noun rather than a pronoun — have to do with the whole? How do all these details relate back to the postulated macrostructure and to the analysis of local spans? A textlinguistic analysis will not automatically deliver to us the meaning and intent of a text and its parts, but it should constrain within plausible bounds our possible interpretations of it.

I posit the formulation in (1):

(1)   TL $\to$ ^{H} $\to$ Text

i.e., "Textlinguistics provides a partial hermeneutic of the text".
Textlinguistics, practiced somewhat as above might with profit be applied to some of the "great books of the Western world" referred to above. Could we, for example, get a new and fresh look at Plato by applying a textlinguistic methodology to the Greek text of the *Dialogues* and of the *Republic*?

3. Text Theory

Textlinguistics was, however, scarcely conceived and born before it was expanded to text theory — the interdisciplinary study of text or at least the study of text against the background of an enriched and much more sophisticated kind of textlinguistics. It became, for example, immediately evident that cognitive and social aspects of text had to be studied whatever interdisciplinary milieu developed. Thus, Teun van Dijk's early partnership with Walter Kintsch, a psychologist, was no fortuitous concourse of personalities. Their experimental work on macrostructures via progressive attrition of text retention on the part of Dutch school children (1977) was of considerable early significance to text theory. Nor

---

2. I refrain here from going into the role of reported speech and variation in quotation formulas to textlinguistic analysis. Janice Ware and I read a joint paper on this frontier question of discourse analysis in 1987; cf. Longacre 1994.

is it an accident that early work on dialogue relations in the United States was carried out by sociologists (e.g. Sacks 1984 and others).

The journal *Text* itself was founded in the hope, which time has justified, of having an interdisciplinary journal devoted to text theory. As mentioned above, special issues, such as those on medical discourse, legal discourse, and the language of prejudice and discrimination have demonstrated the value of the cooperation of the textlinguist with practitioners from other disciplines. It is not always possible to find one person who is competent in two such fields, but joint research and discussion and joint authorship must often be resorted to in order to bridge between two disciplines or professions.

Two conferences at my home university, the University of Texas at Arlington, attempted to encourage such an interdisciplinary milieu. The first, in 1980, took as its topic "Linguistics and the Humanities". Results of this conference were published in three successive issues of *Forum Linguisticum* (1982–1983). The second such conference, in 1985, took as its topic "The text as a focal concern in the humanities". The results of this conference were published in the linguistics journal *Word* (Brend, 1986) and consequently some of the more interdisciplinary papers were not included.

Textlinguistics and text theory can also with profit be applied to Biblical Studies — especially in the somewhat inbred field of Old Testament Studies. While some have talked of a "return from the desert of criticism", textlinguistics and text theory can lead the way in such a return, i.e., a facing away from the questions of putative sources and a facing towards the text itself.

A rather striking example of the latter emerged in a paper by Nicolas Bailey (1992). Nehemiah Chapter 3 is an account of the rebuilding of the walls of Jerusalem by returned Jewish exiles in the fifth century B.C. Critics have latched onto certain differences in the style and grammar of Neh. 3:1–15 and 3:16–32 and have suggested that two authors/sources are involved.[3] At this point Bailey observes that the geography and archaeology have something to say. Crucial is the question of the extent of the city which Nehemiah walled in and the location of the walls. Contemporary Israeli archaeologists have elucidated this problem, and in the process have elucidated our text for us.

The Jerusalem of Solomon's day was essentially the Jebusite stronghold that David captured, plus an extension to the higher land immediately to the north,

---

3. In the English text, Chapter 3 ends with v. 32 and Chapter 4 begins. In the Hebrew, Chapter 3 continues through 4.6 of the English text.

culminating in Solomon's temple mound, which was somewhat smaller than we find today (it having been enlarged by Herod). The whole city then was a narrow walled strip extending over two hills and running from north to south. In Hezekiah's time a refugee population from the north had extensively settled the Western Hill, which Hezekiah proceeded to wall in with his "Broad Wall". This somewhat rectilinear city was destroyed by the Chaldeans in 587 B.C. The question is how much of the wall did Nehemiah rebuild?

Current archaeological investigation suggests that he essentially restored the walls along the line of the Solomonic City; in fact Nehemiah 3:8b could properly be translated: "They left out part of Jerusalem as far as the Broad Wall" — although it is not so translated in even as up-to-date a version as the New International Version.

What then? Essentially Nehemiah enclosed the old city running across the two hills, and including the City of David, the Ophel, and the temple mound. His men began their work at the north end and work crews are described as situated to the south one after the other. The Hebrew text of 3:1–15 says "X restored R, and **on his hand** Y restored S, and **on his hand** Z restored T". But on reaching the southern tip of the narrow oblong city and on rounding the tip the descriptive phraseology changes as the work parties are now described as disposed from south to north. Here the Hebrew text of 3:16–32 runs: "X restored R, and **after him** Y restored S. And **after him**, Z restored T". While the precise rationale of *on his hand* versus *after him* (where *him* refers to the leader of a working group and his followers) is not clear, it seems abundantly clear that the shift in phraseology refers to a shift in descriptive perspective. But this shift of perspective is intelligible if and only if the topography is grasped and the results of current archaeological studies are taken into account. Again, the full understanding of the Neh. 3 text (and an appreciation of its unity) depends not just on the study of the text itself, but on adding insights from geography and archaeology to the study of the text. In the process, the rather strained translation of Neh. 3:8b (in contemporary English versions) can be replaced by a more adequate one — indicating in so many words that Nehemiah did not try to wall in the whole city of the last days of monarchical Judah but intentionally "abandoned" part of it.

While it is a commonplace that the study of one text can be elucidated by the study of a similar related text, text theory suggests that we go further afield and that texts in separate disciplines be allowed to elucidate each other. But whether texts are closely related or relatively distant, a kind of INTERTEXTUALITY is involved.

Let me suggest in (2), therefore, a formulation in which this element of intertextuality is accounted for hermeneutically:

(2) $\text{Text}_i \leftarrow^H \rightarrow \text{Text}_j$

i.e., "a given text may be partially elucidated by reference to another text(s), even if not in the same discipline". I have drawn the hermeneutic arrow here as bidirectional, since the mutual elucidation can work in both directions.

4. Text Theory and the Arts

But what of the implications of text theory for the arts, e.g. music, dance, visual arts, and architecture? Semiotics has made a beginning in this regard, but — as a comprehensive and sprawling discipline — it lacks an adequate theory of text.[4] An adequate theory of text must come by way of textlinguistics and text theory.

But is it not naive and *ad hoc* to make text the measure of everything? Assuredly yes. What then? Let us consider some bidirectional relations of the sort: "X as text; text as X". Thus, if music can be regarded as a kind of text, cannot a text also be compared to a musical composition? And if a painting can be considered to be a kind of text, why cannot a text be considered to be a kind of painting? And if architecture is a kind of "frozen text", why cannot a text be regarded as a kind of building/complex of buildings?

4.1 *Text theory and music*

Textual concepts are not difficult to apply to music. Musical compositions have passages that can be considered to be *introduction, inciting incident, development, climax*, and *denouement* much as in a narrative. A composition has parts which advance it and parts which serve as background. We might with some propriety

---

4. Sydney Lamb is to be commended for inaugurating at Rice University a joint department of linguistics and semiotics. The conference held at the program's inauguration resulted in a volume of articles (Copeland 1984) of considerable relevance in this connection. I mention also in this regard the Halliday festschrift volumes (Steele and Threadgold [eds.] 1987).

search, therefore, for the mainline of development in a composition. Furthermore, one germinal motif (like the opening bars of Beethoven's Fifth Symphony) can be compared in some ways to the macrostucture of a text. In addition, some compositions are spontaneous (improvised) and others are pre-planned — much like unplanned and planned texts. Finally, musical idioms throughout the world, (including the vast world of non-Western music) vary in ways much like the variation observed in texts in different languages.

But what of text as music? A disconcerting aspect of some current text-analysis (including possibly my own!) is the tendency to over-specificity because of dissection according to a particle-oriented view of reality (Pike 1959). Indeed some text analyses are so static that one suspects that a kind of *rigor mortis* has set in. But music is a kind of flowing and less discreet continuum. Taking seriously musical analogies to texts would encourage us to view a text more as a dynamic production. Indeed, such an approach to text-analysis is specifically advocated by de Beaugrande and Dressler as "the procedural approach". Here is where the analogy to music can help save text analysis from *rigor mortis*.

The musical sequence: theme — countertheme — recapitulation, much used in Western music has a rather exact counterpart in text structure, especially in Semitic inclusio/chiastic patterns (Arabic and Hebrew literature), but has also been observed in South American Indian languages (Waltz 1976) and in Australian aboriginal languages (Sayers 1976). Furthermore, the idea that one theme can be dominant while another is echoed or backgrounded (or even nascent), while easily documentable in music, can also be extended to texts. Thus, any one of Arthur Hailey's novels equals (1) a storyline, plus (2) exposé of an institution or industry. The storyline (1) usually predominates, but the background thematic material (2), which is quite pervasive, sometimes becomes dominant for a while as well — or conflates with the storyline.

There is at least one kind of discourse type, the familiar essay, that is often comparable to theme plus variations in music. Such an essay on a topic Q rarely presents a valid logical partitioning of the theme, rather Q_i, Q_j, Q_k ... are presented in succession as variations on the theme. This is illustrated for example in Charles Krauthammer's *Time* essay, "Vacationing on a Return Ticket" where a vacation is presented as an example, often a flight into irresponsibility — and a few examples of such irresponsible jaunts are presented. But always the traveler has a return ticket in his pocket and never intends to live with the situation that he is visiting. Here, I believe that the musical analogue might lead to a perception of the text structure in terms of theme plus variations.

4.2 Text theory and painting

A painting of the more pictorial/anthropomorphic sort can be compared to a text in terms of backgrounding and foregrounding. The whole has an overall macrostructure to which the details must conform. For this reason such paintings are inevitably interpretations or even reconstructions of reality. Furthermore, such a painting has a hierarchical/constituent structure. Certain figures/features are elaborated as sub-wholes which fit into the main whole.

But even the better sort of abstract art is, I suspect, not all that different. A good abstract composition must also have cohesion and prominence. It must subordinate some features to others. It must have a macrostructure of sorts — no matter how difficult it may be to state such a notion in words. And why should we expect it to be stateable in words?

But what of text as painting? Let us return here to an idea voiced in Section 2, where we focus on the linguistic structure of a text in a textlinguistics framework, and mention the feasibility of scalar arrangement of the verb forms/clause types of a discourse type in a given language. The claims were made there that (1) such a scalar arrangement could reflect progressive degrees of departure from the mainline of a story; and (2) this could partially guide microanalysis in that higher-ranking verb forms/clause types in the scale could also be shown to be dominant in the constituent structure of local spans. I have even made the claim (1981) that an optical analogy, the color spectrum, is of relevance here.

Thus, in a story in English, the storyline (active verbs, cognitive events, contingencies) dominates and can be color-coded as red. Background activities and cognitive states can be color-coded as red-orange. Flashbacks — events reported out of sequence, can be color-coded as yellow-orange. Setting (descriptive and explanatory material) can be color coded as yellow. Irrealis sentences — things that didn't/should have/might have happened — can be color-coded as green. And, finally, intrusive author evaluations can be color-coded as blue.

Thinking this way, we conceive of an author as painting a story with various sorts of verb forms/clause types. We can push the analogy further by color-coding a part or all of a story in this fashion, then throwing away the verbal component, and studying the resultant color design. Some such project was once attempted between myself as discourse analyst and Carolyn Dyk, an artist colleague.

4.3 *Text theory and architecture*

What of a building as text? Here the thought of a building as a cohesive whole with lines that lead the eye to its most prominent feature (and avoidance of distracting detail) is not so different from that of a text. Here such facts as that the Parthenon is not built on straight lines but with lines almost imperceptibly bowing outward, is again similar to a requirement of text development: Make everything to the smallest detail subservient to the main thrust of the whole.

But what of text as building? I heard it once remarked that the sermon of a certain preacher kept us so long in the vestibule that we scarcely had time to appreciate the sanctuary — saying in effect that the introduction was much too long and that the body of the sermon was relatively underdeveloped. Or a writer may announce his intention of building only a rude scaffolding in the first part of his work and erecting the main building in the second part. The center of a chiasm in literature can be compared to the keystone of an arch. In fact, running metaphor in terms of architectural motifs often characterizes the discussion of text — even the frequent claim: "I lay a foundation here for what is to follow". Perhaps comparing a text to a building is one of the "metaphors we live by" (Lakoff and Johnson 1980).

Francis Thompson uses the metaphor text-as-building towards the end of the second of his "Sister Songs": a pair of long poems written to two children, Monica and Madeline, who were children of his patron, Wilfred Meynell. He writes at the end of the composite poem:

> As, poised upon this unprevisioned height
>   I lift into its place
> The utmost aery, traceried pinnacle.
> So; it is builded, the high tenement,
>   — God grant! — to mine intent:
> Most like a palace of the Occident,
>   Upthrusting maze on maze
>   Its mounded blaze ...

Down a few lines he likens his poem to a castle guarded by a dragon:

> Yet wail, my spirits, wail!
> So few therein to enter shall prevail.
> Scare fewer could win way, if their desire

> A dragon balked, with involuted spire
> And writhen snout spattered with yeasty fire.

In the next line he sighs for the "appointed knight" who will blow the horn at the portal and gain admission — perhaps the poet-reader who will understand his poetry.

Taking up again the figure of the building, he refers to his poem again as something perceived by glancing through a window:

> Receding labyrinths lessening tortuously
>   In half obscurity
> With mystic images, inhuman, cold
>   That flameless torches hold ...

But, when the one comes who can blow the horn, then

>   Straight
> Open for him shall roll the conscious gate;
> And light leap up from all the torches there,
> And life leap up in every torchbearer ...

As for the appointed knight,
    He threads securely the far intricacies.
    ....
    Until he gain the structure's core, where stands —
        a toil of magic hands —
The unbodied spirit of the sorcerer ...
    ...
It rests exempt, beneath the edifice
    To which itself gave rise;
Sustaining center to that bubble of stone
Which, breathed from it, exists for it alone.

Thus ends Thompson's prolonged passage (51–52) in which he compares his poem to a vast, but rather inaccessible structure sustained at the heart by his spirit and waiting for the arrival of the "appointed knight" who can find his way in.

I have tried to illustrate the "X as text" and "text as X" analogies from domains of the arts in which X is first music, then painting, then architecture. I do not believe that the analogies are superficial. They cut across **worlds**: the world of texts in general (Text-W) and the world of the various Arts (Arts-W).

I believe that just as text theory must be interdisciplinary, with one text illuminating another text across disciplinary lines, so must semiotic theory in general, i.e. one field of study can illuminate another field. I propose therefore a third and final correlation in (3):

(3)   Text-W ← ^{H} → Arts-W

i.e. "the study of texts and the study of the arts can mutually illuminate each other".

References

Bailey, Nicolas A. 1992. Nehemiah 3:1–32: An intersection of the text and the topography. *Journal of Translation and Textlinguistics* 5: 1–12.
de Beaugrande, R., and W. Dressler. 1981. *An Introduction to Textlinguistics*. London: Longmans.
Beekman, John., John Callow, and Michael Kopesec. 1981. *The Semantic Structure of Written Communication*. Fifth Edition. Dallas: Summer Institute of Linguistics.
Borker, Ruth. 1986. 'Moved by the Spirit': constructing meaning in a Brethren breaking of bread service. *Text* 6: 3 (special issue). *The Audience as Co-author*, ed. by Alessandro Duranti, and Donald Brenneis, 317–337.
Brend, Ruth (ed.) 1986. *The Text as Convergence of Concerns*, Second UTA conference on linguistics and the humanities. *Word* 37: 1–2.
Copeland, James A. (ed.). 1984. *New Directions in Linguistics and Semiotics*. Rice University Studies. Houston Texas: Rice University.
Danet, Brenda (ed.) 1984. *Studies of Legal Discourse*. *Text* 4: 1–3 (special issue).
van Dijk, Teun A. 1977. *Text and Context: Explorations in the Semantics and Pragmatics of Discourse*. London: Longmans.
van Dijk, Teun A.. 1980. *Macrostructures: an Interdisciplinary Study of Global Structures in Discourse, Interaction, and Cognition*. Hillsdale, New Jersey: Lawrence Erlbaum Associates.
van Dijk, Teun A., and Walter Kintsch. 1977. Cognitive psychology and discourse. *Current Trends in Textlinguistics*, ed. by W.U. Dressler. Berlin and New York: de Gruyter.
van Dijk, Teun A. and Ruth Wodak (eds.) 1988. *Discourse, Racism and Ideology*. *Text* 8: 1–2 (special issue).

Farmer, Jeff. 1981. The discourse analysis of a piece of transformational-generative argumentation. *Journal of the Linguistic Association of the Southwest* 3: 266–280.

Freeman, Sarah and Monica Heller (eds.) 1987. Medical discourse. *Text* 7.1 (special issue).

Halliday, M. A. K. and Ruqaiya Hasan. 1976. *Cohesion in English.* (English Language Series 9.) London: Longman

Krauthammer, Charles. 1984. Holiday: Living on a return ticket. *Time*, August 27.52

Lakoff, George and Mark Johnson. 1980. *Metaphors We Live by.* Chicago: University of Chicago Press.

Longacre, Robert. 1976. *An Anatomy of Speech Notions.* Lisse: Peter De Ridder Press

Longacre, Robert. 1981. A spectrum and profile approach to discourse analysis. *Text* 1: 337–384.

Longacre, Robert, (ed.) [under Adam Makkai] 1982–1983. *Linguistics and the Humanities. First UTA Conference on Linguistics and the Humanities, Forum Linguisticum* 7.1,2,3 (August 1982, December 1982, April 1983).

Longacre, Robert. 1983. *The Grammar of Discourse.* New York: Plenum Press.

Longacre, Robert. 1985. Discourse peak as zone of turbulence. *Beyond the Sentence*, ed. by Jessica Wirth, 82–98. Ann Arbor: Karoma.

Longacre, Robert. 1989. Two hypotheses regarding text generation and analysis. *Discourse Processes* 12: 413–60.

Longacre, Robert. 1990. *Storyline Concerns and Word-Order Typology in East and West Africa. Studies in African Linguistics*, Supplement 10. Los Angeles: UCLA.

Longacre, Robert. 1994. The Dynamics of Reported Dialoque in Narrative. *Word* 45, 125–143.

Longacre, Robert. 1996. *The Grammar of Discourse.* Second Edition, New York: Plenum Press.

Mann, William C. and Sandra A. Thompson. 1987. *Rhetorical Structure Theory: A Theory of Text Organization.* Marina del Rey: University of Southern California, Information Sciences Institute.

Mann, William C. and Sandra A. Thompson (eds.) 1992. *Discourse Description, Diverse Linguistic Analyses of a Fund-Raising Text.* Amsterdam: John Benjamins.

Pike, Kenneth L. 1959. Language as particle, wave, and field. *The Texas Quarterly* 2: 37–54.
Ricoeur, Paul. 1984–1985. *Time and Narrative* (3 volumes). Chicago: University of Chicago Press.
Sacks, H. 1984. Notes on methodology. *Structures of Social Action: Studies in Conversational Analysis*, ed. by J. Heritage and J.M. Atkinson, 21–24. Cambridge: Cambridge University Press.
Sayers, Barbara. 1976. *The Sentence in Wik-Munkan: A Description of Propositional Relationships*. Pacific Linguistics series 13, no. 44. Canberra: The Australian National University.
Steele, Ross and Terry Threadgold (eds.) 1987. *Language Topics: Essays in Honour of Michael Halliday*. 2 volumes. Amsterdam: John Benjamins.
Thompson, Francis. no date. *Complete Poetical Works of Francis Thompson*. pp. 18–58. New York: The Modern Library (original collection and arrangement by Wilfred Meynell, 1913).
Waltz, Nathan E. 1976. Discourse functions of Guanano sentence and paragraph. *Studies in Indigenous Languages of Colombia, Panama, and Ecuador*, ed. by Robert Longacre and Frances Woods, 21–146. Dallas: Summer Institute of Linguistics Publications #52.

About the author

Robert E. Longacre is Professor Emeritus at the University of Texas at Arlington, where he taught from 1972 to 1993. He completed a doctorate in Linguistics at the University of Pennsylvania in 1955. His primary influences in linguistics came from Zellig Harris of Pennsylvania and Kenneth L. Pike, whom he met at a session of the Summer Institute of Linguistics in 1945. He worked as a field investigator under the SIL from 1946 to 1972, preparing a New Testament translation into the Trique language of Mexico. He has traveled to many parts of the world as a consultant in linguistics and translation. Though he sees himself as reacting somewhat against stratificationalism, he still feels his linguistic work has been enriched by growing up professionally in the same world with Sydney Lamb.

www.ingramcontent.com/pod-product-compliance
Lightning Source LLC
Chambersburg PA
CBHW071434300426
44114CB00013B/1434